Sources of the Self

SOURCES
OF THE
SELF

---

*The Making of the
Modern Identity*

CHARLES TAYLOR

HARVARD UNIVERSITY PRESS
Cambridge, Massachusetts

Library of Congress Cataloging-in-Publication Data

Taylor, Charles, 1931–
Sources of the self : the making of the modern identity /
Charles Taylor.
p.   cm.
Bibliography: p.
Includes index.
ISBN 0-674-82425-3 (alk. paper) (cloth)
ISBN 0-674-82426-1 (paper)
1. Self (Philosophy).   2. Civilization, Modern.   3. Philosophy,
Modern.   4. Ethics.   I. Title.
BD450.T266   1989
126—dc19
88-37229
CIP

To Milou

CONTENTS

PREFACE

I've had a difficult time writing this book. It's taken too many years, and I've changed my mind a few times about what should go into it. In part, this was for the familiar reason that for a long time I wasn't sure what I wanted to say. In part, it was because of the very ambitious nature of the enterprise, which is an attempt to articulate and write a history of the modern identity. With this term, I want to designate the ensemble of (largely unarticulated) understandings of what it is to be a human agent: the senses of inwardness, freedom, individuality, and being embedded in nature which are at home in the modern West.

But I also wanted to show how the ideals and interdicts of this identity—what it casts in relief and what it casts in shadow—shape our philosophical thought, our epistemology and our philosophy of language, largely without our awareness. Doctrines which are supposedly derived from the sober examination of some domain into which the self doesn't and shouldn't obtrude actually reflect much more than we realize the ideals that have helped constitute this identity of ours. This is eminently true, I believe, of the representational epistemology from Descartes to Quine.

In addition, this portrait of our identity is meant to serve as the starting point for a renewed understanding of modernity. This issue, that is, coming to comprehend the momentous transformations of our culture and society over the last three or four centuries and getting these somehow in focus, continues to preoccupy us. The works of major contemporary thinkers such as Foucault, Habermas, and MacIntyre focus on it. Others, while not dealing with it expressly, suppose some picture of what has come about in the stance they take, even if it is one of dismissal, towards past thought and culture. This is no gratuitous obsession. We cannot understand ourselves without coming to grips with this history.

But I find myself dissatisfied with the views on this subject which are now current. Some are upbeat, and see us as having climbed to a higher plateau; others show a picture of decline, of loss, of forgetfulness. Neither sort seems to me right; both ignore massively important features of our situation. We have yet to capture, I think, the unique combination of greatness and danger, of *grandeur et misère,* which characterizes the modern age. To see the full complexity and richness of the modern identity is to see, first, how much we are all caught up in it, for all our attempts to repudiate it; and second, how shallow and partial are the one-sided judgements we bandy around about it.

But I don't think we can grasp this richness and complexity unless we see how the modern understanding of the self developed out of earlier pictures of human identity. This book attempts to define the modern identity in describing its genesis.

I focus on three major facets of this identity: first, modern inwardness, the sense of ourselves as beings with inner depths, and the connected notion that we are 'selves'; second, the affirmation of ordinary life which develops from the early modern period; third, the expressivist notion of nature as an inner moral source. The first I try to trace through Augustine to Descartes and Montaigne, and on to our own day; the second I take from the Reformation through the Enlightenment to its contemporary forms; and the third I describe from its origin in the late eighteenth century through the transformations of the nineteenth century, and on to its manifestations in twentieth-century literature.

The main body of the book, Parts II–V, is taken up with this picture of the developing modern identity. The treatment is a combination of the analytical and the chronological. But because my entire way of proceeding involves mapping connections between senses of the self and moral visions, between identity and the good, I didn't feel I could launch into this study without some preliminary discussion of these links. This seemed all the more necessary in that the moral philosophies dominant today tend to obscure these connections. In order to see them, we have to appreciate the place of the good, in more than one sense, in our moral outlook and life. But this is precisely what contemporary moral philosophies have most trouble admitting. The book therefore begins with a section which tries to make the case very briefly for a picture of the relation between self and morals, which I then draw on in the rest of the work. Those who are utterly bored by modern philosophy might want to skip Part I. Those who are bored by history, if by some mistake they find this work in their hands, should read nothing else.

The whole study is, as I indicated, a prelude to our being able to come to grips with the phenomena of modernity in a more fruitful and less one-sided way than is usual. I didn't have space in this already too big book to paint a full-scale alternative picture of these phenomena. I will have to leave this, as well as the analysis linking the modern identity to our epistemology and philosophy of language, to later works. But I try to set out in the concluding chapter what flows from this story of the emerging modern identity. Briefly, it is that this identity is much richer in moral sources than its condemners allow, but that this richness is rendered invisible by the impoverished philosophical language of its most zealous defenders. Modernity urgently needs to be saved from its most unconditional supporters—a predicament perhaps not without precedent in the history of culture. Understanding modernity aright is an exercise in retrieval. I try to explain in my conclusion why I think this exercise is important, even pressing.

This book has been a long time in preparation, and during this time I have benefited greatly from discussions with colleagues at All Souls College, in Oxford generally, and at McGill, Berkeley, Frankfurt, and Jerusalem, including James Tully, Hubert Dreyfus, Alexander Nehamas, Jane Rubin, Jürgen Habermas, Axel Honneth, Micha Brumlik, Martin Löw-Beer, Hauke Brunkhorst, Simone Chambers, Paul Rosenberg, David Hartman, and Guy Stroumsa. The invitation of Lawrence Freeman and the Benedictine Priory of Montreal to give the John Main Memorial Lectures provided an invaluable occasion to work out the picture of modernity that I am trying to assemble, and the discussions that followed were very helpful.

But I could never have completed the project without the year I spent at the Institute for Advanced Study at Princeton. I am very grateful to Clifford Geertz, Albert Hirschman, and Michael Walzer both for this year of research and for the valuable discussions we had during that time in the unequalled atmosphere of the Institute. I also want to thank the National Endowment for the Humanities, which provided the funds to make that year possible.

I owe a debt of gratitude as well to the Canada Council for granting me an Isaak Killam Fellowship, which made it possible for me to take another year's leave. This proved to be crucial. My thanks go also to McGill University for a sabbatical, and to the Social Sciences and Humanities Research Council of Canada for a Sabbatical Leave Fellowship, which allowed me to complete the manuscript.

I also want to express my thanks to McGill University for a research grant to help in reformatting the manuscript and in preparing the index.

I am very grateful to Mette Hjort for her comments on the manuscript. I would like to thank Alba and Miriam for valuable suggestions, Karen and Bisia for putting me into contact with unfamiliar dimensions of existence, and Beata for her refreshing pragmatism. My thanks go also to Gretta Taylor and Melissa Steele for their help in preparing the final version of the manuscript for publication, and to Wanda Taylor for proofreading and indexing.

I am grateful to Macmillan Publishing Company and to A. P. Watt Ltd., on behalf of Michael B. Yeats and Macmillan London Ltd., for permission to quote lines from W. B. Yeats, "Among Schoolchildren", reprinted from *The Poems of W. B. Yeats: A New Edition,* edited by Richard J. Finneran, copyright 1928 by Macmillan Publishing Company, renewed 1956 by Georgie Yeats; to New Directions Publishing Corporation for permission to quote Ezra Pound's "In a Station of the Metro", from *Personae: Collected Poems of Ezra Pound,* copyright 1926 by Ezra Pound and reprinted by New Directions (1949); to Faber and Faber Ltd. and Random House, Inc., for permission to quote a stanza of the earliest version of "September 1, 1939", © 1940 by W. H. Auden and reprinted from *The English Auden: Poems, Essays, and Dramatic Writings, 1927–1939,* by W. H. Auden, edited by Edward Mendelson; and to Random House, Inc., for permission to quote from Stephen Mitchell's translation of R. M. Rilke's "Panther", © 1982 by Stephen Mitchell and reprinted from *The Selected Poetry of Rainer Maria Rilke.* Lines from Paul Celan, "Weggebeizt", "Kein Halbholz", and "Faden- sonnen" are reprinted from *Gesammelte Werke,* II (1983) by permission of Suhrkamp Verlag; the English translations of these poems are copyright © 1972, 1980, 1988 by Michael Hamburger and are reprinted from *Poems of Paul Celan* by permission of Persea Books and Anvil Press Poetry Ltd. The quotations from Charles Baudelaire, *The Flowers of Evil,* © 1955, 1962 by New Directions Publishing Corporation, are reprinted by permission of New Directions. Excerpts from "In the Middle of Life" by Tadeusz Różewicz and "The Stone" by Zbigniew Herbert are from *Postwar Polish Poetry,* edited and translated by Czesław Miłosz, copyright © 1965 by Czesław Miłosz, and reprinted by Doubleday, a division of Bantam, Doubleday, Dell Publish- ing Group, Inc.

PART I

---

*Identity and
the Good*

1

INESCAPABLE FRAMEWORKS

1.1

I want to explore various facets of what I will call the 'modern identity'. To give a good first approximation of what this means would be to say that it involves tracing various strands of our modern notion of what it is to be a human agent, a person, or a self. But pursuing this investigation soon shows that you can't get very clear about this without some further understanding of how our pictures of the good have evolved. Selfhood and the good, or in another way selfhood and morality, turn out to be inextricably intertwined themes.

In this first part, I want to say something about this connection, before in Parts II–V plunging into the history and analysis of the modern identity. But another obstacle rises in the way even of this preliminary task. Much contemporary moral philosophy, particularly but not only in the English-speaking world, has given such a narrow focus to morality that some of the crucial connections I want to draw here are incomprehensible in its terms. This moral philosophy has tended to focus on what it is right to do rather than on what it is good to be, on defining the content of obligation rather than the nature of the good life; and it has no conceptual place left for a notion of the good as the object of our love or allegiance or, as Iris Murdoch portrayed it in her work, as the privileged focus of attention or will.[1] This philosophy has accredited a cramped and truncated view of morality in a narrow sense, as well as of the whole range of issues involved in the attempt to live the best possible life, and this not only among professional philosophers, but with a wider public.

So much of my effort in Part I will be directed towards enlarging our range of legitimate moral descriptions, and in some cases retrieving modes of thought and description which have misguidedly been made to seem problematic. In particular, what I want to bring out and examine is the richer background languages in which we set the basis and point of the moral obligations we acknowledge. More broadly, I want to explore the background picture of our spiritual nature and predicament which lies behind some of the

3

moral and spiritual intuitions of our contemporaries. In the course of doing so, I shall also be trying to make clearer just what a background picture is, and what role it plays in our lives. Here is where an important element of retrieval comes in, because much contemporary philosophy has ignored this dimension of our moral consciousness and beliefs altogether and has even seemed to dismiss it as confused and irrelevant. I hope to show, contrary to this attitude, how crucial it is.

I spoke in the previous paragraph about our 'moral and spiritual' intuitions. In fact, I want to consider a gamut of views a bit broader than what is normally described as the 'moral'. In addition to our notions and reactions on such issues as justice and the respect of other people's life, well-being, and dignity, I want also to look at our sense of what underlies our own dignity, or questions about what makes our lives meaningful or fulfilling. These might be classed as moral questions on some broad definition, but some are too concerned with the self-regarding, or too much a matter of our ideals, to be classed as moral issues in most people's lexicon. They concern, rather, what makes life worth living.

What they have in common with moral issues, and what deserves the vague term 'spiritual', is that they all involve what I have called elsewhere 'strong evaluation',[2] that is, they involve discriminations of right or wrong, better or worse, higher or lower, which are not rendered valid by our own desires, inclinations, or choices, but rather stand independent of these and offer standards by which they can be judged. So while it may not be judged a moral lapse that I am living a life that is not really worthwhile or fulfilling, to describe me in these terms is nevertheless to condemn me in the name of a standard, independent of my own tastes and desires, which I ought to acknowledge.

Perhaps the most urgent and powerful cluster of demands that we recognize as moral concern the respect for the life, integrity, and well-being, even flourishing, of others. These are the ones we infringe when we kill or maim others, steal their property, strike fear into them and rob them of peace, or even refrain from helping them when they are in distress. Virtually everyone feels these demands, and they have been and are acknowledged in all human societies. Of course the scope of the demand notoriously varies: earlier societies, and some present ones, restrict the class of beneficiaries to members of the tribe or race and exclude outsiders, who are fair game, or even condemn the evil to a definitive loss of this status. But they all feel these demands laid on them by some class of persons, and for most contemporaries this class is coterminous with the human race (and for believers in animal rights it may go wider).

We are dealing here with moral intuitions which are uncommonly deep, powerful, and universal. They are so deep that we are tempted to think of them as rooted in instinct, in contrast to other moral reactions which seem very much the consequence of upbringing and education. There seems to be a natural, inborn compunction to inflict death or injury on another, an inclination to come to the help of the injured or endangered. Culture and upbringing may help to define the boundaries of the relevant 'others', but they don't seem to create the basic reaction itself. That is why eighteenth-century thinkers, notably Rousseau, could believe in a natural susceptibility to feel sympathy for others.

The roots of respect for life and integrity do seem to go as deep as this, and to be connected perhaps with the almost universal tendency among other animals to stop short of the killing of conspecifics. But like so much else in human life, this 'instinct' receives a variable shape in culture, as we have seen. And this shape is inseparable from an account of what it is that commands our respect. The account seems to articulate the intuition. It tells us, for instance, that human beings are creatures of God and made in his image, or that they are immortal souls, or that they are all emanations of divine fire, or that they are all rational agents and thus have a dignity which transcends any other being, or some other such characterization; and that *therefore* we owe them respect. The various cultures which restrict this respect do so by denying the crucial description to those left outside: they are thought to lack souls, or to be not fully rational, or perhaps to be destined by God for some lower station, or something of the sort.

So our moral reactions in this domain have two facets, as it were. On one side, they are almost like instincts, comparable to our love of sweet things, or our aversion to nauseous substances, or our fear of falling; on the other, they seem to involve claims, implicit or explicit, about the nature and status of human beings. From this second side, a moral reaction is an assent to, an affirmation of, a given ontology of the human.

An important strand of modern naturalist consciousness has tried to hive this second side off and declare it dispensable or irrelevant to morality. The motives are multiple: partly distrust of all such ontological accounts because of the use to which some of them have been put, e.g., justifying restrictions or exclusions of heretics or allegedly lower beings. And this distrust is strengthened where a primitivist sense that unspoiled human nature respects life by instinct reigns. But it is partly also the great epistemological cloud under which all such accounts lie for those who have followed empiricist or rationalist theories of knowledge, inspired by the success of modern natural science.

The temptation is great to rest content with the fact that we have such reactions, and to consider the ontology which gives rational articulation to them to be so much froth, nonsense from a bygone age. This stance may go along with a sociobiological explanation for our having such reactions, which can be thought to have obvious evolutionary utility and indeed have analogues among other species, as already mentioned.

But this neat division cannot be carried through. Ontological accounts offer themselves as correct articulations of our 'gut' reactions of respect. In this they treat these reactions as different from other 'gut' responses, such as our taste for sweets or our nausea at certain smells or objects. We don't acknowledge that there is something there to articulate, as we do in the moral case. Is this distinction illegitimate? A metaphysical invention? It seems to turn on this: in either case our response is to an object with a certain property. But in one case the property marks the object as one *meriting* this reaction; in the other the connection between the two is just a brute fact. Thus we argue and reason over what and who is a fit object of moral respect, while this doesn't seem to be even possible for a reaction like nausea. Of course we can reason that it might be useful or convenient to alter the boundaries of what we feel nausea at; and we might succeed, with training, in doing so. But what seems to make no sense here is the supposition that we might articulate a description of the nauseating in terms of its intrinsic properties, and then argue from this that certain things which we in fact react to that way are not really fit objects for it. There seems to be no other criterion for a concept of the nauseating than our in fact reacting with nausea to the things which bear the concept. As against the first kind of response, which relates to a proper object, this one could be called a brute reaction.

Assimilating our moral reactions to these visceral ones would mean considering all our talk about fit objects of moral response to be utterly illusory. The belief that we are discriminating real properties, with criteria independent of our de facto reactions, would be declared unfounded. This is the burden of the so-called 'error theory' of moral values which John Mackie espoused.[3] It can combine easily with a sociobiological standpoint, in which one acknowledges that certain moral reactions had (and have) obvious survival value, and one may even propose to fine-tune and alter our reactions so as to increase that value, as above we imagined changing what we feel nausea at. But this would have nothing to do with a view that certain things and not others, just in virtue of their nature, were fit objects of respect.

Now this sociobiological or external standpoint is utterly different from the way we in fact argue and reason and deliberate in our moral lives. We are all universalists now about respect for life and integrity. But this means not just that we happen to have such reactions or that we have decided in the light of the present predicament of the human race that it is useful to have such reactions (though some people argue in this way, urging that, for instance, it is in our own interest in a shrinking world to take account of Third World poverty). It means rather that we believe it would be utterly wrong and unfounded to draw the boundaries any narrower than around the whole human race.

Should anybody propose to do so, we should immediately ask what distinguished those within from those left out. And we should seize on this distinguishing characteristic in order to show that it had nothing to do with commanding respect. This is what we do with racists. Skin colour or physical traits have nothing to do with that in virtue of which humans command our respect. In fact, no ontological account accords it this. Racists have to claim that certain of the crucial moral properties of human beings are genetically determined: that some races are less intelligent, less capable of high moral consciousness, and the like. The logic of the argument forces them to stake their claim on ground where they are empirically at their weakest. Differences in skin colour are undeniable. But all claims about innate cultural differences are unsustainable in the light of human history. The logic of this whole debate takes intrinsic description seriously, that is, descriptions of the objects of our moral responses whose criteria are independent of our de facto reactions.

Can it be otherwise? We feel the demand to be consistent in our moral reactions. And even those philosophers who propose to ignore ontological accounts nevertheless scrutinize and criticize our moral intuitions for their consistency or lack of it. But the issue of consistency presupposes intrinsic description. How could anyone be accused of being inconsistently nauseated? Some description could always be found covering all the objects he reacts to that way, if only the relative one that they all awake his disgust. The issue of consistency can only arise when the reaction is related to some independent property as its fit object.

The whole way in which we think, reason, argue, and question ourselves about morality supposes that our moral reactions have these two sides: that they are not only 'gut' feelings but also implicit acknowledgements of claims concerning their objects. The various ontological accounts try to articulate these claims. The temptations to deny this, which arise from modern epistemology, are strengthened by the widespread acceptance of a deeply wrong model of practical reasoning,[4] one based on an illegitimate extrapolation from reasoning in natural science.

The various ontological accounts attribute predicates to human beings—like being creatures of God, or emanations of divine fire, or agents of rational choice—which seem rather analogous to theoretical predicates in natural science, in that they (a) are rather remote from our everyday descriptions by which we deal with people around us and ourselves, and (b) make reference to our conception of the universe and the place we occupy in it. In fact, if we go back before the modern period and take the thought of Plato, for example, it is clear that the ontological account underlying the morality of just treatment was identical with his 'scientific' theory of the universe. The theory of Ideas underlay one and the other.

It seems natural to assume that we would have to establish these ontological predicates in ways analogous to our supporting physical explanations: starting from the facts identified independently of our reactions to them, we would try to show that one underlying explanation was better than others. But once we do this, we have lost from view what we're arguing about. Ontological accounts have the status of articulations of our moral instincts. They articulate the claims implicit in our reactions. We can no longer argue about them at all once we assume a neutral stance and try to describe the facts as they are independent of these reactions, as we have done in natural science since the seventeenth century. There is such a thing as moral objectivity, of course. Growth in moral insight often requires that we neutralize some of our reactions. But this is in order that the others may be identified, unmixed and unscreened by petty jealousy, egoism, or other unworthy feelings. It is never a question of prescinding from our reactions altogether.

Moral argument and exploration go on only within a world shaped by our deepest moral responses, like the ones I have been talking about here; just as natural science supposes that we focus on a world where all our responses have been neutralized. If you want to discriminate more finely what it is about human beings that makes them worthy of respect, you have to call to mind what it is to feel the claim of human suffering, or what is repugnant about injustice, or the awe you feel at the fact of human life. No argument can take someone from a neutral stance towards the world, either adopted from the demands of 'science' or fallen into as a consequence of pathology, to insight into moral ontology. But it doesn't follow from this that moral ontology is a pure fiction, as naturalists often assume. Rather we should treat our deepest moral instincts, our ineradicable sense that human life is to be respected, as our mode of access to the world in which ontological claims are discernible and can be rationally argued about and sifted.

1.2

I spoke at the outset about exploring the 'background picture' lying behind our moral and spiritual intuitions. I could now rephrase this and say that my target is the moral ontology which articulates these intuitions. What is the picture of our spiritual nature and predicament which makes sense of our responses? 'Making sense' here means articulating what makes these responses appropriate: identifying what makes something a fit object for them and correlatively formulating more fully the nature of the response as well as spelling out what all this presupposes about ourselves and our situation in the world. What is articulated here is the background we assume and draw on in any claim to rightness, part of which we are forced to spell out when we have to defend our responses as the right ones.

This articulation can be very difficult and controversial. I don't just mean this in the obvious sense that our contemporaries don't always agree in moral ontology. This is clear enough: many people, if asked to give their grounds for the reactions of respect for life discussed above, would appeal to the theistic account I referred to and invoke our common status as God's creatures; others would reject this for a purely secular account and perhaps invoke the dignity of rational life. But beyond this, articulating any particular person's background can be subject to controversy. The agent himself or herself is not necessarily the best authority, at least not at the outset.

This is the case first of all because the moral ontology behind any person's views can remain largely implicit. Indeed, it usually does, unless there is some challenge which forces it to the fore. The average person needs to do very little thinking about the bases of universal respect, for instance, because just about everyone accepts this as an axiom today. The greatest violators hide behind a smoke screen of lies and special pleading. Even racist regimes, like the one in South Africa, present their programmes in the language of separate but equal development; while Soviet dissidents are jailed on various trumped-up charges or hospitalized as 'mentally ill', and the fiction is maintained that the masses elect the regime. Whether one has a theistic or secular foundation rarely comes up, except in certain very special controversies, like that about abortion.

So over wide areas, the background tends to remain unexplored. But beyond this, exploration may even be resisted. That is because there may be—and I want to argue, frequently is—a lack of fit between what people as it were officially and consciously believe, even pride themselves on believing, on one hand, and what they need to make sense of some of their moral reactions, on the other. A gap like this surfaced in the discussion above, where some naturalists propose to treat all moral ontologies as irrelevant stories, without validity, while they themselves go on arguing like the rest of us about what objects are fit and what reactions appropriate. What generally happens here is that the reductive explanation itself, often a sociobiological one, which supposedly justifies this exclusion, itself takes on the role of moral ontology. That is, it starts to provide the basis for discriminations about appropriate objects or valid responses. What starts off in chapter 1 as a hard-nosed scientific theory justifying an error theory of morality becomes in the conclusion the basis for a new 'scientific' or 'evolutionary' ethic.[5] Here, one is forced to conclude, there reigns an ideologically induced illusion about the nature of the moral ontology that the thinkers concerned actually rely on. There is a very controversial but very important job of articulation to be done here, in the teeth of the people concerned, which can show to what extent the real spiritual basis of their own moral judgements deviates from what is officially admitted.

It will be my claim that there is a great deal of motivated suppression of moral ontology among our contemporaries, in part because the pluralist nature of modern society makes it easier to live that way, but also because of the great weight of modern epistemology (as with the naturalists evoked above) and, behind this, of the spiritual outlook associated with this epistemology. So the work I am embarked upon here could be called in large degree an essay in retrieval. Much of the ground will have to be fought for, and I will certainly not convince everybody.

But besides our disagreements and our temptations to suppress, this articulation of moral ontology will be very difficult for a third reason: the tentative, searching, uncertain nature of many of our moral beliefs. Many of our contemporaries, while they remain quite unattracted by the naturalist attempt to deny ontology altogether, and while on the contrary they recognize that their moral reactions show them to be committed to some adequate basis, are perplexed and uncertain when it comes to saying what this basis is. In our example above, many people, when faced with both the theistic and the secular ontologies as the grounds for their reactions of respect, would not feel ready to make a final choice. They concur that through their moral beliefs they acknowledge some ground in human nature or the human predicament which makes human beings fit objects of respect, but they confess that they cannot subscribe with complete conviction to any particular definition, at least not to any of the ones on offer. Something similar arises for many of them on the question of what makes human life worth living or what confers meaning on their individual lives. Most of us are still in the process of groping for answers here. This is an essentially modern predicament, as I shall try to argue below.

Where this is so, the issue of articulation can take another form. It is not merely formulating what people already implicitly but unproblematically acknowledge; nor is it showing what people really rely on in the teeth of their ideological denials. Rather it could only be carried forward by showing that one or another ontology is in fact the only adequate basis for our moral responses, whether we recognize this or not. A thesis of this kind was invoked by Dostoyevsky and discussed by Leszek Kołakowski in a recent work:[6] "If God does not exist, then everything is permitted". But this level of argument, concerning what our commitments really amount to, is even more difficult than the previous one, which tries to show, in the face of naturalist suppression, what they already are. I will probably not be able to venture very far out on this terrain in the following. It would be sufficient, and very valuable, to be able to show something about the tentative, hesitating, and fuzzy commitments that we moderns actually rely on. The map of our moral world, however full of gaps, erasures, and blurrings, is interesting enough.

1.3

The moral world of moderns is significantly different from that of previous civilizations. This becomes clear, among other places, when we look at the sense that human beings command our respect. In one form or another, this seems to be a human universal; that is, in every society, there seems to be some such sense. The boundary around those beings worthy of respect may be drawn parochially in earlier cultures, but there always is such a class. And among what we recognize as higher civilizations, this always includes the whole human species.

What is peculiar to the modern West among such higher civilizations is that its favoured formulation for this principle of respect has come to be in terms of rights. This has become central to our legal systems—and in this form has spread around the world. But in addition, something analogous has become central to our moral thinking.

The notion of a right, also called a 'subjective right', as this developed in the Western legal tradition, is that of a legal privilege which is seen as a quasi-possession of the agent to whom it is attributed. At first such rights were differential possessions: some people had the right to participate in certain assemblies, or to give counsel, or to collect tolls on this river, and so on. The revolution in natural law theory in the seventeenth century partly consisted in using this language of rights to express the universal moral norms. We began to speak of "natural" rights, and now to such things as life and liberty which supposedly everyone has.

In one way, to speak of a universal, natural right to life doesn't seem much of an innovation. The change seems to be one of form. The earlier way of putting it was that there was a natural law against taking innocent life. Both formulations seem to prohibit the same things. But the difference lies not in what is forbidden but in the place of the subject. Law is what I must obey. It may confer on me certain benefits, here the immunity that my life, too, is to be respected; but fundamentally I am *under* law. By contrast, a subjective right is something which the possessor can and ought to act on to put it into effect. To accord you an immunity, formerly given you by natural law, in the form of a natural right is to give you a role in establishing and enforcing this immunity. Your concurrence is now necessary, and your degrees of freedom are correspondingly greater. At the extreme limit of these, you can even waive a right, thus defeating the immunity. This is why Locke, in order to close off this possibility in the case of his three basic rights, had to introduce the notion of 'inalienability'. Nothing like this was necessary on the earlier natural law formulation, because that language by its very nature excludes the power of waiver.

To talk of universal, natural, or human rights is to connect respect for human life and integrity with the notion of autonomy. It is to conceive people as active cooperators in establishing and ensuring the respect which is due them. And this expresses a central feature of the modern Western moral outlook. This change of form naturally goes along with one in content, with the conception of what it is to respect someone. Autonomy is now central to this. So the Lockean trinity of natural rights includes that to liberty. And for us respecting personality involves as a crucial feature respecting the person's moral autonomy. With the development of the post-Romantic notion of individual difference, this expands to the demand that we give people the freedom to develop their personality in their own way, however repugnant to ourselves and even to our moral sense—the thesis developed so persuasively by J. S. Mill.

Of course not everyone agrees with Mill's principle, and its full impact on Western legislation has been very recent. But everyone in our civilization feels the force of this appeal to accord people the freedom to develop in their own way. The disagreement is over the relation of such things as pornography, or various kinds of permissive sexual behaviour, or portrayals of violence, to legitimate development. Does the prohibition of the former endanger the latter? No one doubts that if it does, this constitutes a reason, though perhaps not an ultimately decisive one, to relax social controls.

So autonomy has a central place in our understanding of respect. So much is generally agreed. Beyond this lie various richer pictures of human nature and our predicament, which offer reasons for this demand. These include, for instance, the notion of ourselves as disengaged subjects, breaking free from a comfortable but illusory sense of immersion in nature, and objectifying the world around us; or the Kantian picture of ourselves as pure rational agents; or the Romantic picture just mentioned, where we understand ourselves in terms of organic metaphors and a concept of self-expression. As is well known, the partisans of these different views are in sharp conflict with each other. Here again, a generalized moral consensus breaks into controversy at the level of philosophical explication.

I am not at all neutral on this controversy, but I don't feel at this stage in a position to contribute in a helpful way to it. I would rather try now to round out this picture of our modern understanding of respect by mentioning two other, connected features.

The first is the importance we put on avoiding suffering. This again seems to be unique among higher civilizations. Certainly we are much more sensitive on this score than our ancestors of a few centuries ago—as we can readily see if we consider the (to us) barbarous punishments they inflicted.

Once again, the legal code and its practices provide a window into broader movements of culture. Think of the horrifying description of the torture and execution of a man who had attempted regicide in mid-eighteenth-century France, which opens Michel Foucault's *Surveiller et punir*.[7] It's not that comparable horrors don't occur in the twentieth-century West. But they are now seen as shocking aberrations, which have to be hidden. Even the "clean" legal executions, where the death penalty is still in force, are no longer carried out in public, but deep within prison walls. It's with a shudder that we learn that parents used to bring small children to witness such events when they were offered as public spectacles in earlier times. We are much more sensitive to suffering, which we may of course just translate into not wanting to hear about it rather than into any concrete remedial action. But the notion that we ought to reduce it to a minimum is an integral part of what respect means to us today—however distasteful this has been to an eloquent minority, most notably to Nietzsche.

Part of the reason for this change is negative. Compared for instance to the executioners of Damiens in the eighteenth century, we don't see any point in ritually undoing the terrible crime in an equally terrible punishment. The whole notion of a cosmic moral order, which gave this restoral its sense, has faded for us. The stress on relieving suffering has grown with the decline of this kind of belief. It is what is left over, what takes on moral importance, after we no longer see human beings as playing a role in a larger cosmic order or divine history. This was part of the negative thrust of the utilitarian Enlightenment, protesting against the needless, senseless suffering inflicted on humans in the name of such larger orders or dramas.

But of course this stress on human welfare of the most immediate kind also has religious sources. It springs from the New Testament and is one of the central themes of Christian spirituality. Modern utilitarianism is one of its secularized variants. And as such it connects with a more fundamental feature to Christian spirituality, which comes to receive new and unprecedented importance at the beginning of the modern era, and which has also become central to modern culture. I want to describe this as the affirmation of ordinary life. This last is a term of art, meant roughly to designate the life of production and the family.

According to traditional, Aristotelian ethics, this has merely infrastructural importance. 'Life' was important as the necessary background and support to 'the good life' of contemplation and one's action as a citizen. With the Reformation, we find a modern, Christian-inspired sense that ordinary life was on the contrary the very centre of the good life. The crucial issue was how it was led, whether worshipfully and in the fear of God or not. But the life of the God-fearing was lived out in marriage and their calling. The previous 'higher' forms of life were dethroned, as it were. And along with this went frequently an attack, covert or overt, on the elites which had made these forms their province.

I believe that this affirmation of ordinary life, although not uncontested and frequently appearing in secularized form, has become one of the most powerful ideas in modern civilization. It underlies our contemporary "bour-geois" politics, so much concerned with issues of welfare, and at the same time powers the most influential revolutionary ideology of our century, Marxism, with its apotheosis of man the producer. This sense of the importance of the everyday in human life, along with its corollary about the importance of suffering, colours our whole understanding of what it is truly to respect human life and integrity. Along with the central place given to autonomy, it defines a version of this demand which is peculiar to our civilization, the modern West.

1.4

Thus far I have been exploring only one strand of our moral intuitions, albeit an extremely important one. These are the moral beliefs which cluster around the sense that human life is to be respected and that the prohibitions and obligations which this imposes on us are among the most weighty and serious in our lives. I have been arguing that there is a peculiarly modern sense of what respect involves, which gives a salient place to freedom and self-control, places a high priority on avoiding suffering, and sees productive activity and family life as central to our well-being. But this cluster of moral intuitions lies along only one of the axes of our moral life. There are others to which the moral notions that I have been discussing are also relevant.

'Morality', of course, can be and often is defined purely in terms of respect for others. The category of the moral is thought to encompass just our obligations to other people. But if we adopt this definition, then we have to allow that there are other questions beyond the moral which are of central concern to us, and which bring strong evaluation into play. There are questions about how I am going to live my life which touch on the issue of what kind of life is worth living, or what kind of life would fulfill the promise implicit in my particular talents, or the demands incumbent on someone with my endowment, or of what constitutes a rich, meaningful life—as against one concerned with secondary matters or trivia. These are issues of strong evaluation, because the people who ask these questions have no doubt that one can, following one's immediate wishes and desires, take a wrong turn and hence fail to lead a full life. To understand our moral world we have to see not only what ideas and pictures underlie our sense of respect for others but also those which underpin our notions of a full life. And as we shall see, these are not two quite separate orders of ideas. There is a substantial overlap or, rather, a complex relation in which some of the same basic notions reappear in a new way. This is particularly the case for what I called above the affirmation of ordinary life.

In general, one might try to single out three axes of what can be called, in the most general sense, moral thinking. As well as the two just mentioned— our sense of respect for and obligations to others, and our understandings of what makes a full life—there is also the range of notions concerned with dignity. By this I mean the characteristics by which we think of ourselves as commanding (or failing to command) the respect of those around us. Here the term 'respect' has a slightly different meaning than in the above. I'm not talking now about respect for rights, in the sense of non-infringement, which we might call 'active' respect, but rather of thinking well of someone, even looking up to him, which is what we imply when we say in ordinary speech that he has our respect. (Let's call this kind 'attitudinal'.)

Our 'dignity', in the particular sense I am using it here, is our sense of ourselves as commanding (attitudinal) respect. The issue of what one's dignity consists in is no more avoidable than those of why we ought to respect others' rights or what makes a full life, however much a naturalist philosophy might mislead us into thinking of this as another domain of mere 'gut' reactions, similar to those of baboons establishing their hierarchy. And in this case, its unavoidability ought to be the more obvious in that our dignity is so much woven into our very comportment. The very way we walk, move, gesture, speak is shaped from the earliest moments by our awareness that we appear before others, that we stand in public space, and that this space is potentially one of respect or contempt, of pride or shame. Our style of movement expresses how we see ourselves as enjoying respect or lacking it, as commanding it or failing to do so. Some people flit through public space as though avoiding it, others rush through as though hoping to sidestep the issue of how they appear in it by the very serious purpose with which they transit through it; others again saunter through with assurance, savouring their moments within it; still others swagger, confident of how their presence marks it: think of the carefully leisurely way the policeman gets out of his car, having stopped you for speeding, and the slow, swaying walk over as he comes to demand your licence.[8]

Just what do we see our dignity consisting in? It can be our power, our sense of dominating public space; or our invulnerability to power; or our self-sufficiency, our life having its own centre; or our being liked and looked to by others, a centre of attention. But very often the sense of dignity can ground in some of the same moral views I mentioned above. For instance, my sense of myself as a householder, father of a family, holding down a job, providing for my dependants; all this can be the basis of my sense of dignity. Just as its absence can be catastrophic, can shatter it by totally undermining my feeling of self-worth. Here the sense of dignity is woven into this modern notion of the importance of ordinary life, which reappears again on this axis.

Probably something like these three axes exists in every culture. But there are great differences in how they are conceived, how they relate, and in their relative importance. For the warrior and honour ethic that seems to have been dominant among the ruling strata of archaic Greece, whose deeds were celebrated by Homer, this third axis seems to have been paramount, and seems even to have incorporated the second axis without remainder. The 'agathos' is the man of dignity and power.[9] And enough of this survives into the classical period for Plato to have depicted an ethic of power and self-aggrandizement as one of his major targets, in figures like Callicles and Thrasymachus. For us, this is close to inconceivable. It seems obvious that the first axis has paramountcy, followed by the second. Connected with this, it would probably have been incomprehensible to the people of that archaic period that the first axis should be conceived in terms of an ethic of general principles, let alone one founded on reason, as against one grounded in religious prohibitions which brooked no discussion.

One of the most important ways in which our age stands out from earlier ones concerns the second axis. A set of questions make sense to us which turn around the meaning of life and which would not have been fully understandable in earlier epochs. Moderns can anxiously doubt whether life has meaning, or wonder what its meaning is. However philosophers may be inclined to attack these formulations as vague or confused, the fact remains that we all have an immediate sense of what kind of worry is being articulated in these words.

We can perhaps get at the point of these questions in the following way. Questions along the second axis can arise for people in any culture. Someone in a warrior society might ask whether his tale of courageous deeds lives up to the promise of his lineage or the demands of his station. People in a religious culture often ask whether the demand of conventional piety are sufficient for them or whether they don't feel called to some purer, more dedicated vocation. Figures of this kind have founded most of the great religious orders in Christendom, for instance. But in each of these cases, some framework stands unquestioned which helps define the demands by which they judge their lives and measure, as it were, their fulness or emptiness: the space of fame in the memory and song of the tribe, or the call of God as made clear in revelation, or, to take another example, the hierarchical order of being in the universe.

It is now a commonplace about the modern world that it has made these frameworks problematic. On the level of explicit philosophical or theological doctrine, this is dramatically evident. Some traditional frameworks are discredited or downgraded to the status of personal predilection, like the space of fame. Others have ceased to be credible altogether in anything like their original form, like the Platonic notion of the order of being. The forms of revealed religion continue very much alive, but also highly contested. None forms the horizon of the whole society in the modern West.

This term 'horizon' is the one that is frequently used to make this point. What Weber called 'disenchantment', the dissipation of our sense of the cosmos as a meaningful order, has allegedly destroyed the horizons in which people previously lived their spiritual lives. Nietzsche used the term in his celebrated "God is dead" passage: "How could we drink up the sea? Who gave us the sponge to wipe away the whole horizon?"[10] Perhaps this way of putting it appeals above all to the intellectuals, who put a lot of stock in the explicit doctrines that people subscribe to, and anyway tend to be unbelievers. But the loss of horizon described by Nietzsche's fool undoubtedly corresponds to something very widely felt in our culture.

This is what I tried to describe with the phrase above, that frameworks today are problematic. This vague term points towards a relatively open disjunction of attitudes. What is common to them all is the sense that no framework is shared by everyone, can be taken for granted as *the* framework tout court, can sink to the phenomenological status of unquestioned fact. This basic understanding refracts differently in the stances people take. For some it may mean holding a definite traditionally defined view with the self-conscious sense of standing against a major part of one's compatriots. Others may hold the view but with a pluralist sense that it is one among others, right for us but not necessarily binding on them. Still others identify with a view but in the somewhat tentative, semi-provisional way I described above in section 1.2. This seems to them to come close to formulating what they believe, or to saying what for them seems to be the spiritual source they can connect their lives with; but they are aware of their own uncertainties, of how far they are from being able to recognize a definitive formulation with ultimate confidence. There is alway something tentative in their adhesion, and they may see themselves, as, in a sense, seeking. They are on a 'quest', in Alasdair MacIntyre's apt phrase.[11]

With these seekers, of course, we are taken beyond the gamut of traditionally available frameworks. Not only do they embrace these traditions tentatively, but they also often develop their own versions of them, or idiosyncratic combinations of or borrowings from or semi-inventions within them. And this provides the context within which the question of meaning has its place.

To the extent that one sees the finding of a believable framework as the object of a quest, to that extent it becomes intelligible that the search might fail. This might happen through personal inadequacy, but failure might also come from there being no ultimately believable framework. Why speak of this in terms of a loss of meaning? Partly because a framework is that in virtue of which we make sense of our lives spiritually. Not to have a framework is to fall into a life which is spiritually senseless. The quest is thus always a quest for sense.

But the invocation of meaning also comes from our awareness of how much the search involves articulation. We find the sense of life through articulating it. And moderns have become acutely aware of how much sense being there for us depends on our own powers of expression. Discovering here depends on, is interwoven with, inventing. Finding a sense to life depends on framing meaningful expressions which are adequate. There is thus something particularly appropriate to our condition in the polysemy of the word 'meaning': lives can have or lack it when they have or lack a point; while it also applies to language and other forms of expression. More and more, we moderns attain meaning in the first sense, when we do, through creating it in the second sense.

The problem of the meaning of life is therefore on our agenda, however much we may jibe at this phrase, either in the form of a threatened loss of meaning or because making sense of our life is the object of a quest. And those whose spiritual agenda is mainly defined in this way are in a fundamentally different existential predicament from that which dominated most previous cultures and still defines the lives of other people today. That alternative is a predicament in which an unchallengeable framework makes imperious demands which we fear being unable to meet. We face the prospect of irretrievable condemnation or exile, of being marked down in obloquy forever, or being sent to damnation irrevocably, or being relegated to a lower order through countless future lives. The pressure is potentially immense and inescapable, and we may crack under it. The form of the danger here is utterly different from that which threatens the modern seeker, which is something close to the opposite: the world loses altogether its spiritual contour, nothing is worth doing, the fear is of a terrifying emptiness, a kind of vertigo, or even a fracturing of our world and body-space.

To see the contrast, think of Luther, in his intense anguish and distress before his liberating moment of insight about salvation through faith, his sense of inescapable condemnation, irretrievably damning himself through the very instruments of salvation, the sacraments. However one might want to describe this, it was not a crisis of meaning. This term would have made no sense to Luther in its modern use that I have been describing here. The 'meaning' of life was all too unquestionable for this Augustinian monk, as it was for his whole age.[12]

The existential predicament in which one fears condemnation is quite different from the one where one fears, above all, meaninglessness. The dominance of the latter perhaps defines our age.[13] But even so, the former still exists for many, and the contrast may help us understand different moral stances in our society: the contrast between the moral majority of born-again evangelicals in the contemporary American West and South, on one hand, and their middle-class urban compatriots on the East Coast, on the other.

In a way which we cannot yet properly understand, the shift between these two existential predicaments seems to be matched by a recent change in the dominant patterns of psychopathology. It has frequently been remarked by psychoanalysts that the period in which hysterics and patients with phobias and fixations formed the bulk of their clientele, starting in their classical period with Freud, has recently given way to a time when the main complaints centre around "ego loss", or a sense of emptiness, flatness, futility, lack of purpose, or loss of self-esteem.[14] Just what the relation is between these styles of pathology and the non-pathological predicaments which parallel them is very unclear. In order even to have a serious try at understanding this, we would have to gain a better grasp of the structures of the self, something I want to attempt below. But it seems overwhelmingly plausible a priori that there is some relation; and that the comparatively recent shift in style of pathology reflects the generalization and popularization in our culture of that "loss of horizon", which a few alert spirits were foretelling for a century or more.

1.5

Of course, the same naturalist temper that I mentioned above, which would like to do without ontological claims altogether and just make do with moral reactions, is very suspicious of this talk of meaning and frameworks. People of this bent would like to declare this issue of meaning a pseudo-question and brand the various frameworks within which it finds an answer as gratuitous inventions. Some find this tempting for epistemological reasons: the stripped-down ontology which excludes these frameworks seems to them more in keeping with a scientific outlook. But there are also reasons deep in a certain moral outlook common in our time which push people in this direction. I hope to explain this more clearly below.

But just as with the ontological claims above underlying our respect for life, this radical reduction cannot be carried through. To see why is to understand something important about the place of these frameworks in our lives.

What I have been calling a framework incorporates a crucial set of qualitative distinctions. To think, feel, judge within such a framework is to function with the sense that some action, or mode of life, or mode of feeling is incomparably higher than the others which are more readily available to us. I am using 'higher' here in a generic sense. The sense of what the difference consists in may take different forms. One form of life may be seen as fuller, another way of feeling and acting as purer, a mode of feeling or living as deeper, a style of life as more admirable, a given demand as making an absolute claim against other merely relative ones, and so on.

I have tried to express what all these distinctions have in common by the term 'incomparable'. In each of these cases, the sense is that there are ends or goods which are worthy or desirable in a way that cannot be measured on the same scale as our ordinary ends, goods, desirabilia. They are not just *more* desirable, in the same sense though to a greater degree, than some of these ordinary goods are. Because of their special status they command our awe, respect, or admiration.

And this is where incomparability connects up with what I have been calling 'strong evaluation': the fact that these ends or goods stand independent of our own desires, inclinations, or choices, that they represent standards by which these desires and choices are judged. These are obviously two linked facets of the same sense of higher worth. The goods which command our awe must also function in some sense as standards for us.

Looking at some common examples of such frameworks will help to focus the discussion. One of the earliest in our civilization, and which is still alive for some people today, is that associated with the honour ethic. The life of the warrior, or citizen, or citizen-soldier is deemed higher than the merely private existence, devoted to the arts of peace and economic well-being. The higher life is marked out by the aura of fame and glory which attaches to it, or at least to signal cases, those who succeed in it brilliantly. To be in public life or to be a warrior is to be at least a candidate for fame. To be ready to hazard one's tranquility, wealth, even life for glory is the mark of a real man; and those who cannot bring themselves to this are judged with contempt as "womanish" (this outlook seems to be inherently sexist).

Against this, we have the celebrated and influential counter-position put forward by Plato. Virtue is no longer to be found in public life or in excelling in the warrior *agōn*. The higher life is that ruled by reason, and reason itself is defined in terms of a vision of order, in the cosmos and in the soul. The higher life is one in which reason—purity, order, limit, the unchanging—governs the desires, with their bent to excess, insatiability, fickleness, conflict.

Already in this transvaluation of values, something else has altered in addition to the content of the good life, far-reaching as this change is. Plato's ethic requires what we might call today a theory, a reasoned account of what human life is about, and why one way is higher than the others. This flows inescapably from the new moral status of reason. But the framework within which we act and judge doesn't need to be articulated theoretically. It isn't, usually, by those who live by the warrior ethic. They share certain discriminations: what is honourable and dishonouring, what is admirable, what is done and not done. It has often been remarked that to be a gentleman is to know how to behave without ever being told the rules. (And the "gentlemen" here are the heirs of the former warrior nobility.)

That is why I spoke above of acting within a framework as functioning with a 'sense' of a qualitative distinction. It can be only this; or it can be spelled out in a highly explicit way, in a philosophically formulated ontology or anthropology. In the case of some frameworks it may be optional whether one formulates them or not. But in other cases, the nature of the framework demands it, as with Plato, or seems to forbid it, as with the warrior-citizen ethic he attacked: this does seem to be refractory to theoretical formulation. Those who place a lot of importance on this latter tend to downplay or denigrate the role and powers of theory in human life.

But I want to mention this distinction here partly in order to avoid an error we easily fall victim to. We could conclude from the fact that some people operate without a philosophically defined framework that they are quite without a framework at all. And that might be totally untrue (indeed, I want to claim, always is untrue). For like our inarticulate warriors, their lives may be entirely structured by supremely important qualitative distinctions, in relation to which they literally live and die. This will be evident enough in the judgement calls they make on their own and others' action. But it may be left entirely to us, observers, historians, philosophers, anthropologists, to try to formulate explicitly what goods, qualities, or ends are here discriminated. It is this level of inarticulacy, at which we often function, that I try to describe when I speak of the 'sense' of a qualitative distinction.

Plato's distinction stands at the head of a large family of views which see the good life as a mastery of self which consists in the dominance of reason over desire. One of the most celebrated variants in the ancient world was Stoicism. And with the development of the modern scientific world-view a specifically modern variant has developed. This is the ideal of the disengaged self, capable of objectifying not only the surrounding world but also his own emotions and inclinations, fears and compulsions, and achieving thereby a kind of distance and self-possession which allows him to act 'rationally'. This last term has been put in quotes, because obviously its meaning has changed relative to the Platonic sense. Reason is no longer defined in terms of a vision of order in the cosmos, but rather is defined procedurally, in terms of instrumental efficacy, or maximization of the value sought, or self-consistency.

The framework of self-mastery through reason has also developed theistic variants, in Jewish and Christian thought. Indeed, it is one of them which first spawned the ideal of disengagement. But the marriage with Platonism, or with Greek philosophy in general, was always uneasy; and another, specifically Christian, theme has also been very influential in our civilization. This is the understanding of the higher life as coming from a transformation of the will. In the original theological conception, this change is the work of grace, but it has also gone through a number of secularizing transpositions. And variants of both forms, theological and secular, structure people's lives today. Perhaps the most important form of this ethic today is the ideal of altruism. With the decline of the specifically theological definition of the nature of a transformed will, a formulation of the crucial distinction of higher and lower in terms of altruism and selfishness comes to the fore. This now has a dominant place in modern thought and sensibility about what is incomparably higher in life. Real dedication to others or to the universal good wins our admiration and even in signal cases our awe. The crucial quality which commands our respect here is a certain direction of the will. This is very different from the spirit of Platonic self-mastery, where the issue turns on the hegemony of reason, however much that spirit may overlap in practice with altruism (and the overlap is far from complete). And for all its obvious roots in Christian spirituality, and perfect compatibility with it, the secular ethic of altruism has discarded something essential to the Christian outlook, once the love of God no longer plays a role.

Alongside ethics of fame, of rational mastery and control, of the transformation of the will, there has grown up in the last two centuries a distinction based on vision and expressive power. There is a set of ideas and intuitions, still inadequately understood, which makes us admire the artist and the creator more than any other civilization ever has; which convinces us that a life spent in artistic creation or performance is eminently worthwhile. This complex of ideas itself has Platonic roots. We are taking up a semi-suppressed side of Plato's thought which emerges, for instance, in the *Phaedrus,* where he seems to think of the poet, inspired by mania, as capable of seeing what sober people are not. The widespread belief today that the artist sees farther than the rest of us, attested by our willingness to take seriously the opinions about politics expressed by painters or singers, even though they may have no more special expertise in public affairs than the next person, seems to spring from the same roots. But there is also something quintessentially modern in this outlook. It depends on that modern sense, invoked in the previous section, that what meaning there is for us depends in part on our powers of expression, that discovering a framework is interwoven with inventing.

But this rapid sketch of some of the most important distinctions which structure people's lives today will be even more radically incomplete if I do not take account of the fact with which I started this section: that there is a widespread temper, which I called 'naturalist', which is tempted to deny these frameworks altogether. We see this not only in those enamoured of reductive explanations but in another way in classical utilitarianism. The aim of this philosophy was precisely to reject all qualitative distinctions and to construe all human goals as on the same footing, susceptible therefore of common quantification and calculation according to some common 'currency'. My thesis here is that this idea is deeply mistaken. But as I said above, it is motivated itself by moral reasons, and these reasons form an essential part of the picture of the frameworks people live by in our day.

This has to do with what I called in section 1.3 the 'affirmation of ordinary life'. The notion that the life of production and reproduction, of work and the family, is the main locus of the good life flies in the face of what were originally the dominant distinctions of our civilization. For both the warrior ethic and the Platonic, ordinary life in this sense is part of the lower range, part of what contrasts with the incomparably higher. The affirmation of ordinary life therefore involves a polemical stance towards these traditional views and their implied elitism. This was true of the Reformation theologies, which are the main source of the drive to this affirmation in modern times.

It is this polemical stance, carried over and transposed in secular guise, which powers the reductive views like utilitarianism which want to denounce all qualitative distinctions. They are all accused, just as the honour ethic or the monastic ethic of supererogation was earlier, of wrongly and perversely downgrading ordinary life, of failing to see that our destiny lies here in production and reproduction and not in some alleged higher sphere, of being blind to the dignity and worth of ordinary human desire and fulfilment.

In this, naturalism and utilitarianism touch a strong nerve of modern sensibility, and this explains some of their persuasive force. My claim is here that they are nevertheless deeply confused. For the affirmation of ordinary life, while necessarily denouncing certain distinctions, itself amounts to one; else it has no meaning at all. The notion that there is a certain dignity and worth in this life requires a contrast; no longer, indeed, between this life and some "higher" activity like contemplation, war, active citizenship, or heroic asceticism, but now lying between different ways of living the life of production and reproduction. The notion is never that *whatever* we do is acceptable. This would be unintelligible as the basis for a notion of dignity. Rather the key point is that the higher is to be found not outside of but as a *manner of living* ordinary life. For the Reformers this manner was defined theologically; for classical utilitarians, in terms of (instrumental) rationality. For Marxists, the expressivist element of free self-creation is added to Enlightenment rationality. But in all cases, some distinction is maintained between the higher, the admirable life and the lower life of sloth, irrationality, slavery, or alienation.

Once one sets aside the naturalist illusion, however, what remains is an extremely important fact about modern moral consciousness: a tension between the affirmation of ordinary life, to which we moderns are strongly drawn, and some of our most important moral distinctions. Indeed, it is too simple to speak of a tension. We are in conflict, even confusion, about what it means to affirm ordinary life. What for some is the highest affirmation is for others blanket denial. Think of the utilitarian attack on orthodox Christianity; then of Dostoyevsky's attack on utilitarian utopian engineering. For those who are not firmly aligned on one side or the other of an ideological battle, this is the source of a deep uncertainty. We are as ambivalent about heroism as we are about the value of the workaday goals that it sacrifices. We struggle to hold on to a vision of the incomparably higher, while being true to the central modern insights about the value of ordinary life. We sympathize with both the hero and the anti-hero; and we dream of a world in which one could be in the same act both. This is the confusion in which naturalism takes root.

2

THE SELF IN MORAL SPACE

2.1

I said at the beginning of section 1.5 that the naturalist reduction which would exclude frameworks altogether from consideration cannot be carried through, and that to see why this is so is to understand something important about the place of frameworks in our lives. Having seen a little better what these frameworks consist in, I want now to pursue this point.

In sections 1.4 and 1.5 I have been talking about these qualitative distinctions in their relation to the issue of the meaning of life. But it is plain that distinctions of this kind play a role in all three dimensions of moral assessment that I identified above. The sense that human beings are capable of some kind of higher life forms part of the background for our belief that they are fit objects of respect, that their life and integrity is sacred or enjoys immunity, and is not to be attacked. As a consequence, we can see our conception of what this immunity consists in evolving with the development of new frameworks. Thus the fact that we now place such importance on expressive power means that our contemporary notions of what it is to respect people's integrity includes that of protecting their expressive freedom to express and develop their own opinions, to define their own life conceptions, to draw up their own life-plans.

At the same time, the third dimension too involves distinctions of this kind. The dignity of the warrior, the citizen, the householder, and so on repose on the background understanding that some special value attaches to these forms of life or to the rank or station that these people have attained within them.

Indeed, one of the examples above, the honour ethic, has plainly been the background for a very widespread understanding of dignity, which attaches to the free citizen or warrior-citizen and to an even higher degree to someone who plays a major role in public life. This goes on being an important dimension of our life in modern society, and the fierce competition for this kind of dignity is part of what animates democratic politics.

These distinctions, which I have been calling frameworks, are thus woven in different ways into the three dimensions of our moral life. And this means, of course, that they are of differential importance. I want to explore here a little further just how they interweave through our moral existence.

The first way is the one that I have already discussed. Frameworks provide the background, explicit or implicit, for our moral judgements, intuitions, or reactions in any of the three dimensions. To articulate a framework is to explicate what makes sense of our moral responses. That is, when we try to spell out what it is that we presuppose when we judge that a certain form of life is truly worthwhile, or place our dignity in a certain achievement or status, or define our moral obligations in a certain manner, we find ourselves articulating inter alia what I have been calling here 'frameworks'.

In a sense, this might be thought to offer a sufficient answer to the naturalist attempt to sideline frameworks. We might just reply to whoever propounds this reductive thesis with the ad hominem point that they also make judgements about what is worthwhile, have a sense of dignity, and so on, and that they cannot simply reject the preconditions of these beliefs and attitudes making sense.

But the ad hominem argument doesn't seem to go deep enough. We might think that although almost all the protagonists of naturalist reduction can themselves be caught making the kind of distinctions which presuppose what they are rejecting, this doesn't dispose of the question whether we could in principle do without frameworks altogether—whether, in short, adopting them is ultimately to be seen as an optional stance for human beings, however difficult it in fact has been to avoid them throughout most of previous human history.

What tends to lend credence to the view that they are so optional is just the developing 'disenchantment' of modern culture, which I discussed in section 1.4 and which has undermined so many traditional frameworks and, indeed, created the situation in which our old horizons have been swept away and all frameworks may appear problematical—the situation in which the problem of meaning arises for us. In earlier ages, the reasoning might run, when the major definition of our existential predicament was one in which we feared above all condemnation, where an unchallengeable framework made imperious demands on us, it is understandable that people saw their frameworks as enjoying the same ontological solidity as the very structure of the universe. But the very fact that what was once so solid has in many cases melted into air shows that we are dealing not with something grounded in the nature of being, but rather with changeable human interpretations. Why is it impossible, then, to conceive a person or even a culture which might so understand this predicament as to do altogether without frameworks, that is, without these qualitative discriminations of the incomparably higher? The fact that we may always be able to catch our contemporaries still clinging to some such in their actual lives and judgements does nothing to show that they are grounded on anything beyond ultimately dispensable interpretation.

So runs a currently persuasive argument in favour of the reductive thesis. And this is precisely the thesis I oppose. I want to defend the strong thesis that doing without frameworks is utterly impossible for us; otherwise put, that the horizons within which we live our lives and which make sense of them have to include these strong qualitative discriminations. Moreover, this is not meant just as a contingently true psychological fact about human beings, which could perhaps turn out one day not to hold for some exceptional individual or new type, some superman of disengaged objectification. Rather the claim is that living within such strongly qualified horizons is constitutive of human agency, that stepping outside these limits would be tantamount to stepping outside what we would recognize as integral, that is, undamaged human personhood.

Perhaps the best way to see this is to focus on the issue that we usually describe today as the question of identity. We speak of it in these terms because the question is often spontaneously phrased by people in the form: Who am I? But this can't necessarily be answered by giving name and genealogy. What does answer this question for us is an understanding of what is of crucial importance to us. To know who I am is a species of knowing where I stand. My identity is defined by the commitments and identifications which provide the frame or horizon within which I can try to determine from case to case what is good, or valuable, or what ought to be done, or what I endorse or oppose. In other words, it is the horizon within which I am capable of taking a stand.

People may see their identity as defined partly by some moral or spiritual commitment, say as a Catholic, or an anarchist. Or they may define it in part by the nation or tradition they belong to, as an Armenian, say, or a Québecois. What they are saying by this is not just that they are strongly attached to this spiritual view or background; rather it is that this provides the frame within which they can determine where they stand on questions of what is good, or worthwhile, or admirable, or of value. Put counterfactually, they are saying that were they to lose this commitment or identification, they would be at sea, as it were; they wouldn't know anymore, for an important range of questions, what the significance of things was for them.

And this situation does, of course, arise for some people. It's what we call an 'identity crisis', an acute form of disorientation, which people often express in terms of not knowing who they are, but which can also be seen as a radical uncertainty of where they stand. They lack a frame or horizon within which things can take on a stable significance, within which some life possibilities can be seen as good or meaningful, others as bad or trivial. The meaning of all these possibilities is unfixed, labile, or undetermined. This is a painful and frightening experience.

What this brings to light is the essential link between identity and a kind of orientation. To know who you are is to be oriented in moral space, a space in which questions arise about what is good or bad, what is worth doing and what not, what has meaning and importance for you and what is trivial and secondary. I feel myself drawn here to use a spatial metaphor; but I believe this to be more than personal predilection. There are signs that the link with spatial orientation lies very deep in the human psyche. In some very extreme cases of what are described as "narcissistic personality disorders", which take the form of a radical uncertainty about oneself and about what is of value to one, patients show signs of spatial disorientation as well at moments of acute crisis. The disorientation and uncertainty about where one stands as a person seems to spill over into a loss of grip on one's stance in physical space.[1]

Why this link between identity and orientation? Or perhaps we could put the question this way: What induces us to talk about moral orientation in terms of the question, Who are we? This second formulation points us towards the fact that we haven't always done so. Talk about 'identity' in the modern sense would have been incomprehensible to our forebears of a couple of centuries ago. Erikson[2] has made a perceptive study of Luther's crisis of faith and reads it in the light of contemporary identity crises, but Luther himself, of course, would have found this description reprehensible if not utterly incomprehensible. Underlying our modern talk of identity is the notion that questions of moral orientation cannot all be solved in simply universal terms. And this is connected to our post-Romantic understanding of individual differences as well as to the importance we give to expression in each person's discovery of his or her moral horizon. For someone in Luther's age, the issue of the basic moral frame orienting one's action could *only* be put in universal terms. Nothing else made sense. This is linked, of course, with the crisis for Luther turning around the acute sense of condemnation and irremediable exile, rather than around a modern sense of meaningless-ness, or lack of purpose, or emptiness.

So one part of the answer to our question is historical; certain developments in our self-understanding are a precondition of our putting the issue in terms of identity. Seeing this will also prevent us from exaggerating our differences with earlier ages. For most of us, certain fundamental moral questions are still put in universal terms: those, for instance, which we stated in section 1.1, dealing with people's rights to life and integrity. What differentiates us from our forebears is just that we don't see all such questions as framed in these terms as a matter of course. But this also means that our identities, as defined by whatever gives us our fundamental orientation, are in fact complex and many-tiered. We are all framed by what we see as universally valid commitments (being a Catholic or an anarchist, in my example above) and also by what we understand as particular identifications (being an Armenian or a Québecois). We often declare our identity as defined by only one of these, because this is what is salient in our lives, or what is put in question. But in fact our identity is deeper and more many-sided than any of our possible articulations of it.

But the second facet of the question above is not historical. It is rather: Why do we think of fundamental orientation in terms of the question, Who? The question Who? is asked to place someone as a potiential interlocutor in a society of interlocutors. Who is this speaking? we say over the phone. Or who is that? pointing to some person across the room. The answer comes in the form of a name: 'I'm Joe Smith', often accompanied by a statement of relationship: 'I'm Mary's brother-in-law', or by a statement of social role: 'It's the repair man', or 'the man you're pointing to is the President'. The slightly more aggressive form: 'Who (the hell) do you think you are?' calls for the latter type of answer. To be someone who qualifies as a potential object of this question is to be such an interlocutor among others, someone with one's own standpoint or one's own role, who can speak for him/herself. Of course, I can ask the question, Who?—pointing to someone lying over there in an irreversible coma. But this is obviously a derivative case: beings of whom one can ask this question are normally either actually or potentially capable of answering for themselves.

But to be able to answer for oneself is to know where one stands, what one wants to answer. And that is why we naturally tend to talk of our fundamental orientation in terms of who we are. To lose this orientation, or not to have found it, is not to know who one is. And this orientation, once attained, defines where you answer from, hence your identity.

But then what emerges from all this is that we think of this fundamental moral orientation as essential to being a human interlocutor, capable of answering for oneself. But to speak of orientation is to presuppose a space-analogue within which one finds one's way. To understand our predicament in terms of finding or losing orientation in moral space is to take the space which our frameworks seek to define as ontologically basic. The issue is, through what framework-definition can I find my bearings in it? In other words, we take as basic that the human agent exists in a space of questions. And these are the questions to which our framework-definitions are answers, providing the horizon within which we know where we stand, and what meanings things have for us.

That this is so, that the space in question is one which must be mapped by strong evaluations or qualitative distinctions, emerges from the above discussion. It is not just that the commitments and identifications by which we in fact define our identity involve such strong evaluations, as the above examples make clear, or just that the issue of identity is invariably for us a matter itself of strongly valued good—an identity is something that one ought to be true to, can fail to uphold, can surrender when one ought to. More fundamentally, we can see that it only plays the role of orienting us, of providing the frame within which things have meaning for us, by virtue of the qualitative distinctions it incorporates. Even more, it is difficult to see how anything could play this role which didn't incorporate such distinctions. Our identity is what allows us to define what is important to us and what is not. It is what makes possible these discriminations, including those which turn on strong evaluations. It hence couldn't be entirely without such evaluations. The notion of an identity defined by some mere de facto, not strongly valued preference is incoherent. And what is more, how could the absence of some such preference be felt as a disorienting lack? The condition of there being such a thing as an identity crisis is precisely that our identities define the space of qualitative distinctions within which we live and choose.

But if this is so, then the naturalist supposition that we might be able to do without frameworks altogether is wildly wrong. This is based on a quite different picture, that of human agency where one could answer the question, Who? without accepting any qualitative distinctions, just on the basis of desires and aversions, likes and dislikes. On this picture, frameworks are things we invent, not answers to questions which inescapably pre-exist for us, independent of our answer or inability to answer. To see frameworks as orientations, however, does cast them in this latter light. One orients oneself in a space which exists independently of one's success or failure in finding one's bearings, which, moreover, makes the task of finding these bearings inescapable. Within this picture, the notion of inventing a qualitative distinction out of whole cloth makes no sense. For one can only *adopt* such distinctions as make sense to one within one's basic orientation.

The distinction between the two views can perhaps be put this way: the idea that we invent distinctions out of whole cloth is equivalent to the notion that we invent the questions as well as the answers. We all think of some issues as factitious in this sense. To take a trivial example: if we see a dispute in some society about what is the fashionable way to wear a bowler hat, flat or at a rakish angle, we would all agree that this whole issue might easily not have existed. It would have sufficed that no one have invented the bowler hat. On a more serious level, some atheists take this view towards the dispute among different religions over what one might call the shape of the supernatural—whether we speak in terms of the God of Abraham, or of Brahman, or of Nirvana, and so on. The whole issue area in which these answers make sense didn't need to arise, these atheists believe, and one day might totally disappear from human concern. By contrast, our orientation in space is not the answer to a factitious, dispensable issue. We couldn't conceive of a human life form where one day people came to reflect that, since they were spatial beings, they ought after all to develop a sense of up and down, right and left, and find landmarks which would enable them to get around—reflections which might be disputed by others. We can't conceive of a form in which this question is not always already there, demanding an answer. We can't distance ourselves from the issue of spatial orientation or fail to stumble on it—as with the right angle for bowler hats—or repudiate it, as the atheists imagine we can for religion.

The naturalist view would relegate the issue of what framework to adopt to the former category, as an ultimately factitious question. But our discussion of identity indicates rather that it belongs to the class of the inescapable, i.e., that it belongs to human agency to exist in a space of questions about strongly valued goods, prior to all choice or adventitious cultural change. This discussion thus throws up a strong challenge to the naturalist picture. In the light of our understanding of identity, the portrait of an agent free from all frameworks rather spells for us a person in the grip of an appalling identity crisis. Such a person wouldn't know where he stood on issues of fundamental importance, would have no orientation in these issues whatever, wouldn't be able to answer for himself on them. If one wants to add to the portrait by saying that the person doesn't suffer this absence of frameworks as a lack, isn't in other words in a crisis at all, then one rather has a picture of frightening dissociation. In practice, we should see such a person as deeply disturbed. He has gone way beyond the fringes of what we think as shallowness: people we judge as shallow do have a sense of what is incomparably important, only we think their commitments trivial, or merely conventional, or not deeply thought out or chosen. But a person without a framework altogether would be outside our space of interlocution; he wouldn't have a stand in the space where the rest of us are. We would see this as pathological.

What is, of course, easily understandable as a human type is a person who has decided that he ought not to accept the traditional frameworks distinguishing higher and lower ends, that what he ought to do is calculate rationally about happiness, that this form of life is more admirable, or reflects a higher moral benevolence, than following the traditional definitions of virtue, piety, and the like. This is even a familiar picture. It is the utilitarian ideologue, who has played such a role in our culture. But this person doesn't lack a framework. On the contrary, he has a strong commitment to a certain ideal of rationality and benevolence. He admires people who live up to this ideal, condemns those who fail or who are too confused even to accept it, feels wrong when he himself falls below it. The utilitarian lives within a moral horizon which cannot be explicated by his own moral theory. This is one of the great weaknesses of utilitarianism. But because this horizon can be easily forgotten in favour of the facts and situations one deals with within it, this framework can be disregarded, and the picture is accredited of a framework-less agent. But once one becomes aware of how human agents are inescapably in a space of such moral questions, it springs to light that the utilitarian is very much one of us, and the imagined agent of naturalist theory is a monster.

But the naturalist might protest: Why do I have to accept what emerges from this phenomenological account of identity? For so he might want to describe it, and he wouldn't be entirely wrong. The answer is that this is not only a phenomenological account but an exploration of the limits of the conceivable in human life, an account of its "transcendental conditions". It may be wrong in detail, of course; and the challenge is always there to provide a better one. But if it's correct, the objection that arises for naturalism is decisive. For the aim of this account is to examine how we actually make sense of our lives, and to draw the limits of the conceivable from our knowledge of what we actually do when we do so. But what description of human possibilities, drawn from some questionable epistemological theories, ought to trump what we can descry from within our practice itself as the limits of our possible ways of making sense of our lives? After all, the ultimate basis for accepting any of these theories is precisely that they make better sense of us than do their rivals. If any view takes us right across the boundary and defines as normal or possible a human life which we would find incomprehensible and pathological, it can't be right. It is on these grounds that I oppose the naturalist thesis and say that the horizons in which we live *must* include strong qualitative discriminations.

2.2

I recognize that there is a crucial argument here which I have stated all too briefly. I will return to it below, in the next chapter. But for the moment, I want to pursue something else, viz., the connection that came to light in the above discussion between identity and the good.

We talk about a human being as a 'self'. The word is used in all sorts of ways; and we shall see in Part II that this whole language is historically conditioned. But there is a sense of the term where we speak of people as selves, meaning that they are beings of the requisite depth and complexity to have an identity in the above sense (or to be struggling to find one). We have to distinguish this from all sorts of other uses which have cropped up in psychology and sociology. I remember an experiment designed to show that chimps too have 'a sense of self': an animal with paint marks on its face, seeing itself in the mirror, reached with its paws to its own face to clean it. It somehow recognized that this mirror image was of its own body.[3] Obviously, this involves a very different sense of the term from the one I wish to invoke.

Nor is it sufficient to be a self in the sense that one can steer one's action strategically in the light of certain factors, including one's own desires, capacities, etc. This is part of what is meant by having (or being) an Ego in the Freudian sense, and in related uses. This strategic capacity requires some kind of reflective awareness. But there is an important difference. It is not essential to the Ego that it orient itself in a space of questions about the good, that it stand somewhere on these questions. Rather the reverse. The Freudian Ego is at its freest, is most capable of exercising control, when it has the maximal margin of manoeuvre in relation to the imperious demands of the Superego as well as in the face of the urgings of the Id. The ideally free Ego would be a lucid calculator of pay-offs.

The Ego or Self also enters psychology and sociology in another way, in connection with the observation that people have a 'self-image' which matters to them; that they strive to appear in a good light in the eyes of those they come in contact with as well as in their own. Here there is indeed a sense of self which goes beyond neutral self-observation and calculations of benefits. But in the way this is usually conceived, the importance of image bears no connection to identity. It is seen as a fact about human beings that they care that their image matches up to certain standards, generally socially induced. But this is not seen as something which is essential to human personhood. On the contrary, what is usually studied under this head is what we can identify, outside the sterilized, "value-free" language of social science, as the all-too-human weakness of "ego" and "image" in the everyday sense of these terms (themselves, of course, incorporated into the vernacular from social science). The ideally strong character would be maximally free of them, would not be deterred by the adverse opinions of others, and would be able to face unflinchingly the truth about himself or herself.[4]

By contrast, the notion of self which connects it to our need for identity is meant to pick out this crucial feature of human agency, that we cannot do without some orientation to the good, that we each essentially are (i.e., define ourselves at least inter alia by) where we stand on this. What it is to be a self or person of this kind is difficult to conceive for certain strands of modern philosophy and above all for those which have become enshrined in mainstream psychology and social science. The self, even in this sense, ought to be an object of study like any other. But there are certain things which are generally held true of objects of scientific study which don't hold of the self. To see the conceptual obstacles here, it would help to enumerate four of these.

1. The object of study is to be taken "absolutely", that is, not in its meaning for us or any other subject, but as it is on its own ("objectively").

2. The object is what it is independent of any descriptions or interpretations offered of it by any subjects.

3. The object can in principle be captured in explicit description.

4. The object can in principle be described without reference to its surroundings.

The first two features correspond to a central feature of the great seventeenth-century revolution in natural science, that we should cease trying to explain the world around us in subjective, anthropocentric, or "secondary" properties. I have discussed this elsewhere.[5] But, of course, neither of these features holds of the self. We are selves only in that certain issues matter for us. What I am as a self, my identity, is essentially defined by the way things have significance for me. And as has been widely discussed, these things have significance for me, and the issue of my identity is worked out, only through a language of interpretation which I have come to accept as a valid articulation of these issues.[6] To ask what a person is, in abstraction from his or her self-interpretations, is to ask a fundamentally misguided question, one to which there couldn't in principle be an answer.

So one crucial fact about a self or person that emerges from all this is that it is not like an object in the usually understood sense. We are not selves in the way that we are organisms, or we don't have selves in the way we have hearts and livers. We are living beings with these organs quite independently of our self-understandings or -interpretations, or the meanings things have for us. But we are only selves insofar as we move in a certain space of questions, as we seek and find an orientation to the good.[7]

That the self will fail to exhibit the third feature of the classical object of study is already implicit in its failure on the second. The self is partly constituted by its self-interpretations; this is what made it fail to match the second feature. But the self's interpretations can never be fully explicit. Full articulacy is an impossibility. The language we have come to accept articulates the issues of the good for us. But we cannot have fully articulated what we are taking as given, what we are simply counting with, in using this language. We can, of course, try to increase our understanding of what is implicit in our moral and evaluative languages. This can even be an ideal, one which, for instance, Socrates imposed on his unwilling and frustrated interlocutors in Athens, until they shut him up once and for all. But articulation can by its very nature never be completed. We clarify one language with another, which in turn can be further unpacked, and so on. Wittgenstein has made this point familiar.

But why is this a point specifically about the self? Doesn't it apply to any language, even that of the scientific description of objects? Yes, of course. But it is in the case of the self that the language which can never be made fully explicit is part of, internal to, or constitutive of the "object" studied. To study persons is to study beings who only exist in, or are partly constituted by, a certain language.[8]

This brings us to the fourth feature. A language only exists and is maintained within a language community. And this indicates another crucial feature of a self. One is a self only among other selves. A self can never be described without reference to those who surround it.

This has become an important point to make, because not only the philosophico-scientific tradition but also a powerful modern aspiration to freedom and individuality have conspired to produce an identity which seems to be a negation of this. Just how this happened is a central theme that I will trace in Part II. But I would like to show here how this modern independence of the self is no negation of the fact that a self only exists among other selves.

This point is already implicit in the very notion of 'identity', as we saw above. My self-definition is understood as an answer to the question Who I am. And this question finds its original sense in the interchange of speakers. I define who I am by defining where I speak from, in the family tree, in social space, in the geography of social statuses and functions, in my intimate relations to the ones I love, and also crucially in the space of moral and spiritual orientation within which my most important defining relations are lived out.

This obviously cannot be just a contingent matter. There is no way we could be inducted into personhood except by being initiated into a language. We first learn our languages of moral and spiritual discernment by being brought into an ongoing conversation by those who bring us up. The meanings that the key words first had for me are the meanings they have for *us*, that is, for me and my conversation partners together. Here a crucial feature of conversation is relevant, that in talking about something you and I make it an object for us together, that is, not just an object for me which happens also to be one for you, even if we add that I know that it's an object for you, and you know, etc. The object is for us in a strong sense, which I have tried to describe elsewhere[9] with the notion of 'public' or 'common space'. The various uses of language set up, institute, focus, or activate such common spaces, just as it would appear the very first acquisition of language depends on a proto-variant of it, as seems indicated in the pioneering work of Jerome Bruner.[10]

So I can only learn what anger, love, anxiety, the aspiration to wholeness, etc., are through my and others' experience of these being objects for *us*, in some common space. This is the truth behind Wittgenstein's dictum that agreement in meanings involves agreement in judgements.[11] Later, I may innovate. I may develop an original way of understanding myself and human life, at least one which is in sharp disagreement with my family and background. But the innovation can only take place from the base in our common language. Even as the most independent adult, there are moments when I cannot clarify what I feel until I talk about it with certain special partner(s), who know me, or have wisdom, or with whom I have an affinity. This incapacity is a mere shadow of the one the child experiences. For him, everything would be confusion, there would be no language of discernment at all, without the conversations which fix this language for him.

This is the sense in which one cannot be a self on one's own. I am a self only in relation to certain interlocutors: in one way in relation to those conversation partners who were essential to my achieving self-definition; in another in relation to those who are now crucial to my continuing grasp of languages of self-understanding—and, of course, these classes may overlap. A self exists only within what I call 'webs of interlocution'.[12]

It is this original situation which gives its sense to our concept of 'identity', offering an answer to the question of who I am through a definition of where I am speaking from and to whom.[13] The full definition of someone's identity thus usually involves not only his stand on moral and spiritual matters but also some reference to a defining community. These two dimensions were reflected in the examples which quite naturally came to mind in my discussion above, where I spoke of identifying oneself as a Catholic or an anarchist, or as an Armenian or a Québecois. Normally, however, one dimension would not be exclusive of the other. Thus it might be essential to the self-definition of A that he is a Catholic and a Québecois; of B that he is an Armenian and an anarchist. (And these descriptions might not exhaust the identity of either.)

What I have been trying to suggest in this discussion is that these two dimensions of identity-definition reflect the original situation out of which the whole issue of identity arises.

But this second definition tends to become occluded. Modern culture has developed conceptions of individualism which picture the human person as, at least potentially, finding his or her own bearings within, declaring independence from the webs of interlocution which have originally formed him/her, or at least neutralizing them. It's as though the dimension of interlocution were of significance only for the genesis of individuality, like the training wheels of nursery school, to be left behind and to play no part in the finished person. What has given currency to these views?

In a sense, this will be one of the major themes of later parts, where I will trace some of the history of the modern identity. But I need to say a word about it here in order to overcome a common confusion.

First, it is clear that the most important spiritual traditions of our civilization have encouraged, even demanded, a detachment from the second dimension of identity as this is normally lived, that is, from particular, historic communities, from the given webs of birth and history. If we transpose this discussion out of the modern language of identity, which would be anachronistic in talking about the ancients, and talk instead of how they found their spiritual bearings, then it is plain that the ideal of detachment comes to us from both sides of our heritage. In the writings of the prophets and the Psalms, we are addressed by people who stood out against the almost unanimous obloquy of their communities in order to deliver God's message. In a parallel development, Plato describes a Socrates who was firmly rooted enough in philosophical reason to be able to stand in imperious independence of Athenian opinion.

But it is important to see how this stance, which has become a powerful ideal for us, however little we may live up to it in practice, transforms our position within, but by no means takes us out of, what I have called the original situation of identity-formation. It goes on being true of such heroes that they define themselves not just genetically but as they are today, in conversation with others. They are still in a web, but the one they define themselves by is no longer the given historical community. It is the saving remnant, or the community of like-minded souls, or the company of philosophers, or the small group of wise men in the mass of fools, as the Stoics saw it, or the close circle of friends that played such a role in Epicurean thought.[14] Taking the heroic stance doesn't allow one to leap out of the human condition, and it remains true that one can elaborate one's new language only through conversation in a broad sense, that is, through some kind of interchange with others with whom one has some common understanding about what is at stake in the enterprise. A human being can always be original, can step beyond the limits of thought and vision of contemporaries, can even be quite misunderstood by them. But the drive to original vision will be hampered, will ultimately be lost in inner confusion, unless it can be placed in some way in relation to the language and vision of others.

Even where I believe that I see a truth about the human condition that no one else has seen—a condition that Nietzsche seems to have approached sometimes—it still must be on the basis of my reading of others' thought and language. I see the 'genealogy' underlying their morality, and therefore hold them too to be (unwitting and unwilling) witnesses to my insight. Somehow I have to meet the challenge: Do I know what I'm saying? Do I really grasp what I'm talking about? And this challenge I can only meet by confronting my thought and language with the thought and reactions of others.

Of course, there is a big difference between the situation, on one hand, where I work out where I stand in conversation only with my immediate historic community and where I don't feel confirmed in what I believe unless we see eye to eye, and the case, on the other hand, where I rely mainly on a community of the like-minded, and where confirmation can take the form of my being satisfied that they give unwitting testimony to my views, that their thought and language bespeak contact with the same reality, which I see clearer than they. The gap gets even bigger when we reflect that in the latter case, the 'conversation' will no longer be exclusively with living contemporaries, but will include, e.g., prophets, thinkers, writers who are dead. What is the point of my insisting that the thesis about interlocution holds in spite of this gap?

The point is to insist on what I might call this 'transcendental' condition of our having a grasp on our own language, that we in some fashion confront it or relate it to the language of others. This is not just a recommended policy of the kind that suggests if you check your beliefs against others' you'll avoid some falsehoods. In speaking of a 'transcendental' condition here, I am pointing to the way in which the very confidence that we know what we mean, and hence our having our own original language, depends on this relating. The original and (ontogenetically) inescapable context of such relating is the face-to-face one in which we actually agree. We are inducted into language by being brought to see things as our tutors do. Later, and only for part of our language, we can deviate, and this thanks to our relating to absent partners as well and to our confronting our thought with any partner in this new, indirect way, through a reading of the disagreement. And even here, not *all* the confronting can be through dissent.

I stress the continuity between the later, higher, more independent stance and the earlier, more "primitive" form of immersion in community not just because the second is necessarily ontogenetically prior, and not even just because the first stance can never be adopted across the whole range of thought and language, so that our independent positions remain embedded, as it were, in relations of immersion. I also want to point out how through language we remain related to partners of discourse, either in real, live exchanges, or in indirect confrontations. The nature of our language and the fundamental dependence of our thought on language makes interlocution in one or other of these forms inescapable for us.[15]

The reason why this is an important point to make is that the development of certain modern character forms, of a highly independent individualism, has brought along with it, understandably if mistakenly, certain views of selfhood and language which have denied it or lost it utterly from sight. For instance, the early modern theories of language, from Hobbes through Locke to Condillac, presented it as an instrument potentially inventable by individuals. A private language was a real possibility on these views.[16] This idea continues to bewitch us in this age. We have only to think of the sense of fresh insight we gain, or alternatively, of the resistance and disbelief we feel, when we first read Wittgenstein's celebrated arguments against the possibility of a private language. Both are testimony to the hold of certain deeply entrenched modes of thought in modern culture. Again, a common picture of the self, as (at least potentially and ideally) drawing its purposes, goals, and life-plans out of itself, seeking "relationships" only insofar as they are "fulfilling", is largely based on ignoring our embedding in webs of interlocution.

It seems somehow easy to read the step to an independent stance as a stepping altogether outside the transcendental condition of interlocution—or else as showing that we were never within it and only needed the courage to make clear our basic, ontological independence. Bringing out the transcendental condition is a way of heading this confusion off. And this allows the change to appear in its true light. We may sharply shift the balance in our definition of identity, dethrone the given, historic community as a pole of identity, and relate only to the community defined by adherence to the good (of the saved, or the true believers, or the wise). But this doesn't sever our dependence on webs of interlocution. It only changes the webs, and the nature of our dependence.

Indeed, we can go even further and define ourselves explicitly in relation to no web at all. Certain Romantic views of the self, drawing its sustenance from nature within and the great world of nature without, tend in this direction, as do their debased derivatives in modern culture. And a close cousin to Romanticism is the self of the American Transcendentalists, in a sense containing the universe, but bypassing any necessary relation to other humans. But these grandiose aspirations do nothing to lift the transcendental conditions.

This kind of individualism, and the illusions which go with it, is peculiarly powerful in American culture. As Robert Bellah and his co-authors point out,[17] Americans have built on the earlier Puritan tradition of "leaving home". In early Connecticut, for instance, all young persons had to go through their own, individual conversion, had to establish their own relation to God, to be allowed full membership in the church. And this has grown into the American tradition of leaving home: the young person has to go out, to leave the parental background, to make his or her own way in the world. In contemporary conditions, this can transpose even into abandoning the political or religious convictions of the parents. And yet we can talk without paradox of an American 'tradition' of leaving home. The young person learns the independent stance, but this stance is also something expected of him or her. Moreover, what an independent stance involves is defined by the culture, in a continuing conversation into which that young person is inducted (and in which the meaning of independence can also alter with time). Nothing illustrates better the transcendental embedding of independence in interlocution. Each young person may take up a stance which is authentically his or her own; but the very possibility of this is enframed in a social understanding of great temporal depth, in fact, in a "tradition".

It would be to forget the distinction between the transcendental conditions and our actual stance to think that this enframing in tradition simply makes a mockery of the emphasis on independent, self-reliant individuals. Of course the independence can become a very shallow affair, in which masses of people each try to express their individuality in stereotyped fashion. It is a critique that has often been made of modern consumer society that it tends to breed a herd of conformist individuals. This is indeed a mockery of the pretensions of the culture. But just for that reason we can't conclude that the existence of a traditional culture of independence itself empties individuality of its meaning.

In order to see that the cultural shift to the ideal of self-reliance makes a difference, even in its debased form, we have only to compare it with a quite different culture. It matters that American young people are expected to be independent of their elders, even if this itself is one of the demands of the elders. Because what each young person is working out is an identity which is meant to be his/her own in the special sense that it could be sustained even against parental and social opposition. This identity is worked out in conversations with parents and consociates, but the nature of the conversation is defined by this notion of what an identity is. Compare this with Sudhir Kakar's account of the upbringing of young Indians: "The yearning for the confirming presence of the loved person . . . is the dominant modality of social relations in India, especially within the extended family. This 'modality' is expressed variously but consistently, as in a person's feeling of helplessness when family members are absent or his difficulty in making decisions alone. In short, Indians characteristically rely on the support of others to go through life and to deal with the exigencies imposed by the outside world."[18]

This is plainly a different pattern from the one encouraged in our societies in the West. The fact that both are elaborated in cultural traditions does nothing to lessen the difference. The Indian pattern, on this view anyway, tends to encourage a kind of identity in which it is difficult for me to know what I want and where I stand on an important range of subjects if I am out of phase or not in communication with the people close to me. The Western pattern tries to encourage just the opposite.

From within each, the other looks strange and inferior. As Kakar points out, Western scholars have tended to read the Indian pattern as a kind of "weakness". Indians might read the Western one as unfeeling. But these judgements are ethnocentric and fail to appreciate the nature of the cultural gap.[19] Ethnocentrism, of course, is also a consequence of collapsing the distinction between the transcendental conditions and the actual content of a culture, because it makes it seem as though what we are "really" is separated individuals, and hence that this is the proper way to be.[20]

2.3

I have been trying, in the previous section, to trace the connections between our sense of the good and our sense of self. We saw that these are closely interwoven and that they connect too with the way we are agents who share a language with other agents. Now I want to extend this picture, to show it relates to our sense of our life as a whole and the direction it is taking as we lead it. To set the context for this, I return to my argument about the good, to sum up where I think it stands at this point.

In my introductory remarks I began by declaring that my aim was to explore the background picture which underlies our moral intuitions. And later (section 1.2), I redefined this target as the moral ontology which lies behind and makes sense of these intuitions and responses. As the discussion has proceeded, I have come to describe my goal in different terms again: we can now see it as exploring the frameworks which articulate our sense of orientation in the space of questions about the good. These qualitative distinctions, which define the frameworks, I saw first as background assumptions to our moral reactions and judgements, then as contexts which give these reactions their sense. So I still see them. But these descriptions of their role do not capture how indispensable they are to us. Even the second fails to do this: for though a context which makes sense of a particular range of judgements is indeed indispensable to those judgements, the option might still seem open of not making such valuations at all. As long as the naturalist picture, by which having a moral outlook is an optional extra, continues as plausible, the place of these frameworks in our lives will be obscured. Seeing these qualitative distinctions as defining orientations has altered all this. We can now see that they are contestable answers to inescapable questions.

But the image of spatial orientation which I have been using as an analogy brings out another facet of our life as agents. Orientation has two aspects; there are two ways that we can fail to have it. I can be ignorant of the lie of the land around me—not know the important locations which make it up or how they relate to each other. This ignorance can be cured by a good map. But then I can be lost in another way if I don't know how to place myself on this map. If I am a traveller from abroad and I ask where Mont Tremblant is, you don't help me by taking me blindfolded up in a plane, then ripping the blindfold off and shouting, "There it is!" as we overfly the wooded hill. I know now (if I trust you) that I'm at Mont Tremblant. But in a meaningful sense, I still don't know where I am because I can't place Tremblant in relation to other places in the known world.

In contrast, a native of the region might get lost on a trek in Mont Tremblant Park. She presumably knows well how the mountain relates to the

Rivière Diable, St. Jovite, Lac Carré. But she has ceased to be able to place herself in this well-known terrain as she stumbles around the unfamiliar forest. The traveller in the plane has a good description of where he is but lacks the map which would give it an orienting sense for him; the trekker has the map but lacks knowledge of where she is on it.

By analogy, our orientation in relation to the good requires not only some framework(s) which defines the shape of the qualitatively higher but also a sense of where we stand in relation to this. Nor is this question a potentially neutral one, to which we could be indifferent, taking any answer which effectively oriented us as satisfactory, no matter how distant it placed us from the good. On the contrary, we come here to one of the most basic aspirations of human beings, the need to be connected to, or in contact with, what they see as good, or of crucial importance, or of fundamental value. And how could it be otherwise, once we see that this orientation in relation to the good is essential to being a functional human agent? The fact that we have to place ourselves in a space which is defined by these qualitative distinctions cannot but mean that where we stand in relation to them must matter to us. Not being able to function without orientation in the space of the ultimately important means not being able to stop caring where we sit in it.

We are back here to what I called the second axis of strong evaluation in section 1.4, which concerns questions about what kind of life is worth living, e.g., what would be a rich, meaningful life, as against an empty one, or what would constitute an honourable life, and the like. What I am arguing here is that our being concerned with some or other issue of this range is not an optional matter for us, in just the way that the orientation which defines our identity is not, and ultimately for the same reason. Of course, the kind of issue which arises along this axis varies from person to person and, much more markedly, from culture to culture. I touched on this in section 1.4, particularly in connection with the saliency in our day of questions about the "meaning" of life. But so, of course, do the goods by which people define their identity vary—indeed, to the point where the very term 'identity' is somewhat anachronistic for premodern cultures—which doesn't mean, of course, that the need for a moral or spiritual orientation is any less absolute, but just that the issue cannot arise in the reflexive, person-related terms that it does for us. My point is that the goods which define our spiritual orientation are the ones by which we will measure the worth of our lives; the two issues are indissolubly linked because they relate to the same core, and that is why I want to speak of the second issue, about the worth, or weight, or substance of my life, as a question of how I am 'placed' or 'situated' in relation to the good, or whether I am in 'contact' with it.

Typically, for contemporaries, the question can arise of the 'worthwhileness' or 'meaningfulness' of one's life, of whether it is (or has been) rich and substantial, or empty and trivial. These are expressions commonly used, images frequently evoked. Or: Is my life amounting to something? Does it have weight and substance, or is it just running away into nothing, into something insubstantial? Another way the question can arise for us (below we will see better why) is whether our lives have unity, or whether one day is just following the next without purpose or sense, the past falling into a kind of nothingness which is not the prelude, or harbinger, or opening, or early stage of anything, whether it is just 'temps perdu' in the double sense intended in the title of Proust's celebrated work,[21] that is, time which is both wasted and irretrievably lost, beyond recall, in which we pass as if we had never been.

These are peculiarly modern forms and images, but we recognize the similarity with other forms, some of them also alive today, which go much further back in human history. The modern aspiration for meaning and substance in one's life has obvious affinities with longer-standing aspirations to higher being, to immortality. And the search for this kind of fuller being which is immortality, as John Dunne has shown so vividly,[22] has itself taken a number of forms: the aspiration to fame is to immortality in one form, that one's name be remembered, forever on people's lips. "The whole world is their memorial", as Pericles says of the fallen heroes.[23] Eternal life is another. When St. Francis left his companions and family and the life of a rich and popular young man in Assisi, he must have felt in his own terms the insubstantiality of that life and have been looking for something fuller, wholer, to give himself more integrally to God, without stint.

The aspiration to fulness can be met by building something into one's life, some pattern of higher action, or some meaning; or it can be met by connecting one's life up with some greater reality or story. Or it can, of course, be both: these are alternative favoured descriptions, not necessarily mutually exclusive features. We might think that the second kind of description is more "premodern", that it tends to occur earlier in human history. And in a sense this is true. Certainly earlier formulations of the issue of this second axis invoke some larger reality we should connect with: in some earlier religions, a cosmic reality; in Jewish-Christian monotheism, one transcending the cosmos. In certain early religions, like the Aztec, there was even a notion that the whole world runs down, loses substance or Being, and has to be periodically renewed in sacrificial contact with the gods.

But it would be a mistake to think that this kind of formulation has disappeared even for unbelievers in our world. On what is perhaps a more trivial level, some people get a sense of meaning in their lives from having Been There, i.e., having been a witness to big, important events in the world of politics, show business, or whatever. On a deeper level, some committed leftists see themselves as part of the socialist Revolution, or the march of human History, and this is what gives meaning, or fuller Being, to their lives.

But whatever favoured description, be it incorporating something in one's life or connecting to something greater outside, I use my images of 'contact' with the good, or 'how we are placed' in relation to the good, as generic terms, overarching this distinction and maintaining the primacy of my spatial metaphor.

Thus within certain religious traditions, 'contact' is understood as a relation to God and may be understood in sacramental terms or in those of prayer or devotion. For those who espouse the honour ethic, the issue concerns their place in the space of fame and infamy. The aspiration is to glory, or at least to avoid shame and dishonour, which would make life unbearable and non-existence seem preferable. For those who define the good as self-mastery through reason, the aspiration is to be able to order their lives, and the unbearable threat is of being engulfed and degraded by the irresistible craving for lower things. For those moved by one of the modern forms of the affirmation of ordinary life, it is above all important to see oneself as moved by and furthering this life, in one's work for instance, and one's family. People for whom meaning is given to life by expression must see themselves as bringing their potential to expression, if not in one of the recognized artistic or intellectual media, then perhaps in the shape of their lives themselves. And so on.

I am suggesting that we see all these diverse aspirations as forms of a craving which is ineradicable from human life. We have to be rightly placed in relation to the good. This may not be very obtrusive in our lives if things go well and if by and large we are satisfied with where we are. The believer in reason whose life is in order, the householder (I am talking of course about someone with a certain moral ideal, not the census category) who senses the fulness and richness of his family life as his children grow up and his life is filled with their nurture and achievement, these may be quite unaware of this aspiration as such, may be impatient or contemptuous of those whose lives are made tempestuous and restless by it. But this is only because the sense of value and meaning is well integrated into what they live. The householder's sense of the value of what I have been calling ordinary life is woven through the emotions and concerns of his everyday existence. It is what gives them their richness and depth.

At the other extreme, there are people whose lives are torn apart by this craving. They see themselves, over against the master of himself, as in the grip of lower drives, their lives disordered and soiled by their base attachments. Or they have a sense of impotence: 'I can't get it together, can't shake that habit (hold a regular job, etc.)'. Or even a sense of being evil: 'I can't somehow help hurting them badly, even though they love me. I want to hold back, but I get so distressed, I can't help lashing out'. Over against the dedicated fighter for a cause, they feel themselves on the outside: 'I can't really throw myself into this great cause/movement/religious life. I feel on the outside, untouched. I know it's great, in a way, but I can't feel moved by it. I feel unworthy of it somehow'.

Or alternatively, someone might see in the same everyday life which so enriches the householder only a narrow and smug satisfaction at a pitiable comfort, oblivious to the great issues of life, or the suffering of the masses, or the sweep of history. In recent decades, we have seen the drama repeated that the ones who often react this way turn out precisely to be the children whose growth the householder so cherished. This is just one example, a peculiarly poignant one in our day, of how this aspiration to connection can motivate some of the most bitter conflicts in human life. It is in fact a fundamental drive, with an immense potential impact in our lives.

This craving for being in contact with or being rightly placed in relation to the good can be more or less satisfied in our lives as we acquire more fame, or introduce more order in our lives, or become more firmly settled in our families. But the issue also arises for us not just as a matter of more or less but as a question of yes or no. And this is the form in which it most deeply affects and challenges us. The yes/no question concerns not how near or far we are from what we see as the good, but rather the direction of our lives, towards or away from it, or the source of our motivations in regard to it.

We find this kind of question clearly posed in the religious tradition. The Puritan wondered whether he was saved. The question was whether he was called or not. If called, he was 'justified'. But if justified, he might still be a long way from being 'sanctified': this latter was a continuous process, a road that he could be more or less advanced on. My claim is that this isn't peculiar to Puritan Christianity, but that all frameworks permit of, indeed, place us before an absolute question of this kind, framing the context in which we ask the relative questions about how near or far we are from the good.

This is obviously the case of those secular derivatives of Christianity, which see history in terms of a struggle between good and evil, progress and reaction, socialism and exploitation. The insistent absolute question here is: Which side are you on? This permits of only two answers, however near or distant we may be from the triumph of the right. But it is also true for other conceptions which are not at all polarized in this way.

The believer in disengaged objectification, who sees the mastery of reason as a kind of rational control over the emotions attained through the distance of scientific scrutiny, the kind of modern of whom Freud is a prototypical example and for whom he is often a model, obviously sees this mastery as attained slowly and step by step. Indeed, it is never complete and is always in danger of being undone. And yet behind the more-or-less question of mastery achieved lies an absolute question about basic orientation: the disengaged agent has taken a once-for-all stance in favour of objectification; he has broken with religion, superstition, resisted the blandishments of those pleasing and flattering world-views which hide the austere reality of the human condition in a disenchanted universe. He has taken up the scientific attitude. The direction of his life is set, however little mastery he may have actually achieved. And this is a source of deep satisfaction and pride to him.

The householder, who sees the meaning of life in the rich joys of family love, in the concerns of providing and caring for wife and children, may feel that he is far from appreciating these joys at their full or from giving himself to these concerns unstintingly. But he senses that his ultimate allegiance is there, that against those who decry or condemn family life or who look on it as a pusillanimous second best, he is deeply committed to building over time a web of relationships which gives fulness and meaning to human life. His direction is set.

Or again, someone who sees the fulfilment of life in some form of expressive activity may be far from this fulfilment, but she may nevertheless see herself as striving towards it and approaching it, even though she never fully encompasses what she projects for herself. Of course, in this case, the issue may concern not only her basic stance, as with disengaged objectification, and not only her deepest motivation, as with the householder, but the objective limits of possibility which frame her life. People bent on an artistic career may feel they have it in them to do something significant; or alternatively, they may come to feel one day that they just haven't got what it takes. Or their despair may spring from a sense that some external limitations stand in the way: that people of their class, or race, or sex, or poverty will never be allowed to develop themselves in the relevant ways. Many women in our day have felt so excluded from careers, which they saw as deeply fulfilling (for a whole host of reasons, to do with recognition as well as with expression and the significant achievements for human welfare that these jobs entailed), by external barriers which had nothing to do with their own authentic desires and attitudes. These barriers helped set the direction of their lives, and their relation to what they identified as crucial goods.

This array of examples puts us on the track of why the absolute question not only can arise but inevitably does arise for us. The issue that recurs in different forms in the above cases is the one I put in terms of the direction of our lives. It concerned our most fundamental motivation, or our basic allegiance, or the outer limits of relevant possibilities for us, and hence the direction our lives were moving in or could move in. Because our lives move. Here we connect with another basic feature of human existence. The issue of our condition can never be exhausted for us by what we *are*, because we are always also changing and *becoming*. It is only slowly that we grow through infancy and childhood to be autonomous agents who have something like our own place relative to the good at all. And even then, that place is constantly challenged by the new events of our lives, as well as constantly under potential revision, as we experience more and mature. So the issue for us has to be not only where we *are*, but where we're *going;* and though the first may be a matter of more or less, the latter is a question of towards or away from, an issue of yes or no. That is why an absolute question always frames our relative ones. Since we cannot do without an orientation to the good, and since we cannot be indifferent to our place relative to this good, and since this place is something that must always change and become, the issue of the direction of our lives must arise for us.

Here we connect up with another inescapable feature of human life. I have been arguing that in order to make minimal sense of our lives, in order to have an identity, we need an orientation to the good, which means some sense of qualitative discrimination, of the incomparably higher. Now we see that this sense of the good has to be woven into my understanding of my life as an unfolding story. But this is to state another basic condition of making sense of ourselves, that we grasp our lives in a *narrative*. This has been much discussed recently, and very insightfully.[24] It has often been remarked[25] that making sense of one's life as a story is also, like orientation to the good, not an optional extra; that our lives exist also in this space of questions, which only a coherent narrative can answer. In order to have a sense of who we are, we have to have a notion of how we have become, and of where we are going.

Heidegger, in *Being and Time*,[26] described the inescapable temporal structure of being in the world: that from a sense of what we have become, among a range of present possibilities, we project our future being. This is the structure of any situated action, of course, however trivial. From my sense of being at the drugstore, among the possible other destinations, I project to walk home. But it applies also to this crucial issue of my place relative to the good. From my sense of where I am relative to it, and among the different possibilities, I project the direction of my life in relation to it. My life always has this degree of narrative understanding, that I understand my present action in the form of an 'and then': there was A (what I am), and then I do B (what I project to become).

But narrative must play a bigger role than merely structuring my present. What I am has to be understood as what I have become. This is normally so even for such everyday matters as knowing where I am. I usually know this partly through my sense of how I have come there. But it is inescapably so for the issue of where I am in moral space. I can't know in a flash that I have attained perfection, or am halfway there. Of course, there are experiences in which we are carried away in rapture and may believe ourselves spoken to by angels; or less exaltedly, in which we sense for a minute the incredible fulness and intense meaning of life; or in which we feel a great surge of power and mastery over the difficulties that usually drag us down. But there is always an issue of what to make of these instants, how much illusion or mere 'tripping' is involved in them, how genuinely they reflect real growth or goodness. We can only answer this kind of question by seeing how they fit into our surrounding life, that is, what part they play in a narrative of this life. We have to move forward and back to make a real assessment.

To the extent that we move back, we determine what we are by what we have become, by the story of how we got there. Orientation in moral space turns out again to be similar to orientation in physical space. We know where we are through a mixture of recognition of landmarks before us and a sense of how we have travelled to get here, as I indicated above. If I leave the local drugstore, and turn the corner to find the Taj Mahal staring me in the face, I am more likely to conclude that the movie industry is once again earning its tax write-offs in Montreal than to believe myself suddenly by the Jumna. This is analogous to my distrust of sudden rapture. Part of my sense of its genuineness will turn on how I got there. And our entire understanding beforehand of states of greater perfection, however defined, is strongly shaped by our striving to attain them. We come to understand in part what really characterizes the moral states we seek through the very effort of trying, and at first failing, to achieve them.

Of course, the immediate experience *could* be strong and convincing enough on its own. If it really were all there, Taj, Jumna, the city of Agra, bullocks, sky, everything, I would have to accept my new location, however mysterious my translation. Something analogous may exist spiritually. But even here, your past striving and moral experience would alone enable you to understand and identify this rapturous state. You would recognize it only through having striven in a certain direction, and that means again that you know what you are through what you have become.

Thus making sense of my present action, when we are not dealing with such trivial questions as where I shall go in the next five minutes but with the issue of my place relative to the good, requires a narrative understanding of my life, a sense of what I have become which can only be given in a story. And as I project my life forward and endorse the existing direction or give it a new one, I project a future story, not just a state of the momentary future but a bent for my whole life to come. This sense of my life as having a direction towards what I am not yet is what Alasdair MacIntyre captures in his notion quoted above that life is seen as a 'quest'.[27]

This of course connects with an important philosophical issue about the unity of a life, which has once more been brought to the fore by Derek Parfit's interesting book, *Reasons and Persons*.[28] Parfit defends some version of the view that a human life is not an a priori unity or that personal identity doesn't have to be defined in terms of a whole life. It is perfectly defensible for me to consider (what I would conventionally call) my earlier, say, pre-adolescent self as another person and, similarly, to consider what "I" (as we normally put it) shall be several decades in the future as still another person.

This whole position draws on the Lockean (further developed in the Humean) understanding of personal identity. Parfit's arguments draw on examples which are of a kind inaugurated by Locke, where because of the unusual and perplexing relation of mind to body our usual intuitions about the unity of a person are disturbed.[29] From my point of view, this whole conception suffers from a fatal flaw. Personal identity is the identity of the self, and the self is understood as an object to be known. It is not on all fours with other objects, true. For Locke it has this peculiarity that it essentially appears to itself. Its being is inseparable from self-awareness.[30] Personal identity is then a matter of self-consciousness.[31] But it is not at all what I have been calling the self, something which can exist only in a space of moral issues. Self-perception is the crucial defining characteristic of the person for Locke.[32] It is the vestigial element corresponding to the four features which distinguish the self from an ordinary object that I outlined in section 2.2. All that remains of the insight that the self is crucially an object of significance to itself is this requirement of self-consciousness. But what has been left out is precisely the *mattering*. The self is defined in neutral terms, outside of any essential framework of questions. In fact, of course, Locke recognizes that we are not indifferent to ourselves; but he has no inkling of the self as a being which essentially is constituted by a certain mode of self-concern—in contrast to the concern we cannot but have about the quality of our experiences as pleasurable or painful. We shall see in Part II how this neutral and "bleached" sense of the person corresponds to Locke's aspiration to a disengaged subject of rational control. We have here a paradigm example of what I discussed in the previous section: how the assertion of the modern individual has spawned an erroneous understanding of the self.

This is what I want to call the 'punctual' or 'neutral' self—'punctual' because the self is defined in abstraction from any constitutive concerns and hence from any identity in the sense in which I have been using the term in the previous section. Its only constitutive property is self-awareness. This is the self that Hume set out to find and, predictably, failed to find. And it is basically the same notion of the self that Parfit is working with, one whose "identity over time just involves ... psychological connectedness and/or psychological continuity, with the right kind of cause".[33]

If we think of the self as neutral, then it does perhaps make sense to hold that it is an ultimately arbitrary question how we count selves. Our picking out of enumerable objects in the world can be thought to depend ultimately on the interests and concerns we bring to them. My car to me is a single thing. To a skilled garage mechanic, it may be an assemblage of discrete functioning units. There is no sense to the question what it "really" is, *an sich*, as it were.

But if my position here is right, then we can't think of human persons, of selves in the sense that we are selves, in this light at all. They are not neutral, punctual objects; they exist only in a certain space of questions, through certain constitutive concerns. The questions or concerns touch on the nature of the good that I orient myself by and on the way I am placed in relation to it. But then what counts as a unit will be defined by the scope of the concern, by just what is in question. And what is in question is, generally and characteristically, the shape of my life *as a whole*. It is not something up for arbitrary determination.

We can see this in two dimensions, the past and future "ekstaseis" that Heidegger talks about.[34] I don't have a sense of where/what I am, as I argued above, without some understanding of how I have got there or become so. My sense of myself is of a being who is growing and becoming. In the very nature of things this cannot be instantaneous. It is not only that I need time and many incidents to sort out what is relatively fixed and stable in my character, temperament, and desires from what is variable and changing, though that is true. It is also that as a being who grows and becomes I can only know myself through the history of my maturations and regressions, overcomings and defeats. My self-understanding necessarily has temporal depth and incorporates narrative.

But does that mean that I have to consider my whole past life as that of a single person? Isn't there room for decision here? After all, even what happened before I was born might on one reading be seen as part of the process of my becoming. Isn't birth itself an arbitrary point? There is perhaps an easy answer to this last question. There clearly is a kind of continuity running through my lifetime that doesn't extend before it. But the objector seems to have some point here: don't we often want to speak of what we were as children or adolescents in terms like this: 'I was a different person then'?

But it is clear that this image doesn't have the import of a real counter-example to the thesis I'm defending. And this becomes obvious when we look at another aspect of our essential concern here. We want our lives to have meaning, or weight, or substance, or to grow towards some fulness, or however the concern is formulated that we have been discussing in this section. But this means our *whole* lives. If necessary, we want the future to "redeem" the past, to make it part of a life story which has sense or purpose, to take it up in a meaningful unity.[35] A famous, perhaps for us moderns a paradigm, example of what this can mean is recounted by Proust in his *A la recherche du temps perdu*. In the scene in the Guermantes's library, the narrator recovers the full meaning of his past and thus restores the time which was "lost" in the two senses I mentioned above. The formerly irretrievable past is recovered in its unity with the life yet to live, and all the "wasted" time now has a meaning, as the time of preparation for the work of the writer who will give shape to this unity.[36]

To repudiate my childhood as unredeemable in this sense is to accept a kind of mutilation as a person; it is to fail to meet the full challenge involved in making sense of my life. This is the sense in which it is *not* up for arbitrary determination what the temporal limits of my personhood are.[37]

If we look towards the future, the case is even clearer. On the basis of what I am I project my future. On what basis could I consider that only, say, the next ten years were "my" future, and that my old age would be that of another person? Here too we note that a future project will often go beyond my death. I plan the future for my family, my country, my cause. But there is a different sense in which I am responsible for myself (at least in our culture). How could I justify considering myself in my sixties, say, as another person for this purpose? And how would *his* life get its meaning?

It seems clear from all this that there is something like an a priori unity of a human life through its whole extent. Not quite, because one can imagine cultures in which it might be split. Perhaps at some age, say forty, people go through a horrendous ritual passage, in which they go into ecstasy and then emerge as, say, the reincarnated ancestor. That is how they describe things and live them. In that culture there is a sense to treating this whole life cycle as containing two persons. But in the absence of such a cultural understanding, e.g., in our world, the supposition that I could be two temporally succeeding selves is either an overdramatized image, or quite false. It runs against the structural features of a self as a being who exists in a space of concerns.[38]

In the previous section we saw that our being selves is essentially linked to our sense of the good, and that we achieve selfhood among other selves. Here I have been arguing that the issue of how we are placed in relation to this good is of crucial and inescapable concern for us, that we cannot but strive to give our lives meaning or substance, and that this means that we understand ourselves inescapably in narrative.

My underlying thesis is that there is a close connection between the different conditions of identity, or of one's life making sense, that I have been discussing. One could put it this way: because we cannot but orient ourselves to the good, and thus determine our place relative to it and hence determine the direction of our lives, we must inescapably understand our lives in narrative form, as a 'quest'. But one could perhaps start from another point: because we have to determine our place in relation to the good, therefore we cannot be without an orientation to it, and hence must see our life in story. From whichever direction, I see these conditions as connected facets of the same reality, inescapable structural requirements of human agency.

3

ETHICS OF INARTICULACY

3.1

In the previous chapter I tried to show the crucial place of qualitative distinctions in defining our identity and making sense of our lives in narrative. But what is their place in moral thought and judgement? How do they relate to the whole range of the ethical, to adopt this term, following Williams,[1] for the undivided category of considerations which we employ to answer questions about how we should live? This is, after all, what the great controversies have been about.

The simple answer would be: qualitative distinctions give the reasons for our moral and ethical beliefs. This is not wrong, but it is dangerously misleading—unless we first clarify what it is to offer reasons for moral views.

But this whole complex of issues has been almost irremediably muddled and confused by the widespread acceptance of arguments against the supposed "naturalistic fallacy", or versions of the Humean 'is/ought' distinction. These views were of course underpinned by the prejudices of modern naturalism and subjectivism (ironic as that might appear for adversaries of a "fallacy" misnamed 'naturalistic'). Goods or 'values' were understood as projections[2] of ours onto a world which in itself was neutral—which is why our seeing the world in "value" terms was considered ultimately optional in the view I contested in section 2.3.

This projection could be seen in two ways. It could be something we did or, ideally, something we could bring under voluntary control. This kind of view underlay Hare's prescriptivism:[3] the logic of our value terms is such that we can separate out a descriptive level to their meaning from an evaluative force. We could ideally pick out the same entities—actions, situations, qualities—in a purely descriptive language, void of prescriptive force; and this means that we could devise new value vocabularies, in which prescriptive force was connected with descriptions hitherto left unmarked. Discriminating these two kinds of meaning allows us to be maximally reflective and rational about our value commitments.

But in another version, the projection could be seen as something deeply involuntary, a way we can't help experiencing the world, even though our scientific consciousness shows that value is not part of the furniture of things. Sociobiologists tend to talk in these terms.[4] Values would have a status analogous to the one that post-seventeenth-century science has given to secondary properties, like colour:[5] we know that without sighted agents like ourselves there would be nothing in the universe like what we now identify as colour, although there would be the properties of surfaces of objects which determine the wavelengths of the light they reflect and which are now correlated with our colour perceptions in a law-like way. Values, on this involuntary projection view, would be a "colouration" which the neutral universe inescapably had for us.

On either version, it will be possible to offer non-evaluative descriptions which are extensionally equivalent to each of our value terms. According to the first version, these will encapsulate the "descriptive meaning" of these terms; on the second version, they will give us the underlying reality which triggers off our "coloured" experience of value. In the first case, they define part of what we mean by the value term, the entire "descriptive" part; in the second, they offer the normal causally necessary and sufficient conditions for our wanting to use the value term.

But as has often been argued, most recently brilliantly and economically by Bernard Williams,[6] these descriptive equivalents turn out to be unavailable for a whole host of our key value terms. With terms like 'courage' or 'brutality' or 'gratitude', we cannot grasp what would hold all their instances together as a class if we prescind from their evaluative point. Someone who had no sense of this point wouldn't know how to "go on" from a range of sample cases to new ones.[7] This means, as far as the first version is concerned, that the "descriptive" meaning cannot be separated from the "evaluative"; and for the second version, it shows up the ineptitude of the whole parallel to secondary properties.[8]

But what is involved in seeing the evaluative point of a given term? What kind of understanding do you need to grasp it? There seem to be two orders of considerations, which interlock in most cases to form the background of a term. First, one needs an understanding of the kind of social interchange, the common purposes, or mutual needs, how things can go well or badly between people in the society where this term is current. And second, one needs to grasp what I have been calling the qualitative discriminations that the people concerned make; one needs to get a sense, in other words, of their perceptions of the good.

For some terms, just one set of considerations may suffice—at least to give one a functional approximation of its sense. Thus one could argue that a great many of our socially defined obligations, including some of the most serious ones, like those forbidding killing, injury, lying, and the like, are shaped in part by the functional requirements of any human society. Social life, with the minimum of trust and solidarity it demands, couldn't consist with unrestricted violence and deceit. Everybody understands this as part of the point of these rules, and hence as part of the background by which we understand the terms—e.g., 'murder', 'honesty', 'assault',—in which they are couched. This background helps to explain and justify the apparent exceptions, such as capital punishment for criminals, or lying to enemies, which are made to these exclusions in different societies.

Most people in our society also see these restrictions as justified by a perception of the good. They have some notion of the sanctity or dignity of human life, bodily integrity, and the aspiration to truth which these infringements violate—notions of the range that I discussed in section 1.1. But it would be possible to understand many of the rules of our society, even to feel the obligation to follow them, without any such intuition of the good. There are, indeed, much less serious rules which have an analogous background which many people do accept without any sense that their infringement would be a violation. These are a subset of the minimal rules of politeness. (I say 'a subset', because some of the rules of etiquette of any society are tied up with its notions of dignity, which is precisely why they are often opaque to outsiders.) I can see quite well how it helps things along to say 'please' and 'sorry' in the right places—and I know how to throw in functional equivalents where I can't say these words—even though I set no great value on the whole practice, even admire those brave enough to flout it. To the extent that some of our moral rules have this kind of background, we find them maximally easy to understand across cultural gaps, even when another people's notions of the good might be utterly strange to us.

In contrast, there are virtue terms which apply to features of our lives as individuals, where the understanding of social interaction is close to irrelevant, but where everything depends on grasping a certain vision of the good. The excellences of aesthetic sensibility, say, those shown by a great performer, are of this kind. As are perhaps those definitive of a Nietzschean superman.

But the great mass of our terms seem to require that we bring to bear both kinds of background. There are virtue terms like 'kindness' or 'generosity' which define the qualities they do partly against the background of the social interchange characteristic of a given society and partly in the light of a certain understanding of personal dedication. There are social rules, like those governing our behaviour in a socialist commune, where the norms of social interchange are profoundly marked by the aspiration to certain goods: e.g., absolute equality without regard to rank or sex, autonomy of individuals, solidarity. Only against this background can we understand why the question whether A takes out the garbage and B washes the dishes, or vice versa, can be a *moral* issue here. Some features of the rules of any society are of this kind. These are the aspects that are hardest to understand for outsiders.

But once we have made clear the conditions of intelligibility of our value terms, there still seems to be room for a more sophisticated version of the is/ought or fact/value distinction. Up to now, we have encountered three attempts to formulate some view to the effect that values are not part of reality, but in some form our projection. The first was discussed in section 1.1; it tries to assimilate our moral reactions to visceral ones. The second represents our notions of the good as opinions on an issue which is ultimately optional, and I tried to refute this in my discussion of the conditions of identity in 2.1. The third is the thesis that value terms have descriptive equivalents, and we have just seen in this section how erroneous this is.

But if, as we have just seen, our language of good and right makes sense only against a background understanding of the forms of social interchange in a given society and its perceptions of the good, then can one not say after all that good and right are merely relative, not anchored in the real? To say this would be to fall into an important confusion. Certainly what emerges from this is that good and right are not properties of the universe considered without any relation to human beings and their lives. And to the extent that our natural science since the seventeenth century has been developing on the basis of a conception of the world which is maximally freed from anthropocentric conceptions, what Williams has called the "absolute" conception,[9] we can say that good and right are not part of the world as studied by natural science.

But from there, it is an unjustified leap to say that they therefore are not as real, objective, and non-relative as any other part of the natural world. The temptation to make this leap comes partly from the great hold of natural science models on our entire enterprise of self-understanding in the sciences of human life. But the ascendancy of these models is one of the great sources of illusion and error in these sciences, as has been demonstrated time and again.[10] In a sense, however, premodern notions of science have also contributed to this over-hasty inference. For Plato, in his way, the ultimate concepts of ethics and those fundamental to explanation in the sciences were the same, viz., the Ideas. It is easy to see their fundamental role in science as the guarantee of their ontological status as real and objective standards of good. So when they lose this role, as they do in the modern age irrevocably, the temptation is strong to conclude that they have lost all claim to objective ontological status as well.

Platonism and the natural science model are thus objectively allied in creating a false picture of the issue of moral goods. We have to free ourselves of both and examine the question again. What needs to be said can perhaps best be put in a rhetorical question: What better measure of reality do we have in human affairs than those terms which on critical reflection and after correction of the errors we can detect make the best sense of our lives? 'Making the best sense' here includes not only offering the best, most realistic orientation about the good but also allowing us best to understand and make sense of the actions and feelings of ourselves and others. For our language of deliberation is continuous with our language of assessment, and this with the language in which we explain what people do and feel.[11]

This is an important point for my purposes, and so I want to pause to examine it a bit more closely. What are the requirements of 'making sense' of our lives? These requirements are not yet met if we have some theoretical language which purports to explain behaviour from the observer's standpoint but is of no use to the agent in making sense of his own thinking, feeling, and acting. Proponents of a reductive theory may congratulate themselves on explanations which do without these or those terms current in ordinary life, e.g., 'freedom' and 'dignity',[12] or the various virtue terms mentioned before which resist splitting into "factual" and "evaluative" components of meaning. But even if their third-person explanations were more plausible than they are, what would be the significance of this if the terms prove ineradicable in first-person, non-explanatory uses? Suppose I can convince myself that I can explain people's behaviour as an observer without using a term like 'dignity'. What does this prove if I can't do without it as a term in my deliberations about what to do, how to behave, how to treat people, my questions about whom I admire, with whom I feel affinity, and the like?

But what does it mean 'not to be able' to do without a term in, say, my deliberations about what to do? I mean that this term is indispensable to (what now appears to me to be) the clearest, most insightful statement of the issues before me. If I were denied this term, I wouldn't be able to deliberate as effectively, to focus the issue properly—as, indeed, I may feel (and we frequently do) that I was less capable of doing in the past, before I acquired this term. Now 'dignity', or 'courage', or 'brutality' may be indispensable terms for me, in that I cannot do without them in assessing possible courses of actions, or in judging the people or situations around me, or in determining how I really feel about some person's actions or way of being.

My point is that this kind of indispensability of a term in a non-explanatory context of life can't just be declared irrelevant to the project to do without that term in an explanatory reduction. The widespread assumption that it can comes from a premiss buried deep in the naturalist way of thinking, viz., that the terms of everyday life, those in which we go about living our lives, are to be relegated to the realm of mere appearance. They are to be taken no more seriously for explanatory purposes than the visual experience of the sun going down behind the horizon is in cosmology.[13] But this assimilation is untenable. We can see excellent reasons why my perception of the horizon at sunset ought to be sidelined in face of the evidence of, e.g., satellite observations. But what ought to trump the language in which I actually live my life? This is not (quite) a rhetorical question, because we do sometimes offer accounts of what people are about in their likes, dislikes, deliberations, and so forth which purport to be more perceptive, shorn of certain delusions or limitations of vision that affect the people themselves. But these are also terms in which the individuals can live their lives. Indeed, we frequently offer them to the people concerned as an improvement on their own self-understandings. What is preposterous is the suggestion that we ought to disregard altogether the terms that can figure in the non-explanatory contexts of living for the purposes of our explanatory theory. This is the more untenable in that the languages of the two kinds of contexts overlap and interpenetrate. As I said above, the terms we use to decide what is best are very much the same as those we use to judge others' actions, and these figure again for the most part in our account of why they do what they do.

Theories like behaviourism or certain strands of contemporary computer-struck cognitive psychology, which declare "phenomenology" irrelevant on principle, are based on a crucial mistake. They are "changing the subject", in Donald Davidson's apt expression.[14] What we need to *explain* is people living their lives;[15] the terms in which they cannot avoid living them cannot be removed from the explanandum, unless we can propose other terms in which they could live them more clairvoyantly. We cannot just leap outside of these terms altogether, on the grounds that their logic doesn't fit some model of "science" and that we know a priori that human beings must be explicable in this "science". This begs the question. How can we ever know that humans can be explained by any scientific theory *until* we actually explain how they live their lives in its terms?

This establishes what it means to 'make sense' of our lives, in the meaning of my statement above. The terms we select have to make sense across the whole range of both explanatory and life uses. The terms indispensable for the latter are part of the story that makes best sense of us, unless and until we can replace them with more clairvoyant substitutes. The result of this search for clairvoyance yields the best account we can give at any given time, and no epistemological or metaphysical considerations of a more general kind about science or nature can justify setting this aside. The best account in the above sense is trumps. Let me call this the BA principle.

It seems to me that the various theories of moral judgements as projections, and the attempts to distinguish 'value' from 'fact', fall afoul of this BA principle. In fact we find ourselves inescapably using terms whose logic cannot be understood in terms of this kind of radical distinction. If we live our lives like this, what other considerations can overrule this verdict?

Of course, the terms of our best account will never figure in a physical theory of the universe. But that just means that our human reality cannot be understood in the terms appropriate for this physics. This is the complement to the anti-Aristotelian purge of natural science in the seventeenth century. Just as physical science is no longer anthropocentric, so human science can no longer be couched in the terms of physics. Our value terms purport to give us insight into what it is to live in the universe as a human being, and this is a quite different matter from that which physical science claims to reveal and explain. This reality is, of course, dependent on us, in the sense that a condition for its existence is our existence. But once granted that we exist, it is no more a subjective projection than what physics deals with.

Perhaps it would clarify the application of this argument to the main theme of this section if I formulated a terse polemical attack on the position I am contesting. It is addressed to all those who are influenced by a naturalist-inspired metaphysical picture, say, of humans as objects of science, or as part of a disenchanted universe, to adopt a basically non-realist position about the strongly valued goods I have been discussing—all the way from the cruder 'error theory' of Mackie, where values are seen as metaphysically "queer",[16] to the more refined view of Williams (who is not a non-realist in the ordinary sense, and is difficult to class), through Simon Blackburn's 'quasi-realism'.[17]

The attack falls into two phases, to which I add a third for good measure, or perhaps to heap insult on injury.

1. You cannot help having recourse to these strongly valued goods for the purposes of life: deliberating, judging situations, deciding how you feel about people, and the like. The 'cannot help' here is not like the inability to stop blinking when someone waves a fist in your face, or your incapacity to contain your irritation at Uncle George sucking his dentures, even though you know it's irrational. It means rather that you need these terms to make the best sense of what you're doing. By the same token these terms are indispensable to the kind of explanation and understanding of self and others that is interwoven with these life uses: assessing his conduct, grasping her motivation, coming to see what you were really about all these years, etc.

2. What is real is what you have to deal with, what won't go away just because it doesn't fit with your prejudices. By this token, what you can't help having recourse to in life is real, or as near to reality as you can get a grasp of at present. Your general metaphysical picture of "values" and their place in "reality" ought to be based on what you find real in this way. It couldn't conceivably be the basis of an *objection* to its reality.

The force of this argument is obscurely felt even by non-realists. It comes in the confused sense that espousing the projection view ought to have a devastating effect on first-order morality. This is the sense that everyone has before they are got to by philosophical rationalization, that what they count with as they live—goods and the demands they make—is flatly incompatible with a projection view. To go along with this sense, a projectivist would have to reject morality altogether, as this is usually understood, i.e., as a domain of strong evaluation. But most non-realists are reluctant to take this route. They themselves are committed to some morality, and they also have some distant sense of my point 1, that one *couldn't* operate this way. Even Mackie doesn't follow through on his error theory and propose that we stop moralizing or do so quite differently.

So they try instead to show how a non-realist theory is compatible with our ordinary moral experience. This is the point of Blackburn's 'quasi-realism', which he defines as "the enterprise of showing how much of the apparently 'realist' appearance of ordinary moral thought is explicable and justifiable on an anti-realist picture".[18] But here they impale themselves on the other horn of a dilemma. They make non-realism *compatible* with moral experience by making this experience somehow *irrelevant* to it, by making the determinants of this issue of the status of the good lie elsewhere. But that runs against my point 2.

If non-realism can't be *supported* by moral experience, then there are *no* good grounds to believe it at all. The non-realist would have to get down to the detail of the moral life, and show in particular cases how a projective view made more sense of them, if he were to convince us. But we have seen how the logic of our moral language resists this kind of splitting.[19]

3. In fact, most non-realists adopt an incoherent mixture of both routes, impaling themselves moderately on both horns. While insisting on their compatibilist thesis, they also tend to argue for a more sociobiological (as in some respects, Mackie) or consequentialist (Blackburn)[20] cast of first-order moral theory. Not that even this follows strictly, for there really ought to be no place for what we understand as moral obligation at all. But one can still justify some rules as more conducive to survival and general happiness, which we can assume are widely sought ends. Hence in some sense, these rules are obviously a "good thing". The trick is then to forget or fudge the fact that non-realism undermines morality, and adopt these rules as the content of one's moral theory. As we shall see later (section 3.3), there can be strong (if unadmitted) moral reasons for adopting an ethic of this kind, and this in turn can contribute to the projectivist conviction. For some people, the motivation runs in both directions, even if in both cases by a set of invalid inferences.

But once this is said, is not the door still open to another kind of subjectivism, this time a species of relativism? Human societies differ greatly in their culture and values. They represent different ways of being human, we might say. But perhaps there is no way, in the end, of arbitrating between them when they clash. Perhaps they are quite incommensurable, and just as we recognize in general that the existence of certain goods is dependent on the existence of humans, so we might be forced to recognize that certain goods are only such granted the existence of humans within a certain cultural form.

Unlike the other attempts to relativize the good that I discussed above, I think this is a real possibility. There may be different kinds of human realization which are really incommensurable. This would mean that there would be no way of moving from one of these to the other and presenting the transition without self-delusion as either a gain or a loss in anything. It would just be a total switch, generating incomprehension of one's past—something that could in principle only come about through intimidation and brainwashing. I think this is a real possibility, but I doubt if it is true.

Of course, there is another very poignant sense in which we may be unable to choose between cultures. We may indeed be able to understand the transition in terms of gain and loss, but there may be some of both, and an overall judgement may be hard to make. Some moderns see our predicament in relation to earlier societies somewhat in this way. They have little doubt that we have a better science, that we have explored more fully the human potential for self-determining freedom. But this, they think, has gone along with an irretrievable loss in our attunement to our natural surroundings and our sense of community. Although for obvious reasons they are beyond being able to choose again for themselves, these moderns may genuinely believe that their lot is no better than their forebears'—as may emerge in their reluctance to induct still premodern societies into our civilization.

But this last predicament is no real relativization, unlike the previous situation of incommensurability. For it presupposes that we can, in principle, understand and recognize the goods of another society as goods-for-everyone (and hence for ourselves). That these are not combinable with our own home-grown goods-for-everyone may indeed be tragic but is no different in principle from any of the other dilemmas we may be in through facing incombinable goods, even within our own way of life. There is no guarantee that universally valid goods should be perfectly combinable, and certainly not in all situations.

Even our understanding of the transition from a previous society in terms of gains and losses has analogues in our reflection within our own culture. Thus we tend to believe that our culture has gained relative to its pre-seventeenth-century predecessor in having a superior model of science. This model is superior partly in respect of the critical self-awareness it entails. In the light of this criticism, previous theories do not stand up. But we take the same critical stance to certain ideas and practices in our own culture. We have a sense of gain through critical examination when we overcome some of the confusions which are the product of our own culture. In these kinds of cases, our mode of assessment across cultures is not so different from our way of arbitrating within our culture. Commensurability seems to have been attained. It is a question of fact how far it can be extended. It may be that our contact with certain cultures will force us to recognize incommensurability, as against simply a balance of goods- and bads-for-everyone that we cannot definitively weigh up. But we certainly shouldn't assume this is so a priori.

Until we meet this limit, there is no reason not to think of the goods we are trying to define and criticize as universal, provided we afford the same status to those of other societies we are trying to understand. This does *not* mean of course that all our, or all their, supposed goods will turn out at the end of the day to be defensible as such; just that we don't start with a preshrunk moral universe in which we take as given that their goods have nothing to say to us or perhaps ours to them.

3.2

There is one great oversimplification in the discussion of the previous sections that I'd now like to lift. I spoke in the previous chapter, for instance, of different types: people who believe in rational mastery, or a rich conception of family life, or expressive fulfilment, or fame. But in fact a great many of us moderns are moved by all these goods and more. The type descriptions above rang a bell, if they did, because they evoke people who take the particular goods in question not as the *only* orienting framework of their lives but as the most important and serious one. Most of us not only live with many goods but find that we have to rank them, and in some cases, this ranking makes one of them of supreme importance relative to the others. Each of the goods I am talking about here is defined in a qualitative contrast, but some people live according to a higher-order contrast between such goods as well. They recognize the value of self-expression, of justice, of family life, of the worship of God, of ordinary decency, of sensitivity, and a host of others; but they consider one of these—perhaps their relation to God, or perhaps justice—as of overriding importance. This is not to say that they give it unflinching priority in their deliberations and decisions. There may be all sorts of considerations, ranging from a sense of their own limits to the recognition that the other goods are valuable also, which restrain them from this. They may find themselves accused of half-heartedness by other more single-minded adherents to the same good: Why do they not spend more time in prayer? Or why do they not dedicate their whole lives to the struggle for justice in society? But nevertheless as far as they themselves are concerned, this good has an incomparable place in their lives.

For those with a strong commitment to such a good, what it means is that this above all others provides the landmarks for what they judge to be the direction of their lives. While they recognize a whole range of qualitative distinctions, while all of these involve strong evaluation, so that they judge themselves and others by the degree they attain the goods concerned and admire or look down on people in function of this, nevertheless the one highest good has a special place. It is orientation to this which comes closest to defining my identity, and therefore my direction to this good is of unique importance to me. Whereas I naturally want to be well placed in relation to all and any of the goods I recognize and to be moving towards rather than away from them, my direction in relation to this good has a crucial importance. Just because my orientation to it is essential to my identity, so the recognition that my life is turned away from it, or can never approach it, would be devastating and insufferable. It threatens to plunge me into a despair at my unworthiness which strikes at the very roots of my being as a person. Symmetrically, the assurance that I am turned towards this good gives me a sense of wholeness, of fulness of being as a person or self, that nothing else can. While all the goods I recognize, however much they may admit of lesser or greater attainment, allow for a yes/no question concerning the direction of my life in relation to them, if I am strongly committed to a highest good in this sense I find the corresponding yes/no question utterly decisive for what I am as a person. For people who understand their lives this way, there is a qualitative discontinuity between this one good and the others; it is incomparably above them, in an even more striking fashion than they are seen as incomparably more valuable than a life which lacks them. Thus I may see expressive fulfilment as incomparably more worthwhile than the ordinary things we all desire in life; but I see the love of God or the search for justice as itself incommensurably higher than this fulfilment. A higher-order qualitative distinction itself segments goods which themselves are defined in lower-order distinctions.

Even those of us who are not committed in so single-minded a way recognize higher goods. That is, we acknowledge second-order qualitative distinctions which define higher goods, on the basis of which we discriminate among other goods, attribute differential worth or importance to them, or determine when and if to follow them. Let me call higher-order goods of this kind 'hypergoods', i.e., goods which not only are incomparably more important than others but provide the standpoint from which these must be weighed, judged, decided about.

But then it would appear that we all recognize some such; that this status is just what defines the 'moral' in our culture: a set of ends or demands which not only have unique importance, but also override and allow us to judge others. There has been a common tendency in modern philosophy to define morality by a kind of segregation, though the definition of the boundary has varied. Kant defines the moral in terms of the categorical imperative, and this in turn by universalizability or by our being members of a kingdom of ends.[21]

Habermas in our day identifies a set of issues which have to do with universal justice and hence with the universal acceptability of norms, which are the domain of a discourse ethic; and he gives these a superior status to issues concerning the best or most satisfactory life.[22] In both these cases, and in many others, the 'moral' encompasses a domain significantly narrower than what ancient philosophers defined as the 'ethical'. Bernard Williams, in an attempt to challenge this special status, has offered his own description of what he sees as a common thread through much of modern moral philosophy: a definition of the 'moral' in terms of the notion of obligation.[23] And Hegel, who also wanted to challenge "morality", had his own account of the difference.[24]

What justifies this kind of segregation, or whether it can ever be justified, is a big issue of ethical theory. Of course there will always be ranking of goods. The most comprehensive ethical theory, that which most eschews the hiving off of a special class of ends or issues as uniquely crucial, must incorporate some notion of the relative importance of goods. Aristotle's, the greatest of all comprehensive theories in the tradition, is a case in point. But this leaves open how we are actually going to square off different competing ends in the changing situations of life. In some predicaments, an end of generally lower rank may have exceptional urgency. By contrast, segregating theories insulate their higher goods from figuring in the same deliberative process. On Kant's theory, considerations of happiness should be silent when we find ourselves addressed by a categorical imperative. And the 'moral' is often defined as what has overriding force, against the merely 'prudential'.[25]

I will take up this issue of the status of the moral in the next section. Here I want to pursue further the nature of 'hypergoods' and the difficulties they pose for the thesis I've been developing.

Hypergoods are generally a source of conflict. The most important ones, those which are most widely adhered to in our civilization, have arisen through a historical supersession of earlier, less adequate views—analogous to the critical supersession of premodern by modern science that I mentioned at the end of the last section. Hypergoods are understood by those who espouse them as a step to a higher moral consciousness.

To take perhaps the most salient example of modern culture, many accept as their highest good (or perhaps we should say at this stage, principle of right) a notion of universal justice and/or benevolence, in which all human beings are to be treated equally with respect, regardless of race, class, sex, culture, religion. But we who stand within this framework are aware that it was not always recognized, that this universal ethic replaced earlier ones which were in various respects restricted, and that this was accomplished through a number of hard-fought and painfully won stages. In this regard, the principle of universal and equal respect is like our modern conception of science, with which it has some close intellectual connections and affinities. And as with our science, the sense that it arose through a historical supersession of less adequate views goes along with its serving as a standard of criticism of contemporary beliefs and practices.

So the principle of equal respect is not only defined through its historical genesis in early modern times as a negation of hierarchical conceptions of society; it also continues on, finding new applications—as for instance today, in relations between the sexes, challenging certain 'patriarchal' forms of life which were originally left unchallenged by its early modern protagonists.

This example offers us the picture of a hypergood in which our awareness of its being incomparably higher than others builds on an understanding of its having superseded earlier, less adequate views and thus still serving as a standard by which contemporary views can be criticized and sometimes found wanting. It seems that this is generally true of what are recognized as hypergoods in our civilization. To take two other crucial origin points of such goods, Platonism in one way, and the Judaeo-Christian religious revelations in another, both have been defined as historical supersessions—of the Homeric-inspired honour ethic and of various forms of idolatry, respectively—and both remain as sources of radical criticism of existing practices and beliefs.

An ethical outlook organized around a hypergood in this way is thus inherently conflictual and in tension. The highest good is not only ranked above the other recognized goods of the society; it can in some cases challenge and reject them, as the principle of equal respect has been doing to the goods and virtues connected with traditional family life, as Judaism and Christianity did to the cults of pagan religions, and as the author of the *Republic* did to the goods and virtues of agonistic citizen life. And that is why recognizing a hypergood is a source of tension and of often grievous dilemmas in moral life.

To have a hypergood arise by superseding earlier views is to bring about (or undergo) what Nietzsche called a 'transvaluation of values'.[26] The new highest good is not only erected as a standard by which other, ordinary goods are judged but often radically alters our view of their value, in some cases taking what was previously an ideal and branding it a temptation. Such was the fate of the warrior honour ethic at the hands of Plato, and later of Augustine, and later still in the eyes of the modern ethic of ordinary life. And as Nietzsche so well saw, a transvaluation is not necessarily a once-for-all affair. The older condemned goods remain; they resist; some seem ineradicable from the human heart. So that the struggle and tension continues.

There are two extreme strategies whereby all hint of a dilemma may be avoided here. The first is to go all the way, in total consistency, and deny entirely the credentials of any goods which stand in the way of the hypergood. This is the stance that Plato's Socrates seems to be taking in the

Republic, where the normal fulfilments of family life and property are denied the guardians in the name of social harmony. Let us call this the uncompromisingly 'revisionist' stance.

Against this, the other possible strategy is propounded by Aristotle. This is to affirm all goods. And indeed, regarding the goods we have come to recognize, which are bound up with the mode of social interchange which has developed among us, in the way in which I described in the last section, and which reflect the most sensitive insights of those who live within this mode: who is to say that these are worthless? Where, after all, can one stand to decide what the good for human beings is, unless within the (or a) human life form, taking note of the goods that people tend to seek within this form? The good life must thus be understood as one which somehow combines to the greatest possible degree all the goods we seek. These are not, to be sure, of equal value; and Aristotle recognizes that some are of higher rank than others—e.g., contemplation *(thewria),* and the kind of common deliberation which maximally develops *phronēsis.* These touch more centrally on what we are as rational life, and thus their absence would void a life of much of its value. But their paramountcy is to be understood in terms of high priority, not as offering a critical perspective from which other lesser ones can be denied altogether.

We could say that what plays the role of a 'hypergood' in Aristotle's theory is the "supreme good" *(teleion agathon)* itself; but this is the *whole* good life, i.e., all the goods together in their proper proportions.

This 'comprehending' strategy has powerful arguments on its side. But it is hard to follow it either, in totality. It involves respecting all the goods which are internal to practices which humans develop in their different societies. By 'internal' goods, I mean those whose point must be understood against the background of a certain mode of social interchange in the manner I discussed in the previous section.[27] But if we ever could have done this, we are plainly too far gone in our recognition of hypergoods to go the whole comprehending route. We are too aware that there have been and are societies and modes of social interchange which are vicious or are incompatible with justice or human dignity. And we are not encouraged along the Aristotelian path by the thought that the Philosopher himself justified slavery, not to speak of a subordinate place for women. This is not to say that moral indignation against Aristotle himself is in order on this score, but just that we can see all too well how these institutions could look perfectly all right in that society while we now see them as unconscionable and as fit objects for reform or abolition.

But we can readily see from all this that the place of these hypergoods in our lives cannot but provoke an epistemological malaise, which in turn feeds the naturalist temper and the various reductive theories that I have been contending against. Even when one gets beyond the cruder reductionist theories, those which see values as simple projections onto a neutral world, even after we have come to accept that our evaluative outlooks have their proper place within our experience, as we dwell in the world within a certain form of life, there is still room for a more sophisticated naturalism. This would understand our valuations as among the perceptions of the world and our social existence which are inseparable from our living through and participating in our form of life. Granted the mode of social interchange, granted that this mode is organized around certain goods which we cherish and that it in turn makes other qualities and conditions of value to us, we cannot but perceive our lives in terms of certain qualitative distinctions. Or rather, the only way to prescind from these would be to stand altogether outside this mode of life; grasping the world in terms of these values is inseparable from participating in this way of living.

This sophisticated naturalism could agree that the distinctions marked by our value words were as real as any others, certainly not mere projections. Coming to learn them would be seen as attaining a kind of 'knowledge'.[28] But whatever truths were to be found here would nevertheless in a crucial sense be relative to the given form of life. To the extent to which these goods appear not to be so from the standpoint of another way of living, or even appear sometimes to be wrong or evil, there is no way of adjudicating the dispute. Each side has to be judged right from its own point of view, but there is no standpoint beyond the two from which the issue could be arbitrated.

Of course, I accept this as a possibility: this is the one I described with the term 'incommensurability'. But I am talking here about a mode of naturalism which would make such culture-relativity a fatality, an in-principle limit. Precisely because it conceives the 'objectivity' of our valuations entirely in terms of their embedding in our different ways of life, it allows in principle no purchase from which the goods enshrined in a given way of life can be shown as wrong or inadequate.

But something like this is what is involved in the claims to critical supersession that are made on behalf of hypergoods. When we stand within the moral outlook of universal and equal respect, we don't consider its condemnation of slavery, widow-burning, human sacrifice, or female circumcision only as expressions of our way of being, inviting a reciprocal and equally valid condemnation of our free labour, widow-remarriage, bloodless sacrifice, and sex equality from the societies where these strange practices flourish. We do find ourselves sometimes thinking in these terms, in our reflective moments, under the impress not only of naturalist epistemology but also of our anti-colonialist sympathies (ironically, another offshoot of the principle of universal respect). But the moral outlook makes wider claims, and this by its very nature. For it engenders a pitiless criticism of all those beliefs and practices within our society which fail to meet the standard of universal respect. It ruthlessly sets aside the goods involved in these peccant practices. It is hard to see why this critical radicalism should suddenly fail when we get to the boundaries of our society—boundaries which are hard to draw in any case—and condone the often much more severe lapses we find in premodern civilizations, for instance. If we cannot accept hiring practices which don't ensure that women get their share of the jobs, how can we accept polygamy, purdah, female circumcision, let alone the killing of "fallen" women by their male relatives in order to save the family honour?

Can we save the objectivity of these cross-cultural critical claims that are involved in what I have been calling hypergoods? Of course I don't mean, Can we show all such claims to be right? Many of them are undoubtedly wrong and deeply ethnocentric and insensitive. What I mean is, Can we show how any claim of this kind could be valid? Or are all such claims unreceivable in principle because they run against the very bases of our valuations, as our sophisticated naturalism would have it?

To see how these claims can be valid, we have to administer another dose of the same argument that levered us out of the cruder naturalism. Faced with the view that all valuation is simply projection of our subjective reactions onto a neutral world, we had recourse to what might be called moral phenomenology, but which also can be seen as an examination of the inescapable features of our moral language. I tried to show in section 2.1 that orientation to the good is not some optional extra, something we can engage in or abstain from at will, but a condition of our being selves with an identity. And in the last section I invoked the arguments, made familiar by followers of Wittgenstein,[29] to the effect that our language of valuation cannot for the most part be construed as expressing our reactions to features of the world, our life, or society which are or could be identified in neutral terms. The logic of, e.g., virtue terms like courage or generosity is such that they have to be construed as picking out projectible properties, just as 'red' or 'square' do, an essential feature of which is precisely their value.

Of course, it is clear that an essential condition of the existence of such properties is that there are human beings in the world, with a certain form of life, and kinds of awareness, and certain patterns of caring. But these properties are no less real features of the world which does contain humans than any "neutral" properties are.

The underlying consideration which makes this argument compelling could be put this way: How else to determine what is real or objective, or part of the furniture of things, than by seeing what properties or entities or features our best account of things has to invoke? Our favoured ontology for the micro-constitution of the physical universe now includes quarks and several kinds of force, and other things I understand only dimly. This is very different from how our ancestors conceived these things. But we have our present array of recognized entities because they are the ones invoked in what we now see as the most believable account of physical reality.

There is no reason to proceed differently in the domain of human affairs, by which I mean the domain where we deliberate about our future action, assess our own and others' character, feelings, reactions, comportments, and also attempt to understand and explain these. As a result of our discussions, reflections, arguments, challenges, and examinations, we will come to see a certain vocabulary as the most realistic and insightful for the things of this domain. What these terms pick out will be what to us is real here, and it cannot and should not be otherwise. If we cannot deliberate effectively, or understand and explain people's action illuminatingly, without such terms as 'courage' or 'generosity', then these are real features of our world.

Our tendency has been to be derailed by the thought that such features wouldn't figure in an absolute account of the universe. Both naturalism and the Platonic precedent combine to give this consideration great weight. But should it weigh with us? Only if we have reason to believe that an absolute account, one that prescinds from anthropocentric properties, in particular from the meanings that things have for us, offers the best explanation, not only of the extra-human universe (that much seems now fairly clear), but of human life as well. And this seems not only undersupported as an assertion but highly implausible in the light of what we know both about human beings and the resources of explanations in absolute—say, physical or chemical— terms.[30] Unless we make a wild conjecture of this kind, we will be disposed to accept that the world of human affairs has to be described and explained in terms which take account of the meanings things have for us. And then we will naturally, and rightly, let our ontology be determined by the best account we can arrive at in these terms. We will follow what I called above the BA principle (section 3.1).

If naturalism and the Platonic precedent shouldn't deter us from following this principle to the point of allowing for courage and generosity, nor should they frighten us away from what I have been calling hypergoods, if these turn out to be really ineliminable from our best account. Hypergoods tend to be more epistemologically unsettling and to trigger off the reactions which naturalism and the Platonic precedent nourish in us, and that for two reasons.

The first is that they present us with a good which challenges and displaces others. The picture of moral life in which a hypergood figures is one where we are capable of growth from a 'normal', or 'original', or 'primitive', or 'average' condition, in which we acknowledge and orient ourselves by a certain range of goods, to a recognition of a good which has incomparably greater dignity than these. Our acceptance and love of this good makes us re-evaluate the goods of the original range. We judge them differently and perhaps experience them quite differently, to the point of possible indifference and, in some cases, rejection.

For Plato, once we see the Good, we cease to be fascinated by and absorbed in the search for honour and pleasure as we were before, and we will even altogether want to renounce certain facets of these. On a Christian view, sanctification involves our sharing to some degree God's love *(agapē)* for the world, and this transforms how we see things and what else we long for and think important. Or again, the move from a prerational and parochial perspective to one in which we recognize the right of all humans to equal respect transforms our entire way of seeing historical cultures and their practices. What previously was endowed with the highest prestige may now seem narrow, tawdry, exploitative. We can no longer feel awe before it. On the contrary what now inspires this sentiment is the moral law itself and its universal demands. We feel ourselves lifted out of the ruck of unthinking custom, and becoming citizens of a wider republic, a kingdom of ends.

The fact that the perspective defined by a hypergood involves our changing, a change which is qualified as 'growth', or 'sanctification', or 'higher consciousness', and even involves our repudiating earlier goods, is what makes it so problematic. It is problematic right off because controversial, critical of where 'ordinary', or 'unregenerate', or 'primitive' moral understanding is. And this actual struggle and disagreement, the seemingly ineradicable absence of unanimity about these hypergoods, has always been a potent source of moral scepticism. This perennial worry understandably strengthens the naturalist reaction in this case. Who is to say that the critics, the protagonists of 'higher' morality, are right against 'ordinary' consciousness, or "l'homme moyen sensuel"? This suspicion is all the stronger in the modern world because of what I described in section 1.3 as the affirmation of ordinary life. The rejection of the supposedly "higher" activities, contemplation or citizen participation, or of "higher" levels of dedication in the form of monastic asceticism, in favour of the ordinary life of marriage, children, work in a calling conferred a higher dignity on what had previously been relegated to a lower status. This unleashed a powerful tendency in our civilization, one which has taken ever new forms. Some of these involved turning against the very religious tradition which had inaugurated this tendency and defending "natural" desire and fulfilment against the demands of sanctification, now seen as specious and destructive.

And then Nietzsche took this attack a stage further and tried to break out of the whole form of thought he defined as 'moral', i.e., all forms which involve the rejection of the supposedly "lower" in us, of our will to power, and to come to a more total self-affirmation, a yea-saying to what one is. Enlightenment naturalism also frequently portrayed religious moralities of the "higher" not only as the source of self-repression but also as the justification of social oppression, as the supposed carriers of the "higher", be they priests or aristocrats, exercise their natural right to rule the "lower" orders for the latter's own good. Neo-Nietzschean thinkers have extended this critique and tried to show how various forms of social exclusion and domination are built into the very definitions by which a hypergood perspective is constituted, as certain models of religious order excluded and dominated women,[31] as ideals and disciplines of rational control excluded and dominated the lower classes (as well as women again),[32] as definitions of health and fulfilment exclude and marginalize dissidents,[33] as other notions of civilization exclude subject races,[34] and so on.

Of course, the argument is complicated by the fact that all of these attacks, with the exception of Foucault's, are overtly (and, in fact, I believe Foucault's are as well, though unadmittedly) committed to their own rival hypergoods, generally in the range of our third example above, connected to the principle of universal and equal respect. But this doesn't reduce the perplexity and uncertainty we feel here. It seems that at least some of the hypergoods espoused so passionately must be illusory, the projection of less admirable interests or desires. Why then shouldn't all of them be so?

So indeed they might be. But it is wrong to think that we have stumbled on an a priori argument showing this to be so. The revelation that some hypergoods have been woven into relations of dominance, and this against the express pretensions made on their behalf, no more shows that all claims of this kind are irreceivable (and the more so in that the critical stance is often—or always—from the perspective of a rival hypergood) than does the success of the absolute standpoint in physics. There is still no substitute for the BA principle here as elsewhere. We can only look: perhaps we will find that we cannot make sense of our moral life without something like a hypergood perspective, some notion of a good to which we can grow, and which then makes us see others differently.

But, it will be objected, it is not just a matter of looking but also of arguing, of establishing that one view is better than another. And this raises the difficult question of practical reason. Is there any rational way for A to convince B that his hypergood perspective is superior? And if not, then how does A rationally convince himself? Or is it all just a matter of sub-rational hunches and feelings (as naturalists have been claiming all along)?

Here again our understanding has been clouded by a naturalist epistemology and its focus on the natural science model. Because following the argument in favour of a theory in natural science requires that we neutralize our own anthropocentric reactions, we too easily conclude that arguments in the domain of practical reason ought not to rely on our spontaneous moral reactions. We ought to be able to convince people who share absolutely none of our basic moral intuitions of the justice of our cause, or else practical reason is of no avail. Certain modern doctrines have tried to take up this challenge,[35] but we perhaps don't need to examine their inadequacies in detail to see that the challenge cannot be met. The error is in thinking that it ought to be. Once we make this error, we cannot but despair of practical reason, and we are then readier to surrender to naturalist reduction.

But if our moral ontology springs from the best account of the human domain we can arrive at, and if this account must be in anthropocentric terms, terms which relate to the meanings things have for us, then the demand to start outside of all such meanings, not to rely on our moral intuitions or on what we find morally moving, is in fact a proposal to change the subject. How then does practical reasoning proceed? How do we rationally convince each other or ourselves?

Practical reasoning, as I have argued elsewhere,[36] is a reasoning in transitions. It aims to establish, not that some position is correct absolutely, but rather that some position is superior to some other. It is concerned, covertly or openly, implicitly or explicitly, with comparative propositions. We show one of these comparative claims to be well founded when we can show that the *move* from A to B constitutes a gain epistemically. This is something we do when we show, for instance, that we get from A to B by identifying and resolving a contradiction in A or a confusion which A relied on, or by acknowledging the importance of some factor which A screened out, or something of the sort. The argument fixes on the nature of the transition from A to B. The nerve of the rational proof consists in showing that this transition is an error-reducing one. The argument turns on rival interpretations of possible transitions from A to B, or B to A.[37]

This form of argument has its source in biographical narrative. We are convinced that a certain view is superior because we have lived a transition which we understand as error-reducing and hence as epistemic gain. I see that I was confused about the relation of resentment and love, or I see that there is a depth to love conferred by time, which I was quite insensitive to before. But this doesn't mean that we don't and can't argue. Our conviction that we have grown morally can be challenged by another. It may, after all, be illusion. And then we argue; and arguing here is contesting between interpretations of what I have been living.

If hypergoods arise through supersessions, the conviction they carry comes from our reading of the transitions to them, from a certain understanding of moral growth. This is always open to challenge: the attacks on hypergoods as repressive and oppressive constitute only the most virulent of such challenges. When Nietzsche wants to launch his out-and-out attack on morality, he does this by offering an account of the transition to it, the rise of slave morality. 'Genealogy' is the name for this kind of probing. No one can fail to recognize that, if true, Nietzsche's genealogies are devastating. That is because genealogy goes to the heart of the logic of practical reasoning. A hypergood can only be defended through a certain reading of its genesis.

The bad model of practical reasoning, rooted in the epistemological tradition, constantly nudges us towards a mistrust of transition arguments. It wants us to look for 'criteria' to decide the issue, i.e., some considerations which could be established even outside the perspectives in dispute and which would nevertheless be decisive. But there cannot be such considerations. My perspective is defined by the moral intuitions I have, by what I am morally moved by. If I abstract from this, I become incapable of understanding any moral argument at all. You will only convince me by changing my reading of my moral experience, and in particular my reading of my life story, of the transitions I have lived through—or perhaps refused to live through.

But then the force of this bad, external model is increased by something else, which is the second of the two main reasons which breed suspicions about hypergoods. These often make essential reference to beings or realities which transcend human life, as Plato does to the Idea of the Good, or theistic views do to God, and some Romantic-derived views do to Nature as a great source. These are problematic in themselves, and seen in the light of the Platonic precedent they seem doubly so: for these beings play no part in our natural science explanations today. If we are consistent in our adhesion to the BA principle, this fact shouldn't disturb us; but a worry arises from another quarter. It seems as though invoking these realities implies something about the order of argument. If you're a Platonist you must be saying: first realize that the world is ordered for the good, and then deduce from this fact that you ought to embrace certain moral reactions, internalize certain moral intuitions. And a theist must be saying: first realize that there is a God; he is good, creator, etc.; and *then* you will see that you ought to worship him, obey him, etc. And this was indeed a common way of conceiving argument in this domain in the days when the Platonic precedent was still unchallenged. Some philosophers thought you could prove the existence of God from facts about the world, accessible to all, regardless of moral perspective.

But the acceptance of God or the Good has no necessary connection with this order of argument. And from our modern perspective, where the Platonic synthesis of scientific explanation and moral insight lies irrecoverably shattered by the rise of natural science, it seems more and more implausible. But nothing prevents a priori our coming to see God or the Good as essential to our best account of the human moral world. There is no question here of our ever being able to come to recognize this by prescinding from our moral intuitions. Rather our acceptance of any hypergood is connected in a complex way with our being *moved* by it. It is necessary to add 'in a complex way', because we never think of these things entirely on our own and monologically, however certain moral views may exhort us to do so. We may accept something as a good although we are relatively unmoved by it, because at the lowest, we think very little about it and glide along in conformity with our milieu; or because we revere and look up to established authority; or perhaps best, because we choose certain figures as authoritative for us, sensing in them that they are moved by something authentic and great, even though we don't fully understand it or feel it ourselves. But through all these complex chains of intermediation, the connection between seeing the good and being moved by it cannot be broken. Our authorities, or the founders of our traditions, those who give these goods their energy and place in our lives, *they* felt them deeply.

This intrinsic connection between seeing and feeling in this domain has, of course, been grist to reductionist mills. It is easy to rush in with the standard subjectivist model: the good's importance reposes just in its moving us so. But this model is false to the most salient features of our moral phenomenology. We sense in the very experience of being moved by some higher good that we are moved by what is good in it rather than that it is valuable because of our reaction. We are moved by it seeing its point as something infinitely valuable. We experience our love for it as a well-founded love. Nothing that couldn't move me in *this* way would count as a hypergood. Of course, I could be wrong. The whole thing could be just a projection of some quite ordinary desire which confers this seemingly exalted status on some object, surrounds it with a halo of the higher. Indeed, I could be. But I could also be right. The only way to decide is by raising and facing this or that particular critique. Is there a transition out of my present belief which turns on an error-reducing move? Do I have to recognize, for instance, that previously unavowed fears and desires of a descreditable kind have been lending lustre to this good, which it quite loses when these are factored out? What successfully resists all such critique is my (provisionally) best account. There is nothing better I could conceivably have to go on. Or my critics either for that matter. So says the BA principle.

Now the fact that, in applying this principle, I may come to a belief in God, a being who infinitely transcends my moral experience and understanding, doesn't mean that my rational confidence in this belief is grounded in considerations which take no account of this moral experience. It isn't, and with the demise of the Platonic synthesis, it couldn't any longer be.

The predicament of practical reason resembles the most primitive context in which I acquire factual knowledge, that of perception. My confidence in my awareness of my perceptual surroundings rests in large part on the quite inarticulate sense I have of enjoying a sure perceptual purchase on things, a sense which enframes all my particular perceivings. A typical response when we encounter something surprising, unsettling, or seemingly wrong is to stop, shake our heads, concentrate, set ourselves to command a good view, and look again. All these manoeuvres, which we often do without focally attending to them, draw on our implicit know-how about getting good perceptual purchase When we then look again, we give greater credence to this second perception, not because we have discovered that these manoeuvres work as tricks, but precisely because we have the sense that we now have a better prise on the situation. Our sense that the transition was a purchase-improving one is what underlies our present confidence.

The idea that we ought to prescind altogether from this background confidence of purchase is as unjustified as the corresponding demand in the moral field that we step outside moral intuitions. This would mean checking the trustworthiness of this confidence against something else. But this something else would have to be quite outside the perceivable, and thus gives us an impossible task. Classical epistemology was always threatening to drive into this cul-de-sac and therefore fall into the despair of scepticism. Of course, in one case as in the other, our confidence *on a particular occasion* may be misplaced. But we discover this only by shifting out of one purchase into another, more adequate one. My blithe, unthinking assurance that I know the path gives way to my careful and attentive grip on my surroundings after I trip. My conceited confidence that there is only one moral issue at stake here gives way to an appreciation of the legitimacy of other demands as I mature. I read both these transitions as gains, and thus I embrace the later views over the earlier ones. But in neither case can I do anything with the suggestion that it might all be illusion and that I ought to defend myself against this possibility by stepping altogether outside any reliance either on intuition or on sense of purchase. This demand is in its nature impossible. The most reliable moral view is not one that would be grounded quite outside our intuitions but one that is grounded on our strongest intuitions, where these have successfully met the challenge of proposed transitions away from them.

3.3

We can now see better the point of the answer I gave some time back to the question, What role do our qualitative discriminations play in our moral thinking? I said then (section 3.1) one thing that they do is provide reasons, but that this has to be understood in a different way than usual. As long as the wrong, external model of practical reason holds sway, the very notion of giving a reason smacks of offering some external considerations, not anchored in our moral intuitions, which can somehow show that certain moral practices and allegiances are correct. An external consideration in this sense is one which could convince someone who was quite unmoved by a certain vision of the good that he ought to adopt it, or at least act according to its prescriptions. This is the kind of reason which a naturalistic picture of human life might seem to offer utilitarianism or some ethic of 'material' welfare; or the kind of support that theories like Hare's prescriptivism derive from considerations about the logic of moral language.[38] But once one thinks in this way in connection with, say, a theistic view, then one is heading towards a totally wrong picture of the situation, one which had some relevance to an earlier age, as I argued above, but has none to ours. The belief in God, say, offers a reason not in this sense but as an articulation of what is crucial to the shape of the moral world in one's best account. It offers a reason rather as I do when I lay out my most basic concerns in order to make sense of my life to you. And we can see right off from this why the perception of a hypergood, while offering a reason, at the same time helps define my identity.

Nor do our qualitative distinctions offer reasons in another sense which is often evoked in the literature of moral philosophy. In this sense, we give a reason for a certain moral principle or injunction when we show that the act enjoined has some crucial property which confers this force on it. I say: "you ought to do A", and when you ask why, I add: "because A = B", where 'B' allegedly offers a description of an act-form which we're morally committed to. So typical fillings for 'B' would be: 'obeying the law', or 'conducing to the greatest happiness of the greatest number', or 'saving your integrity'. We say that B gives a reason because we hold that the act picked out by the A-description is only enjoined because it also bears the B-description. Were this identity to fail, A would no longer be a moral obligation. Thus a utilitarian will argue that I ought generally to pay my taxes, because this conduces to the general happiness. But in exceptional circumstances, where public revenues are being terribly misused, this identity fails, and I don't have to pay. A = B is an obligation-conferring identity. It is in its nature to work asymmetrically. B makes A obligatory, not vice versa. We can call B in this case a 'basic' reason.

This form of argument is very frequent in ethics. We often ask what makes a given action right, and we are answered with a basic reason. But it is a big issue in moral philosophy how systematically our moral ends or obligations can be related to a small list of basic reasons. There has been a tendency to breathtaking systematization in modern moral philosophy. Utilitarianism and Kantianism organize everything around one basic reason. And as so often happens in such cases, the notion becomes accredited among the proponents of these theories that the nature of moral reasoning is such that we ought to be able to unify our moral views around a single base. John Rawls, following J. S. Mill, rejects what he describes as the "intuitionist" view, which is precisely a view which allows for a plurality of such basic criteria.[39] But to see how far this is from being an essential feature of moral thinking we have only to look at Aristotle's ethical theory. Aristotle sees us pursuing a number of goods, and our conduct as exhibiting a number of different virtues. We can speak of a single "complete good" *(teleion agathon),* because our condition is such that the disparate goods we seek have to be coherently combined in a single life, and in their right proportions. But the good life as a whole doesn't stand to the partial goods as a basic reason. There is no asymmetrical conferral of their status as goods. A good life should include, inter alia, some contemplation, some participation in politics, a well-run household and family. These should figure in their right proportion. But we can't say informatively that contemplation is a good because it figures in the good life. It is much more that this life is good because, in part, it includes contemplation. This drive towards unification, far from being an essential feature of morality, is rather a peculiar feature of modern moral philosophy. I will try to offer some explanation of this, along with other features, below.[40]

What is relevant to my argument here is that articulating a vision of the good is not offering a basic reason. It is one thing to say that I ought to refrain from manipulating your emotions or threatening you, because that is what respecting your rights as a human being requires. It is quite another to set out just what makes human beings worthy of commanding our respect, and to describe the higher mode of life and feeling which is involved in recognizing this. It is true that clarification on the second is closely related to the definition of the basic reasons we invoke in the first kind of claim. Our conceptions of what makes humans worthy of respect have shaped the actual schedule of rights we recognize, and the latter has evolved over the centuries with changes in the former. But they are nonetheless distinct activities. They offer reasons in quite different senses.

Our qualitative distinctions, as definitions of the good, rather offer reasons in this sense, that articulating them is articulating what underlies our ethical choices, leanings, intuitions. It is setting out just what I have a dim grasp of when I see that A is right, or X is wrong, or Y is valuable and worth preserving, and the like. It is to articulate the moral point of our actions. That is why it is so different from offering an external reason. I can only convince you by my description of the good if I speak for you, either by articulating what underlies your existing moral intuitions or perhaps by my description moving you to the point of making it your own. And that is also why it cannot be assimilated to giving a basic reason. Relative to the most basic action-description, we can still strive to make clear just what is important, valuable, or what commands our allegiance, as with the above example of respecting human rights. This isn't a step to a more basic level, because there is no asymmetry. But we can see how articulating the good may help further definitions of what is basic.

So we can see the place that qualitative discriminations have in our ethical life. Prearticulately, they function as an orienting sense of what is important, valuable, or commanding, which emerges in our particulate intuitions about how we should act, feel, respond on different occasions, and on which we draw when we deliberate about ethical matters. Articulating these distinctions is setting out the moral point of the actions and feelings our intuitions enjoin on us, or invite us to, or present as admirable. They have this place as much in the broader domain of goods that we pursue across the whole range of our lives, as in the more special domain of higher goods, which claim a status of incomparably greater importance or urgency.

In a way, it may seem totally unnecessary to say what I have just said. Isn't it just a truism? But in fact this whole study from the beginning has been struggling to make this point. What I first described as 'frameworks' I presented as offering background assumptions to our moral reactions, and later as providing the contexts in which these reactions have sense. Then I went on to argue that living within these frameworks was not an optional extra, something we might just as well do without, but that they provided a kind of orientation essential to our identity. What seemed to make it necessary to say all this was the resistance put up by the naturalist temper which permeates much of our philosophic thought, not only within the academy but in our society at large. The mode of thought which surfaces in contemporary sociobiology wants us to think of our moral reactions outside of any sense-making context, as on all fours with visceral reactions like nausea.[41] On a more sophisticated level, we have the picture of values as projections on a neutral world, something which we normally though unconsciously live within but could perhaps abstain from. It has been necessary to describe all this at length in order to rescue our awareness of the crucial importance of these distinctions from a kind of bewitchment.

Up to now I have been talking about the naturalistic sources of this bewitchment. But it is in fact stronger and more firmly rooted in modern culture. And to see this, we have to look not so much at the various reductive theories of values which have had an impact on modern social science and moral theory, but at certain central features of this modern moral theory itself.

Much of this philosophy strives to do away with these distinctions altogether, to give no place in moral life to a sense of the incomparably higher goods or hypergoods. Utilitarianism is the most striking case. A good, happiness, is recognized. But this is characterized by a polemical refusal of any qualitative discrimination. There is no more higher or lower; all that belongs to the old, metaphysical views. There is just desire, and the only standard which remains is the maximization of its fulfilment. The critic can't help remarking how little utilitarians have escaped qualitative distinctions, how they in fact accord rationality and its corollary benevolence the status of higher motives, commanding admiration. But there is no doubt that the express theory aims to do without this distinction altogether.

What motivates this curious blindness? In part, the naturalist temper, as I have described above. And then, of course, the epistemological assumptions that go so well with this temper. These tend to allow the natural sciences a paradigm status for all forms of knowledge, including that of human affairs, as I discussed in the previous section. Then such things as 'higher' goods must appear very strange entities indeed. Wherever can they fit in the furniture of the universe, as revealed, say, by physics?[42]

But naturalism also exercises a more subtle and pervasive influence on moral thinking, one that affects our thinking about the whole form of an ethical theory. I mentioned in the beginning of the first chapter the tendency in contemporary philosophy to give a very narrow focus to morality. Morality is conceived purely as a guide to *action*. It is thought to be concerned purely with what it is right to do rather than with what it is good to be. In a related way the task of moral theory is identified as defining the content of obligation rather than the nature of the good life. In other words, morals concern what we *ought* to *do;* this excludes both what it is good to do, even though we aren't *obliged* (which is why supererogation is such a problem for some contemporary moral philosophy),[43] and also what it may be good (or even obligatory) to *be* or *love,* as irrelevant to ethics. In this conception there is no place for the notion of the good in either of two common traditional senses: either the good life, or the good as the object of our love or allegiance. (I want to speak about this latter in the next chapter.)

Moral philosophies so understood are philosophies of obligatory action. The central task of moral philosophy is to account for what generates the obligations that hold for us. A satisfactory moral theory is generally thought to be one that defines some criterion or procedure which will allow us to derive all and only the things we are obliged to do. So the major contenders in these stakes are utilitarianism, and different derivations of Kant's theory, which are action-focussed and offer answers exactly of this kind. What should I do? Well, work out what would produce the greatest happiness of the greatest number. Or work out what I could choose when I have treated other people's prescriptions as if they were my own.[44] Or think what norm would be agreed by all the people affected, if they could deliberate together in ideal conditions of unconstrained communication.[45]

We can see how moral theory so conceived doesn't have much place for qualitative distinctions. It is in the business of offering what I called above basic reasons. Our qualitative distinctions are useless for this; they give us reasons in a quite different sense. Articulating them would be indispensable if our aim were to get clearer on the contours of the good life, but that is not a task which this theory recognizes as relevant. All we need are action-descriptions, plus a criterion for picking out the obligatory ones.

But it is not just that the distinctions are of no use for the particular goals that this moral theory sets itself. There is a tendency among philosophers of this cast of thought to deny them any relevance altogether, or even in some cases to deny them intellectual coherence, or reality, to reduce them to the status of projections, as we have seen. Whence this exclusion?

The motives are complex, as I now want to explore. Naturalism is only one of them, but it does make its contribution. Articulating our qualitative distinctions is setting out the point of our moral actions. It explains in a fuller and richer way the meaning of this action for us, just what its goodness or badness, being obligatory or forbidden, consists in. It is possible to know, for instance, as a child sometimes does, that a certain act is forbidden, but not to understand yet what kind of badness it exhibits. Later one may learn that it is something dishonourable, or perhaps mean-spirited, in distinction from other forbidden things, which are ruled out just because they're dangerous, or because we can't now pull them off. Many of our virtue terms belong to these richer languages of what I have been calling qualitative discriminations. The child or the outsider can be told what not to do, can be given a description of what to avoid which they can understand, before they can understand just what is wrong. We can get a sufficient grasp of the commandment, 'Thou shalt not kill', or can obey the order, 'Don't talk like that to Granddad!' before we can grasp articulations about the sanctity of human life, or what it means to respect age. These two stages can't be completely prised apart, because outside of the background articulated at the second stage we generally aren't able to project properly to new cases: to see, e.g., what exclusions there are to the ban on killing (if we accept a view which allows some) or grasp what other persons are worthy of respect. This is the point I made in section 3.1. But it is sometimes possible to give people at least a good first approximation of how to behave in external action terms. E.g., you tell the new arrival: 'Just remember, when you see someone with a red headdress, bow three times'.

To move from external action descriptions to the language of qualitative distinctions is to move to a language of "thick description", in the sense of this term that Clifford Geertz has made famous,[46] that is, a language which is a lot richer and more culturally bound, because it articulates the significance and point that the actions or feelings have within a certain culture.

But that is just what naturalism strives to avoid. One of the defining characteristics of naturalism, as I am using the term,[47] is the belief that we ought to understand human beings in terms continuous with the sciences of extra-human nature. Just as these last have progressed by turning away from anthropocentric language, by excluding descriptions which bear on the significance of things for us, in favour of 'absolute' ones, so human affairs ought to be maximally described in external, non-culture-bound terms. Thinkers of a naturalist temper, when considering ethics, naturally tend to think in terms of action. This temper has helped contribute to the dominance of moral theories of obligatory action in our intellectual culture.

But this is not all, of course. The dominance is overdetermined, as I suggested above, and there are also *moral* motives for this exclusion. I mentioned one in the discussion of hypergoods in the previous section. The various offshoots of the modern affirmation of ordinary life have engendered a suspicion of the claims made on behalf of 'higher' modes of life against the 'ordinary' goals and activities that humans engage in. The rejection of the higher can be presented as a liberation, as a recovery of the true value of human life. Of course, the moral value attaching to this liberating move itself presupposes another context of strong good. But with that curious blindness to the assumptions behind their own moral attitudes, utilitarians and modern naturalists in general can just focus on the negation of the older distinctions and see themselves as freeing themselves altogether from distinctions as such.

There is also a closely related way in which the rejection of qualitative distinctions can be seen as a liberation, which we can understand if we explore moral phenomenology a bit further. I mentioned in section 2.2 that we cannot but crave to be rightly placed in relation to the goods we recognize. But precisely this craving can be the source of much suffering, or alternatively of self-delusion, or smug self-satisfaction. That is, I can feel the demand to incorporate the good in my life as crushing; it is a demand that I feel utterly unable to live up to, which I constantly measure up badly on, and which leads to an overwhelming depreciation of myself. This, besides being uncomfortable, can be immensely restricting and even destructive. To break my allegiance to this good can therefore be experienced as a liberation, and this is what it is often represented as in much of the human potential literature of our day.[48] In particular, Christianity has been attacked ever since the Enlightenment for laying a crushing burden on those in whom it inculcates a sense of sin; or, in contemporary language, for "laying a guilt trip" on its devotees. To break with a good to which one cannot really subscribe is of course a liberation in anyone's language. The issue is whether flight is the only answer to unhealthy guilt. But we can readily see how, in a confused way, the possibility of such a liberation could seem to accredit the rejection of qualitative distinctions as such. (Though generally not, it must be said, in the popular writings concerned today with human potential; these usually espouse their own crucial distinctions, around such goods as fulfilment or self-expression.)

Alternatively, of course, my craving to be well placed to the good can make me a prey to illusions, can either lead me to espouse a standard on which I measure well, but which I cannot ultimately really defend, or can make me blind to how poorly I actually do compare. And to illusion is often added a certain smug satisfaction in contrasting myself to others. How much of my ability to live with myself comes from the repetition of such consoling thoughts as: at least I'm not like those (wastrels, weaklings, blackguards, philistines, rightists, leftists, etc.)? Reflecting on all this can strengthen the sense that turning away from all these notions of the good is somehow a liberation.

So metaphysical, epistemological, and moral considerations run together here. But we have not exhausted the moral considerations. As well as the affirmation of ordinary life, there is the modern notion of freedom. The ancient notion of the good, either in the Platonic mode, as the key to cosmic order, or in the form of the good life à la Aristotle, sets a standard for us in nature, independent of our will. The modern notion of freedom which develops in the seventeenth century portrays this as the independence of the subject, his determining of his own purposes without interference from external authority. The second came to be considered as incompatible with the first. The conflict was originally conceived in theological terms. Late mediaeval nominalism defended the sovereignty of God as incompatible with there being an order in nature which by itself defined good and bad. For that would be to tie God's hands, to infringe on his sovereign right of decision about what was good.[49] This line of thought even contributed in the end to the rise of mechanism: the ideal universe from this point of view is a mechanical one, without intrinsic purpose.[50] But with the modern era, something analogous begins to be transferred onto humans. Normative orders must originate in the will. This is most evident in the seventeenth-century political theory of legitimacy through contract. As against earlier contract theories, the one we find with Grotius and Locke starts from the individual. Being in a political order to which one owes allegiance presupposes, on this view, that one has given it one's consent. Rightful submission cannot arise just by nature, as classical theories assume. The most radical development of this line of thought in moral philosophy had to await Kant.

But in the meantime the new conception of freedom, which arose partly from an anthropological transfer of the prerogatives of God, already has some role in the formation of utilitarian thought and its proto-doctrines. Hobbes's political atomism is plainly linked with his nominalism and with his view that the good is determined for each person by what he desires,[51] both doctrines plainly owing a lot to late mediaeval defences of theological decisionism. Political right is made by fiat.[52] And in mature utilitarianism, the stress on modern freedom emerges in the rejection of paternalism. Each person is the best judge of his own happiness. The rejection of the idea that our good is founded in some natural order is seen by utilitarians as the repudiation of paternalism. Not only is it justified on epistemological-metaphysical grounds and not only is it appropriate as an affirmation of the value of ordinary life, but it is also seen as establishing the individual's freedom to determine the goals of his or her own life and own definition of happiness.

This powerful array of motives converges, however mistakenly, to discredit qualitative distinctions, to make them appear as intellectually suspect and morally sinister, and to establish a model of moral thinking which tries to do without them altogether. Thence arise some of the perplexities and fudgings of utilitarianism, such as the difficulty in understanding what the moral motivation is that it appeals to, the relation between hedonism as a motivational theory and the benevolence that utilitarian practice seems to suppose, and the like. But the force of these motives is great enough to outweigh the intellectual discomfort of these unsolved puzzles; somewhere, utilitarians feel, there must be answers, and meantime they plunge forward into their homogeneous universe of rational calculation. (And the sense of power and control which comes from this latter is, of course, another powerful motive for accepting the theory.)

But utilitarianism is not the only philosophy responsible for this climate of modern thought. Kant's theory in fact rehabilitates one crucial distinction, that between actions done from duty and those done from inclination. This is grounded on a distinction of motives: the desire for happiness versus respect for the moral law. Kant deliberately takes this stance in opposition to utilitarian thought, the *"Glückseligkeitslehre"* of which he speaks in scathing terms. Following Rousseau, he breaks with the utilitarian conception of our motives as homogeneous. He returns to the Augustinian insight that there are radically different qualities of the will; what is of ultimate moral importance is just this issue of the quality of one's will.[53]

But nevertheless Kant shares the modern stress on freedom as self-determination. He insists on seeing the moral law as one which emanates from our will. Our awe before it reflects the status of rational agency, its author, and whose being it expresses. Rational agents have a status that nothing else enjoys in the universe. They soar above the rest of creation. Everything else may have a price, but only they have 'dignity' *(Würde)*.[54] And so Kant strongly insists that our moral obligations owe nothing to the order of nature. He rejects vigorously as irrelevant all those qualitative distinctions which pick out higher and lower in the order of the cosmos or in human nature. To take these as central to one's moral views is to fall into heteronomy.

It has therefore been easy for the followers of Kant to take this rejection of qualitative distinctions in the order of being for a rejection of any distinction at all, and to forget or put into the shade Kant's doctrine of the dignity of rational agents. This has been the easier given the connection between the affirmation of modern freedom and the rejection of such distinctions that the naturalist Enlightenment gives currency to; and it is aided and abetted by all the epistemological and metaphysical doubts that it has entrenched in our modern outlook.

This mixture of Kantian and naturalist conceptions has yielded the picture of the human agent so familiar in much contemporary moral philosophy. Iris Murdoch captures it in a memorable description: "How recognizable, how familiar to us is the man so beautifully portrayed in the *Grundlegung,* who confronted even with Christ turns away to consider the judgement of his own conscience and to hear the voice of his own reason. Stripped of the exiguous metaphysical background which Kant was prepared to allow him, this man is with us still, free, independent, lonely, powerful, rational, responsible, brave, the hero of so many novels and books of moral philosophy".[55]

No one can gainsay the power of this ideal among our contemporaries, and thanks to the confusion mentioned above it has greatly served to strengthen the modern moral philosophies of obligatory action, which I described earlier, and which tend to sideline these qualitative distinctions, where they do not deny them a place altogether. The focus is on the principles, or injunctions, or standards which guide *action,* while visions of the good are altogether neglected. Morality is narrowly concerned with what we ought to *do,* and not also with what is valuable in itself, or what we should admire or love. Contemporary philosophers, even when they descend from Kant rather than Bentham (e.g., John Rawls), share this focus. Moral philosophy should concern itself with determining the principles of our action. Or where it sees itself in a strictly "meta-ethical" role, it should concern itself with the language in which we determine extra-philosophically the principles of our action. Its starting point should be our intuitions about what actions are right (Rawls), or some general theory about what morality is, conceived in prescriptive, i.e., action-guiding, terms (Hare). The idea that moral thought should concern itself with our different visions of the qualitatively higher, with strong goods, is never even mooted. Awareness of their place in our moral lives has been so deeply suppressed that the thought never seems to occur to many of our contemporaries.

Their conception of freedom and their epistemological suspicion of strong goods bind together utilitarians and naturalists of all sorts, as well as Kantians, in this suppression. And in this another motive concurs as well. A central feature of Enlightenment morality, in which it shows its roots in Christianity, is the stress on practical benevolence. This was a crucial theme with Bacon, where it was still expressed in Christian terms, and he passed it on to his more secular spiritual successors. Our scientific effort should not serve simply to create objects of contemplation for us, but should serve to "relieve the condition of mankind".[56] Practical charity is enjoined on us. The Enlightenment took this up in intensified form, and it has become one of the central beliefs of modern Western culture: we all should work to improve the human condition, relieve suffering, overcome poverty, increase prosperity, augment human welfare. We should strive to leave the world a more prosperous place than we found it.

This can seem to give independent justification to the exclusive focus on action in much of contemporary moral theory. This focus can be represented as being a sign of moral earnestness, of benevolent determination. Those who are concerned about what is valuable, what one should love or admire, are worried about the state of their own souls. They are self-absorbed, prone to narcissism, and not committed to altruistic action, the improvement of the lot of mankind, or the defence of justice. Utilitarians frequently slide into moral arguments in defence of their ethical theory.[57]

We can begin to appreciate how heavily overdetermined is this vogue of theories of obligatory action. Not only the epistemological and metaphysical predilections of naturalism are at work here, but also strong moral motives. I have spoken about three: the defence of ordinary life and desire against the (supposedly specious) demands of "higher" goods, the modern conception of freedom, and one reading of the demands of benevolence and altruism. But the desire for a fully universal ethic can also play a role. The goods that we articulate in qualitative distinctions are frequently those of a particular cultural group and are embedded in their way of life. If the aim is to avoid above all parochial ethical principles, then one has another reason to sideline these distinctions. This is undoubtedly an important factor in Habermas's positions.[58] Williams in turn, in the penetrating discussion that closes his book,[59] argues that the exclusive focus on obligation in much modern moral philosophy has its own peculiar motivation in the attachment to a hypergood (as I would call it) of purity.

Various combinations of these motives tend to bring Kantians and utilitarians together around theories of obligatory action and, relatedly, lead them to share a procedural conception of ethics. I am using the word 'procedural' here in opposition to 'substantive'. These terms can be applied to forms of ethical theory by derivation from their use to describe conceptions of reason. I call a notion of reason substantive where we judge the rationality of agents or their thoughts and feelings in substantive terms. This means that the criterion for rationality is that one get it right. Plato has a conception of this kind. You couldn't be fully rational, in his book, and believe for instance that Democritus was right about the natural world or that the best life was the one where you fulfilled the most sensual desires. By contrast, a procedural notion of reason breaks this connection. The rationality of an agent or his thought is judged by how he thinks, not in the first instance by whether the outcome is substantively correct. Good thinking is defined procedurally. Descartes offers a paradigm example of this with his model of clear and distinct thought. We end up with the assurance that this will give us substantive truth, but only after we have gone through the argument proving the existence of a veracious God. Correct thinking is not *defined* by substantial truth, because defining it is the prelude to raising the question whether its results are trustworthy.

Practical reason was understood by the ancients substantively. To be rational was to have the correct vision, or in the case of Aristotle's *phronēsis*, an accurate power of moral discrimination. But once we sideline a sense or vision of the good and consider it irrelevant to moral thinking, then our notion of practical reasoning has to be procedural. The excellence of practical reasoning is defined in terms of a certain style, method, or procedure of thought. For the utilitarians, rationality is maximizing calculation. *Zweck-rationalität* is the crucial form. For the Kantians the definitive procedure of practical reason is that of universalization.

Beyond the common weight of modern epistemology on them, it is clear how for both the stress on the procedural is bound up with their allegiance to modern freedom. To make practical reason substantive implies that practical wisdom is a matter of seeing an order which in some sense is in nature. This order determines what ought to be done. To reverse this and give primacy to the agent's own desires or his will, while still wanting to give value to practical reason, you have to redefine this in procedural terms. If the right thing to do still has to be understood as what is rationally justifiable, then the justification has to be procedural. It can't be defined by the particular outcome, but by the way in which the outcome is arrived at.

This modern idea of freedom is the strongest motive for the massive shift from substantive to procedural justifications in the modern world. We can see the rise of social contract theory in the same light. Instead of defining legitimacy substantively in terms of the kind of regime or some conception of the good society, we define it by the procedure of its inauguration. It's all right, thought Grotius, no matter what its form, as long as it comes about through consent. And if we leap from the earliest to the most recent such theory, Habermas's conception of a discourse ethic is founded in part on the same consideration. The idea that a norm is justified only to the extent that all could uncoercedly accept it is a new and interesting variant of the procedural idea. It owes something to Kant but offers a "dialogical" procedure in place of Kant's, which each agent could carry out on his or her own. But this change seems a step forward precisely because it involves a fuller acceptance of the free self-determination of diverse people. In a way, it unites both Kantian universality and the Benthamite refusal to decide for other people what is right for them.[60]

And so we sketch the portrait of a wide trend in modern moral philosophy. Having excluded qualitative distinctions for epistemological and moral reasons so effectively, indeed, that it has almost suppressed all awareness of their place in our lives, it proposes a view of moral thought focussed simply on determining the principles of action. To the extent that it accords practical reason an important role in determining these, that it considers that the right action should always be in some strong sense rationally justifiable, it adopts a procedural conception of reason. One of its central issues is how we should understand practical reason, how we should rationally determine what we ought to do.

But this suppression leaves perplexing gaps in the theory. It has no way of capturing the background understanding surrounding any conviction that we ought to act in this or that way—the understanding of the strong good involved. And in particular, it cannot capture the peculiar background sense, central to much of our moral life, that something incomparably important is involved. So this reappears in an odd form, for instance in a definition of moral reasoning, as a reasoning of a particular form whose outcomes have a special priority over others. What this priority consists in is left unexplained. For Hare, it belongs logically to the moral. This is just what we mean by 'moral'.[61] For Habermas, the priority to a discourse ethic is a product of maturation both ontogenetically and in the history of culture.[62] But clearly there is a gaping hole here. We might be tempted to put it this way: they leave us with nothing to say to someone who asks why he should be moral or strive to the "maturity" of a 'post-conventional' ethic. But this could be misleading, if we seemed to be asking how we could convince someone who saw none of the point of our moral beliefs. There is nothing we can do to "prove" we are right to such a person. But imagine him to be asking another question: he could be asking us to make plain the point of our moral code, to articulate what's uniquely valuable in cleaving to these injunctions. Then the implication of these theories is that we have nothing to say which can impart insight. We can wax rhetorical and propagandize, but we can't say what's good or valuable about them, or why they command assent.

Or else we can take up the question, 'Why should I be moral?' in the way Hare does in his book *Moral Thinking*.[63] The only kind of answer that Hare can conceive of offering here is one in prudential terms. He tries to show that it is in someone's *interest* to be brought up with the right moral principles. Within his philosophy, the question I articulated can't be addressed at all.

This conception of the moral is strangely skewed. It tries to account for the incomparable weight of certain considerations, which we should see in terms of the incomparable status of certain goods, by segregating off a domain of the 'moral' and hermetically sealing it from other considerations (section 3.2). 'Moral' defines a certain kind of reasoning, which in some unexplained way has in principle priority. It is not clear how moral considerations can function with others in a single deliberative activity; we cannot see why these higher considerations should usually be given priority and also why they might be denied this in certain circumstances. For this kind of deliberation would presuppose that we see them all as goods, with different levels of importance.

But at the same time this segregating boundary can't just be dropped. It is the only way a procedural ethic has of marking some considerations as incomparably higher. The more we are really (if inarticulately) moved by a hypergood, the more fiercely we have to defend this boundary, however inadequate our explanation of it may be. For instance, in Habermas's case, the boundary between questions of ethics, which have to do with interpersonal justice, and those of the good life is supremely important, because it is the boundary between demands of truly universal validity and goods which will differ from culture to culture. This distinction is the only bulwark, in Habermas's eyes, against chauvinistic and ethnocentric aggression in the name of one's way of life, or tradition, or culture. It is thus crucial to maintain it.

The more one examines the motives—what Nietzsche would call the 'genealogy'—of these theories of obligatory action, the stranger they appear. It seems that they are motivated by the strongest moral ideals, such as freedom, altruism, and universalism. These are among the central moral aspirations of modern culture, the hypergoods which are distinctive to it. And yet what these ideals drive the theorists towards is a denial of all such goods. They are caught in a strange pragmatic contradiction, whereby the very goods which move them push them to deny or denature all such goods. They are constitutionally incapable of coming clean about the deeper sources of their own thinking. Their thought is inescapably cramped.

A common slogan of Kant-derived moral theories in our day serves also to justify the exclusion of qualitative distinctions. This is the principle of the priority of the right over the good. In its original form, as a Kantian counter-attack against utilitarianism, as an insistence that morality couldn't be conceived simply in terms of outcomes but that moral obligation also had to be thought of deontologically, it can be seen as one moral theory among others and, in its anti-utilitarian thrust, highly justified. But it also can be used to downgrade not just the homogeneous good of desire-fulfilment central to utilitarian theory but also any conception of the good, including the qualitative distinctions underlying our moral views. Rawls, for instance, seems to be proposing in *A Theory of Justice* that we develop a notion of justice starting only with a "thin theory of the good", by which he means what I am calling weakly valued goods.[64] But this suggestion is on the deepest level incoherent. Rawls does, of course, manage to derive (if his arguments in rational choice theory hold up) his two principles of justice. But as he himself agrees, we recognize that these are indeed acceptable principles of justice because they fit with our intuitions. If we were to articulate what underlies these intuitions we would start spelling out a very "thick" theory of the good. To say that we don't "need" this to develop our theory of justice turns out to be highly misleading. We don't actually spell it out, but we have to draw on the sense of the good that we have here in order to decide what are adequate principles of justice. The theory of justice which starts from the thin theory of the good turns out to be a theory which keeps its most basic insights inarticulate, as emerges, for instance, in Michael Sandel's critique.[65]

Where 'good' means the primary goal of a consequentialist theory, where the right is decided simply by its instrumental significance for this end, then we ought indeed to insist that the right can be primary to the good. But where we use 'good' in the sense of this discussion, where it means whatever is marked out as higher by a qualitative distinction, then we could say that the reverse is the case, that in a sense, the good is always primary to the right. Not in that it offers a more basic reason in the sense of our earlier discussion, but in that the good is what, in its articulation, gives the point of the rules which define the right.[66]

This is what has been suppressed by these strange cramped theories of modern moral philosophy, which have the paradoxical effect of making us inarticulate on some of the most important issues of morality. Impelled by the strongest metaphysical, epistemological, and moral ideas of the modern age, these theories narrow our focus to the determinants of action, and then restrict our understanding of these determinants still further by defining practical reason as exclusively procedural. They utterly mystify the priority of the moral by identifying it not with substance but with a form of reasoning, around which they draw a firm boundary. They then are led to defend this boundary all the more fiercely in that it is their only way of doing justice to the hypergoods which move them although they cannot acknowledge them.

And from this frequently follows another of the strange cramps they put in moral thinking, the tendency to unify the moral domain around a single consideration or basic reason, e.g., happiness or the categorical imperative, thus cramming the tremendous variety of moral considerations into a Procrustes bed.[67] And there are other cramps as well. The notion that morality is exclusively concerned with obligations has had a restricting and distorting effect on our moral thinking and sensibility. Williams shows[68] how badly distorting this is, and how it fails to cope with all that aspect of our moral thinking which concerns aspirations to perfection, heroism, supererogation, and the like. Once more, in Procrustean fashion, this is either assimilated to a foreign mould or rejected.

All this in answer to the question why it is necessary to belabour the obvious fact that qualitative distinctions have an inexpungable place in our moral life and thinking. We have to fight uphill to rediscover the obvious, to counteract the layers of suppression of modern moral consciousness. It's a difficult thing to do. But what is the point of doing it?

4

MORAL SOURCES

4.1

In a way, this is to ask: What is the point of articulacy about the good? We
tend to have a prejudice in favour of articulacy in our culture (at least in the
academy), and so the question may not seem to need an answer. But in fact
there have been cogent reasons put forward, or at least hinted at, for a saving
inarticulacy in this domain. Some things perhaps ought to be passed over in
silence. Ludwig Wittgenstein, among others, certainly thought so.

And so the question needs an answer. The obvious point to begin with is
that the goods I have been talking about only exist for us through *some*
articulation. The rather different understandings of the good which we see in
different cultures are the correlative of the different languages which have
evolved in those cultures. A vision of the good becomes available for the
people of a given culture through being given expression in some manner.
The God of Abraham exists for us (that is, belief in him is a possibility)
because he has been talked about, primarily in the narrative of the Bible but
also in countless other ways from theology to devotional literature. And also
because he has been talked *to* in all the different manners of liturgy and
prayer. Universal rights of mankind exist for us because they have been
promulgated, because philosophers have theorized about them, because
revolutions have been fought in their name, and so on. In neither case, of
course, are these articulations a sufficient condition of belief. There are
atheists in our civilization, nourished by the Bible, and racists in the modern
liberal West. But articulation is a necessary condition of adhesion; without it,
these goods are not even options.[1]

But it is clear that the notions of 'language' and 'articulation' are being
used in an unusually broad and encompassing sense here. A sense of the good
finds expression not only in linguistic descriptions but also in other speech
acts—as with the example above of prayer. And if we follow this example
further, into liturgy, we see that expression goes beyond the bounds of
language as normally and narrowly conceived. The gesture of ritual, its
music, its display of visual symbols, all enact in their own fashion our relation

to God. Indeed, we can come to hold that prose language description is the most impoverished medium, that it cannot come close to capturing what we can sense and relate to in other ways, as proponents of a negative theology believe. And it is clear that for centuries in the Western church, the principal media in which the mass of believers came to understand their faith were, alongside narrative, those of ritual and visual presentation in church frescos and illuminated windows.

But this makes us raise our question again in a new form: Why articulacy in the narrow sense? Why try to *say* what the underlying sense of the good consists in? Why make it articulate in descriptive language? Why try to find formulations for it which can figure in moral thinking?

There is, of course, a one-line Socratic answer to this. It emerges from a particular ethical view, or range of views, which sees reason, in the sense of the logos, of linguistic articulacy, as part of the telos of human beings. We aren't full beings in this perspective until we can say what moves us, what our lives are built around.

I confess that I share some version of this conception. But without prejudice to this more general issue of the value of the unexamined life as such, what I want to examine now is the more particular importance of articulacy for our sense of the good. In this I may also be following a Socratic idea. The central notion here is that articulation can bring us closer to the good as a moral source, can give it power.

The understanding of the good as a moral source has also been deeply suppressed in the mainstream of modern moral consciousness, although it was perfectly familiar to the ancients. I have been speaking of the good in these pages, or sometimes of strong good, meaning whatever is picked out as incomparably higher in a qualitative distinction. It can be some action, or motive, or style of life, which is seen as qualitatively superior. 'Good' is used here in a highly general sense, designating anything considered valuable, worthy, admirable, of whatever kind or category.

But in some of these distinctions, there is something which seems to deserve the attribution in a fuller sense. To take Plato's theory as an example: the distinction between higher and lower actions, motivations, ways of living turns on the hegemony of reason or desire. But the hegemony of reason is understood substantively. To be rational is to have a vision of rational order, and to love this order. So the difference of action or motivation has to be explained by reference to a cosmic reality, the order of things. This is good in a fuller sense: the key to this order is the Idea of the Good itself. Their relation to this is what makes certain of our actions or aspirations good; it is what constitutes the goodness of these actions or motives.

Let us call this kind of reality a 'constitutive good'. We can then say that for Plato the constitutive good is the order of being, or perhaps the principle of that order, the Good. But we can see right away that this plays another role in addition to constituting or defining what good action is. The Good is also that the love of which moves us to good action. The constitutive good is a moral source, in the sense I want to use this term here: that is, it is a something the love of which empowers us to do and be good.

But spelling this out puts the discussion of the previous sections in a new light. In the argument of the last chapters, I have been concentrating on qualitative distinctions between actions, or feelings, or modes of life. The goods which these define are facets or components of a good life. Let us call these 'life goods'. But now we see, in Plato's case, that the life goods refer us to some feature of the way things are, in virtue of which these life goods are goods. This feature constitutes them as goods, and that is why I call them constitutive.

The constitutive good does more than just define the content of the moral theory. Love of it is what empowers us to be good. And hence also loving it is part of what it is to be a good human being. This is now part of the content of the moral theory as well, which includes injunctions not only to act in certain ways and to exhibit certain moral qualities but also to love what is good.[2]

This obviously takes us far beyond the purview of the morals of obligatory action. These theories balk even at acknowledging life goods; they obviously have no place at all for a constitutive good which might stand behind them. I argued at the end of the previous chapter that the refusal of these theories to accept qualitative distinctions, while understandable, was based on a confusion; that they themselves were motivated by goods of this kind. In other words, I argued that they were grounded on an unadmitted adherence to certain life goods, such as freedom, altruism, universal justice. And indeed, if the argument of the previous chapters is anywhere near right, it is hard to see how one could have a moral theory at all or, indeed, be a self, without some such adherence.

Can an analogous point be made about constitutive goods? Do they too form part of the unacknowledged baggage of modern, or indeed of all, moral theories? Or is this Platonic notion of a good as the object of empowering love something which belongs to the remote past?

It is obvious that Platonism is not alone in conceiving a constitutive good as source in this way. Christian and Jewish theism do as well. It was natural for Christian Platonists like Augustine to see God as occupying the place of Plato's Idea of the Good. The image of the sun serves for both, with of course the major difference that the love which empowers here is not just ours for God, but also his *(agapē)* for us. But what happens when, as in modern humanist views, we no longer have anything like a constitutive good external to man? What can we say when the notion of the higher is a form of human life which consists precisely in facing a disenchanted universe with courage and lucidity?

It seems to me that one can still speak of a moral source here. There *is* a constitutive reality, namely, humans as beings capable of this courageous disengagement. And our sense of admiration and awe for these capacities is what empowers us to live up to them. This is something which comes to clear recognition in the humanist theory of Kant. The motive which enables us to live according to the law is the sense of respect *(Achtung)* that we experience before the moral law itself, once we understand it as emanating from rational will. Our recognition that rational agency stands infinitely above the rest of the universe, because it alone has dignity, brings with it an awe which empowers us morally. In Kant's theory, rational agency is the constitutive good.

I don't want for a minute to underplay the tremendous importance of this internalizing move of modern humanism, which recognizes no more constitutive goods external to us. It involves a veritable revolution in moral consciousness. It would be tempting to mark it by describing it as the definitive rejection of constitutive goods. Certainly it does away with these in the traditionally recognizable sense, for which Platonism and Christian theology provided the paradigm models.

I don't suppose it matters exactly what terms we use here. I wouldn't mind adopting the convention of the previous paragraph; except that we risk losing from view the continuing role of moral sources. As the Kantian case shows, an entirely immanent view of the good is compatible with recognizing that there is something the contemplation of which commands our respect, which respect in turn empowers. Whatever fills this role is playing the part of a moral source; it has an analogous place in the ethical life of Kantians to that of the Idea of the Good among Platonists. The move to an immanent ethic doesn't mean that this role stops being played.

But it might be objected, that's all very true of Kant—but it is so only because he was still insufficiently modern, had not yet gone all the way along the road to disenchantment, or discarded all the remnants of Christian theology and ancient philosophy.[3] How about the other view I evoked above, which sees our dignity in the courage and lucidity of our stance to a meaningless universe? My point is that something analogous still functions here in the crucial role. That is, those who hold this view have a sense of the dignity of human beings, which consists precisely in their ability to stand unconsoled and uncowed in face of the indifferent immensity of the world and to find the purpose of their lives in understanding it and transcending in this way by far their own insignificant locus and being. Pascal already gave voice to this with his image of the thinking reed. Man can be annihilated by the universe, but his greatness in relation to it consists in his going down knowingly. Something inspires our respect here, and this respect empowers. Or if it fails utterly to move us, then it cannot be that we accept that conception of the good. This humanism is less far from the Kantian than it may think.

Or course, another important change has occurred with the immanentization: the empowering motive has changed from love to respect. Or perhaps we might say that from the mixture of love and awe which the God of Abraham commanded, only some of the latter is left in face of our own powers of disengagement. Here is another reason to mark this by a break in our vocabulary. And once again, I don't mind such a break, provided we don't lose the continuity from view. I don't mind if one says that modern immanent humanism has no more place for constitutive goods, that nothing functions quite like the moral sources of premodern theories. But what remains true is that something still functions analogously. That is, there is something relation to which defines certain actions and motives as higher, viz., our capacities as 'thinking reeds'; and our contemplation of this can inspire a motive which empowers us to live up to what is higher.

But this is precisely what we are tempted to forget in the climate of modern moral philosophy. The eclipse of our whole awareness of qualitative distinctions carries with it the neglect of this whole dimension of our moral thought and experience.

For this reason, I shall elect to speak still of moral sources even in connection with modern immanentist theories, and even of the most severely disenchanted kind. I will try to do justice to the differences and not fall into too seamless a picture of the continuities. But all things considered, I think this danger is the lesser one in our times.

If we return to the issue of articulacy, we can see that one of the important discontinuities is that we often feel ourselves less able than our forebears to be articulate. I mentioned in the first chapter how people are often at a loss to say what underpins their sense of the respect owed to people's rights (section 1.1), and later (1.4) how traditional frameworks have become problematic for us, and how much our articulations are exploratory. Iris Murdoch, who defends a view which has plainly drawn a great deal from Plato, stresses that the good is something which is "non-representable and indefinable."[4]

And it emerges, too, in the way that empowering images and stories function in our time. Some of the most powerful have their roots in religious and philosophical doctrines which many moderns have abandoned. One may not be able to substitute for the theological or metaphysical beliefs which originally underpinned them; but the images still inspire us. Or perhaps better, they go on pointing to something which remains for us a moral source, something the contemplation, respect, or love of which enables us to get closer to what is good. Murdoch's theory of the "sovereignty of 'good' ", just mentioned, is a case in point. No one today can accept the Platonic metaphysic of the Ideas as the crucial explanation of the shape of the cosmos. And yet the image of the Good as the sun, in the light of which we can see things clearly and with a kind of dispassionate love, does crucial work for her. It helps define the direction of attention and desire through which alone, she believes, we can become good.[5]

Another example, this time from the Jewish and Christian religious traditions, has been explored by Michael Walzer.[6] The story of the Exodus has inspired movements of reform and liberation throughout the centuries, even those which claimed to reject the theological outlook which the original story proclaims. Sometimes some clear alternative secular theory has been substituted, e.g., a Marxist picture of humanity's advance towards socialism. But it is also clear that the story has tremendous power even for those who have no definite notion of a God or a History which is freeing them from bondage. To see one's story in this light can be inspiring and empowering, even though one might be puzzled if asked to state what underlying doctrine about humans, or God, or history one relies on to make sense of this. The fact is, seeing one's life in this pattern carries tremendous moral power. Even where the theology is lost, the story marches on. Northrop Frye shows how the Bible as a whole has been a tremendous source of such empowering stories in Western history.[7]

So articulating the good is very difficult and problematic for us. Is that a reason for eschewing it? In one way perhaps it might be, as I shall mention in a minute. But first there seem to be very strong reasons in favour of articulacy wherever a constitutive good serves as a moral source. Moral sources empower. To come closer to them, to have a clearer view of them, to come to grasp what they involve, is for those who recognize them to be moved to love or respect them, and through this love/respect to be better enabled to live up to them. And articulation can bring them closer. That is why words can empower; why words can at times have tremendous moral force.

And of course not just any articulation will do. Some formulations may be dead, or have no power at this place or time or with certain people. And in the most evident examples the power is not a function of the formulation alone, but of the whole speech act. Indeed, the most powerful case is where the speaker, the formulation, and the act of delivering the message all line up together to reveal the good, as the immense and continuing force of the gospel illustrates. A formulation has power when it brings the source close, when it makes it plain and evident, in all its inherent force, its capacity to inspire our love, respect, or allegiance. An effective articulation releases this force, and this is how words have power.

Words may have power because they tap a source hitherto unknown or unfelt, as we see with the Exodus, with Isaiah, with the Gospels; or they may restore the power of an older source that we have lost contact with, as with St. Francis or Erasmus. Or they may have power in another way, by articulating our feelings or our story so as to bring us in contact with a source we have been longing for. This may come about through the recasting of our lives in a new narrative, as with Augustine's *Confessions,* or through seeing our struggle through the prism of the Exodus, as with the civil rights movement in America in the 1960's,[8] or in innumerable less famous and fateful places in which people understand their lives through a new story.

The tremendous force of certain stories has to be understood in the light of the discussion above in section 2.3, where I talked of our striving to make sense of our lives in narrative as somehow related to the good. One way in which people do this is to relate their story to a greater pattern of history, as the realization of a good, whether it be the traditional *Heilsgeschichte* of Christianity, or that of the Progress of mankind, or the coming Revolution, or the building of a peaceful world, or the retrieval or continuance of our national culture. It's almost as though these schematic historical narratives exercised a force of attraction of their own. The secret of their strength is their capacity to confer meaning and substance on people's lives. Just what gives them this is a matter of further inquiry. But that some schemata, including the above mentioned, have this power seems beyond question.

But then we can readily see why some people distrust articulation as a source of delusion or fear it as a profanation, as I mentioned above. It is not mainly because there are so many dead formulations, so many trite imitations, although this is one of the reasons why one may prefer silence—Karl Kraus is perhaps a case in point.[9] What is worse is that the whole thing may be counterfeited. This is not to say that words of power themselves may be counterfeit. But the act by which their pronouncing releases force can be rhetorically imitated, either to feed our self-conceit or for even more sinister purposes, such as the defence of a discreditable status quo. Trite formulae may combine with the historical sham to weave a cocoon of moral assurance around us which actually insulates us from the energy of true moral sources. And there is worse: the release of power can be hideously caricatured to enhance the energy of evil, as at Nuremberg. As for the narrative constructions of our lives, there is no need to speak at length about the possibilities of delusion which attend us here.

There are good reasons to keep silent. But they cannot be valid across the board. Without any articulation at all, we would lose all contact with the good, however conceived. We would cease to be human. The severest injunctions to silence can only be directed to certain classes of articulation, and must spare others. The issue is to define which ones. Our question then returns about articulations in descriptive prose of our sense of qualitative distinctions. These are the ones which modern moral philosophy tends to suppress. Should we try to recover them for moral thought, or are they best left in implicit limbo?

4.2

One might think straight off that we have an obvious reason to articulate them in the very modern predicament of perplexity and conflict between rival notions of the good. If one wants to reason about them, doesn't one have to spell them out? Or put negatively, isn't inarticulacy a crippling handicap to seeing clearly in this domain?

I think it is, and I am very sympathetic to this argument. But a proponent of silence might be unconvinced. If articulation can only banalize at best, and at worst feeds our love of self-display and self-delusion, then it cannot improve our epistemic plight. And isn't there a danger of ironing out too quickly what is paradoxical in our deepest moral sense, of reconciling too quickly the conflicts, making a synthesis of what cannot easily be combined, in short of making our moral predicament look clearer, more unified, more harmonious, than it really is?

I am very aware of these dangers; at least I aspire to be. In another situation, they might provide good reasons for silence. But I think the silence of modern philosophy is unhealthy. It is powered, I argued above, partly by metaphysical and epistemological reasons which I believe invalid and largely by moral or spiritual reasons: the affirmation of ordinary life, and the modern conception of freedom, which indeed I want to endorse under some version, but cannot under this one. The reason is that this version is deeply confused. It reads the affirmation of life and freedom as involving a repudiation of qualitative distinctions, a rejection of constitutive goods as such, while these are themselves reflections of qualitative distinctions and presuppose some conception of qualitative goods. Lastly, when a theory of this range is inspired (inarticulately) by a hypergood, it cannot but distort our deliberative predicament and draws a rigid boundary between the 'moral' and the 'non-moral' or (in Habermas's case) between 'ethical' considerations and those relating to the 'good life', which badly occludes their relation, and above all, prevents us from asking one of the crucial questions of modern moral thought: to what extent the "revisionist" claims made on behalf of hypergoods ought to be accepted at all (see section 3.2).

The existence of this cast of thought and its importance in our culture create an overwhelming case for articulation of the good. It suppresses so many questions and hides so many confusions that one cannot but experience it as intellectually asphyxiating, once one has escaped, even partially, from its spell.

Of course a complex position of this kind, whose parts interlock so well as to form a kind of fortress, in which the different epistemological, metaphysical, and moral motives buttress each other while hiding their joint operation, will inspire attack from many sides. Not all will be concerned to articulate the underlying notions of the good. There is an influential line of attack today, which can loosely be called neo-Nietzschean, and of which the late Michel Foucault propounded an influential variant, which has its own strong reasons to deny articulation. The neo-Nietzchean position attacks the procedural ethic mainly for its implicit moral inspirations:[10] for the conception of freedom it defends, and for its attachment to a hypergood and consequent radical revisionism. In this it resembles my critique, because we both want to show that this modern philosophy *has* moral motives, instead of being uniquely determined by epistemic ones. But there the convergence ends. The neo-Nietzschean type of theory sees no value in this articulation other than the polemical one of unmasking the pretensions of modern moral philosophy and, indeed, of much of moral philosophy in general. It sees no value in this articulation itself. On the contrary, it has espoused its own version of projection theory. If intellectual positions are closely tied up with moral ones, this is because both are to be seen as orders which we have imposed on reality, following a line of thinking drawn largely from *The Gay Science*.[11] No position is to be seen as more or less justified than any other. All are ultimately based on fiat. Such are the "regimes of truth" of which Foucault spoke. Needless to say, I find this view as deeply implausible as its empiricist cousins. The point of view from which we might constate that all orders are equally arbitrary, in particular that all moral views are equally so, is just not available to us humans. It is a form of self-delusion to think that we do not speak from a moral orientation which we take to be right. This is a condition of being a functioning self, not a metaphysical view we can put on or off. So the meta-construal of the neo-Nietzschean philosopher—'in holding my moral position, I am imposing (or collaborating in the imposition of) a regime of truth on the chaos, and so does everyone'—is just as impossible as the meta-construal of the empiricist—'in holding my moral position, I am projecting values on a neutral world of facts, and so does everyone'. Both are incompatible with the way we cannot but understand ourselves in the actual practices which constitute holding that position: our deliberations, our serious assessments of ourselves and others. They are not construals you could actually make of your life while living it. They clash, in other words, with the best available account of our moral life. And what meta-considerations can overrule our best account of our actual moral experience? The neo-Nietzschean position falls afoul of the BA principle, just as the crasser forms of naturalism do.[12]

Oddly enough—or ironically—the neo-Nietzschean theory is open to the same kind of criticism as that which we both, it and I, level against mainstream moral philosophy: that of not coming quite clean about its own moral motivations. Only here the problem is not that it denies having any, as with modern meta-ethical theories which claim only epistemological grounds, but that it accords them a false status. It claims a kind of distance from its own value commitments, which consists in the fact that it alone is lucid about their status as fruits of a constructed order, which lucidity sets it apart from other views and confers the advantage on itself of being free from delusion in a way that the others aren't. This is, of course, strikingly similar to the claim made by naturalist theories, those which see that values are "merely" projections. The claim in one and the other case is unfounded, and is only kept aloft by a certain lack of self-lucidity, which keeps the relevant meta-construal from connecting with the terms in which we cannot but live our actual moral experience.

Of course neo-Nietzschean theories, just as those of obligatory action, have their own complex of underlying epistemological and moral motives. One of these is particularly worth noting, because it has led to some important insights. Writers in this stream have made us especially aware how visions of good may be connected to certain forms of domination. This was obvious in certain cases, e.g., the warrior ethic of fame and glory plainly exalted men and gave a subordinate and largely ancillary role to women. But various forms of more lofty, seemingly universal spiritual outlooks may also foster inequality and the suppression of supposedly lesser beings. Neo-Nietzscheans build here on insights which were put forward in the Romantic era. Allegiance to certain kinds of hypergoods leads to a suppression of 'nature', and this introduces relations of domination within us.[13] These relations then become fatally reflected in those between people. Thinkers of the Frankfurt school drew on this source as well as on Nietzsche.

There is obviously much truth, and of a very crucial sort, in this charge. Certain variants, at least, of the ideals of rational disengaged freedom and universal justice seem to exalt male ways of being over female.[14] And I have mentioned other examples in section 3.2.

But as with the theories of obligatory action, it is a confusion to infer from this either that views of the good are all simply enterprises of domination or that we can consider them all arbitrarily chosen. This would be to fail to recognize the manner in which one's own position or, indeed, that of any human being, is powered by a vision of the good.

In face of both these constricting meta-views, there is a great need for undistorted articulacy about the visions of the good that actually underlie our moral reactions, affinities, and aspirations. It would first of all help us to see our way clearer in the ongoing debate between different moral visions which murmurs or rages around us and frequently in us. In fact, getting clear on the nature of mainstream theory and neo-Nietzscheanism would itself be a step forward in this debate. If, as I argued above, the way in which we advance in practical reason is by showing how one view supersedes another by emerging out of it through an error-reducing move, then the theories of morality which are inspired by a vision of the good which they deny richly deserve supersession, and moving beyond them would be sheer gain. The different forms of naturalistic or Nietzschean ethics, or theories of universal right, which would emerge from this would be all the stronger and more persuasive for having put behind them the deep incoherence and self-illusion which this denial involves.

But the debate would also be advanced, because we would be able to address its central and most problematic issues in a less distorted fashion.

A cluster of these turn in modern culture on the tension or even conflict between our commitment to certain hypergoods, in particular the demands of universal and equal respect and of modern self-determining freedom, on one hand, and our sense of the value of what must apparently be sacrificed in their name, on the other. There are a number of different conflicts of this kind. In some cases, what seems threatened is the good of community; in others friendship, or else our traditional identity, seems in danger. In still other situations of conflict, the goods of sensuality and sexual fulfilment are in tension with our higher goals.

Of course, we might experience these as we do any conflict arising from incompatible goods, forcing a decision on us as to the the proper "trade-off" point. But in talking of tension, I'm referring rather to a conflict of moral outlook in the modern world; between a view which gives unchallenged primacy to the hypergood, on one hand, and a view which sees the kind of sacrifice of other, "lower" goods which this entails as utterly unacceptable, on the other. This latter outlook arises from the modern affirmation of ordinary life and has developed into a host of forms, from Romantic-inspired defence of harmony with "nature", within and without, to Nietzschean attacks on the self-destructive character of "morality" (see section 3.2).

A series of disputes of this form runs through modern culture, between what appear to be the demands of reason and disengaged freedom, and equality and universality, on one hand, and the demands of nature, or fulfilment, or expressive integrity, or intimacy, or particularity, on the other. The lines are drawn in rather different ways by the various disputants, and there are crucial disagreements between the different definitions of what must not be sacrificed—between, say, religious advocates of the acceptance of human limits, and sensualist flower children—but the disputes have a similar form and are all linked in some way or other to the great intramural debate of the last two centuries, pitting the philosophy of the Enlightenment against the various forms of Romantic opposition.

Now I believe that both the mainstream form of moral philosophy, which shuns any articulation of goods, and the various strands of neo-Nietzschean thought impede clear thinking on these issues. The mainstream form can't deal with the clash between hypergoods and "ordinary" goods. Concentrating on the principles of action, and having a penchant for a unitary conception of the 'moral', based on a single criterion, it can't even properly conceive of the kind of diversity of goods which underlies the conflict. Where there is some sense of the special status of the hypergood, this is disguised in some doctrine about the special logical properties of moral language or the presuppositions of discourse.

As for the neo-Nietzschean outlooks, they dissolve the conflict by discrediting hypergoods. But they do this by means of a meta-doctrine which sees moral views simply as imposed orders. This doctrine is not only unsustainable but also hides from view the ways in which the protest against the sacrifice and mutilation demanded by one hypergood may be animated by another quite different hypergood. In this respect, Nietzsche himself has a much richer and more believable philosophy, offering as he did the counter-ideal of the superman and the hypergood of unreserved yea-saying.

The articulation of goods, which both these popular philosophies hamper owing to their ultimately confused meta-construals of our moral thinking, is an essential condition of seeing clearly in this whole range of disputes.

And not only here. These philosophies have not only occluded the goods which they are inspired by; they also contribute to a profound skew in the whole modern debate, in the direction of what we could call subjectivism. The goods they (unadmittedly) express and exalt are all human-centred: freedom, active benevolence, universal rights. But another major debate rages in our culture about whether we need to acknowledge claims from non-human nature. Does the "self-forgetful pleasure" that we can take "in the sheer alien pointless independent existence of animals, birds, stones, and trees" bring us closer to the moral good, as Iris Murdoch claims?[15] Some strands of the ecological movement have made this a central issue. In another form: does wilderness have a claim on us, a demand for its preservation, not one grounded on long-term prudence, hedging our bets to hold onto what might pay off eventually for humans, but for its own sake?[16] Or to leap to a quite different domain, is there a non-instrumental good in making the truth manifest? Is it a good thing to do (here it is really inappropriate to speak of obligation) even when it can't possibly contribute to any other good (relieve suffering, end injustice) and may very likely exact a terrible cost from the teller? Why do we admire Mandelstam, for instance, whose 1932 poem about Stalin cost him his freedom, and eventually his life?[17]

I am not neutral, of course; I accept all three of these 'extra-human' claims (and more). But I believe that even those who are agnostic on these issues will agree that the philosophies I am criticizing here prejudge them irrevocably. This they do not because they are inspired by one side but because this inspiration is hidden, where it can't come up for debate. The human-centredness is then unassailable. It appears in the (supposed) defining characteristics of moral theory, such as the maximization of general happiness, or action on a maxim that can be universalized, or action on a norm that all participants could accept in unconstrained debate. The claims of the non-human (or at the very outside, of the non-animate)[18] cannot be heard in frameworks of this kind.

This is another one of those cramps which philosophies of obligatory action, and I would also claim neo-Nietzschean theories, put in our moral thinking, of which I spoke at the end of the last chapter (section 3.3). In general, they are blinkers which prevent us from acknowledging the force of goods, leave us unmoved by them, or, if we are moved, induce us to misidentify this as some non-moral emotion. The negative focus on the good as a source of crushing guilt or, alternatively, of a smug sense of superiority ends up making us unwilling to admit how a constitutive good can interpellate us, move us, empower us.

All this speaks strongly in favour of the attempt to articulate the good in some kind of philosophical prose.

4.3

That is what I want to try to do in what follows. But to do so is not easy. It will not after all be a matter of just recording for examination already stated positions. Sometimes these may be available, but often it will be a question precisely of articulating what has remained implicit, the moral outlook which underlies certain of those modern philosophies which have made it a point of honour not to admit to any such outlook. One has not just to record but to invent language here, rather presumptuously claiming to say better than others what they really mean.

But there is one great recourse here, and that is history. The articulation of modern understandings of the good has to be a historical enterprise; and this not just for the usual reasons valid for any such enterprise, viz., that our present positions are always defined in relation to past ones, taking them either as models or as foils. There is ample evidence of both in the modern world—from the civic humanist tradition which has defined itself in relation to the paradigm models of the ancient republic and polis to the philosophy of the Enlightenment which defines itself in opposition to a past dominated by religion and tradition. The very fact of this self-definition in relation to the past induces us to re-examine this past and the way it has been assimilated or repudiated. Very often, understanding how this has in fact come about gives us insight into contemporary views which would not be otherwise available. In understanding our differences from the ancients, we have a better idea what our assimilation of their paradigms of self-rule actually amount to for us; and in looking more closely at the "traditions" which our Enlightenment thought supposedly repudiated, and at the forms that repudiation took, we may come to see the difference between the two opposed terms in a new light, and consequently to take a new view on contemporary philosophy.[19]

But the recourse to the past is even more necessary in the case of these modern naturalist views which suppress their own underlying visions of the good. Tracing their development from earlier religious or metaphysical views through the partial repudiation of these is not only important in order to define more clearly what kind of a transformation gave rise to them. We also have to recur to these earlier views in order to get some model of the kind of sense of the good which was still openly avowed then, but is suppressed from awareness now. For instance, I believe that the modern naturalist-utilitarian hostility to 'higher' goods and defence of ordinary, sensuous happiness emerge from what I have been calling the affirmation of ordinary life, which in early modern times brought about a similar repudiation of supposedly 'higher' modes of activity in favour of the everyday existence of marriage and the calling. The original form of this affirmation was theological, and it involved a positive vision of ordinary life as hallowed by God. This life itself is seen as having a higher significance conferred on it by God, and this is what grounds the affirmation. But modern naturalism not only can't accept this theistic context; it has divested itself of all languages of higher worth. Nevertheless I want to claim that some such sense of the worth of the ordinary still animates it and provides the powerful moral motive for its widespread acceptance. In articulating this suppressed element, we are forced to turn to its predecessor; and also to raise the question to what degree it is still living from the spiritual insights of this predecessor which it claims to have utterly repudiated. For it draws on a somewhat similar spiritual energy, of which it nevertheless has no account itself. Can it offer an account consistent with its own metaphysical premisses? Or is it really drawing implicitly on something it explicitly rejects? The strength of biblical spiritual imagery even in the most secularist quarters of our lay civilization should perhaps make us suspicious, as it did Nietzsche—even though we might not draw the same conclusion he did.

In any case, what this shows is that the path to articulacy has to be a historical one. We have to try to trace the development of our modern outlooks. And since we are dealing not just with philosophers' doctrines but also with the great unsaid that underlies widespread attitudes in our civilization, the history can't just be one of express belief, of philosophical theories, but must also include what has been called 'mentalités'. We have to try to open out by this study a new understanding of ourselves and of our deepest moral allegiances.

4.4

It is my hunch that when we do, we shall see our moral predicament as both more complex and more potentially conflictual than we do at present. In particular, I believe that we shall find that we are and cannot but be on both sides of the great intramural moral disputes I mentioned earlier between the espousal of hypergoods and the defence of those goods which are to be sacrificed in their name.

This may seem a rather wild claim. Greater articulacy can surely show that we *are* unwittingly on both sides, but how could it show that we must be? Couldn't we then choose in greater lucidity to repudiate one?

The 'must' here doesn't arise from any external argument, which I have tried to show can be of no weight here. Rather it has to do with our identity. In fact, our visions of the good are tied up with our understandings of the self. We have already seen one facet of this connection in the close link discussed in section 2.1 between identity and moral orientation. We have a sense of who we are through our sense of where we stand to the good. But this will also mean, as we shall see in detail later, that radically different senses of what the good is go along with quite different conceptions of what a human agent is, different notions of the self. To trace the development of our modern visions of the good, which are in some respects unprecedented in human culture, is also to follow the evolution of unprecedented new understandings of agency and selfhood.

In fact, the discussion in Chapter 2 suggests a connection between four terms: not just (a) our notions of the good and (b) our understandings of self, but also (c) the kinds of narrative in which we make sense of our lives, and (d) conceptions of society, i.e., conceptions of what it is to be a human agent among human agents. As I shall try to illustrate in Part II, these evolve together, in loose "packages", as it were. Our modern senses of the self not only are linked to and made possible by new understandings of good but also are accompanied by (i) new forms of narrativity and (ii) new understandings of social bonds and relations.

Typical modern forms of narrativity include stories of linear development, progress stories in history, or stories of continuous gain through individual lives and across generations, rags-to-riches stories, which have no ending point. And they include construals of life as growth, not just through childhood and adolescence, but through the later phases as well. Rather than seeing life in terms of predefined phases, making a whole whose shape is understood by unchanging tradition, we tell it as a story of growth towards often unprecedented ends. This is to mention only widely familiar forms, and not the most imaginative innovations of our times, such as the kind of unity through narration which Proust created for his life, which has struck such a deep chord in contemporary imagination. And of course there is the spiral picture of history, from innocence to strife and then to a higher harmony, borrowed from Christian divine history and the millennial movements but secularized by Marxism and a host of other theories, and immensely powerful in its hold on modern thought and feeling.

Along with these forms of narrativity go new understandings of society and forms of living together. Corresponding to the free, disengaged subject is a view of society as made up of and by the consent of free individuals and, corollary to this, the notion of society as made up of bearers of individual rights. This is perhaps one of the most deeply entrenched images of society that modern civilization has thrown up. It begins with the famous seventeenth-century theories of social contract, but it develops and mutates, and emerges, inter alia, today in a perhaps debased form on the interpersonal level in the contemporary notion of a love "relationship" between two independent beings. Connected to an expressivist self-understanding is the picture of society as a nation, drawn together by similar expressive roots, which because they define our common human potentiality allegedly have a command on our allegiance and devotion. Modern nationalism has in turn developed its own forms of historical narrative, as Benedict Anderson has shown.[20] These multiple connections are part of what is suppressed from view by those contemporary modes of thought which have no place for the good. They are quite unaware of the way in which our modern sense of the self is bound up with and depends on what one can call a 'moral topography'.[21] They tend to think that we have selves the way we have hearts and livers, as an interpretation-free given. And of course, they have no sense at all of the inverse relation.

Once these connections are drawn, it may not be so easy to repudiate certain moral visions. That is, their repudiation, while one still defines oneself as a certain kind of agent, may turn out to be a sham; one still goes on living by them. And yet it may not be so easy genuinely and authentically to see oneself in other terms. This sense of self may still be part of the best available account whereby we can make sense of ourselves as we act, feel, and think. The BA principle can also function as a test for the genuineness of our moral stands.[22]

If this turns out to be so, then the moral conflicts of modern culture rage within each of us. Unless, that is, our greater lucidity can help us to see our way to a reconciliation. If I may give expression to an even farther-out hunch, I will say that I see this as the potential goal and fruit of articulacy. We have to search for a way in which our strongest aspirations towards hypergoods do not exact a price of self-mutilation. I believe that such a reconciliation is possible; but its essential condition is that we enable ourselves to recognize the goods to which we cannot but hold allegiance in their full range. If articulacy is to open us, to bring us out of the cramped postures of suppression, this is partly because it will allow us to acknowledge the full range of goods we live by. It is also because it will open us to our moral sources, to release their force in our lives. The cramped formulations of mainstream philosophy already represent denials, the sacrifice of one kind of good in favour of another, but frozen in a logical mould which prevents their even being put in question. Articulacy is a crucial condition of reconciliation.

Of course, if reconciliation is impossible, then articulacy will buy us much greater inner conflict. This might be thought a risk. But even in this case, we would have at least put an end to the stifling of the spirit and to the atrophy of so many of our spiritual sources which is the bane of modern naturalist culture.

In any case, whatever the outcome, I now want to turn in the succeeding pages to trace the historical development of some of the connections between my four terms which have gone to make up the modern identity.

PART II

Inwardness

5

MORAL TOPOGRAPHY

Our modern notion of the self is related to, one might say constituted by, a certain sense (or perhaps a family of senses) of inwardness. Over the next chapters, I want to trace the rise and development of this sense.

In our languages of self-understanding, the opposition 'inside-outside' plays an important role. We think of our thoughts, ideas, or feelings as being "within" us, while the objects in the world which these mental states bear on are "without". Or else we think of our capacities or potentialities as "inner", awaiting the development which will manifest them or realize them in the public world. The unconscious is for us within, and we think of the depths of the unsaid, the unsayable, the powerful inchoate feelings and affinities and fears which dispute with us the control of our lives, as inner. We are creatures with inner depths; with partly unexplored and dark interiors. We all feel the force of Conrad's image in *Heart of Darkness*.

But strong as this partitioning of the world appears to us, as solid as this localization may seem, and anchored in the very nature of the human agent, it is in large part a feature of our world, the world of modern, Western people. The localization is not a universal one, which human beings recognize as a matter of course, as they do for instance that their heads are above their torsos. Rather it is a function of a historically limited mode of self-interpretation, one which has become dominant in the modern West and which may indeed spread thence to other parts of the globe, but which had a beginning in time and space and may have an end.

Of course, this view is not original. A great many historians, anthropologists, and others consider it almost a truism. But it is nevertheless hard to believe for the ordinary layperson that lives in all of us. The reason this is so is that the localization is bound up with our sense of self, and thus also with our sense of moral sources.[1] It is not that these do not also change in history. On the contrary, the story I want to tell is of such a change. But when a given constellation of self, moral sources, and localization is *ours,* that means it is the one from *within* which we experience and deliberate about our moral situation. It cannot but come to *feel* fixed and unchallengeable, whatever our knowledge of history and cultural variation may lead us to believe.

So we naturally come to think that we have selves the way we have heads or arms, and inner depths the way we have hearts or livers, as a matter of hard, interpretation-free fact. Distinctions of locale, like inside and outside, seem to be discovered like facts about ourselves, and not to be relative to the particular way, among other possible ways, we construe ourselves. For a given age and civilization, a particular reading seems to impose itself; it seems to common sense the only conceivable one. Who among us can understand our thought being anywhere else but inside, 'in the mind'? Something in the nature of our experience of ourselves seems to make the current localization almost irresistible, beyond challenge.

What we are constantly losing from sight here is that being a self is inseparable from existing in a space of moral issues, to do with identity and how one ought to be. It is being able to find one's standpoint in this space, being able to occupy, to *be* a perspective in it.[2]

But isn't there some truth in the idea that people always are selves, that they distinguish inside from outside in all cultures? In one sense, there no doubt is. The really difficult thing is distinguishing the human universals from the historical constellations and not eliding the second into the first so that our particular way seems somehow inescapable for humans as such, as we are always tempted to do.

I can't pretend to have a general formula for making this distinction. If I did, I would have solved the greatest intellectual problem of human culture. I even suspect that no satisfactory general formula can be found to characterize the ubiquitous underlying nature of a self-interpreting animal. But the distinction can nevertheless be hinted at through a few illuminating examples.

When moderns read of, say, shamanistic cultures where they are alleged to believe that the human person has three souls and that one of them can travel outside and even remain there for a time,[3] they find it hard to know what to make of this information. Does it mean that these people don't share our sense of the unity of the person or the link/identity of a person with his or her body, that they don't count persons in the same way as we do? But we don't have to suppose anything so bizarre. We can probably be confident that on one level human beings of all times and places have shared a very similar sense of 'me' and 'mine'. In those days when a paleolithic hunting group was closing in on a mammoth, when the plan went awry and the beast was lunging towards hunter A, something similar to the thought 'Now I'm for it' crossed A's mind. And when at the last moment, the terrifying animal lurched to the left and crushed B instead, a sense of relief mingled with grief for poor B was what A experienced. In other words, the members of the group must have had very much the same sense that we would in their place: here is one person, and there is another, and which one survives/flourishes depends on which person/body is run over by that mammoth.

But alongside these strands of continuity, which would probably make even our remote ancestors comprehensible to us, there are baffling contrasts when we try to understand human agency in its moral and spiritual dimension. This is driven home to us in our puzzlement at the three souls of the Buriats of northern Siberia. But our modern notion of the self is just as much a historically local self-interpretation which would also be opaque and perplexing to outsiders. It is probable that in every language there are resources for self-reference and descriptions of reflexive thought, action, attitude (these resources would go beyond referring expressions and would include forms like the archaic Indo-European middle voice). But this is not at all the same as making 'self' into a noun, preceded by a definite or indefinite article, speaking of "the" self, or "a" self. This reflects something important which is peculiar to our modern sense of agency. The Greeks were notoriously capable of formulating the injunction *'gnōthi seauton'*—'know thyself'—but they didn't normally speak of the human agent as *'ho autos'*, or use the term in a context which we would translate with the indefinite article.[4]

A similar distinction could probably be made between the perennial and the specifically modern in regard to the distinction inside/outside. There is a sense of "inside" which designates the thought or desires or intentions which we hold back for ourselves, as against those which we express in speech and action. When I refrain from saying what I think about you, the thought remains inner, and when I blurt it out, then it is in the public domain. This distinction seems to be a common theme to many different cultures, one which is woven into a richer notion of what 'inner' and 'outer' mean, which expresses in each case the specific moral/spiritual vision of the civilization. Thus there is something quite immediately understandable and familiar to us in the *'batin'*/*'lair'* distinction which Clifford Geertz reports from Java.[5] As Geertz describes it, *'batin'* "consists in the fuzzy, shifting flow of subjective feeling in all its phenomenological immediacy"; and *'lair'* "refers to that part of human life which, in our culture, strict behaviourists limit themselves to studying—external actions, movements, postures, speech".[6] Geertz stresses at the same time how different this conception is from its Western analogue, particularly in the fact that it is not related to individuals in quite the same way[7] or connected to the soul/body distinction in the way we're familiar with. What appears to be a universally familiar human distinction between inner and outer has been here woven into a spiritual doctrine which is quite strange and unfamiliar.

Nevertheless, just as with our notion of the self, the fact that one facet of such doctrines is always familiar to us contributes to our layperson's difficulty in recognizing that the whole localization is really very different to ours and hence, obversely, that our modern notions of inner and outer are indeed strange and without precedent in other cultures and times.

In order to see how strange and different it is, it will be useful to trace its genesis from a previously dominant localization. I find a paradigm statement of this in Plato.

6

PLATO'S SELF-MASTERY

6.1

Plato's moral doctrine, as he sets it out in the *Republic,* for instance, seems quite familiar to us. We are good when reason rules, and bad when we are dominated by our desires. Of course many people disagree with this view today, but it seems perfectly comprehensible to us. Indeed, it is plain that many disagreed with it in Plato's day, as the strenuous arguments in his works attest. This appearance of a familiar and understandable doctrine is partly valid, but it covers up a deeper change which I want to bring out.

In the terms set out above, Plato offers us a view of moral sources. He tells us where we can go to accede to a higher moral state. And we might say that the site he shows us is the domain of thought. The translation I have just made of 'thought' for 'reason' is not entirely innocent. I will argue below that the transformation I want to describe between ancient and modern can be reflected in this shift of vocabulary. But for the moment, I will act as though it were innocent, to allow us to see Plato as situating moral resources in the domain of thought. This is where we have to go to have access to a higher moral condition.

What we gain through thought or reason is self-mastery. The good man is 'master of himself' (or 'stronger than himself', *kreittō autou,* 430E). Plato sees the absurdity of this expression unless one adds to it a distinction between higher and lower parts of the soul. To be master of oneself is to have the higher part of the soul rule over the lower, which means reason over the desires (*'to logistikon'* over *'to epithumetikon'*).

And so we become good when reason comes to rule, and we are no longer run by our desires. But the shift in hegemony is not just a matter of one set of goals taking over the priority from another. When reason rules, a quite different kind of order reigns in the soul. Indeed, we can say that order reigns there for the first time. By contrast, the realm of desire is that of chaos. The good souls enjoy order *(kosmos),* concord *(xumphonia),* and harmony *(harmonia),* where the bad are torn every which way by their desires and are in perpetual conflict. Plato even describes them as suffering from a kind of 'civil war' *(stasis)*.[1] And later on, in his graphic description of democratic and tyrannical man, Plato imprints indelibly on the reader's mind the miseries of remorse and inner self-destructive conflict that they suffer.

Besides being at one with himself, the person ruled by reason also enjoys calm, while the desiring person is constantly agitated and unquiet, constantly pulled this way and that by his cravings. And this in turn is connected to a third difference. The good person is collected, where the bad one is distraught. The first enjoys a kind of self-possession, of centring in himself, which the other wholly lacks, driven as he is by endless desire. Plato constantly stresses the unlimited nature of desire. The curse of one ruled by his appetites is that he can never be satisfied; he is dragged ever onward. The desiring element, says Plato, is 'by nature insatiable' (442A, *physei aplēstotaton*).

The mastery of self through reason brings with it these three fruits: unity with oneself, calm, and collected self-possession.

Plato helped set the form of the dominant family of moral theories in our civilization. Over the centuries, it has seemed self-evident to many that thought/reason orders our lives for the good, or would if only passion did not prevent it. And the background connections underlying this view have remained much the same: to consider something rationally is to take a dispassionate stance towards it. It is both to see clearly what ought to be done and to be calm and self-collected and hence able to do it. Reason is at one and the same time a power to see things aright and a condition of self-possession. To be rational is truly to be master of oneself.

This outlook has been dominant but never unchallenged. Although Christian theology incorporated much Platonic philosophy, and sanctity and salvation came to be expressed in Platonic-derived terms of purity and the "beatific vision", nevertheless the Christian emphasis on the radical conversion of the will could never be finally accommodated in this synthesis. There were recurrent revolts by Christian thinkers against some or other aspect of the marriage with Greek philosophy, and from time to time the thesis would be pressed that reason by itself could just as well be the servant of the devil, that indeed, to make reason the guarantor of the good was to fall into idolatry. Luther speaks graphically of reason as "that whore".

And partly deriving from this tradition of Christian resistance to Greek philosophy, our modern age has seen a number of rebellions against the moral philosophy of reason. From some Romantics in one way, from Nietzsche in another, down to the Frankfurt school which borrowed from both, the notion has been developed that rational hegemony, rational control, may stifle, desiccate, repress us; that rational self-mastery may be self-domination or enslavement. There is a 'dialectic of Enlightenment', in which reason, which promises to be a liberating force, turns into its opposite. We stand in need of liberation from reason.

The challenge in the name of freedom is specifically modern; but the hegemony of reason was not uncontested among the ancients. In a sense, Plato can be seen as the key figure in the establishment of this dominant moral philosophy. In the process, other moralities, other maps of our moral sources, had to be either discredited or annexed and subordinated. There is, for instance, a warrior (and later warrior-citizen) morality, where what is valued is strength, courage, and the ability to conceive and execute great deeds, and where life is aimed at fame and glory, and the immortality one enjoys when one's name lives for ever on men's lips. The higher moral condition here is where one is filled with a surge of energy, an access of strength and courage—e.g., on the battlefield—and is able to sweep all before one. It is not only different from but quite incompatible with the reflective and self-collected stance of rational contemplation. Indeed, in some more primitive cultures, this access is seen as a kind of possession or mania. The great warrior is carried away by a kind of madness on the field of battle; he runs 'berserk'. The word is taken from primitive Scandinavian culture, but something of the same condition was visible among the early Celts.

This is an utterly different view from Plato's about the site of moral sources, about where one has to go to accede to a higher condition. It has something in common with another rival view, one which exalts a state of manic inspiration in which poets create. (As Socrates says in the *Apology*, poets make their works not by wisdom but "by some instinct and possessed by the god *'enthusiazontes'* ", 22C.)

The author of the *Republic*[2] has to deal with both these views in order to establish his own. His line is to discredit the second one almost entirely, or at least to make us very wary of it, and to subordinate the first. This latter operation is accomplished in the *Republic* by identifying a third element in the soul, between desire and reason, viz., 'spirit' *(thumos)*, whose proper role is to be the auxiliary of reason, analogous to the warrior function in society, which should be properly subordinate to political leadership.

Plato's work should probably be seen as an important contribution to a long-developing process whereby an ethic of reason and reflection gains dominance over one of action and glory. The latter is never set aside altogether. In spite of Plato's attempts to discredit glory as a life goal, since a concern for it is focussed on mere appearances and not reality, the relation of subordination he maps in the picture of the ordered tripartite soul is a better model for what has emerged in Western society, i.e., a sort of containment of the ethic of action and glory, uneasily held in the hegemony of a higher morality of reason or purity. The post-Crusade model of the Christian knight offers a well-known example.

But what is interesting from our point of view here, in relation to different kinds of localization, is the way in which this rise towards dominance of the ethic of reason seems to have brought with it a different understanding of the agent. This perhaps offers us a way of interpreting the features of Homeric psychology which Bruno Snell and others have commented on.

Snell[3] remarked on the absence in Homer of words that could happily be translated by our 'mind', or even by 'soul' in its standard post-Platonic meaning, that is, a term designating the unique locus where all our different thoughts and feelings occur. Homeric *'psychē'* seems to designate something like the life force in us, what flees from the body at death, rather than the site of thinking and feeling. If one asks 'where' such things go on in Homer's account of his heroes, no single answer can be given. Rather there seems to us to be a fragmentation: some things happen in the *'thumos'*, others in the *'phrenes'*, others again in the *'kradiē'*, *'ētor'*, or *'ker'*, still others in the *'noos'*. Some of these sites can be loosely identified with bodily locations; for instance, *'kradiē'*, *'etor'*, and *'ker'* seem to be identified with the heart, and *'phrenes'* with the lungs. Richard Onians[4] also makes a strong case for *'thumos'* being originally sited in the lungs. In parallel to the multiplicity of 'mind' locations, bodily references are also usually to what we would think of as parts. The term *'soma'*, Snell argues, refers to the corpse. References to the living body are to, e.g., the 'limbs', 'skin', etc., varying as appropriate with the context.

Snell also noted that the Homeric hero was frequently carried to the greatest heights of action by a surge of power infused into him by a god. And indeed, the same could be said for some of his great mistakes. Agamemnon excuses his unfair and unwise treatment of Achilles by referring to the 'madness' *(menos)* visited on him by the god. But contrary to our modern intuitions, this doesn't seem to lessen the merit or demerit attaching to the agent. A great hero remains great, though his impressive deeds are powered by the god's infusion of energy. Indeed, there is no concession here; it is not that the hero remains great *despite* the divine help. It is an inseparable part of his greatness that he is such a locus of divine action.

As Adkins puts it, Homeric man is revealed "as a being whose parts are more in evidence than the whole, and one very conscious of sudden unexpected accesses of energy".[5] To the modern, this fragmentation, and the seeming confusion about merit and responsibility, are very puzzling. Some[6] have been tempted to make light of Snell's thesis, and to deny that Homeric man was all that different from us in his way of understanding decision and responsibility.

The debate can easily fall prey to cross-purposes unless some crucial distinctions are taken into account, and that is what I was trying to do above. If we return to the example above of the paleolithic hunters, it seems very likely that they, just as much as Homeric warriors—and ourselves—had the familiar sense of themselves as single agents among others: I am the one whose fate is being decided in that mammoth charge or in that spear-thrust of my adversary. And similarly, they must have shared our familiar understanding of the decisions they were called upon to take. Some things are up to me: Do I dodge the beast? Do I fight or flee?

What this vocabulary betokens, I want to argue, is a quite different notion of moral sources, of where one has to go to accede to moral power. As with all such cultures which are very different from our own, it is extremely difficult to give a positive description of it, even if one could live among Homeric warriors as an anthropologist. With only a few texts at one's disposal, the task becomes virtually impossible.

But it may be possible to say something negatively about this outlook, defining it by what it is not, viz., the conception of mind and responsibility which eventually overcame it. And if we once again take Plato's theory as a culminating statement of this ultimately victorious view, the points of contrast stand out. Plato's view, just because it privileges a condition of self-collected awareness and designates this as the state of maximum unity with oneself, requires some conception of the mind as a unitary space. The temptation to place certain thoughts and feelings in a special locus comes from the special nature of those thoughts and feelings. They are different from, perhaps even incompatible with, what we ordinarily feel. What we experience in moments of heightened inspiration can have this character. And today, we are still tempted by talk of special localization, but of another character: we speak of a person being 'carried away', or 'beside herself', swept off as it were to someplace outside. In a sense, what we feel when we are in a towering rage seems incommensurable with what we feel when we have calmed down; the people and events are quite transformed in aspect. And a similar change can occur when we fall in or out of love. The landscape of experience changes so much that we are easily tempted to use images of a change of locale to describe the transition.

For a view of the moral life which finds the highest sources in these special states, as in a condition of the highest inspiration, the description of experience in terms of special locales will seem the deepest and most revealing. We stress the special nature of these states by marking their lack of continuity with ordinary thought and feeling. But if, in contrast, the highest condition for us is one in which we are reflective and self-collected, then to be in a special state, discontinuous with the others, is a kind of loss of centring, a falling off, something which has to be overcome. Our privileged condition, that of rational reflection, is defined as one in which we understand and can thus survey all others. For the moralist of reason, the privileged condition is not a special state in the sense of being out of communication with all the others, but is on the contrary the one in which all thoughts and feelings are under purview, as we achieve the centring on ourselves that rational hegemony brings. Special, non-communicating states are thus lapses; they are obstacles to reason and represent failure to achieve the heights of reason.

In other words, the soul is de jure, in principle, one; it is a single locus. The experience of it as comprising a plurality of loci is an experience of error and imperfection. The unicity of locus, and hence the new notion of the soul as this single site of all thought and feeling—as against the 'psychē' as life-principle—is an essential concomitant of the morality of rational hegemony. The soul *must* be one if we are to reach our highest in the self-collected understanding of reason, which brings about the harmony and concord of the whole person.

Plurality of locus, on the other hand, accommodates quite well to a moral outlook in which the infusion of higher power is the source of the higher. I find it hard, like everyone, to give a convincing picture of the outlook of Homeric man, but I don't think it was an accident that fragmentation and divine infusion of power belonged together, or that both were set aside in the Platonic formulation of the view which comes to dominate.

6.2

But this is all the prehistory of the story I want to tell. The centring or unification of the moral self was a precondition of the transformation which I will describe as an internalization, but the centring is not this internalization itself. Without the unified self which we see articulated in Plato's theory, the modern notion of interiority could never have developed. But it took a further step to bring it about.

One could, of course, use the language of 'inside/outside' to formulate the opposition of the Platonic to the warrior ethic. For what the former considers crucial is the disposition of the soul, not external success. Indeed, Plato in some dialogues (e.g., the *Gorgias*) argues forcefully that one is better off being a just man, even if one suffers terribly for one's virtue, than one is inflicting injustice, however successfully. And this is the doctrine that the *Republic* is meant to establish, that the just life is the most advantageous—even in the absence of success in the world of action and power. In fact, the truly wise, just—and thus happy—person is disinterested in the world of power. He has to be forced back to take his part in ruling the just state.

Thus if we think of the external as the realm of action in the polis, and the internal as that of the soul's disposition, then we could express the doctrine of the hegemony of reason in contrast to that of glorious action as an exaltation of the internal over the external. (Of course, we aren't yet at the point Kant will bring us to, where the right is a matter of inner intention, regardless of external action, so that any pattern of action could consist with the absence of true goodness—i.e., of a good will. In Plato's view the virtuous man *acts* in a characteristically different pattern from the vicious one. But external *success* may escape him.)

But in fact, Plato does not use the inside/outside dichotomy to make his point.[7] We have to wait until Augustine before a theory of this kind, where the goods of the soul are stressed over those of worldly action, is formulated in terms of inner and outer. I shall be returning to this below.

The oppositions which are crucial to Plato are those of soul as against body, of the immaterial as against the bodily, and of the eternal as against the changing. It is these which carry the main weight in Plato's formulations. And given the nature of his theory, they obviously say more and better what he wanted to convey than inner/outer could.

But this latter is not just less informative than the standard Platonic oppositions; there is another sense in which Plato may have considered it misleading. That is because of his whole conception of reason and the rule of reason. The notion of reason is closely connected to that of order. The soul ruled by reason is an ordered one, enjoying concord and harmony, as we have seen. The soul by its nature needs or tends towards a certain kind of order, one where reason is paramount, just like the body needs and tends towards the order we identify as health. The health analogy plays an important role for him. In Book IV, for instance, he argues that bodily health too is a matter of the proper elements ruling and being ruled, and sickness is where this order is inverted. So "virtue . . . would be a kind of health and beauty and good condition of the soul, and vice would be disease, ugliness and weakness" (444D–E).

Reason is the capacity to see and understand. To grasp by reason is to be able to "give reasons", or "give an account" (*logon didonai*, 534B). So to be ruled by reason is to be ruled by the correct vision or understanding. The correct vision or understanding of ourselves is one which grasps the natural order, the analogue of health. One feature of this natural order is the requirement itself that reason should rule; and so there is a self-affirming aspect of reason's hegemony. But the correct order also establishes priorities among our different appetites and activities, distinguishes between necessary and unnecessary desires (558–559), and the like. So reason can be understood as the perception of the natural or right order, and to be ruled by reason is to be ruled by a vision of this order.

Plato offers what we can call a substantive conception of reason. Rationality is tied to the perception of order; and so to realize our capacity for reason is to see the order as it is. The correct vision is criterial. There is no way one could be ruled by reason and be *mistaken* or wrong about the order of reality. It makes no sense for Plato to imagine a perfectly rational person who would nevertheless have quite erroneous views about the order of things or the morally good—who might believe, for instance, in a Democritan universe of accidentally concatenating atoms, or might hold that the end of life was accumulating power or wealth. But the order with which reason is thus criterially connected is not just the one we might be tempted to call 'internal', that between the different goals, appetites, and elements in the soul. More fundamental is the connection with the order of things in the cosmos. This is related to the right order of the soul as whole is to part, as englobing to englobed. But it is not more important just for this reason. The real point is that it is only on the level of the whole order that one can see that everything is ordered for the good.

The vision of the good is at the very centre of Plato's doctrine of moral resources. The good of the whole, whose order manifests the Idea of the Good, is the final good, the one which englobes all partial goods. It not only includes them but confers a higher dignity on them; since the Good is what commands our categorical love and allegiance. It is the ultimate source of strong evaluation, something which stands on its own as worthy of being desired and sought, not just desirable given our existing goals and appetites. It provides the standard of the desirable beyond the variation of de facto desire. In the light of the Good, we can see that our good, the proper order in our souls, has this categoric worth, which it enjoys as a proper part of the whole order.

Thus the good life for us is to be ruled by reason not just as the vision of correct order in our souls but also and more fundamentally as the vision of the good order of the whole. And we cannot see one of these orders without the other. For the right order in us is to be ruled by reason, which cannot come about unless reason reaches its full realization which is in the perception of the Good; and at the same time, the perception of the Good is what makes us truly virtuous. The love of the eternal, good order is the ultimate source and the true form of our love of good action and the good life. The surest basis for virtue is the perception of this order, which one cannot see without loving. That is why philosophy is the best safeguard of virtue.

Philosophers love the eternal truth, as against ordinary men who are lovers of spectacles and the arts or are just men of action (476B–C). Instead of looking for beautiful sights and sounds, philosophers look for beauty itself, something that remains always the same, while beautiful objects vary and change, and "wander between generation and destruction" ("planōmenēs hupo geneseōs kai phthoras", 485B). But people who thus love the eternal,

Plato argues, cannot help but be morally good; they will necessarily have all the virtues (486–487), because the love of order will itself bring order (cf. 442E). Again later, he argues:

> For surely, Adeimantus, the man whose mind is truly fixed on eternal realities has no leisure to turn his eyes downward upon the petty affairs of men, and so engaging in strife with them to be filled with envy and hate, but fixes his gaze upon the things of the eternal and unchanging order, and seeing that they neither wrong nor are wronged by one another, but all abide in harmony as reason bids, he will endeavour to imitate them and, as far as may be, to fashion himself in their likeness and assimilate himself to them. Or do you think it possible not to imitate the things to which anyone attaches himself with admiration? (500B–C)

Reason reaches its fulness in the vision of the larger order, which is also the vision of the Good. And this is why the language of inside/outside can in a sense be misleading as a formulation of Plato's position. In an important sense, the moral sources we accede to by reason are not within us. They can be seen as outside us, in the Good; or perhaps our acceding to a higher condition ought to be seen as something which takes place in the "space" between us and this order of the good. Once reason is substantively defined, once a correct vision of the order is criterial to rationality, then our becoming rational ought not most perspicuously to be described as something that takes place in us, but rather better as our connecting up to the larger order in which we are placed.

And Plato does turn to an image of this kind at the culmination of his great allegory of the Cave. Some people think, he says, that education is a matter of putting true knowledge into a soul that doesn't have it. The model here would be the virtues and capacities of the body, which Plato agrees should be seen as things we acquire by habit and practice. We incorporate them in us, as it were, and put them where they didn't exist before. But the specific virtue of thought (*hē de tou phronēsai*, 518E) doesn't come to be in this way. Rather we should see ourselves as having something like a capacity of vision which is forever unimpaired, and the move from illusion to wisdom is to be likened to our turning the soul's eye around to face in the right direction. Some people, the lovers of sights and sounds and beautiful spectacles, are focussed entirely on the bodily and the changing. Making those people wise is a matter of turning the soul's gaze from the darkness to the brightness of true being (518C). But just as the physical eye can only be turned by swivelling the whole body, so the whole soul must be turned to attain wisdom. It is not a matter of internalizing a capacity but rather of a conversion (*periagōgē*, 518E). For Plato the key issue is what the soul is directed towards. That is why he wants to formulate his position in terms of the oppositions bodily/immaterial, changing/eternal, for these define the possible directions of our awareness and desire. Not only is the inner/outer dichotomy not useful for this purpose, but it actually tends to obscure the fact that the crucial issue is what objects the soul attends to and feeds on. The soul as immaterial and eternal ought to turn to what is immaterial and eternal. Not what happens within it but where it is facing in the metaphysical landscape is what matters.

At the same time, the image of the soul's eye helps to clarify Plato's notion of reason. Reason is our capacity to see being, illuminated reality. Just as the eye cannot exercise its function of seeing unless there is reality there and it is properly illuminated, so reason cannot realize its function until we are turned towards real being, illuminated by the Good. That is why reason has to be understood substantively, and why the vision of the true order is criterial for rationality.

6.3

To return to my point at the beginning of this chapter, Plato's moral theory seems in some ways very familiar and understandable to us. This is so when we describe it as calling for a kind of self-mastery, which consists in reason ruling over desires, a self-control which contrasts to being dominated by one's appetites and passions. We instinctively feel we understand what this moral theory is about, whether we agree with it or not. We see it as one of our contemporary options.

But it begins to seem strange when we understand that the rule of reason is to be understood as rule by a rational vision of order—or better, since for Plato the logos was in reality as well as in us, we should speak of rule by a vision of rational order. The question of which element in us rules translates immediately into a question of what the soul as a whole attends to and loves: the eternal order of being, or else the changing play of sights and sounds and the bodily perishable. To be ruled by reason means to have one's life shaped by a pre-existent rational order which one knows and loves.

The transformation which I want to call 'internalization' consists in a replacement of this understanding of the dominance of reason by another, more readily accessible to our minds, in which the order involved in the paramountcy of reason is *made,* not found. The representative figure of this modern view, to be contrasted to Plato, is Descartes; or, at least, he is who I want to talk about in this connection. But before we turn to him, a few words about the historic impact of the Platonic model.

This model remained dominant in the ancient world. Throughout the revisions of Plato which the other schools descending from Socrates wrought, the same basic understanding of the rule by reason continues. Aristotle, for instance, rebels against the tight connection Plato made between awareness of right order in our lives and of the order of the cosmos. It seems as though the second is an essential condition of the first, at least as he sets things out in the *Republic*. Aristotle finds this unacceptable. Our grasp of the cosmic order is a kind of science in the strong sense of a knowledge of the unchanging and eternal. Our grasp of the right order and priority of ends in life cannot be of this kind. It is an understanding of the ever-changing, in which particular cases and predicaments are never exhaustively characterized in general rules. The practically wise man *(phronimos)* has a knowledge of how to behave in each particular circumstance which can never be equated with or reduced to a knowledge of general truths. Practical wisdom *(phronēsis)* is a not fully articulable sense rather than a kind of science.

And yet for Aristotle, this practical wisdom is a kind of awareness of order, the correct order of ends in my life, which integrates all my goals and desires into a unified whole in which each has its proper weight. Aristotle takes over the medical analogy from Plato and sees the good life as like health, where each element must be held between the limits of too much and too little for the balance and well-being of the whole. And the good order of my life is essentially connected with my being rational, both in that as rational life reason is the most important determinant of my ends, and also in that it is through one of the excellences of reason, *phronēsis*, that I can determine my life by this order.

Moreover, although Aristotle distinguishes the knowledge of the eternal order from our awareness of the right order of life, they both remain essential to the good life. *Theōria*, or contemplation of the unchanging order, is one of the highest activities of man, one which brings him close to the divine. The complete good of human life as rational doesn't simply consist in ethical excellence; it also includes the excellences of science. And the fulfilment of these requires a grasp of the cosmic order. Attending to both orders is thus constitutive of the human good.

But the link between the two orders is also ontological. The good life for human beings is as it is because of humans' nature as rational life. Humanity is part of the order of beings, each with its own nature. Each kind of thing, moved by the love of God, strives to reach its perfection and hence fulfils its nature. As agents, striving for ethical excellence, humans thus participate in the same rational order which they can also contemplate and admire in science.

The Stoics broke with both Plato and Aristotle by rejecting altogether the value of contemplation. Man is to be understood as a rational animal, but the reason he is called on to realize is purely practical. Reason shows us what the good life is. The vicious person is moved by passions, and passions can be understood as false opinions about the good. The wise person is fully free of these.

But for the Stoics too rationality is a vision of order. It is not only that wisdom involves seeing through the falseness of the goods which ordinary men's passions relate to. This negative understanding was the flip side of a positive insight. The Stoic sage saw the goodness of the whole order of things and loved it. He had a powerful vision of the providence of God, who has disposed everything for the best. It is this positive love which liberates him from caring for the particular advantageous or unfavourable outcomes which hold most men in hope and fear, pain and pleasure. One can say that, because the Stoic sage comes to love the goodness of the whole, and because this vision is the fulfilment of his nature as a rational being, he responds to each new event with equal joy as an element of this whole, rather than with satisfaction or dismay at success or setback in his particular life-plan.

And so in a sense the Stoics take Plato's part against Aristotle, in that a vision of the cosmic order becomes an essential condition of true virtue and practical wisdom. That is why the Stoic teachers insisted that their physics was the ground of their ethics. Only unlike Plato, there is no value in this knowledge of the cosmos for its own sake, no value in mere contemplation; the whole point of science is to make men better.

I would like to argue that even the limit case, the Epicureans, remain within the bounds of the Platonic model in an important sense. Epicurus is the limit case because he denies what is most essential for Plato, viz., the very notion of a rational order in the cosmos on which humans can model themselves. On the contrary, the path of wisdom is to see through all such false illusions of order or divine purpose and to focus on the pleasures that human life offers. But seeing these pleasures aright involves seeing the correct order of valuation among them. And both here and in the cosmos, reason is understood as the capacity to see the order which is there; only in this limit case, what reason sees in the cosmos for the Epicurean is the lack of order, or one resulting purely from chance, the drift of atoms in the void. This may sound at the present stage of the argument like mere sophistry. I have no desire to overlook the immense difference between Epicurus' disenchanted view of the cosmos and the Platonic notions of order. The analogy I am pointing to, however, will come out much more clearly after I have looked at Descartes.

7

"IN INTERIORE HOMINE"

7.1

On the way from Plato to Descartes stands Augustine. Augustine's whole outlook was influenced by Plato's doctrines as they were transmitted to him through Plotinus. His encounter with these doctrines played a crucial role in his spiritual development. He could liberate himself from the last shackles of the false Manichaean view when he finally came to see God and the soul as immaterial. Henceforth, for Augustine, the Christian opposition between spirit and flesh was to be understood with the aid of the Platonic distinction between the bodily and the non-bodily.

Along with this duality, Augustine took on the full panoply of related oppositions, of course. The higher realm was also that of the eternal as against the merely temporal, of the immutable in contrast to the ever-changing.

And he also took over the Ideas. These are now the thoughts of God and hence can remain eternal even in this new theistic context. Augustine was deeply impressed by the account of the making of the world in the *Timaeus*, for all its important differences with orthodox Christian belief. He stresses the likeness, and was one of the founders of the line of Christian thought that sees Plato as the 'Attic Moses'. The Christian God can still make things on the model of the Ideas, because they are his own thoughts, eternal like him. Augustine can even take over the Platonic-Pythagorean sense of the ontological foundation of creation in numbers.[1]

The doctrine of creation ex nihilo is thus married with a Platonic notion of participation. Created things receive their form through God, through their participation in his Ideas. Everything has being only insofar as it participates in God. Augustine, in explaining the Christian notion of the ontological dependence of things in Platonic terms, here as elsewhere makes a synthesis with striking new possibilities. The conception of an order of creation made according to God's thoughts merges with the great Johannine image of creation through the Word, and hence links Platonism with the central Christian doctrine of the Trinity. If everything participates in God and everything is in its own way like God, then the key principle underlying everything is that of Participation or Likeness itself. But the archetype of Likeness-to-God can only be God's Word itself, begotten from him and of one substance with him, i.e., the Second Person of the Trinity, by whom all things were made.

In any case, whether this synthesis works or not, Augustine gives us a Platonic understanding of the universe as an external realization of a rational order. Things should be understood ultimately as like signs, for they are external expressions of God's thoughts. Everything which is, is good (Manichaean error is totally repudiated); and the whole is organized for the good. Here is another of those crucial junction points where Jewish theism and Greek philosophy can be stitched together. The affirmations of Genesis 1, "and God saw that it was good", are linked to the Platonic doctrine of the Idea of the Good, only the place of that all-structuring Idea is now taken by God himself (either the First or Second Persons of the Trinity). Augustine takes over the image of the sun, central to Plato's discussion of the Idea of the Good in the *Republic*, which both nourishes things in their being and gives the light to see them by; but now the ultimate principle of being and knowledge together is God. God is the source of light, and here is another junction point, linking up with the light in the first chapter of John's Gospel.

So the created world exhibits a meaningful order; it participates in God's Ideas. God's eternal law enjoins order. It calls on humans to see and respect this order.[2] For Augustine as for Plato, the vision of cosmic order is the vision of reason, and for both the good for humans involves their seeing and loving this order. And similarly, for both what stands in the way is the human absorption with the sensible, with the mere external manifestations of the higher reality. The soul must be swivelled around; it has to change the direction of its attention/desire. For the whole moral condition of the soul depends ultimately on what it attends to and loves. "Everyone becomes like what he loves. Dost thou love the earth? Thou shalt be earth. Dost thou love God? then I say, thou shalt be God".[3]

Of course, in agreeing with Plato about the pivotal importance of the direction of our attention and love, Augustine alters the balance between these in what turns out to be a decisive way. It is love and not attention which is the ultimately deciding factor. And that is why the Augustinian doctrine of the two directions is usually expressed in terms of the two loves, which can ultimately be identified as charity and concupiscence. I want to return to this below.

For the moment, I only want to bring out the striking elements of continuity between the two doctrines. And that only in order to point out this first important difference, from my point of view here: that this same opposition of spirit/matter, higher/lower, eternal/temporal, immutable/

changing *is* described by Augustine, not just occasionally and peripherally, but centrally and essentially in terms of inner/outer.[4] For instance, in *de Trinitate*, XII.1, he distinguishes between the inner and outer man. The outer is the bodily, what we have in common with the beasts, including even our senses, and the memory storage of our images of outer things. The inner is the soul. And this is not just one way of describing the difference for Augustine. It is in a sense the most important one for our spiritual purposes, because the road from the lower to the higher, the crucial shift in direction, passes through our attending to ourselves as *inner*.

Let one very famous line stand for many: "Noli foras ire, in teipsum redi; in interiore homine habitat veritas" ("Do not go outward; return within yourself. In the inward man dwells truth").[5] Augustine is always calling us within. What we need lies *'intus'*, he tells us again and again. Why this striking difference from Plato?

The short answer is that inward lies the road to God. But it is extremely valuable for my purposes to unpack this answer at greater length.

I pointed above to the parallel between God and the Idea of the Good, in that both provide the ultimate principle of being and knowledge; and both are portrayed with the same central image of the sun. Part of the force of the image in both philosophies is that the highest reality is very difficult, indeed in a sense impossible, to contemplate directly. But for Plato, we find out about this highest principle by looking at the domain of objects which it organizes, that is, the field of the Ideas. What we saw above in the image of the eye of the soul was the doctrine that the power of seeing doesn't have to be put into it; rather it just has to be *turned*. Facing the right field is what is decisive. We may have to struggle to rise to this, but the struggle is over the direction of our gaze.

For Augustine, too, God can be known more easily through his created order and in a sense can never be known directly, except perhaps in a rare condition of mystical rapture (such as Paul experienced, for instance, on the road to Damascus). But our principal route to God is not through the object domain but 'in' ourselves. This is because God is not just the transcendent object or just the principle of order of the nearer objects, which we strain to see. God is also and for us primarily the basic support and underlying principle of our knowing activity. God is not just what we long to see, but what powers the eye which sees. So the light of God is not just 'out there', illuminating the order of being, as it is for Plato; it is also an 'inner' light. It is the light "which lighteth every man that cometh into the world" (John 1:9). It is the light in the soul. "Alia est enim lux quae sentitur oculis; alia qua per oculos agitur et sentiatur; haec lux qua ista manifesta sunt, utique intus in anima est" ("There is one light which we perceive through the eye, another by which the eye itself is enabled to perceive; this light by which [outer things] become manifest is certainly within the soul").[6] The link between Plato's light metaphors and St. John has brought about an important turning.

Augustine shifts the focus from the field of objects known to the activity itself of knowing; God is to be found here. This begins to account for his use of the language of inwardness. For in contrast to the domain of objects, which is public and common, the activity of knowing is particularized; each of us is engaged in ours. To look towards this activity is to look to the self, to take up a reflexive stance.

But this understates the case. There is a less radical kind of turning to the self which was a relatively common topic among ancient moralists. Foucault has mentioned the importance of the theme of "the care of oneself".[7] The call to a higher moral life could be phrased in terms of a call to give less concern to the external things that people normally care for: wealth, power, success, pleasure; and more concern for one's own moral condition. But 'care of self' here meant something like the care of one's soul. The point of call was to show how foolish it is to be very concerned about the state of one's property, for instance, and not at all about the health of one's own soul. It is analogous to the comment someone might make today to a busy executive who is driving himself beyond all limits: "Why try so hard to make an extra million when you'll give yourself a heart attack in the process?" This advice might also be couched in the terms: "Take care of yourself".

This injunction calls us to a reflexive stance, but not a radically reflexive one. The stance becomes radical (this is a term of art I want to introduce here) when what matters to us is the adoption of the first-person standpoint. This could perhaps take a bit of explaining, in view of the place it will hold in my argument.

The world as I know it is there for me, is experienced by me, or thought about by me, or has meaning for me. Knowledge, awareness is always that of an agent. What would be left out of an inventory of the world in one of our most 'objective' languages, e.g., that of our advanced natural sciences, which try to offer a "view from nowhere", would be just this fact of the world's being experienced, of its being *for* agents, or alternatively, of there being something that it is like to be an experiencing agent of a certain kind.[8] In our normal dealings with things, we disregard this dimension of experience and focus on the things experienced. But we can turn and make this our object of attention, become aware of our awareness, try to experience our experiencing, focus on the way the world is *for* us. This is what I call taking a stance of radical reflexivity or adopting the first-person standpoint.

It is obvious that not all reflexivity is radical in this sense. If I attend to my wounded hand, or begin (belatedly) to think about the state of my soul instead of about worldly success, I am indeed concerned with myself, but not yet radically. I am not focussing on myself as the agent of experience and making this my object. Similarly, I can muse in general terms about there being a dimension of experience, as I did in the previous paragraph, without adopting the first-person standpoint, where I make *my* experience my object. Radical reflexivity brings to the fore a kind of presence to oneself which is inseparable from one's being the agent of experience, something to which access by its very nature is asymmetrical: there is a crucial difference between the way I experience my activity, thought, and feeling, and the way that you or anyone else does. This is what makes me a being that can speak of itself in the first person.

The call to take care of oneself as emanating from an ancient sage, or as addressed to a modern executive, is not an appeal to radical reflexivity. It is a call to concern ourselves with the health of one very important thing (our soul for the ancients, the body for the modern) as against being completely absorbed in the fate of something much less important (our property or power). But in either case, what this leads us to focus on, i.e., the causes and constituents of (psychic or bodily) health and sickness, bears no special relation to a first-person standpoint. Thus we today have a science of what it is to be healthy which is impersonally available, and in no way requires for its understanding that we assume the first-person stance. A similar point could be made about the ancients' lore of the soul. Of course the identity of knower and known is very relevant to my *caring* about the soul/body in question: the whole point of the appeal is that it points up the absurdity of my not caring for my own soul (or body). But this identity is of no importance in learning and defining what it is to care for this soul (body).

Augustine's turn to the self was a turn to radical reflexivity, and that is what made the language of inwardness irresistible. The inner light is the one which shines in our presence to ourselves; it is the one inseparable from our being creatures with a first-person standpoint. What differentiates it from the outer light is just what makes the image of inwardness so compelling, that it illuminates that space where I am present to myself.

It is hardly an exaggeration to say that it was Augustine who introduced the inwardness of radical reflexivity and bequeathed it to the Western tradition of thought. The step was a fateful one, because we have certainly made a big thing of the first-person standpoint. The modern epistemological tradition from Descartes, and all that has flowed from it in modern culture, has made this standpoint fundamental—to the point of aberration, one might think. It has gone as far as generating the view that there is a special domain of "inner" objects available only from this standpoint; or the notion that the vantage point of the 'I think' is somehow outside the world of things we experience.

For those of us who are critical of the modern epistemological tradition, it may on one hand seem that Augustine has a lot to answer for. And for those still captured by this tradition (and the two classes overlap considerably), it may on the other hand be hard to appreciate his achievement, since we tend to read *all* reflexivity as radical. But somewhere between these two reactions lies a just appreciation of the change he wrought. This was to make a turn to the self in the first-person dimension crucial to our access to a higher condition—because in fact it is a step on our road back to God—and hence to inaugurate a new line of development in our understanding of moral sources, one which has been formative for our entire Western culture.

In reaction against what we have thus become, particularly through the reified and self-focussed forms of modern subjectivism, we may depreciate this; or in our imprisonment within modern subjectivism, we may fail to notice it. But Augustine needs to be rescued from identification both with his successors and with his predecessors. And that is what I am trying to do in placing him between Plato and Descartes. Augustine makes the step to inwardness, as I said, because it is a step towards God. The truth dwells within, as we saw above, and God is Truth. One way in which this shows itself is in our attempt to prove God's existence. Augustine offers us such a proof in the dialogue *On Free Will,* Book II. He tries to show his interlocutor that there is something higher than our reason, which thus deserves to be called God. The proof turns on the insight that reason recognizes that there is a truth which is criterial for it, i.e., a standard on which it regulates itself, which is not its own making, but beyond it and common to all.

One can imagine making a proof of this kind without recourse to the first-person standpoint. Someone today, for instance, might argue for the existence of binding inter-subjective standards on the grounds of what we actually accept in argument. The proof would point to our habits of discourse and the standards we appealed to and accepted there. This kind of argument is common among the followers of Wittgenstein. Augustine, however, does couch his argument reflexively. He appeals to our first-person experience in thinking.

Thus he starts by showing his interlocutor that he does know something, that he does grasp some truth. Augustine feels he must answer the sceptic, because the pivotal argument that our judgements of truth repose on standards binding on all reasoners would be unhinged if the sceptic could prove that we really know nothing. But in order to prove that we know something, Augustine makes the fateful proto-Cartesian move: he shows his interlocutor that *he* cannot doubt his own existence, since "if you did not exist it would be impossible for you to be deceived".[9] As Gilson points out, Augustine makes frequent use of this proto-cogito.[10]

Augustine's use of this is very different from that of his illustrious successor; it doesn't have such a pivotal importance, and he isn't so concerned to use it to establish mind-body dualism—something Augustine didn't believe needed as much argument.[11] But what it does do, besides giving us at least one truth to show for ourselves, is establish us in the first-person standpoint. It is a feature of this certainty, that it is a certainty *for me;* I am certain of *my* existence: the certainty is contingent on the fact that knower and known are the same. It is a certainty of self-presence. Augustine was the inventor of the argument we know as the 'cogito', because Augustine was the first to make the first-person standpoint fundamental to our search for the truth.

Having shown his interlocutor that he knows that he exists, indeed, that he lives, and that he has intelligence, Augustine gets him to agree that there is a hierarchy among these three. Something which exists and lives is higher than something which just lives, and something which also has intelligence is higher still. The grounds for this are that the higher in each case includes the lower as well as itself. But later on, another ground for superiority enters, this time allowing us to show the superiority of reason to sense: this is that the higher is the judge of the lower. With our reason, we determine what of our sensible experience is really trustworthy. What judges must be higher, so reason is king. Nothing is superior to reason in human nature.[12]

It is this same principle which will allow us to show that something is higher than reason itself. To bring us to this conclusion, Augustine shows that our particular activities of thinking and sensing bear on a common world of objects. The things in the world we perceive with our senses are examples of such common realities. But there are even higher common objects, those which are available to all reasoners. The truths of number and wisdom are of this kind (these are for Augustine, as a good Platonist, closely linked together). There are truths of wisdom, such that humans ought to live justly, or the worse ought to be subjected to the better, or the incorrupt is better than the corrupt, the eternal better than the temporal, and the inviolable better than the violable.[13] These are not truths that each person makes on his own; they represent common standards. We do not judge these and ask whether, for example, the eternal ought to be superior to the temporal, or whether seven plus three ought to equal ten; there is no question that one *is* superior, and that ten *is* the sum. "Knowing simply that these *truths* are so one does not examine them with a view to their correction but rejoices to have discovered them . . . We pass judgement on our minds in accordance with truth as a standard, while we cannot in any way pass judgement on truth".[14] Hence we see that there is something superior to the human mind. QED: God = truth exists.

Moreover, this truth is a common reality in an even stronger sense than the objects we see and touch. For unlike the latter, where we may have to jostle each other to get a good look or shove people aside to touch, truth can be enjoyed by all together. From this store, those who take always leave as much for the others.[15]

Augustine's proof of God is a proof from the first-person experience of knowing and reasoning. I am aware of my own sensing and thinking; and in reflecting on this, I am made aware of its dependence on something beyond it, something common. But this turns out on further examination to include not just objects to be known but also the very standards which reason gives allegiance to. So I recognize that this activity which is mine is grounded on and presupposes something higher than I, something which I should look up to and revere. By going inward, I am drawn upward.

But it may seem strange that Augustine goes to all this trouble to establish that there are higher standards common to all thinkers, something which Plato already had laid out in the Ideas. Was it simply that he felt he had to meet a stronger sceptical challenge? This is how we would tend to look at things with our post-Cartesian eyes. But to see this as Augustine's principal preoccupation is to assume that the sceptical challenge of his day was couched in the form familiar to us: How can one get beyond first-person experience and conclude to a world out there? But this was neither how the challenge was put nor how people thought to answer it before Augustine. The relation of historical causation seems rather to be the reverse: the idea of seeing scepticism as the question whether I can get beyond 'my' inner world is much more a product of the revolution which Augustine started, but which only bore this fruit many centuries later.

The reasons Augustine took this path seem to me to be rather that his concern was to show that God is to be found not just in the world but also and more importantly at the very foundations of the person (to use modern language); God is to be found in the intimacy of self-presence. God as Truth gives us the standards, the principles of right judgement. But he gives them to us not just through the spectacle of a world organized by the Ideas but more basically by that "incorporeal light . . . by which our minds are somehow irradiated, so that we may judge rightly of all these things".[16]

The idea that God is to be found within emerges with greater force out of Augustine's account of our search for self-knowledge. The soul is present to itself, and yet it can utterly fail to know itself; it can be utterly mistaken about its own nature, as Augustine thought that he himself had been when he was a Manichaean. So we can search to know ourselves; and yet we wouldn't know where to begin looking or be aware that we had found ourselves unless we already had some understanding of ourselves. Augustine faces the problem of how we can both know and not know, as Plato did in the Meno, and he solves it with a similar (and obviously derived) recourse to "memory".

But Augustine's 'memory' is rather different from Plato's. In his mature philosophy, it has broken altogether away from the conception of an original vision of the Ideas, crucial to the Platonic theory. In fact, Augustine's concept gets extended and comes to include matters that have nothing to do with past experience, including just those principles of the intelligible order which we have been discussing and which are somehow within us, in the sense that we are capable of formulating them and making them explicit, even though they were never presented explicitly to us in the past. Augustine, by taking the Platonic notion of memory and cutting it from its roots in the theory of prenatal experience (a doctrine hard to square with Christian orthodoxy), developed the basis for what later became the doctrine of innate ideas. Deep within us is an implicit understanding, which we have to think hard to bring to explicit and conscious formulation. This is our *'memoria'*. And it is here that our implicit grasp of what we are resides, which guides us as we move from our original self-ignorance and grievous self-misdescription to true self-knowledge.

But what is at the basis of this memory itself? At its root, constituting this implicit understanding, is the Master within, the source of the light which lights every man coming into the world, God. And so at the end of its search for itself, if it goes to the very end, the soul finds God. The experience of being illumined from another source, of receiving the standards of our reason from beyond ourselves, which the proof of God's existence already brought to light, is seen to be very much an experience of inwardness. That is, it is in this paradigmatically first-person activity, where I strive to make myself more fully present to myself, to realize to the full the potential which resides in the fact that knower and known are one, that I come most tellingly and convincingly to the awareness that God stands above me.

At the very root of memory, the soul finds God. And so the soul can be said to "remember God"—Augustine can give a new meaning to an old biblical expression. When I turn to God, I am listening to what is deep in my "memory"; and so the soul "is reminded to turn to the Lord as to the light by which it was somehow touched even when turned away from him".[17]

But the way within leads above. When we get to God, the image of place becomes multiple and many-sided. In an important sense, the truth is *not* in me.[18] I see the truth 'in' God. Where the meeting takes place, there is a reversal. Going within memory takes me beyond.

Here is a striking place where Augustine has built on a Platonic doctrine to a novel purpose. For Plato in the *Meno,* the doctrine of reminiscence, besides answering the difficult question of how you ever know what you seek, underscores the thesis that knowledge of the Ideas isn't put into us by training. The capacity is there. Augustine takes this point up. Properly speaking, we are not taught the important principles of reason; the teacher only awakens them in us. But while for Plato, the 'within' was only a way of recurring to a 'before', for Augustine, it is the path to an 'above', and indispensable as the road thither. As Gilson put it, Augustine's path is one "leading from the exterior to the interior and from the interior to the superior".[19]

So we come to God within. The clear difference between Augustine's imagery and Plato's, for all the continuity of metaphysical theory, reposes on a major difference of doctrine. Augustine takes our focus off the objects reason knows, the field of the Ideas, and directs it onto the activity of striving to know which each of us carries on; and he makes us aware of this in a first-person perspective. At the end of this road we see that God's is the power sustaining and directing this activity. We grasp the intelligible not just because our soul's eye is directed to it but primarily because we are directed by the Master within.

God is behind the eye, as well as the One whose Ideas the eye strives to discern clearly before it. He is found in the intimacy of my self-presence. Indeed he is closer to me than I am myself, while being infinitely above me; he is "interior intimo meo et superior summo meo".[20] God can be thought of as the most fundamental ordering principle in me. As the soul animates the body, so God does the soul. He vivifies it. "As the soul is the life of the flesh, so God is the blessed life of the man".[21]

This doctrine is the basis of Augustine's attempts to discern the image of the Trinity in the soul and its activity.[22] The first trinity is that of mind, knowledge, and love (mens, notitia, et amor). The mind comes to know itself and, in that, love itself. The same basic idea underlies the second trinity, of memory, intelligence, and will (memoria, intelligentia, et voluntas). In this, the basic movement of the trinity in the soul is made even clearer. 'Memory' is the soul's implicit knowledge of itself. Something is in my memory when I know it even though I am not thinking of it or focussing on it. But to make this explicit and full knowledge, I have to formulate it. In the particular case of the soul, the true latent knowledge I have of myself will be overlaid by all sorts of false images. To dissipate these distorted appearances and get to the truth, I have to draw out the implicit knowledge within (which also comes from above). This comes about in the word (verbum) that I formulate inwardly, and this constitutes intelligentia. But to understand my true self is to love it, and so with intelligence comes will, and with self-knowledge, self-love.

The parallels with the Christian doctrine of the Trinity, particularly with the Father's begetting of the Word, need no stressing. But what is striking here for our purposes is that man shows himself most clearly as the image of God in his inner self-presence and self-love. It is a kind of knowledge where knower and known are one, coupled with love, which reflects most fully God in our lives. And indeed, the image of the Trinity in us is the process whereby we strive to complete and perfect this self-presence and self-affirmation. Nothing shows more clearly than these images of the Trinity how Augustinian inwardness is bound up with radical reflexivity, and they also begin to make clear how essentially linked is this doctrine of inwardness to Augustine's whole conception of the relation of man to God.

We can best see this if we relate this doctrine to another major difference with Plato. I mentioned above that Augustine too sees the soul as potentially facing two ways, towards the higher and immaterial, or towards the lower and sensible. And these two directions of attention are also two directions of desire. Augustine speaks of two loves. But within this similarity to Plato there is a tremendous difference in the way that knowing and loving are related. In Augustine, perhaps inevitably as a Christian thinker, there is a developed notion of the will. Where for Plato, our desire for the good is a function of how much we see it, for Augustine the will is not simply dependent on knowledge.

Two important changes underlay this developing doctrine of the will, and they were taken further by Augustine's successors. The first had already been brought about by Stoic thinkers. They gave a central place to the human capacity to give or withhold assent, or to choose. Humans will have the same sensuous impulses *(hormētikai phantasiai)* as animals, Chrysippus argues, but they are not forced to act on them. They are capable of giving or withholding consent from what impulses urge them to. The wise man will know that pain is to be borne and will not be rushed into seeking relief at all costs. We are not masters of our *phantasiai*, but we do control our all-things-considered rational intention *(synkatathesis)*. Much later on, Epictetus developed a similar doctrine using the Aristotelian term 'prohairesis', which one might translate 'moral choice'. What impulses may impinge is beyond our power, but my *prohairesis* is utterly under my control. Charles Kahn quotes this passage from the *Discourses:*[23] "The tyrant says: 'I will put you in bonds.' 'What are you saying? put *me* in bonds? You will fetter my leg, but not even Zeus can conquer my prohairesis' ".

The singling out of this power of choice or assent is one source of the developing notion of the will, and there is already an important change in moral outlook in making this the central human faculty. What is morally crucial about us is not just the universal nature or rational principle which we share with others, as with Plato and Aristotle, but now also this power of assent, which is essentially in each case mine ('*jemeinig,*' to use Heidegger's term). Western Christian moral sensibility took up and accentuated this side of Stoic thought. From this, the idea can grow that moral perfection requires a personal adhesion to the good, a full commitment of the will. We shall see later how important this demand became in the early modern period.

The second change emerged out of a Christian outlook and was given paradigmatic formulation by Augustine. It posits that humans are capable of two radically different moral dispositions. The teleological theory of nature underlying Greek moral philosophy supposes that everyone is motivated by a love of the good, which can be sidetracked to evil through ignorance (the view that Plato attributes to Socrates) or distortive training and bad habits (Aristotle). Augustine's doctrine of the two loves allows for the possibility that our disposition may be radically perverse, driving us to turn our backs even on the good we see. Indeed, that is precisely the predicament of all of us, owing to the sin of Adam. The will must first be healed through grace before we can function fully on the Socratic model.

The further development of the doctrine of the will in Western Christendom and its successor culture weaves together these two master ideas, not without some tension and difficulty: the will as our power to confer or withhold all-things-considered assent, or choice; and the will as the basic disposition of our being. According to the first facet, we speak of people as strong- or weak-willed; according to the second, we speak of them as of good or ill will.

Both of these changes complicate the simpler "Socratic" model according to which we always act for the good we see; and above all, the second introduces a potential conflict between vision and desire. This is not to say that the will is declared quite independent of knowledge, or that Augustine believed in the possibility that we might see in full clarity the glory of God and not respond in love. This kind of limit case is invoked, of course, in the Judaeo-Christian legend of Lucifer, but it has never been attributed by Christian theology as a power to humans. It does mean, however, that in the zone in which we live, of half-understanding and contrary desires, the will is as much the independent variable, determining what we can know, as it is the dependent one, shaped by what we see. The causality is circular and not linear.

For the linear theories which descend from Socrates, as well as for modern rationalists, the phenomenon of weakness of the will—'akrasia'—is a major intellectual problem; for Augustine, it was no problem, but rather the central crisis of moral experience. That is why he seized so eagerly on the passage from St. Paul's Epistle to the Romans (7:19–25): "For the good that I would I do not: but the evil which I would not, that I do", as he relates in the Confessions.[24] In Augustine's Christian outlook, as we saw, the perversity in the will can never be sufficiently explained by our lack of insight into the good; on the contrary, it makes us act below and against our insight, and prevents this from becoming fuller and purer.

This perversity can be described as a drive to make ourselves the centre of our world, to relate everything to ourselves, to dominate and possess the things which surround us. This is both cause and consequence of a kind of slavery, a condition in which we are in turn dominated, captured by our own obsessions and fascination with the sensible. So we can see that evil cannot be explained simply by lack of vision but involves something also in the dimension of the soul's sense of itself. Reflexivity is central to our moral understanding.

But this is not all. If reflexivity were only the source of evil, then the remedy might easily be to turn away from the self, to become absorbed fully in the impersonal Ideas. Connecting the self with evil and suffering can also lead us in this direction, as Buddhist doctrine shows us. But for Augustine, it is not reflexivity which is evil; on the contrary, we show most clearly the image of God in our fullest self-presence. Evil is when this reflexivity is enclosed on itself. Healing comes when it is broken open, not in order to be abandoned, but in order to acknowledge its dependence on God.

And so the discovery which dissipates the perversity of the will, and which the rectifying of this perversity makes possible, is that of our dependence on God in the very intimacy of our own presence to ourselves, at the roots of those powers which are most our own. We see here that the stress on reflexivity, on the inward path, is not only for the benefit of intellectuals, trying to prove the existence of God; the very essence of Christian piety is to sense this dependence of my inmost being on God. And just as in our perverse condition of sin, our desire for the good was so much less than our insight; in being turned towards God, our love for him goes beyond the measure of any order, however good. When it comes to God, the right measure is to love without measure.[25] So both for better and for worse, the will leaps beyond the desire appropriate to a cosmos ordered for the Good. There is something gratuitious in love as well as in the refusal of love; and this, of course, is at the heart of the Judaeo-Christian outlook. It matches the gratuitous creation of the world by God, which is so crucially different from its analogue in Plotinus, the emanation of the lower from the higher, following its own essence.

We might say that where for Plato the eye already has the capacity to see, for Augustine it has *lost* this capacity. This must be restored by grace. And what grace does is to open the inward man to God, which makes us able to see that the eye's vaunted power is really God's.

7.2

We can thus see the crucial importance of the language of inwardness for Augustine. It represents a radically new doctrine of moral resources, one where the route to the higher passes within. In this doctrine, radical reflexivity takes on a new status, because it is the 'space' in which we come to encounter God, in which we effect the turning from lower to higher. In Augustine's doctrine, the intimacy of self-presence is, as it were, hallowed, with immensely far-reaching consequences for the whole of Western culture. This exclamation from the *Confessions* movingly sums up Augustinian piety: "God the light of my heart, and the bread that nourishes my soul, and the power which weds my mind to my inmost thoughts".[26]

Some of the consequences are very relevant to our understanding of Descartes and the transposition he wrought in the Augustinian tradition. Augustine is the originator of that strand of Western spirituality which has sought the certainty of God within. There is a certain family of 'proofs' of the existence of God whose basic form is typically Augustinian. The démarche which is common to them all is something like this: my experience of my own thinking puts me in contact with a perfection, which at one and the same time shows itself to be an essential condition of that thinking and also to be far beyond my own finite scope and powers to attain. There must then be a higher being on which all this depends, i.e., God. In the version we examined from Augustine, the perfection in question was that of eternal, unchanging truth, which operates as a common standard for our thought. This is both something essentially presupposed in our thinking and yet manifestly not our own product, argues Augustine.

But the famous (or infamous) ontological argument of Anselm, which Descartes took over, can also be understood as a basically 'Augustinian' proof. Here we start from the idea in the mind, that of the most perfect being. I think the underlying intuition is that this is not an idea we just happen to have, but one which must occur to us. The notion that the idea must occur is the properly 'Augustinian' intuition: we can only understand ourselves if we see ourselves as in contact with a perfection which is beyond us. But if the idea must be, then the reality must exist, because the notion of a most perfect being lacking existence is a contradiction. The fact that this latter part of the argument scarcely convinces should not divert us from understanding the kind of spiritual stance which underlies it.

And the same spirit inhabits Descartes's own proof, in the third Meditation. I find in myself the idea of a being who is "souverainement parfait et infini". But this is not an idea which I might fail to have, understanding myself as I do. That is, it couldn't be that, understanding myself as finite first, I then constructed by my own powers of conception the idea of a being who would represent the negation of myself and hence would be infinite. On the contrary, it works the other way around. I wouldn't have the notion of myself as finite unless I already had implanted within me this idea of infinity and perfection. But to understand myself as doubting and wanting is to see myself as lacking in some respect, and hence as finite and imperfect. So my most basic and unavoidable modes of self-understanding presuppose the idea of infinity. "For how could I know that I doubt and that I desire, that is, that I lack something and am not quite perfect, if I had no idea in myself of a being more perfect than I, by comparison with whom I can know the defects of my nature".[27]

Here is what I described as the basically Augustinian démarche: I can only understand myself in the light of a perfection that goes far beyond my powers. How is it that this light is cast upon my thought? It is beyond my powers to have produced it myself. Descartes argues; so it must have come from a being who really enjoys these perfections.

In a sense, we can contrast the temper of these Augustinian proofs with those that Thomas formulated. The latter argue to God from the existence of created reality (or what the proofs show to be created reality). They pass, as it were, through the realm of objects. The Augustinian proof moves through the subject and through the undeniable foundations of his presence to himself. Descartes was not alone in embracing the Augustinian path at the beginning of the modern era. In a sense those two centuries, the sixteenth and seventeenth, can be seen as an immense flowering of Augustinian spirituality across all confessional differences, one which continued in its own way into the Enlightenment, as the case of Leibniz amply illustrates. Indeed, I will argue that its impact is still potent today, and that it in a sense matches the outlook and identity of moderns. But more of this below.

For the moment, I want to mention a few other points at which Augustine anticipated Descartes. I have already spoken of the many formulations of a sort of proto-cogito. But what is also interesting to note is that the word itself is not only used but singled out for comment by Augustine. To focus on my own thinking activity is to bring to attention not only the order of things in the cosmos which I seek to *find* but also the order which I *make* as I struggle to plumb the depths of memory and discern my true being. In the *Confessions*, Augustine reflects how our thoughts "must be rallied and drawn together again, that they may be known; that is to say, they must as it were be collected and gathered together from their dispersions: whence the word 'cogitation' is derived".[28] And Augustine goes on to point out the etymological link between *'cogitare'* and *'cogere'* = 'to bring together' or 'to collect'. This understanding of thinking as a kind of inner assembly of an order we construct will be put to a revolutionary new use by Descartes.

There are other points of anticipation as well. As I mentioned above, the conception of innate ideas is already there in germ in Augustine's 'memory'—he even uses the image of the ring whose imprint remains in the wax.[29] So is the idea that the soul is better known to itself than the body. And even the (bad) argument that the soul should eliminate from its idea of itself anything derived from the senses, because it knows these things differently than it knows itself, anticipates a notorious Cartesian reasoning.

But in spite of all this, Descartes brought about a revolutionary change. And the transformation in the doctrine of moral resources from Augustine to Descartes is no less momentous than that which Augustine wrought relative to Plato.

8

DESCARTES'S DISENGAGED REASON

Descartes is in many ways profoundly Augustinian: the emphasis on radical reflexivity, the importance of the cogito, the central role of a proof of God's existence which starts from 'within', from features of my own ideas, instead of starting from external being, as we see in the Thomistic proofs, all put him in the stream of revived Augustinian piety which dominated the late Renaissance on both sides of the great confessional divide.

But Descartes gives Augustinian inwardness a radical twist and takes it in a quite new direction, which has also been epoch-making. The change might be described by saying that Descartes situates the moral sources within us.

We saw that the language of inner/outer doesn't figure in Plato or indeed in other ancient moralists. One reason for this was that gaining mastery of oneself, shifting the hegemony from the senses to reason, was a matter of changing the direction of our soul's vision, its attention-cum-desire. To be ruled by reason was to be turned towards the Ideas and hence moved by love of them. The locus of our sources of moral strength resides outside. To have access to the higher is to be turned towards and in tune with this cosmic order, which is shaped by the Good.

Augustine does give a real sense to the language of inwardness. But this is not because he sees the moral sources as situated within us any more than Plato did. Augustine retains the Platonic notion of an order of things in the cosmos which is good. True, this doesn't suffice for us, because we have to be healed of sin to love this order as we should. And this healing comes to us within. But it does not come from a power which is ours. On the contrary, we turn to the path within only to accede beyond, to God.

The internalization wrought by the modern age, of which Descartes's formulation was one of the most important and influential, is very different from Augustine's. It does, in a very real sense, place the moral sources within us. Relative to Plato, and relative to Augustine, it brings about in each case a transposition by which we no longer see ourselves as related to moral sources outside of us, or at least not at all in the same way. An important power has been internalized.

I will follow each of these transpositions in turn. First, in relation to Plato, Descartes offers a new understanding of reason, and hence of its hegemony over the passions, which both see as the essence of morality.

Some change became inevitable, once the cosmic order was no longer seen as embodying the Ideas. Descartes utterly rejected this teleological mode of thinking and abandoned any theory of ontic logos. The universe was to be understood mechanistically, by the resolutive/compositive method pioneered by Galileo. This shift in scientific theory, as we would call it today, involved a radical change in anthropology as well. Plato's theory of the Ideas involved a very close relation between scientific explanation and moral vision. One has the correct understanding of both together, one might say, or of neither. If we destroy this vision of the ontic logos and substitute a very different theory of scientific explanation, the entire account of moral virtue and self-mastery has to be transformed as well.

The account of scientific knowledge which ultimately emerges on the Galilean view is a representational one. To know reality is to have a correct representation of things—a correct picture within of outer reality, as it came to be conceived. Descartes declares himself "assuré que je ne puis avoir aucune connaissance de ce qui est hors de moi, que par l'entremise des idées que j'ai eu en moi" ("certain that I can have no knowledge of what is outside me except by means of the ideas I have within me").[1] And this conception of knowledge comes to seem unchallengeable, once an account of knowledge in terms of a self-revealing reality, like the Ideas, was abandoned.

A representation of reality now has to be constructed. As the notion of 'idea' migrates from its ontic sense to apply henceforth to intra-psychic contents, to things "in the mind", so the order of ideas ceases to be something we *find* and becomes something we *build*. Moreover, the constraints on its construction include but go beyond its correctly matching external reality. As Descartes argued forcefully, representations attain the status of knowledge not only by being correct but also by carrying certainty. There is no real knowledge where I have a lot of ideas in my head which happen to correspond to things out there, if I have no well-grounded confidence in them. But for Descartes, well-grounded certainty comes from the matter presenting itself to us in a certain light, one where the truth is so clear as to be undeniable, what he calls 'évidence'. "Toute science est une connaissance certaine et évidente" is the opening sentence of his *Regulae ad directionem ingenii*.

The order of representations has to be developed in such a way as to generate certainty, through a chain of clear and distinct perceptions. This is the point of the rules laid out in the *Regulae* and of those later formulated in the *Discours*. In the latter work, for instance, we are told to divide up our problems "en autant de parcelles qu'il se pourroit, & qu'il seroit requis pour les mieux resoudre" ("into as many parts as possible, and as seemed requisite in order that it might be resolved in the best manner possible").[2] And the following rule tells us to conduct our thoughts in order, building from the simpler to the complex, "et supposant mesme de l'ordre entre ceux qui ne se precedent point naturellement les uns les autres" ("assuming an order, even if a fictitious one, among those which do not follow a natural sequence relatively to one another").[3]

The order of representations must thus meet standards which derive from the thinking activity of the knower. It is an order collected and brought together to meet, inter alia, certain subjective demands. Thinking which is such a construction or gathering is rightly designated by *'cogitare'*, with its etymological links to notions like gathering and ordering.[4]

This very different view of knowledge and the cosmos means that Descartes's dualism of soul and body will be strikingly different from Plato's. For Plato, I realize my true nature as a supersensible soul when I turn towards supersensible, eternal, immutable things. This turning will no doubt include my seeing and understanding the things which surround me as participating in the Ideas which give them being.

For Descartes, in contrast, there is no such order of Ideas to turn to, and understanding physical reality in terms of such is precisely a paradigm example of the confusion between the soul and the material we must free ourselves from. Coming to a full realization of one's being as immaterial involves perceiving distinctly the ontological cleft between the two, and this involves grasping the material world as mere extension. The material world here includes the body, and coming to see the real distinction requires that we disengage from our usual embodied perspective, within which the ordinary person tends to see the objects around him as really qualified by colour or sweetness or heat, tends to think of the pain or tickle as in his tooth or foot. We have to objectify the world, including our own bodies, and that means to come to see them mechanistically and functionally, in the same way that an uninvolved external observer would.

We are helped in this if we focus clearly on what it is to understand the reality which surrounds us, as in the examination of the piece of wax in the second Meditation, whereby we are brought to see the role of pure understanding: that in fact "nous ne concevons les corps que par la faculté d'entendre qui est en nous, & non point par l'imagination ny par les sens, & que nous ne les connoissons pas de ce que nous les voyons, ou que nous les touchons, mais seulement de ce que nous les concevons par la pensée" ("bodies are not properly speaking known by the senses or by the faculty of the imagination, but by the understanding only, and . . . they are not known from the fact that they are seen or touched, but only because they are understood").[5] But we also have to clear up our understanding of matter and stop thinking of it as the locus of events and qualities whose true nature is mental. And this we do by objectifying it, that is, by understanding it as "disenchanted", as mere mechanism, as devoid of any spiritual essence or expressive dimension. We have to cease seeing the material universe as a kind of medium, in which psychic contents like heat and pain, or the supposed Forms or Species of scholastic tradition, could be lodged or embodied or manifest themselves.

But this involves more than just the rejection of the traditional ontology; it also does violence to our ordinary, embodied way of experiencing. We have to disengage ourselves from this, for Descartes, irremediably confused and obscure way of grasping things. To bring this whole domain of sensations and sensible properties to clarity means to grasp it as an external observer would, tracing the causal connection between states of the world or my body, described in primary properties, and the 'ideas' they occasion in my mind. Clarity and distinctness require that we step outside ourselves and take a disengaged perspective.[6]

There is something at first sight paradoxical here. In one way, the Cartesian dualism seems more austere and severe than Plato's, since it no longer admits that the bodily can be a sort of medium in which the spiritual can appear. The Plato of the *Symposium* is utterly undercut, and this kind of presence of the eternal in the temporal repudiated. Yet in another way, Cartesian dualism *needs* the bodily as the Platonic did not. Not that Descartes doesn't conceive our entering into a disembodied condition after death, but rather that in our present condition, the way to realize our immaterial essence is by taking a certain stance to the body. Where the Platonic soul realizes its eternal nature by becoming absorbed in the supersensible, the Cartesian discovers and affirms his immaterial nature by objectifying the bodily.

That is why Descartes is right to consider his theory of the substantial union of soul and body as closer than Plato's conception of their relationship—even though he rather misidentified Plato's theory. The Cartesian soul frees itself not by turning away but by objectifying embodied experience. The body is an inescapable object of attention to it, as it were. It has to support itself on it to climb free of it. By analogy with Weber's famous description of Protestant spirituality as an "innerworldly asceticism", we could describe Descartes's dualism as showing the way to an 'innerworldly liberation' of the soul.

But this different ontology, and hence different theory of knowledge, and thus revised conception of dualism cannot but result in a very different notion of the self-mastery wrought by reason. This cannot mean what it meant for Plato, that one's soul is ordered by the Good which presides over the cosmic order which one attends to and loves. For there is no such order. Being rational has now to mean something other than being attuned to this order.

The Cartesian option is to see rationality, or the power of thought, as a capacity we have to *construct* orders which meet the standards demanded by knowledge, or understanding, or certainty. In Descartes's case, of course, the standards in question are those of *'evidence'*. If we follow this line, then the self-mastery of reason now must consist in this capacity being the controlling element in our lives, and not the senses; self-mastery consists in our lives being shaped by the orders that our reasoning capacity constructs according to the appropriate standards.

The place of this new notion of reason in Descartes's theory of knowledge is familiar enough. What is less appreciated is that it underlay his ethics as well. In his famous correspondence with the princess Elisabeth, Descartes sets out a moral view which is quite reminiscent of ancient Stoicism. In particular, it seems to give central importance to an ideal resembling the Stoic *autarkeia*.[7] He even propounds a doctrine which sounds closely analogous to Epictetus' that our only concern should be the state of our *'prohairesis'*, i.e., that in us which directs our conduct. For Descartes, the point is to be made in terms of the will. We see this, for instance, in a famous passage of his letter to Christina of Sweden:

> outre que le libre arbitre est de soy la chose la plus noble qui puisse estre en nous, d'autant qu'il nous rend en quelque façon pareils à Dieu & semble nous exempter de luy estre suiets, & que, par consequent, son bon usage est le plus grand de tous nos biens, il est aussi celuy qui est le plus proprement nostre & qui nous importe le plus, d'où il suit que ce n'est que de luy que nos plus grands contentemens peuvent proceder.

> Now freewill is in itself the noblest thing we can have because it makes us in a certain manner equal to God and exempts us from being his subjects; and so its rightful use is the greatest of all the goods we possess, and further there is nothing that is more our own or that matters more to us. From all this it follows that nothing but freewill can produce our greatest contentments.[8]

It is from the hegemony of reason itself that our greatest contentment comes. But there has been a radical shift of interpretation in relation to the Stoics. For these, the hegemony of reason was that of a certain vision of the world, in which everything which happens comes from the providence of God. The wise man, seeing this, is able to accept and rejoice in whatever happens qua event in this providential order and is cured from the false opinion that these events matter qua promotions or frustrations of his individual needs or desires. For Descartes, the hegemony means what it naturally tends to mean to us today, that reason controls, in the sense that it instrumentalizes the desires.

Descartes does have a conception of providence, and indeed one very close to the Stoics.[9] But this doesn't prevent him from having a very different notion of what the mastery of reason consists of. I said that for the Stoics the hegemony of reason was that of a certain vision of the world, because for them the move from slavery to the passions to rational self-possession was accounted for entirely in terms of the acquisition of insight into the order of things. The passions are construed as wrong opinions. To be moved by fear and lust is to be enthralled by false views about what is really worth fleeing or possessing. Epictetus says at one point in the *Discourses* that the crucial thing for us is the nature of our opinions *(dogmata)*; and later he says that what makes the soul impure is its bad judgements *(krimata)*.[10]

In a general sense this intellectualism is common to all the ethical theories which come down from the Greeks. The hegemony of reason is that of a vision of order. The rational man for Plato is moved by the cosmic order; whereas for Aristotle what is important ethically is a sense (not theoretically stateable, but grasped by *phronēsis*) of the proper order among the ends we pursue. The Stoics were extreme in simply identifying passions with opinions, but all the great ancients looked on them as encapsulating insight or its lack. Freeing oneself from passion was a matter of altering insight. Aristotle was far from agreeing with the Stoics that the passions should simply be stilled definitively; on the contrary, they were good and useful in their proper place. The Aristotelian account of what it is for a passion to be in its proper place, however, was that it be aroused only on the appropriate occasion. This may be brought about by training, but what it amounts to is the passion's being infused with, and thus docile to, rational insight into what is appropriate.

Augustine's doctrine of the two loves added a new dimension to this picture. Insight could be powerless because of a perversity of the will; and a transformation of the will might now be necessary for further insight. But the fulness of perfection is still described in terms of insight into the good.

Descartes introduces an account of a radically different kind. Rational mastery requires insight, of course; and in a curious way, Descartes follows the Stoics in founding his ethics on a "physics". As he says to Chanut, "La notion telle quelle de la Physique . . . m'a grandement servy pour établir des fondemens certains en la Morale" ("What little knowledge of physics I have tried to acquire . . . has been a great help to me in establishing sure foundations in moral philosophy").[11] But the insight is not into an order of the good; rather it is into something which entails the emptiness of all ancient conceptions of such order: the utter separation of mind from a mechanistic universe of matter which is most emphatically not a medium of thought or meaning, which is expressively dead.

Insight is essential to the move we can call, following Weber, 'disenchanting' the world. We could also call it neutralizing the cosmos, because the cosmos is no longer seen as the embodiment of meaningful order which can define the good for us. And this move is brought about by our coming to grasp this world as mechanism. We saw above how we escape the confused experience of everyday sensations by seeing the causal-functional connections between body-state and idea. We demystify the cosmos as a setter of ends by grasping it mechanistically and functionally as a domain of possible means. Gaining insight into the world as mechanism is inseparable from seeing it as a domain of potential instrumental control.

This connection between knowledge and control was already evident to Descartes, and he gave expression to it in a famous passage of the *Discours:*

> Elles [quelques notions generales touchant la physique] m'ont fait voir qu'il est possible de parvenir à des connoissances qui soient fort utiles a la vie, & qu'au lieu de cete philosophie speculative, qu'on enseigne dans les escholes, on en peut trouver une pratique, par laquelle, connoissant la force & les actions du feu, de l'eau, de l'air, des astres, des cieux & de tous les autres cors qui nous environnent, aussy distinctement que nous connoissons les divers metiers de nos artisans, nous les pourrions employer en mesme façon a tous les usages ausquels ils sont propres, & ainsi nous rendre comme maistres & possesseurs de la Nature.

> For they [some general notions concerning Physics] caused me to see that it is possible to attain knowledge which is very useful in life, and that, instead of that speculative philosophy which is taught in the Schools, we may find a practical philosophy by means of which, knowing the force and the action of fire, water, air, the stars, heavens and all other bodies that environ us, as distinctly as we know the different crafts of our artisans, we can in the same way employ them in all those uses to which they are adapted, and thus render ourselves the masters and possessors of nature.[12]

The new model of rational mastery which Descartes offers presents it as a matter of instrumental control. To be free from the illusion which mingles mind with matter is to have an understanding of the latter which facilitates its control. Similarly, to free oneself from passions and obey reason is to get the passions under instrumental direction. The hegemony of reason is defined no longer as that of a dominant vision but rather in terms of a directing agency subordinating a functional domain.

That is why Descartes develops a quite new theory of the passions. The Stoics' was the most influential theory of the tradition. They classified the passions according to the implicit (and erroneous) opinions about the good and bad that they contained. Descartes's classification is influenced by this universally quoted model. But it soon becomes evident that his principle of explanation is fundamentally different. Passions are seen not as opinions but as functional devices that the Creator has designed for us to help preserve the body-soul substantial union. Passions are emotions in the soul, caused by movements of the animal spirits, which have as their function to strengthen the response which the survival or well-being of the organism requires in a given situation.[13]

The sight of a dangerous animal, for instance, will typically have three kinds of consequences. It may trigger off a reflex of flight. This is the only consequence which occurs in animals, which must be understood as complex machines. With man it will also bring about the rational recognition that he ought to make himself scarce. The man is rationally motivated to do what his animal reactions have perhaps already started. But then passion will strengthen the response, because the animal spirits connected with the perception of the animal and the flight reflex also incite fear in the soul. This serves to beef up the already existing rational movement towards flight. This extra élan is often useful. Indeed, in a situation of threat by a dangerous animal, the extra drive given by fear may provide the vital margin as I clear a six-foot fence that I normally could not.

Descartes sums it up: "L'usage de toutes les passions consiste en cela seul, qu'elles disposent l'ame à vouloir les choses que la nature dicte nous estre utiles, & à persister en cette volonté: comme aussi la mesme agitation des esprits, qui a coustume de les causer dispose le corps aux mouvemens qui servent à l'execution de ces choses" ("The customary mode of action of all the passions is simply this, that they dispose the soul to desire those things which nature tells us are of use, and to persist in this desire, and also bring about that same agitation of spirits which customarily causes them to dispose the body to the movement which serves for the carrying into effect of these things").[14]

Reason rules the passions when it can hold them to their normal instrumental function. The hegemony of reason for Descartes is a matter of instrumental control.

That is why Descartes doesn't call on us to get rid of our passions. On the contrary, he admires "les plus grandes âmes" who "ont des raisonnements si forts & si puissans que, bien qu'elles ayent aussi des passions, & mesme souvent de plus violentes que celles du commun, leur raison demeure neantmoins tousiours la maistresse" ("great souls . . . whose reasoning powers are so strong and powerful, that although they also have passions, and often even more violent than is common, nonetheless their reason remains sovereign").[15] The idea that our passions might be not only strong but "violent" is not only unthinkable from a Stoic perspective but shocking even for those other strands of traditional ethical thought which didn't accept the extreme Stoic goal of a complete liberation from passion. But it makes sense from the new Cartesian perspective, where what matters is instrumental control. If this is what mastery means, then the strength of the subordinate element is no problem; indeed, the stronger it is the better, so long as it is properly steered by reason.

Thus he says to Elisabeth: "Le vray usage de nostre raison pour la conduite de la vie ne consiste qu'a examiner & considerer sans passions la valeur de toutes les perfections, tant du corps que de l'esprit, . . . afin qu'estant ordinairement obligez de nous priver de quelques unes, pour avoir les autres, nous choisissions tousiours les meilleures." But once the rational order of priorities is imposed, there is no reason whatever why we should try to free ourselves of passion. On the contrary, "il suffit qu'on les rende suiettes a la raison, & lorsqu'on les a ainsy apprivoisées, elles sont quelquefois d'autant plus utiles qu'elles penchent plus vers l'exces" ("The true function of reason, then, in the conduct of life is to examine and consider without passion the value of all perfections of body and soul that can be acquired by our conduct, so that since we are commonly obliged to deprive ourselves of some goods in order to acquire others, we shall always choose the better . . . It is enough to subject one's passions to reason; and once they are thus tamed they are sometimes useful precisely to the degree that they tend to excess").[16]

The endorsement of instrumental control means that Descartes constantly enjoins efficacious action for what we want, alongside detachment from the outcome. The proper stance is a detached engagement, as the previous quote prescribes: that we try to attain the best, but that we be satisfied with what we get. Thus the passage about "les grandes âmes" quoted above continues: "Elles font bien tout ce qui est en leur pouvoir pour se rendre la Fortune favorable en cette vie, mais neantmoins elles l'estiment si peu, au regard de l'Eternité, qu'elles n'en considerent quasi les evenemens que comme nous faisons ceux des Comedies" ("They do everything in their power to make fortune favour them in this life, but nevertheless they think so little of it, in relation to eternity, that they view the events of this world as we do those of a play").[17]

The new definition of the mastery of reason brings about an internalization of moral sources. When the hegemony of reason comes to be understood as rational control, the power to objectify body, world, and passions, that is, to assume a thoroughly instrumental stance towards them, then the sources of moral strength can no longer be seen as outside us in the traditional mode—certainly not in the way that they were for Plato, and I believe also for the Stoics, where they reside in a world order which embodies a Good we cannot but love and admire. Of course, Augustine's theism remains, which finds our most important source in God. And this was vitally important for Descartes—it is sheer anachronism to read back into his mind what later Deists and unbelievers did with his conception of reason.[18] But on the human, natural level, a great shift has taken place. If rational control is a matter of mind dominating a disenchanted world of matter, then the sense of the superiority of the good life, and the inspiration to attain it, must come from the agent's sense of his own dignity as a rational being. I believe that this modern theme of the dignity of the human person, which has such a considerable place in modern ethical and political thought, arises out of the internalization I have been describing.[19]

It will become an explicitly central theme with Kant more than a century later. But Descartes's ethical theory is already moving in its orbit. We can see this in the great emphasis he places on the satisfactions of self-esteem in describing the rewards of the good life.[20] And it comes out even more clearly in the central place he gives to 'générosité', this crowning virtue of the honour ethic of the seventeenth century, now transposed into the crucial motivational basis for an ethic of rational control.

The use of this term is at first sight puzzling in a 'neo-Stoic' morality. The ethic which prized honour, glory, fame, which made concern for reputation a high duty, was always a main target of Stoic criticism. And, indeed, in this respect, the Stoics followed Plato, and were joined by Augustine, who sees nothing but *libido dominandi* in these worldly concerns. This ethic nevertheless had its defenders in the Renaissance. Machiavelli is a spectacular case, but there were thoroughly "mainstream" currents which upheld it. We see one in the France of Descartes's day, which found expression, for instance, in the early works of Corneille. It was in a sense the natural ethic of aristocrats, and the modern challenge to it becomes interwoven with the rise of a 'bourgeois' ethic—a theme I will return to below.

But all this does little to explain Descartes's use of the term. On the question of fame he is an orthodox Stoic, classing "les honneurs, les richesses & la santé" together as goods that don't depend on us and that we have to be able to do without.[21] The explanation is more interesting. The ethic of rational control, finding its sources in a sense of dignity and self-esteem, transposes *inward* something of the spirit of the honour ethic. No longer are we winning fame in public space; we act to maintain our sense of worth in our own eyes. There is a shift in the virtue terms. Earlier Stoic thought, alongside freedom from passion, stresses the harmony and serenity of the good soul. To make our mind (*hēgemonikon*) conformable to nature, says Epictetus, is to make it "elevated, free, unrestrained, unimpeded, faithful, modest".[22] For Seneca, the soul no longer touched by accidents of fortune is like the upper part of the universe, which rides serenely above the tempest-filled lower air. It is a "sublimis animus, quietus semper et in statione tranquilla collocatus". The highest virtue is a "sublimitas et sanitas et libertas et concordia et decor animi".[23]

Descartes continues this theme of inner peace. He writes to Christina of "le repos d'esprit & la satisfaction interieure que sentent en eux-mesmes ceux qui sçavent qu'ils ne manquent iamais à faire leur mieux" ("the repose of mind and interior satisfaction felt by those who never fail to do their best").[24] But another theme is also heard. He speaks now of strength and force. The "grandes âmes" have "des raisonnemens si forts & si puissans" that they can ride herd even on "violent" passions. They are to be contrasted, in a revealing phrase with "les . . . ames . . . basses & vulgaires" who "se laissent aller à leurs passions" ("base and vulgar souls . . . who let themselves go with their passions").[25]

The themes of strength and self-control also figured in the Stoic tradition. The early writers spoke of the good soul's "tension" *(tonos)*, almost as we might speak of the tonus of a muscle. An eclectic writer like Cicero (significantly, a Roman under a still republican regime) can also put great emphasis on self-control as a virtue of "manly" strength.[26] But Descartes makes strength of will the central virtue. Following virtue, he says to Elisabeth, is "having a firm and constant will to do what we judge the best"; and he propounds the same doctrine to Christina of Sweden.[27] In the treatise on *The Passions of the Soul,* he describes strong souls as those "in whom the will can by nature conquer the passions with the greatest ease." A strong soul fights passions "with its own arms"; "Ce que je nomme ses propres armes sont des jugemens fermes & determinez touchant la connoissance du bien & du mal, suivant lesquels elle a resolu de conduire les actions de sa vie" ("That which I call its proper arms consists of the firm and determinate judgements respecting the knowledge of good and evil, in pursuance of which it has resolved to conduct the actions of its life").[28]

Strength, firmness, resolution, control, these are the crucial qualities, a subset of the warrior-aristocratic virtues, but now internalized. They are not deployed in great deeds of military valour in public space, but rather in the inner domination of passion by thought.[29]

This explains the crucial place that Descartes gives to the motive of 'generosity'. This was the frequently used term for the central motive of the honour ethic. Although the word was already beginning to take on its modern meaning of open-handedness, it mainly referred to that strong sense of one's own worth and honour which pushed men to conquer their fears and baser desires and do great things. We might say that the generous man was a "great soul" (cf. "les grandes âmes" of the letter to Elisabeth), except that the term for this—'magnanimous'—has gone through an analogous slide since the seventeenth century towards its modern meaning: something like a being ready to forgive, to make allowances for others.[30]

Generosity figured prominently in the tragedies of Corneille, particularly the earlier ones, whose heroes were above all moved by the search for honour and glory. Rodrigue in *Le Cid* explains to Chimène why he owes it to their

love to follow the demands of honour and kill her father; for otherwise, "Qui
m'aima généreux me haïra infame" ("She who loved me when generous
would hate me when infamous"; III.iv.890). And perhaps one of the best
descriptions of the quality is Cleopatra's speech in *Pompée:*

> Les Princes ont cela de leur haute naissance
> Leur âme dans leur sang prend des impressions
> Qui dessous leur vertu rangent les passions.
> Leur générosité soumet tout à leur gloire.

> Princes have this from their noble birth.
> Their souls are shaped by their blood
> To order their passions below their virtue.
> Their generosity submits everything to their glory. (II.i.370–373)

This common concern for the key virtue of the honour ethic has been
remarked among the semi-contemporaries Corneille and Descartes.[31] There
is unquestionably a connection, but it doesn't come from their describing the
same social reality, as Gustave Lanson implies. Nor is the Cornelian character
as close to the Cartesian ideal as Cassirer seems to argue. What we have is a
virtually total transposition of the notion of generosity from the defence of
honour in warrior societies (portrayed by Corneille) to the Cartesian ideal of
rational control.[32]

Because this ideal is no longer powered by a vision of order, but is rather
powered by a sense of the dignity of the thinking being, generosity is the
appropriate emotion. And it is not only appropriate, but essential; it is the
motor of virtue. So true generosity

> qui fait qu'un homme s'estime au plus haut point qu'il se peut legitime-
> ment estimer, consiste seulement, partie en ce qu'il connoist qu'il n'y a rien
> qui veritablement luy appartiene que cette libre disposition de ses
> volontez, ny pourquoi il doive estre loüé ou blasmé sinon pour ce qu'il en
> use bien ou mal; & partie en ce qu'il sent en soy mesme une ferme &
> constante resolution d'en bien user, c'est à dire de ne manquer jamais de
> volonté, pour entreprendre & executer toutes les choses qu'il jugera estre
> les meilleures. Ce qui est suivre parfaitement la vertu.

> which causes a man to esteem himself as highly as he legitimately can,
> consists alone partly in the fact that he knows that there is nothing that
> truly pertains to him but this free disposition of his will, and that there is
> no reason why he should be praised or blamed unless it is because he uses
> it well or ill; and partly in the fact that he is sensible in himself of a firm
> and constant resolution to use it well, that is to say, never to fail of his
> own will to undertake and execute all the things which he judges to be the
> best—which is to follow perfectly after virtue.[33]

In other words, generosity is the emotion which accompanies my sense of my human dignity. In its true form it incorporates a correct understanding of what this dignity consists in, as well as a sense that I am living up to it. This sense of esteem then fuels my continued commitment to virtue, partly in that it makes me disdain and lose interest in all the things that don't really matter, and partly in that it impels me to realize even more fully the highest good in my life. Generosity is "comme la clef de toutes les autres vertus, & un remede general contre tous les dereglements des Passions" ("the key of all other virtues, and a general remedy for all the disorders of the passions").[34] This central place accorded to the (admittedly purified) key virtue of the honour ethic, occupying the spot that earlier theories of the moral tradition often gave to temperance, reveals how Descartes has placed the notions of dignity and esteem at the heart of his moral vision.

Descartes's ethic, just as much as his epistemology, calls for disengagement from world and body and the assumption of an instrumental stance towards them. It is of the essence of reason, both speculative and practical, that it push us to disengage. Obviously, this involves a very different concept of reason from Plato's. Just as correct knowledge doesn't come anymore from our opening ourselves to the order of (ontic) Ideas but from our constructing an order of (intra-mental) ideas according to the canons of *évidence;* so when the hegemony of reason becomes rational control, it is no longer understood as our being attuned to the order of things we find in the cosmos, but rather as our life being shaped by the orders which we construct according to the demands of reason's dominance, i.e., the "jugements fermes et déterminés touchant la connaissance du bien et du mal" which we have resolved to live by.

Of course, at various points these standards will demand that we take account of and conform to the dispositions of things which we find in the world, or in our own natures—as the Cartesian learns to reshape his passions according to the purposes they were designed for. But this will not be because this disposition essentially and of itself commands the love of all rational knowers, but rather because taking account of it is the rational thing to do, where this term is now defined by the standards imposed on the orders we construct in order to live by them. So just as the rational search for knowledge requires that we construct orders of representations, one of the constraints on which is that they match or conform to the disposition of things out there—the other being that they offer certainty, so practical reason demands that we use the things in the world, including our own dual nature, so as to maintain and enhance rational control, and this will frequently require that we conform or adapt ourselves to the disposition of things and the design of our bodily being.

But what is now utterly out of the question is the notion that the disposition of things can be any longer the *measure* of rationality, that the ultimate criterion of rationality be conformity with this order itself. Conformity is now demanded, where it is, as part of a strategy whose ultimate standards or goals lie elsewhere.

We could say that rationality is no longer defined substantively, in terms of the order of being, but rather procedurally, in terms of the standards by which we construct orders in science and life. For Plato, to be rational we have to be right about the order of things. For Descartes rationality means thinking according to certain canons. The judgement now turns on properties of the activity of thinking rather than on the substantive beliefs which emerge from it.

Of course, Descartes holds that his procedure will result in substantively true beliefs about the world. But this is something which has to be established. Indeed, to establish it is one of the most important goals of Descartes's philosophy. We make the link between procedure and truth with the proof that we are the creatures of a veracious God. The procedure is not simply *defined* as the one which leads to substantive truth. It could have been leading us entirely astray, if we had been victims of a malicious demon. Rationality is now an internal property of subjective thinking, rather than consisting in its vision of reality. In making this shift, Descartes is articulating what has become the standard modern view. In spite of the wide disagreements over the nature of the procedure, and despite all the scorn which has been heaped on him from the dominant empiricist trend in modern scientific culture, the conception of reason remains procedural.

The move from substance to procedure, from found to constructed orders, represents a big internalization relative to the Platonic-Stoic tradition of ethics. Plainly the whole Cartesian project owes a great deal to its Augustinian roots and the enhanced place this tradition gave to inwardness.

But plainly also there has been a transposition of this tradition as well. Cartesian internalization has transmuted into something very different from its Augustinian source. For Augustine, the path inward was only a step on the way upward. Something similar remains in Descartes, who also proves the existence of God starting from the self-understanding of the thinking agent. But the spirit has been altered in a subtle but important way. Following Augustine's path, the thinker comes to sense more and more his lack of self-sufficiency, comes to see more and more that God acts within him.

In contrast, for Descartes the whole point of the reflexive turn is to achieve a quite self-sufficient certainty. What I get in the cogito, and in each successive step in the chain of clear and distinct perceptions, is just this kind of certainty, which I can generate for myself by following the right method. This power to give ourselves the certainty we seek seems to have been the key insight in Descartes's decisive moment of inspiration, on that cold November night in winter quarters in Germany.

Of course, the chain of reasoning shows that I rely on a veracious God for my knowledge of the external world. But note how different this is from the traditional Augustinian order of dependence. The thesis is not that I gain knowledge when turned towards God in faith. Rather the certainty of clear and distinct perception is unconditional and self-generated. What has happened is rather that God's existence has become a stage in *my* progress towards science through the methodical ordering of evident insight. God's existence is a theorem in *my* system of perfect science. The centre of gravity has decisively shifted.

The step from the imperfect self to a perfect God, so essentially Augustinian in its source, is in the process of mutating into something else. It is not carried out so as to make God appear at the very roots of the self, closer than my own eye. On the contrary, it is the sure *inference,* from powers that I can become quite certain of possessing, to their inescapable source. The Cartesian proof is no longer a search for an encounter with God within. It is no longer the way to an experience of everything in God. Rather what I now meet is myself: I achieve a clarity and a fulness of self-presence that was lacking before. But from what I find here reason bids me infer to a cause and transcendent guarantee, without which my now well-understood human powers couldn't be as they are. The road to Deism is already open.

But not yet taken. We have to stop ourselves from seeing Descartes anachronistically. He is not only not a closet atheist, he is also no eighteenth-century Deist. We can go further and say that Cartesianism, for all its focus on self-sufficient knowledge and will, was not even unequivocally on the Catholic or Jesuit side, against the Protestants or Jansenists, in the debate on the roles of nature and grace. The Cartesian sense of the continual tendency to fall into darkness and confusion ("lorsque ie relâche quelque chose de mon attention, mon esprit se trouvant obscurcy & comme aveuglé par les images des choses sensibles"; "when I slightly relax my attention, my mind, finding its vision somewhat obscured and so to speak blinded by images of sensible objects")[35] could be seen as a sign of our fallen nature. Descartes could be and was taken up by some of the thinkers of Port Royal—Arnauld, for instance.[36]

In short, Descartes had no intention to *replace* the Augustinian ascent with his theory of knowledge. But this ascent could not be conceived in quite the same way after Cartesianism. As a result, the Augustinian tradition develops along new paths in the modern world—some of which I will explore below.

However, the truth behind the anachronistic judgements—as well as the contemporary critical reaction of Pascal[37]—is that this new conception of inwardness, an inwardness of self-sufficiency, of autonomous powers of ordering by reason, *also* prepared the ground for modern unbelief. It may even provide part of the explanation for the striking fact about modern Western civilization as against all others: the widespread incidence of unbelief within it. But this takes us too far ahead of the argument; first we must look further at the impact of Descartes in his century.

9

LOCKE'S PUNCTUAL SELF

9.1

Descartes's disengaged subject, like his procedural notion of rationality, is not just an idiosyncratic conception. For all the challenges and disagreements to his dualism in modern thought, with the central idea of disengagement he was articulating one of the most important developments of the modern era. Recent research has shown the tremendous importance of the mode of thinking roughly designated 'neo-Stoic' in the late sixteenth and early seventeenth centuries, associated with Justus Lipsius, and in France with Guillaume du Vair. As the name implies, these thinkers were inspired by classical Stoicism, but with a number of important differences. These included not only soul-body dualism but also an increasing emphasis on a model of self-mastery which prepares the Cartesian transposition to the model of instrumental control.

More significantly, neo-Stoicism was bound up with a broad movement among political and military elites towards a wider and more rigorous application of new forms of discipline in a host of fields: first in the military, of course, as one sees with the reforms of William of Orange, which had world-historical consequences in the Netherlands' revolt against Spain; but also later in various dimensions of the civil administration, which grew with the new aspirations and capacities of the 'absolutist' state, regulating trade, labour, health conditions, mores, even routines of piety.[1] The spread of these new modes of discipline through a host of institutions—armies, hospitals, schools, workhouses—has been vividly, if somewhat one-sidedly, traced by Michel Foucault in his *Surveiller et punir*.[2]

What one finds running through all the aspects of this constellation—the new philosophy, methods of administration and military organization, spirit of government, and methods of discipline—is the growing ideal of a human agent who is able to remake himself by methodical and disciplined action. What this calls for is the ability to take an instrumental stance to one's given properties, desires, inclinations, tendencies, habits of thought and feeling, so that they can be *worked on,* doing away with some and strengthening others, until one meets the desired specifications. My suggestion is that Descartes's picture of the disengaged subject articulates the understanding of agency which is most congenial to this whole movement, and that is part of the grounds for its great impact in his century and beyond.

The subject of disengagement and rational control has become a familiar modern figure. One might almost say it has become one way of construing ourselves, which we find it hard to shake off. It is one aspect of our inescapable contemporary sense of inwardness. As it develops to its full form through Locke and the Enlightenment thinkers he influenced, it becomes what I want to call the 'punctual' self.

The key to this figure is that it gains control through disengagement. Disengagement is always correlative of an 'objectification', if I may introduce this as another term of art. Objectifying a given domain involves depriving it of its normative force for us. If we take a domain of being in which hitherto the way things are has set norms or standards for us, and take a new stance to it as neutral, I will speak of our objectifying it.

The great mechanization of the scientific world picture of the seventeenth century, which Descartes helped to carry out, was an objectification in this sense. On the previously dominant view, the cosmic order was seen as the embodiment of the Ideas. The physical world around us takes the shape it does in order to body forth an order of Ideas. This can be taken itself as an ultimate in explanation, as it is by Plato, as ordered for the Good; or it can be integrated into Christian theology, and the Ideas understood as the thoughts of God. But in either case, the order is seen to be what it is because it exhibits Reason, Goodness; in the theological variant, the Wisdom of God. There is, in a sense, a double teleology. First, the things which surround us take the form they do in order to exemplify ideas or archetypes. The Renaissance doctrines of "correspondences" belong to this level. The notion that the king in the realm corresponds to the lion among animals, or the eagle among birds, and so on, gets its sense from the notion that the same Ideas must manifest themselves in all domains. On the second level, the ensemble of Ideas itself takes the form that it does in order to exhibit some perfection. On the Platonic-influenced conception which had been handed down through neo-Platonism and the pseudo-Dionysius, and which was dominant in medieaeval and early modern Europe, these perfections included those of reason. In other words, what we would consider today as the perfections of *description* or *representation,* of an order of perspicuous presentation, were considered perfections of *being.* The Platonic Idea is a self-manifesting reality. Things are as they are in order to conform to a pattern of rational self-manifestation, in which the One turns into the Many, in which all possible niches are occupied (Lovejoy's "principle of plenitude"), and the like. An order conceived after this fashion I want to call a 'meaningful' order, or one involving an 'ontic logos'.

It is plain that an order of this kind sets the paradigm purposes of the beings within it. As humans we are to conform to our Idea, and this in turn must play its part in the whole, which among other things involves our being 'rational', i.e., capable of seeing the self-manifesting order. No one can understand this order while being indifferent to it or failing to recognize its normative force. Indifference is a sign that one has not understood, that one is in error, as Epicureans and other atomists were widely condemned as being by the premodern mainstream.

The move to mechanism neutralizes this whole domain. It no longer sets norms for us—or at least it does not set norms in the traditional way. Nor was this simply a side effect of a move prompted by purely epistemological considerations. On the contrary, part of the impetus for the new science came from an anti-teleological morality. The source of this was theological: the nominalist revolt against Aristotelian realism, by figures like William of Occam, was motivated by a sense that propounding an ethic founded on the supposed bent of nature was attempting to set limits to the sovereignty of God. God must preserve the fullest freedom to establish good and bad by fiat. The further developments of this Occamist line of thought played an important role in the scientific revolution of this century, as has often been remarked.[3] In the end, a mechanistic universe was the only one compatible with a God whose sovereignty was defined in terms of the endless freedom of fiat.

One of the strongest motives underlying the rise of mechanism was thus originally its link with 'control', at first in relation to God. But then the beneficiary comes to be seen as human as well, and with the actual seventeenth-century revolution, motives come to be inextricably intertwined. Mechanism is plainly still linked with a certain theology for Descartes. He pushes God's sovereignty to the point of holding that even what we understand as the "eternal verities", such as the axioms of mathematics, are made by divine fiat.[4] But at the same time, he sees the new science as one which will make us "masters and possessors" of the earth.[5] And this instrumental control is not just valued for itself but is identified (perhaps following Bacon) as a criterion of scientific truth, as it must be if the world is really machine-like.

The modern figure I call the punctual self has pushed this disengagement much further, and has been induced to do so by the same mix of motivations: the search for control intertwined with a certain conception of knowledge. The disengagement is carried further in being turned towards the subject himself. Descartes already starts this movement. It involves taking a stance to ourselves which takes us out of our normal way of experiencing the world and ourselves. We can see what this means if we return to the examples which played a central role in Descartes's thought: secondary properties, and bodily sensations.

The mistake of obscure and confused thought is to see these as 'in' the bodies concerned. The normal, unreflecting person thinks of colour or sweetness as being in the dress or the candy; places the pain in the tooth, the tingling in the foot. The real ontological locus of all these, Descartes asserts, is in the mind. They are all ideas which are, indeed, brought about by certain properties of dress, candy, tooth, foot, but their place is in the mind. In this, they are like the ideas of primary qualities—figure, number, size. But unlike these, they fail to represent anything in the object. The body isn't red in the way it is square.

To see things this way is to have a clear and distinct understanding of them.[6] But this involves withdrawing from our normal way of being in the world. As we live normally through them, our experiences of the red dress or of a toothache are the ways in which these objects are there for us. The red dress is present for me, through my seeing it; the tooth insistently clamours that *it* is in pain. I attend to the object through the experience, as Merleau-Ponty and Michael Polanyi have variously described it.[7] What Descartes calls on us to do is to stop living 'in' or 'through' the experience, to treat it itself as an object, or what is the same thing, as an experience which could just as well have been someone else's. In doing this, I suspend the 'intentional' dimension of the experience, that is, what makes it the experience *of* something. I take note, of course, that this experience makes a claim to be of something, or that it inescapably suggests to us its (supposed) intentional object. But I treat it on all fours with quite non-intentional experiences like inner sensations; and as in the case of these, I relate it no longer to a putative object but to an external cause. In objectifying the experience, I no longer accept it as what sets my norm for what it is to have knowledge of these properties.

Of course, this withdrawn stance, although it can certainly alter our way of experiencing things, is not simply another way of experiencing them. There is a confusion about this in the whole Cartesian-empiricist tradition. Descartes and his empiricist successors sometimes talk as though the focus on "immediate" experience were brought about through a more exact awareness of our actual first-person experience. But there is no way I can *experience* my toothache as a mere idea in the mind, caused by decay in the tooth, sending signals up the nerves to the brain (or through the animal spirits to the pineal gland). And since the very nature of disengagement is to withdraw from the ordinary first-person experience, it would be surprising if I could. Disengagement involves our going outside the first-person stance and taking on board some theory, or at least some supposition, about how things work. This is what Descartes does in this case, when he supposes that pains and observed secondary qualities are ideas in the mind which are *caused* by various (primary) properties of the organ or object. Once we disengage and no longer live in our experience, then some supposition has to be invoked to take up the interpretive slack, to supply an account in the place of the one we are forgoing. For Descartes and his empiricist successors, the suppositions are (naturally) mechanistic.

In view of its transposition of first-person experience into an objectified, impersonal mode, it might seem surprising to class the stance of disengaged control as a modified figure of Augustinian inwardness. But the paradox is merely superficial. Radical reflexivity is central to this stance, because we have to focus on first-person experience in order so to transpose it. The point of the whole operation is to gain a kind of control. Instead of being swept along to error by the ordinary bent of our experience, we stand back from it, withdraw from it, reconstrue it objectively, and then learn to draw defensible conclusions from it. To wrest control from "our appetites and our preceptors",[8] we have to practise a kind of radical reflexivity. We fix experience in order to deprive it of its power, a source of bewitchment and error.

We can see the connections adumbrated above: between disengagement and objectification, on one hand, and a kind of power or control, on the other; between this and the ideal of a correct procedure, a proper way of assembling or constructing our thoughts, which defines rationality; and lastly between rationality and the attaining of knowledge. These connections have become so strong in certain departments of modern culture that they might seem the only possible construal. But a little examination should show that it is not always true that the road to surer knowledge lies through disengagement and procedural reason.

To take everyday instances, when we see something surprising, or something which disconcerts us, or which we can't quite see, we normally react by setting ourselves to look more closely; we alter our stance, perhaps rub our eyes, concentrate, and the like. Rather than disengaging, we throw ourselves more fully into the experience, as it were. There is a kind of search which involves being "all there", being more attentively 'in' our experience. A more important context is the one in which we try to get clearer on what we feel about some person or event. This involves reflexivity and self-awareness, but precisely not of the disengaging kind. Rather we think of that person or event, we allow our feelings full reign, precisely as the way we experience the person concerned.

To attempt to disengage from our feelings involves something quite different. Here as above, we try to withdraw from the intentional dimension.

Perhaps you find Aunt Mabel's sense of humour irritating. It seems strained and pushy, calculated to take over and grab attention. But you tell yourself that you're overreacting. It's just something about you, which makes you react like this to a perfectly normal way of being. You try to strangle the reaction by treating it as just a reaction, not a valid perception of annoying features. We do something similar when we decide that we oughtn't to feel guilty for something we do or feel and treat the spasms like some irrational holdover from our childhood training. Disengagement and what we might call engaged exploration are two quite different things. They carry us in contrary directions and are extremely difficult to combine.

The point of this contrast is to see that the option for an epistemology which privileges disengagement and control isn't self-evidently right. It requires certain assumptions. If the great age of rationalism and empiricism launched itself on the "way of ideas", it was because it took certain things for granted. Epistemically, as has just been mentioned, it was based in part on a belief in mechanism as against the universe of meaningful order, of the ontic logos. To see the world as the embodiment of Ideas is to see knowledge as attained by attuning the soul's gaze. We get to it by engaging more fully with this order, turning the eye of the soul towards it in Plato's image; in Aristotle's formulation, we come to knowledge when the *eidos* of our *nous* and that of the object are one. The picture of our attaining knowledge is that of our coming to discern the pattern through careful attention, as we see in the famous image of the arrested rout.[9]

But this is not the whole story. The move to self-objectification requires more than a belief in a mechanistic physics. Certain thinkers of the late seventeenth century, like Cudworth and Leibniz, each in his own way, took on board mechanism while trying to retain or rebuild a teleological view of the subject. The further step in disengagement from self involved a rejection of all such attempts. It was powered by a radical rejection of teleology, of definitions of the human subject in terms of some inherent bent to the truth or to the good, which might give justification to an engaged exploration of the true tendencies of our nature.

Locke took the really uncompromising stance, the one which set the terms in which the punctual self was to be defined through the Enlightenment and beyond. He went beyond Descartes and rejected any form of the doctrine of innate ideas. This is usually seen as an epistemologically grounded move. Locke is here following a more Baconian or a more Gassendian model of what science is than the overdrawn rationalism of Descartes. In this he aligns himself with the model which will triumphantly emerge from the long intellectual revolution, instantiated paradigmatically by Newton.

This is undoubtedly part of the truth. But here I want to bring out another side. In rejecting innateness, Locke is also giving vent to his profoundly anti-teleological view of human nature, of both knowledge and morality. The motives for this are complex and have much to do with the winning of a certain kind of control.

In respect of knowledge, Locke aligns himself against any view which sees us as naturally tending to or attuned to the truth, whether it be of the ancient variety, that we are qua rational beings constitutionally disposed to recognize the rational order of things; or of the modern variety, that we have innate ideas, or an innate tendency to unfold out thought towards the truth. At the same time that Locke is developing the views he will publish in the *Essay*, Ralph Cudworth is trying to define a post-Cartesian Christian Platonism. "Knowledge," he claims, "is an Inward and Active Energy of the Mind it self, and the displaying of its own Innate Vigour from within, whereby it doth Conquer, Master and Command its Objects, and so begets a Clear, Serene, Victorious, and Satisfactory Sense within it self".[10] Cudworth is sure "that the Soul is not a meer Rasa Tabula, a Naked and Passive Thing, which has no innate Furniture of Activity of its own, nor any thing at all in it, but what was impressed upon it from without".[11]

But the "Universal Rationes, or Intelligible Natures and Essences of All Things"[12] which Cudworth claims we can generate from our inward activity are seen by Locke as being so many gratuitous syntheses, accredited by custom and authority, but in no wise grounded in reason. They are of a piece with the inventions of those "Peripatetick wranglers" which he denounces in his *Essay* (4.6.11).[13]

Locke proposes to suspend judgement on these traditional ideas and examine their foundations before accepting them. The underlying notion is that our conceptions of the world are syntheses of the ideas we originally received from sensation and reflection. But under the influence of passion, custom and education, these syntheses are made without awareness and without good grounds. We come to believe things and accept notions which seem solid and inescapable, but which have no validity. But since these notions are the vehicles of all our thoughts, we find it hard to accept that they are called into question.

> Vague and insignificant forms of speech, and abuse of language, have so long passed for mysteries of science; and hard and misapplied words, with little or no meaning, have, by prescription, such a right to be mistaken for deep learning and height of speculation, that it will not be easy to persuade either those who speak or those who hear them, that they are but the covers of ignorance, and hindrance of true knowledge. (*Essay*, Epistle, p. 14)

The crucial first task is therefore one of demolition, and Locke speaks of his ambition as "to be employed as an under-labourer in clearing the ground a little, and removing some of the rubbish that lies in the way to knowledge" (ibid.).

Locke proposes to demolish and rebuild. This in itself is not new; it is just what Descartes propounded. More generally, the attack on the errors inculcated by custom and ordinary education is at least as old as Plato. Even the proposal to reconstruct on the basis of sense experience is not entirely new: the Aristotelian-Thomistic tradition also makes sensation primary in our knowledge of the world. What is radical is the extent of the disengagement he proposes.

We do not reject custom like Plato in order to follow the inherent bent in us towards reason. Nor do we make sense experience primary in order to discern through this experience the forms of the things we encounter. Nor do we accept any innate principles. The demolition is not stopped in principle by our placing our trust in any of the prereflective activities of the mind. Its ultimate stopping place is the particulate ideas of experience, sensation and reflection. And these are to be taken as rock bottom, because they aren't the product of activity at all. "In this part the understanding is merely passive; and whether or not it will have these beginnings, and as it were materials of knowledge, is not in its own power" (2.1.25; see also 2.30.3, where Locke says that the mind is "wholly passive in respect of its simple ideas"). It is not in our power either to create or to destroy a simple idea (2.2.2).

This is a more thoroughgoing disengagement than that from the experience of secondary properties and bodily sensations, which Locke also takes over from Descartes. It touches our entire mental activity. And like the earlier disengagement, it isn't the fruit of a new mode of first-person experience, but rather relies on an objectifying theory of the mind. And in this case, as in the previous one, the theory is deeply indebted to the regnant mechanistic outlook.

Locke *reifies* the mind to an extraordinary degree. First, he embraces an atomism of the mind; our understanding of things is constructed out of the building blocks of simple ideas. Metaphors to do with constructing and assembling stuff are very prominent in Locke, and not just in the usual mode, where one speaks of 'constructing' a theory or a view. Ideas are 'materials', and man's "power, however managed by art and skill, reaches no farther than to compound and divide the materials that are made to his hand" (2.2.2). And after speaking in 2.12.1 of the formation of complex ideas out of simple, Locke says: "This shows man's power, and its ways of operation, to be much the same in the material and intellectual world. For the materials in both being such as he has no power over, either to make or to destroy, all that man can do is either to unite them together, or to set them by one another, or wholly separate them".

In another reifying image, the brain is likened to "the mind's presence-room" (2.3.1); in still another, to a dark room (2.11.17). All this contributes to a central confusion which affects not only Locke but the whole tradition of the "theory of ideas": these are sometimes treated as inert objects in the mind, and sometimes as propositional entities. The idea is sometimes seen as a quasi-object that can be moved around and sometimes as an entity which could only be adequately described in a 'that . . .' clause. As has often been remarked, this lay behind the problem which all the empiricists had with "general ideas": was our idea of a triangle in general itself to be thought of as isosceles or scalene or equilateral? Locke tried to maintain that even the ideas in our minds which have general import are themselves particulars (4.17.8). The deep muddle has its source in the entire 'building block' theory of thinking.

Second, the atoms themselves come into existence by a quasi-mechanical process, a kind of imprinting on the mind through impact on the senses. Ideas "are produced in us . . . by the operation of insensible particles on our senses" (2.8.13; in 4.2.11, Locke speaks of "globules"). And third, a good part of the assembly of these atoms is accounted for by a quasi-mechanical process of association (2.23).

The aim of this disassembly is to reassemble our picture of the world, this time on a solid foundation, by following reliable rules of concatenation. Aside from the findings of mathematics or truths established by deduction, over the far greater extent of our knowledge which is empirical, the rules concerned are those of probable evidence, as Locke helped to define them, especially in Book IV. In effecting this double movement of suspension and examination, we wrest the control of our thinking and outlook away from passion or custom or authority and assume responsibility for it ourselves. Locke's theory generates and also reflects an ideal of independence and self-responsibility, a notion of reason as free from established custom and locally dominant authority.

I have borrowed the term 'self-responsibility' from Husserl[14] to describe something that Locke shares with Descartes (to whom Husserl applied the term) and which touches on the essential opposition to authority of modern disengaged reason. What we are called upon to do by both these writers, and by the tradition they establish, is to think it out ourselves. As with Descartes, knowledge for Locke isn't genuine unless you develop it yourself:

For, I think, we may as rationally hope to see with other Mens Eyes, as to know by other Mens Understandings. So much as we our selves consider and comprehend of Truth and Reason, so much we possess of real and true Knowledge. The floating of other Mens Opinions in our brains makes us not a jot more knowing, though they happen to be true. What in them was Science, is in us but Opinatrety, whilst we give up our assent to reverend Names, and do not, as they did, employ our own Reason to understand those Truths, which gave them reputation . . . In the Sciences, every one has so much, as he really knows and comprehends: What he believes only, and takes upon trust, are but shreds. (1.4.23)

Plato, of course, says something analogous. Really knowing is different from just believing something. For the former, you have to be able to "give an account",[15] to say why it's so. And this involves breaking with a lot of accepted, conventional beliefs of your society. But what is different with the moderns is that the requirement to work it out oneself is more radical and exclusive, and this in virtue of their very notion of reason.

Plato enjoins us to stand out against custom and "opinion" in order to arrive at the truth. But the truth at which we arrive is a vision of the order of things. It is not absolutely excluded in principle that our best way of getting there might be to be guided by some authority—not, indeed, the corrupt and erroneous one of popular opinion, but by someone with wisdom. Once we have science, of course, we can dispense with guidance, but it might help us to come to this independent condition.

By contrast the modern conception of reason is procedural. What we are called on to do is not to become contemplators of order, but rather to construct a picture of things following the canons of rational thinking. These are differently conceived by Descartes and Locke, but on this basic notion of reason they are one. The aim is to get to the way things really are, but these canons offer our best hope of doing that. Rationality is above all a property of the process of thinking, not of the substantive content of thought.

This is the distinction that Locke is hammering at in the passage quoted above. But the procedure is a radically reflexive one, as we have seen. It essentially involves the first-person standpoint. It involves disengaging from my own spontaneous beliefs and syntheses, in order to submit them to scrutiny. This is something which in the nature of things each person must do for himself. We are not just independent once we have achieved science; our whole path there must be radically independent, if the result is to be science.

That is why this model of reason is radically and intransigently exclusive of authority. In Locke's case, this requirement of disengaged reason is further strengthened by the Protestant principle of personal adhesion. Earlier in the passage I have just quoted Locke assures us that "I have not made it my business, either to quit, or follow any Authority in the ensuing Discourse: Truth has been my only aim" (1.4.23). And that is why Locke will speak often of the issue of reason in terms of the dramatic opposition of slavery and freedom. Freedom is difficult; it is hard to strike out on one's own, following one's own process of thought. But those who fail to do so, those ordinary, insouciant creatures who get carried along with the current, are under subjection. Locke delivers a stern warning to those who belong to the elite but are happy to shirk this responsibility to think. "They who are blind, will always be led by those that see, or else fall into the Ditch: and he is certainly the most subjected, the most enslaved, who is so in his Understanding" (4.20.6).

And the whole *Essay* is directed against those who would control others by specious principles supposedly beyond question, like the ones that are allegedly "innate". Speaking of "those who affected to be masters and teachers", Locke says:

> For having once established this tenet—that there are innate principles, it puts their followers upon the necessity of receiving *some* doctrines as such; which was to put them off from the use of their own reason and judgement, and put them on believing and taking them upon trust without further examination; in which posture of blind credulity, they might be more easily governed by, and made useful to some sort of men, who had the skill and office to principle and guide them. (1.3.25)

This anti-teleological objectifying view of the mind doesn't only rule out theories of knowledge which suppose an innate attunement to the truth; it also is directed against moral theories which see us tending by nature towards the good—in the first place, of course, the major traditions which came down from the ancients, Platonic, Aristotelian, and Stoic. Disengagement has to transform our theory of motivation as well. Locke, like other anti-teleological theorists before him, and following Gassendi, adopts a hedonist theory. Pleasure and pain are for us good and evil. "Things then are good or evil, only in reference to pleasure or pain" (2.20.2). And they motivate us. "Pleasure and pain and that which causes them,—good and evil, are the hinges on which our passions turn" (2.20.3). But following his objectifying view of the mind, Locke puts this ancient theory through a reifying transposition. What moves us is not directly the prospect of good, i.e., pleasure, but 'uneasiness' (2.21.31). Locke thinks of desire as a kind of uneasiness. "All pain of the body, of what sort soever, and disquiet of the mind, is uneasiness" (ibid.). Desire for something is then seen as a species of this genus. It is an uneasiness aroused by the absence of some good. But not all things which are good for us provoke uneasiness in their absence, not even all the things which we know are good for us. The greater good in view doesn't always move us. If it did, argues Locke, we would clearly spend the greater part of our efforts ensuring our eternal salvation (2.21.38).

What must happen for a good to motivate us is that it must come to arouse an uneasiness in us. It moves us only through its connection with this disquiet. "Good and evil, present and absent, it is true, work upon the mind. But that which *immediately* determines the will, from time to time, to every voluntary action, is the *uneasiness of desire*" (2.21.33, emphasis in original). Locke characteristically shows how this must be so by invoking a quasi-mechanical argument: "Another reason why it is uneasiness alone determines the will, is this: because it alone is present and, it is against the nature of things that what is absent should operate where it is not" (2.21.37). His theory is grounded on the well-known mechanical principle excluding action at a distance.

Thus Locke carries disengagement to unprecedented lengths: even our motivated action to what brings us pleasure is not rock bottom in the order of assembly. It has to arise through a connection being established with an inner state, which is itself without any intrinsic object. We see the remote origins of modern reductive psychology and the theory of reinforcement. Where twentieth-century psychologists speak of 'habits', Locke speaks of the association that each of us makes between inner unease and certain goods as our 'relish' (2.21.56).

This can be and has been the basis of a purely determinist theory of motivation, which sees people as invariably impelled by their strongest desires. Locke seems to be heading in this direction in 2.21.46, where he says that the "most pressing" uneasiness naturally determines the will. But as with the theory of knowledge, the reification is meant to make control possible. Locke introduces the will. The mind has "a power to suspend the execution of any of its desires; and so all, one after another; is at liberty to consider the objects of them, examine them on all sides, and weigh them with others" (2.21.53, also 48). We can determine, following rational canons of evidence, what is the greatest good, and will ourselves to seek it. Moreover, this will reform our relish so that it will gain motivational weight. Thus

> a man may suspend the act of his choice from being determined for or against the thing proposed, till he has examined whether it be really of a nature, in itself and its consequences, to make him happy or not. For, when he has once chosen it, and thereby it is become part of his happiness, it raises desire, and that proportionably gives him uneasiness. (2.21.57)

To stand thus back from ourselves and our existing 'relish', just as in the case of our notions and beliefs, allows us the possibility to remake ourselves in a more rational and advantageous fashion. We are creatures of ultimately contingent connections: we have formed certain habits. But we can break from them and re-form them.

> Fashion and the common opinion have settled wrong notions, and education and custom ill habits, the just values of things are misplaced, and the palates of men corrupted. Pains should be taken to rectify these;

and contrary habits change our pleasures, and give us a relish to what is necessary and conducive to our happiness. (2.21.71)

Radical disengagement opens the prospect of self-remaking.

As to the rational goals of such remaking, Locke is clear that it should follow the law laid down by God, which he also calls at times the Natural Law. This is not only what we ought to do morally, but it is also what conduces to our greatest happiness, as is evident when we think of the "unspeakable" joys and equally terrible pains that God holds out as rewards and punishments. Indeed, according to Locke's definition, it is the highest moral course, just *because* it is that laid down by a lawgiver who can attach pains to his commands.

> Moral good and evil . . . is only the conformity or disagreement of our voluntary actions to some law, whereby good or evil is drawn on us, from the will and power of the law-maker; which good or evil, pleasure or pain, attending our observance or breach of the law by the decree of the law-maker, is that we call reward and punishment. (2.28.5)

Locke thereby places himself in the tradition of theological voluntarism, which as we have seen was closely interwoven with the rise of mechanism, and his command theory of the natural law aligns him with Pufendorf, and an influential stream of thought in his time. But Locke unites voluntarism with hedonism, as Tully remarks.[16] What this position amounts to as a moral outlook, I will take up below.

Here I want to look at it in its aspect as a new, unprecedentedly radical form of self-objectification. The disengagement both from the activities of thought and from our unreflecting desires and tastes allows us to see ourselves as objects of far-reaching reformation. Rational control can extend to the re-creation of our habits, and hence of ourselves. The notion of 'habit' has undergone a shift: it no longer carries its Aristotelian force, where our *'hexeis'* are formed against the background of a nature with a certain bent. Habits now link elements between which there are no more relations of natural fit. The proper connections are determined purely instrumentally, by what will bring the best results, pleasure, or happiness.

The subject who can take this kind of radical stance of disengagement to himself or herself with a view to remaking, is what I want to call the 'punctual' self. To take this stance is to identify oneself with the power to objectify and remake, and by this act to distance oneself from all the particular features which are objects of potential change. What we are essentially is none of the latter, but what finds itself capable of fixing them and working on them. This is what the image of the point is meant to convey, drawing on the geometrical term: the real self is "extensionless"; it is nowhere but in this power to fix things as objects.

This power reposes in consciousness. And thus Locke in his discussion of personal identity in *Essay* 2.27 refuses to identify the self or person with any substance, material or immaterial, but makes it depend on consciousness.

> For as far as any intelligent being can repeat the idea of any past action with the same consciousness it had of it at first, and with the same consciousness it has of any present action; so far it is the same personal self. For it is by the consciousness it has of its present thoughts and actions, that it is a *self to itself* now, and so will be the same self, as far as the same consciousness can extend to actions past and to come; and would be by distance of time, or change of substance, no more two persons, than a man by wearing other clothes today than he did yesterday, with a long or short sleep between; the same consciousness uniting those distant actions into the same person, whatever substances contributed to their production. (2.27.10, emphasis in original)

Or again:

> It is plain, consciousness, as far as ever it can be extended—should it be ages past—unites existences and actions very remote in time into the same person, as well as it does the existences and actions of the immediately preceding moment: so that whatever has the consciousness of present and past actions, is the same person to whom they both belong. (2.27.16)

This radically subjectivist view of the person[17] is defended by Locke through a series of bizarre thought experiments, e.g., of the same consciousness inhabiting different bodies, or two consciousnesses sharing the same, or bodies exchanging consciousness, which are the basis for Parfit's speculations, which I invoked in section 1.2.[18] But the question begged is revelatory here. It is assumed that something we call consciousness or self-consciousness could be clearly distinguished from its embodiment, and the two allowed to separate and recombine in various thought experiments, that our self-awareness is somehow detachable from its embodiment. We are asked to imagine something supposedly strange but clear under the description of a prince waking up in the body of a cobbler. But what distinguishes this from the case of a cobbler waking up with amnesia about his past life, and the strange sense that he remembers another's experiences, as people allegedly have of the experiences of persons long dead?[19]

The perfectly detachable consciousness is an illusion, I would claim, but it is a shadow cast by the punctual self. The stance of detachment generates the picture of ourselves as pure independent consciousness, which underpins and justifies this stance and is the basis of the radical promise of self-control and -remaking it holds out. The close connection between Locke's subjectivist doctrine of the person and the prospect of self-making emerges in the discussion of this chapter, where Locke tells us that 'person', which is our name for the self, "is a forensic term, appropriating actions and their merit; and so belongs only to intelligent agents, capable of a law, and happiness and misery" (2.27.26). The same person as X is the being who can rightly be rewarded or punished for X's doings and failings: "In this personal identity is founded all the right of reward and punishment; happiness and misery being that for which every one is concerned for himself, and not mattering what becomes of any substance, not joined to, or affected with that consciousness" (2.27.18). Locke is acknowledging in his own way here what I argued in Part I (section 2.2): the close connection between our notion of the self and our moral self-understanding. Locke's person is the moral agent who takes responsibility for his acts in the light of future retribution. The abstracted picture of the self faithfully reflects his ideal of responsible agency.

9.2

Not only Locke's epistemology but his radical disengagement and reification of human psychology were immensely influential in the Enlightenment. Part of this is undoubtedly due to the relative closeness of fit between his views on knowledge and the triumphant Newtonian model, at least in relation to the Cartesian alternative. But this is not the whole story. The tremendous strength of Locke's punctual self through the Enlightenment and beyond comes also from the central place of the disengaged, disciplinary stance to the self in our culture. I mentioned earlier the rise of disciplinary practices over a wide range in this period in the military, hospitals, and schools as well as the related practices of methodical bureaucratic control and organization.

Locke's theory was not, of course, the only possible justification of such practices. They began to spread well before it was devised. This distinction is an important one to make, because the practices are sometimes confusedly identified with this philosophy in contemporary debates about modernity. But an identification of this kind is absurd; it confuses quite different kinds of things: on one hand, the development of new powers of self-control and -remaking, requiring a new disengaged stance to the self, and on the other, a particular theory, which pictures the self as capable in principle of a kind of total disengagement. The latter as a theory is up for confirmation or refutation (I am satisfied that it richly deserves the latter); but the former we either bring off or don't (and we certainly have, for better or worse—and for richer).

But at the same time, the relationship has been close between these two. The theory is certainly one that is congenial to the practices, that would recommend itself to those deeply committed to them, that would rationalize them, justify them, and also hold out rather far-reaching hopes for their efficacy in human affairs. This theory has undoubtedly contributed to their all-conquering march through contemporary culture.

What probably made Locke the great teacher of the Enlightenment was his combination of these two factors: that he offered a plausible account of the new science as valid knowledge, intertwined with a theory of rational control of the self; and that he brought the two together under the ideal of rational self-responsibility. Many things have been declared authoritatively true, both in science and in practice, which have no real title to the name. The rational, self-responsible subject can break with them, suspend his adhesion to them, and by submitting them to the test of their validity, remake or replace them.

Holding the package together is an ideal of freedom or independence, backed by a conception of disengagement and procedural reason. This has given Locke's outlook its tremendous influence, not only in the eighteenth century, but right through to today. Even those who reject many of Locke's doctrines feel the power of his model. We can see it in one way in some contemporary discussions about identity, as I have mentioned.[20] And it permeates modern psychology. Besides the obvious developments in modern learning theory,[21] it is the basis, I believe, of the mature Freudian conception of the ego, which belongs to the 'structural' model. This ego is in essence a pure steering mechanism, devoid of instinctual force of its own (though it must draw power from the id to function). Its job is to manoeuvre through the all-but-unnavigable obstacle course set by id, super-ego, and external reality. Its powers are incomparably less than Locke's punctual self, but like its ancestor it is fundamentally a disengaged agent of instrumental reason.

Thus if we follow the theme of self-control through the vicissitudes of our Western tradition, we find a very profound transmutation, all the way from the hegemony of reason as a vision of cosmic order to the notion of a punctual disengaged subject exercising instrumental control. And this, I would argue, helps to explain why we think of ourselves as 'selves' today.

The crucial capacity for the great ancient moralists was that of seeing the order—in the cosmos (for Plato) or in the priority of human goals (for the Stoics). Introspection had no significance for the first, and wasn't thought to be crucial for the second. The Stoics give us an argument about reason, nature, and self-sufficiency to convince us that we shouldn't set any store by ordinary satisfactions; they don't ask us to examine ourselves.

By contrast, the modern ideal of disengagement requires a reflexive stance. We have to turn inward and become aware of our own activity and of the processes which form us. We have to take charge of constructing our own representation of the world, which otherwise goes on without order and consequently without science; we have to take charge of the processes by which associations form and shape our character and outlook. Disengagement demands that we stop simply living in the body or within our traditions or habits and, by making them objects for us, subject them to radical scrutiny and remaking.

Of course the great classical moralists also call on us to stop living in unreflecting habit and usage. But their reflection turns us towards an objective order. Modern disengagement by contrast calls us to a separation from ourselves through self-objectification. This is an operation which can only be carried out in the first-person perspective. It doesn't tell us, like Stoicism, to be aware of what is worthwhile for humans as such or, like Plato, to focus on the properties of reason and desire and their relation to what we know about the happy life. It calls on me to be aware of *my* activity of thinking or *my* processes of habituation, so as to disengage from them and objectify them. Indeed, the whole (strange and ultimately questionable) picture of myself as objectified nature which this modern turn has made familiar to us only became available through that special kind of reflexive stance I am calling disengagement. We had to be trained (and bullied) into making it, not only of course through imbibing doctrines, but much more through all the disciplines which have been inseparable from our modern way of life, the disciplines of self-control, in the economic, moral, and sexual fields. This vision is the child of a peculiar reflexive stance, and that is why we who have been formed to understand and judge ourselves in its terms naturally describe ourselves with the reflexive expressions which belong to this stance: the 'self', the 'I', the 'ego'.

That at least is part of the story. Another is that this self which emerges from the objectification of and separation from our given nature cannot be identified with anything in this given. It can't be easily conceived as just another piece of the natural world. It is hard for us simply to *list* souls or minds *alongside* whatever else there is. This is the source of a continuing philosophical discomfort in modern times for which there is naturally no analogue among the ancients. Various solutions have been tried—reductionism, 'transcendental' theories, returns to dualism—but the problem continues to nag us as unsolved. I will not tackle this problem here. My point is rather that this ungrounded 'extra-worldly' status of the objectifying subject accentuates the existing motivation to describe it as a self. All other appellations seem to place it somewhere in the roster of things, as one among others. The punctual agent seems to be nothing else but a 'self', an 'I'.

Here we see the origin of one of the great paradoxes of modern philosophy. The philosophy of disengagement and objectification has helped to create a picture of the human being, at its most extreme in certain forms of materialism, from which the last vestiges of subjectivity seem to have been expelled. It is a picture of the human being from a completely third-person perspective. The paradox is that this severe outlook is connected with, indeed, based on, according a central place to the first-person stance. Radical objectivity is only intelligible and accessible through radical subjectivity. This paradox has, of course, been much commented on by Heidegger, for instance, in his critique of subjectivism, and by Merleau-Ponty. Modern naturalism can never be the same once one sees this connection, as both these philosophers argue. But for those who haven't seen it, the problem of the 'I' returns, like a repressed thought, as a seemingly insoluble puzzle.[22]

For us the subject is a self in a way he or she couldn't be for the ancients. Ancient moralists frequently formulated the injunction 'Take care of yourself', as Foucault has recently reminded us.[23] And Epictetus persuades us that all that really matters to us is the state of our own *hēgemonikon,* or ruling part, sometimes translated 'mind', or 'will'. They can sometimes *sound* like our contemporaries. But in reality, there is a gulf between us and them. The reason is that the reflexivity that is essential to us is radical, in the sense of this term that I introduced in Chapter 7. Disengagement requires the first-person stance.

This is what distingushes the classical writers from followers of Descartes, Locke, Kant, or just about anyone in the modern world. The turn to oneself is now also and inescapably a turn to oneself in the first-person perspective— a turn to the self as a self. That is what I mean by radical reflexivity. Because we are so deeply embedded in it, we cannot but reach for reflexive language.

10

EXPLORING "L'HUMAINE CONDITION"

I have been following one strand of the internalization which has gone into making the modern identity. This took me from Plato through the inward turn of Augustine to the new stance of disengagement which Descartes inaugurates and Locke intensifies. To follow this development is to trace the constitution of one facet of the modern self. Adopting the stance of disengagement towards oneself—even if one doesn't push it to the Lockean extreme of punctuality—defines a new understanding of human agency and its characteristic powers. And along with this come new conceptions of the good and new locations of moral sources: an ideal of self-responsibility, with the new definitions of freedom and reason which accompany it, and the connected sense of dignity. To come to live by this definition—as we cannot fail to do, since it penetrates and rationalizes so many of the ways and practices of modern life—is to be transformed: to the point where we see this way of being as normal, as anchored in perennial human nature in the way our physical organs are. So we come to think that we 'have' selves as we have heads. But the very idea that we have or are 'a self', that human agency is essentially defined as 'the self', is a linguistic reflection of our modern understanding and the radical reflexivity it involves. Being deeply embedded in this understanding, we cannot but reach for this language; but it was not always so.

But this is only one strand. I took as my guiding thread the successive understandings of the moral ideal of self-mastery. This was the basis of the contrast between Plato and Descartes. But the line of development through Augustine has also generated models of self-exploration which have crucially shaped modern culture.

Augustine's inward turn was tremendously influential in the West; at first in inaugurating a family of forms of Christian spirituality, which continued throughout the Middle Ages, and flourished again in the Renaissance. But then later this turn takes on secularized forms. We go inward, but not necessarily to find God; we go to discover or impart some order, or some meaning or some justification, to our lives. In retrospect, we can see

Augustine's *Confessions* as the first great work in a genre which includes Rousseau's work of the same title, Goethe's *Dichtung und Wahrheit*, Wordsworth's *Prelude*—except that the Bishop of Hippo antedates his followers by more than a millennium.

To the extent that this form of self-exploration becomes central to our culture, another stance of radical reflexivity becomes of crucial importance to us alongside that of disengagement. It is different and in some ways antithetical to disengagement. Rather than objectifying our own nature and hence classing it as irrelevant to our identity, it consists in exploring what we are in order to establish this identity, because the assumption behind modern self-exploration is that we don't already know who we are.

There is a turning point here whose representative figure is perhaps Montaigne. There is some evidence that when he embarked on his reflections, he shared the traditional view that these should serve to recover contact with the permanent, stable, unchanging core of being in each of us. This is the virtually unanimous direction of ancient thought: beneath the changing and shifting desires in the unwise soul, and over against the fluctuating fortunes of the external world, our true nature, reason, provides a foundation, unwavering and constant.

For someone who holds this, the modern problem of identity remains unintelligible. Our only search can be to discover within us the one universal human nature. But things didn't work out this way for Montaigne. There is some evidence that when he sat down to write and turned to himself, he experienced a terrifying inner instability. "Mon esprit . . . faisant le cheval eschappé . . . m'enfante tant de chimères et monstres fantasques les uns sur les autres, sans ordre et sans propos" ("My spirit . . . playing the skittish and loose-broken jade . . . begets in me so many extravagant Chimeraes, and fantasticall monsters, so orderlesse, and without any reason, one hudling upon an other").[1] His response was to observe and catalogue his thoughts, feelings, responses ("J'ai commencé de les mettre en rolle"; "I have begun to keep a register of them").[2] And from this emerged a quite different stand towards the impermanence and uncertainty of human life, an acceptance of limits, which drew on both Epicurean and Christian sources.

It is not that the aspiration to stability is altogether abandoned. Montaigne is certainly acutely aware of the mutability of all things, and above all human life:

> il n'y a aucune constante existence, ny de nostre estre, ny de celui des objects. Et nous, et nostre jugement, et toutes choses mortelles, vont coulant et roulant sans cesse . . . Nous n'avons aucune communication à l'estre, par ce que toute humaine nature est tousjours entre le naistre et le mourir, ne baillant de soy qu'une obscure apparence et ombre, et une

incertaine et debile opinion. Et si, de fortune, vous fichez vostre pensée a vouloir prendre son estre, ce sera ne plus ne moins que qui voudrait empoigner l'eau.

there is no constant existence, neither of our being, nor of the objects. And we, and our judgement, and all mortall things else do uncessantly rowle, turne, and passe away . . . We have no communication with being; for every humane nature is ever in the middle between being borne and dying; giving nothing of itself but an obscure apparence and shadow, and an uncertaine and weak opinion. And if perhaps you fix your thought to take its being; it would be even, as if one should go about to grasp the water.[3]

Perpetual change is not only in us, but everywhere: "Le monde n'est qu'une branloire perenne. Toutes choses y branlent sans cesse: la terre, les rochers du Caucase, les pyramides d'Aegypte, et du branle public et du leur. La constance mesme n'est autre chose qu'un branle plus languissant. ("The world runnes all on wheeles. All things therein moove without intermission; yea the earth, the rockes of Caucasus, and the Pyramides of AEgypt, both with the publike and their own motion. Constancy it selfe is nothing but a languishing and wavering dance").[4]

But nevertheless, or perhaps just because of this, Montaigne proposes to describe himself. Indeed, the point of the sentence just quoted is to justify his kind of self-description, which doesn't seek the exemplary, the universal, or the edifying but simply follows the contours of the changing reality of one being, himself. This life, however, "basse et sans lustre", will reveal as much as any other, because "chaque homme porte la forme entiere de l'humaine condition" ("every man beareth the whole stampe of humane condition").[5]

Montaigne strives to come to a certain equilibrium even within the ever-changing by identifying and coming to terms with the patterns which represent his own particular way of living in flux. So although "we have no communication with being," Montaigne sought, and found some inner peace in, his "maistresse forme" ("my Mistris forme").[6] Self-knowledge is the indispensable key to self-acceptance. Coming to be at home within the limits of our condition presupposes that we grasp these limits, that we learn to draw their contours from within, as it were.

In this new sense, shorn of pretensions to universality, nature can once again be our rule.

J'ai pris . . . bien simplement et cruement pour mon regard ce precepte ancien: que nous ne sçaurions faillir à suivre nature, que le souverain precepte c'est de se conformer à elle. Je n'ay pas corrigé, comme Socrates, par force de la raison mes complexions naturelles, et n'ay aucunement troublé par art mon inclination.

I have ... taken for my regard this ancient precept, very rawly and simply: That "We cannot erre in following Nature": and that the soveraigne document is, for a man to conforme himselfe to her. I have not (as Socrates) by the power and vertue of reason, corrected my natural complexions, nor by Art hindered mine inclination.[7]

It is in this spirit that we have to understand the precept: "Mener l'humaine vie conformément à sa naturelle condition" ("lead my life conformably to its naturall condition").[8] To live right is to live within limits, to eschew the presumption of superhuman spiritual aspirations. But the limits which are relevant for me are mine; to live by some universal model is another one of those chimaeric goals which Epicurean wisdom and Christian humility should warn us to avoid.

To attain his just measure, Montaigne took his distance from the excesses of moral rigour as much as from those of passion.

Je me deffens de la temperance comme j'ai faict autrefois de la volupté. Elle me tire trop arriere, et jusques à la stupidité. Or je veus estre maistre de moy, à tous sens. La sagesse a ses excès, et n'a pas moins besoin de moderation que la folie.

As I have heretofore defended my selfe from pleasure, so I now ward my selfe from temperance: it haleth me too far back, and even to stupidity. I will now every way be master of my selfe. Wisdom hath hir excesses, and no lesse need of moderation, then follie.[9]

Montaigne repudiates the superhuman standards so often held up by the moral tradition.

A quoy faire ces pointes eslevées de la philosophie sur lesquelles aucun estre humain ne se peut rassoir, et ces regles qui excedent nostre usage et nostre force?

To what purpose are these heaven-looking and nice points of Philosophy, on which no humane being can establish and ground it selfe? And to what end serve these rules, that exceed our use and excell our strength?[10]

The source of this is pride and an empty self-satisfaction: "toute cette nostre suffisance, qui est au-delà de la naturelle, est à peu près vaine et superflue" ("All our sufficiency, that is beyond the naturall, is well nigh vaine and superfluous").[11] We have to discover the human balance: "J'estime pareille injustice prendre à contre coeur les voluptez naturelles que de les prendre trop à coeur" ("I deeme it an equall injustice, either to take naturall sensualities against the hart, or to take them too neere the hart").[12] And Montaigne anticipates Pascal in warning against the terrible consequences of this presumptuous rigorism:

Entre nous, ce sont choses que j'ay tousjours veuës de singulier accord: les opinions supercelestes et les meurs sousterraines . . . Ils veulent se mettre hors d'eux et eschapper à l'homme. C'est folie; au lieu de se transformer en anges, ils se transforment en bestes . . . Ces humeurs transcendantes m'effrayent, commes les lieux hautains et inaccessibles.

Super-celestiall opinions, and under-terrestriall manners, are things, that amongst us, I have ever seen to be of singular accord . . . They will be exempted from them and escape man. It is meere folly, insteade of transforming themselves into Angels, they transchange themselves into beastes . . . Such transcending humours affright me as much, as steepy, high and inaccessible places.[13]

Montaigne, like Lucretius, has an idea of nature which is no longer a vehicle for the demands of moral perfection, but which can be used to free us from what is excessive and tyrannical in these demands. The battle is not the Epicurean one with the fear of the gods and their punishment, but rather with the contempt and depreciation of our natural being which these presumptuous standards engender and express. This contempt is often directed at our bodily being. But "c'est tousjours à l'homme que nous avons affaire, duquel la condition est merveilleusement corporelle" ("It is man with whom we have always to doe, whose condition is marvelously corporall").[14]

A quoy faire desmembrons nous en divorce un bastiment tissu d'une si joincte et fraternelle correspondance? Au rebours, renouons le par mutuels offices.

To what end doe wee by a divorce dismember a frame contexted with so mutuall, coherent and brotherly correspondency. Contrariwise, let us repaire and renue the same by enterchangeable offices.[15]

The fight is in a sense to come to accept what we are. And in this regard, as we shall see, Montaigne inaugurates one of the recurring themes of modern culture.

We seek self-knowledge, but this can no longer mean just impersonal lore about human nature, as it could for Plato. Each of us has to discover his or her own form. We are not looking for the universal nature; we each look for our own being. Montaigne therefore inaugurates a new kind of reflection which is intensely individual, a self-explanation, the aim of which is to reach self-knowledge by coming to see through the screens of self-delusion which passion or spiritual pride have erected. It is entirely a first-person study, receiving little help from the deliverances of third-person observation, and none from "science".

The contrast with Descartes is striking, just because Montaigne is at the point of origin of another kind of modern individualism, that of self-discovery, which differs from the Cartesian both in aim and method. Its aim is to identify the individual in his or her unrepeatable difference, where Cartesianism gives us a science of the subject in its general essence; and it proceeds by a critique of first-person self-interpretations, rather than by the proofs of impersonal reasoning. What it ends up with is an understanding of my own demands, aspirations, desires, in their originality, however much these may lie athwart the expectations of society and my immediate inclinations.

> Il n'est personne, s'il s'escoute, qui ne descouvre en soy une forme sienne, une forme maistresse, qui luicte contre l'institution, et contre la tempeste des passions qui lui est contraire.

> There is no man (if he listen to himselfe) that doth not discover in himselfe a peculiar forme, a swaying forme, that wrestleth against the institution, and against the tempests of passions which are contrary unto him.[16]

Descartes is a founder of modern individualism, because his theory throws the individual thinker back on his own responsibility, requires him to build an order of thought for himself, in the first person singular. But he must do so following universal criteria; he reasons as anyone and everyone. Montaigne is an originator of the search for each person's originality; and this is not just a different quest but in a sense antithetical to the Cartesian. Each turns us in a sense inward and tries to bring some order in the soul; but this likeness is what makes the conflict between them particularly acute.

The Cartesian quest is for an order of science, of clear and distinct knowledge in universal terms, which where possible will be the basis of instrumental control. The Montaignean aspiration is always to loosen the hold of such general categories of "normal" operation and gradually prise our self-understanding free of the monumental weight of the universal interpretations, so that the shape of our originality can come to view. Its aim is not to find an intellectual order by which things in general can be surveyed, but rather to find the modes of expression which will allow the particular not to be overlooked.

As Hugo Friedrich put it, where Montaigne tried to bring the particularity of human feeling to expression, Descartes "lays a neatly ordered net of classification . . . over the soul".[17] The very nature of the Montaignean enterprise must lead it to fight free of this. At bottom, the stance towards the self is flatly opposed in these two enterprises. The Cartesian calls for a radical disengagement from ordinary experience; Montaigne requires a deeper engagement in our particularity. These two facets of modern individuality have been at odds up to this day.

But Montaigne's study in its own way has to be just as radically reflexive as that of Descartes. We have to turn inward.

Le monde regarde tousjours vis à vis; moy, je replie ma veue au dedans, je la plante, je l'amuse là. Chacun regarde devant soy; moy, je regarde dedans moy.

The world lookes ever for-right, I turne my sight inward, there I fix it, there I ammuse it. Every man lookes before himselfe, I looke within my selfe.[18]

A study of the particular not framed from the start in a general doctrine: Montaigne was aware how easily it could miscarry. He was aware too of how the reality studied was susceptible of being shaped by the terms employed:

Je n'ay pas plus faict mon livre que mon livre m'a faict, livre consubstantiel à son autheur, d'une occupation propre, membre de ma vie; non d'une occupation et fin tierce et estrangere comme tous autres livres.

I have no more made my booke, then my booke hath made me. A booke consubstantiall to his Author: Of a peculiar and fit occupation. A member of my life. Not of an occupation and end, strange and forraine, as all other bookes.[19]

Montaigne sought through laborious self-examination the penetrating grasp of the particular, which can arise spontaneously in a deep friendship. Montaigne had lived one such, and he was aware of the link; indeed, he attributed his undertaking the study to the loss of his friend, La Boétie, as though it were but a second best: "Luy seul jouyssoit de ma vraye image, et l'emporta. C'est pourquoy je me deschiffre moy-mesme si curieusement" ("He alone partook of my true image, and carried it off with him. That is why I so curiously decipher myself").[20] The self is both made and explored with words; and the best for both are the words spoken in the dialogue of friendship. In default of that, the debate with the solitary self comes limping far behind. Epicurus may have also had some insight of this range, who gave such a central place to the conversation among friends.

But one has to resist the temptation to read Montaigne anachronistically; a temptation which is strong precisely because he pioneered so much that is important to us now. The search for the self in order to come to terms with oneself, which Montaigne inaugurates, has become one of the fundamental themes of our modern culture; or so I would claim. His goal still resonates with us: "C'est une absolue perfection, et comme divine, de sçavoir jouyr loiallement de son estre" ("It is an absolute perfection, and as it were divine for a man to know how to enjoy his being loyally").[21] And this gives us another reason to think of ourselves in reflexive terms. There is a question about ourselves—which we roughly gesture at with the term 'identity'—which cannot be sufficiently answered with any general doctrine of human nature. The search for identity can be seen as the search for what I essentially am. But this can no longer be sufficiently defined in terms of some universal description of human agency as such, as soul, reason, or will. There still remains a question about me, and that is why I think of myself as a self. This word now circumscribes an area of questioning. It designates the kind of being of which this question of identity can be asked.

In order to conjure the demon of anachronism, we have to remind ourselves that the full modern question of identity belongs to the post-Romantic period, which is marked by the idea, central to Herderian expressivism, that each person has his or her own original way of being. I will discuss this at some length later. Montaigne served as a paradigm figure to illustrate another way in which Augustinian inwardness has entered modern life, and he helped to constitute our understanding of the self.

And, of course, Augustinian self-examination reverberated throughout the Renaissance in all sorts of forms, among followers of both major confessions. Self-exploration was part of the discipline of both Jesuits and Puritans, among others. Its importance to the latter, of course, is more readily recognized, because it is arguably one of the sources of modern English literature, in particular, of the novel. But it was a striking phenomenon in its own right. Calvin, taking up Augustine's doctrine of sin in a single-minded and remorseless fashion, made God's transformation of the will through grace the key to salvation. The Puritan was encouraged to scrutinize his inner life continually, both to descry the signs of grace and election and to bring his thoughts and feelings into line with the grace-given dispositions of praise and gratitude to God. What was remarkable about this discipline is that it wasn't meant only for a small elite of spiritual athletes, but for all Christians. It remained, of course, the property of an elite, but of one more broadly based than any earlier period had seen. In New England, it would appear, "almost every literate Puritan kept some sort of journal".[22] Concerning England, Lawrence Stone writes: "From the seventeenth century onwards there bursts on to paper a torrent of words about intimate thoughts and feelings set down by large numbers of quite ordinary English men and women, most of them now increasingly secular in orientation".[23] From Bunyan to Pepys to Boswell, and arguably even to Rousseau, the Protestant culture of introspection becomes secularized as a form of confessional autobiography, while at the same time helping to constitute the new form taken by the English novel in the eighteenth century at the hands of Defoe, Richardson, and others.[24]

11

INNER NATURE

Thus by the turn of the eighteenth century, something recognizably like the modern self is in process of constitution, at least among the social and spiritual elites of northwestern Europe and its American offshoots. It holds together, sometimes uneasily, two kinds of radical reflexivity and hence inwardness, both from the Augustinian heritage, forms of self-exploration and forms of self-control. These are the ground, respectively, of two important facets of the nascent modern individualism, that of self-responsible independence, on one hand, and that of recognized particularity, on the other.

A third facet must also be mentioned. We might describe this as the individualism of personal commitment. I mentioned in Chapter 7 the legacy of the Stoic conception of the will, in its aspect of our power to give or withhold consent—Chrysippus' *'synkatathesis'*, or Epictetus' *'prohairesis'*. To make this the central human moral power is to open the way to an outlook which makes commitment crucial: No way of life is truly good, no matter how much it may be in line with nature, unless it is endorsed with the whole will. The Augustinian heritage was hospitable to this outlook— Augustine identified the force of sin precisely as the inability to will fully.[1] The appeal of the various purified ethical visions of Renaissance humanism, of Erasmus, for instance, or of the later neo-Stoics, was partly that they offered such an ethic of the whole will against the more lax and minimal rules demanded by society at large.

And one of the driving forces of the Protestant Reformation, as central almost as the doctrine of salvation by faith, was the idea that this total commitment must no longer be considered the duty only of an elite which embraced 'counsels of perfection', but was demanded of all Christians indiscriminately.[2] This was the ground for the reformers' vigorous rejection of all the supposedly special vocations of monasticism.

This three-sided individualism is central to the modern identity. It has helped to fix that sense of self which gives off the illusion of being anchored in our very being, perennial and independent of interpretation. We can see its principal features coming to be in these two centuries. I want to look at two of these here.

The first concerns modern localizations. One facet of these has already been my central theme in these chapters: the growth of forms of inwardness, correlative of the increasing centrality of reflexivity in spiritual life, and the consequent displacement of moral sources. But what may seem to common sense even more basic and unchallengeable is the location in general of the properties and nature of something 'in' that thing, and in particular, the location of thought 'in' the mind. A new way of distinguishing and ordering things comes to be conveyed by this too familiar preposition, a way which comes to seem as fixed and ineradicable from reality as the preposition is from our lexicon.

Thought and feeling—the psychological—are now confined to minds. This follows our disengagement from the world, its 'disenchantment', in Weber's phrase. As long as the order of things embodies an ontic logos, then ideas and valuations are also seen as located in the world, and not just in subjects. Indeed, their privileged locus is in the cosmos, or perhaps beyond it, in the realm of Ideas in which both world and soul participate. This is the disposition of things which underlies the theories of knowledge of Plato and Aristotle. When Aristotle says that "actual knowledge is identical with its object",[3] or "the activity of the sensible object and that of the percipient sense is one and the same activity, and yet the distinction between their being remains",[4] he is operating with a conception of knowing which is far removed from the representational construal that becomes dominant with Descartes and Locke.[5] Knowledge comes when the action of the Forms in shaping the real coincides with its action in shaping my intelligence *(nous)*. True knowledge, true valuation is not exclusively located in the subject. In a sense, one might say that their paradigm location is in reality; correct human knowledge and valuation comes from our connecting ourselves rightly to the significance things already have ontically. In another sense, one might say that true knowledge and valuation only arise when this connection comes about. In either case, these two—to us—"psychological" activities are ontically situated.

An example is cited by Walter Ong in his book on Ramus. In traditional discussions of rhetoric, they spoke of the 'praise' of words (sometimes *'laus'*, sometimes 'honos/honor', sometimes also *'lumen'* of words).[6] The 'praise' was attributed here to the objects worthy of praise. Where we think of an activity of subjects, exercised on or in relation to certain objects—here an activity of valuation—the tradition seems to put the valuation in the objects themselves. Or perhaps better, it is somehow both in the worthy objects and in the activity of praising them.

Ong quotes lines like these: "the chief prayse and cunning of our poet is in the discreet using of his figures"; or this, from the *Merchant of Venice:*

> How many things by season season'd are
> To their right praise and true perfection![7] (5.1.108–109)

It would be misleading to speak, as I began to above, of the valuation being "in" the worthy object. For it is not "in" this in the same sense as for us it is "in" the mind of the praiser or in his activity of lauding the object. The whole understanding of localization is utterly different within a theory of ontic logos. The point might best be made by saying that these straddle what we think of as the gap between subject and object. Our activity of praising (when right) is continuous with the valuation in things, just as knowledge in its actuality is with the actuality of the object. The significance of being objects of praise inhabits, as it were, praiseworthy things. It can almost be thought of as something which emanates from them. (Hence the use of the term *'lumen'* interchangeably with *'laus'*, above.)

The paradigm case of this relation is, of course, the glory of God. We glorify God; so glory is something we would seem to be bestowing. But in doing this we are only responding to God's glory.[8] The same term *('doxa')* designated a property of God, and what we confer. The two join when our praising is 'straight' or 'right' (i.e., when we have *'orthē doxa'*).

All this changes when we disengage from the world, and when therefore theories of ontic logos cease to be meaningful for us. This whole traditional kind of localization ceases to make sense. The world consists of a domain of objects to which we can respond in varying ways. We develop certain ideas about them, and we take various evaluative responses towards them. We may think of these valuations as founded or unfounded, as against being ultimately arbitrarily chosen. That is, we may still be objectivists about value—although many have drawn subjectivist conclusions from the new ontology. But where the valuations are founded, they are so in a new way. For instance, a modern may think an object valuable because it fulfils a function in God's design. The valuation is then objective. But it is not a significance expressed or embodied in the object in the way characteristic of theories of ontic logos. The valuation is now unambiguously not in the object but in *minds,* ours or God's.

And so we have not just a new localization of thought, valuation—even feeling, as we shall see—but a new kind of localization. The two world-views are incommensurable. They don't determine similar maps within which we can pick out different places; they determine altogether different notions of place. For the modern disengaged subject, thought and valuation are in the mind in a new and stronger sense, because minds are now the *exclusive* locus of such realities, which can therefore now be called 'psychic' in a new sense.

The facts that we are ready to apply this term without hesitation to them, that we find the older localization rather weird and hard to understand, that it rather appears to us as a fuzzy lack of localization, all show how much we are now within the new self-understanding, defined by this new, exclusive localization.

This defines a new understanding of subject and object, where the subject is, as it were, over against the object. Indeed, we could say that the very notions of subject and object in their modern sense come to be within this new localization. The modern sense is one in which subject and object are separable entities. That is, in principle—though perhaps not in fact—one could exist without the other. For Descartes, there could have been minds without bodies. Within this framework, a set of problems arises about the relationship of the two entities which are in principle self-subsistent.

But this way of seeing things made no sense on the older view. Aristotle's *nous* couldn't exist without a world of Forms. That is, there is no coherent supposition of its independent existence which we can formulate within Aristotle's understanding of things. Nor could the world of particular things exist without Forms, and hence quite independent of thought.

The modern idea of a subject as an independent existent is just another facet of the new, strong localization. We can now think of ideas as being 'in' this independent being, because it makes sense to see them as here and *not elsewhere*. And reciprocally, the notion of a separation requires some new sense of locale. The shift from Platonic Ideas to Cartesian 'ideas' is perhaps the most eloquent illustration of the change I've been describing. For the first, Ideas are ontic, the basis of reality; for the second, they are contents of the mind.

The shift can be thought of as a new subjectivism. This is Heidegger's description, and we can see why. It can be so called because it gives rise to the notion of a subject in its modern sense; or otherwise put, because it involves a new localization, whereby we place 'within' the subject what was previously seen as existing, as it were, between knower/agent and world, linking them and making them inseparable.

The opposition of subject to object is one way in which the new strong localization arises. Another is the fixing of a clear boundary between the psychic and the physical. Our modern ideas of the psychosomatic or of psycho-physical correlations depend on this boundary. We can illustrate this by taking another traditional example and seeing how hard it is for us to make sense of it.

Melancholia is black bile. That's what it means. Today we might think of the relationship expressed in this term as a psycho-physical causal one. An excess of the substance, black bile, in our system tends to bring on melancholy. We acknowledge a host of such relationships, so that this one is easily understandable to us, even though our notions of organic chemistry are very different from those of our ancestors.

But in fact there is an important difference between this account and the traditional theory of humours. On the earlier view, black bile doesn't just cause melancholy; melancholy somehow resides in it. The substance embodies this significance. This is what links it, for instance, to Saturn, which also embodies this meaning.[9]

Black bile produces melancholy feelings, because these manifest what it is, its ontic-logical status. The psychic is one of the media in which it manifests itself, if one likes, but black bile *is* melancholy, and not just in virtue of a psycho-physical causal link.

The theory of humours depended on a conception of ontic logos. When this goes, we are forced to a new, sharper localization. Melancholy feelings are now 'in' the mind. The only way left to state something like the traditional theory is in terms of a psycho-physical correlation. Too much black bile makes us melancholy.

This way of sorting things out makes it natural for us to talk of the 'mental' and the 'physical' as though they were two exclusive categories.[10] Natural, but not inevitable. Much modern philosophy has striven against this kind of dualism. But this is a mode of thought we easily fall into. The onus of argument, the effort, falls to those who want to overcome dualism. This is another way of measuring the strength of our modern conceptions of self and locus: by the way the common sense of our age distributes the onus of persuasion.

This modern dualism can generate its own kind of naturalist, mechanistic monism, of course—though here the dualism is more repressed than properly overcome, since this outlook still depends on a sense of ourselves as disengaged subjects, as I argued earlier. But if we do adopt some such naturalist outlook, we might be willing to say, in another easily understandable sense, that my melancholy was 'in' my black bile (assuming we could hold on to some modern endocrinological transform of the traditional theory of humours). We would be helped in this by another converging development of the modern conception, another shift to strong localization.

On the post-Cartesian conception of the physical universe, the nature of a thing can be localized 'in' the thing, again in a strong sense without proper analogue in the earlier views. Aristotle's Forms are often said to be "in" the things they inform, in contrast to Plato's, because he doesn't allow them an independent existence in some immaterial realm, as Plato seems to do. But they are not "in" them in the strong modern sense.

For instance, the Form of Man is something which is not in you or in me only. It is what lies behind the humanity of all of us, what gets passed from my parents to me, and then to my children. In an important sense, the Form is prior to the particular cases; it brings them about; they conform to it. The crucial difference with our contemporary outlook comes out when we look at the relation between the Form and the particular it informs. It is not embedded in them in the sense that its existence is dependent on them. There is no particular, or group of particulars, of which this is true. Any particular human can disappear; the Form goes on. But perhaps this just means that we're considering too small a unit? How about the whole human race, that is, the ensemble of all individuals from the beginning? But even this doesn't constitute a particular on which the Form depends for its existence. Forms are not independent entities; they exist within an order of Forms. They cannot therefore be considered as ontically totally dependent on the particulars they inform. That is why the unity of a Form is not just a matter of there being converging particulars, why the Forms can also inform intelligences *(nous)*, and why knowledge consists in the same activity *(energeia)* linking intelligence and object. It was the remains of this outlook, incidentally, which made the idea of evolution, the formerly inconceivable idea that species could come to be and pass away, seem so disturbing and incredible at first.

By contrast, the modern conception does localize the nature in the thing. That is, what we can identify as the nearest analogue to an Aristotelian nature, the forces or causes which make an entity function as it does, can be considered as 'in' the entity concerned—not, of course, in the sense that the behaviour of the thing may not depend on a field of forces which geographically extends beyond its boundaries, but in the sense that this 'nature' is ontically entirely dependent on the existence of particulars which exemplify it. If they disappear, it disappears. Their nature is whatever causes operate in them. This is a profoundly nominalist conception: there is no identity criterion of a 'nature' other than the similarity of causes operating in a number of entities, and each such identified 'kind' of thing is ontologically independent of all the others. It may causally depend on them, but its nature isn't defined by its place in the whole, as with a theory of ontic logos.

Here is another kind of strong localization which arises with the modern view. It dovetails with the ones I described earlier. If I don't want to think of myself as a 'mind', I can think of my psychological properties as inhering 'in' me as an organism. The causal properties inducing melancholy feelings would be 'in' the black bile, in this modern nominalist sense.

But this is entirely different from the older theory of humours. For the black bile of a modern localization would just be the physical substance. It is no longer the embodiment of the significance 'melancholy'. The feeling can no longer have its seat in a substance in *that* sense, but only in the sense that it finds in this substance its cause.

The modern localization doesn't only arise on the ashes of ancient *theories*. It is not just philosophers who see the world differently. What we find formulated in the theory of humours was not just a school doctrine but a widespread self-understanding. It was not only educated people who saw psychic life this way. Well into the eighteenth century, even into the nineteenth, ordinary people understood their emotional life in part in terms of humours. Even today, we speak of people as 'phlegmatic' or 'sanguine'. And in a host of other ways, we can see that the boundary between the psychic and the physical had not yet been sharply drawn.

The popular belief in magic reflects this. It requires such an open boundary. The magic which deals in such things as love potions or spells to produce or cure disease in cattle is not just an alternative technology to modern medicine. It relies on a notion that certain powers have their seat in certain substances or in certain speech acts, in the premodern sense of this relation. There is no room for this in a 'disenchanted' world, as Weber's term ('*entzaubert*') implies.

That the power inhabits the thing was not just a matter of the causal properties of the latter, but partook to some degree also of the way a significance inhabits its expression or a soul inhabits the body it animates (on a pre-Cartesian understanding of this relation). The revolution which produced the modern idea of the psyche and its strong localization had not only to sweep aside traditional theories of ontic logos; it had also to undermine and replace a deeply rooted popular way of understanding human life and its place in nature, that which underlay and made possible a serious belief in magic.

Once we take this change in 'mentality' across its whole scope, we can see that it was not just a matter of magic fading away before science. The new disengagement was carried by profound changes in spiritual outlook. One of the most powerful forces working against magic, and for the disenchanted view of the world, was the Protestant Reformation, which was profoundly suspicious of such meddling with occult forces. Magical practices couldn't be allowed as a proper use of divine power, because that would be to assume human control over this, which was against the very principle of the Reformation. Indeed, the Catholic sacraments were often assimilated to magic practices by Reformers and condemned in similar terms. The power must be diabolic, if it existed at all; Protestants accentuated the traditional Christian suspicion of magic.

Keith Thomas has shown that this stance went back to the proto-Reformation movement of the Lollards in the fourteenth century. Here is one of their statements from 1395:

> That exorcisms and hallowings, made in the Church, of wine, bread, and wax, water, salt and oil and incense, the stone of the altar, upon vestments, mitre, cross, and pilgrims' staves, be the very practice of

necromancy, rather than that of the holy theology. This conclusion is proved thus. For by such exorcisms creatures be charged to be of higher virtue than their own kind, and we see nothing of change in no such creature that is so charmed, but by false belief, the which is the principle of the devil's craft.[11]

Magical practices underwent a decline in Protestant societies, as Thomas explains, and there is some evidence that the decline occurred faster in Catholic societies which were affected by Jansenism. Disenchantment was driven by and connected with a new moral/spiritual stance to the world, as we shall see below in discussing the Protestant background to Baconian science. It was connected to a new piety, and what we see emerging is a new notion of freedom and inwardness, which this piety fostered.

The decline of the world-view underlying magic was the obverse of the rise of the new sense of freedom and self-possession. From the viewpoint of this new sense of self, the world of magic seems to entail a thraldom, an imprisoning of the self in uncanny external forces, even a ravishing or loss of self. It threatens a possession which is the very opposite of self-possession. For our contemporaries who are very secure in the modern identity or even feel imprisoned within it, playing with the occult can provide a pleasant frisson for the contented, or perhaps even seem to offer a way of escape for those who feel oppressed by disenchantment. But things must have been very different as this identity was emerging.

Perhaps this can help account for that puzzling phenomenon, the European witchcraft craze, which stretches from about the fifteenth to the mid-seventeenth century and which contrasts so oddly with the detached scepticism of the early Middle Ages. It is oddly incongruous that Aquinas, for instance, sounds much more "modern" on this issue than does, say, Bodin. Perhaps the obsessional concern with witches, and the spectacular rise of belief in and sense of threat from them, can be partly understood as a crisis arising in the transition between identities. The aspect of possession, of ravishment, perhaps became even more important and obsessional just at the time and to the degree that the identity was emerging which would break our dependence on orders of ontic logos, and establish a self-defining subject. The witchcraft craze, lying between a period in which people accepted without resistance their insertion in a universe of meaningful order and a period in which that universe was definitively shattered, could be a response to the fragility of the emerging identity as it was establishing itself, a function of its immaturity and lack of solidity.

Both disengagement and this understanding of the nature of things as within them helped to generate a new notion of individual independence. The disengaged subject is an independent being, in the sense that his or her paradigm purposes are to be found within, and not dictated by the larger order of which he or she is a part. One of the fruits of this is the new political atomism which arises in the seventeenth century, most notably with the theories of social contract of Grotius, Pufendorf, Locke, and others. Contract theory as such wasn't new in this century, of course. There is a rich background to it in the tradition. It had its roots in Stoic philosophy and mediaeval theories of rights. Moreover, there had been an important development of theories of consent in the late Middle Ages, most notably around the conciliar movement in the church. And the sixteenth century saw the contract theories of the great Jesuit writers like Suarez.

Nevertheless, there was something importantly new in the seventeenth-century theories. Previously the issue of consent had been put in terms of a people establishing government by contract. The existence of the community was something taken for granted in all earlier versions. Even writers like Gerson, who go back to the original Stoic idea that men were first of all solitary wanderers *(solivagi)*, understood the consent which founds political authority as the consent of a community.[12] For a post-seventeenth-century reader, an obvious question arises: How does the community get started? Where does it get its authority to determine the nature of political authority over its constituent individuals? Before the seventeenth century this issue is not raised. The big innovation of contract theorists from Grotius on is that they do address it; it now begins to appear self-evident that it has to be addressed.

The new theories add to the traditional contract founding government a second one, which precedes it: a contract of association. This is a universal agreement which founds a political community and confers on it the power to determine a form of government. The shift between these two kinds of contract theory reflects a shift in the understanding of the human moral predicament. Previously that people were members of a community went without saying. It didn't need to be justified relative to a more basic situation. But now the theory starts from the individual on his own. Membership of a community with common power of decision is now something which needs to be explained by the individual's prior consent. Of course, each may be seen as a social being in another sense. Locke's picture of the state of nature seems to involve a lot of interchange between people. But what cannot now be taken for granted anymore is a community with decisional powers over its members. People start off as political atoms.

Underlying this atomist contract theory, we can see two facets of the new individualism. Disengagement from cosmic order meant that the human agent was no longer to be understood as an element in a larger, meaningful order. His paradigm purposes are to be discovered within. He is on his own. What goes for the larger cosmic order will eventually be applied also to political society. And this yields a picture of the sovereign individual, who is 'by nature' not bound to any authority. The condition of being under authority is something which has to be-*created*.

The question is, what can create it? To us the obvious answer seems to be consent. But this wasn't the only answer offered in the seventeenth century. What gave this answer its plausibility for its adherents was the force of another facet of individuation, the stress on personal commitment. This was especially important in Calvinist, particularly Puritan, societies. Here the notion that the believer should be personally committed, along with the view that only a minority were truly saved or regenerated, led to an increasing emphasis on an association of the saved. And this tended to be seen, at least in the early, more revolutionary days, as an association which would not be congruent with the existing groups and societies in which people found themselves, because all these would be split between regenerate and damned.

So the godly must be ready to break with family, with local community, with political society, in order to cleave to the community of the saved. "Vicinity and neighborhood will fail and alliance and kindred will fail but grace and religion will never fail. If we adjoin ourselves unto [godly men] for their virtue and goodness, they will not separate themselves from us for calamities and trouble".[13] Puritanism brought about at first a downgrading of natural, given, inherited communities in favour of one which came about through personal commitment. The society of the godly ought to be one of willed consent. Some went to great lengths, including crossing the ocean to the wilds of New England, to separate themselves from the ungodly and set up a Christian society.

The irony is, of course, that having set up such a separate society, Puritans began to see themselves as a tribe of the saved among heathen peoples. This was one reason for their strong identification with the ancient Israelites. And they tended to believe that the children of the saved would be saved themselves, so that family and community became once more poles of virtually unquestioned allegiance. But something important had nevertheless changed. The central significance of personal commitment meant that all these communities were now understood in a more consensual light. Marriage comes to be seen more as a free contractual relation between the parties.[14]

The importance that Puritans gave to the idea of covenant, the agreement between God and his people, begins to develop into an understanding of society as based on a covenant between its members. In a godly community founded on personal commitment, the two could be seen as facets of one and the same covenant.

This new sense of the role of contract and consent, so salient among Puritans, also was growing in other milieus, though perhaps nowhere else with the same explicitness and emphasis. And this, combined with the idea of the free, disengaged individual, helped produce the doctrines of consent of this century. To those influenced by this notion of personal commitment, it seemed obvious that the only thing which could create authority was the consent of the individual. His will and his purposes are his own. Only he can bind them to something bigger and create the obligation to obey.

Where doctrines of personal commitment were less developed, there had to be other ways of coping with the challenge of atomism. The erosion of the sense of authority as something natural, something given in the order of things or the community, required some answer to the question, What has brought about legitimate submission? The idea that there may be no legitimate authority is obviously too dangerous to be tolerable. The doctrine of the divine right of kings provided an alternative to contract theory in the seventeenth century. Divine right was a quintessentially modern doctrine, unlike previous mediaeval doctrines of the divine constitution of authority. Divine right assumed atomism; that is, it took for granted that there were no natural relations of authority among men, and it then argued that only a special grant of divine power to kings could avoid the chaos of anarchy. The earlier doctrines had assumed that human communities had authority, and they invoked God's endorsement of the political dispositions made of this authority, whatever they might be—republican or monarchical. The seventeenth-century doctrine started from atomist premises, and it required God's intervention specifically establishing kings as his lieutenants on earth.

When Bossuet argues for this doctrine, he argues a need for an authority which is above society. His picture of society shows it as incapable of cohesion on its own. Its hierarchical arrangement, the very element which to earlier ages was a source of cohesion, is now seen as a cause of tension. Precisely because there are higher and lower social estates, with all the rivalry that this entails, political power cannot reside within society, but has to be above it. For if power reposed with any estate, this would be disadvantageous, and also demeaning, for the others. For Bossuet, royal power is a condition of everyone's dignity as much as it is of social peace.[15]

We inherit atomism from the seventeenth century. Not that we still espouse social contract theories (although various transposed versions are still popular).[16] But we still find it easy to think of political society as created by will or to think of it instrumentally. In the latter case, even though we no longer understand the origins of society as reposing in agreement, we nevertheless both understand and evaluate its workings as an instrument to attain ends we impute to individuals or constituent groups.

And we inherit from this century our theories of rights, the modern tendency to frame the immunities accorded people by law in terms of subjective rights. This, as I said above (section 1.3), is a conception which puts the autonomous individual at the centre of our system of law. From

Locke comes an influential gloss on this, what Brough Macpherson has called 'possessive individualism',[17] a conception of the most basic immunities we enjoy—life, liberty—on the model of the ownership of property. This construction reflects the extreme stance of disengagement towards one's own being of the Lockean punctual self. The continuing force of this individualism is a sign of the enduring attraction of this self-understanding.

The atomism/instrumentalism complex belongs to those ideas I spoke about above which are somehow easier for us, in that they benefit from the onus of argument, or at least explanation. This is not to say that we are imprisoned within it. Quite the contrary: there are a number of influential doctrines in the modern world which have tried to recapture a more holistic view of society, to understand it as a matrix for individuals rather than as an instrument. And some of these have been important for our political practice. But they have remained burdened with the onus of explanation. Atomist views always seem nearer to common sense, more immediately available. Even though they don't stand up very well in argument (at least, so I believe), even though a modicum of explanation is enough to show their inadequacy, nevertheless this explanation is continually necessary. It's as though without a special effort of reflection on this issue, we tend to fall back into an atomist/instrumental way of seeing. This seems to dominate our unreflecting experience of society, or at least to emerge more easily when we try to formulate what we know from this experience. It's a naturally favoured idea, benefiting from a built-in ever-renewed initial plausibility.

This occurs in spite of the fact that modern political life has generated powerful counter-ideas. In particular, there is the understanding of society which has been described as "civic humanist". This draws on the ancient republic or polis for its model. It came to the fore briefly in fifteenth-century Italy,[18] played some role in the troubles which led to the English Civil War, and then was central to the great revolutions of the eighteenth century in America and France which have helped to shape modern politics.

The notion of citizen virtue, as we see it defined in Montesquieu and Rousseau, can't be combined with an atomist understanding of society. It assumes that the political way of life, in devotion to which Montesquieu's 'virtue' consists, is in an important sense prior to the individuals. It establishes their identity, provides the matrix within which they can be the kinds of human beings they are, within which the noble ends of a life devoted to the public good are first conceivable. These political structures can't be seen simply as instruments, means to ends which could be framed without them.

We might argue that a constituent tension in modern Western democracies which descend from the Anglo-Saxon or French models of the eighteenth century is that between the consequences of an atomist-instrumental kind of politics, on one hand, and the demands of citizen-participation politics, on the other. In this tension, the natural favour the first idea enjoys has played some role. But the citizen understanding, however recessive and distorted and relegated to the background it may be, still is needed to capture an essential part of our practice as citizen republics.[19]

There is a third feature of the modern identity, in addition to its characteristic localizations and atomism, which I'd like to mention briefly here. This is the significance given to what I want to call our 'poietic' powers. I could use the word 'productive' here, but I'm not talking about economic activity, and therefore to avoid confusion I prefer to coin this neologism. What I am getting at is the new centrality of constructed orders and artifacts in mental and moral life.

We saw this in one way with the new notions of procedural reason, both speculative and practical. Knowledge comes not from connecting the mind to the order of things we find but in framing a representation of reality according to the right canons. Descartes's insight that our knowledge of things is our own construct was the basis for his deep confidence, which seems to have preceded the arguments that articulate its justification, that we could attain certainty. This must be attainable, because we can reflect on our own activity of thinking: because thinking is something we *do,* we can achieve certainty about it.

Descartes's representational model of knowledge was taken up by the empiricists. Building also on Hobbes, they emphasized further the constructive dimension of our knowledge of the world. Hobbes, and later Locke, followed by his disciples in the eighteenth century, thought of our world picture as almost literally put together out of building blocks—which were ultimately the sensations or ideas produced by experience.

In the moral domain, Locke also builds on Descartes's model of rational control and defines a task of self-remaking which falls to the punctual self. Rather than following the telos of nature, we become constructors of our own character.

This emphasis on constructive activity leads to a new understanding of language, which one can see again arising in Hobbes and Locke. It is an offshoot of the nominalist theories: words are ultimately given their meaning arbitrarily through definitions which attach them to certain things or ideas. But the function of language is to aid the construction of thought. We need language to build an adequate picture of things. We couldn't match the world with a painstaking combination of individual bits of perception, individual ideas. Through language, we can combine them in whole bunches, in whole classes, and this alone makes it possible to have genuine knowledge.[20]

It follows, of course, that words can also be terribly dangerous. They can be that through which we utterly lose contact with reality, if they are not properly anchored in experience through definitions. That is why both Hobbes and Locke are wary of them and at times almost obsessionally anxious that our words not run away with us. This fear of losing control is the natural outgrowth of the role given to language here: to help us to master and marshall our thoughts. As Condillac says later, developing the Lockean doctrine, language gives us "empire sur notre imagination".[21]

This centring on the constructive powers of language undergoes a further crucial development in the late eighteenth century. Language and in general our representational powers come to be seen not only or mainly as directed to the correct portrayal of an independent reality but also as our way of manifesting through expression what we are, and our place within things. And on the new understanding of ourselves as expressive beings, this manifestation is also seen as a self-completion. This expressive revolution identifies and exalts a new poietic power, that of the creative imagination. I will return to this below; here I want to say only that this new shift further increases the importance of our poietic capacities. They are seen as even more central to human life. And this is the basis for the growing interest and fascination in them in all their forms—in language and artistic creation—which rises at times almost to obsession in our century.

12

A DIGRESSION ON
HISTORICAL EXPLANATION

But this expressive facet of the modern identity has a deeper background which I have barely touched on. I am eager now to go on to this, but before I do, there is an issue about what I've been doing which needs to be clarified.

I've been talking about the rise of (one aspect of) the modern identity. What relation does my study have to a historical explanation of this identity?

Some might think that this work *is* proffered as a historical explanation; and in that case it is bound to appear as an uncommonly bad one. By and large, I have been dwelling on certain developments in philosophy and religious outlook, with an odd glance at aspects of popular mentality. I have barely mentioned the great changes in political structures, economic practices, and military and bureaucratic organization which marked the period. Surely the modern identity would be unthinkable without these.

Am I perhaps offering an "idealist" account, one which relegates all these institutional and structural changes to a subordinate role, following on and seconding epochal changes in ideas and moral outlook? This would be crazy.

To begin with, even remaining on the level of "ideas", or culture, I have not begun to touch on all the currents that have gone together to make the modern identity. I have spoken of some important changes in philosophy and religion. But what is striking is the way in which such a monumental change in self-understanding is fed from a multitude of sources. Other developments could have been mentioned in the Renaissance.

To take one example, there is the famous landmark that everyone cites: Pico's *Oration* on the dignity of man, which affirms an exceptional position for human beings in the universe. They are free, in that they are not, as other things are, tied to a determinate nature, but rather have the power to assume any nature. Pico has God address Adam thus:

> Neither a fixed abode nor a form that is thine alone nor any function peculiar to thyself have we given thee, Adam, to the end that according to thy longing and according to thy judgement thou mayest have and possess what abode, what form, what functions thou thyself shalt desire. The

nature of all other beings is limited and constrained within the bounds of laws prescribed by Us. Thou, constrained by no limits, in accordance with thine own free will, in whose hand We have placed thee, shalt ordain for thyself the limits of thy nature. We have set thee at the world's center that thou mayest from thence more easily observe whatever is in the world. We have made thee neither of heaven nor of earth, neither mortal nor immortal, so that with freedom of choice and with honor, as though the maker and molder of thyself, thou mayest fashion thyself in whatever shape thou shalt prefer.[1]

This seems to prepare the way, even while remaining within the Renaissance Platonic order of ontic logos, for a later decisive break with it. It seems to prepare the way for a stage where the ends of human life will no longer be defined in relation to a cosmic order at all, but must be discovered (or chosen) within. This although Pico is still very far himself from such a step. The order of being is still a geocentric and hierarchical one ("we have set thee at the world's center"), and man's power to assume any nature is the power either to debase or exalt himself. The passage continues: "Thou shalt have the power to degenerate into the lower forms of life, which are brutish. Thou shalt have the power, out of thy soul's judgement, to be reborn with the higher forms, which are divine".[2] Man's ends are still set by a cosmically realized order of good.

Or again, there was a new emphasis in the Renaissance on human action, on man's role in completing God's creation and bringing the cosmos to its full nature. We see this with Nicholas of Cusa, for instance, and later with Bovillus. And one can argue that the emphasis on production of Renaissance magi like Dee and Paracelsus helped lay the groundwork for the Baconian revolution.[3] Here again, we have what looks like a preparation for the new within the bounds of the old. The new understanding of the place of human productive power within the cosmic order prepares the subversion and utter rejection of this whole conception of cosmic order.

And of course currents well beyond the boundaries of philosophy and science helped prepare the modern identity. The new importance of human poietic powers is reflected and foreshadowed in the great prestige of the visual and plastic arts in the Italian Renaissance, something which had no precedent among the ancients. This is the way we look at it today, but it is also the way people looked at it at the time. The writings of Vasari and Alberti, for instance, give expression to their sense that their age is remarkable for the great discoveries (partly rediscoveries) it has made in the visual arts. Indeed, the rediscovery of nature, in which the Italian Renaissance believed itself to have rejoined the ancients in spirit, after the "middle ages" inaugurated by barbarian destruction, was realized as much—indeed, perhaps preeminently—in visual art as in literature. And when Florentine neo-Platonism begins to become the dominant view, it is quite understandable that some artists begin to see their work within its framework: visual art has a vocation to make the Ideas manifest. This notion Plato would have found incomprehensible and repellent: making Ideas manifest is for dialectic alone.

Michaelangelo is deeply imbued with the neo-Platonic idea that earthly beauty is the mortal veil through which we see divine grace. The artist, both writer and painter/sculptor, makes this hidden reality shine through the veil. Leonardo is looking for "reasons" in nature: "Nature is full of an infinity of reasons which have never been in experience".[4] Later in the century, the claim was made that the activity of forming things in art brings us to a "perfect knowledge of the intelligible objects".[5] And the classical revival of the Italian seventeenth century, according to Panofsky, makes an appeal again to a neo-Platonic vision in order to define the true nature of art against both mannerist and naturalist deviations.[6]

But Renaissance visual art can be seen as preparing the emergence of the modern identity in a more direct way than merely by enhancing the importance of the poietic. The Renaissance aspiration to imitate nature leads to a more realistic and full portraiture, to free-standing sculpture no longer "consubstantial" with its architectural context.[7] We can, of course, take Gombrich's point[8] that our judgements of realism are relative to a tradition and context. Nevertheless, the important point is that there was an intention to "let things be", to give the reality of nature priority over the shapes of the iconographic tradition.

This freeing of nature from the iconographic tradition also carries consequences for the place of the subject. The artist who sets himself to imitate nature sees himself as standing over against the object. There is a new distance between subject and object, and they are clearly situated relative to each other. By contrast, the reality manifested in the earlier iconic tradition has no such determinate situation; it can't be definitvely placed, either within or without. In the new art, space becomes important, and position in space. The artist is looking at what he depicts from a determinate point of view. With the achievement of perspective, the depicted reality is laid out as it appears from a particular situation.

As Panofsky puts it, the painted surface loses the materiality it possesses in the high Middle Ages. Instead of being an opaque and impervious surface, it becomes like a window through which we see reality as it appears from that perspective. He quotes Alberti: "Painters should know that they move on a plane surface with their lines and that, in filling the areas thus defined with colours, the only thing they seek to accomplish is that the forms of the things seen appear on this plane surface as if it were made of transparent glass". And even more explicitly, Alberti says: "I describe a rectangle of whatever size I please, which I imagine to be an open window through which I view whatever is to be depicted there".[9]

So the "freeing" of the object also carries with it a "freeing" of the subject, in the form of a greater self-consciousness, a new distance and separation from the object, a sense of standing over against and no longer being englobed by what is depicted. As Panofsky describes it,[10] the new distance "at one and the same time objectifies the object and personalizes the subject". Didn't this also in its way prepare the ground for the more radical break, in which the subject frees himself decisively by objectifying the world? The separation by which I stand over against the world perhaps helps prepare for the deeper rupture where I no longer recognize it as the matrix in which my life's ends are set. The stance of separation helps overcome that profound sense of involvement in the cosmos, that absence of a clear boundary between self and world, which was generated by and contributed to sustaining the premodern notions of cosmic order.[11]

And at the same time, the new self-consciousness about the depiction of reality and the sense of breaking new ground in this reinforce awareness of the role of human poiesis and enhance its importance.[12]

But does that mean that this study only fails to be a historical explanation because it isn't wide enough? That it would be an adequate account if only I could mention all the currents of cultural life that helped prepare the modern identity? This would be indeed to take an "idealist" view, relegating all the institutional and structural changes to a subordinate place as mere consequences.

What I'm doing has to be seen as distinct from historical explanation, and yet relevant to it. It's distinct because I'm asking a different question. The question to which an explanation is the answer would be, e.g., what brought the modern identity about. It's a question about diachronic causation. We want to know what were the precipitating conditions, and this leads us to some statement of the features peculiar to Western civilization in the early modern period which made it the case that this particular cultural shift occurred here. A similar question can be asked about the rise of capitalism, the industrial revolution, the rise of representative democracies, or any of the other major features particular to emerging modern Western civilization—however much they may have spread since. (And the answers to these different questions would obviously be related.)

This is the really ambitious question. I think it is difficult at this stage (this is an understatement!) to offer a satisfactory, fully fleshed-out answer. Over-simple and reductive variants of Marxism seem to have a clear answer: the precipitating conditions lie in the breakdown of the previous ("feudal") mode of production, and the rise of the new ("capitalist") one. But this seems to me either question-begging or terribly implausible, depending on how one takes it. I will try to offer some general considerations below why this is bound to be so. For the moment I confess to lacking (I am not alone) a very clear and plausible diachronic-causal story.

But there is a second, less ambitious question. It is an interpretive one. Answering it involves giving an account of the new identity which makes clear what its appeal was. What drew people to it? Indeed, what draws them today? What gave it its spiritual power? We articulate the visions of good involved in it. What this question asks for is an interpretation of the identity (or of any cultural phenomenon which interests us) which will show why people found (or find) it convincing/inspiring/moving, which will identify what can be called the 'idées-forces' it contains. This can, up to a point, be explored independently of the question of diachronic causation. We can say: in this and this consists the power of the idea/identity/moral vision, however it was brought to be in history.

But of course these two orders of question can't be entirely separated. The answer to the less ambitious one has an important bearing on the answer to the more ambitious one. To understand wherein the force of certain ideas consists is to know something relevant to how they come to be central to a society in history. This is undoubtedly one of the things we have to understand in order to answer the diachronic-causal question. One reason why vulgar Marxism is so implausible is that its reductive accounts of, say, religious or moral or legal-political ideas seem to give no weight at all to their intrinsic power. But all historiography (and social science as well) relies on a (largely implicit) understanding of human motivation: how people respond, what they generally aspire to, the relative importance of given ends and the like. This is the truth behind Weber's celebrated affirmation that any explanation in sociology has to be "adequate as to meaning".[13] The trouble with vulgar Marxisms is that, when they don't neglect this point altogether and rely on some incomprehensible 'structural' determination which bypasses human motivation altogether,[14] their implicit picture of human motivation is unbelievably one-dimensional.

The reciprocal relation also holds: any insight we might have into the diachronic-causal genesis of an idea will help us to identify its spiritual centre of gravity. Just because the two questions can't be fully separated, I have to acknowledge that by entering onto the less ambitious while staying away from the more, my discussion will at times be halting, and may at other times take too much for granted. I don't see any way to avoid this danger altogether without setting out to offer a complete diachronic-causal explanation, which I am unable to encompass. All I can do is apologize in advance for the incomplete nature of this study.

But apart from this unavoidable incompleteness, I don't believe that an interpretive study of this kind has anything to apologize for. In some Marxist circles, a focus on this question is taken as in principle "idealist". As I said above, this term might rightly be applied as a reproach, if the underlying thesis were that somehow an interpretive study of idées-forces was *sufficient* to answer the diachronic-causal question. But it is not clear who has ever held such a thesis. (If there were such a thing as a vulgar Hegelian, he would hold it.) The confusion arises because reductive Marxism seems to want to allow *no* causal role *at all* to idées-forces, which is the equal and opposite absurdity to "idealism"; and worse, this kind of Marxism has trouble recognizing that there is a third possibility between these extremes. But in this middle ground lies all adequate historical explanation. One has to understand people's self-interpretations and their visions of the good, if one is to explain how they arise; but the second task can't be collapsed into the first, even as the first can't be elided in favour of the second.

In order to avoid too great misunderstanding, I'd like to say a word about how I see diachronic causation in general. The kinds of ideas I'm interested in here—moral ideals, understandings of the human predicament, concepts of the self—for the most part exist in our lives through being embedded in practices. By 'practice', I mean something extremely vague and general: more or less any stable configuration of shared activity, whose shape is defined by a certain pattern of dos and don'ts, can be a practice for my purpose. The way we discipline our children, greet each other in the street, determine group decisions through voting in elections, and exchange things through markets are all practices. And there are practices at all levels of human social life: family, village, national politics, rituals of religious communities, and so on.

The basic relation is that ideas articulate practices as patterns of dos and don'ts. That is, the ideas frequently arise from attempts to formulate and bring to some conscious expression the underlying rationale of the patterns. I say this is the basic relation, not because it's the only one, but because it's the one through which others arise and can be understood. As articulations, ideas are in an important sense secondary to or based on patterns. A pattern can exist just in the dos and don'ts that people accept and mutually enforce, without there being (yet) an explicit rationale. And as children, we learn some of the most fundamental patterns at first just as such. The articulations come later.

There can of course be ideas without a corresponding pattern. I may be devising and propounding a utopian vision of the self-management of a perfect anarchist community, which is practised nowhere, and for all we know may never be. Our modern culture is full of such ideas which transcend existing reality. But this is a derivative phenomenon. Revolutionary projects can only be formulated in opposition to what exists. They are put forward as what ought to supersede the status quo. They imply, and make no sense without, some interpretation—in this case, generally derogatory—of what exists. That is what I meant by saying that the basic role of such ideas is as formulations of existing practices. If we articulate any rationale at all, it *must* involve an interpretation of current practice; it *may* also be projecting something new and untried.

The ways in which ideas can interweave with their practices are various. There can be a perfectly stable relation of mutual reinforcement, where the idea seems to articulate the underlying rationale of the dos and don'ts in an adequate and undistortive fashion; and then the idea can strengthen the pattern and keep it alive, while the experience of the pattern can constantly regenerate the idea.

But then it can come to appear to some people that the dominant ideas distort the practice and that perhaps as a consequence the practice itself is corrupt. They may demand rectification. From the standpoint of the conservatives, it will appear that the protesters are (at best) inventing a new practice. But however one describes it, the result of the struggle will be change, perhaps a split into two communities with separate practices—the case of Western Christendom in the sixteenth century.

Or it can be that the whole practice and its rationale come to seem repugnant, and there can be a demand for what is self-consciously seen as a transfer of allegiance to a new practice—as when whole Untouchable communities in India convert to Buddhism or Islam.

These are cases where the genesis of change can be identified with new ideas. But change can come about in other ways as well. Ideas and practices may come to be out of true with each other, because one or the other fails to reproduce itself properly. Some of the original rationale may be lost, just through drift or through the challenge of some new insight; or the practice may alter as it is inadequately handed down.

And above all, practices may be constrained or facilitated, may take on less or more space, for a whole host of reasons which are unconnected to their rationales. A given ritual practice may become terribly costly and demand big sacrifices which it didn't entail before. Or it may face rivals in a new situation. Or it may be greatly facilitated because of changed circumstances. It may gain or lose prestige, owing to a change in the social surroundings—say, a rise in social standing of the group which mainly practises it. And so on. All this will deeply affect the fate and the nature of the corresponding ideas.

It is clear that change can come about in both directions, as it were: through mutations and developments in the ideas, including new visions and insights, bringing about alterations, ruptures, reforms, revolutions in practices; and also through drift, change, constrictions or flourishings of practices, bringing about the alteration, flourishing, or decline of ideas. But even this is too abstract. It is better to say that in any concrete development in history, change is occurring both ways. The real skein of events is interwoven with threads running in both directions. A new revolutionary interpretation may arise partly because a practice is under threat, perhaps for reasons quite extraneous to the ideas. Or a given interpretation of things will gain force because the practice is flourishing, again for idea-extraneous reasons. But the resulting changes in outlook will have important consequences of their own. The skein of causes is inextricable.

The modern identity arose because changes in the self-understandings connected with a wide range of practices—religious, political, economic, familial, intellectual, artistic—converged and reinforced each other to produce it: the practices, for instance, of religious prayer and ritual, of spiritual discipline as a member of a Christian congregation, of self-scrutiny as one of the regenerate, of the politics of consent, of the family life of the companionate marriage, of the new child-rearing which develops from the eighteenth century, of artistic creation under the demands of originality, of the demarcation and defence of privacy, of markets and contracts, of voluntary associations, of the cultivation and display of sentiment, of the pursuit of scientific knowledge. Each of these, and others, has contributed something to the developing set of ideas about the subject and his or her moral predicament which I am examining in this book. There have been strains and oppositions between these practices and the ideas they vehicle, but they have helped to constitute a common space of understanding in which our current ideas of the self and the good have grown.

We very often can't fully understand these ideas if we think them in isolation from the practices. For instance, an important relation links the Lockean notion of "possessive individualism" I described earlier and the economic practices of capitalist, market society. But this relation mustn't be confused with a unidirectional causal one. It is just as important to note the way in which this self-understanding smoothed the way for an extension of market relations as it is to point to the way that the increased penetration of markets made it natural for people to see themselves this way. The causal arrow runs in both directions.

What is more, the balance between the two directions may change with time. In the case of some of the crucial idées-forces discussed here, the facilitation may be mainly from idea to economic practice in the early period, where the ideas found their original source in religious and moral life. This seems to be the case with possessive individualism, which emerges before the explosive development of market relations in the industrial revolution. But in the later phase, when some of the new ideas originating among the social elite became the common property of the whole society, the preponderant direction was often reversed. It is clear for instance that the forceful imposition of proletarian status on masses of ex-peasants who were chased off the land into the new centres of industrialization preceded and caused the acceptance of atomistic self-consciousness (frequently combated by new formulations of working-class solidarity)[15] by so many of their descendants today.

This is in fact merely one example of a general process by which certain practices of modernity have been imposed, often brutally, outside their heartlands. For some of them this seems to have been part of an irresistible dynamic. It is clear that the practices of technologically oriented science helped endow the nations where they developed with a cumulative technological advantage over others. This, combined with the consequences of the new emphasis on disciplined movement which I described earlier, gave European armies a marked and increasing military edge over non-Europeans from the seventeenth until about the mid-twentieth century. And this combined with the consequences of the economic practices we call capitalism allowed the European powers to establish a world hegemony for a time.

This has obviously had tremendous importance for the spread of these practices. This kind of success virtually enforces their generalization, since no society can stand against those who have such an edge. We are incapable of fully chronicling, let alone understanding, all the practices which have been forced to the wall in the rush to gain the military disciplines and technological-economic capacities which all societies need to survive. But obviously the "pay-off" of these practices has had a crucial effect on the development of both European and non-European societies, and the prestige of the self-understandings associated with them—as these have been interpreted—has had a fateful importance for the development of cultures.

All this, which would have to be a central part of any answer to the question of historical causation, won't figure in my analysis, except at the boundaries. I shall be concentrating on the interpretive question and trying to articulate the modern identity in its various phases. This discussion should be a warning to the reader not to mistake this study for a historical explanation. But it also has to serve as a warning to me not to lose from sight the context of practices in which this identity developed, and the powerful forces shaping them. Pressures so massive on the history of a civilization as those I have been describing have to be kept in mind even when they are not—rightly not—the focus of attention. I hope I will succeed in doing this in what follows.

PART III

---

*The Affirmation
of Ordinary Life*

13

"GOD LOVETH ADVERBS"

13.1

I want now to turn to a second major aspect of the modern identity. In Part II, I traced the development of a multifaceted notion of the self. It is a self defined by the powers of disengaged reason—with its associated ideals of self-responsible freedom and dignity—of self-exploration, and of personal commitment. These powers—at least the first two—requiring a radical reflexivity, are the basis for a certain conception of inwardness. But they still don't explain the full stretch of the modern idea of the inner: in particular, they can't explain our sense of "inner depths"—the master image of Conrad's novel is still outside our purview.[1]

To understand this, we have to look at another development, the rise of our modern notions of nature, and their roots in what I call the affirmation of ordinary life.

'Ordinary life' is a term of art I introduce[2] to designate those aspects of human life concerned with production and reproduction, that is, labour, the making of the things needed for life, and our life as sexual beings, including marriage and the family. When Aristotle spoke of the ends of political association being "life and the good life" *(zēn kai euzēn)*, this was the range of things he wanted to encompass in the first of these terms; basically they englobe what we need to do to continue and renew life.

For Aristotle the maintenance of these activities was to be distinguished from the pursuit of the good life. They are, of course, necessary to the good life, but they play an infrastructural role in relation to it. You can't pursue the good life without pursuing life. But an existence dedicated to this latter goal alone is not a fully human one. Slaves and animals are concerned exclusively with life. Aristotle argues in the *Politics*[3] that a mere association of families for economic and defence purposes is not a true polis, because it is designed only for this narrow purpose. The proper life for humans builds on this infrastructure a series of activities which are concerned with the good life: men deliberate about moral excellence, they contemplate the order of things;

of supreme importance for politics, they deliberate together about the common good, and decide how to shape and apply the laws.

Aristotle manages to combine in his 'good life' two of the activities which were most commonly adduced by later ethical traditions as outranking ordinary life: theoretical contemplation and the participation as a citizen in the polity. These were not unanimously favoured. Plato looked with a jaundiced eye on the second (at least in its normal form of competing for office). And the Stoics challenged both. But these authors still gave ordinary life a lesser status in the order of ends. For the Stoics, the sage should be *detached* from the fulfilment of his vital and sexual needs. These might indeed be "preferred" *(proēgmena)*, in the sense that when other things are equal they should be selected, but fundamentally their status was that of *"adiaphora"*, things ultimately indifferent. One must be detached from them in a way that one was not from wisdom and the whole order of things which the wise love. One gladly gives them up because one is following this order.

But the influential ideas of ethical hierarchy exalted the lives of contemplation and participation. We can see a manifestation of the first in the notion that philosophers should not busy themselves with the mere manipulation of things, and hence with the crafts. This was one source of resistance to the new experimental science which Bacon advocated. Scholarly humanism was imbued with this hierarchical notion, which was also linked to a distinction between the true sciences, which admitted of demonstration, and lower forms of knowledge, which could only hope to attain to the 'probable', in the sense the word had then, e.g., the forms of knowledge practised by alchemists, astrologers, miners, and some physicians.[4]

We see the second idea returning in early modern times with the various doctrines of civic humanism, first in Italy and later in northern Europe. Life as a mere householder is inferior to one which also involves participation as a citizen. There is a kind of freedom citizens enjoy which others are deprived of. And in most variants, too, great a striving for or possession of riches was felt to be a danger to the free life of the republic.[5] If the means of mere life bulk too big, they endanger the good life.

The citizen ethic was in some ways analogous to, and could at times even partially fuse with, the aristocratic ethic of honour, whose origins lay in the life of warrior castes (as indeed the ancient citizenship ideals did also). This found a variety of expressions, e.g., the ideal of 'corteisie' in mediaeval French Romance[6] and, as I discussed earlier, the ethic of 'generosity' in the seventeenth-century sense. It involved a strong sense of hierarchy, in which the life of the warrior or ruler, which turned on honour or glory, was incommensurable to that of men of lesser rank, concerned only with life.[7] Willingness to risk life was the constitutive quality of the man of honour. And it was frequently thought that a too great concern with acquisition was incompatible with this higher life. In some societies, engaging in trade was considered a derogation of aristocratic status.

The transition I am talking about here is one which upsets these hierarchies, which displaces the locus of the good life from some special range of higher activities and places it within 'life' itself. The full human life is now defined in terms of labour and production, on one hand, and marriage and family life, on the other. At the same time, the previous 'higher' activities come under vigorous criticism.

Under the impact of the scientific revolution, the ideal of *theōria*, of grasping the order of the cosmos through contemplation, came to be seen as being vain and misguided, as a presumptuous attempt to escape the hard work of detailed discovery. Francis Bacon constantly hammers home the point that the traditional sciences have aimed at discovering some satisfying overall order in things, rather than being concerned to see how things function: "I find that even those who have sought knowledge for itself, and not for benefit and ostentation, or any practical enablements in the course of life, have nevertheless propounded to themselves a wrong mark—namely, satisfaction (which men call Truth) and not operation".[8]

The consequence has been that they have been without fruit, not just in the sense that they have yielded no useful, applicable technology but also in that the knowledge they offer is specious; for technological gain is the criterion of genuine knowledge.

> Of all the signs there is none more certain or more noble than that taken from fruits. For fruits and works are as it were sponsors and sureties for the truth of philosophies. Now, from all these systems of the Greeks and their ramifications through particular sciences, there can hardly after the lapse of so many years be adduced a single experiment which tends to relieve and benefit the condition of man, and which can in truth be referred to the speculations and theories of philosophy.[9]

To relieve the condition of man: this is the goal. Science is not a higher activity which ordinary life should subserve; on the contrary, science should benefit ordinary life. Not to make this the goal is not only a moral failing, a lack of charity, but also and inextricably an epistemological failing. Bacon has no doubt that the root of this momentous error is pride. The old science amounts to "prescribing laws to nature": "We want to have all things as suits our fatuity, not as fits the Divine Wisdom, not as they are found in nature. We impose the seal of our image on the creatures and works of God, we do not diligently seek to discover the seal of God on things".[10]

The Baconian revolution involved a transvaluation of values, which is also the reversal of a previous hierarchy. What was previously stigmatized as lower is now exalted as the standard, and the previously higher is convicted of presumption and vanity. And this involved a revaluation of professions as well. The lowly artisan and artificer turn out to have contributed more to the advance of science than the leisured philosopher.[11]

And indeed, an inherent bent towards social levelling is implicit in the affirmation of ordinary life. The centre of the good life lies now in something which everyone can have a part in, rather than in ranges of activity which only a leisured few can do justice to. The scope of this social reversal can be better measured if we look at the critique launched against the other main variant of the traditional hierarchical view, the honour ethic, which had its original roots in the citizen life. This was closely connected with the social stratification of the age and particularly with the distinction between aristocrats and commoners, and so the challenge turns out to have an important social dimension. But this was not immediately evident.

The ethic of honour and glory, after receiving one of its most inspiring expressions in the work of Corneille, is subjected to a withering critique in the seventeenth century. Its goals are denounced as vainglory and vanity, as the fruits of an almost childish presumption. We find this with Hobbes as well as with Pascal, La Rochefoucauld, and Molière. But the negative arguments in these writers are not new. Plato himself was suspicious of the honour ethic, as concerned with mere appearances. The Stoics rejected it; and it was denounced by Augustine as the exaltation of the desire for power, the *libido dominandi*, which was one of a trinity of disordered passions, along with sexual desire and the craving for gain. A writer like Pascal was really reformulating the uncompromising Augustinian critique.[12]

But what eventually gives this critique its historical significance as an engine of social change is the new promotion of ordinary life. In the latter part of the century, the critique is taken up and becomes a commonplace of a new ideal of life, in which sober and disciplined production was given the central place, and the search for honour condemned as fractious and undisciplined self-indulgence, gratuitously endangering the really valuable things in life. A new model of civility emerges in the eighteenth century, in which the life of commerce and acquisition gains an unprecedentedly positive place.

As Albert Hirschman shows,[13] a conception arose of "le doux commerce" as a property of civilized nations. In contrast to the aristocratic search for military glory, which was seen as wildly destructive and as frequently turning to the piratical quest for plunder, commerce is a constructive and civilizing force, binding men together in peace and forming the basis of "polished" mores. The ethic of glory is confronted here with a fully articulated alternative view, of social order, political stability, and the good life.[14]

This "bourgeois" ethic has obvious levelling consequences, and no one can be blind to the tremendous role it has played in constituting modern liberal society, through the founding revolutions of the eighteenth century and beyond, with their ideals of equality, their sense of universal right, their work ethic, and their exaltation of sexual love and the family. What I have been calling the affirmation of ordinary life is another massive feature of the modern identity, and not only in its "bourgeois" form: the main strands of revolutionary thought have also exalted man as producer, one who finds his highest dignity in labour and the transformation of nature in the service of life. The Marxist theory is the best known but not the only case in point.

The transition I have been talking about is easy to identify negatively, in terms of the ethics it (partly) displaced. But for my purposes here, it is important to understand the positive new valuation it put on ordinary life. The displaced traditional views were connected with conceptions of moral sources. The idea that our highest activity was contemplation was contingent on a view of the world order as structured by the Good; the ethic of honour saw the love of fame and immortality as the source of great deeds and exemplary courage. Both could offer a positive account of what made their favoured version of the good life really a higher form of existence for man. What was the corresponding account for the various ethics of ordinary life?

To see this aright we have to return to a theological point of origin. The affirmation of ordinary life finds its origin in Judaeo-Christian spirituality, and the particular impetus it receives in the modern era comes first of all from the Reformation. One of the central points common to all Reformers was their rejection of mediation. The mediaeval church as they understood it, a corporate body in which some, more dedicated, members could win merit and salvation for others who were less so, was anathema to them. There could be no such thing as more devoted or less devoted Christians: the personal commitment must be total or it was worthless.

The rejection of mediation was closely connected to their rejection of the mediaeval understanding of the sacred. This flowed from the most fundamental principle of the Reformers, perhaps even more basic than salvation by faith alone, which was that salvation was exclusively the work of God. Fallen man was utterly helpless and could do nothing by himself. The point of harping on the helplessness and depravity of mankind was to throw into the starkest relief the power and mercy of God, who could bring about a salvation which was utterly beyond human power and, what is more, still wanted to rescue his unworthy creature beyond all considerations of justice. The powerful idea which moved those who threw themselves into the successive Protestant movements over three centuries (and even today in some revival movements) was that of an unaccountable salvation by an almighty and merciful God, against all rational human hope and utterly disregarding our just deserts. Those who deeply embraced the new faith were moved by an overwhelming sense of awe and gratitude, and in certain circumstances this became a tremendously potent motive force behind revolutionary change.

What this saving action seemed to call for was first and foremost our recognition, our acknowledgement: both of the fact of salvation and of its being exclusively God's gift. Humans can do nothing to earn or bring about this gift, so fundamentally all they can do is acknowledge it. This is what it is to have faith. In the logic of Reformed theology, even this minimal participation, even faith, is a gift of God; but it is the kind of participation which, unlike the good works of Catholic piety, has built in a recognition of our own nullity, of our own zero contribution to God's saving action.

This faith seemed to require an outright rejection of the Catholic understanding of the sacred, and hence also of the church and its mediating role. The Catholic theology of the sacraments, particularly the sacrament of the altar, whereby a power has been given to the church to bring about communion between God and humans, even at the hands of sinful priests, was an abomination. The issue was not even the sinfulness of the priests; this just dramatized the real point, which was the idea that God's response was in a sense imprisoned, tied to an action which it was in men's power to perform: the Mass. This whole theology could only be a presumptuous and blasphemous refusal to acknowledge the sole and entire contribution of God to our salvation. It was an arrogant attempt to fetter God's unlimited sovereignty. It was thus quite incompatible with what Protestants defined as faith.

Along with the Mass went the whole notion of the sacred in mediaeval Catholicism, the notion that there are special places or times or actions where the power of God is more intensely present and can be approached by humans. Therefore Protestant (particularly Calvinist) churches swept away pilgrimages, veneration of relics, visits to holy places, and a vast panorama of traditional Catholic rituals and pieties. And along with the sacred went the mediaeval Catholic understanding of the church as the locus and vehicle of the sacred. As a consequence of this, in turn, the central mediating role of the church ceased to have any meaning.

If the church is the locus and vehicle of the sacred, then we are brought closer to God by the very fact of belonging and participating in its sacramental life. Grace can come to us mediately through the church, and we can mediate grace to each other, as the lives of the saints enrich the common life on which we all draw. Once the sacred is rejected, then this kind of mediation is also. Each person stands alone in relation to God: his or her fate—salvation or damnation—is separately decided.

The rejection of the sacred and of mediation together led to an enhanced status for (what had formerly been described as) profane life. This came out in the repudiation of the special monastic vocations which had been an integral part of mediaeval Catholicism. The celibate life under vows had been seen both by Protestants and by their Catholic opponents as part of the economy of the sacred in the Catholic church. (That this was a theological misperception doesn't detract from its sociological truth.) This was partly because of the connection between priesthood and celibacy, and partly because of the role of religious in an economy of mutual mediation: monks and nuns prayed for everyone, just as the laity worked, fought, and governed for the whole. Both traditional Catholic and Protestant reformers shared the (mistaken) view these vocations supposed a hierarchy of nearness to the sacred, with the religious life being higher/closer than the secular. There was an intense consciousness of the dependence of laypeople on the life of prayer and renunciation of religious through the mutual mediation of the church, but the reciprocal dependence was lost sight of. The result was a lesser spiritual status for lay life, particularly that of productive labour and the family.

In rejecting the sacred and the idea of mediation Protestants also rejected this hierarchy, not only because its foundation was repudiated as incompatible with faith but also because it went against the nature of religious commitment as they understood it. Where a mediated salvation is no longer possible, the personal commitment of the believer becomes all important. Salvation by faith thus not only reflected a theological proposition about the inanity of human works but also reflected the new sense of the crucial importance of personal commitment. One no longer belonged to the saved, to the people of God, by one's connection to a wider order sustaining a sacramental life, but by one's wholehearted personal adhesion.

The very institution of monastic special vocations seemed to flout both the unmediated nature and the wholeheartedness of the Christian commitment. On the degenerate, hierarchical understanding of the monastic life then prevalent, I as a layman am as it were only half-involved in my salvation: both because I need to draw on the merits of those who are more fully dedicated to the Christian life, through the mediation of the church, and because in accepting this lower level of dedication, I am settling for less than a full commitment to the faith. I am a passenger in the ecclesial ship on its journey to God. But for Protestantism, there can be no passengers. This is because there is no ship in the Catholic sense, no common movement carrying humans to salvation. Each believer rows his or her own boat.

Thus by the same movement through which the Protestant churches rejected a special order of priesthood in favour of the doctrine of the priesthood of all believers, they also rejected the special vocation to the monastic life and affirmed the spiritual value of lay life. By denying any special form of life as a privileged locus of the sacred, they were denying the very distinction between sacred and profane and hence affirming their interpenetration. The denial of a special status to the monk was also an affirmation of ordinary life as more than profane, as itself hallowed and in no way second class. The institution of the monastic life was seen as a slur on the spiritual standing of productive labour and family life, their stigmatization as zones of spiritual underdevelopment. The repudiation of monasticism was a reaffirmation of lay life as a central locus for the fulfilment of God's purpose. Luther marks their break in his own life by ceasing to be such a monk and by marrying a former nun.

What is important for my purpose is this positive side, the affirmation that the fulness of Christian existence was to be found within the activities of this life, in one's calling and in marriage and the family. The entire modern development of the affirmation of ordinary life was, I believe, foreshadowed and initiated, in all its facets, in the spirituality of the Reformers. This goes as much for the positive evaluation of production and reproduction as for the anti-hierarchical consequences of the rejection of sacramental authority and higher vocations.

13.2

The foundation for this new radical revaluation of ordinary life was, of course, one of the most fundamental insights of the Jewish-Christian-Islamic religious tradition, that God as creator himself affirms life and being, expressed in the very first chapter of Genesis in the repeated phrase: "and God saw that it was good". Life in a calling could be a fully Christian life, because it could be seen as participating in this affirmation of God's. In this sense, of course, the Reformers were only drawing the radical consequences from a very old theme in Christendom. It was after all the monks themselves who had pioneered the notion of living the life of prayer in work.

But the specificity of this Judaeo-Christian affirmation of life has often been lost from view. In particular, the contrast with ancient pagan philosophy tends to be forgotten. Christianity, particularly in its more ascetic variants, appears a continuation of Stoicism by other means, or (as Nietzsche sometimes says) a prolongation of Platonism. But for all the strong resemblances to Stoicism—for instance, in its universalism, its notion of providence, its exalting self-abnegation—there is a great gulf. In fact, the meaning of self-abnegation is radically different. The Stoic sage is willing to give up some "preferred" thing, e.g., health, freedom, or life, because he sees it genuinely as without value since only the whole order of events which, as it happens, includes its negation or loss, is of value. The Christian martyr, in giving up health, freedom, or life, doesn't declare them to be of no value. On the contrary, the act would lose its sense if they were not of great worth. To say that greater love hath no man than this, that a man give up his life for his friends, implies that life is a great good. The sentence would lose its point in reference to someone who renounced life from a sense of detachment; it presupposes he's *giving up* something.

Central to the Judaeo-Christian notion of martyrdom is that one gives up a good in order to follow God. What God is engaged in is the hallowing of life. God first called Israel to be a "holy nation" (Exodus 19:6). But the hallowing of life is not antithetical to its fulness. On the contrary. Hence the powerful sense of loss at the heart of martyrdom. It only becomes necessary because of sin and disorder in the world: because, e.g., a Nebuchadnezzar or an Antiochus Epiphanes requires that Israelites worship idols or otherwise violate the Torah. Or, to turn to the paradigm Christian case, that Christ's teaching led to his crucifixion was a consequence of evil in the world, of the darkness not comprehending the light. In the restored order that God is conferring, good doesn't need to be sacrificed for good. The eschatological promise in both Judaism and Christianity is that God will restore the integrity of the good.

This is, of course, what makes the death story of Jesus so different from that of Socrates, however much they have been put in parallel. Socrates tries to prove to his friends that he is losing nothing of value, that he is gaining a great good. In his last request to Crito, to pay his debt of a cock to Asclepius,[15] he seems to imply that life is an illness of which death is the cure (Asclepius being the god of healing whom one rewards for cures). Socrates is serenely untroubled. Jesus suffers agony of soul in the garden, and is driven to despair on the cross, when he cries, "Why hast thou forsaken me?" At no point in the Passion is he serene and untroubled.

The great difference between Stoic and Christian renunciation is this: for the Stoic, what is renounced is, if rightly renounced, ipso facto not part of the good. For the Christian, what is renounced is thereby affirmed as good—both in the sense that the renunciation would lose its meaning if the thing were indifferent and in the sense that the renunciation is in furtherance of God's will, which precisely affirms the goodness of the kinds of things renounced: health, feedom, life. Paradoxically, Christian renunciation is an affirmation of the goodness of what is renounced. For the Stoic, the loss of health, freedom, life does not affect the integrity of the good. On the contrary, the loss is part of a whole which is integrally good and couldn't be changed without making it less so. Stoics are drawn to images like that of the shadow which is needed to set off the brilliance of the light. In the Christian perspective, however, the loss is a breach in the integrity of the good. That is why Christianity requires an eschatological perspective of the restoral of that integrity, even though this has been variously understood.

The contrast has tended to be lost from view. This is because the Christian picture didn't just displace the ancient one but came to enter a partnership, which led to a fusion, or rather a number of alternative fusions, of which the

Augustinian and Thomistic are the two most famous and influential in Western Christendom. There were strong reasons supporting a convergence. One of the most powerful was Plato's idea of the Good, a connection which Augustine clinched for Western mediaeval culture. Plato also offered a justification for seeing all being as good, and this helped Augustine to go beyond his Manichaean phase.

The reading of the goodness of things in terms of Plato's order of Ideas, which we owe to the Greek fathers as well as to Augustine, was one of the most influential and important syntheses which helped to form Western civilization—analogous to, and indeed in its later stages influenced by, similar fusions made by Islamic and Jewish thinkers. It was facilitated by Plato's creation story in the *Timaeus,* and it issues in the powerful and widely recurring idea of creatures as the signs of God, embodiments of his Ideas. Through it the notion of an ontic logos was welded for centuries into the very centre of Christian theology, so that for many people in modern times the challenge to this notion has seemed indistinguishable from atheism.

But naturally this synthesis has also been the locus of tensions, disputes, and ultimately painful ruptures in Christian civilization. Nominalists and later Reformers protested against the notion of a cosmic order, as did great numbers of others, concerned to defend above all God's sovereignty as creator and preserver. A basically Stoic theodicy, explaining away suffering and loss as a necessary and integral part of a good order, is always creeping back, with Leibniz, for example, and is always being vigorously combated, as by Kant and even more sharply by Kierkegaard.

The Pauline opposition of spirit and flesh is repeatedly being pulled out of its hinges and aligned with the Platonic-derived opposition between the immaterial and the bodily. Augustine is one of the principal offenders in this respect, but lots of others have made similar elisions on their own, most notably Descartes and the whole band of rationalists and empiricists influenced by him. And just as repeatedly this elision has been protested against. We shall read an example shortly from the Puritan preacher William Perkins.

The Platonic reading of the spirit/flesh opposition also justifies a certain notion of hierarchy, and this along with pre-Christian notions of renunciation helps to credit a view of ascetic vocations as "higher". This is the distorted notion of the monastic vocation, as the fully Christian life in contrast to the lay state as a half effort, against which the Reformers rebelled. The monastic vocation was perceived by them as a slur on the lay life, while its meaning in Christian terms ought to have been an affirmation of its value. Obviously, the misperception was not exclusively, or even primarily, on the part of the Reformers. Monasticism itself was in a bad way, as other critics, e.g., Erasmus, testify.

The Protestant Reformation involved among other things a challenge to this synthesis. As a result, certain of the original potentialities of Christian faith, which tended to be neutralized in the amalgam with ancient metaphysics and morals, were allowed to develop. The crucial potentiality here was that of conceving the hallowing of life not as something which takes place only at the limits, as it were, but as a change which can penetrate the full extent of mundane life. Perhaps the first important realization of this potentiality in the broader tradition was in Rabbinic Judaism, at the very beginning of the present era, in the Pharasaic idea of a way of living the law which thoroughly permeated the details of everyday life.[16] But the Protestant Reformation brought about an extension of this form of spirituality which was unprecedented in Christendom.

Once this potentiality was realized, it took on a life of its own. Its influence, in other words, was felt beyond the boundaries of Protestant Europe and not necessarily most strongly within these boundaries. It was felt in Catholic countries, and then later also in secularized variants. Its impact was the greater in that it dovetailed nicely with the anti-hierarchical side of the gospel message. The integral sanctification of ordinary life couldn't consist with notions of hierarchy, at first of vocation and later even of social caste. The gospel notion that the orders of this world, the spiritual as much as the temporal, are reversed in the kingdom of God, that the foolishness of the children of God is stronger than the wisdom of the wise, had its effect in discrediting earlier notions of superiority and accrediting the new spiritual status of the everyday.

For ordinary life to encompass this spiritual purpose, it had of course to be led in the light of God's ends, ultimately to the glory of God. This meant, of course, that one fulfil God's intentions for life, avoiding sin, debauchery, excesses of all sorts. But it also meant that one live it for God. Sin has made humans deviate from this ultimate purpose.

God placed mankind over creation and made the things of the world for human use. But humans are there in turn to serve and glorify God, and so their use of things should serve this final goal. The consequence of sin is that humans come to be concerned with these things not for God's sake but for themselves. They come to desire them as ends and no longer simply as instruments for God's purposes. And this upsets the whole order of things. Humans were meant to bring the rest of creation to God. But when they turn to make creatures themselves the end, then both mankind and the creatures are thrown out of their proper relation to the Creator.

This basically Augustinian idea was central to Puritan thought.

Man had originally an Empire and Dominion over these creatures here below ... But sin hath inverted this Order, and brought confusion upon earth. Man is dethroned, and become a servant and slave to those things that are made to serve him, and he puts those things in his heart, that God hath put under his feet.[17]

This disorders the creation: "Man was the mean betwixt God and the Creature to convey all good with all the constancy of it, and therefore when Man breaks, Heaven and Earth breaks all asunder, the Conduit being cracked and displaced there can be no conveyance from the Fountain".[18] The regeneration which comes with grace restores the right order. Mankind turns from things back to God. But this most emphatically doesn't mean a life of asceticism in the traditional sense. Humans are meant to enjoy the things which God has put there for them—only the enjoyment must partake of a certain spirit. We must enjoy things while remaining detached from them. We should be seeking God's glory in our "eating and drinking, sleeping and recreating".[19]

So to take their proper place in God's order, humans had to avoid two opposite deviations. They must spurn the monkish error of renouncing the things of this world—possessions, marriage—for this amounts to scorning God's gifts, which they should instead be bringing back to him through worshipful use. "God hath given us Temporals to enjoy ... We should therefore suck the sweet of them, and so slack our Thirst with them, as not to be Insatiably craving after more".[20] Moreover, asceticism is not only a deviation from God's plan but the fruit of pride, born of the presumption which makes us think that we can contribute to our regeneration, which is typical of Papism.[21]

The other error was to become absorbed in things, take them for our end, which happens "when we refer not all to the glory of God, and our own, and other's eternal good, and welfare".[22] It was not the use of things which brought evil, Puritan preachers constantly repeated, but our deviant purpose in using them: "Yet wee must know it is not the *World* simply that draws our heart from God and goodnesse, but the *love* of the world".[23] Or to put the same point in another way, we should love the things of this world, but our love should as it were pass through them to their creator. "Hee doth not forbid mercy or love to Beasts or Creatures, but hee would not have your love terminated in them".[24] Where the world becomes master, then everything goes awry: "Where the world hath got possession in the heart, it makes us false to God, and false to man, it makes us unfaithfull in our callings, and false to Religion it selfe. Labour therefore to have the world in its owne place, under thy feet . . . Labour . . . to know the world that thou maiest detest it".[25] We must in one sense love the world, while in another sense detesting it. This is the essence of what Weber called the Puritan's "innerworldly asceticism".[26] The answer to the absorption in things which is the result of sin is not renunciation but a certain kind of use, one which is detached from things and focussed on God. It is a caring and not caring, whose paradoxical nature comes out in the Puritan notion that we should use the world with "weaned affections". Use things, "but be not wedded to them, but so weaned from them, that you may use them, as if you used them not".[27]

And this is not a second-best solution, inferior to a straight renunciation: the kind of thing that St. Paul seems to hint at when he says, 'It is better to marry than to burn", and "I say therefore to the unmarried, . . . 'It is good for them if they abide even as I' " (1 Corinthians 7:8–9). Rather, using the world with weaned affections is the only way of restoring the right order. The asceticism must be within the practices of ordinary life.

Thus ordinary life is to be hallowed. But this doesn't come about in the manner of the Catholic tradition, by connecting it to the sacramental life of the church; rather it comes about within this life itself, which has to be lived in a way which is both earnest and detached. Marriage and a calling are not optional extras; they are the substance of life, and we should throw ourselves into them purposefully. But all the while our hearts should be elsewhere.

> There is another combination of vertues strangely mixed in every lively holy Christian, And that is, Diligence in worldly businesses, and yet deadnesse to the world; such a mystery as none can read, but they that know it. For a man to [take] all opportunities to be doing something, early and late, and loseth no opportunity, go any way and bestir himselfe for profit, this will he doe most diligently in his calling: And yet bee a man dead-hearted to the world . . . though hee labour most diligently in his calling, yet his heart is not set upon these things.[28]

And so we can appreciate the full seriousness of the Puritan idea of the calling. In addition to the general calling to be a believing Christian, everyone had a particular calling, the specific form of labour to which God summoned him or her. Whereas in Catholic cultures, the term 'vocation' usually arises in connection with the priesthood or monastic life, the meanest employment was a calling for the Puritans, provided it was useful to mankind and imputed to use by God. In this sense, all callings were equal, whatever their place in the social hierarchy, or in what we think of as the hierarchy of human capacities. As John Dod says:

> Whatsoever our callings be, we serve the Lord Christ in them . . . Though your worke be base, yet it is not a base thing to serve such a master in it. They are the most worthy servants, whatsoever their imploiment bee, that do with most conscionable, and dutifull hearts and minds, serve the Lord, where hee hath placed them, in those works, which hee hath allotted unto them.[29]

Joseph Hall makes substantially the same point:

The homeliest service that we doe in an honest calling, though it be but to plow, or digge, if done in obedience, and conscience of God's Commandement, is crowned with an ample reward; whereas the best workes for their kinde (preaching, praying, offering Evangelicall sacrifices) if without respect of God's injunction and glory, are loaded with curses. God loveth adverbs; and cares not how good, but how well.[30]

Hall captures the essence of the transvaluation implicit in affirming the ordinary. The highest life can no longer be defined by an exalted *kind* of activity; it all turns on the *spirit* in which one lives whatever one lives, even the most mundane existence.

Perkins takes on the hierarchical preconceptions of his audience with a shocking directness:

Now if we compare worke to worke, there is a difference betwixt washing of dishes, and preaching of the word of God: but as touching to please God none at all . . . As the Scriptures call him carnall which is not renewed by the spirit and borne again in Christs flesh, and all his workes likewise . . . whatsoever he doth, though they seem spirituall and after the law of God never so much. So contrariwise he is spirituall which is renewed in Christ, and all his workes which spring from faith seeme they never so grosse . . . yea deedes of matrimonie are pure and spirituall . . . and whatsoever is done within the lawes of God though it be wrought by the body, as the wipings of shoes and such like, howsoever grosse they appeare outwardly, yet are they sanctified.[31]

Perkins clearly meant to shock in this passage, and in doing so to drive home the doctrine of the sanctification of the ordinary.

Thus labour in a calling was a spiritually serious business, something we should give ourselves to not just intermittently but earnestly and unremittingly. Puritans exhorted their hearers to shun idleness. This was partly because it bred temptation. "A heart not exercised in some honest labour works trouble out of itself".[32] "An idle man's brain becometh quickly the shop of the devil".[33] But this was not the only reason. Or rather, this was the negative side of a positive reason, which was that it was largely through such work that sanctification took place.

For Robert Sanderson, the gifts of God to each one of us are the manifestations of his spirit in us. They impose the duty to use them.

This manifestation of the Spirit . . . imposeth on every man the necessity of a Calling . . . O then up and be doing: Why stand ye all the day Idle? . . . in the Church, he that cannot style himself by any other name than a Christian, doth indeed but usurp that too. If thou sayest thou art of the body: I demand then, what is thy office in the Body? . . . If thou hast a Gift get a calling.[34]

But all this business would be spiritually of no avail, if the intention were wrong. The aim must be to serve God. What did this mean concretely? Negatively, it meant that one not engage in work primarily for some other, merely self-related, purpose. "They profane their lives and callings that imploy them to get honours, pleasures, profites, worldly commodities etc. for thus we live to another end then God hath appointed, and thus we serve ourselves, and consequently, neither God, nor man".[35] As Hall puts it,

> These businesses of his Calling the Christian follows with a willing and contented industry, not as forced to it by the necessity of humane Laws, or as urged by the law of necessity, out of the . . . fear of want; nor yet contrarily, out of an eager desire of enriching himself in his estate, but in a conscionable obedience to that God who hath made man to labour as the sparks to fly upward.[36]

The concomitant of this was that we enjoy the fruits of our labour only with moderation, conscious that we need these fruits to live and continue God's work, but at no point allowing them to take on importance for themselves, to go beyond the instrumental significance which God has appointed for them.

Positively, it meant that we see the purpose of our lives as "to serve God in the serving of men in the works of our callings".[37] The middle phrase in this involved formula reminds us that a central feature of any valid calling was that it be of benefit to humans. Perkins's definition of the calling was "a certaine kind of life, ordained and imposed on man by God, for *the common good*".[38] The theological background to this doctrine, as we saw, was that the creator intends the preservation of the creature. Humans serve God's purposes in taking the appointed means to preserve themselves in being. This doesn't mean that we are called upon to preserve others at our own expense; there is no question of renunciation. Rather we are called upon to serve both ourselves and others as being equally humans and God's creatures.

And beyond this, our work must be the occasion of our dedicating ourselves more fully to God. Perkins insists that both the general and the particular callings "must be joyned, as body and soul are joyned in a living man".[39] For Robert Bolton, the Christian should "ever go about the affaires of his Calling with a heavenly mind, seasoned, and sanctified with habitual prayer . . . pregnant with heavenly matter and meditation".[40]

We see here the basis for one strand of Weber's thesis about Protestantism as the nurturing ground of capitalism. Weber thought that the Puritan notion of the calling helped to foster a way of life focussed on disciplined and rationalized and regular work, coupled with frugal habits of consumption, and that this form of life greatly facilitated the implantation of industrial capitalism. There may be some quarrel on the latter half of this thesis, that is, concerning the degree to which this new work culture was widespread among capitalists and their workers, or whether it was or was not essential to capitalism's development. But the first half of the claim seems well founded. A spiritual outlook which stressed the necessity of continuous disciplined work, work which should be of benefit to people and hence ought to be efficacious, and which encouraged sobriety and restraint in the enjoyment of its fruits surely must be recognized as one of the formative influences of the work ethic of modern capitalist culture, at least in the Anglo-Saxon world.

The Puritan idea of the sanctification of ordinary life had analogous consequences for their understanding of marriage. On one hand, this took on new spiritual significance and value for its own sake; on the other, it too must never become an end in itself, but serve the glory of God.

As to the first point, the rehabilitation of married life starts with the first Reformers, and is part of their rejection of monasticism. I have already mentioned Luther's marriage to a former nun. In his prayer book of 1549, Archbishop Cranmer adds a third reason to the two traditional ones for marriage, viz., the avoidance of fornication and the procreation of legitimate children. The new one is the "mutual society, help and comfort, that the one ought to have of the other, both in prosperity and adversity".[41]

With Puritanism this developed into an emphasis on the intrinsic spiritual value of the marriage relationship, and of the love and companionship which it involved. It was God's will that husband and wife should love one another. Benjamin Wadsworth, an American divine, holds that spouses "should endeavour to have their affections really, cordially and closely knit, to each other". Otherwise God's law is broken. For "the indisputable Authority, the plain Command of the Great God, requires Husbands and Wives, to have and manifest very great affection, love and kindness to one another".[42] This new sense of the sanctification of married love even led to some extravagant formulations, such as the declaration of Jeremy Taylor that "the marital love is a thing pure as light, sacred as a temple, lasting as the world".[43]

But at the same time, this love must not be merely centred on itself; it cannot be at the expense of our love of God. When we take too much pleasure in any creature, "where we exceedingly delight in Husbands, Wives, Children," John Cotton warned, it "much benumbs and dims the light of the Spirit". Man and wife forget their maker when they are "so transported with affection" that they aim "at no higher end than marriage itself". What is required is that "such as have wives look at them not for their own ends, but to be better fitted for Gods service, and bring them nearer to God".[44] And so we must also moderate our affections. We should constantly remember that marriage ceases at death.

It should be obvious that this aspect of Puritan belief has also been an important influence on the development of modern culture. It contributed to a central feature of this culture, which we see in the growth of a new ideal of companionate marriage in the later seventeenth century in England and America, which in turn is ancestral to our whole contemporary understanding of marriage and sexual love. I will return to this below.

13.3

I have been discussing the Puritan strand of Protestantism, in England and America. My reason for doing this is that these churches developed a peculiarly strong and radical version of what I have been calling the affirmation of ordinary life, and that this in turn has generated one of the central ideas of modern culture, an idea which was given a terse formulation by the greatest of Puritan poets:

> To know
> That which before us lies in daily life
> Is the prime wisdom.[45]

But there were obviously other strands of Protestantism, such as the different Continental Calvinist churches and, even more distantly, the Lutherans, not to speak of German Anabaptists, which either did not develop the same doctrine of the calling and marriage or did so with a somewhat different emphasis or intensity.

I by no means want to imply that the Calvinist was the only direction one could go on the basis of the fundamental principles of the Reformation: that salvific action is solely of God, that justification is by faith, and that a wholehearted personal commitment is called for. Nor do I mean to say that within Calvinism, Anglo-Saxon Puritanism was the only logical development. On the contrary, there was something peculiar to Calvinists, and more particiularly to Puritans; and it is worthwhile bringing this out, because it too has had a powerful impact on modern culture.

Calvinism is marked out by a militant activism, a drive to reorganize the church and the world. This is its striking difference from Lutheranism. It is just as valid a response to the central doctrine of justification by faith, and the commitment that this calls for, to consider external forms of lesser moment and to see the crucial issue as one concerning the soul's relation to God. The rejection of the Catholic sacred can lead to a relativization of outer ceremony in favour of inner commitment. There are many branch lines which can be travelled on this route, and some of them lead to antinomianism, to religious tolerance and latitudinarianism, or to doctrines of inner light. Some of these radical theories surface again within the English Puritan tradition, to the dismay of orthodox Calvinists. But in a moderate form, this spirit enabled the established Lutheran churches to accept without demur a wide variety of church orders, both episcopal and not, and to retain much of the traditional Catholic ceremonial.

The route travelled by Calvinism was quite different. Everywhere it insisted on reorganizing the church along lines imperatively dictated by the new theology; these lines, moreover, were very much the same across international boundaries, until the big battles within English Puritanism in the seventeenth century. And it aspired generally to more, to a far-reaching regulation of the conduct of those who lived under church discipline. Calvinist movements aspired to build a new, proper order of things.

Commentators have often felt it a paradox that a church which so firmly believed in salvation by faith and predestination generated such tremendous revolutionary activism, as though a belief in predestination ought logically to produce only a fatalistic quietism. But Calvinist activism is not really paradoxical or even hard to understand. It would indeed be paradoxical if activism were meant to *bring about* the salvation of those whose lives were thus reordered. But that would be an absurd and blasphemous aim.

As Calvin writes in his commentary on the Epistle to the Romans, the duty of a Christian pastor is "by bringing men into the obedience of the Gospel, to offer them as it were in sacrifice unto God". It is not "as papists have hitherto proudly bragged, by the offering up of Christ to reconcile men unto God".[46] In other words, while humans can do nothing to bring about reconciliation, the reconciled person feels the imperative need to repair the disorder of things, to put them right again in God's plan. His desire and effort in this direction are only the fruit of God's reconciling action in him; they flow from his regeneration. This is indeed what properly results from this regeneration. To the Calvinist, it seemed self-evident that the properly regenerate person would above all be appalled at the offence done to God in a sinful, disordered world; and that therefore one of his foremost aims would be to put this right, to clean up the human mess or at least to mitigate the tremendous continuing insult done to God.

That is why there is no contradiction in a Calvinist church order seeking to control the behaviour even of the unregenerate. If the aim were to effect their salvation, this would of course be senseless. Nothing can save those foreknown to damnation. But this is not the goal. The purpose is rather to combat a disorder which continuously stinks in God's nostrils.

This is the source of that tremendous revolutionary energy, which ended up fomenting rebellion or civil disorder in a number of European states, which unleased a civil war in England, and which issued in the judicial execution of a king and plans for a new ecclesial and political order, not to speak of its consequences in the American colonies.

Michael Walzer is surely right in arguing that one of the driving motives in the specifically Calvinist and especially Puritan brand of reformation was horror at disorder: at a social disorder, in which undisciplined gentry and the unemployed and rootless poor, the underclass of rogues, beggars, and vagabonds, pose a constant threat to social peace; at personal disorder, in which licentious desires and the hold of intemperate practices make impossible all discipline and steadiness of life; and at the connection between the two disorders and the way they feed on each other.

What was needed was personal discipline first, individuals capable of controlling themselves and taking responsibility for their lives; and then a social order based on such people. This gives an additional reason why continuous work in a calling was essential. Those so engaged have "settled courses"; they are mutually reliable. They can form the basis of a stable social order.[47] And moreover, the social order formed by such individuals is more and more seen as based properly on contract. For it is an order of those who have taken on a discipline by personal commitment and who have chosen their walk of life in the same way. It is an order of those who rule themselves in their own personal lives. More and more, freely agreed contract is seen as the only proper bond between such people.

Here is another, well-documented place where Puritanism plays a foundational role in modern culture. But the initial thrust was not at all towards democracy, but rather to a kind of elite rule. The godly, the disciplined, ought to rule over themselves through agreement, but over the unregenerate through force if necessary. The proper order of the church was "an order left by God unto his church, whereby men learn to frame their wills and doings according to the law of God, by instructing and admonishing one another, yea, and by correcting and punishing all willful persons and contemners of the same".[48] The saints control themselves, they admonish each other, but they rule the ungodly coercively.

This throws into relief another extraordinary thing about Calvinism, and about Puritanism in particular: its strong affinity for ancient Israel (which had the fortunate consequence of greatly reducing anti-Semitism in societies dominated by this brand of theology). This seems paradoxical in a faith which starts from a central focus on the Epistle to the Romans, with its revolutionary thesis that salvation by the law is to be put aside in favour of salvation by faith. What could be further from Jewish practice, in ancient Israel or in modern times alike?

But again the paradox disappears, once one sees that the law, for Puritans, was not at all for salvation. They could as a people feel constituted by God's law, exactly like the people portrayed in the Old Testament, just because they felt so strongly the imperative to rectify the disorder in the world. Their theology of predestination told them that the elect were a few rescued from the mass of the ungodly. Thus they could feel like a people beleaguered and embattled, just as ancient Israel had been. They could find inspiration, hope, and promise of ultimate triumph in the Old Testament. The sombre side of this is that they could also be unfeeling and unmerciful to those defined as standing without. This weakness became catastrophic when such communities lived on a racial frontier. But the identification as the people of God's law was a source of tremendous strength.

13.4

The Puritan theology of work and ordinary life provided a hospitable environment for the scientific revolution. Indeed, much of Bacon's outlook stems from a Puritan background. The support given to the Baconian vision by Puritans has often been commented upon.[49] The Baconian programme begins to attract wide support in the 1640's. Good reasons for this spontaneous alliance are not hard to identify. There was a profound analogy in the way the proponents of both Baconian science and Puritan theology saw themselves in relation to experience and tradition. Both saw themselves as rebelling against a traditional authority which was merely feeding on its own errors and as returning to the neglected sources: the Scriptures on one hand, experimental reality on the other. Both appealed to what they saw as living experience against dead received doctrine—the experience of personal conversion and commitment, or that of direct observation of nature's workings. One can even say that the paradigm authority figure against which both rebellions were levied was the same. Aristotle was seen both as the father of traditional physics and medicine (with Galen) and as the philosophical mentor of the scholastic theologians.

John Webster, later a chaplain in the Parliamentary army, takes up the Baconian theme that science must serve to benefit mankind: "Surely natural philosophy hath a more noble, sublime and ultimate end, than to rest in speculation, abstractive notions, mental operations and verball disputes"; it should serve "not onely to know natures power in the causes and effects, but further to make use of them for the general good and benefit of mankind, especially for the conservation and restauration of the health of man, and of those creatures that are usefull for him".[50] We recognize Bacon's double thesis in this passage: the old science is epistemically useless (ending merely in the speculative, the verbal, in unresolvable disputes), and it has turned its back on its proper, moral end of enabling beneficent works.

And as Christopher Hill has argued,[51] there were social reasons why the new science appealed to those attracted by the new theology. These were generally men of the middling sort. We saw above their sense that the order they sought was under threat both from the undisciplined among the landed classes and from the rootless underclass of beggars and vagabonds. The new faith was stronger among artisans, tradesmen, and small landholders. These classes were developing a new confidence and self-reliance, which both encouraged and was entrenched by their new religion of personal commitment. This was one of the factors which underlay the civil war of the 1640's.

But these social developments also created an audience for the new science. The Baconian revolution shifted the central goal of science from contemplation to productive efficacy. And this was at the same time and inseparably a shift against the hierarchy of social valuation, in favour of the productive artisan classes against those classes which prided themselves in leisure. The new science gave a new cachet to getting one's hands dirty in the mechanic arts. Later in the century Boyle and Locke took pride in describing themselves (perhaps somewhat disingenuously) as "underbuilders" and "under-labourers". The combined philosophical-cum-social shift in evaluation had deep appeal for artisan and merchant classes which were becoming conscious of their new achievements and aspiring to a new dignity and influence in society. The appeal was all the greater in that their religious faith also stressed the value of work and the equal dignity of all callings. It is not surprising that there was some convergence between the new science, the new religion, and the new revolutionary spirit which convulsed England in the 1640's.

But this convergence is of course a phenomenon of the time only. The scientific revolution easily survived the Restoration. Indeed, it properly took off under Charles, with his patronage of the new Royal Society. The Society found its supporters well outside the ranks of former roundheads, while some of those who had been sympathetic to the Commonwealth, like Boyle, prudently kept their distance.

The connection between Puritanism and modern science which is of more lasting interest is on a deeper level. It comes through in the religious outlook which suffuses Bacon's works. The shift in the goal of science from contemplation to productive efficacy was based on a biblical understanding of humans as stewards in God's creation. They do God's work in labouring to complete and preserve the things of creation, and first of all themselves. We might say that where Protestant theology had made the circumspect and sober use of the things which surround us to the ends of our preservation and the glory of God, the spiritually correct way to be in the world, Bacon develops a view of the physical universe which makes this essential to the *epistemically* correct way as well. Science and circumspect, productive use are intrinsically connected, both because use is the proper test of science and because it requires science to be responsibly carried out. Our aim must be to use things in the way God intended, and this has yet to be (re)discovered in our fallen condition. Scientific probing is part of the pious man's effort to use things according to God's purposes.

Baconian science, in other words, gains a pious purpose within the framework of Puritan spirituality: not only in the obvious way—that it ought to be directed to the general benefit of mankind, the condition of any proper calling—but also in that it is the search for God's purposes. As John Durie was to put it later, the purpose of knowledge is "to make use of the Creatures for that whereunto God hath made them".[52]

So conceived, Baconian science is the avenue not only to right service of God in our use of his creation but also to his greater glory, as we come to understand his purposes and can render him knowledgeable and fitting praise for the marvels of his design. Bacon devised a conception of the world which ensured that these two pious duties coincided.

This means that the instrumental stance towards the world has been given a new and important spiritual meaning. It is not only the stance which allows us to experiment and thus obtain valid scientific results. It is not only the stance which gives us rational control over ourselves and our world. In this religious tradition, it is the way we serve God in creation. And that in two respects: first, it is the stance we must assume to work in our callings to preserve ourselves and God's order; but second, it is also what protects us against the absorption in things which would wrench us away from God. We must constantly remember to treat the things of creation merely as instruments and not as ends valuable in themselves. Richard Sibbes enjoins us to "use [the world] as a servant all thy dayes, and not as a Master"; and he tells us, as I quoted above, "Labour therefore to have the world in its owne place, under thy feet".[53] *Instrumentalizing* things is the spiritually essential step.

The tremendous importance of the instrumental stance in modern culture is overdetermined. It represents the convergence of more than one stream. It is supported not just by the new science and not just by the dignity attaching to disengaged rational control; it has also been central to the ethic of ordinary life from its theological origins on. Affirming ordinary life has meant valuing the efficacious control of things by which it is preserved and enhanced as well as valuing the detachment from purely personal enjoyments which would blunt our dedication to its general flourishing.

That is why Puritanism contributed to the demise of the old conceptions of meaningful order, based on an ontic logos. Not that this came about all at once. Indeed, Perry Miller has shown how a Platonic-derived notion of God ordering the world after the Ideas became implanted in the New England mind, partly under the influence of Ramus. But it is interesting to note that this conception itself had undergone the transformation which made the instrumental central. Our grasp of this order was referred to by the term *'technologia'*, and the unity of God's order was seen not as a structure to be contemplated but as an interlocking set of things calling for actions which formed a harmonious whole. The harmony between its parts was captured in the term *'eupraxia'*; it was more a matter of the coherence of the occasions for action than of the mutual reflection of things in an order of signs. In Samuel Mather's statement:

> All the Arts are nothing else but the beams and rays of the Wisdom of the *first Being* in the Creatures, shining, and reflecting thence, upon the glass of man's understanding . . . Hence there is an affinity and kindred of Arts . . . which is according to the . . . subordination of their particular ends . . . One makes use of another, one serves to another, till they all reach and return to *Him,* as Rivers to the Sea, whence they flow.[54]

As Miller says,[55] one can see the origins not only of Transcendentalism but also of pragmatism in this outlook. It is the source both for Emerson and for Henry Adams.

Making the instrumental stance central could not but transform the understanding of the cosmos from an order of signs or Forms, whose unity lies in their relation to a meaningful whole, into an order of things producing reciprocal effects in each other, whose unity in God's plan must be that of interlocking purposes. This is in fact what we see emerging in the eighteenth century. But first we shall have to see what became of this theology of ordinary life.

14

RATIONALIZED CHRISTIANITY

14.1

I want in this and the ensuing chapters to trace the way in which the affirmation of ordinary life has shaped the modern identity. A crucial stage in this story has been the fusion of the ethic of ordinary life and the philosophy of disengaged freedom and rationality: a bringing together of the outlook derived from the Reformers (partly through Bacon) with that so influentially formulated by Descartes. We already saw the affinity between the two in the previous chapter: they shared common opponents in the defenders of the older, hierarchical views of order, and came together in endorsing the instrumental stance to self and world.

The combination, which comes about first in England, has ended up generating what is perhaps the dominant outlook of modern Western technological society. This and the responses to it—most notably in the currents of thought and sensibility loosely called 'Romantic'—have largely shaped modern culture, and are crucial components of our images of the self and of our moral ideals.

In its early forms, the fusion retains something of the original theological outlook surrounding the affirmation of ordinary life. Then towards the end of the eighteenth century, a mutation occurs and a naturalist variant arises, sometimes fiercely anti-religious, with the writers of the radical Enlightenment. I will look at this development later. In the next few chapters, I will be talking about the earlier phase, and the scatter of positions roughly called 'Deist'.

Locke was a crucial figure in this phase—and indeed, in this whole development, granted his immense influence on virtually all strands of the Enlightenment. His was one of the earliest embodiments of the synthesis. One of the most important articulators of disengaged freedom—indeed, one who carried it to new lengths of self-objectification, as we saw above—he remained in some sense a believing Christian, and one deeply influenced by the Puritan affirmation of ordinary life. This is often less than fully appreciated today, because we tend to look at Locke with the hindsight of an age sceptical of religious faith. When one adds that this scepticism is often intellectually nourished by arguments which claim descent from Locke, the temptation is great to see Locke's Christianity as largely a residual attachment to the past or perhaps even as a protective colouration in an age when open unbelief invited reprisal. Though Locke was not without his accusers in his own time,[1] this reading is wrong, and in an important sense anachronistic. Locke was certainly not fully orthodox theologically, but his faith was not peripheral to this position. It was seriously meant. And moreover, not to see this is to misunderstand badly the nature of the moral position he espoused. Since this has had a great importance as a stage in the formation of our modern outlook, this misinterpretation has more than historical relevance; it can rebound on our self-understanding.

Following the predominant view in the Puritan strand of Christian spirituality, Locke inclined to theological voluntarism. The moral good for humans, their moral obligations, is founded in God's commands, not in any bent which can be apprehended in nature independent of our recognition that we are the recipients of God's commands. Locke speaks of the Law of Nature, and he gives credit to "the judicious Hooker",[2] but this law is not grounded in the fashion of the Thomistic-Aristotelian tradition Hooker drew on. The Law of Nature is normative for us, in Locke's eyes, *because* it is God's command. In this he is espousing a view which was not uncommon at the time. Pufendorf adopted a similar theory.[3]

What easily misleads his readers, particularly of the *Second Treatise*, into classing Locke with the traditional conception running from Stoics to Thomists and defended in his day by the Cambridge Platonists, and in his own fashion by Grotius, is Locke's insistence that the law is also known by reason. It is not, as one might think a purely voluntaristic law ought to be, known exclusively by revelation. Locke reconciles the two, because he thinks that we are in fact able to read God's purposes fairly easily from the actual nature of his creation. This turns, as we shall see below, on his making preservation the central point of the law.

But the particular way in which Locke links divine commands and human reason turns on the fact that, while being a theological voluntarist, he was also a hedonist. For humans good is pleasure, pain evil (2.28.5).[4] God's law is the law to follow, precisely because it is attended with such superlative rewards and punishments. Following the logic of this hedonism, God's law is normative for us not because he is our creator or infinitely good but because he proffers a totally credible threat of overwhelming retribution to the disobedient. Locke doesn't follow this logic consistently. In the *Second Treatise*, he seems to assume that we are bound to obey God because he made us, and the purposes of the maker are normative for the artifact. In fact, for Locke, the stark issue I posed—do we obey God because he commands us, or because he punishes us?—couldn't arise. This is because his very conception of law requires penalties.[5] Unless a law is attended with penalties, it cannot bind a rational creature. Speaking of the commands of Christ, in *The Reasonableness of Christianity,* he says: "If there were no punishment for the transgressors of them, his laws would not be the laws of a king, that had no authority to command, and power to chastise the disobedient; but empty talk, without force and without influence".[6] This is an odd doctrine, because it's all too easy to see how these two reasons to obey, say, a human tyrant may diverge. People in the entourage of the late Joseph Stalin used to try to anticipate his desires. A correct move in this game might have been a way to stay alive. It was thus not the dictator's *having commanded* something which made it imperative, but rather the prospect of a visit to the Lubyanka if one didn't do it.

Be that as it may, this amalgam of voluntarism and hedonism enables Locke to see the Law of Nature both as divine command *and* as the dictate of reason. The reason in question is instrumental. Once we see that we are creatures of an omnipotent lawgiver, the rational thing to do is to obey. No other pain or pleasure could compensate for those which he will administer.[7]

In fact, Locke thinks not only that obeying God is the (instrumentally) rational thing to do but even that (theoretical) reason can discern the content of God's will. Although we in fact learn of God's law through revelation, we could in principle reach similar conclusions by reason alone. Locke believes that reason shows us clearly that our world was created by God. And he believes that the basic purposes of God in the creation can be read off this creation.[8] His creatures strive instinctively to preserve themselves, and therefore we can conclude that preservation is God's intent. But although this is in principle possible through reason, in fact humans only learn God's law through its whole extent by revelation. Humans' shortcomings, their sloth, passions, fears, superstitions, their susceptibility to being imposed on by unscrupulous elites, all ensure that they fail to realize their capacity in principle to work it all out, and God's proclamations come to the rescue.[9]

This amalgam was profoundly repugnant to many people then as now. It offended religious sensibilities that the following of God's law and the achieving of the highest pay-off of pleasure should be motivationally aligned. It offended moral sensibilities that virtue should be seen as something mercenary.

> The philosophers, indeed, showed the beauty of virtue: they set her off and drew men's eyes and approbation to her; but leaving her unendowed, very few were willing to espouse her . . . But now there being put into the scales, on her side, "an exceeding and immortal weight of glory", interest is come about to her; and virtue now is visibly the most enriching

purchase, and by much the best bargain . . . It has another relish and efficacy to persuade men, that if they live well here, they shall be happy hereafter. Open their eyes to the endless unspeakable joys of another life; and their hearts will find something solid and powerful to move them . . . Upon this foundation, and upon this only, morality stands firm, and may defy all competition.[10]

The motives of morality and maximization are more often considered rivals, with the latter cast in the role of principal impediment to the former. Locke's hedonism, together with his picture of government, and the opinion of one's milieu as also exacting conformity under threat of punishment, made some perceive him as a moral relativist.[11] And this impression was strengthened for many by his energetic rejection of innate ideas, since this seemed to rule out any inherent bent to the good in humans and hence undercut the very basis of morality.[12]

To see Locke in this way was to see him through the prism of a certain conception of moral sources, sources which he seemed to be denying. I will return to the reaction which sprang from this. But for now, it is important to see that Locke doesn't have to be understood in this light. Both his shocked contemporaries and those today for whom the entire theistic outlook has lost its credibility in face of naturalism converge in seeing Locke as a subverter of this outlook.

14.2

But this is not how he saw himself. We have to understand his position in the light of his own sense of moral sources, not just in the context of those he negated. What could inspire in him a sense of the moral law, God's law, as something higher, commanding awe and respect, not just prudent compliance?

We should start with the content of the Law of Nature. This, says Locke, is preservation. He sets this out in the often-quoted passage in the *Second Treatise*. Reason, which is the Law of Nature, "teaches all Mankind, who will but consult it, that . . . no one ought to harm another in his Life, Liberty or Possessions". The reason for this is that men are made by God, and hence "they are his Property, whose Workmanship they are, made to last during his, not one anothers Pleasure". It follows, affirms Locke, that "every one as he is bound to preserve himself, and not quit his Station wilfully; so by the like reason when his own Preservation comes not in competition, ought he, as much as he can, to preserve the rest of Mankind".[13]

The argument here seems to be that, since God gave us life, we go against his will in ending life; unless, of course, this is necessary for its general preservation, which is why we may kill criminals. But in the *First Treatise*, discussing our right to use the other creatures in the world for our own purposes, Locke offers another rationale. As beings designed by God with a strong urge to self-preservation, we can infer that our preservation must have been his intent. We read the purpose off the design.

> God having made Man, and planted in him, as in all other Animals, a strong desire of Self-preservation, and furnished the World with things fit for Food and Rayment and other Necessaries of Life, Subservient to his design, that Man should live and abide for some time upon the Face of the Earth, and not that so curious and wonderful a piece of Workmanship by its own Negligence, or want of Necessaries, should perish again, presently after a few moments continuance: God, I say, having made Man and the World thus, spoke to him, (that is) directed him by his Senses and Reason, as he did the inferior Animals by their Sense, and Instinct, which he had placed in them to that purpose to the use of those things, which were serviceable for his Subsistence, and given him as the means of his Preservation . . . For the desire, strong desire of Preserving his Life and Being having been Planted in him, as a Principle of Action by God himself, Reason, which was the voice of God in him, could not but teach him and assure him, that pursuing that natural Inclination he had to preserve his Being, he followed the Will of his Maker.[14]

In making our preservation the central point of God's will for us, Locke is following the Protestant affirmation of ordinary life; and that in the two aspects I described above. First, the activity designed to acquire the means to life is given central importance and dignity. God wants us to be productive, and this means that we should give ourselves energetically and intelligently to some useful task. Locke integrates into his own thought something like the Puritan notion of the calling, as John Dunn has shown.[15] The fact that God calls us to our particular line of work gives this a higher significance for us, but this entails a duty on our part to work hard at it and also as effectively as possible.

God gives the world to mankind in common, Locke argues in Chapter V of the *Second Treatise,* but he "hath also given them reason to make use of it to the best advantage of Life, and convenience".[16] Since "he gave it to them for their benefit, and the greatest Conveniences of Life they were capable to draw from it", he obviously "gave it to the use of the Industrious and Rational".[17] It is these two properties that God intends us to exhibit. The first requires us to work hard, the second to be efficacious, to bring about "Improvement".

The second facet of Puritan doctrine stressed the need to work for the common good. This was indeed built into the definition of a valid calling, that it be useful for the community or mankind in general; and the requirement that one be industrious and rational came not only from the need to avoid idleness and be about God's purposes: these latter also included conferring benefits on mankind. For Locke, too, the injunction to improve was aimed not only at the increased "conveniencies" of the improver but also at the general good. That is wHy improvement can play an important part in Locke's justification of private property in land. "For the provisions serving to the support of humane life, produced by one acre of inclosed and cultivated land, are (to speak within compasse) ten times more, than those which are yeilded by an acre of Land, of an equal richnesse, lyeing wast in common. And therefor he, that incloses Land and has a greater plenty of the conveniencys of life from ten acres, than he could have from an hundred left to Nature, may truly be said, to give ninety acres to Mankind".[18]

This then is what God calls us to: to act strenuously, and also efficaciously, to meet our needs, but with an eye also to the common good.[19] This is what Locke means by acting rationally; or rather it englobes the somewhat different senses in which he seems to use this word in his work. John Dunn,[20] followed by Neal Wood,[21] has distinguished two senses in which Locke speaks of people as being differentially rational. In the first and more englobing sense, one is rational to the extent that one sees the law of nature (= law of reason) and tries to live up to it. In the second sense, the term is reserved for those capable of using knowledge and reflection to increase their efficacy. We might speak of moral and intellectual rationality. Then we might say that to live up to the whole demands of God is to be morally rational, but these also include the requirement that we be as intellectually rational as we can.

This is how we ought to live: to be industrious and rational in meeting our own needs and hence, through the improvements which result, help to meet the needs of others. Locke's picture of the ordered human life helped to prepare the way for the conception of the high Enlightenment for which Halévy coined the term 'harmony of interests'. There is a way of life which can conciliate self-service and beneficence. A key feature of it is that our service of self takes productive form, as against being furthered at the expense of invading others' rights and property. If this is the "bourgeois" ideal, then we have to think of Locke as one of the seminal figures who helped to formulate and spread it.

He is in fact a crucial hinge figure in the evolution of the ethic of ordinary life from its original theological formulation to the modern, "bourgeois" naturalist one, which has both facilitated and been entrenched by the rise of capitalism. But it is premature to think of Locke as an apologist of capitalism. He obviously approved of the new developments in agriculture, such as the introduction of fallow crops, the draining of fens and marshes, manuring, and stockbreeding, which marked his century. He must have had these, among others, in mind in talking about 'improvements'. And these, of course, only came to pass because landowners began to function like entrepreneurs. But he doesn't seem to have had any particular brief for large-scale commerce and industry.

But his ethical outlook was plainly an endorsement of the serious, productive, pacific improver of any class and against the aristocratic, caste-conscious pursuit of honour and glory through self-display and the warrior virtues. Locke continued and further developed the inversion of the old hierarchy of values which the ethic of ordinary life entailed. His attitude towards science echoes that of Bacon: those whose discoveries have contributed to human welfare deserve praise over those who have merely added new general maxims or wide-ranging hypotheses of the traditional, Aristotelian science. "For, notwithstanding these learned Disputants, these all-knowing Doctors, it was to the unscholastick Statesman, that the Governments of the World owed their Peace, Defence, and Liberties; and from the illiterate and contemned Mechanick (a Name of Disgrace) that they received the improvements of useful Arts" (3.10.9). As with Bacon, a judgement of intellectual value goes hand in hand with an inversion of social prestige.

This was how it ought to be, but in fact it is rarely like that. Men are diverted from this path by sloth, covetousness, passion, ambition. Not only do they fail to live up to this ideal; they frequently fail to recognize it, misled as they are by their superstitions, by bad education and customs, by partisan spirit, and by their own bad passions. Locke had certainly shed the belief in original sin in anything like its orthodox sense that he had inherited from his Puritan background.[22] But he had substituted a naturalized variant, an inherent penchant of human beings to egocentricity and personal power. This *was* innate: we see it in very young children.

> We see Children as soon almost as they are born (I am sure long before they can speak) cry, grow peevish, sullen, out of humour, for nothing but to have their *Wills*. They would have their Desires submitted to by others; they contend for a ready compliance from all about them . . .
>
> Another thing wherein they shew their love of Dominion, is their desire to have things to be theirs; They would have *Propriety* and possession, pleasing themselves with the Power which that seems to give, and the Right they thereby have, to dispose of them, as they please.[23]

If we add to this the human tendencies to laziness and pride, as long as we are not trained early in good habits, and if we take account of the bad effects of education in most societies, then it is small wonder that the Law of Nature is rarely integrally obeyed.

The ideal would be a much higher and better and ultimately even more advantageous way to be. But we can't somehow get it together. This is where God comes in. Through his revelation, he makes his law known to us, in an unmistakable fashion, one which is bound to make a deep impression on us. This happens particularly through Jesus Christ, who attests to his status as God's messenger through the miracles he performs. God thus spectacularly overcomes the difficulties we have in knowing his Law.

But this is not all. By publishing his will as a *law,* that is, as attended by pains and rewards, he gives us an overwhelming *motive* to seek this idea. So revelation not only helps us to know what is good but gives us a tremendous motivational shove, as it were, in the right direction. God's legislative action and its proclamation help to lift us out of the ruck in which we would otherwise wallow helplessly.

If one might be tempted to complain that the downside risk of eternal damnation is a rather high price to pay for God's help in this, the answer lies partly in the fact that only a law, and that means a rule attended with punishment for transgression, will do the trick. Shorn of the threat of punishment, God's words to us would lack force and influence.[24] But on top of this, God has been merciful. The rules of the game established by the Christian revelation are that those who have faith in Christ and repent and sincerely attempt to amend their lives, will be saved. So now full compliance is not a necessary condition of eternal reward, but only the sincere attempt at it, coupled with faith.[25]

Seen from this perspective, the legislative, self-proclaiming God is a great benefactor to mankind. I believe that this is how Locke saw him, and that this was the basis of a genuine and deeply felt piety. Today this may be hard to credit, because the contemporary scene is dominated on one side by unbelievers and on the other by believers from whom this kind of faith seems at best flat and even repugnant (I confess to being in this latter category). But it would be anachronistic to conclude from this that Locke's faith was either insincere or peripheral to his life.

On the contrary, if one starts from a vision of humans as potentially rational but with an inherent penchant for irrationality and evil, doomed on their own resources even to frustrate their own best potentiality, one can see that their condition cried out for a God who would pull them beyond it. God alone gives sense and hope to a human condition which is otherwise the source of irremediable despair and potentially endless self-destruction. God has to exist for humans to give some order to their life. That is why Locke was induced to except atheists from his otherwise wide rule of toleration. Such people had spurned the very basis of human civil life.

In so lifting us, God uses our self-love. It is a basic fact about humans that they desire pleasure and seek to avoid pain. This is not a failing but an unalterable feature of their make-up (2.20.2–3, 2.21.42, 2.28.5). But there are irrational, destructive and wrong forms of self-love, and a rational, moral form. God helps to lift us from the first to the second. But the basic self-love which makes this operation possible, our fear of endless pain and our desire for "unspeakable" joys, is not evil. It is made by God and therefore good. Locke is already preparing the ground for the later Enlightenment doctrine of the innocence of natural self-love; but he himself was too aware of the innate sources of depravity in man to propound a similar view.

In this connection, the alignment of following God's will with maximizing our pleasure, so shocking to the mainstream of Christian theology, is fully in keeping with the providential design of things. God, like a super-player in a game of rational choice, instrumentalizes our instrumental reason by giving us a law which brings us into line with his purpose of general conservation. We are following God's purpose in maximizing, when we do it properly.

Theologically, this embracing of human nature in its limitations mimics an important feature of Reformation theology, which had also been followed by Bacon. In breaking with the monastic "counsels of perfection", the Reformers stressed the ungodly motivation of pride that led people to try to transcend the ordinary lay condition.[26] Humans should accept with humility the nature God has given them. The Lockean acceptance of Gassendian hedonism, the fact that we are impelled by nature to maximize pleasure, can be presented in a similar light. Rather than aspire to a self-abnegating altruism for which we are not made, we should accept our nature and fulfil God's purpose in it. Locke's psychology could be seen as a new transposition of the theology of ordinary life, on the way to its naturalistic successor doctrine.[27]

In this version, we come to God through reason. That is, the exercise of rationality is the way we take part in God's plan. The ethic of ordinary life, as we saw in the previous chapter, while rejecting supposedly "higher" activities, makes the crux of the moral life depend on the manner in which we live our ordinary life. "God loveth adverbs", as Joseph Hall put it. In Locke's new transposition of the ethic, the crucial adverbs are shifting. Where in the pure Reform variant, it was a matter of living *worshipfully* for God, now it is becoming a question of living *rationally*. But with Locke, we are still in a transitional stage. It is still a question of following God's will, but this is now understood in terms of rationality. Rising from passion, blind prejudice, and unthinking custom to reason confers the two related transformations: it gives our own productive life order and dignity, and it releases us from egoism and destructiveness to benefit others. Disengaged procedural reason raises us from destruction to beneficence because it breaks the shackles of illusion, blind custom, and superstition, and in doing so lifts us from wild disordered egoism to the productive search for happiness which confers benefits on others as well. Reason releases the constructive, beneficent potentiality of self-love. This high view of the morally transformatory power of reason emerges from the logic of Locke's theory. He himself doesn't thematize it, but it will be developed into one of the major organizing ideas of the Enlightenment.

We need moral rationality, of course, but also intellectual rationality. Indeed, from this standpoint, we can see what links these two together. They are tied together by the primacy of instrumental, maximizing reason. This is the point of purchase within us which God uses to lift us up to our full potential. We are morally rational when we allow ourselves to be so lifted. But this same maximizing reason demands that we be intellectually rational. That means that the proper end of intellectual rationality is usefulness to our life-purposes. The *Essay,* says Locke, aims "at Truth and Usefulness". Indeed, "he fails very much of that Respect he owes the Publick, who prints, and consequently expects Men should read that, wherein he intends not they should meet with anything of Use to themselves or others" (Epistle, p. 9). And when we are tempted to regret that our comprehension of things falls so far short of their "vast Extent", we should reflect that "the Author of our Being" has bestowed on us "whatsoever is necessary for the Conveniences of Life, and the Information of Vertue (2 Peter 1:3)". "We shall not have much Reason to complain of the narrowness of our Minds, if we will but employ them about what may be of use to us; for of that they are very capable" (1.1.5).

In following these two biddings of our instrumental reason—accepting God's law and acquiring and reflecting on knowledge for use—we participate in God's plan. Instrumental rationality, properly conducted, is of the essence of our service of God. In thus making reason central, Locke was plainly stepping outside the orthodox Reformed theology; this was of a piece with his rejection of original sin. But he was just as far from those traditional views which accorded a high place to human reason, and which Reform theology had attacked. The reason spoken of in these earlier theologies was substantive: it was what enabled us to see the order of the good by our natural light. And it was what culminated—for that theology which was born of the marriage with Hellenistic Platonism, where the highest expression of reason was contemplation—in the beatific vision. Locke shares, indeed builds on, the Reformers' rejection of these views. The rationality in question is now procedural: in practical affairs, instrumental; in theoretical, involving the careful, disengaged scrutiny of our ideas and their assembly according to the canons of mathematical deduction, and empirical probability. This is how we participate in God's purposes. Not through blind instinct, like the animals, but through conscious calculation, we take our place in the whole. Of course, this means that we unlike animals have to rise to become aware of this whole and of the sovereign purpose guiding it. But this is precisely what we do when learning to follow God's law.

Thus seen from the inside, Locke's "reasonable" religion is not just a swallowing of religious obligation in egoism, as it too easily can appear to critics, or just a step on the road to naturalism (however much it may have turned out *objectively* to be such). It offers a new understanding of what it is to serve God, one which recaptures the old terms in a new significance. The goodness and wisdom of God are now understood as those appropriate to the designer of a universe, contrived so as to conduce to the continued conservation of its animate and rational inhabitants. This was not a sharp break with tradition. It had always been considered part of God's providence that his creation allowed for the thriving of the many living things within it, and the psalmist praises him, "that thou mayest give them their meat in due season" (Psalm 104:27). The God of Abraham sees being and life as good.

But in the new vision, which Locke helped to prepare, and consistent with the new centrality of ordinary life, it is the preservation of this latter which now takes on prime importance. The goodness and the providence of God are shown above all in his designing the world for the preservation of its denizens, and particularly so that the various parts of it conduce to reciprocal conservation. Eternal life, in a world beyond, is something superadded to this benefit; but it is so fitted on that it too conduces to the proper running of this earthly order, in that it takes the form of rewards and punishments which impel us to obey the law of preservation—indeed, without which we would have no overriding reason to do so.

Locke helped to define and give currency to the growing Deist picture, which will emerge fully in the eighteenth century, of the universe as a vast interlocking order of beings, mutually subserving each other's flourishing, for whose design the architect of nature deserves our praise and thanks and admiration. Cumberland was also developing a vision of this kind in Locke's time.[28] I will return to this interlocking order below.

Within this vision of creation, as we, recognizing the awesome and overwhelming force of God's retribution which leaves us no rational choice, line ourselves up with his law, we do not act in the spirit of the prudent servants of the capricious tyrant, who are concerned simply to maximize advantage in an amoral context. On the contrary, we do so in a spirit of admiration and wonder and gratitude. For in thus exercising reason, we see ourselves as taking up our proper place in God's plan. Instrumental rationality is our avenue of participation in God's will. Rather than seeing this as an abasement of God's will to the status of a factor in our game, we see it as the exalting of our reasoning to the level of collaborator in God's purpose.[29]

This form of Christian faith thus incorporates modern disengagement and procedural rationality in itself. And in so doing it incorporates the moral sources they connect with. If we look for the constitutive goods of this outlook, if we ask what it is whose vivid presence to our understanding empowers us to act for the good, two features spring to mind: the goodness and wisdom of God as shown in the interlocking order, and our disengaged reason as our way of participating in God's purpose. But this picture of disengaged reason is linked as we saw to a conception of human dignity. In particular, it incorporates a sense of self-responsible autonomy, a freedom from the demands of authority.

And so this too is integrated into religious belief. It is a central idea of Deism as it develops that God relates to humans as rational beings, that God's purposes fully respect humans' autonomous reason. And so we get works by self-professed followers of Locke, like Toland's *Christanity Not Mysterious* and Tindal's *Christianity as Old as the Creation*. Locke still had reservations about this; he was too conscious of human frailty. But that is what Lockean religion came to mean.[30]

But if the Deism Locke inspired is not simply a cover for naturalism, this is not to say that some large piece of the orthodox tradition hasn't been jettisoned. First, it is clear that the place of mystery in this religion shrinks to the vanishing point. God's providence becomes more and more scrutable, however much the engineering detail may escape us. Many writers still gesture to higher purposes we don't understand, but the logic of the position drives towards rational transparency. This is just the obverse side of the integration of autonomous reason. Toland's title—*Christianity Not Mysterious*—said it in a shockingly direct way, which earned him persecution and his book a condemnation of burning by the public hangman. Tindal spells out even further the rational comprehensibility of God's purposes. Indeed, they are nothing else except the "common Interest, and mutual Happiness of his rational Creatures".[31] God is kind enough to make our acting for our present happiness the way of securing our future goods;[32] which is to say that the rewards and punishments of a future life endorse the path which produces the most mutual happiness in this. Since humans cannot act other than under the impulsion to seek happiness, this system of rewards is indeed, the best suited for them. As for the details of God's will for us, we only have to look into the "Book of Nature" to see what relations we stand in, and what they require. Only a tyrant would impose commands which do not flow from these relations.[33] In Tindal, we find the basic ideas of Locke's theology, but pushed to their logical conclusion and freed from all the anxious and conflicted sense of human imperfection and obduracy which marked the outlook of the older man. We now have a reasonable Christianity, without tears.

More fundamentally, the place for grace tends to disappear. If the good of man that God calls to becomes more and more available to human rational scrutiny, it also becomes more and more encompassable with human powers.

These two changes are linked. There are two great traditional streams of doctrine about grace and nature in Christian thought. We can best describe them by relating them to a conception of the human natural good, that is, the good that non-depraved human beings can discern on their own and at least set themselves to accomplish. Through most of the first millennium and a half of Christian history, this natural good was defined in the terms laid down by the great pagan philosophers.

There are two ways in which the human natural good was seen as needing supplementation by grace: (1) God calls humans to something more than the natural good, to a life of sanctity, which involves participation in God's salvific action. This takes us beyond the excellences defined by the natural good. In the language of Thomism, beyond the natural virtues stand the "theological" ones—faith, hope, and charity. (2) Human will is so depraved by the Fall that humans require grace even to make a decent attempt at and perhaps even properly to discern the natural good, let alone to go beyond it.

The overwhelming mainstream of Christian theologies up to the modern time contained some variants of both (1) and (2); but there were radical differences depending on which was dominant. Where (1) is and (2) is not interpreted radically, grace is seen to "perfect nature, not to destroy it", as Aquinas put it.[34] The striving after natural perfection is not an obstacle to sanctification, and the great ancient moralists are seen in a positive light (as with Erasmus). Where (2) is interpreted radically, there is suspicion and hostility to the search for natural perfection, and at the extreme the ancient moralists are denounced (as with Luther).

The early modern period was dominated by gigantic battles in which radical interpretations of (2)—let me call them 'hyper-Augustinian' views—played a leading part, not only in the Reformation movements themselves but also in the struggle between Jansenists and their opponents in France, between Arminians and strict Calvinists in Holland, and later in America, and so on.

The rise of Enlightenment Deism is usually seen as a conflict, ultimately victorious, with such hyper-Augustinian views. And there were indeed battle lines drawn between these two. The high French Enlightenment, including Rousseau, saw itself as aligned against the terrible misanthropic effects of the doctrine of original sin. The Scottish Enlightenment waged a continuing fight against the forces of pure radical Calvinism in the Church of Scotland, which tried to silence some of its major figures, e.g., Hutcheson and Hume. Enlightenment Deism ends up suppressing any place for grace of type 2, in the teeth of orthodox opposition, and then naturalism takes over from there.

It comes to be thought, not only by the protagonists to this struggle but by later commentators, that these two positions, hyper-Augustinianism and Enlightenment Deism (succeeded by naturalism), exhaust the space of possibilities. This mistake is the easier to make in that this Deism finds some of its roots in Reform theology, as we see with the case of Locke.

What gets forgotten here is the way in which Deism also suppresses any role for grace of type 1. And this in spite of the fact that, in their battle with hyper-Augustinianism, Deists drew heavily on writers of the Erasmian tradition. Indeed, many of their arguments against the picture of a Deity imposing senseless demands on his creatures to make clear his sovereignty, their insistence that God wills our good as we can understand good, are drawn from this tradition. Tindal follows Whichcote. But between this latter and the former, something crucial is dropped. The good that God wills comes more and more to centre on natural good alone. Even eternal reward comes to be seen as just a lot more of the same—and distributed so as to support and prod the production of natural good down here.

Locke has still not gone all the way towards this Deism. In particular, there are vestiges of hyper-Augustinianism in his assessment of human weakness. But it is clear on closer examination that there is not much room left for grace here. There is some reference in the *Reasonableness* to God's spirit helping us.[35] But the main thing God does in revelation is make *clear* what the law is, thus motivating us more strongly to the good; and second, in the case of the Christian revelation, he softens the rules about punishment and allows faith to compensate for our involuntary failings.[36] But the first type of role has virtually vanished in Locke's scheme. In the successor doctrines inspired by him, the last vestiges disappear.[37]

15

MORAL SENTIMENTS

15.1

I have been drawing a portrait of what we could call Lockean Deism. But there is another and rather different kind, which develops partly in opposition to it. Shaftesbury is the founder of this variant. It crystallizes around a rival moral outlook, which comes to be known as the theory of moral sentiments, expounded in a set of influential writings by Francis Hutcheson.

The difference between the two variants can be explained in terms of, perhaps even largely traced to, the kinds of orthodox Christianity out of which they respectively emerge. The Lockean has Puritan roots, which means its background is in a hyper-Augustinian theology. It rebels against this but retains important features of it. Locke's rather jaundiced view of the human propensity for illusion, folly, and destructive behaviour is as it were a naturalistic transposition of the doctrine of original sin. More important, he shares with the Puritans theological voluntarism. God's law is what he decides it is, and God's law determines the good. God cannot be seen as bound by a good which would be already implicit in the bent of the nature he has created.

Following this theological outlook, God's law is doubly external to us fallen creatures. First, we cannot identify the good with the bent of our own natures; we have rather to discover what God's sovereign decrees are in relation to us (although Locke thought that the actual tendency of our nature to preservation gives us a shrewd hint about God's intentions, as we saw in the previous chapter). And second, this law runs against the grain of our depraved wills. It has to be imposed on an unwilling nature, if it is to be followed at all, until we are fully sanctified by grace.

The affinity and historical connections between this theology and empiricist mechanism have often been noted. This theological outlook itself pushed towards the adoption of the mechanistic world picture, as I described above.[1] God's sovereignty was best safeguarded in face of a creation without purposes of its own. But the disengaged subject resembles the Deity in this respect. Disengagement, as we saw, operates by objectifying the domain in

248

question, rendering it neutral. The disengaged subject of empiricist mechanism takes over some of the prerogatives accorded God in Occamist theology. Indeed, in some ways the new outlook can be seen as a kind of anthropological transposition of this theology.

Among other things, it inherits a command theory of law and morality. In the now neutralized world of the psyche, there is only de facto desire; there is no longer a place for a higher good, the object of a strong evaluation, within nature itself. "Whatsoever is the object of any man's appetite or desire, that is it which he for his part calleth good", as Hobbes put it.[2] An ethic can be constructed taking simply this de facto desire as its basis: the higher good just is the maximization of de facto goals. This will be utilitarianism. The only other alternative is to retain some kind of command theory. This is, of course, what Hobbes does in his political theory. The link to the old theology is evident in the description of the state as a "mortal god".[3]

In this mechanized, and perhaps even atheist, transposition, law is still external to us in the two senses above. English seventeenth-century philosophy seems to us dominated by the rise of empiricism. But the Erasmian tradition was still alive and fighting, most notably in a group of thinkers loosely referred to as the "Cambridge Platonists", e.g., Henry More, Ralph Cudworth, Benjamin Whichcote, John Smith.[4] They vigorously opposed a religion of external law, in the name of one which saw humans as intrinsically attuned to God. Humans approach God in fear, as an inscrutable lawgiver whose judgements are utterly beyond human comprehension and may already, indeed, have condemned us, regardless of our present aspirations to reform.

> The spirit of true Religion is of a more free, noble, ingenuous and generous nature . . . It [divine love] thaws all those frozen affections which a Slavish fear had congealed and lock'd up, and makes the Soul most chearfull, free, and nobly resolved in all its motions after God.[5]

Smith opposes a religion of fear, one of "a constrained and forced obedience to God's Commandments", which he sees as one of servility, and which treats God as a harsh and capricious tyrant and "begets . . . a forc'd and dry devotion, void of inward Life and Love".

> Religion is no sullen Stoicism or oppressing Melancholy, is no enthralling tyranny exercised over those noble and vivacious affections of Love and Delight . . . but it is full of a vigorous and masculine delight and joy, and such as advanceth and ennobles the Soul, and does not weaken or disspirit the life and power of it.[6]

Smith puts his contrast as a religion of fear versus one of love, a servile or forced devotion versus a free one. Religion is "the Mother and Nurse" of a "truly-noble and divine Liberty". But he also uses other images which will have a tremendous career in modern culture:

> There are a sort of Mechanical Christians in the world, that not finding Religion acting like a living form within them, satisfie themselves only to make an Art of it . . . But true Religion is no Art, but an inward Nature that conteins all the laws and measures of its motion within it self.[7]

The organic versus the artificial, the living versus the mechanical: Cassirer was right to see in the Cambridge Platonists one of the originating sources of later Romanticism. It's as if the battle lines are already drawn, and Smith has seen the crucial affinity of mechanism with the whole religious outlook he is attacking.

Another expression which points forward to a central feature of contemporary culture is 'inward Nature'. Smith is once more attacking the crux of voluntarism, which makes God's will something quite external to the bent of nature:

> If it could be supposed that God should plant a Religion in the Soul that had no affinity or alliance with it, it would grow there but as a strange slip. But God when he gives his Laws to men, does not by virtue of his Absolute dominion dictate any thing at randome, and in such an arbitrarious way as some imagine.[8]

The major plea of voluntarism was that an "arbitrarious" will *had* to be attributed to God, or else we fail to recognize his absolute sovereignty. To hold a doctrine of natural good was itself a denial of God's power, an affront to the honour of God.

To this the Cambridge thinkers replied that voluntarists were projecting their own "Peevishness and Self-will" onto God, as though he were a human tyrant "easily entic'd by Flatteries".[9] As Whichcote put it, "There is that in God that is more beautiful than power, than will and Sovereignty, viz. His righteousness, His good-will, His justice, wisdom and the like".[10]

The Cambridge thinkers couched their opposition to voluntarism in a teleological doctrine of nature as tending towards the good, grounded in the Platonic school, hence the term they are usually known by. As Cassirer has pointed out, their roots were in the Platonism of the Renaissance, as developed in the fifteenth century by Ficino and Pico. This was a Platonism very influenced by Plotinus. It was a doctrine in which love played a central part; not only the ascending love of the lower for the higher, Plato's *erōs*, but also a love of the higher which expressed itself in care for the lower, which could easily be identified with Christian *agapē*. The two together make a vast circle of love through the universe.[11] Nothing more at odds with the new mechanical philosophy can be conceived. In their natural science, Cudworth and his allies were fighting a rear-guard action against the future.[12]

But the driving motive of their "Platonism" was a religious and moral one, and in this domain something new is creeping in. A brand of Augustinian inwardness is transposing the "Platonism" into something different. This is what is reflected in Smith's use of the expression 'inward Nature'. But in order to see better what this amounted to, we have to take the story forward, to the variety of Deism which built on this Erasmian orthodoxy.

In effect, we can arrive at this by putting this theology through a transposition defined by two crucial principles of Deism: (1) the central place accorded to the human subject as an autonomous reasoner and (2) the sidelining of grace. What emerges out of this, in the particular circumstances of the turn of the century in England, is Shaftesbury. The third Earl probably got his allegiance to autonomous reason from his tutor, Locke, but much of the inspiration for his very anti-Lockean moral views came from the Cambridge Platonists. His first publication was an edition of Whichcote's sermons.

His inspiration, I say, rather than his doctrine. Of all the traditional philosophical views, Shaftesbury was closest to the Stoics. His masters were Epictetus and Marcus. The highest good for humans is to love and take joy in the whole course of the world. Someone who achieves this love reaches a perfect tranquillity and equanimity; he is proof against all the buffetings of adverse fortune; and above all, he can love those around him constantly and steadily, undiverted by his own pain and disappointments, or his own partial interests. He attains "a generous affection, an exercise of friendship uninterrupted, a constant kindness and benignity".[13] Moreover, this love carries itself the greatest intrinsic satisfaction. Since by nature we love the ordered and beautiful, the highest and most complete order and beauty is an object of the greatest joy. "For 'tis impossible that such a divine order should be contemplated without ecstasy and rapture".[14]

But since we have a natural tendency to love the whole, the goal we seek might be put negatively, as clearing away the obstacles to this love, which arise from our believing that the world is in some way imperfect and bad.[15] As with his Stoic mentors, Shaftesbury thinks that what separates us from this peace and equanimity is our false opinions, whereby we see some things in the universe as evils and imperfections. Right opinions make us capable of loving providence.[16] I must love whatever happens, and see it all as fitted to me and orderly with respect to the whole, even "the sack of cities and the ruin of mankind".[17]

We can spare ourselves the details of how Shaftesbury tries to convince himself and us that all these disasters really fit the order of things. In fact, he doesn't give us many details. But some of the principles—that good needs a foil in evil, that partial blemishes work for the whole, that the universe has to proceed by general laws—become standard in eighteenth-century providen-tialism, of the kind which Voltaire savagely satirized in *Candide*. The real argument of Shaftesbury is not at this Panglossian level at all, however. The crucial consideration is the Stoic one, that nothing ought to distress us, or matter to us, except the state of our own mind, or will or self. "My own concern is for truth, reason and right *within myself*".[18] Shaftesbury makes his own the Epictetan distinction between things which depend on me and those which don't, and embraces the injunction to concern myself only with the first.[19] Once this is in order, not even my imminent death ought to distress me, and Shaftesbury takes up the beautiful image of Epictetus, that one part giving thanks to the master of the banquet.[20] Or, more heroically put:

> Everything wastes and is perishing; everything hastens to its dissolution ... Mortalities must every day be expected—friends dropping off, accidents and calamities impending, diseases, lamenesses, deafness, loss of sight, of memory, of parts ... All is misery, disappointment and regret. In vain we endeavour to drive away these thoughts; in vain we strive by humour and diversion to raise ourselves; which is but to fall the lower. He and he alone is in any degree happy, who can confront these things; who can steadily look on them without turning away his sight; and who, knowing the sum and conclusion of all, waits for the finishing of his part, his only care in the meanwhile being to act that part as becomes him and to preserve his mind entire and sound, unshaken and uncorrupt; in friendship with mankind, and in unity with that original mind with respect to which nothing either does or can happen but what is most agreeable and conducing, and what is of universal good.[21]

God figures in this, too, but as with the Stoics it is God as the framer of this order. He is rather different from the God of Abraham, of revelation. Shaftesbury sees him more as the mind that not only designs but moves and animates the whole. Theocles, the character in the dialogue *The Moralists* who truly speaks for Shaftesbury, thus addresses Him:

> O mighty Genius! sole animating and inspiring power! author and subject of these thoughts! thy influence is universal, and in all things thou art inmost. From thee depend their secret springs of action. Thou movest them with an irresistible unwearied force, by sacred and inviolable laws, framed for the good of each particular being, as best may suit with the perfection, life and vigour of the whole ... thou who art original soul, diffusive, vital in all, inspiriting the whole.[22]

The goal of loving and affirming the order of the world could also be described as bringing our particular minds into harmony with the universal one: "the particular mind should seek its happiness in conformity with the general one, and endeavour to resemble it in its highest simplicity and excellence".[23]

This conception is what enables Shaftesbury to pose the issue of theism versus atheism in the surprising and disconcerting way he does in his *Inquiry*. He takes it basically as a *cosmological* question. The theist is the one who believes "that everything is governed, ordered, or regulated for the best, by a designing principle or mind, necessarily good and permanent".[24] The paradigm atheists are Epicureans. What it really turns on is the order or lack of it in the cosmos. To grasp the universe as a single entity, like a tree, whose parts sympathize,[25] and which is ordered for the best, is what puts us on the path to God.

We can see why Shaftesbury was unalterably opposed not only to hyper-Augustinian Christianity but to its offshoot in Lockean Deism. He utterly rejected a conception of God's law as external. The highest good doesn't repose in any arbitrary will, but in the nature of the cosmos itself; and our love for it isn't commanded under threat of punishment, but comes spontaneously from our being. Sometimes he echoes closely the words of the Cambridge writers in denouncing a religion which would describe God as a jealous being, and man as submitted to his will through fear of punishment. "How comes it then . . . that according as the Deity is represented to us, he should more resemble the weak, womanish, and impotent part of our nature, than the generous, manly and divine?"[26] A religion of fear, in which man is motivated by the prospect of reward and punishment, stifles true piety, which is "to love God for his own sake".[27] This kind of religion suffers from "mercenariness and a slavish spirit".[28]

Locke's theology deserves this stinging epithet as well. But Locke is also reproached for something worse: he has continued the work of Hobbes and denied our natural bent towards the good. According to this view, nothing is good or bad, admirable or contemptible intrinsically, but only in relation to some law or rule under which it is made to fall, backed by penalties; "that all actions are naturally indifferent; that they have no note or character of good or ill in themselves; but are distinguished by mere fashion, law, or arbitrary decree".[29]

Nothing could be more wrong. It is as absurd to say that virtue and vice, honour and dishonour, could be a matter of arbitrary decree, as "that the measure or rule of harmony was caprice or will, humour or fashion".[30] Shaftesbury recurs again and again to this analogy with music—and with architecture and painting—in defending against this Hobbes-Locke thesis of natural indifference: let me call it the extrinsic theory of morality. Right and wrong are just as fixed to standards in nature as are harmony and dissonance.[31] Something like a harmony or proportion of numbers is to be found in all these fields. In *Advice,* the true artist is said to be one who is not "at a loss in those numbers which make the harmony of a mind. For knavery is mere dissonance and disproportion".[32] He has to have an eye or ear "for these interior numbers".[33] And "the real honest man . . . instead of outward forms of symmetries, is struck with that of inward character, the harmony and numbers of the heart and beauty of the affections".[34]

What did Shaftesbury mean in using these as terms of moral description? It's not entirely clear to us, and perhaps it wasn't fully so to him. Plainly there is some Platonic-Pythagorean background to it all, which presumably came down to him through Ficino and the Cambridge Platonists. But does it mean that he is likening moral insight to mathematical? This was a line of thought explored by some thinkers of this period, people like Samuel Clarke, for instance, the collaborator of Newton, and William Wollaston,[35] who were also trying to argue against the extrinsic theory. They spoke of certain acts being "fitting"—e.g., the grateful return of favours for benefits conferred—as though this were something like a logical truth, whose contradictory would be senseless. Grotius seemed to be invoking principles of this kind in the Introduction to his *de Jure Belli ac Pacis.*[36] Some clung to this form of rationalism, because it seemed the only way to defeat the extrinsic theory.

The term 'rationalist' can be applied in one sense to Shaftesbury. He did accept one of the main principles of Deism mentioned above: he allows no form of religious authority which cannot be made convincing to autonomous reason.[37] In this way he does participate in the general movement towards the Enlightenment, along with his tutor. This was of a piece with the Whig politics he shared with both tutor and grandfather. But I don't think he was a rationalist in the sense that Clarke was. The key analogy behind his number and proportions seems to be not so much mathematical necessity as the requirements of orderly wholes. The good life, the good character, was one in which everything took its right space and proportion, no more, no less. The key concept was therefore something like the original Platonic or Stoic one of a whole of things, ordered for the good. One finds the standards by which to live, the firm criteria in nature of the right, through a grasp of the whole order in which one is set. The good person loves the whole order of things.

Here we have a rival to Lockean Deism, which embraces autonomous reason and sidelines grace but which has an utterly different view of moral sources. Instead of finding these in the dignity of a disengaged subject, objectifying a neutral nature, it seeks them in the inherent bent of our nature towards a love of the whole as good. Lockean self-disengagement is not just an error, it is a sure way of making these sources invisible, of losing contact with them and hence with the good. That is why Shaftesbury has to combat the extrinsic theory as an abomination. It stands in the way of a re-engagement with our own love of the whole.

It sounds as though this counter-Lockean Deism, at least as we see it in Shaftesbury, takes the form purely of a return to ancient models, to Plato and above all to the Stoics. We could see it as part of the recovery of "paganism", which some have seen as an essential strand in the Enlightenment.[38] But this would be too quick. In fact Shaftesbury's philosophy, for all its Stoic inspiration, is crucially shaped by a modern, one might say 'post-Christian', mode of thought. This is what we have to examine in order to understand the impact of his theory in his century and beyond.

There are two important respects in which Shaftesbury's language is modern which I would like to bring out here. This is not to say that there weren't many other aspects of this thought which bespoke his time, but that these two were of special importance in the formation of the alternative to Lockean Deism. They are both reflected in one key term that Shaftesbury uses. He speaks often of 'natural affection'. The thesis that we by nature love the whole is expressed by saying that our natural affections would carry beyond our immediate family and entourage to a disinterested love of all mankind, if we rightly understood our situation.[39] Natural affection is what holds societies together, and rightly understood it would bind the whole species. It is part of everyone's innate endowment, along with the sense of right and wrong, and this is what is forgotten by the proposers of the extrinsic theory.[40]

The two features which I find reflected in this term are (1) the internalization, or we might say 'subjectivization', of a teleological ethic of nature; and (2) the transformation of an ethic of order, harmony, and equilibrium into an ethic of benevolence. It's not clear in each case how much Shaftesbury's thought itself reflected these changes. What is certain is that they were what his language suggested to his contemporaries and were fully evident in the moral sense theories that he helped inspire.

1. The ancient theories that Shaftesbury drew on, those of Plato and the Stoics, weren't expressed in the language of inwardness. And as I argued above, this was not simply a semantic accident.[41] We love the good, and the good we love is in the order of things, as well as in the wise soul, aligned with nature. But the second of these orders is not self-sufficient: we only can have order in the soul in seeing and loving the order of things. For Plato this means having a vision of the Good; for the Stoics this means seeing and affirming the course of the world. This is what differentiates their ethic from that of the Epicureans, who were in this respect the odd men out among ancient moralists. For the great theories which played a dominant role in the European tradition, the soul's good involves loving the cosmic good.

But supposing we ask: Why do we love the cosmic good? The answer is simple: we are rational beings. Reason is understood substantively: rationality is the power to grasp the order of things, itself a reflection of reason. No other 'motivational postulate' is necessary. It is in the nature of rational beings to love rational order when they see it. The problem is their inability to see it. They are blinded by their focus on sensible things; or they have false opinions *(dogmata)* which take the form of passions.

The focus is not inward, on the motivation 'in' the psyche, as we would say. Rather the cosmic good is loved, because it is essentially loveable, and that's all that need be said.

Christian thought introduces a change, well articulated in Augustine. This natural bent to love the good can fail; we suffer through the Fall from a perversion of the will. There are potentially two loves in us, a higher one and a lower one, charity and concupiscence. As we were made by God, we love the good; but as we have become, we are drawn to evil. It may not be enough just to make the good evident to us; the will may have to be transformed by grace. This change is connected, as we saw above, with the development in Augustine and in the culture that succeeded him of a language of inwardness.

By the time we get to Shaftesbury's age, following the great Renaissance transpositions and intensifications of inwardness I described earlier, this language has become inescapable. One can't help thinking in these terms. Shaftesbury constantly expresses his Stoic convictions and sentiments in terms of a turn inward, or a concern for what is within.[42] And he frequently speaks of the mind as a self, taking both these terms to be virtually synonymous with Epictetus' *'hēgemonikon'*.[43]

But there is a further step to modern subjectivization. This is where we come to offer a wholly different answer to the question above, why do we love the cosmic (or any other) good? This answer points not to the intrinsic loveability of the object but to certain inclinations implanted in the subject. It is an answer of this kind that the word 'affection' suggests to a modern. The explanation turns on a feature of the lover's motivation.

This is not to say that a 'modern' explanation has to see goods as merely 'subjective', as shadows cast by the subject on a neutral universe, which is what the 'projection' theories of ethics I discussed in Part I hold. This has obviously been a major tendency of modern accounts, one of their major temptations, we might say. But this is not the only possible reason for an inward turn.

There has been a strand of Christian thought, as we have recurrently seen, which has not accommodated easily to the ordered cosmos as the measure of the good. For Luther, man was to be understood not primarily as *animal rationale,* but as *homo religiosus.* Humans long for God. Within this perspective, it is quite possible to conceive that our starting point in the search for the highest good might lie within—in our longing and our sense of incompleteness. This after all is just a transposition of Augustine's favoured path to a proof of the existence of God, through an awareness of my imperfection. Pascal was the first to explore this disquiet in thoroughly modern times, which remain relevant today. In the next chapter, we shall see a Deist theory which makes our inner motivation central, but which is nevertheless not projectivist.

And even outside a theistic perspective, it is quite possible to conceive that the best theory of the good, that which gives the best account of the worth of things and lives as they are open to us to discern, may be a thoroughly realist one—indeed, that is the view I want to defend, without wanting to make a claim about how things stand for the universe 'in itself' or for a universe in which there were no human beings. A realistic view is perfectly compatible with the thesis that the boundaries of the good, as we can grasp it, are set by that space which is opened in the fact that the world is there for us, with all the meanings it has for us—what Heidegger called 'the clearing'.[44]

Once a thesis of one of these kinds is accepted, then insofar as we can account at all for the existence of this space in which the good appears, it cannot simply be in terms of the universe as a self-manifesting reality; it has also to be in terms of our own make-up. The ancient view now tends to appear naive. We are tempted to say that its naivety consists in explicating the good in terms of the universe *'an sich'*. But this is anachronistic. The majority tradition among the ancients didn't raise the question to which a theory of good in things *an sich* is one answer. This presupposes that we sharply separate mind from nature. But the very concept of *'eidos'* or Form resists this separation. The very essence of things is an entity closely related to mind *(nous)* and reason *(logos)*.[45] The Ideas for Plato are not just objects waiting to be perceived; they are self-manifesting; the Idea of Ideas is itself a source of light, following his master image. The logos is ontic.

But for us moderns, the question insistently arises. Even where a Pascalian motive isn't present, the mechanistic picture of the universe and the disengaged stance of the subject conspire to make a separation, even a gulf, between mind and world. Whatever the answer, even for those who like certain Romantics tried to put Spirit back in Nature—indeed, especially for the Romantics—the crucial issue concerns the nature of the subject. And this, among others, takes the form of the question, What is it about the subject which makes him recognize and love the good? This could no longer be answered simply by the ancient term 'rational', meaning equipped to see the ratio in things, a response which perfunctorily closes the issue.

Where this question is appropriate, then an inquiry into the nature and conditions of the good takes us just as much inward as outward; as well as the constitution of things, we have to examine our own desires, aspirations, inclinations and feelings. This is what the full thrust of subjectivization amounts to, and where desires and aspirations become the crucial loci of examination. It becomes conceivable that good and evil can turn on the nature of our sentiments. Even those Romantics who aspired to rediscover Spirit in Nature learn the nature of Spirit through an inward turn.

Once this internalization takes place, then clearly, projectivism becomes a major temptation, and the issue between projectivists and realists comes to be a dominant one. But we are not quite there yet, at the threshold of the eighteenth century. This is the moment when the internalization of moral theory is established and becomes part of the wider culture. This is the century in which sentiment becomes important as a moral category, in a host of ways, including an influential theory of the moral sentiments.

Shaftesbury himself seems to me too close to the ancient Stoic model to have himself taken this step, at least fully and unambiguously. But his term 'affection' strongly suggests internalization. And he does speak sometimes of a 'moral sense',[46] which came to be a key term in the later theory of sentiment. Whether willingly or no, he certainly contributed to the development of this theory. This is one way in which at least his mode of expression gave his ancients-derived theory a modern twist.

2. The other is also suggested in the word 'affection'. The ancient theories which Shaftesbury drew on make harmony and equilibrium of the soul their major goal. Even when dealing with the way we treat others, balance and order are crucial. Justice and temperance are the primary virtues which ought to preside over our dealings with others. The injunction of the Stoic writer is well known,[47] that in commiserating with another for his misfortune, we ought indeed to *talk* consolingly, but not be *moved* by pity.

This is one respect in which Christianity was radically different from pagan thought. The highest virtue was a kind of love, unstinting giving, whose paradigm exemplar gave his life for others. The centre of gravity of the moral life shifts. These two moral outlooks were fitted together in Christian culture, not always in easy union, naturally, but perhaps most harmoniously in the famous Thomistic doctrine that superadds the three "theological" virtues to the natural ones.

With the affirmation of ordinary life, *agapē* is integrated in a new way into an ethic of everyday existence. My work in my calling ought to be for the general good. This insistence on practical help, on doing good for people, is carried on in the various semi-secularized successor ethics, e.g., with Bacon and Locke. The principal virtue in our dealing with others is now no longer just justice and temperance but beneficence. With the internalization of ethical thought, where inclinations are crucial, the motive of benevolence becomes the key to goodness.

Shaftesbury is part way along in this shift. He still speaks like his ancient mentors of the good life as producing "a constant complacency, constant security, tranquillity, equanimity";[48] and Theocles describes in *The Moralists* how the good man "becomes in truth the architect of his own life and fortune, by laying within himself the lasting and sure foundations of order, peace, concord".[49] But in the former of these places, the three items listed above are preceded by "a generous affection, an exercise of friendship uninterrupted, a constant kindness and benignity". Doing good also has crucial importance for Shaftesbury. He is too much of a modern, too much of a product of the age of Locke, let alone his close experience of him as tutor, for it to be otherwise.

Nevertheless, he still breathes the air of Stoic calm and equilibrium, or longingly aspires to do so. We have to await his successors to see benevolence promoted to the main virtue.

All this we can see worked out in the moral sense theory, which Shaftesbury helped inspire, and whose major spokesman was Francis Hutcheson.

15.2

Hutcheson was a fierce opponent of the extrinsic theory, and in this he took his lead from Shaftesbury. His *Inquiry into the Original of Our Ideas of Beauty and Virtue* is subtitled in part: "in which the Principles of the late Earl of Shaftesbury are Explain'd and Defended, against the Author of the *Fables of the Bees*". Mandeville, the author of this latter work, had made himself the centre of a storm of controversy by attempting to show how what were normally considered vices tended to the good of society, on grounds which are later integrated into mainstream thought by Adam Smith, grounds that we would class today as 'economic'. The work seemed like an attack on the very validity of the virtue/vice distinction.

But in fact Hutcheson doesn't spend that much time on Mandeville. Much more serious opponents are moralists of the extrinsic school, who believe indeed that good is really distinguished from bad, but who make this depend ultimately on self-love or self-interest, once we take into account the full consequences of our actions, including divine rewards and punishments. This class includes the ancient Epicureans and their modern followers (in which class Hutcheson places Hobbes and La Rochefoucauld), but it also contains certain "Christian Moralists of this Scheme", who are unnamed, but among whom it is not hard to recognize Locke.[50]

This seems to Hutcheson very wrong, and as we shall see, damagingly wrong. He is not even tempted to adopt this extrinsic view, because it seems to fly in the face of the most obvious human experience. We are obviously moved by something other than egoism, some generous motives, when we act morally. And we often morally admire a gallant enemy, loyal to his cause, and despise his traitorous colleague, however useful to us. The extrinsic account of our desires and affections is not really credible, because it makes "the most generous, kind and disinterested of them, to proceed from Self-Love, by some subtle Trains of Reasoning, to which honest Hearts are often wholly Strangers".[51]

Goodness and generosity are natural to us. He might have been tempted in an earlier generation to say 'innate', but he has internalized enough of the Lockean psychology to shy away from this. So he claims that these sentiments are ones we naturally grow to have, just as we develop to our normal stature and shape.[52]

But how to explain these impulsions in terms of our psychology? Hutcheson builds on Lockean concepts and grounds them in a moral sense. A sense is what delivers ideas to us; it operates passively, and its deliverances are not to be gone behind or questioned. Just because they come passively, without any interpretation on our part, ideas are to be taken as brute data, as the building blocks of knowledge.[53] So Locke. Hutcheson defines a sense as what delivers ideas in this meaning.[54] The utter un-derivability of our moral judgements and motivations from any merely prudential ones is then enshrined in the thesis that we have a moral sense: "Some Actions have to Men an immediate Goodness", and that through "a superior Sense, which I call a Moral one".[55] The reductive extrinsic theory is stopped dead in its tracks. Moral reactions can't by their definition be further explained.

This is perhaps a dangerous way to attain this end. By grounding moral judgements in brute data, Hutcheson opens the possibility, of treating them like any other de facto reaction, of disengaging from them and considering them mere projections. This kind of account could be grist to the mill of a projectivist theory, where moral properties would be assimilated to secondary properties, unanchored in reality, but a regular part of our experience in virtue of our constitution. This assimilation has been the basis for a projectivist 'error' theory in our day, as I described in Part I.[56] And Hutcheson himself at times seems to be espousing the analogy.[57] A standard feature in the analysis of secondary properties is that they are correlated with primary qualities and thought to be part of the subjective 'colouration' attending our experience of these latter. What makes them 'subjective' on this view is that they depend on our make-up, and might just as well be quite different, if our senses were differently constituted.

Hutcheson, seemingly following some such analogy, allows that the moral sense can be seen as equally adventitiously hooked up to the world. He allows the supposition that God could have hooked us up differently, e.g., so as not to feel benevolently towards others[58] or even to take delight in their torments.[59] Hutcheson introduces these possibilities in order to laud the goodness of God for having chosen the existing dispensation—proving God's benign providence is one of his principal goals. But he fails to see how wide this opens the door to relativism, and how problematic this makes his judgement about the moral goodness of the Deity.[60]

However much this psychology may open the door to relativism and naturalism—an avenue which Hume perhaps began to explore—this is clearly not the way intended by Hutcheson. Whether he has a right to it or not, he has a very clear and strong idea of the goodness of the Deity, anterior to his choice of senses to endow us with. What is good is the way it works out for us. We are beings who seek happiness, and this is defined in the standard Lockean way, more or less in terms of pleasure.[61] The fortunate thing is that (1) our moral sense pushes us to benevolence and (2) benevolence is what works most for our happiness.

(1) is a central doctrine of Hutcheson. He is thoroughly modern in this regard. "All the actions which are counted as amiable any where . . . always appear as Benevolent, or flowing from the Love of others, and Study of their Happiness." And the "Actions our moral Sense would most recommend to our Election, as the most perfectly Virtuous" are "such as appear to have the most universal unlimited Tendency to the greatest and most extensive Happiness of all the rational Agents, to whom our influence can extend".[62] Hutcheson even attempts to bring the classical four virtues into line with this modern hegemony of benevolence. Thus justice is redefined as "a constant study to promote the most universal happiness in our power, by doing all good offices as we have opportunity which interfere with no more extensive interest of the system".[63]

As to (2), Hutcheson is a convinced believer in the perfectly interlocking universe, which God has designed for the mutual good and happiness of its inhabitants. Things work together for the best.

> How can any one look upon this World as under the Direction of an evil Nature, or even question a perfectly good Providence? How clearly does the Order of our Nature point out to us our true Happiness and Perfection, and lead us naturally as the several Powers of the Earth, the Sun, and Air, bring Plants to their Growth, and the Perfection of their Kinds? . . . We may see, that Attention to the most universal Interest of all sensitive Natures, is the Perfection of each individual of Mankind: . . . Nay, how much of this do we actually see in the World? What generous Sympathy, Compassion, and Congratulation with each other?[64]

Consequently, there is no clash of interests. Each person serves himself best by serving the whole: "His constant pursuit of publick Good is the most probable way of promoting his own Happiness".[65] This, of course, is what those extrinsic theorists claim who want to base morals on self-interest. Hutcheson doesn't differ with them on this. He agrees with Cumberland and Pufendorf that "Reflection on the Circumstances of Mankind in this World would have suggested, that a universal Benevolence and social Temper, or a Course of such external Actions, would most effectually promote the external Good of every one".[66] He even agrees with them that it is very important to get people to see that there is such a harmony of interests.[67]

What he cannot agree with is that seeing this harmony is what in fact motivates us to benevolence. Why does he want so strongly to make this point? Writing from the perspective of the twentieth century, where the issue of the foundation of ethics has become so perplexed and disputed, we might think that we saw the extrinsic theory as a denial of morality, fraught with the projection theories which developed from it. This is how David Fate Norton approaches Hutcheson, for instance.[68] There is some truth in this; after all the *Inquiry* was meant to answer Mandeville, who was certainly perceived as a subverter of morality.

But most of the extrinsic theorists he wants to criticize were plainly not rejecting morality, and he allows that they are not. He even admits that their principal empirical argument, that of the harmony of interests, is valid and needs to be made known. The big issue is elsewhere. It is a question of moral sources. The extrinsic theorists have totally misidentified the very mainsprings of moral action. They are denying that, the vivid recognition of which empowers us to the moral life. This is to put it in my terms, of course, but Hutcheson seems to be acknowledging something very similar.

In Hutcheson's mind, taking the extrinsic view, or in any way failing to recognize the benevolence in our nature, stifles and cripples our moral sentiments. There is one obvious way in which this can happen, of course, and that is if we believe that our interest is opposed to helping others. This specious deterrent must be set aside, and that is why we have to convince people that self-love is not opposed to benefiting others. We have to get "this noble Disposition"—"our natural Propensity to Benevolence"—"loose from these Bonds of Ignorance, and false Views of Interest".[69]

This is purely an external deterrent, so to speak, and has nothing to do with what I am calling moral sources. But Hutcheson also holds that not believing in our own moral inclinations dampens them, and recognizing them gives them strength. In acknowledging the mainsprings of good in us, we rejoice in them, and this joy makes them flow the stronger. This is why it is crucial to establish his doctrine of the moral sense, and this is why the misanthropic extrinsic theory has to be combated.

In the Preface to his *Essay on the Nature and Conduct of the Passions and Affections,* Hutcheson justifies inquiring into the passions, which some might think as "too subtle for common Apprehension, and consequently not necessary for the Instruction of Men in Morals, which are the common business of Mankind". But in fact certain notions are already current about the passions (the extrinsic theory), "to the great Detriment of many a Natural Temper; since many have been discouraged from all Attempts of cultivating kind generous Affections in themselves, by a previous Notion that there are no such Affections in Nature, and that all Pretence to them was only Dissimulation, Affectation, or at best some unnatural Enthusiasm".[70]

To be good, it is important to identify our own sources of goodness. And not only in ourselves but in our fellow humans and, of course, in the God who designed all this. We have to believe in the goodness of human nature. Or else,

> when upon any small Injury's, or sudden Resentment, or any weak superstitious Suggestions, our Benevolence is so faint, as to let us run into any odious Conceptions of Mankind . . . as if they were wholly Evil, or Malicious, or as if they were a worse Sort of Beings than they really are; these Conceptions must lead us into malevolent Affections, or at least weaken our good ones, and make us really Vitious.[71]

Seeing the goodness of human beings makes us better. And that is why it is important to grasp that "Every Passion or Affection in its moderate Degree is innocent, many are directly amiable, and morally good: we have Senses and Affections leading us to publick Good, as well as to private; to Virtue, as well as to other sorts of Pleasure".[72]

But if seeing the good in ourselves and in others releases this good and intensifies it, the effect will be all the greater if we extend our gaze and see that the whole universe is good and springs from the all-embracing benevolence of the creator. In the passage I quoted above about the harmonious order of the world, in which Hutcheson remarks on the "generous Sympathy, Compassion and Congratulation with each other" we see in it, he continues: "Does not even the flourishing State of the inanimate Parts of Nature, fill us with joy? Is not thus our Nature Admonished, exhorted and commanded to cultivate universal Goodness and Love, by a Voice heard thro' all the Earth, and Words sounding to the Ends of the World?"[73]

But most of all,

> A constant regard to God in all our actions and enjoyments, will give a new beauty to every virtue, by making it an act of gratitude and love to him; and increase our pleasure in every enjoyment, as it will appear an evidence of his goodness; it will give a diviner purity and simplicity of heart, to conceive all our virtuous dispositions as implanted by God in our hearts, and all our beneficent offices as our proper work, and the natural duties of that station we hold in this universe, and the services we owe to this nobler country.[74]

Thus for Hutcheson our moral sources—the goods reflection on which morally empowers us—are first, our own benevolence, and then the source in turn of this, the universal benevolence of God—"the AUTHOR of our Nature", as Hutcheson often styles him. For all his acceptance of Lockean psychological terms, his inspiration is clearly Shaftesbury, and through him his roots go back to the Erasmian tradition of the Cambridge school. He shares their fierce opposition to an ethic of extrinsic law. But with Hutcheson, this tradition has gone through the two transformations which were only hinted at in Shaftesbury's language: Our bent towards the good (1) is thoroughly internalized in *sentiment* and (2) takes the form above all of universal *benevolence*.

These two changes bring him closer than Shaftesbury to Lockean Deism. The internalization to sentiments is what allows him to couch his theory in Lockean psychology. The stress on benevolence places him in a line that runs from the Puritans through Bacon and Locke to the utilitarians.

Indeed, Hutcheson often sounds like a utilitarian, and he plainly did a lot to prepare the ground for this school. "That action is best", he declares, "which accomplishes the greatest Happiness for the greatest Numbers".[75] The purpose of God is said to be "the universal happiness", which he brings about impartially.[76] He was even one of the pioneers of rational choice theory, proposing mathematical calculations of, e.g., the morality of an action, the "Quantity of publick Good produc'd" by a person, and the like.[77] Moreover, in his refutation of the rationalists, he puts forward as uncompromising a definition of reason as instrumental as one can find anywhere:

> He acts reasonably, who considers the various Actions in his Power, and forms true Opinions of their Tendencies; and then chuses to do that which will obtain the highest degree of that, to which the Instincts of his Nature incline him, with the smallest Degree of those things from which the Affections in his Nature make him averse.[78]

Hutcheson's Deism is thus in some way close to Locke's. The most important notion Hutcheson and Locke share is that of the great interlocking universe, in which the parts are so designed as to conduce to their mutual preservation and flourishing.

> It was observed above, how admirably our Affections were contrived for good in the whole . . . they all aim at good, either private or publick: and by them each particular Agent is made, in great measure, subservient to the good of the whole. Mankind are thus insensibly linked together, and make one great System, by an invisible Union. He who voluntarily continues in this Union, and delights in employing his Power for his Kind, makes himself happy: He who does not continue this Union freely, but

affects to break it, makes himself wretched; nor yet can he break the Bonds of Nature.[79]

The two kinds of Deism share some such vision; and they share the inspiration which this vision provides. To that extent, their respective senses of moral sources overlap. But where they differ is in how we take our place in this order. For the Lockean, we do so through the exercise of disengaged reason. For the Deism which comes from Shaftesbury (and also from Leibniz, as we shall see in Chapter 16), though disengaged reason is not repudiated, we participate in God's plan through a re-engagement: we have to recover the movement towards the good within us, and allow it to take its proper shape. We turn within to retrieve the true form of our natural affection or our benevolent sentiments; and in doing that we give them their full force.

And thus in this respect the moral sources of the two variants radically differ. In one case, we find them in the dignity of the disengaged, self-responsibly clairvoyant, rational, controlling subject. In the other case, we also look for them in the sentiments we find within. When Deism was at its height, in the first half of the century, this difference may not always have seemed significant. But it becomes of crucial importance later, with the developing conception of nature as an inner source. With Rousseau and the Romantics, it flares up into one of the deepest oppositions of our culture.

But in order to understand this better, I want to look first at this new conception of an interlocking order, as well as at the new conception of nature as within us, and then turn to examine the radical, unbelieving Enlightenment. This will set the scene for the Rousseauian challenge which still reverberates through our culture.

16

THE PROVIDENTIAL ORDER

16.1

We ordinarily tend to look on eighteenth-century Deism simply as a staging area on the way to the secular, unbelieving Enlightenment. In a sense, this isn't wrong as a perspective. Deism did prepare the way for the radical Enlightenment. It turned out to have explored some of the arguments which were taken further into unbelief. But in another way, this perspective can be very misleading, because it is often taken as implying that Deistic views were simply half-hearted unbelief, that those who propounded them had already all but abandoned a religious perspective and were largely keeping up appearances. What differentiated them from their atheist successors is then thought to be simply a lack of courage.

There was, of course, lots of dissimulation in the eighteenth century on this score. It wasn't easy to declare yourself an unbeliever, and very few did. The costs could be very high. But it is very wrong to see all those we can classify as Deists as either dissemblers or only half-committed to their views. And this mistake is crippling, if we want to understand this period; it obscures our picture of religious and irreligious alike. Or so I want to claim. That is because it hides from us the force of these Deist views as religious beliefs. But unless we see what they had going for them, how they could convince and even inspire those who held them, we will miss something crucial in the whole context in which they rose and fell.

Paradoxically, the best way to appreciate this point is to take seriously the cliché that Deism is halfway on the road to the radical Enlightenment, because then we will see how coming to understand what could inspire the former will give us insight into the latter.

So we should ask what could move people in the religious outlook we find expressed in Hutcheson or, more radically perhaps, in Tindal. What would lead one to praise and be thankful to God, if one saw his work the way they did? The answer is obviously his goodness, his benevolence. And this was expressed in his having made a world in which the purposes of the different beings inhabiting it, and particularly of the rational beings, so perfectly interlock. The world was designed so that each in seeking his or her good will also serve the good of others. The fullest human happiness, on Hutcheson's view, is attained when we give full reign to our moral sentiments and feelings of benevolence. But it is just then that we do most to contribute to the general happiness.

God's goodness thus consists in his bringing about our good. His beneficence is explained partly in terms of our happiness. But what is striking about these Deist views is that the converse relation, so central to the religious tradition, seems to be lacking. It is after all a central tenet of the Judaeo-Christian religious tradition that God loves and seeks the good of his creatures. But this good in turn has always been defined as consisting in some relation to God: in our loving him, serving him, being in his presence, contemplating him in the beatific vision, or something of this kind.

What is striking about Deist views is that the human good in terms of which God's benevolence is defined is so self-contained. It is not that the reference to God is wholly absent, but it seems to be subordinate to a conception of happiness which is defined purely in creaturely terms. Happiness is the attaining of the things we by nature desire, or pleasure and the absence of pain. The rewards of the next life seem to be considered just as more intense and longer-lasting versions of the pleasures and pains of this. Moreover, God's having set up this system of recompense in the next world seems to be designed at least partly to underpin the interlocking system in this one.

Humans are indeed moved to the height of goodness, on Hutcheson's view, only by a sense of love and gratitude to God:

> Thus as the calm and most extensive determination of the soul towards the universal happiness can have no other center of rest and joy than the original independent omnipotent Goodness; so without the knowledge of it, and the most ardent love and resignation to it, the soul cannot attain to its own most stable and highest perfection and excellence.[1]

So the soul needs God to be integrally good. This is an entirely traditional view. But what our goodness seems to consist in is a "determination . . . towards the universal happiness"; and what God's goodness consists in seems to be his fostering this same end. A purely self-contained, non-theocentric notion of the good, happiness, plays a central role in this outlook; and the lineaments of our right relationship to God—gratitude, love, resignation—are all defined in terms of it.

A similar point should be made about the crucial virtue on Hutcheson's view, namely benevolence. This takes the place and continues the function of the earlier theological virtue of charity. The notion that the godly person is one who gives of himself or herself is continued in this new ethic, in which all the traditional virtues are redefined, as we saw above, and related to benevolence.[2] But the content of this disposition is defined in terms of human happiness.

The crucial thing here is thus the focus on the human. It is human happiness that really matters in the universe. It is this which is the object of God's prodigious efforts (or at least part-object: he is concerned with his other creatures a well). This is sheer presumptuousness from the standpoint of one important strand of Christian thought—and there were lots of people in this century who were more than willing to point this out. Humans are there for God, not vice versa.[3] In this respect, Deism seems a total break with the religious tradition. But in other respects it was deeply rooted in it. Disentangling these strands will help us to understand its motivations.

Very deep in all religious traditions where there is a god, or gods, at all, lies the idea that god's purposes are distinct from ours. The Greek religious tradition required that one maintain the boundary between god and man, immortal and mortal. The gods are powerful beings, wondrous and awe-inspiring, but whose friendship or good disposition cannot be taken for granted. They often have to be propitiated. Right up to the end, the cults of paganism retained their traditional purpose of averting or propitiating divine anger.[4] But a god whose friendship had been won would "hold his hand" above his devotee in protection.[5] Divine-human relations had something of the character of those between patrons and clients, except that the class of immortals was incomparably and awesomely above its mortal servants.

In the Hebrew Bible, the transcendent and inscrutable nature of God's purposes is even more strongly marked: "For my thoughts are not your thoughts, my ways are not your ways—it is Yahweh who speaks. Yes, the heavens are as high above the earth as my ways are above your ways, my thoughts above your thoughts" (Isaiah 55:8–9; JB). Humans are not owed a full explanation, but are called on to obey. David Hartman has shown how the tremendous interpretive freedom accorded the rabbinic community in Judaism combines nevertheless with a sense of the ultimacy of God's decisions. In the midrash in which Moses expresses horror at the gruesome martyrdom suffered by Rabbi Akiva, one of the greatest of all scholars, God sternly replies: "Be silent, for such is My decree".[6]

Man's goals and God's seem far apart. At the same time they are drawn together in both traditions, but in rather different ways. The great philosophical formulations, principally influenced by Plato, drew pagan religion towards a loftier and more unitary notion of Deity. God, when he is spoken of in the singular, 'ho theos', has risen far above Homer's libidinous, squabbling family on Olympos. He is the God who made or emanates in the cosmos and is identified with its order and harmony. But in this philosophy, the goals of mankind have also been redefined upward. Humans too, as rational beings, are characterized above all by a love for this order. At their best, they converge with God in loving one and the same thing, the cosmic order. For some this emerges in the primacy of contemplation. For the Stoics, it takes the form of willing acceptance of whatever occurs. Shaftesbury seems to return to a position close to this. But in general, Deism has affinities with this ancient philosophical religion, with which many thinkers in the eighteenth century felt a strong sympathy, against its Christian supplanter.

The drawing together of God and man took a quite different form among the Hebrews. There the separation of God from the cosmos remains strong. God's holiness *(kodesh)* contrasts with the merely profane in the universe.[7] But surprisingly, God calls on Israel to be his people. At the beginning, this involved something like a patron-client relation, in this respect like all the surrounding peoples who had "their" gods. But it also involved something more, that Israel become a "holy people" (Exodus 19:6, Leviticus 20:7), that is, a people consecrated to God, hence themselves set apart from among the nations.

> You must lay them [the nations] under ban. You must make no covenant with them nor show them any pity . . . For you are a people consecrated [*kadosh*] to Yahweh your God; it is you that Yahweh our God has chosen to be his very own people out of all the peoples on the earth. (Deuteronomy 7:2, 6, JB; also Leviticus 20:26)

In other words, it was a people called to live God's way; not to live by the ordinary ways of other peoples, "paying their dues" to a tutelary deity, but to live by a law given by God. Israel became, in a sense, a theocracy.

The convergence thus takes the form of humans being drawn into God's purposes. But there is also a movement the other way, as it were. God wills and furthers the good of his people. This, of course, fits with the "normal", widely recognized patron-client model. But there is a difference. That the dedication to God goes beyond mere "paying of dues" is reflected in the story of the Akedah, Abraham's readiness to sacrifice Isaac at God's command. God asks for a total giving, and in return "the Lord provides" (Genesis 22:14).

Further, the notion develops with the prophets that service to God involves justice and help to the oppressed. "What are your endless sacrifices to me? says Yahweh. I am sick of holocausts of rams and the fat of calves . . . Your hands are covered with blood, wash, make yourselves clean. Take your wrongdoing out of my sight. Cease to do evil. Learn to do good, search for justice, help the oppressed, be just to the orphan, plead for the widow" (Isaiah 1:11, 16–17; JB).

This is the point at which the convergence between God and man seems similar to that in pagan philosophy. In doing God's will, humans are called to high ethical standards. Many pious Jews, and later many Christians, saw the close analogy,[8] as did some pagans as well. As mentioned in Chapter 7, Plato later won the title of 'Attic Moses'.

Analogy there certainly is, which accounts for the incorporation of so much Greek philosophy into both Judaism and Christianity. But there is also a difference, which I discussed in Chapter 13. Sanctification in the Judaeo-Christian tradition (being a *'tsadik'*, or a 'saint') does indeed involve embracing a higher morality. But this is not defined only in terms of certain "higher" activities, or love of the order of things. These don't exhaust what it means to be dedicated to the cause of God. Moreover, this cause includes an affirming of life, which incorporates what I have called ordinary life. What differentiates God from humans in this respect is the fulness, the force of the affirmation—something humans can't match on their own, but which they can participate in by following God.

This participation in the Jewish case is defined by the Torah. In the Christian case, the key notion is that of *agapē*, or charity, God's affirming love for the world (John 3:16), which humans through receiving can then give in turn. In either case, there is something beyond morality, as it were, viz., participation in God's affirming power.

It is this extra dimension which Deism drops from view. This brings it closer to the pagan philosophical model. But this human-centred view also has its roots in the Christian tradition. It can be drawn from the very radicalism of the New Testament challenge to "pharisaic" orthodoxy: e.g., "the Sabbath was made for man, and not man for the Sabbath" (Mark 2:27), or "they [the scribes and the pharisees] bind heavy burdens and grievous to be borne, and lay them on men's shoulders" (Matthew 23:4). It can be grounded on the view of God as humbling himself to rescue mankind, which is one of the dominant strands of interpretation of the Incarnation.[9]

More immediately, the human-centred outlook drew, as one might imagine, on the polemic against certain hyper-Augustinian views. We find the argument among the Cambridge Platonists, for instance, that it was demeaning to God to suppose that he should be concerned in his dealings with us with anything but our good—as though he might need our service or might actually desire to be paid honour for his own satisfaction.[10] Tindal makes a similar point in his *Christianity as Old as the Creation*: we shouldn't think of God as injured by human wrongdoing. It is wrong and demeaning to God to think that he punishes us to restore his own honour. He does it purely for our sake.[11] The continuity is there, but what has changed radically between Whichcote and Tindal is the content of the human good for which God is thought to act. In Whichcote's understanding it includes "deification", the raising of human nature to participate in the divine.[12] For Tindal, the human good which God endeavours to promote has shrunk to the "common Interest, and mutual Happiness of his rational Creatures".[13]

The change is not insignificant. In terms of the discussion of Chapter 14, we can say that the first kind of role for grace mentioned there, that which consists in our being called to a good which transcends the natural, is totally undercut. For this only made sense in that extra dimension of God's affirming power I spoke of above. And of course the second role, that which figures in hyper-Augustinian theologies which stress the moral incapacity of our fallen nature, was being directly denied. So grace begins to disappear altogether. Orthodox Christians were not mistaken in thinking that something crucial had been dropped.

But we have also to see how the Deist focus on human happiness could be represented as simply carrying further, and doing fuller justice to, this crucial insight of Erasmian Christianity, that God's greatness consists in his not needing us to exist for him, and that therefore it finds its purest expression in his being disposed to think exclusively of our good. God is capable of disinterested love, argues Tindal, in a way that we aren't. We can only love him because he's good to us.[14] The belief that God doesn't put any further demands on us than the proper fulfilment of our own nature can be represented as a more uncompromising working out of the basic insight that God's goodness consists in his seeking our good. Paradoxically, the very uncompromising nature of God's affirmation of mankind can serve to justify dispensing humans from participating in it; and the superhuman strength of this affirming power can serve to declare it beyond the human purview.

We can see the extrapolation of another leading idea here as well. Tindal's view of human destiny is infinitely more modest than Whichcote's. The Deist conception of nature and happiness is in the direct line of succession from the Reformation affirmation of ordinary life, as indeed we saw in earlier chapters. The human good, the happiness which God has designed for us, is purely a matter of the fulfilment of our natural desires and sentiments. It has no more place for the higher activities of ancient moral theories than it has for the higher destinies of the Greek fathers, or any other classical theologians.

What I want to bring out here is the way in which the Deist rewriting of Christian faith, around the picture of a natural order designed inter alia for a self-contained human good, stands in two lines of theological development: the Erasmian definition of God's goodness in terms of his beneficence to mankind; and the anti-hierarchical affirmation of ordinary life. Both of these lines were drawn in the course of a hard-fought polemic: the first against the theologies of human incapacity and predestination; the second against the (supposedly) presumptuous claims to higher moral powers or spiritual destinies. This should help us to understand how Deist views, however much they subverted or abandoned crucial aspects of Christian faith, could be seen as fuller and more uncompromising expressions of what that faith entailed. In relation to the opponent in each polemic, they could appear as the more full-blooded response. Until, that is, they were in turn trumped in this respect by frankly unbelieving theories, an important part of whose appeal, I believe, came precisely from their apparently more uncompromising fulfilment of aspirations which were deeply embedded in the very religious tradition they were denying. But this only comes to light, I think, when one appreciates what Deism had going for it as a religious view. I shall return to this below.

It was, of course, precisely these "Christian" features which made Deism unlike the pagan philosphical models its spokesmen sometimes admired, as I noted in the previous chapter. It was also too human-centred, too concerned with merely human good, to fit the ancient model. But what made the affinity in spite of this was the fact that once more a cosmic *order* was at the centre of spiritual life.

The idea that God designs things for the human good took the form of a belief in good order of *nature*. Providence was understood in general terms; it was reflected in the regular disposition of things. The Deists had no more place for the "particular providences", God's interventions in the stories of individuals and nations, which were at the centre of much popular piety and were extremely important to the orthodox—and to a contemporary popular movement like Methodism, for instance.

Deism didn't hold that God constantly intervenes miraculously in order to make things work out well for us. On the contrary, the thinkers of this stamp took up the Reformers' belief that the "age of miracles" was past, and eventually took it even further, to scepticism about the founding miracles of the New Testament. This was a serious matter, because following Locke many orthodox thinkers argued that the Christian revelation showed itself to be genuine in the miracles Christ performed. These made his claims truly believable. Hence the challenge of Hume and others to the believability of the miracle stories themselves touched a sensitive nerve.

But in the Deist outlook, the miracle stories of the New Testament had lost their point. There they stand as interventions of the divine affirming power saving people from specific outcomes generated in and by a fallen world. In this sense, they are emblematic concrete instances of God's whole saving action in the Incarnation. The healings take place through a forgiveness of sins.[15] But in the Deist perspective, the goodness of God manifests itself in the beneficence of the regular order of things. It is not the fallenness of the world but its perfection of design which now becomes crucial. People need not to be saved from a reigning disorder, but rather to learn to conform properly to the design of things.

Indeed, on this view God can't intervene to interrupt the regular operations of the world, at least not too frequently, on pain of frustrating his own purposes. The order would cease to be a regular one, and the benefits which flow from this would cease. This is how Hutcheson, among others, meets the principal challenge of theodicy. He was confident that the various ills that people suffer in this world could be explained as the necessary side effects of the regular production of good. For instance, we suffer pain, because it has been designed as a very effective signalling system of malfunction. Without the pain of burning, we might not know to withdraw our hand from the fire when we are distracted elsewhere, and the like. It's an unfortunate side effect of this that we actually suffer. Couldn't God have designed a painless signalling system? Plainly this wouldn't have worked, argues Hutcheson. You need something which not only warns people but also stimulates them to take remedial action. Even as things are, we see that fever and racking sores don't always deter people from vice.[16]

Well then, how about God intervening in the system whenever the unfortunate feature isn't required? Suppose he made pain milder for more virtuous people, who don't need to be goaded into reformation. That, thinks Hutcheson, is ruled out because then there would no longer be, properly speaking, an order of things. One of the benefits of an order is that we can count on it; this is what allows us to achieve our good through the exercise of our characteristic powers, those of instrumental reason. If God were constantly to adjust the laws to particular cases, then this "would immediately supercede all contrivance and forethought of men, and all prudent action",[17] not to speak of the fact that removing all obstacles to their well-being would allow no more place for active virtue.

The design of an order for the good of instrumentally rational creatures leaves God no choice, as it were, but to establish laws which he will leave to operate without interference. He shows his goodness in refraining from miracles.

So the paramountcy of order excludes miraculous interventions. But it also marginalizes history. The 'historical' nature of Judaism, Christianity, Islam—that is, the fact that allegiance and piety are focussed on key historical events: Sinai, the Incarnation, the giving of the Quran—is intrinsically connected with their recognition of the extra dimension. These events are the eruptions of God's affirming power in human life, and its continued force in our lives requires that we maintain unbroken continuity with these moments through tradition. Once the notion of order becomes paramount, it makes no more sense to give them a crucial status in religious life. It becomes an embarrassment to religion that it should be bound to belief in particular events which divide one group from another and are in any case open to cavil. The great truths of religion are all universal. Reason extracts these from the general course of things. A gap separates these realities of universal import from the particulate facts of history. These latter cannot support the former.

"Zufällige Geschichtswahrheiten können der Beweis von notwendigen Vernunftwahrheiten nie werden" ("Contingent historical truths can never serve as proof for necessary truths of reason"), as Lessing put it.[18]

Short of jettisoning these beliefs altogether, one could still give them some justification as part of a pedagogy of the human race, which in its earliest phases probably needed such stories to get it to accept the high spiritual outlook which a more philosophical age can understand directly. Such was Lessing's view.[19] But the mature religion which eventually emerges is stripped down to the bare essentials. In its most general formulation, it can be reduced to three propositions: the existence of a Creator God, his Providence, and the fact of an afterlife with rewards and punishments.[20] Revelation, which was intrinsically connected to historical religion, becomes unnecessary, because these "truths" were held available to reason alone. True religion was ultimately natural religion.

I hope the preceding discussion will have made clearer the appeal of this Deism. One facet—which I discussed in Chapter 9—is the force of the ideal of self-responsible reason. Here was a fully rational religion, which made no appeals to historically grounded authority. This is often given exclusive attention in discussions of Deism today. My argument here has been intended to show that there was another facet to its motivation, that it also drew on certain ideals whose roots are deep in the Christian tradition itself.

16.2

This latter element in the motivation explains why, for all the elements of continuity, the order admired by the Deists of this century is very different from that of the ancient tradition.

Alexander Pope's *Essay on Man* gives eloquent expression to this vision of order. In continuity with a long tradition, he sees it as a "great chain of being":

> Vast chain of Being! which from God began,
> Natures ethereal, human, angel, man.
> Beast, bird, fish, insect, what no eye can see,
> No glass can reach; from Infinite to thee,
> from thee to Nothing.

Or again:

> All are but parts of one stupendous whole,
> Whose body Nature is, and God the soul[21]

This sounds like the familiar concept, which had been invoked over many centuries. And in some senses it is. Lovejoy has shown how far the notion of the great chain of being goes back.[22] What he has called "the principle of plenitude" is invoked by Pope a little later in this same epistle.[23] And in this Pope is not exceptional; this side of the traditional view was very much alive. Locke had also taken as given that God had created beings to fill all the possible levels of existence. And Hutcheson invoked the same idea in his theodicy, in the chapter I just quoted from above:[24] the universe must contain some imperfection, because God will create beings right down to the point where the superiority of good over bad is at vanishing point. Leibniz's espousal of this principle is celebrated.[25]

But there is an important difference. Pope's statement that "All Nature is but Art, unknown to thee",[26] already hints at it. The order we are being asked to admire here is not an order of expressed or embodied meanings. What makes the collection of entities that make up the world an order is not primarily that they realize an interrelated whole of possibilities—although something of that lingers on, as we see, in the principle of plenitude.[27] The principal thing that makes the entities in the world into an order is that their natures *mesh*. The purposes sought by each, of the causal functions which each one exercises, interlock with the others so as to cohere into a harmonious whole. Each in serving itself serves the entire order.

This new vision is presented by means of another traditional image:

> Look round our World; behold the chain of Love
> Combining all below and all above.[28]

The chain of love figures prominently in Ficino's Platonism, which had a wide influence through the Renaissance and up to the period we're now looking at, through the Cambridge Platonists, and then Shaftesbury. In the very next line, Pope refers to "plastic Nature", a key term of the Cambridge school, as it was of the Romantics later. But for Ficino, the chain functioned within the context of a neo-Platonic theory of emanation: the higher loves the lower which emanates from it, and the lower loves the higher, of which it is in a sense an emanation or expression. Plato's doctrine of love in the *Symposium* is essential to this theory.

But the chain of love for Pope is rather that interconnection of mutual service which the things in this world of harmonious functions render to each other. There was, of course, a traditional "organicism" in the old views of order: the different things in the universe depend on each other and support each other. But where that mutual dependence once flowed from the fact that each holds its ordered place in a whole, which would otherwise revert to chaos (see Ulysses' speech in Shakespeare's *Troilus:* "Take but degree away, untune that string, / And hark what discord follows"; 1.3.109–110), now the support takes direct efficient-causal form: e.g., things *feed* each other. The lines about the chain of love continue:

> See plastic Nature working to this end,
> The single atoms each to other tend,
> Attract, attracted to, the next in place
> Formed and impelled its neighbour to embrace.
> See Matter next, with various life endued,
> Press to one centre still, the general Good.
> See dying vegetables life sustain,
> See life dissolving vegetate again:
> All forms that perish other forms supply,
> (By turns we catch the vital breath, and die)
> Like bubbles on the sea of Matter born,
> They rise, they break, and to that sea return.
> Nothing is foreign: Parts relate to whole;
> One all-extending, all-preserving Soul
>
> Connects each being, greatest with the least;
> Made Beast in aid of Man, and Man of Beast;
> All served, all serving: nothing stands alone;
> The chain holds on, and where it ends, unknown.

Further on, he praises God:

> God in nature of each being founds
> Its proper bliss, and sets its proper bounds:
> But as he framed a Whole, the Whole to bless,
> On mutual Wants built mutual Happiness:
> So from the first, eternal ORDER ran,
> And creature linked to creature, man to man.[29]

This new order of interlocking natures arises to take the place of an order predicated on an ontic logos. As the metaphysical basis of the earlier view erodes, in particular with the growing success of mechanistic science, the new vision can step into the vacuum. It is fully compatible with the modern conception of the nature of a thing as made up of the forces which operate within it. Each thing is seen as having its own purpose or bent. The goodness of the order consists in the fact that these don't run athwart each other, but mesh.

Leibniz's was the most influential formulation of the idea of an order made up of elements of this kind. These are described by him as "monads". They can be seen as particulars which have, to a higher or lower degree, a purpose which they are bent to encompass. Leibniz thus combines something of Aristotelian teleology, in the notion that the nature of a thing provides for its unfolding in a certain fashion, with the modern idea that the nature of a thing is within it. Because the forms are internal, in a way that they are not with Aristotle, the harmony of the world has to be "pre-established" by God.[30]

Like its predecessor the meaningful cosmos, the new order of meshing natures can also provide the foundation for moral and social order. Thanks to providence, the way of the world is good. We can place entire confidence in it.

> Such is the World's great harmony, that springs
> From Order, Union, full Consent of things:
> Where small and great, where weak and mighty, made
> To serve, not suffer, strengthen, not invade;
> More powerful each as needful to the rest,
> And, in proportion as it blesses, blest;
> Draw to one point, and to one centre bring
> Beast, Man or Angel, Servant, Lord or King.[31]

Our superficial view that all is not right has to be corrected:

> All Chance, Direction, which thou canst not see;
> All Discord, Harmony not understood;
> All partial Evil, universal Good:
> And, spite of Pride, in erring Reason's spite,
> One truth is clear, WHATEVER IS, IS RIGHT.[32]

Nature is fundamentally concord, beneficence. The way to be good is to act according to nature. This can be framed into an extremely conservative doctrine; and certainly the slogan with which Pope ends the passage I've just quoted sounds quietistic in the extreme. For all Pope's attacks on the Stoics, he sometimes seems to come close to them (and in this he perhaps shows the influence of Shaftesbury, who was much more of an ancient Stoic than he was a Christian). But the demand to live according to nature could also be radical; it could be interpreted as requiring a far-reaching change in social arrangements. In part, the shift from Deism to the unbelieving Enlightenment involved the slide to a more radical interpretation. But before looking at this transition, I want to examine more closely what was involved in the notion of living according to nature.

This is a deceptively familiar formula. We still seem to be in the territory of ancient philosophy. And the fact that acting according to nature can also be described as acting according to reason only increases the sense that there is nothing radically new here. But just as the natural order described in terms of the principle of plenitude and the chain of love looked much less new than it really was, so here. There is a deep change in what it is to live according to nature which separates the eighteenth century from its ancient sources. I think that this has to be brought out if we are to understand what made Deism a popular view, what then brought about its supersession, and, in fact, if we are to understand the whole dynamic of modern moral ideas.

For the ancients, life according to nature is life according to reason. *Kata physin = kata logon.* What we are by nature is rational life, and hence acting by reason is the key to the good for us. But what it is to live according to reason is in turn spelled out by some notion of order, which ranks different activities in a hierarchical order. This may be ultimately linked to a hierarchical order in the cosmos, as it is with Plato; or it may be simply an order of our goals, as it is also with Plato, but also with Aristotle and the Stoics. But in each case, reason enables us to rank our activities and pursue some in preference to others, just because they rank higher according to reason. The activities involving reason are by their very nature higher than those which involve mere desire. So for Aristotle, our life reaches closest to the divine when we contemplate the unchanging; and the citizen life, where we deliberate together and exercise and develop prudence, is higher than the life of production and consumption; and this in turn is higher than mere sensual pleasure; though all these are goods.

Of course, this generalization is a little too sweeping to be true. The Epicureans notoriously stood aside from this general identification of reason with a hierarchy of goals or actions. Human ends could be reduced to one: pleasure. But even Epicurus was enough a child of his culture that he reintroduced something like hierarchical distinctions between pleasures, discriminating those which were more worthwhile because longer lasting and less accompanied by pain and trouble. But still, the Epicureans had the makings of a radical levelling of goals; that is why they were invoked often in the centuries which led up to the Enlightenment.

But if we neglect the Epicureans, we can see that the ethic of ordinary life which arises in the modern age stands in sharp contrast to the mainstream of ancient thought. Certain activities are singled out—here work in a calling, and family life—not in virtue of their hierarchical rank in the light of man's rational nature, but rather because of God's plan. These activities are marked as significant, because they define how God intends us to live, what he designed us for when he made us. It follows that to see what we ought to do we need an insight not into the hierarchical order of nature but into the purposes of God. It follows further that what we are called to do is not simply to act according to some natural ranking, but to carry out the marked activities in full acknowledgement of their marked character.

This ethic thus involves two kinds of contrast. The first is with a set of wrong views, which fail to appreciate the marked character of the activities of ordinary life; such, for instance, as the views of traditional ethics themselves, which rank other things higher. The second contrast is with a wrong way of living these activities, that is, living them in a way which fails to acknowledge their significance for God's plan, as when we live them for ourselves or just in view of pleasure and gain, and not for the sake of God, worshipfully. We can see here the background to two features of this ethic which came out in the earlier discussion: its rejection of the old hierarchy of activities, and the definition of the crucial moral issue as one of *how* one fulfils one's calling and lives one's married life. It is not so much a matter of what acts are special to the good person, but rather how one carries out what everyone does. God loveth adverbs.

The long slide from orthodox theologies of ordinary life to Deist visions of nature took place within this basic mould. The crucial activities are not identified by a vision of natural hierarchy, but they are marked by the purpose for which humans were made. Now, however, this is less and less a matter of God's inscrutable purposes which are shown to us in revelation, and more and more something we read off the design of nature itself. From this point of view, Deism does appear as a mere staging ground; at a later stage the design of nature itself will suffice to mark the activities of ordinary life.

But now we can see how 'living according to nature' can take on a sense quite different from the ancient one. It doesn't mean at all living according to the hierarchy of goals of (substantive) reason. It means, rather, living according to the design of things. In other words, what makes the proper way of life good is not that it reflects the inherent rank of certain activities as rational, but that it follows the design of nature, according their proper significance to those activities marked as significant by this design. This design, as we saw, aims at concord through interlocking purposes. What it marks are, for each kind of thing, the purposes which bring the thing into mesh with all the others. This is how we define living by nature now. What we have is an ethic, not of hierarchical reason, but of marked activities, fully continuous with the theological ethic which gave rise to it.

And this involves, as before, two kinds of contrast. There is a contrast with views, principally the old hierarchical ones, which fail to see which activities are marked. Here the eighteenth-century philosophy of natural order continues the affirmation of ordinary life in endorsing our natural inclinations to pleasure and away from pain, and our normal impulse of self-love. Pope sees "two principles in human nature reign", self-love and reason. But they shouldn't be opposed:

> Let subtle schoolmen teach these friends to fight,
> More studious to divide than to unite;

> And Grace and Virtue, Sense and Reason split,
> With all the rash dexterity of wit.
> . . . . .
> Self-love and Reason to one end aspire,
> Pain their aversion, Pleasure their desire;
> But greedy That, its object would devour,
> This taste the honey, and not wound the flower:
> Pleasure, or wrong or rightly understood,
> Our greatest evil, or our greatest good.

And against the Stoics, he praises the life of strenuous exertion, as moved by passion we strain after what we desire.

> In lazy Apathy let Stoics boast
> Their Virtue fixed; 'tis fixed as in a frost;
> . . . . .
> The rising tempest puts in act the soul,
> Parts may it ravage, but preserves the whole.
> On life's vast ocean diversely we sail,
> Reason the card, but Passion is the gale;
> Nor God alone in the still calm we find,
> He mounts the storm, and walks upon the wind.[33]

The second contrast is with the wrong ways of living out our marked goals. And this now turns on reason. But this is instrumental reason. It has nothing to do with a vision of natural hierarchy. In Pope's image, reason is there to guide passion, but passion provides all the motive force. Instrumental reason intervenes in two ways, however, which are not clearly compatible with each other.

First, it shows us that the best policy, for the maximization of our own gains, is to fit into our proper place in the interlocking order. Everything is made so that the good of each serves the good of all; so our best interest must be to act for the general good. But second, this whole itself is a magnificent creation of instrumental reason, now that of God, which has encompassed a universal maximization. Our powers of reason, which enable us to see this, can lift us to a grasp of the whole and in this way bring us to want more than our particular interest.

These two routes bring us from a narrow focus on immediate gratification for ourselves alone to a well-considered commitment to the long-term, general good. We have seen in previous chapters that an important controversy raged about these, with moralists of the extrinsic view only allowing for the first. The major stream of Deism encompassed both. It was certainly important to realize "that true SELF-LOVE and SOCIAL are the same",[34] but we also are endowed with the capacity for sympathy, for a general benevolence, and this is what is awakened by a rational perception of the whole order of nature.

> Self-love thus pushed to social, to divine,
> Gives thee to make they neighbour's blessing thine.
> Is this too little for thy boundless heart?
> Extend it, let thy enemies have part:
> Grasp the whole worlds of Reason, Life, and Sense,
> In one close system of Benevolence:
> Happier as kinder, in whate'er degree,
> And height of Bliss but height of Charity.[35]

Thus living according to nature once more is equivalent to living according to reason. But this now means living in full appreciation of the interlocking design. Minimally, this can mean only drawing the full strategic benefit from one's knowledge of the design. More fully, it generally meant finding one's highest satisfaction in furthering the design itself. In this latter and more common version, it was closely parallel to the theistic view it emerged from: the good life requires that in carrying out the activities which have been marked as significant, one espouse the spirit of whatever has so marked them. In the theistic variant, this latter phrase designates God; in Deism it slides towards designating Nature's design. But in either case, humans are called to a broader perspective, to embrace the whole. What was charity now merges into benevolence.

So negatively, living according to the design of nature means avoiding three kinds of deviance: (1) The first is defined by the traditionally recognized vices: sloth, sensuality, disorder, violence. But the exclusion of these is now often justified in terms of instrumental reason, rather than the hierarchical superiority of order and stability over agitation and passion—as Pope made clear in his anti-Stoic passage. (2) We have to avoid the error of downgrading ordinary life, or natural self-love, in the name of supposedly "higher" activities or more exalted or spiritual motives, in particular a hierarchical conception of reason which would oppose it to self-love ("let subtle schoolmen teach these friends to fight"). (3) We have to avoid the error of condemning natural self-love as irremediably sinful. We need to see that the search for happiness is in itself innocent. It is part of the design, marked by it as significant. We must reject all ascetic moralities.

Eschewing these three has us pursuing our happiness in a rational way. But in addition, as we have just seen, living according to reason and nature demands that we rise to the viewpoint of the whole and concern ourselves for the general happiness. Benevolence must be added to the rational pursuit of happiness if we are to live fully by nature's design—although according to the extrinsic view, this involves no additional requirement, since beneficence is just the best strategy for personal happiness.

So in spite of the similarity of language with the ancients, we have an ethic based no longer on inherent hierarchy but rather on marked activities. Reason is still important, and those beings who possess it are still ranked higher in the chain of being. But it doesn't suffice to determine the good by serving as the benchmark by which activities are ranked. Rather these get their significance from the design. The importance of (instrumental) reason then comes from its being the way that we are intended to play our part in this design.

And reason is not alone and unchallenged even in this role. Rational understanding can be considered our only way of coming to grasp and appreciate the design. But this design is not only a fact about our relation to the whole; it is also visible in our own make-up—for instance, in the inclinations and tendencies of our own nature. And our access to this can be more direct than through a rational apprehension of our make-up. We can have access to our design through our own desires and feelings.

The shift from the exclusively rational mode of access to one which also gave a place to feeling is what we saw in the move from Locke through Shaftesbury to Hutcheson's theory of moral sentiments. This comes to be more and more the dominant stream of Deist thought. Our way of contact with the design of nature lies also within us, in the natural sentiments of sympathy and benevolence.

This allows us to explain better the move to subjectivization or internalization which I described in Chapter 15. For the ancients, it was enough to answer the question of why the proper form of life was my good by pointing out that I was rational life. This set the hierarchy of activities, in terms of which this proper life is designated as such; and a rational being cannot help but love and approve this way of being. But now something is the proper way of life in virtue of how things, including me, are designed; and this design includes my being provided with certain inclinations, desires, sentiments. Knowing the good isn't just a matter of apprehending a hierarchical order. It requires rather that I come to know my own inclinations. This is not because I am adopting a subjective morality or one based on mere projection. Things are not simply right because I incline to them. What is right is what fits a design, of which my sentiments are an integral part.

This is how Hutcheson reasons. Our moral sentiments are an integral part of the whole providential order. Things would go much less well without them.[36] It is not just because they indicate some things as right that these are right. It is because they do so as part of the whole order. To see Hutcheson as projectivist is to take him anachronistically, or at least out of his context.

Once you sweep away the providentialism, then the deep and worrying question arises. It does with Hume. But this is to denature Hutcheson.

What I've been describing here, in the shift from the ancient to the modern notions of life according to nature, is a massive change in our understanding of the constitutive good. The providential design of nature, as against the hierarchical order of reason, now takes the central place. The different notions of moral sources are relative to this: whether these lie in reason alone or also in our feelings. Which we choose will depend on which we think gives us access to the design.

Whatever we choose, it represents an internalization relative to the ancient model. Even if we opt with Lockean Deism to make reason our sole mode of access, this is now instrumental reason, and it starts from facts about our own inclinations, what brings us pleasure and pain. And if we follow Hutcheson, the turn inward is even more evident. For it is through consulting our sentiments that we can really come to endorse and rejoice in the design of things.

This form of Deism understandably tends to become predominant as the century advances.[37] And the option more and more for feeling brings about a revolution in the philosophical understanding of sentiment. We can perhaps trace it in the change of vocabulary: the word 'sentiment' itself, partly replacing 'passion', bespeaks the rehabilitation the life of feeling has gone through.

Underlying this is a very deep change in moral psychology. For the ancients, the passions were understood primarily through their relevance to the moral life. This was seen to lie principally in their being implicit appreciations of the goodness or badness of some end or state of affairs. The Stoics simply defined them as 'opinions'. But even Aristotle, who is far from sharing this reductive view, sets as a moral goal a condition wherein our passions will be perfectly docile to our understanding of the good; so that the good person will be moved only when and to what degree he should. The passions will be guided by *phronēsis*.

With Descartes, as we saw, there is a first change. The relevance of the passions is now not so much as implicit appreciations but in their function in the whole soul-body union. Here for the first time we are in the modern framework, where what is relevant is the design. Our goal must be to subordinate the passions to their proper functions. But we come to understand what these are purely through disengaging reason. The lived experience of the passions teaches us nothing; it can only mislead. Our passions should in the end function only as cold disengaged understanding shows us they ought to.

With the eighteenth-century theory of the sentiments, we have another profound change. It is still a matter of the design, but at least one paradigm route of access to this is through feeling. Now sentiments become *normative*. We find out what is right at least in part by coming to experience our normal sentiments. This may involve our overcoming the distortive effects of vice or false opinion—Hutcheson constantly points out how the extrinsic theory makes us fail to appreciate our moral sentiments, and this dampens them. We may have to use our reason to correct these distortions, as Hutcheson says. But this doesn't take away from the fact that our entire access to this domain of good and evil depends on our moral sense, just as my correcting for distorted colour perception by taking account of my diseased condition doesn't take away from the fact that I only grasp colour through my sense of sight.[38]

Sentiment is now important, because it is in a certain way the touchstone of the morally good. Not because feeling that something is good makes it so, as the projective interpretation holds; but rather because undistorted, normal feeling is my way of access into the design of things, which is the real constitutive good, determining good and bad. This sentiment can be corrected by reason when it deviates, but the insight it yields cannot be substituted for by reason. It is no longer just an implicit appreciation of things, which must be brought into line with the independently available hierarchy of reason. Nor is it just the affective concomitant of a function which is well understood and awaits normalization by disengaged reason. It is itself part measure of the good, and reason must take account of it. It enjoys an unprecedented status in the moral life, which neither the ancient nor the Cartesian theory accorded it.

The new place of sentiment completes the revolution which has yielded a modern view of nature as normative, so utterly different from the ancient view. For the ancients, nature offers us an order which moves us to love and instantiate it, unless we are depraved. But the modern view, on the other hand, endorses nature as the source of right impulse or sentiment. So we encounter nature paradigmatically and centrally, not in a vision of order, but in experiencing the right inner impulse. Nature as norm is an inner tendency; it is ready to become the voice within, which Rousseau will make it, and to be transposed by the Romantics into a richer and deeper inwardness.

THE CULTURE OF MODERNITY

17.1

I have been tracing a movement, indeed, a massive shift in the notion of the constitutive good connected with nature: from a hierarchical notion of reason to a conception of providential design, which marks certain activities as significant. These activities included those which had been affirmed in the preceding theology of ordinary life. But the Deist shift, which gave more and more weight to the perfectly interlocking natural order, opened the way for a new and unprecedented role for sentiment.

I have been tracing all this through the writings of philosophers: from the ancient moralists, through Descartes and Locke, to Shaftesbury and Hutcheson. But what is striking about this change is that it takes place over the whole culture. In this respect, it is parallel to (and interwoven with) the increasingly wide diffusion of the principles of autonomy and the practices of self-examination which I talked about at the end of Part II. In the one case as in the other, philosophers helped articulate the change; and no doubt this articulation added force and impetus to it. But they did not originate it, much less bring it about unaided.

To appreciate this, I want to look outside philosophy to certain broad movements of the culture of the seventeenth and eighteenth centuries: to the new valuation of commerce, to the rise of the novel, to the changing understanding of marriage and the family, and to the new importance of sentiment.

I have already mentioned the new value put on commercial activity and money-making in the eighteenth century. The idea arose of "le doux commerce", and business activity was supposed to make for more "polished" and "gentle" mores.[1]

The rise of this new valuation of commercial life can also be traced in the recession of the aristocratic honour ethic, which stressed glory won in military pursuits. Of course, this didn't come about without a struggle; and one of the crucial running controversies of the eighteenth century, at least in England, was this battle between the two ethical outlooks. The "bourgeois" outlook stressed the goods of production, an ordered life, and peace—in short, accented the activities of ordinary life; the other stressed the virtues of the citizen life, of the search for fame and renown, and gave a central place to the warrior virtues.[2]

The new valuation is reflected in the coming to be of the very category of the 'economic' in its modern sense. The eighteenth century saw the birth of political economy, with Adam Smith and the Physiocrats. Louis Dumont[3] has shown what a shift of outlook was required before it could become conceivable that there be an independent science of this 'economic' aspect of social existence. In terms of a categorization drawn from Marx, economics focusses on the interchange between humans and nature as a domain with its own laws, distinct from (even though potentially disturbed by) what happens in the domains in which humans relate to each other through politics and culture. The isolation of this domain cannot be seen just as a 'scientific' discovery that people stumbled on. It reflects the higher value put on this dimension of human existence, the affirmation of ordinary life.

In addition, the new science was grounded on the notion, utterly absent in previous ages, that the events in this domain form a self-regulating system. This was the great innovation of the Physiocrats, taken over by Smith, and it might be considered the founding move of modern economics. Indeed, the very notion we have today of 'the economy' or 'a (national) economy' supposes some such system. This innovation reflects another facet of the moral outlook I've been examining. The self-regulating system of production and exchange is a prime manifestation of the interlocking providential order of nature; it binds the productive, that is, those who follow the designated human vocation, into a mutually sustaining harmony.

17.2

Another well-known development of this century, the rise of the modern novel, also manifests the new consciousness, and in more than one way.

(i) First, the new type of novel written by Defoe, Richardson, and Fielding both reflected and further entrenched the egalitarian affirmation of ordinary life. It is not just that its subjects were often middle class; or that the works exalted entrepreneurial virtues (Defoe) or dealt somewhat moralistically with the issues of love and marriage (Richardson). The very form of writing involved an equalization. What Erich Auerbach has called the 'Stiltrennung' of the classical tradition involved a difference of style between tragedy and comedy, which also marked a difference between subjects. Tragedy portrayed the heroic dimensions of the lives of exalted figures in the appropriate style. Quite another one was reserved for the everyday reality of common people. This difference of level is still evident in Shakespeare in his differential treatment of the socially low figures that bring comic relief. And it was central to French classicism of le grand siècle, which revived all the ancient rules.

The Christian tradition, of course, provided an influential alternative: the Gospels treat the doings of very humble people along with those of the great with the same degree of seriousness. Indeed, events of the greatest importance for human salvation come about through the actions of fishermen. Auerbach shows the considerable impact this had on mediaeval and early modern literature.[4] This was certainly evident in some of the writings inspired by Puritanism, like Bunyan's *Pilgrim's Progress*.

It is this alternative tradition which triumphs in the modern novel, and definitively. The very form of narration, relating the—sometimes minute—particulars of life, puts all events and lives on the same stylistic footing. It is the modern novel, which more and more has come to set our standards of narrative literature, which has made the older separation of styles seem strange and alien to us.[5]

(ii) The new modern novel stands out against all previous literature in its portrayal of the particular. It departs from traditional plots and archetypical stories and breaks with the classical preference for the general and universal. It narrates the lives of particular people in their detail. As Ian Watt points out,[6] its characters have ordinary proper names—unlike those of Bunyan, for instance, which are personified qualities.

This is not to say that the novel is unconcerned with the general and that all reference to archetypes drops out. It would hardly have gripped readers over the last two and a half centuries if this were so. And James Joyce has shown in our time how the great archetypical myths of the tradition can be reintegrated into it. But the general or typical now emerges out of the description of particular, situated people in their peculiarity, people with first names and surnames (even if one of the latter is the un-Irish-sounding 'Daedelus').

This change surely both expresses and reinforces the demise of the view of the world as the embodiment and archetypes, the world of the ontic logos, whose philosophical articulation I've been tracing. The nature of a thing, I have argued, is now seen as within it in a new sense. We have to scrutinize the particular to arrive at the general. This was not just a principle of natural philosophers, but part of the way people came to understand their lives. Any other mode of narration now seems strange to us.

(iii) But the death of archetypes also brought with it a new time-consciousness, and the novel is a good place to observe this as well. Various writers[7] have pointed out the weak sense of anachronism that our forebears had. In the Middle Ages, the Holy Family would be portrayed in painting and glass windows in contemporary dress. The Virgin Mary might be dressed like a Tuscan merchant's daughter. This seems strangely incongruous to us today yet must have then been quite natural. It is hard for us fully to understand this mentality, but one of its components must have been a sense of time as the locus for the recurrent embodiment of archetypes, not themselves temporally placed.

We feel the incongruity when Mary has the features of a thirteenth-century Tuscan rather than of a first-century Jew, because to us she is this particular woman, whose placing in history is crucial to what she was. But in a mentality in which there were such, the Mother of God easily gravitates towards an archetype; and as such she is equidistant from, and hence equally belongs to, all ages.

With the term 'archetype' I am gesturing at a mode of consciousness which is very complex and rich and which took many forms beyond those reflected in a Platonic theory of Ideas. We find another mode of it in the religious tradition, where one event can be a 'type' or prefiguration of another which happens long after it.[8] Thus the sacrifice of Isaac was seen as a 'type' of the sacrifice of Christ. In this outlook, the two events are linked through something outside history, where their symbolic affinity reflects some deeper identity in regard to Divine Providence.[9] Something other than their causal relations in time connects them; in spite of the immense temporal gap, there is a sense in which they are simultaneous. History embodies the extra-temporal.

But this sense of what it is to exist in time is undermined by the decline of an ontic logos and by the new self-understanding as disengaged reason. One consequence of objectifying the world has been the development of the idea of a "homogeneous, empty time",[10] the time of physics, whose events are related diachronically purely by efficient causal relations, and synchronically by mutual conditioning. This has come to pose an unavoidable, but also at times apparently unanswerable, question of how we relate our own lives to this time. Much of the most innovative philosophy of the last hundred years, from Bergson to Heidegger, has been occupied with an attempt to answer or reformulate this question. Various narrations have emerged from this over the last two centuries, the ones that have tried to give an account of the origins of humanity and human culture; and this task has always been undertaken, since the eighteenth century, against the background of homo-geneous world time.

This objectification of time has had its effect on literature, as Benedict Anderson argues,[11] in making it normal and easy for us to envisage (provisionally) unconnected events as occurring simultaneously in the same story-space. The reader is made into an omniscient observer, able to hold these independently unfolding trains of events together.

But the new time sense has also changed our notion of the subject: the disengaged, particular self, whose identity is constituted in memory. Like any other human being at any time, he can only find an identity in self-narration. Life has to be lived as a story, as I argued in Part I. But now it becomes harder to take over the story ready-made from the canonical models and archetypes. The story has to be drawn from the particular events and circumstances of this life; and this in two interwoven senses.

First, as a chain of happenings in world time, the life at any moment is the causal consequence of what has transpired earlier. But second, since the life to be lived has also to be *told,* its meaning is seen as something that unfolds through the events. These two perspectives are not easy to combine, at least not once they are formulated intellectually and become a problem for philosophy. For the first seems to make the shape of a life simply the *result* of the happenings as they accumulate; whereas the second seems to see this shape as something already latent, which emerges through what comes to pass.

But they are obviously both inescapable. We are made what we are by events; and as self-narrators, we live these through a meaning which the events come to manifest or illustrate. Was Napoleon "made" by the siege of Toulon, or did this just give him the occasion to demonstrate his tactical insight, daring and charisma, in short, his "genius" and thus "destiny" in a Europe wracked with conflict?

This mode of life-narration, where the story is drawn from the events in this double sense, as against traditional models, archetypes, or prefigurations, is the quintessentially modern one, that which fits the experience of the disengaged, particular self. It is what emerges in modern autobiography, starting with the great exempla by Rousseau and Goethe. And it is what determines the narrative form of the modern novel. That is why the particular details of circumstances and happenings, and their order in time, become the stuff of the story. This is what Watt calls the 'formal realism' of the novel, embodying "the premise, or primary convention, that the novel is a full and authentic report of human experience".[12] This mode has been consubstantial with the modern novel from its beginnings in the eighteenth century until very recently. And it reaches one of its characteristic expressions in the Bildungs-roman, where the double-sided emergence of a life-shape from the events becomes the explicit theme of the work.

17.3

Starting among the wealthier classes in the Anglo-Saxon countries and in France in the late seventeenth century, we see a growing idealization of marriage based on affection, true companionship between husband and wife, and devoted concern for the children. I believe that this is to be understood as an aspect of the new sense of the significance of ordinary life—indeed, as one of the major loci of this new understanding.

The new understanding of marriage naturally goes along with further individualization and internalization. The companionate marriage, like the Puritan one which preceded it, presupposes a higher degree of personal and emotional commitment than was demanded earlier. And so it comes to be seen as something that we have to enter into voluntarily. From this period on, there is a steady decline in the power wielded by parents and by wider kinship groups in the choice of marriage partner, and more and more the choice is seen as the couple's. As ever, the stress on individuation and personal commitment leads to a greater place for contractual agreement. And in some societies, this even leads to a greater tolerance for divorce.

In this revolution in family life, the two major facets of the growing moral consciousness are interwoven. The rebellion against the patriarchal family involves an assertion of personal autonomy, and voluntarily formed ties, against the demands of ascriptive authority. But the rebellion is fired by the sense that what is at stake is a fulfilment that nature has made centrally significant.[13]

When St.-Preux, tutor of Julie in Rousseau's *Nouvelle Héloïse,* has won the heart of his ward, he finds their union opposed by the implacable opposition of her father. He is moved to an impassioned declaration of the rights of love.

> Quel que soit l'empire dont vous abusez, mes droits sont plus sacrés que les vôtres; la chaîne qui nous lie est la borne du pouvoir paternel, même devant les tribunaux humains; et quand voux osez réclamer la nature, c'est vous seul qui bravez ses lois.

> How despotic soever may be the empire you assume my rights are infinitely more sacred. The chain by which we are united marks the extent of paternal dominion, even in the estimation of human law, and whilst you appeal to the law of nature, you yourself are trampling upon its institutions.[14]

This whole development leads to a progressive withdrawal of the family from the control of the wider society. People today are always appalled to learn, for instance, how much the pre-eighteenth-century village presumed to control of its members' lives, even what we would consider today their intimate family affairs. Take, for instance, the "charivari" that henpecked husbands had to undergo, not to speak of fornicators. Charivaris were noisy manifestations of public collective ridicule. In France, for instance, a husband who had beaten his wife, or who did women's work, or who was cuckolded, could be the target of one of these. Presumably this was because he was allowing an inversion of the proper, patriarchal order. This couldn't be seen just as a matter between himself and his wife; it was everybody's business, because the order was a shared one within which all individuals lived.

With the breakdown of this idea of a larger order and the assertion of individual independence, the new value of the intimate personal relation gains ground. People demand and win privacy for the family. The new need for privacy is reflected in the very organization of domestic space. The pre-seventeenth-century home allowed for very little. Parents were always in the presence of their children among the poor; and the whole family was under the eye of servants among the rich. Houses now begin to be built to provide private space; corridors allow servants to circulate without seeing or being seen, private dining rooms are installed, and the like.

Philippe Ariès sums up the all-pervasive nature of earlier society:

> The historians taught us long ago that the King was never left alone. But in fact, until the end of the seventeenth century, nobody was ever left alone. The density of social life made isolation virtually impossible, and people who managed to shut themselves up in a room for some time were regarded as exceptional characters: relations between peers, relations between people of the same class but dependent on one another, relations between masters and servants—these everyday relations never left a man by himself.[15]

These two changes, the companionate marriage and the demand for privacy, rose together. The family based on affection had to be formed by affinity. It could not be the fruit exclusively of the dynastic and property arrangements that were so important for the old lineage. And it could flourish only in intimacy, which ruled out the open, goldfish bowl world of traditional society.[16]

17.4

And this change is linked to a third. In the eighteenth century, again in the Anglo-Saxon countries and France, who seem to be the pioneers in this regard, sentiment takes on a greater importance. And thus the sentiments of love, concern, and affection for one's spouse come to be cherished, dwelt on, rejoiced in, and articulated. Something similar occurs with the affection of parents for children. And partly as a result, childhood takes on an identity as a separate phase of the life cycle, with its own peculiar feelings and needs. And as a further consequence, child-rearing becomes a subject of absorbing interest to the literate public. We are on our way to the spiritual age of Dr. Spock.

The nature of this change has often been misunderstood. Some critics have taken the historians of family life to have been making the preposterous claim that before modern times, people didn't really love their children and never married for love. It is easy to show that these views are absurd. Obviously human beings of all ages and climes have cared for their children; and even the striking differences from today in the place given to family and property considerations in making marriages in the old days is less significant when one reflects that this probably only concerned the rich and propertied. Most peasants probably at least tried to marry spouses they were attracted to.

But this misses the nature of the change. It is not the actual place of affection but the sense of its importance. What changes is not that people begin loving their children or feeling affection for their spouses, but that these dispositions come to be seen as a crucial part of what makes life worthy and significant. Whereas previously these dispositions were taken as banal, except perhaps that their absence in a marked degree might cause concern or condemnation (just as today some mild degree of benevolent sentiment for my neighbours, in the absence of a good reason for hostility, is taken for granted; but its marked absence—a virulent hatred of them without good cause—would occasion critical remark), now they are seen as endowed with crucial significance. The change in sensibility, in other words, is precisely the one whose philosophical expression I have been tracing: it concerns what aspects of life are marked as significant. The difference lies not so much in the presence/absence of certain feelings as in the fact that much is made of them. It is of course true that beginning to make something of them also alters these dispositions. But this is far from saying that they didn't exist at all before.[17]

What seems to have happened is that, in the latter part of the century, in the upper and middle classes of anglophone and French societies, the affectionate family undergoes an intensification and comes to be seen self-consciously as a close community of loving and caring, in contrast to relations with more distant kin and outsiders, which are correspondingly seen as more formal or distant. The family is on the way to becoming that "haven in a heartless world"[18] which it has come to be for so many in the last two centuries. Of course this last development presupposes industrialization, the break-up of earlier primary communities, the separation of work from home life, and the growth of a capitalist, mobile, large-scale, bureaucratic world, which largely deserves the epithet 'heartless'. But the paradigms of family sentiment and self-enclosure were laid down before industrialization swept the mass of the population in its train, and in classes which were not brutally displaced.

On the contrary, it is first the middle-class family which, conscious of the strength and rightness of the feelings of love and solicitude which bind it together, lays new kinds of demands on its members. Fliegelman[19] notes how in the latter part of the century the scriptural injunction on children to obey their parents is supported in a new way. This is not just the command of God and the path of filial duty but also now a demand of love, because disobedience threatens to break a parent's heart. He points out how frequently Jacob's cry on being asked to part with Benjamin, that should mischief befall "then shall ye bring down my gray hairs with sorrow to the grave" (Genesis 42:38), was echoed in the literature of the period.

The eighteenth-century family, in Ariès's view,[20] organized "itself around the child and raised the wall of private life between the family and society". It thus "satisfied a desire for privacy and also a craving for identity: the members of the family were united by feeling, habits, and their way of life. They shrank from the promiscuity imposed by the old sociability". Children were now in a sense more restricted. "The solicitude of family . . . deprived the child of the freedom he had hitherto enjoyed among adults . . . But this severity was the expression of a very different feeling from the old indifference: an obsessive love which was to dominate society from the eighteenth century on".

Jan Lewis, in her fascinating study of the Virginia gentry in the age of Jefferson, places a similar change somewhat later. The prerevolutionary upper strata had an ideal of domestic tranquility, a family life which was warm and affectionate but at the same time simple and restrained. The family was seen as "a counterpoint to a tumultuous world, and activity in that world was considered significant and exciting". In the early nineteenth century, we see something quite different. Men and women look for full emotional support from their spouses and children; they look to build a haven in an otherwise inhospitable world.

Of course, there are special factors at work here. Virginia was declining economically relative to other areas, and in particular, its gentry class was painfully maladapted to face the entrepreneurial demands of the new national economy. We can perhaps see why these people especially needed a haven. But while this new family culture may have filled a crying need here—even as it was to do in a different way for the newly industrialized workers later—it is only if we lose sight of the actual quality of this culture that we will fail to see what is new and unprecedented in it: it didn't have to be this which met the need; other people in other ages have faced decline and disruption in other ways. What is special to this period is that the cultural mutation to the self-enclosed family of feeling was available, was already taking place across the whole Atlantic world. This is a mutation out of which our present civilization emerges. We still see love, family—or at least "relationships"—as central human fulfilments.

This was a culture which put a high value on feeling and on its full expression. Where their eighteenth-century forebears had tried "to control emotion, fearing the disruptive effects of unbridled feeling", where they had as a consequence "expressed themselves formally, using the form to shape and check the feeling", early-nineteenth-century Virginians sought to give the fullest and most sincere expression to what they felt. Their letters show them straining beyond the formal conventions and striving to share their thoughts and their own individual sentiments. This sharing was an essential part of the fulfilment, the "heart's ease" that they sought in close family ties.[21]

The importance of family emerges in another facet of Lewis's study. In the nineteenth century the hope of immortality as a consolation for death takes on a different form. What comes to be frequently stressed is the reunion with loved ones beyond the grave. "Heaven was defined as a family reunion where those separated by death would be rejoined, never more to part".[22]

The transformation in sensibility of Virginian gentry in this period was just a reflection in microcosm of what was taking place or would soon be taking place in all Western societies and across all classes. Sentiment takes on moral relevance. For some it even becomes the key to the human good. Experiencing certain feelings now comes to be an important part of the good life. Among these is married love. But it is not the only one, as we have already seen. Moral sentiments also became significant, as did those of benevolence. Later aesthetic feelings of affection became central to the cult of *Empfindsamkeit*.

17.5

This moral consecration of sentiment becomes strong and unmistakable in England and then France in the latter half of the eighteenth century. The literature of the time both made it visible and contributed immensely to its intensification and propagation. The novels of Richardson, *Pamela* and *Clarissa,* with their long and exalted descriptions of noble sentiments, were devoured by an enthusiastic public, which must have found their own developing moral outlook confirmed, as well as strengthened and defined, in them.

Richardson was translated into French, and his works made a tremendous sensation in France as well. But the novel which helped more than any other to define and spread the new outlook there was undoubtedly Rousseau's *La Nouvelle Héloïse.* The novel, the story of a young idealistic tutor in love with his charge but forbidden to marry her because her father saw him as an unsuitable match, touched a theme similar to *Clarissa*'s. But it doesn't take the same tragic turn. On the contrary, the lovers see that their love would be profaned by a sexual fulfilment which violated the demands of duty and heroically transmute it into a more noble companionship.

The interest of Rousseau's novel is less in the story as a set of events than in the portrayal and evocation of strong and noble sentiments: love, benevolence, the devotion to virtue. The overpowering picture which emerges is that we are somehow ennobled by strong, true, uncorrupted feeling, as Julie and St.-Preux are by their love, which they have kept pure by sacrificing its immediate fulfilment to the demands of duty.[23]

The impact of *La Nouvelle Héloïse* when it came out in 1761 is hard to imagine in this more jaded age. Copies were snapped up, and many of those who read it were literally overpowered with emotion. Rousseau received a flood of letters from readers who were "ravished", "in transports", in "ecstasy", moved to "délices inexprimables" and "larmes délicieuses". The Baron Thiébault came to the end of the book, "ne pleurant plus, mais criant, hurlant comme une bête" ("no longer weeping, but crying out, howling like a beast"). François, a cornet in the cavalry, was so moved by his reading "que je crois que dans ce moment j'aurais vu la mort avec plaisir" ("I believe that in that moment I would have looked upon death with pleasure"). The readers were not only overwhelmed but morally uplifted. Madame Rolland thought that any woman who could read the book without being made morally better must have a soul of mud.[24]

The story of Julie and St.-Preux was inspiring because they had attained to a nobility and purity of sentiment in spite of the crossing of their love—or perhaps it was because this love was unfulfilled in the normal way. Their love was great and exemplary, and this was partly because it had called for a certain heroism to live up to it. This is a heroism of renunciation, and it is fuelled by the sense that life attains greatness this way, that one has lived on a bigger and fuller scale than would have been possible otherwise. Something like this, of course, is what inspires heroism at any time; the difference was that here it was not undying fame that moved the lovers but a certain nobility and purity of feeling. Love transmuted by renunication and suffering seems to offer the way to the highest in life, to an exaltation of sentiment which ordinary happiness cannot bring. "Rien n'est bon que d'aimer", and "rien n'est vrai que de souffrir" ("nothing is good but loving"; "nothing is true but suffering"); these twin slogans capture the animating vision of the cult of sensibility.[25]

It was fatally easy for this cult to slide from heroism to self-indulgence. The renunciation, the loss, instead of rousing us to self-transcendence, is savoured in melancholy. The age of sentiment was also one of melancholy, which was also defined and propagated by English writers, who were also translated and had a great impact on the Continent. In this case, it was Young's poem "Night Thoughts" and Gray's "Elegy Written in a Country Churchyard", which did most to shape the mood. But the term has already shifted somewhat in meaning. It no longer bears the sense of an excess of one humour. It rather refers to a mood, a feeling. It is what one experiences when one can take a certain distance from the sadness and loss in one's life and see it as a story, under a kind of closure. Seen this way, it takes on a meaning, it can exhibit a style, a beauty, even a distinction. There is something tremendously consoling about melancholy, a beguiling pleasure, which can make suffering strangely enjoyable, a source of "les rêveries mélancoliques et les voluptueuses tristesses" ("melancholy revery and voluptuous sadness").[26]

This recourse had been available in all ages. But it was only in an age which valued sentiment that melancholy could be cherished. If distinction attached to the loftiness of one's sentiments, and if the highest were inseparable from renunciation and suffering, then the very savouring in melancholy of a nobly felt misfortune could be seen as admirable. Not everyone would have the sensibility to feel such misfortune, and those who did must be superior beings.

The conditions had been created for the tremendous success of Goethe's *The Sorrows of Young Werther,* which was published in 1774 and instantly translated into English and French. Werther is driven to suicide by his inability to attain ordinary happiness in this world. His tragic flaw is precisely his extreme sensibility. He can be pitched from elation to despair in an instant. He feels everything too strongly. Werther rapidly became an archetype: the young man suffering from *Weltschmerz,* or *le mal du siècle,* driven first into melancholy, and then to death. And the ectypes were not only found in literature. A young man shot himself with a pistol before Rousseau's tomb in Ermenonville. He didn't leave his name, only a confession of his despair: "Ne refusez pas une sepulture, aux lieux que je vous demande, au malheureux rêveur mélancolique . . . Ah! qu'il est malheureux l'homme sensible . . . C'est l'amour malheureux, la mélancolie, le goût des rêveries, ma sensibilité qui m'ont perdu" (" Do not deny burial, at the place where I have asked you, to the unfortunate, melancholy dreamer . . . Ah! how unhappy is the sensitive man . . . unhappy love, melancholy, a taste for dreaming, my sensitivity . . . all have been my downfall").[27] Through the lines of this unfortunate youth there breathes the sense of an exceptional, even admirable destiny. This is what the cult of sensibility made possible.

17.6

The moral importance of sentiment emerges clearly from another angle if we look at the growth of the feeling for nature in the eighteenth century. This is evident in all sorts of ways. In France it is particularly marked from about mid-century among the aristocratic and monied classes. We see it in the increased vogue of living in the country, in the pleasure taken in country walks, in the growing popularity of the rustic idyll and the *"bergerade",* even in its more absurd pretences, of which the best known is the Petit Trianon, where Marie Antoinette and her ladies played at being shepherdesses and milkmaids.[28] But perhaps we see it best of all in the retreat of the formal French garden before the *'jardin anglais'*, which was supposed to put us in touch with unforced nature.[29]

There was something quite new in this return to nature. The vogue of the bucolic idyll may hide this, because it draws on models which go back to Virgil and Horace: the underlying idea that the life of simple, rustic people is closer to wholesome virtue and lasting satisfactions than the corrupt existence of city-dwellers. These stereotypes were renewed and reinforced in the eighteenth century by a number of developments: various forms of primitiv-ism, nourished partly by tales of "uncivilized" people abroad; the promotion of ordinary life; and the serious concern with agronomy which spread from England. But this re-evaluation of rustic life was still distinct from the new feeling for nature, even though some of the same people may have had a hand in furthering both—Rousseau is a case in point, with his (seeming) espousal of primitivism and his affirmation of ordinary life.

This new orientation to nature was not concerned directly with the virtues of simplicity or rusticity, but rather with the sentiments which nature awakens in us. We return to nature, because it brings out strong and noble feelings in us: feelings of awe before the greatness of creation, of peace before a pastoral scene, of sublimity before storms and deserted fastnesses, of melancholy in some lonely woodland spot. Nature draws us because it is in some way attuned to our feelings, so that it can reflect and intensify those we already feel or else awaken those which are dormant. Nature is like a great keyboard on which our highest sentiments are played out. We turn to it, as we might turn to music, to evoke and strengthen the best in us.

Girardin, who built the garden at Ermenonville where Jean-Jacques Rousseau was buried, says at the end of a description of woods, river, and fields: "C'est dans de semblables situations que l'on éprouve toute la force de cette analogie entre les charmes physiques et les impressions morales . . . on voudrait y rester toujours, parce que le coeur y sent toute la vérité et l'énergie de la nature" ("It is in such situations that one witnesses the full force of the analogy between physical beauty and moral impressions . . . one would like to remain there forever, because the heart then feels all the truth and energy of nature").[30] Thomas, one of the writers cited by Mornet, loved the "vastes forêts", because they "reposent et agrandissent l'âme"; while for Marquis de Mirabeau, the beauties of nature demand a sublime soul "pour soutenir un commerce intime avec sa silencieuse majesté" ("vast forests" . . . "rest and elevate the soul"; "to sustain an intimate exchange with its silent majesty").[31] The Marquis de Langle, however, is in a quite different state after visiting the Lake of Thun: "Le jour oú je vis pour la première fois ce beau lac faillit être le dernier de mes jours: mon existence m'échappait; je me mourais de *sentir*, de *jouir*: je tombais dans l'anéantissement" ("The day when I first saw this beautiful lake was almost my last: my existence was slipping from me; I was dying with *feeling*, with *delight*: I was falling into nothingness").[32]

The new wave of 'English' gardens were built with this relation in view. The aim was to awaken and nourish certain sentiments. The art of building gardens had a basic principle, according to the Prince de Ligne: "Cherchons à parler à l'âme" ("Let us endeavour to speak to the soul"). And for Hirschfeld it was : "Remuons fortement l'imagination et le sentiment" ("Let us stir up the imagination and feelings"). Gardens can be built to awaken all sorts of emotions: some may be gay, others offer a sweet melancholy, others will be romantic, and others again majestic. The art of gardens is a "metaphysic", which makes us able "par la manière de diriger les terrains, de se donner, à sa volonté, des sentiments et des pensées" ("by the way one lays out the grounds, to give oneself, at will, feelings and thoughts"). Gardens can thus make us better: "La théorie des jardins nous mène à l'humanité et à la bienfaisance" ("the theory of gardens leads us to humanity and beneficence").[33]

In fact, the gardens of the late eighteenth century were used for all sorts of purposes in addition to making people better. Many were designed to evoke and sustain the pleasant melancholy of the lonely dreamer. The park at Ermenonville even had an Altar of Revery. And their means included more than nature. They also evoked nostalgic melancholy by constructing tombs, temples, statues, pagodas, and also fresh ruins, which sometimes suggested foreign lands and far-away times. They played the full gamut of emotions, from the most exalted to the most sensational. And some were meant to evoke a frisson before the fearful and uncanny. But always the point lay in the *feelings*.

To see how new this is, we can perhaps usefully contrast it with earlier views of nature which also in some way relied on notions of a certain attunement or correspondence between natural phenomena and human affairs. We see this kind of correspondence in Shakespeare, for instance, where great natural disorders accompany and portend crimes in the human domain. The night in which Duncan is murdered was an unruly one, with "lamentings heard i' th' air; strange screams of death", and it remains dark even though day should have started. On the previous Tuesday a falcon had been killed by a mousing owl; and Duncan's horses turned wild in the night, "Contending 'gainst obedience, as they would / Make war with mankind".[34]

Nature is here in some way in tune with human affairs. But the relation is utterly different and in fact incompatible with the modern one which we inherit from the eighteenth century. Shakespeare draws on some notion of order based on an ontic logos, more precisely on the correspondences of

Renaissance thought. The same hierarchical order manifests itself in the different domains, the human, the avian, the animal; and so these are attuned: the disorder in one is reflected in the others. Duncan's murder is the negation of all hierarchy, as is the killing of a falcon by the lowly mouse owl or the rebellion of animals against mankind.

There is a parallel with the late-eighteenth-century experience of nature, but the underlying conception is beginning to change. The old cosmology still lingers, linking physical and moral realms, and a "tamed and ordered" version of it, "smoothed to a neo-classical decency", still informs some of the poetry of place and nature.[35] But an alternative understanding is developing which threatens to replace this cosmology. According to this, the meaning that the natural phenomena bear is no longer defined by the order of nature in itself or by the Ideas which they embody. It is defined through the effect of the phenomena on us, in the reactions they awaken. The affinity between nature and ourselves is now mediated not by an objective rational order but by the way that nature resonates in us. Our attunement with nature no longer consists in a recognition of ontic hierarchy, but in being able to release the echo within ourselves.

Nature has become a vast reservoir of what T. S. Eliot called 'objective correlatives'[36] to human sentiments and moods. It is now a great multilevel keyboard, capable of striking the most varied music from the human soul. Rational order is no longer the necessary mediating concept.

That is why French neo-Classicism had to resist the new return to nature so firmly. As the dominant aesthetic of 'le grand siècle', its rules defined by Boileau, it also invoked nature as a standard, but in a sense which made this equivalent to invoking reason.

> Aimez donc la raison; que toujours vos écrits
> Empruntent d'elle seule et leur lustre et leur prix.

Therefore love reason; that your writings will always draw from her alone both their lustre and their worth.[37]

For Boileau and his followers, of course, reason had to be understood partly as the procedural, constructive, ordering power defined by Descartes. But it also incorporated some of the old substantive sense, where nature itself embodies reason. Art must obey reason, because the mind must construct its mimesis by rational canons, but also because nature itself has its orders and proportions.

The gardens of Le Nôtre, who did his greatest work for and under Louis XIV, are the perfect embodiment of neo-Classicism. They involved imposing an order of constructive reason on nature—drawing straight lines down long vistas, balanced and symmetrical, as we see at Versailles. But they also reflected an order, in which the Sun King was the central power which secured a hierarchy endorsed by nature and God.

The 'jardin anglais' is a protest, a rebellion against all this. It is a place we go to encounter nature. But this encounter allows no more sense to the old ontic reason. And it demands that we reject the abstract, constructed orders of procedural reason. Its aim is to allow unforced nature to awaken in us the response of unforced feeling.

Now what previously passed for monstrous, for disorder, could awaken astonishment, awe. It could be what now came to be called 'sublime'.[38] Mme. Necker protested in the name of the old order when she said

> Nous sommes bien loin encore de cet amour de la nature qui fait reconnaître la perfection dans les justes proportions, dans le rapport des effets avec nos goûts et non dans l'étonnement qu'elle nous cause.

> We are still very far from that love of nature that recognizes perfection in its just proportions, in the relation of its effects to our taste and not in the astonishment it causes us.[39]

But the new love of nature turns precisely on what it awakens in us.

This is still recognizably continuous with the meaning of nature for us today. The experience evoked by Shakespeare, the premisses of Le Nôtre's designs, are no longer available to us as living options. Mornet puts it well:

> Du jardin architectural nous aboutissons au jardin état d'âme. Cela marque l'étape décisive. Après Rousseau, la nature devient décidément ce qu'elle est pour nos âmes modernes, la vie confuse et profonde où s'épuise et s'épanche tout l'inexprimable de nous-mêmes.

> From the architectural garden we come to the state-of-soul garden. This marks the decisive step. After Rousseau, nature becomes decidedly what it is for us moderns, a deep and confused life, where all that is unexpressible in us is poured out.[40]

This is another way of saying that this relation to nature is predicated on the modern identity. It allows us to measure to what extent the late eighteenth century has already crossed over the watershed and stands on the same side with us.

In this relation, nature or the world surrounding us can no longer be seen as the embodiment of that order in relation to which we define what constitutes us as rational beings. This is the kind of relation to which Plato gives paradigm expression. Our being rational is identified with our being attuned with the order of things, potentially capable of seeing and loving it. This basic structural relationship continues powerful throughout the whole premodern period, in a host of forms. The background evoked by Shakespeare is one of them.

But in the feeling for nature which we see emerging in the eighteenth century and since, this is fundamentally broken and then forgotten. A quite different sense of human identity is operative here. Nature that can move us and awaken our feelings is no longer tied to us by a notion of substantive reason. It is no longer seen as the order which defines our rationality. Rather we are defined by purposes and capacities which we discover within ourselves. What nature can now do is awaken these: it can awaken us to feeling against the too pressing regulative control of an analytic, disengaging, order-imposing reason, now understood as a subjective, procedural power.

In other words, this modern feeling for nature which starts in the eighteenth century presupposes the triumph of the new identity of disengaged reason over the premodern one embedded in an ontic logos. Descartes and Locke have already won out against Plato and the theories of meaningful order. Our own nature is no longer defined by a substantive rational ordering of purposes, but by our own inner impulses and our place in the interlocking whole. This is why our sentiments can have a value which earlier philosophy couldn't allow them. And the primacy of disengaging reason can explain why it could seem important to emphasize this value: precisely in order to rescue our sentiments from ethical marginalization in the extrinsic theory of Lockean Deism. This is what moved Hutcheson, and the later cult of sensibility has travelled a great deal farther down this same road.

This new notion of resonance didn't exclude the reinvention, as we see with the Romantics, of a cosmology of correspondences and meaningful order. For Schelling, in a sense also for Novalis, and of course for the anti-Romantic Hegel, the 'meaning' of nature is determined by an objective order, which Hegel even describes as 'rational'. But these theories are on a fundamentally new footing. They are based on an expressivist theory of nature and human life. They incorporate the notion of resonance in a subject. Indeed, they take this further, and see Nature itself as the expression of a Subject. The 'meaning' of natural phenomena as they resonate within us reflects a meaning really expressed in them, by God or a world spirit. Deism slides easily into pantheism. But these theories all remain on the modern side of the watershed, because the access to this meaning requires that we turn within. That is because a single current of life runs through world and self. So Coleridge could say, "In looking at objects of Nature while I am thinking . . . I seem rather to be seeking, as it were *asking*, a symbolical language for something within me that already and forever exists, than observing anything new." And Wordsworth: "I was often unable to think of external things as having external existence, and I communed with all that I saw as something not apart from, but inherent in, my own immaterial nature." Or as Novalis succinctly stated: "Nach innen geht der geheimnisvolle Weg" ("Inward goes the way full of mystery").[41]

It follows that the language needed to interpret the order of nature is not one we read off a publicly available gamut of correspondences; it has to take shape out of the resonances of the world within us. It is a "subtler language",[42] as we will see below.

The new love of nature, associated with the cult of sensibility, is a revealing indicator of profound cultural change. It shows what inroads the modern identity has made at this time among the educated classes, well beyond the range of influence of professional philosophy. Laurence Sterne defines sensibility as "the Eternal fountain of our feeling . . . the divinity which stirs within".[43] This phrase, not from the pen of a philosopher but from one of the most popular writers of his day, captures both the centrality of feeling and its link to the sense that our moral sources are within us, in an inner nature which marks what is significant for us.

17.7

In a parallel way, feeling is given a new importance in the religious revivals of the period, among Pietists, Methodists, and Chassidim. The Pietist movement, which begins in the late seventeenth century in Germany with Spener and Francke, turns away from the orthodox Protestant emphasis on doctrinal correctness and seeks rather to bring about a "new Birth", whose fruits will be a deep piety and a holy life. This was one of the crucial moulding influences on Wesleyan Methodism.

Although Count Zinzendorf and the German Pietists tended to be anti-rational in a way that Wesley was not, all these movements made conviction and devotion more central than learning and theology. This was their transposition of the Reformation demand of total personal commitment, but in the climate of the eighteenth century this fervour took the form of displays of strong emotion. Something similar was evident in the Great Awakening in America, though the theological background was more orthodox Calvinist there.

How is all this to be related to the more secular ways of exalting sentiment that I've been describing? It's difficult to say, but probably the influence went in both directions. In an age in which human goodness begins to be defined in terms of appropriate feelings, it was natural for piety to take such emotional form. And reciprocally, the hallowing of deep emotional expression in religious life may have opened the way at a later phase—in spite of the rather harsh evangelical outlook on child-rearing[44]—to a more effusive life of the emotions within the family.[45]

PART IV

The Voice of Nature

18

FRACTURED HORIZONS

18.1

All this raises tantalizing questions of historical causation, which I don't feel myself competent to answer. What does seem clear is that the philosophical changes I described earlier are carried by and articulate a large-scale transformation in common assumptions and sensibility. What we can describe as a new moral culture radiates outward and downward from the upper middle classes of England, America, and (for some facets) France. In making the transition to new societies and strata, it is frequently transformed; so that what we end up with is a family of resembling moral cultures, or certain civilization-wide traits with important variations among nations and social classes. Thus the Anglo-French "Enlightenment" culture resonated in Germany in a quite original way;[1] and the modern self-enclosed family is often quite differently lived in different classes.

But through all the variations, some common themes are visible. It is a culture which is individualist in the three senses I invoked earlier: it prizes autonomy; it gives an important place to self-exploration, in particular of feeling; and its visions of the good life generally involve personal commitment. As a consequence, in its political language, it formulates the immunities due people in terms of subjective rights. Because of its egalitarian bent, it conceives these rights as universal.

At the same time, this culture accords significance to productive work and also to the family, which is ideally a close community of love, in which the members find an important part of their human fulfilment. In certain sub-cultures of today, the family may be displaced by the sexual liaison, or "relationship", as the proper locus of this fulfilment, but the centrality of love remains. It makes feelings morally crucial, and makes much of their exploration and expression. And universal benevolence, or at least fair dealing, is its most important social virtue.

This is not even a complete thumbnail sketch. There are other crucial features, such as the new relation to nature, which I discussed in the last part, and the premium put on eliminating suffering, and the importance of self-expression, which I have omitted, or barely mentioned, because I want to lay down some necessary background before introducing them. But there is enough here to raise the issues I will explore at this point.

The really large-scale issue concerns the relation of this whole moral culture to its economic and social "base". I wish I could say something insightful and valid on this score, but it is beyond my capacity, and well beyond the scope of this work. It seems clear that the rise of this culture was complexly related to the changes in economic practices, administrative structures and methods, and disciplines that I have mentioned earlier, in a way which I only sketchily indicated at the end of Part II. In some way, the very success of the new theologies and neo-Stoic philosophy in bringing some stable order to the lives of important milieus in European society, along with the changes to more effective economic and administrative practices—such as agricultural improvements, better-disciplined armies, more effective social control—all helped to accredit the sense of living in a well-regulated interlocking order, to which humans are attuned by their natural endowments, and in which the pursuance of the ends of ordinary life through instrumental reason plays a central part. It is this sense of confidence in the natural order which quite naturally found religious expression in Deism, that is, in a theology which would make this order of interlocking natures the key to its understanding of God and his goodness, and hence the basis of its piety.

But all this in no way authorizes the attribution of a unilinear causal relation of "base" and "superstructure" between these economic and social developments and the moral culture. The relationship is plainly circular, however we may come to conceive it in more refined terms. That is, elements of the culture were constitutive to the developments—as, e.g., individual autonomy was to the new forms of economic enterprise and political authority—while in return these elements were entrenched and propagated by the forward march of these developments.

A similar circular relation seems to be integral to any satisfactory answer to a second issue about historical causation, which I do want to look at here. This concerns the relation between the modern moral culture and the philosophical formulations that I was examining earlier. Plainly there is no clear-cut historical priority here either. The culture didn't spread outward from the formulations of epoch-making philosophers. It is sometimes hard to resist writing as though that were so; and philosophers are probably particularly bad at resisting. But this is not really out of professional vanity. No one really thinks that disengagement entered the culture from the pen of Descartes, or individualism from that of Locke. Obviously these are influential thinkers; but they are just as much articulating something which is already in train as they are helping to define its future direction and form. To see that they are doing both these things will save us from the equal and opposite error of thinking them merely epiphenomenal. If Locke didn't invent individualism, or the picture of the mind as a tabula rasa, it is clear that his formulations of both of these became normative for broad movements of thought in the eighteenth century.

But the temptation to give the priority to the philosophical formulation comes from the fact that it *is* a formulation. The movement through the culture is something diffuse and ambiguous, hard to pick out and define. It takes the best resources of that skilled form of historiography we call the *histoire des mentalités* to get some kind of conceptual hold on it. Descartes and Locke offer us pithy sentences which seem to encapsulate it all. And so it is easy to lose sight of the continuing flow between the thinker and his culture.[2]

And this is the more damaging in that we lose our grasp of the relationship between the identification of life goods and the defining of constitutive goods, to use the terms I introduced above (section 4.1). In a broad movement of culture, we see emerging new notions and senses of the good life: for instance, the close, loving family, or the expression of feeling, or the ideals of benevolence. These will also figure, more rigourously defined, in the writings of philosophers, but philosophers will in addition try to articulate the constitutive goods which underlie them.

So alongside the cult of sentiment, or the unstructured sense that feeling is important, we have the philosophical theories of moral sense, with their elaborate views of human psychology, and its relation—or non-relation—to providential order. These are in a circular relation somewhat similar to the one between "base" and "superstructure" I described above. Neither has absolute priority, and neither is fully independent of the other. As I argued in Part I, articulating a constitutive good is making clear what is involved in the life good one espouses. Unreflecting people in the culture, who are drawn to certain life goods, may have nothing to offer in the way of description of constitutive good, but that doesn't mean that their sense of what is worth pursuing isn't shaped by some unstructured intuitions about their metaphysical predicament, about their moral sources being within or without, for example.

We glimpsed something of this implicit relation in Part III, in the discussion of the new orientation to nature. I tried to show how this reflected, in a way presupposed, something like the modern internalized identity, with all that this entails for our understanding of constitutive good. This is not to say that those who were enraptured by mountain lakes or gave themselves to melancholy revery in an English garden had formulated any notion of a disengaged subject for themselves, or even had picked one up from one of the main philosophical schools. It means only that the movement of culture which shaped their outlook and feelings required some such understanding to make sense, and undercut the sense that premodern views had supposed. Thus this movement, however it arose, provided a congenial climate within which explicit formulations of the modern identity could arise, and which it in turn could modify or direct.

That is why we cannot consider the life goods in a culture as self-contained, as without internal relation to various possible articultions of constitutive goods. It is why we can speak of some articulations as the ones which fit, which capture the spirit of a certain unreflecting practice. But at the same time articulations can also alter practice. The life good itself becomes something different when one is induced to see the constitutive good differently.

All of this makes the relationship rather hard to state. To relate it to the transformations I have been discussing, I quite naturally defined the moral culture which has been emerging in terms of certain life goods, e.g., autonomy, the significance of family life, benevolence. One of the important articulations of constitutive goods which stands behind this emergence in the eighteenth century is what I have called the Deist notion of natural order. But this broad movement was, of course, not dependent on this outlook. What one can say is that this philosophy caught the spirit of some of the changes, and in turn deeply influenced the form they took.

The lack of dependence soon becomes evident in the fact that the Deist order loses all credit, and the broad movement carries on. But this is where we are easily tripped up by our language. It now sounds as though the movement of culture was after all self-contained, not inwardly related to certain articulations. The whole illusion lies in the definite description. Not "the" movement, but some particular variant(s) of the major life goods, emerges out of the demise of Deism. The movement of life goods evolves out of the Deist formulation, but in the process it becomes something different, which is to say it moves into the orbit of other formulations.

To see this relationship—and not to make the philosophy something independently efficacious, or to conceive the transformation of moral culture as pursuing its own path independent of its epiphenomenal formulations—is what it takes to come to grips with the history of our moral sources which I'm trying to trace here. For Deism—and as we shall see in a minute, the radical Enlightenment as well—has been a historically efficacious formulation. It has had a *"Wirkungsgeschichte"*.[3] Even though it has been left behind by the movement of modern moral culture, it has helped to determine the direction and shape of this movement. It could not contain it within its definitions, but neither was it irrelevant to it. It has left its mark.[4]

But this puts me before another issue of causation, which it is harder for me to evade. Deism appears as the first step on the road which next led to the unbelieving Enlightenment of figures like Helvétius, Bentham, Holbach, and

Condorcet. And beyond them the road seems to lead to modern secular culture. That's why, as I argued earlier, understanding the motives for Deism is so important. It promises, or threatens, to give us the key to the whole modern development we gesture at with the word 'secularization'.

This is a term which is much used to describe modern society; and it is sometimes even offered as partial explanation for features of this society. But it is more a locus of questions than a source of explanations. It describes a process which is undeniable: the regression of belief in God, and even more, the decline in the practice of religion, to the point where from being central to the whole life of Western societies, public and private, this has become sub-cultural, one of many private forms of involvement which some people indulge in.

The second change—the decline in practice—has been more widespread than the first: many people go on believing in God, or in some higher reality, even though they engage in no formal religious practice. But in regard to earlier ages, and most of the history of mankind, it is perhaps the change in belief which is the more striking. Even though many writers of the seventeenth and early eighteenth centuries thought that they had to argue against "atheists" (Mersenne thought there were fifty thousand in Paris in his day!—but he certainly couldn't have meant what we mean by the word),[5] we can tell from their arguments and tone that unbelief was close to inconceivable for them. The spiritual dimension in human life just seemed inexplicable to them in the absence of a God. Whichcote says, "Man in the use of his Reason, by Force of Mind and Understanding, may as well know, that there is a God that governs the World, as he may know, by the Use of his Eyes, there is a Sun". And he continues: "It is as natural and proper for Mind and Understanding to tend towards God, as for heavy things to tend towards their Center: For God is the Center of immortal Souls".[6] It is clear from both tone and context, indeed, from Whichcote's whole way of reasoning, that this is not polemical hype, but a genuine expression of how things seemed to him. Even in the latter part of the eighteenth century, in the era of the high Enlightenment, genuine atheism was very rare, as the celebrated anecdote of Hume at dinner chez Holbach testifies. Hume is said to have expressed doubt that there were any real atheists in the world. "Look around you", the Baron replied, "and count the guests". There were eighteen at table. "Not bad", said Holbach. "I can show you fifteen atheists right off. The other three haven't yet made up their minds".[7] The very tone of this statement, as well as Hume's opening remark, tells us how outré it was then to be a total unbeliever.

It is clear we live in a totally different climate. What happened? To invoke secularization here is just to redescribe the problem, not to offer an answer. It may seem like an answer, because of our entertaining unstructured beliefs about the inevitability of the decline in religious faith. There are two kinds of factors which are often thought to make this inevitable. Sometimes it is thought that the large-scale institutional changes of the modern world—industrialization, technological change in everyday life, concentration and mobility—conspire to undermine all traditional forms of allegiance and belief, from tribal custom to group identity, including religious belief.

But this explanation won't resist close examination. Obviously, industrialization, technological change, and mobility have undermined many features of earlier forms of life. How could it be otherwise? And undoubtedly in our civilization they have contributed to the spread of unbelief. But it is far from clear that of themselves they must undermine religious belief (as against provoking changes in the forms it takes, as any major social transformation will do). The evidence of non-Western societies is perhaps not yet fully in, but it doesn't indicate an unambiguous causal effect of these major "modernizing" institutional changes. It rather appears as though each civilization will live through these changes in its own characteristic way. In at least some sectors in the West, it seems that unbelief was bound up with what was understood culturally as 'modernity', and *that* is why these changes have helped to spread it here.

The other factor which is thought to lead inevitably to unbelief is the spread of science and education. Here the ideological prejudice shows more clearly on the surface. People who hold this usually simply take for granted that religious belief is irrational and unenlightened or unscientific. If we step back from this prejudice, we can remember how much of the development of modern science was from the beginning bound up with a religious outlook—starting from the roots of mechanism in nominalist theology; and we can see how today, too, scientific questioning can just as well inspire a kind of piety as it can unbelief.

I don't feel able to offer an explanation of the scope that these theories of secularization lay claim to. But I think something more can be said about what the change we call by this name has amounted to. This can be seen as an effort to clarify the explanandum for any adequate theory of secularization.

The crucial change, as I intimated above, is that people no longer feel, like Whichcote, that the spiritual dimension of their lives was incomprehensible if one supposed there was no God. To most of our forebears it seemed strange and bizarre, not to say wicked, to deny the existence of God. How can we understand this?

In the language I have been using in this work, we can say that God was in some way or other bound up with the only moral sources they could seriously envisage. 'Moral sources' has been my term of art for constitutive goods insofar as we turn to them in whatever way is appropriate to them—through contemplation, or invocation, or prayer, or whatever—for moral empowerment. An "age of belief" is one in which all credible moral sources involve God.

Within such an age, there are a great variety of sources, and God may enter into them very differently. We see this reflected in the recognizably different forms of Christian spirituality. For some people, the very fact that their lives had a moral dimension, the fact that they were moved not simply by de facto desires but also by spiritual aspirations, straining to something higher, pointed irresistibly to a Deity. No other explanation seemed credible. Whichcote was obviously one such. He borrows the Platonic notion that our spiritual aspirations give us some sense of what created them and guides them, just as our eyes tell us what makes vision possible. So Reason, our higher part, comes to acknowledge God just as naturally as our eyes do the sun. The other image invoked in the passage I quoted above, that of gravity, is even more telling. Our mind and understanding, the set of our aspirations, "tend towards God", just as heavy things tend towards the earth.

This sense underlies the Augustinian approach to proving the existence of God, which proceeds via a radical reflection on my own spiritual nature. My longing for perfection, coupled with my manifest imperfection, points to the higher being who planted this aspiration in me.

But there were other ways of sensing the undeniability of God. The link could be indirect, as it were, through a notion of order. My existence as a moral agent may seem to me dependent on the existence of an order of things, in human society and perhaps also in nature, and this in two ways: I am aware of having learnt what it is to be a spiritual being from my society or church; and the order itself in its goodness calls forth a sense of awe and gratitude which empowers me. The order is a moral source for me. But the goodness of the order in turn is inseparable from a notion of providence; I can only see it as rooted in God. And so by this route as well, I find God to be as undeniable as the spiritual dimension of my existence.

This spiritual route lies behind the attempts to prove the existence of God through the order of the world, most evidently in arguments from design. But just as with the Augustinian proofs, we have to get behind the arguments as exercises in what we would recognize as strict proof—in which light they appear pretty flimsy to us today—and try to sense the spiritual outlook they articulate.[8]

Of course, nothing prevented people from feeling that God was undeniable in both these ways. Obviously, many did. But equally obviously some leaned heavily to one side or the other. The stricter and more revolutionary strands of Calvinist Puritanism, with their suspicion of pre-Christian philosophies of the cosmos, their indictment of the existing social order, and their acute sense of inner struggle, were obviously firmly planted in the inward route. The Deist theories described above, in which the providential order plays such an important role, gravitate to the outer path.

A study of the different temperaments in American Protestantism in the prerevolutionary era, Philip Greven's *The Protestant Temperament,* is very illuminating in this connection.[9] Greven distinguishes 'evangelical', 'moderate', and 'genteel' forms of spirituality. The last, as the name implies, was especially prominent among the social elites of the colonies. What distinguished genteel piety from the first two, which were largely committed to the inward route, was the way in which it was inseparable from solidarity with established institutions and participation in their rituals. Greven speaks of their conviction "that religious experience and religious worship were public expressions of the harmonious gathering of the whole community, joined together in the institutions, and the rituals and ceremonies, which symbolized the essential unity of both this world and the next. Their piety was synonymous with the act of worship, and thus was always directed outwardly by visible signs of communion with both worlds". As he puts it, "the piety of the genteel became a public act, not an inner preoccupation".[10]

These people inevitably seem to us less deep, less serious, less really pious than their evangelical or moderate critics. This may be unfair. But what is clear is that they in their own way could be as utterly convinced theists (or perhaps Deists, in a minority of cases) as those who struggled inwardly with sin and grace.

It is just this unshakeable rootedness in belief which seems strange to us today. Even in societies where a majority of people profess some belief in God or a divine principle, no one sees it as *obvious* that there is a God. This is what ultimately we have to be able to explain (though not, I hasten to add, in the course of this study).

Some people assume that the explanation ought mainly to point to the removal of obstacles. They assume that our present uncertainty reflects the real epistemic predicament, the way the question of God really is for us humans. No one can know for sure, hence what needs explanation is how people of earlier, more benighted ages could have been unaware of this. We have to understand the blinkers that narrowed their vision. Secularization is explained by the gradual removal of these. A view like this obviously encouraged the theory that unbelief arises inevitably from science and education, which I attacked above.

In a sense I want to concur that our present tentativeness, our loss of a rooted certainty, represents an epistemic gain. But for a quite different reason. I don't think there is such a thing as our real epistemic predicament in relation to God, just sans phrase. Our sense of the certainty or problematicity of God is relative to our sense of moral sources. Our forebears were generally unruffled in their belief, because the sources they could envisage made unbelief incredible. The big thing that has happened since is the opening of other possible sources. In a predicament where these are plural, a lot of things look problematic that didn't before—and not just the existence of God, but also such "unquestionable" ethical principles as that reason ought to govern the passions. Who knows whether further transformations in the available moral sources may not alter all these issues again out of all recognition? I want to argue that our present predicament represents an epistemic gain, because I think that the alternative moral sources which have opened for us in the past two centuries represent real and important human potentialities. It is possible to argue, as many have done, that they are largely based on illusion. But even if I am right and we are in a better epistemic predicament as a consequence, this still doesn't authorize us to talk of "the real" epistemic predicament.

What this means for the explanation of secularization is that the issue shifts from the removal of blinkers to the question how these new sources became available. This is the cultural shift which we have to understand. Secularization doesn't just arise because people get a lot more educated, and science progresses. This has some effect, but it isn't decisive. What matters is that masses of people can sense moral sources of a quite different kind, ones that don't necessarily suppose a God.

The limited effect of "Enlightenment" on its own becomes clear when we try to see what it is for new sources to become 'available'. I confess that this is a very difficult question. But it's obvious that availability here can't mean that another quite different position is logically conceivable or even that it is there in the tradition. In this sense, a range of pagan views, those of the ancient philosophers, were "available" through most of the mediaeval and early modern periods. Only a tiny minority actually adopted one or another of them—in their "pagan" form, that is, involving a denial of the God of Abraham; influential schools of thought were built on Christianized variants. There was a tiny handful of atheists influenced by Epicureanism—the Chevalier de Méré seems to have been such. Shaftesbury came very close to being an ancient Stoic. Spinoza, for his part, invented his own original form of "pagan" philosophy out of the resources of Cartesianism.

We are tempted with hindsight to see these people as the wave of the future, and to suspect their contemporaries who were inspired by the same ancient sources while professing Christianity of concealing their unbelief. But this is anachronistic. Spinoza and Shaftesbury—but not the Chevalier de Méré—become major cultural reference points during the Romantic period. Spinoza ceases then to be a disturbing, shocking outsider, like Hobbes, who mainly serves as a kind of benchmark of disquieting error, a focus against which to direct right-thinking argument. For Goethe and others of his generation, Spinoza is a seer.

But Spinoza himself would have been rather astonished to hear the doctrines for which he was admired. He emerges as a forerunner of that great quasi-pantheistic sense of a cosmic spirit running through the whole of nature and coming to expression in mankind, which seized the imagination of a whole generation, both Weimar Classicists and Romantics, in Germany. Here we do make contact with a developing conception of moral sources which was truly available in a stronger sense. Pure Spinozism was not on. Shaftesbury becomes immensely influential for rather similar reasons: his sense of the unity of nature, his doctrine of plastic powers, his being perceived as the originator of moral sense theory, all made him an inspiration to the Germans of the Romantic epoch. The austere follower of Epictetus is forgotten.

18.2

I am getting ahead of my main story in talking about the Romantics; but the point of these remarks has been to try to come closer to understanding what makes moral sources really available. Obviously being expounded in well-known and even revered books wasn't enough. Why not? Some elements of an answer are at hand. There were important respects in which the pagan authors failed to capture early modern moral experience: the dimension of *agapē,* later sliding into benevolence or altruism, was wholly absent from the pre-Christian writers, as was the affirmation of ordinary life. And the dimension of post-Augustinian inwardness in all its ramifications of self-control and self-exploration wasn't there either. The most subversive of ancient philosophies, Epicureanism, also repudiated any belief in providence, which meant one had to renounce all recognition of a beneficent order. On the other side, the actual doctrines of the ancients who believed in cosmic order, uniting as they did the moral and the explanatory in theories of ontic logos, fell increasingly on the defensive before the advancing mechanistic science.

Identifying these inadequacies may help in describing the alternative moral sources which actually do begin to emerge in the eighteenth century, and which define our contemporary situation. I think we can, without too great oversimplification, range these under two heads or, one might better say, two "frontiers" of moral exploration. The first lies within the agent's own powers, those of rational order and control initially, but later, as we shall see, it will also be a question of powers of expression and articulation. The second lies in the depths of nature, in the order of things, but also as it is reflected within, in what wells up from my own nature, desires, sentiments, affinities.

We've traced both these frontiers far enough to see how they could emerge as alternatives. Learning to be the disengaged subject of rational control, and eventually a punctual self, is accompanied, even powered by, a sense of our dignity as rational agents. We saw how with Descartes and Locke, and later we shall see in a new emphasis with Kant, this dignity becomes itself a moral source. In all these writers, this dignity is placed in a theistic perspective. The awesome powers of human reason and will are God-made and part of God's plan; more, they are what constitutes the image of God in us. But insofar as the sources now lie within us, more particularly, within certain powers we possess, the basis is there for an independent, i.e., non-theistic morality.

Similarly, we have seen the notion of providential order develop towards the picture of nature as a vast network of interlocking beings, which works towards the conservation of each of its parts, where this age-old principle is now understood as conducing to the life and happiness of the sentient creatures which it contains. It is not only this order which marks ordinary fulfilments as significant. We have access to this fact not only through reason but through our feelings as well. We are aware of this significance through our inner nature. In that the good to which nature conduces is now a purely natural, self-contained good, and in that the proximate moral source is a self-subsistent order of interlocking beings, to whose principles we have access within ourselves, the stage is set for another independent ethic, in which nature itself will become the prime moral source, without its Author.

In each case, the stimulus existed within Christian culture itself to generate these views which stand on the threshold. Augustinian inwardness stands behind the Cartesian turn, and the mechanistic universe was originally a demand of theology. The disengaged subject stands in a place already hollowed out for God; he takes a stance to the world which befits an image of the Deity. The belief in interlocking nature follows the affirmation of ordinary life, a central Judaeo-Christian idea, and extends the centrally Christian notion that God's goodness consists in his stooping to seek the benefit of humans.

What arises in each case is a conception which stands ready for a mutation, which will carry it outside Christian faith altogether. But being ready isn't sufficient to produce the mutation. That seems to have required an additional stimulus. The mutation became necessary when and to the extent that it seemed to people that these moral sources could only be properly acknowledged, could only thus fully empower us, in their non-theistic form. The dignity of free, rational control came to seem genuine only free of submission to God; the goodness of nature, and/or our unreserved immersion in it, seemed to require its independence, and a negation of any divine vocation. What is involved in these changes, particularly the second, is what

I want to examine in subsequent chapters of this book; indeed, it constitutes a major theme of the ensuing discussion.

But I make this sketch now in order to go some steps towards answering the question of what makes an alternative 'available', in the meaning of the act. Why the dignity of disengagement, and the wellsprings of nature, and not Epicurus' *ataraxia,* or Stoic *apatheia*? Or Spinoza's *amor intellectualis Dei,* for that matter? Well, clearly it has something to do with a source capturing the important life goods to which people have come to subscribe. The fact that no ancient view gives a place to benevolence in the modern sense severely restricts their appeal, as I said above. But it has also to relate these life goods to constitutive goods which are recognizable within the spiritual life which people have been leading. Active benevolence can also be inspired by a certain reading of the *Bhagavad Gita,* as Gandhi demonstrated much later on, but this wouldn't have meant very much to our eighteenth-century forebears, beyond a few rare, original spirits.

Of course, what brings about these two features is the interesting explanatory question. Why do certain life goods become prominent, virtually undeniable, in a given age? We may never be able to generate more than suggestive partial hints towards an answer to this question. Certainly, the underlying development of social, economic, and political forms plays a part; for example, the first stages in the rise of capitalism and the modern bureaucratic state were crucial to the story we've been following. But these can never provide sufficient reasons. The outcome crucially depends on the kind of moral culture these forms are interwoven with. Reading this moral culture will also give us the limits within which sources with the second feature must fall. But these limits in the nature of things cannot be exactly traced.

But although I can't offer "the historical explanation", a study of this kind can make an essential contribution to one such. As I argued in Chapter 12, any identification of the political and social causes of secularization would have to be complemented by some insight into what made the alternative sources powerful, what made them seem good and compelling. In a way, I have been elaborating one part of the answer to this question through the preceding chapters: the rise of forms of Christian spirituality which made disengaged reason and interlocking order central. The other part we need will come only with an understanding of the moral impulses which drove some people beyond the threshold, towards unbelieving forms of these master ideas. That is what I want to explore in the succeeding chapters.

In any case, what emerges from this discussion is that an account of secularization cannot simply relate the removal of obstacles to enlightenment. What has to be explained is the cultural mutation by which alternative sources to the theistic became available. And this means that we try to define just what this mutation and these alternatives were. What is indispensable is some interpretive work, exhibiting the nature and force of the goods. This is what I am beginning to embark on in speaking of the two frontiers. But before I follow out the exploration of these frontiers and the further mutations that have occurred on them, I want to say a little more here about the general predicament that has arisen for us.

Modern moral culture is one of multiple sources; it can be schematized as a space in which one can move in three directions. There are the two independent frontiers and the original theistic foundation. The fact that the directions are multiple contributes to our sense of uncertainty. This is part of the reason why almost everyone is tentative today, why virtually no one can have the rooted confidence in their outlook that we see, for instance, in Whichcote.

But this is not all. The two modern directions are inherently problematic. That is why I prefer to call them 'frontiers' for exploration. They are problematic partly because they have been experienced as contestable since their original opening. This might seem to follow naturally from the fact that they were opened in contestation, in a challenge to the reigning theistic outlook. But I also mean that they are inherently contestable in a way that the theistic outlook is not. Theism is, of course, contested as to its truth. Opponents may judge it harshly and think that it would be degrading and unfortunate for humans if it were true. But no one doubts that those who embrace it will find a fully adequate moral source in it.

The other two sources suffer a contestation on this score. The question is whether, even granted we fully recognize the dignity of disengaged reason, or the goodness of nature, this is in fact enough to justify the importance we put on it, the moral store we set by it, the ideals we erect on it. Of course, certain theists have hastened to call this into question from the very beginning of our modern Kulturkampf. They have said that human dignity is a pitiable thing without God, that the demands of nature turn to violence and disorder without faith, and the like. But these doubts are not only raised by theists. From their very inception explorers on these two frontiers have felt the question of adequacy pressing on them.

We might say that all positions are problematized by the fact that they exist in a field of alternatives. But whereas faith is questioned as to its truth, dignity and nature are also called into question in respect of their adequacy if true. The nagging question for modern theism is simply: Is there really a God? The threat at the margin of modern non-theistic humanism is: So what?

This is what turns these sources into frontiers of exploration. The challenge of inadequacy calls forth continually renewed attempts to define what the dignity that inheres in us as rational or expressive beings, or the good involved in our immersion in nature, consists in. This, and not just the predicament of rivalry and contestation, is what makes modern moral outlooks so tentative and exploratory. And many theists join the search, as they try to relate their faith to the fact of modern unbelief.

But the relations between these three sources are even more complicated than I have yet suggested. Since the two independent modern frontiers grow out of mutations in forms of Christian spirituality, they go on being counterposed to theistic variants. There can be, and are, theistic explorations of the dignity of rational agency or the goodness of nature. That is what the image of three-dimensional space was meant to capture. One can advance in one dimension at any level in the other two; one can explore the length of the space at any depth, or its width at any point along the axis of length. The three directions can be seen as rivals, but also as complementary.

Thus some people claim utter insensitivity to one or other direction. Some theists affect to find nothing but presumptuous illusion in modern talk of the dignity of man. Other people seem closed to even the possibility of belief in God. They come close to being the mirror images of the traditional theists of two centuries ago—though no one in our pluralistic age can reach quite that degree of unruffled confidence. These are people whose moral lives are deeply woven into a non-theistic variant of one (or perhaps both) of the other sources.

The utter non-meeting of minds between such anti-humanist theists and complacent agnostics testifies to the contestation and rivalry in modern culture. But at the same time, the three frontiers are related; and this comes out in the mutual influence and interchange between them. In a way this was already evident in the negative interchanges. The very anti-humanism of much evangelical religion today, or of figures like Cardinal Ratzinger, has been defined by the views targeted as rivals. But there is also positive influence and interchange. Christian faith has been transformed by incorporating aspirations which were first developed on the fringes of or quite outside the Christian church. For instance, the central emphasis on reducing suffering, which was pioneered by the radical Enlightenment, by anti-clerical figures like Bentham and Beccaria, became a constitutive feature of nineteenth-century reforming evangelical Anglicanism. More subtly, contemporary notions of faith have been transformed by such ideals as expressive integrity, sexual equality, and world economic justice. In a more complex and untraceable fashion, the "decline of Hell", the steady growth of the belief that salvation is universal, which we see in the eighteenth and nineteenth centuries, not only in Deism but even within revival movements—Wesley's rejection of Calvinist predestinariansim is a case in point—reflects inextricably both orthodox religious sensibility and secular rationalist critique.[11]

It may appear that the influence is all one way, that religious groups have been forced to take on board bits of the secular humanist culture to survive.

But secular humanism also has its roots in Judaeo-Christian faith; it arises from a mutation out of a form of that faith. The question can be put, whether this is more than a matter of historical origin, whether it doesn't also reflect a continuing dependence. This is one of the issues I want to take up in what follows. My belief, baldly stated here, is that it does.

What I want to do in the ensuing chapters is follow, with highly selective attention, the continuing development of these frontiers, the mutations that occur on them, and their relations. The principle of selection is my goal of illuminating the modern identity as we live it today and the understandings of moral sources it incorporates. My claim will be that the expository device of the three frontiers remains valid, even though the original form in which they were opened has been radically challenged. Along with the power of rational control, we now also recognize one of expressive articulation, whose proper exercise is sometimes seen as antithetical to that of the first. The conception of nature as good has been challenged by visions of it as a source of amoral, even wild and irrational, energy. I will argue that in spite of this, the notion of frontiers of exploration of moral sources, situated respectively in our own powers and in nature, remains illuminating and useful.

In tracing this, I will try to bear in mind what I discussed earlier in this chapter: the circular relation between life goods and the articulations of constitutive goods which underlie them. The mutations out of which secularization emerges are a good case in point. They are powered by the sense that certain life goods can be more integrally realized if they are related to a non-theistic source; but in the change, the life good itself is, of course, reinterpreted.

In the next two chapters, I will look at two big constellations of ideas which either immediately or over time have helped generate forms of unbelief. Each combines the two frontiers in a characteristic way: one joins a lively sense of our powers of disengaged reason to an instrumental reading of nature; the other focusses on our powers of creative imagination and links these to a sense of nature as an inner moral source. These forms stand as rival, and the tension between them is one of the dominant features of modern culture.

In Chapter 19, I will turn to the genesis of the first constellation, to the mutation by which the thought of the radical, unbelieving Enlightenment emerged out of Deism. I'm thinking here of the materialist and utilitarian writers like Bentham, Holbach, Helvétius, and Condorcet.

My rather lengthy discussion of secularization has been meant to prepare the way for this transition. Perhaps it was not unnecessary. The explanation in terms of enlightenment, of the removal of the barriers to reason, is particularly tempting in this case, partly because this was the explanation espoused by the radical philosophes about themselves. What distinguished these writers from their Deist predecessors, besides their rejection of God and providence, was their uncompromising stance of disengaged reason. They were all very much followers of Locke, looking at human nature as neutral, malleable stuff, waiting to be moulded to a form that would produce universal happiness. They studied human beings according to the canons of natural science as then understood. If, carried along by their self-image, we think that this is what 'science' and 'reason' require, then we will see this as just another step in the unfolding of enlightenment, and the rejection of God will seem like an inevitable corollary.

But if their scientism seems something less than the quintessence of rationality, then it too will demand explanation, and we will pay attention to the moral motifs in their work. I want briefly to explore these, and hope that when I have done so, it will be evident that these provide an important insight into the motivations of the radical Enlightenment.

19

RADICAL ENLIGHTENMENT

19.1

The radical Aufklärer[1] had no use for the notion of providence, or a providential order; at least they thought they didn't. Their ethic was purely based on utility. We start from the fact that people desire happiness or pleasure and the absence of pain. The only issue is how to maximize happiness. The principle of utility is "that principle which approves or disapproves of every action whatsoever, according to the tendency which it appears to have to augment or diminish the happiness of the party whose interest is in question".[2]

On this view, we can't draw our judgements of right and wrong from any conception of the order of things, either the ancient hierarchical one of reason or the modern one of providential design. The crucial judgement for any action concerns its consequences; we can't be diverted from this to consider how it fits with any pre-existing order. And so any appeals to a Law of Nature, or the "Law of Reason, Right Reason, Natural Justice, Natural Equity, Good Order", or the like, have to be set aside.[3]

Instead of looking at the world as a providential order, we can look at it, and indeed, at our own natures, as a neutral domain, which we have to understand in order to master it, and whose causal relations we have to make use of in order to produce the greatest amount of happiness. We have to carry Lockean disengagement through to its fullest and understand human psychology not in terms of its supposed inherent bents to good or bad, but through a neutral, causal-genetic examination. "Nul individu ne naît bon, nul individu ne naît méchant. Les hommes sont l'un ou l'autre, selon qu'un intérêt conforme ou contraire les réunit ou les divise" ("No one is born good, no one is born bad. Men are one or the other, according to whether mutual or opposing interests unite or divide them"), says Helvétius, dismissing both the moral sense of Shaftesbury and the belief in innate goodness of Rousseau.[4] Our character is formed by the associations which have been set up in our history. These either incline us to serve the general happiness or do not, and on this basis we are judged good or bad. But we *are* neither by nature; we can be *made* one or the other. This is the only relevant issue.

So the radical utilitarians rejected the constitutive good of Deism, the providential order; but at the same time, they were if anything even more strongly committed to the life goods this order had underpinned. Three of these stand out, as central to their outlook:

1. The ideal of self-responsible reason. This entailed, as we saw, a freedom from all authority, and was linked with a notion of dignity.
2. The notion that the ordinary fulfilments that we seek by nature, the pursuit of happiness in the characteristic human way, through production and family life, have a central significance; that is, they not only are what we desire but are worthy of being pursued and furthered.
3. The ideal of universal and impartial benevolence.

In a way, this constellation—rejecting the constitutive goods, and cleaving nevertheless to the life goods—is not surprising. For these life goods were, as we saw, carried by the whole broad movement of modern culture in these centuries. They didn't just come on the scene with the philosophies of interlocking design; nor did they depend exclusively on these philosophies for their credibility. Moreover, this picture of the order of nature was itself under some strain. It was in fact too good, too serenely satisfied with the way things were, to be generally believed.

This was so in two ways, in fact. The first was that in portraying everything as designed for the best, it strained the credulity of anyone who was forced to take disaster and suffering seriously. This is the aspect of the doctrine, best known in the Leibnizian formulation, that this is the best of all possible worlds, which was made famous in the character of Dr. Pangloss in Voltaire's *Candide*. Voltaire's sardonic portrayal said more than volumes of philosophical argument. For those who did want to argue, the Lisbon earthquake of 1757, which took some 70,000 lives, seemed unanswerable.

What strained the credulity of others was the picture of a world in which virtue and self-interest came so neatly together. The struggle between good and evil seemed to have been resolved into a misunderstanding. "Pleasure, or wrong or rightly understood / Our greatest evil, or our greatest good". If the first objection might be called anti-Panglossian, we might call this the anti-levelling one.

This anti-levelling attack will be taken up by Rousseau and Kant. The radical utilitarians were oblivious of it, and went further towards levelling all moral distinctions even than their predecessors. But they did take up the anti-Panglossian objection. In a sense, they proposed to save the life goods of Deism from the distortions and discredit of Deism itself.

For the radical Aufklärer not only went on espousing the three goods mentioned above. They believed themselves to be defending them more fully and effectively in demolishing what had been supposed to be their foundation. The stance of radical disengagement could be presented as a more uncompromising fulfilment of self-responsible reason. The focus on utility alone promised a more single-minded pursuit of happiness. And disengaged reason was meant to sweep away the obstacles to a universal and impartial promotion of well-being. The point of accepting the principle of utility, says Bentham, is to make it "the foundation of that system, the object of which is to rear the fabric of felicity by the hands of reason and of law".[5]

That attachment to the ideal of self-responsible reason played a crucial role in the radicalization of the Enlightenment is fairly obvious. It entered into the very definition of what it was to be a 'philosophe' in France—that one be an autonomous thinker. As Diderot wrote in his Encyclopedia article on the Chaldeans, "l'homme est né pour penser de lui-même". The lead-up to this line reads: "One must be oneself very little of a philosopher not to feel that the finest privilege of our reason consists in not believing anything by the impulsion of a blind and mechanical instinct, and that it is to dishonour reason to put it in bonds as the Chaldeans did". In the article on eclecticism, he expounds his ideal:

> The eclectic is a philosopher who, trampling underfoot prejudice, tradition, venerability, universal assent, authority—in a word, everything that overawes the crowd—dares to think for himself, to ascend to the clearest general principles, to examine them, to discuss them, to admit nothing save on the testimony of his own reason and experience.[6]

But the obvious importance of this ideal tends to accredit an oversimple view of the radical Enlightenment, one moreover which has sometimes been tempting as a self-portrait of philosophes. We could think that the move from Deism to materialism, from providentialism to utilitarianism, was entirely powered by epistemological reasons—that a more careful, responsible examination of the evidence, a fuller independence from time-honoured beliefs and pieties, inevitably led the bravest and most consistent thinkers to shed the last vestiges of the old spiritual beliefs, in God, immortality, providential guidance, the immateriality of the soul. From this self-portrait arises that facile view, which I questioned in the previous chapter, that secularization all flows naturally from the progress of science and reason.

But this is a radically one-sided and inadequate view. It leaves out of account the force of attraction of the other two life goods, the pursuit of happiness and benevolence, and the image of nature which underlay them. It depends on a dubious a priori thesis that the "unprejudiced" rational study of the evidence, independent of one's moral or spiritual intuitions, tells in favour of atheism (or at least agnosticism) and a materialist view of life and mind. On this view, what distinguished Descartes as a practitioner of self-responsible reason from his Encyclopaedist heirs was simply that he stopped halfway on a road they travel to the end. Descartes artificially limits the scope of his radical inquiry, most expressly in his provisional acceptance of established morality and religion;[7] his successors simply lift these limits.[8]

I argued in the previous chapter that this understanding is terribly anachronistic; that for many people in the premodern age the existence of a God seemed inseparable from the moral dimensions of their lives. The Augustinian tradition articulates this sense of connection, frequently in the form of 'proofs' of God's existence. Descartes fits squarely in this tradition. One shouldn't just assume that for him his certainty of himself and his own power to reason cogently could be so detached from his relation to God that he could weigh the issue of God's existence in the same way as that of some bit of the external world. Even less should one assume that he could weigh the issue of God's existence *subsequent* to the existence of the world, as one among many possible explanations for the universe, as Deists and atheists did in the eighteenth century. The order of argument in the *Méditations* is predicated on the opposite assumption. The veracious God provides the necessary guarantee to my reasoning power. Moreover, the very proof offered shows that the two are inseparable. It is my awareness of myself as imperfect, something which is brought forcefully home to me in the state of doubt, which Descartes sees as inseparable from my idea of a perfect being, which in turn I cannot have unless there is a God.[9] Whatever we think of the cogency of this 'proof', it bespeaks the fundamentally Augustinian intuition that the very capacity to aspire to truth is rooted in the soul's relation to God.

In the light of this intuition, refraining from submitting God to the same treatment as the objects of physical science is not an arbitrary limitation or a hypocritical failure of nerve; rather, it belongs to the very nature of self-responsible reason to recognize my dependence on him. Something very big has to change in our spiritual intuitions before we can speak as Laplace did in the famous anecdote of his conversation with Napoleon. After he had explained his theory of determinism to the Emperor, the latter is alleged to have asked: "Et Dieu? M. Laplace, Que faites-vous de Dieu?" To which the scientist coolly replied: "Sire, je n'ai pas eu besoin de cette hypothèse" ("And God? M. Laplace, what do you make of God?" "Sire, I have not needed this hypothesis"). The a priori of followers of the radical Enlightenment is that Laplace's stance is somehow more "rational" than Descartes's; that there is such a thing as what the evidence shows to reason, in abstraction from any view about its moral and spiritual foundations. It is my thesis throughout these pages that this belief in the deliverances of unsituated reason is an illusion, that the move from Descartes to Laplace involves a shift in what was seen to be the nature and moral place of reason.

But to see this, we have to recognize that the thinkers of the radical Enlightenment embraced materialism and atheism not just as the ultimate deliverance of self-responsible reason but also as the way of being integrally true to the demand of nature. Holbach, in his *Système de la nature*, presents one of the first great statements of uncompromisingly monistic materialism. Man, like everything else in the universe, is an entirely physical being. The moral dimension in man is simply his physical existence considered "sous un certain point de vue, c'est-à-dire relativement à quelques-unes de ses façons d'agir" ("from a certain point of view, that is relative to some of his ways of acting").[10] But Holbach goes beyond the bare statement of monism. Materialism means that physics can offer us a reading of human life, by opening us to the profound analogies between the operations of beings at all levels. Just as matter in motion tends to continue in a straight line unless diverted and exercises an attraction drawing all other bodies to it, so living beings have an inherent drive to preserve themselves:

> La conservation est donc le but commun vers lequel toutes les énergies, les forces, les facultés des êtres semblent continuellement dirigés. Les physiciens ont nommé cette tendance ou direction gravitation sur soi; Newton l'appelle force d'inertie; les moralistes l'ont appelée dans l'homme l'amour de soi, qui n'est que la tendance à se conserver, le désir de bonheur, l'amour du bien-être et du plaisir . . . Cette gravitation sur soi est donc une disposition nécessaire dans l'homme et dans tous les êtres, qui, par des moyens divers, tendent à persévérer dans l'existence qu'ils ont reçue, tant que rien ne dérange l'ordre de leur machine ou sa tendance primitive.

> Self preservation is thus the common goal towards which all energies, forces, and human faculties seem continuously directed. Scientists have named this tendency or direction gravitation to a centre. Newton calls it force of inertia, moralists have called it in man self-love, which is but the tendency to preserve oneself, the desire for happiness, the love of well-being and pleasure . . . This gravitation is thus a necessary disposition in man and all beings, who, by diverse means, tend to persevere in the existence they have received, as long as nothing disturbs the order of their machine or its primitive tendency.[11]

Holbach believes that this monistic view must win our conviction once we have really freed ourselves from the false systems which our imagination has spawned. It is the ultimate resting point of critical reason. But the Spinozistic vision of all beings striving to maintain themselves is also the basis for the morality he wants to embrace. The picture of man as striving by necessity to preserve and expand his happiness is not just the correct result of detached reflection; it is also the true basis of the moral life. It needs to be rescued not only from false spiritualist explanatory theories but also from the false depreciation that it has suffered at the hands of religion and metaphysics, which have called on men to deny these impulses in the name of purely imaginary goods and satisfactions.

> Que l'homme cesse de chercher hors du monde qu'il habite, des êtres qui lui procurent un bonheur que la nature lui refuse: qu'il étudie cette nature, qu'il apprenne ses lois, qu'il contemple son énergie et la façon immuable dont elle agit; qu'il applique ses découvertes à sa propre félicité, et qu'il se soumette en silence à des lois auxquelles rien ne peut le soustraire.

> Let man cease to search outside of the world he lives in, for beings that provide him with a happiness which nature refuses him: let him study nature, that he learn its laws, that he contemplate its energy and the immutable way it acts; let him apply his discoveries to his own felicity, and submit in silence to laws from whose binding force nothing can remove him.[12]

The materialist picture of human beings as driven by necessity to self-preservation and satisfaction is sternly defended by Holbach not just as the correct conclusion of observing reason but also as the deliverance of ultimately undistorted moral insight. This latter comes to climactic expression in the last chapter of the work in the voice of Nature herself, calling to us humans:

> O vous, dit-elle, qui, d'après l'impulsion que je vous donne, tendez vers le bonheur dans chaque instant de votre durée, ne résistez pas à ma loi souveraine. Travaillez à votre félicité; jouissez sans crainte, soyez heureux
> . . .
> Vainement, ô superstitieux! cherches-tu ton bien-être au delà des bornes de l'univers où ma main t'a placé. Vainement le demandes-tu à ces fantômes inexorables que ton imagination veut établir sur mon trône éternel . . . vainement comptes-tu sur ces déités capricieuses dont la bienfaisance t'extasie, tandis qu'elles ne remplissent ton séjour que de calamités, de frayeurs, de gémissemens, d'illusions. Ose donc t'affranchir du joug de cette religion, ma superbe rivale, qui méconnaît mes lois. C'est dans mon empire que règne la liberté . . . Reviens donc, enfant transfuge, reviens à la nature! Elle te consolera, elle chassera de ton coeur ces craintes qui t'accablent, ces inquiétudes qui te déchirent, ces transports qui t'agitent, ces haines qui te sépare de l'homme que tu dois aimer.

O you, says she, who, according to the inclination that I give you, tend towards happiness in every instant of your existence, do not resist my sovereign law. Work towards your happiness; Enjoy without fear, be happy . . .

In vain, o superstitious one! do you seek your well-being beyond the limits of the universe where my hand has placed you. In vain do you ask it of these inexorable fantoms which your imagination wishes to establish on my eternal throne . . . in vain do you trust in these capricious deities whose beneficence sends you into ecstasy; while they fill your sojourn with dread, with wailing, with illusions. Therefore dare to free yourself from the yoke of this religion, my proud rival, that does not recognize my laws. In my dominion reigns liberty . . . Come back then, child, deserter, come back to nature! She will console you, she will chase from your heart these fears which overwhelm you, these worries which tear at you, these outbursts which agitate you, these hatreds which separate you from man whom you should love.[13]

This affirmation of the rights of nature was in an important respect continuous with the Deist endorsement of the fulfilments of ordinary life. Both defend the pursuit of happiness against the demands of a false transcendence of nature. The difference was that the basis of this endorsement in Deism was a providential view of nature, which marked these fulfilments as those appointed for human beings; whereas for Enlightenment naturalism the basis was the radical negation of any such providential order. The naturalists saw themselves as enhancing these goods by negating their supposed foundation.

But for all the sharp discontinuity here, the way in which they affirmed these goods was continuous with the way they had been affirmed before. In Chapter 16, I described how the Deist notion of living by the design of nature excluded three kinds of deviance: (1) living by sloth, sensuality, disorder, or violence; (2) downgrading ordinary life, in the name of supposedly "higher" activities; and (3) condemning natural self-love as sinful.

The radical utilitarians saw themselves as fighting at least (2) and (3) more effectively than did their predecessors. If Deism had defended the innocence of ordinary human desire from the hyper-Augustinian charge of thorough-going perversion through sin, this could be done all the more effectively in completely rejecting the religion within which the notion of sin took its sense. If Deism had defended the value of ordinary life against the supposedly higher goals of traditional ethics, naturalism could do this all the more uncompromisingly by stressing the centrality of physical pleasure and fulfilment. Indeed, one fends off both the ascetic demands of the religious battle against sin and the supposed prestige of the more "spiritual" goals, by stressing the physical nature of human desire.

Helvétius declaims roundly: "La douleur et le plaisir physique est le principe ignoré de toutes les actions des hommes" ("Physical pain and pleasure are the unknown principles of all human actions").[14] Bentham declares the principal opponent of the principle of utility to be the "principle of asceticism". He tells us that this has been embraced by two classes of men. One was a "set of moralists, the other a set of religionists". The first was animated by "hope, the aliment of philosophic pride: the hope of honour and reputation at the hands of men". The other was moved by "fear, the offspring of superstitious fancy: the fear of future punishment at the hands of a splenetic and revengeful Deity". The philosophers in their pride wanted to rise above and discard gross pleasures, "that is, such as are organical, or of which the origin is easily traced up to the organical". In order to mark the distinction, they didn't even want to use the name 'pleasure' for their higher aims.[15]

It is remarkable how, in his denunciation of pride, Bentham fits into a well-explored turn of argument, which has served the ethic of ordinary life against the claims of a hierarchical ethics since its original theological form; in the evocation of a "splenetic and revengeful Deity", he stands in a long line which goes back to Erasmian Christianity.[16] But he thinks to take these further, to defend more integrally the equal value and goodness of desire, by affirming its physical nature. In radicalizing their rejection of deviations (2) and (3), the utilitarians thus relaxed or at least altered their view of (1). Sensuality was given a new value. The promotion of ordinary life, already transposed by Deists into an affirmation of the pursuit of happiness, now begins to turn into an exaltation of the sensual.

This turn has profoundly marked modern culture. Where John Smith could speak of "the Epicurean herd of Brutish men, who have drowned all their own sober Reason in the deepest Lethe of Sensuality",[17] and be generally understood and approved by his generation, we are ready to take a quite different view. Sensual fulfilment has itself become marked as significant. This seems to be one of the irreversible changes brought about by the radical Enlightenment.

Diderot, in his *Supplément au voyage de Bougainville*, presents a dialogue between a Tahitian host, Orou, and his guest, a European priest, to whom he offers the sexual favours of his wife and daughters. The priest at first declines, and this is the occasion of an extended discussion of the faults and merits of the two utterly different sexual mores. Diderot puts into the mouth of Orou a devastating attack on the anti-sensual morality of Western Christianity and an eloquent plea for the naturalness of sexual fulfilment. Nature herself seems to cry out against our repressive morality, which is blind to the significance that she has conferred on sensual life.

Je ne sais que c'est que la chose que tu appelles religion; mais je ne puis qu'en penser mal, puisqu'elle t'empêche de goûter un plaisir innocent, auquel nature, la souveraine maîtresse, nous invite tous; de donner l'existence à un de tes semblables; . . . de t'acquitter envers un hôte qui t'a fait un bon accueil, et d'enrichir une nation, en l'accroissant d'un sujet de plus.

I don't know what this thing is you call religion, but I can only think badly of it, since it prevents you from tasting an innocent pleasure, to which nature, the sovereign mistress, invites us all; to give existence to one like you; . . . to do your duty towards a host who has given you a good welcome, and to enrich a nation, by bestowing upon it one subject more.[18]

Sensualism was what made Enlightenment naturalism radical. Taking one's stand in raw human desire was a way of calling to account all the established systems of law, politics, and particularly religion. Do they require the suppression of the universal and necessary demands of nature? Have they created a series of imaginary crimes, whereby actions which are in themselves indifferent or good are proscribed as sins?[19] Very few systems of law, and no religions, can pass this test. Those which fail deserve to be swept away, and in the minds of the more optimistic, for instance Condorcet, this is what the future holds in store for humanity. Diderot was perhaps less confident, but he surely endorsed the sentiments of interlocutor A in the *Supplément:* "Que le code des nations serait court, si on le conformait rigoureusement a celui de la nature! Combien de vices et d'erreurs épargnés à l'homme! ("How short would be the code of nations, if it conformed rigourously to that of nature! How many vices and errors would man be spared!")[20]

If the good of the pursuit of happiness could be defended and enhanced by exploiting an established *via negativa,* then so, the radical Aufklärer seemed to believe, could that of universal and impartial benevolence. But this is usually even further from explicit statement than is the previous argument. We have already seen the basis for this belief in Locke, who seems himself to have held some implicit connection between rationality and an impartial concern for mankind. The link is suggested in the fact that so many of the errors that reason frees us from are themselves the grounds for restricting our efforts for the good or even for inflicting suffering—as superstition justifies fanaticism and persecution, and custom teaches us to work for the benefit only of our country or party, while bad education can make us quite misconceive the good.

The radical Enlightenment seems to have believed even more strongly in the beneficent fruits of rational understanding. Being freed from the confusion sown by wrong principles of morals, liberated from superstition and parochial customs, we are really capable of seeing the whole picture, of conceiving properly and impartially the universal good. And from this it was assumed that we would want to encompass it. Not that this was stated as a thesis; it is rather an unspoken assumption, implicit in the diagnosis of what has gone wrong in history up to now. Moved by the fears and blinded by the superstitions of religion, humans have been terribly cruel; victims of false beliefs about the good, they have done themselves and others great involuntary harm; locked into a parochial allegiance by custom, they have treated outsiders callously. Let these errors be overcome, and they will act beneficently. "Espérons tout du progrés des lumières" ("Let us hope for everything from the progress of enlightenment"), as Holbach writes in his *Politique naturelle*.[21]

The radical Aufklärer were often unclear just how strong a thesis this was because they confused it with another one which was a central part of their doctrine about human happiness. This was the view that there was a potential harmony of interests between human beings. In a properly organized world, one where human happiness was best served, the felicity of each would consist with and even conduce to the felicity of all. Holbach's Nature affirms this clearly in her call to man in the final chapter of the *Système de la nature*. Condorcet asks rhetorically: "L'intérêt mal entendu n'est-il pas la cause la plus fréquente des actions contraires au bien générâl?" (Is not our interest badly understood the most frequent cause of action against the general good?")[22]

It followed that in the perfect condition, everyone would understand and act in full cognizance of this harmony, that each would seek happiness in what made for general happiness. As Condorcet describes the radiant future,

> Cette conscience de sa dignité qui appartient á l'homme libre, une éducation fondée sur une connaissance approfondie de notre constitution morale, ne doivent-elles pas rendre communs à presque tous les hommes, ces principes d'une justice rigoureuse et pure, ces mouvements habituels d'une bienveillance active, éclairée, d'une sensibilité délicate et généreuse, dont la nature a placé le germe dans nos coeurs, et qui n'attendent, pour se développer, que la douce influence des lumières et de la liberté?

> Shouldn't that consciousness of dignity that belongs to the free man, the education built on a deepened knowledge of our moral constitution, make these principles of a pure and rigourous justice, these habitual movements of an active benevolence, enlightened with a delicate and generous sensibility, the germ of which nature has placed in our hearts, common to almost all men; which principles, to be developed, require only the gentle influence of enlightenment and of freedom?[23]

But it is one thing to describe human motivation in a condition of realized harmony; quite another to attribute to people today a love of mankind which would lead them to work for the good of humanity regardless of the cost to themselves. Here was no benevolence based on the recognition of convergent interests; rather the enlightened trail-blazer of the present most often knowingly sacrifices his own well-being to that of future generations, as he risks the ridicule of the ignorant masses and the persecution of priests and rulers. But this kind of selfless benevolence was also thought to be the fruit of enlightenment, albeit rarely explicitly stated or clearly distinguished from the thesis of harmony.

Naturally this conviction didn't come so much from an observation of human affairs as it did from a sense of the human moral predicament, the locus of moral sources. There obviously also entered into it some implicit autobiographical reflections. The Aufklärer felt the goodness of their own motivations, and felt this to be linked with their rational insight. There is a revealing cri de coeur of Bentham: "Is there one of these my pages in which the love of humankind has for a moment been forgotten? Show it me, and this hand shall be the first to tear it out".[24]

A close connection between benevolence and scientific reason isn't particularly evident to us in the latter half of the twentieth century. But we have to remember how much easier it was to believe in it in the eighteenth. We have to recover the emotional force of Voltaire's repeated injunction, "Ecrasez l'infame"; to recall the cruelties inflicted by persecutors in the name of religion; and not to forget those inflicted in the draconian punishments imposed by law in the name of order. In giving central significance to sensual pleasure and pain, and in challenging all the different conceptions of order, the utilitarians made it possible for the first time to put the relief of suffering, human but also animal, at the centre of the social agenda. This has had truly revolutionary effects in modern society, transforming not only our legal system but the whole range of our practices and concerns.[25]

Another insight, too, seemed to support the connection between benevolence and scientific reason. Disengaged rationality seems to separate us from our own narrow, egoistic standpoint and make us capable of grasping the whole picture. It is what allows us to become "impartial spectators" of the human scene. The growth of scientific rationality can therefore be experienced as a kind of victory over egoism. We are no longer imprisoned in the self; we are free to pursue the universal good.[26]

So the motives of the radical Aufklärer can't be seen exclusively as the advancing of scientific reason. This was part of a constellation in which moral motives played a central, even dominant, part. They were spurred to disengagement and scientific reason by the sense that they were affirming the unadulterated demands of nature and freeing universal benevolence from its prison of superstition and error.

In one way, this is obvious. It leaps at you from their writings. In another way, it is problematic, and this because of a central feature of their doctrine. That is that this obvious fact about their motivations and aspirations can't be easily stated within the terms allowed by their theories of human nature. These, in their insistence on the physical nature of the moral life or on the reduction of all human motivation to pleasure, in their zeal to root out all religious and metaphysical doctrines about "higher" or "spiritual" aspirations, to leave them absolutely no ontological space, seemed also to abolish the space for what I have been calling 'strong evaluation', the recognition that certain goals or ends make a claim on us, are incommensurable with our other desires and purposes.

The utilitarianism of Bentham or Helvétius illustrates this clearly. These thinkers recognized only one good: pleasure. Moreover, even this was not defined as a strongly valued good. The whole point was to do away with the distinction between moral and non-moral goods and make all human desires equally worthy of consideration. It is only upon the principle of asceticism, Bentham tells us, "and not from the principle of utility, that the most abominable pleasure which the vilest of malefactors ever reaped from his crime would be to be reprobated, if it stood alone". (Fortunately, he reassures us, "the case is, that it never does stand alone; but is necessarily followed by such a quantity of pain ... that the pleasure in comparison of it, is as nothing".)[27] With the sidelining of the question of strong evaluation, the very issue about the significance of our ordinary desires can no longer find expression; and a similar fate befalls benevolence as a moral ideal.

This makes utilitarianism a very strange intellectual position. Built into its denunciation of religion and earlier philosophical views, built into its sense of rationality as an operating ideal, built into its background assumption that the general happiness, and above all the relief of suffering, crucially *matters*, and emerging in the sense that reason liberates us for universal and impartial benevolence, is a strong and at times impassioned commitment to the three goods which I enumerated above. But in the actual content of its tenets, as officially defined, none of this can be said; and most of it makes no sense.

The austere disengagement, the neutralization even of the human psyche ("nul individu ne naît bon, nul individu ne naît méchant"), is partly espoused as a radical way of undercutting the hyper-Augustinian picture of man as sinful; the approach is radical because it suppresses the very question to which original sin is one answer. The moral conclusion that is meant to emerge from this negation is that ordinary human—even sensual—happiness is the only significant good, and that it ought to be pursued wholeheartedly and unremittingly. This is the goal which animated the life and thought of the utilitarians; and neutralization was also partly meant to allow this end to be pursued more effectively and clairvoyantly by the application of unadulterated instrumental reason. But this very neutralization erases the terms in which their moral motivation could be formulated and avowed.

Something similar can be said of the materialism of a Holbach or a Diderot, which of course was combined with a form of utilitarianism. In Holbach's case, the reduction of the moral to the physical, the assimilation of human desire to a kind of gravity, seems to leave no room for strong evaluation: our self-preservation, our search for satisfaction, engage us and command our actions by unalterable necessity; they englobe and render homogeneous all human striving. But just as clearly, Holbach wants to retain this moral dimension. The great speech of nature in the last chapter of his *Système,* from which I've already quoted, makes this clear. Nature promises us, her children, that she will punish wrongdoing even where the powers of the world do not. But her punishments consist in part in the shame and remorse we feel, in that we become "despicable" in our own eyes, when we act against justice or temperance.[28] These reactions presuppose a moral consciousness, or at least some sense of strong evaluation. Plainly Holbach doesn't think that reason bids us sweep this away altogether, but the monochrome picture of humanity as part of the striving of nature doesn't seem to leave any room for it.

The problem is that Holbach needs the reductive view as much as he needs morality. His whole strategy against religion and traditional metaphysics depends on denying the supposed qualitative distinction between human desire and the brute movements of inanimate nature, which are outside the purview of judgements of right. And yet he needs just as much a certain horizon of moral understanding, if this picture of suffering and desiring human nature is going to move us to benevolent action—to relieving the pain, righting the injustice, rearing the fabric of felicity—as a noble cause, one that lays a claim on us as humans.

The importance of this moral horizon becomes glaringly evident as soon as we see that it is not the only possible one, that materialism or hedonism can form part of a quite different moral outlook. For instance, they could be the basis of a despairing amoralism. Or else, they could be the basis of a reductive morality, in which aspiration to honour and altruism have no place. Diderot senses this reductive spirit in Helvétius' work, and he dedicates his extensive notes on the refutation of the latter's posthumous *de l'Homme* to attacking it.

Speaking of the philosophes themselves, "nos contemporains et nos amis", who put themselves at risk attacking priests and kings, he asks:

Comment résoudrez-vous en dernière analyse à des plaisirs sensuels, sans un pitoyable abus des mots, ce généreux enthousiasme qui les expose à la perte de leur liberté, de leur fortune, de leur honneur même et de leur vie?

How could you equate in the last analysis to sensual pleasure, without a pitiful abuse of words, this generous enthusiasm which exposes them to the loss of their liberty, of their fortune, of their honour itself and their life?[29]

More dangerous was a morality of purely egoistic gratification, which could find a basis in radical materialism. Both Holbach and Diderot saw a view of this kind in La Mettrie's work, and attacked it energetically.

On assure qu'il s'est trouvé des philosophes et des athées qui ont nié la distinction du vice et de la vertu, et qui ont prêché la débauche et la licence dans les moeurs. L'auteur qui vient tout récemment de publier *L'Homme Machine* a raisonné sur les moeurs comme un vrai frénétique.

We are assured that there have been philosophers and atheists who have denied the distinction between virtue and vice, and who have preached debauchery and licence in their morals. The author who has recently published *L'Homme Machine* has argued concerning morals like a frenzied madman.[30]

Even if we think that Holbach and Diderot are unjust to La Mettrie, the fact remains that they are on to a live issue, and one that for a variety of reasons was more salient in France than in England. In the Anglo-Saxon countries generally, the force of the ethic of ordinary life and benevolence was such, not only among intellectuals but in the whole society, that it carried over from theistic or deistic to unbelieving forms almost without interruption.

But France went through a quite different evolution. The seventeenth century saw a strong tension between ethical outlooks which drew on ancient philosophy, principally Stoicism and Epicureanism, on one hand, and a hyper-Augustinian Jansenism on the other.[31] In the latter part of his reign, Louis XIV favoured the increasing domination of a clerical, triumphalist Catholicism and a stern moralism. After his death, aristocratic society of the Regency period swung to the opposite extreme of frivolity and moral laxity. In these conditions, Deism developed its own forms in France, evolving much more clandestinely, passionately anti-clerical and anti-Catholic, and often inspired by the work of Spinoza.

One of the crucial developments which provided the background for the Encyclopaedists in France was the merging of this French Deism with the English varieties. We might speak of the importation of English Deism into France and the corresponding transformation of French thought. In a sense, the two intellectual cultures grew together in the eighteenth century, came close to fusion, and the result was what we know as the Enlightenment, a bilingual product of the two societies (or more accurately England, Scotland, France, and America).

In France, Voltaire was the major architect of this fusion, principally through his *Lettres philosophiques* of 1734, though others also played a part: Montesquieu, for instance, in his praise of English politics. With the fusion, the themes of English Deism become current in France as well. The Abbé de Saint-Pierre coins the term *'bienfaisance'*,[32] which is then taken up by Voltaire and others and occupies a central place in the outlook of the philosophes.

But important differences of emphasis naturally remain. In France, the struggle against religion, in paticular Catholic Christianity, takes on over-whelming importance, at times threatening to crowd out other crucial aspirations. It was essential to show its falseness, its misanthropy, its destructiveness. It was important to prove again and again what Bayle had first asserted, that an atheist can be a virtuous person,[33] but this merges into the attempt to demonstrate that religion must make you bad.

At the same time, something of the older anti-Catholic Deism remained, that of the *'libertins'*. The evolution of this word is significant. At first, it meant simply a free-thinker, one who was intent on thinking independently of the premisses of religious authority; later, around the turn of the century, it slides towards its modern meaning, of one who is loose in his morals. Part of the evolution can be explained as a result of the adverse propaganda that free-thinkers were subject to in these centuries. But partly it has to do with the fact that some free-thinkers, Saint-Evremond for instance, did take on a neo-Epicurean ethic of personal pleasure, which was rather far removed from the austere sense of social responsibility for human welfare which was central to English Deism.

All this meant that it was easier in the French context to take seriously the issue between a purely egoistic materialism and one predicated on universal benevolence. Perhaps Holbach and Diderot were a little unfair to La Mettrie. But Sade at the end of the century showed how the utter rejection of all social limits could be embraced as the most consistent and thoroughgoing liberation from traditional religion and metaphysics. Morals, law, and virtue are to be thrown off.

Les moeurs sont-elles donc plus importantes que les religions? . . . Rien ne nous est défendu par la nature . . . [Les lois], ces freins purement populaires n'ont rien de sacré, rien de légitime aux yeux de la philosophie, dont le flambeau dissipe toutes les erreurs, ne laisse exister dans l'homme sage que les seules aspirations de la nature. Or rien n'est plus immoral que la nature; jamais elle ne nous imposa de freins, elle ne nous dicta jamais des lois.

Are mores then more important than religions? . . . Nothing is forbidden us by nature . . . [Laws], those popular restraints, hold nothing sacred, nothing legitimate in the eyes of philosophy, whose flame dispels all errors and leaves in the mind of the wise man only the aspirations of nature. But nothing is more immoral than nature; she has never imposed limits upon us, nor has she dictated us laws.[34]

What Sade's views bring out, as a foil, is the usually invisible background of Enlightenment humanism, what I have called above the moral horizon of their thought. Just embracing some form of materialism is not sufficient to engender the full ethic of utilitarian benevolence. One needs some background understanding about what is worthy of strong evaluation: in this case, it concerns the moral significance of ordinary happiness and the demand of universal beneficence. Then one has reason to respond to the supposed facts about human desire and happiness in the classical fashion of Enlightenment universalism. By itself materialism gives us no more reason to go in this direction than to embrace Sadian egoism, as the counter-Enlightenment has erroneously claimed. Just to be a materialist is to have an underdetermined ethical position.

Of course, an issue arises whether the specific background of Enlightenment humanism just sketched is ultimately compatible with materialism, and if so of what sort—whether this background doesn't require some richer ontology of the human person and nature, if we are to make sense of it. But that is a different issue. Even if this materialist humanism turns out to be inconsistent, this still doesn't establish that some other position, say Sade's, is right.

But it does raise the question of whether and how this humanism can make sense of the moral horizon it relies on, how it can give a sense to the universal value of ordinary human fulfilment and to the requirement of beneficence; more specifically, can it conciliate whatever does make sense of this horizon with the reductive thrust of its attack on religion and metaphysics? Materialists often think these questions are easy to answer, because of the confusion I mentioned above. They think that if we can show some ultimate harmony of interests, that in the best of societies, the fulfilment of each passes through the fulfilment of all; or if we can show that humans are moved by sympathy, that they take pleasure in each other's well-being, then the problem is resolved.

But this is not at all the case. It may be that things would be wonderfully harmonious in the perfectly engineered society, but why should I work for its distant realization today, even at the cost of my life and well-being? Perhaps humans are generally moved by sympathy, but what if right now, relative to these adversaries, I am not? The underlying claim on which these arguments confusedly rely is that they have somehow shown the moral *superiority* of what they describe. The harmonious society is not only nicer for those lucky enough to inhabit it (if ever there are such); it is an ideal, something higher which commands the allegiance of all of us. It is an object of strong evaluation. Similarly, sympathy is treated not just as a de facto motivation but as a strongly valued one: something you ought to feel, an impulse whose unrestricted force in us is part of a higher way of being. The moral argument relies on the stronger claim. But the metaphysical or "scientific" argument only established the weaker, de facto one and, indeed, trumpets the inability of reason to establish anything stronger. Here resides the confusion and tension.

Thus it has often been remarked that the psychology of utilitarianism is somewhat at odds with its ethic. According to the first, we are all "under the governance of two sovereign masters, pain and pleasure".[35] This means presumably that we are determined to act for our own pleasure, and to avoid pain to ourselves. But in the moral theory, pain and pleasure are the criteria of right action, not as they affect us, but as they touch everyone. We are to seek the greatest happiness of the greatest number. Of course, we can be *conditioned* to find our happiness in the general well-being. Bentham wanted to foster in society a "culture of benevolence"[36] in which this would generally be the case. Or it can work out that there is an underlying "harmony of interests". (Although they might protest to the contrary, utilitarian thinkers assumed a great deal of convergence of interests; most notably in accepting something like the Smithian view, that egocentric activity when productively oriented redounds to the general good.) And undoubtedly in these cases things would work out better for society as a whole. But this doesn't answer the question, Why ought I to seek it?

Theories of Enlightenment materialist utilitarianism are hard to bring into focus. They have two sides—a reductive ontology and a moral impetus—which are hard to combine. This helps explain the paradoxical fact which I invoked above: the rooting of these theories in the ethic of ordinary life and benevolence is from one point of view terribly obvious; while from another it has to be articulated and defended against the grain of these theories themselves. It is the reductive ontology which makes the difficulty. When this is in the foreground, the self-image of Enlightenment naturalism as a theory powered exclusively by disengaged reason tends to gain credit.

This image also gains credibility later on, in the nineteenth century, when religious faith has been displaced as the single dominant moral source and the new predicament of a plurality of such sources has fully developed, in the way I described in the previous chapter. Since all outlooks now seem tentative and uncertain in a way that religious faith in earlier times never did, it becomes entirely possible that some lose this faith through being overborne by the prestige of the naturalist reading of scientific reason. In this case, the biography of such a convert would fit the self-image: first, he rejects religion because he "sees" that it is incompatible with (what he takes to be) scientific rationality tout court; then he takes on the best remaining alternative, viz., utilitarianism or some other form of Enlightenment humanism. This kind of thing seems to have happened a lot in the nineteenth century and in part of the twentieth. Or perhaps more cautiously, an ideal type of this description came close to fitting reality in this period.

But the original eighteenth-century context that we have been discussing here was prior to any such plurality. It is much more likely here that the original conversion was as much powered by some ethic of the good life (and in the case of the Encyclopaedists, the ethic of ordinary fulfilment and beneficence) as by the demands of self-responsible reason.

It would follow, from all that has been described in the preceding pages, that a clear awareness of the moral motivation is liable to have been more in evidence earlier, and in France, than later, and in the English-speaking cultures. This might help explain why the virtually total suppression of any acknowledgement of the dimension of the good has been so much in evidence in contemporary Anglo-Saxon philosophy, as I pointed out in Chapter 3.

The rationalist self-image, and the occulting of moral motivation, is the dominant trend in Enlightenment naturalism. It grows from the most common reaction to the unclear focus described above: to suppress the problem and fudge it over with the aid of various theories of harmony and sympathy. The resulting theories are all strangely inarticulate. Classical utilitarianism is perhaps the first to exhibit a feature which afflicts a host of contemporary theories, as we saw in Part I: they are debarred by the ontology they accept from formulating and recognizing their own moral sources. Their commitment to the goods which drive them occasionally emerges in direct invocations; such is the declaration from Bentham I quoted above about the love for humankind which he claimed animated him. But for the most part, these underlying moral sources emerge only through rhetoric of argument; and above all through the denunciations of the religious and philosophical errors which bring such great suffering on mankind. This means that the place of the moral sources in this philosophy, and in the later ones which resemble it in this regard, is strange. Constitutive goods, when invoked in a certain fashion, are empowering, as I argued in Part I. I have been speaking of goods insofar as they empower as 'moral sources'. In the moral views I have been discussing up to now, be they Platonic, or theistic, or Cartesian, or Deist, or whatever, these sources have been recognized. They have functioned openly, as it were. It is clear to all concerned why it is important to be aware of them and have reverence or gratitude or respect for them, as appropriate. We saw how vital it was in Hutcheson that we come to see and appreciate our own moral sentiments; and also that we see and feel gratitude for God's providential order. This appreciation is part of what morality enjoins, not some reflection external to it.

But now none of this can be openly recognized. How can utilitarians have access to their moral sources? What are the words of power they can pronounce? Plainly these are the passages in which the goods are invoked without being recognized. These include the few passages of direct invocation I instanced above. But they mainly consist of the polemical passages in which error, superstition, fraud, and religion are denounced. What they are denounced for lacking, or for suppressing, or for destroying expresses what we who attack them are moved by and cherish.

This becomes a recognizable feature of the whole class of modern positions which descends from the radical Enlightenment. Because their moral sources are unavowable, they are mainly invoked in polemic. Their principal words of power are denunciatory. Much of what they live by has to be inferred from the rage with which their enemies are attacked and refuted. Marxism is an excellent case in point.

This self-concealing kind of philosophy is also thereby parasitic. In the case of the radical Enlightenment, doubly so. First, it is parasitic on its adversaries for the expression of its own moral sources, its own words of power, and hence for its continuing moral force. But second, since it undermines all previous formulations of the constitutive good which could ground the life goods it recognizes, without putting any in its place, it also lives to some degree on these earlier formulations. We saw how utilitarianism continues and builds on an existing turn of argument, in, e.g., denouncing certain philosophies for the pride with which they elevate certain goals over our common and sensual fulfilments. The invocation of pride made sense within the original Christian context, in contrast to the humility which is proper to those who are all equally children of God. This is denied, but no new context is provided. Nietzsche's challenge brought out the unavowed borrowing from Christianity that underpins this naturalist humanism and at the same time showed how vulnerable this makes it.

Classical utilitarianism lives off moral insights which are widespread in the culture, but which it itself has given no justified place to and perhaps cannot give a place to. And this is the second facet of its parasitism. It not only needs enemies to generate its words of power; sometimes it draws its moral ideals, if not directly from its enemies, at least from a moral culture which they have better articulated.

The utilitarian Enlightenment is in this way shot through with contradiction. I mean pragmatic contradiction. It does not necessarily bring together incompatible propositions; but it speaks from a moral position which it can't acknowledge. This is not necessarily fatal. The goods it lives on but denies have become solidly entrenched in the culture. We saw that Deism did not invent them or give them currency in the first place. Its demise, or that of any other particular formulation, will not abolish them. They are there to feed even those views which cannot recognize them. So eighteenth-century utilitarianism had a big future ahead of it, one that may not yet be exhausted.

But the self-concealment, the parasitic relation to earlier views, and above all the fact that its words of power are mainly denunciatory point to another disability: this kind of view can only attract in opposition. It lives off the horrors of those it attacks. We saw above how it gained plausibility in an eighteenth century which still saw religious persecution and savage legal penalties. It could live from the infamy it proposed to crush. In the attack, the goods can be taken for granted and not thematized, and attention is focussed on the abuses which threaten them in the existing order.

But when one moves from opposition to government, from attack to building a new order, then it has repeatedly been manifest how thin and at the same time how threatening the utilitarian outlook is. Thin, because building requires some sense of the goods one is for and not only what one is against. Threatening, because the refusal to define any goods other than the official one of instrumental efficacy in the search for happiness can lead to appalling destruction in a society's way of life, a levelling and suppression of everything which doesn't fit in that tunnel vision, of which the modern consequences of bureaucratic rationality offer ample testimony, all the way from the Poor Law Act of 1834 to the catastrophe of Chernobyl.

Of course the mere fact that a position may be at its inception parasitic on moral sources it cannot itself acknowledge doesn't prove that it is unfit to build a new world. It may have resources which are yet to flower. It appears that utilitarianism, however, is incapable of this development. It has philosophically debarred itself from acknowledging other goods. This is the kind of philosophy which can only serve in opposition. Perhaps more than one modern philosophy has this character. Hegel believed he discerned just this in the outlook of the radical Jacobins: incapable of building a new society, they could turn only to destruction. And perhaps the same alternatives of terror and/or spiritual exhaustion are the inevitable fate of Marxism, as in the killing fields of Cambodia or the mendacious cynicism of contemporary Prague. I will return to this issue in the conclusion.

19.2

But the case of utilitarianism in no way shows that this path of suppressing the problem of coherence and stifling its own articulacy is the only one open to Enlightenment naturalism. There is obviously another one, which involves taking up the challenge of making sense of one's own moral horizon. This was defined by the three life goods I enumerated above: self-responsible reason, the pursuit of happiness, and benevolence. In the Deist perspective, these were related to a supporting constitutive good, the providential interlocking order. But this was becoming less and less believable, was going the way of earlier conceptions of cosmic order, and was in any case roundly rejected by naturalism.

The task is obviously to articulate some alternative perspective within which these goods can make sense. Something of this has been done in the succeeding two centuries, but we see only the beginning hints of it in the period we've been looking at, notably in the work of Diderot and Hume.

But if we retreat to the level of ideal types, something can be said about the crucial features of this perspective. It has to give a renewed sense to the notion that the ordinary fulfilments of human beings have a special significance, so that someone who lives for these fulfilments clairvoyantly and undistortedly is living a higher life than one, say, who undergoes mortifications in the name of some religious ideal. And in addition, this significance makes a universal demand such that, for instance, I may be called upon to work for a future world in which these fulfilments will be maximized, even though I can have no direct part in it. This significance can't reside in some providentially given or cosmically significant order in nature as a whole.

The significance can only be seen as one which arises for human beings, one which is in a sense given by them. But it can't be seen as arbitrarily conferred by individuals. Something so conferred could just as arbitrarily be withdrawn, and this wouldn't consist with the intuition that human life *has* this significance, whether we recognize it or not. So, that life has this significance amounts to this: that human beings cannot but see it as thus significant, to the extent that they have an undistorted and illusion-free grasp on their lives. This means that we can envisage a biographical development, from a stage where we fail to see this significance to a stage where it dawns on us, which consists in our overcoming some blindness or illusion; but no development in the opposite direction could amount to a gain in insight. Put another way, the limit that we see ourselves tending towards, to the extent that we move to overcome distortions and illusions in our lives, is an understanding of life with this significance. Before we arrive at this limit, which presumably means forever, this construal will remain a more or less plausible presumption; but what other moral view is more strongly based than this?

If this presumption is correct, then this construal will be part of the best available account of our moral lives, along the lines of the discussion in Part I (section 3.2); and hence will also be essential in third-person explanations of our action and feelings. But that will also mean that the significance we recognize here will really function like a constitutive good, that it will be available as a moral source, in this case, something the undistorted recognition of which empowers us to do the good.

It is widely thought that no constitutive good could have such a fragile ontological foundation as this, a niche simply in our best self-interpretation. Unless it is grounded in the nature of the universe itself, beyond the human sphere, or in the commands of God, how can it bind us? But there is no a priori truth here. Our belief in it is fed by the notion that there is nothing between an extra-human ontic foundation for the good on one hand, and the pure subjectivism of arbitrarily conferred significance on the other. But there is a third possibility, the one I have just outlined, of a good which is inseparable from our best self-interpretation. Ironically, mainstream naturalism itself, in its blindness to self-interpretation, tends to accredit the stark alternative and hence to perpetuate its own confusion and incoherence about morality.

This indicates that to clarify and articulate its own sources would not be without problems for mainstream naturalism. That the recognition of such a constitutive good figured in our best self-interpretation would have to be integrated into its understanding of human life and action, which would put paid to its penchant for reductive accounts. And the very recognition of the importance of self-interpretation would detach it from its exclusive focus on disengaged reason.

Nor does the recognition that there can be a constitutive good, lodged not in the universe *an sich* but arising in our experience of it, entail that there really *is* such a good. It shows only that the issue can't be settled a priori. It is a question of fact (a) whether our best, most illusion-free interpretation does involve an acknowledgment of the significance of human life, and (b) whether this significance is best explained in a quite non-theistic, non-cosmic, purely immanent-human fashion. The answer to (a) seems to me unquestionably 'yes', but my hunch is that the answer to (b) is 'no'. It all depends on what the most illusion-free moral sources are, and they seem to me to involve a God. But all this remains to be argued out.

This exploration of the logical space for a naturalistic articulation of the good will help in understanding some of the articulation which has been taking place. The attacks on religion and traditional ethics for their depreciation or condemnation of ordinary human desire appear in a new light against the background of an intuition about the significance of life. We can see the full force of the positive insight here. In rebutting the "calumnies" against nature, in accepting without reserve matter and desire, we finally accord them their full dignity, and this empowers us to realize to the full the goodness and significance of these desires. The insight we struggle through to is that of the innocence of nature. But this insight doesn't leave everything as it was. It has potentially transformatory power, because recognizing the goodness of ordinary desires empowers us to live this goodness more integrally. The recognition as it were releases the force of this goodness, releases it from the crushing weight of its depreciation by religion and ethics.

In drawing this picture, I have borrowed heavily from later writers, and most notably from Nietzsche. Clearly his '*Ja-sagen*' provides a full model for what I have been describing here as the transforming power of the recognition of goodness. To be able to articulate it as Nietzsche did, one needed the full resources of Romantic expressivism, which I will be discussing in the next chapter. And in the course of articulating it, Nietzsche, taking a fateful turn against the Enlightenment, declared benevolence the ultimate obstacle to self-affirmation.

But I nevertheless think that this Nietzchean model helps us to understand something of what went on, confusedly and implicitly, in the eighteenth-century naturalist Enlightenment. That the moral energy and excitement attending the naturalist rejection of religion and traditional ethics comes from this sense of empowerment, of releasing nature and desire from a stultifying thraldom, releasing them to a fuller affirmation.

The rejection/release had two sides: the negation of religion and metaphysics, and the affirmation of the goodness and significance of nature. The language that seemed necessary for the first left no place for the second, so the second could hardly be said. It starts off as an inarticulate source of excitement, of inspiration. The mainstream of naturalism seems to have remained stuck there. The problem is denied, the inarticulable remains semi-repressed, and not surprisingly the negative side takes on the crucial importance. At the end of the road the Enlightenment impulse can turn into a mere cynical unmasking; the revolutionary impulse is defined above all by the aspiration to destroy the established order.

But some strands of naturalism take another route. They try to move towards articulacy, and thus to a more direct and open, hence fuller, release of the stultified powers of nature and desire. This meant modifying the exclusive focus on disengagement, and ultimately a marriage of naturalism and expressivism, of which I will speak further below.

In the period of the high Enlightenment, only the first, most hesitating, and preparatory steps were taken in this direction. Diderot is an important figure in this regard, his thought richly sensitive to the constitutive tension of naturalism[37] and containing many proto-Romantic themes. And in a curious way, so is Hume.

Hume is perhaps worth looking at a little further in this connection. He denies the entire providential view of the world. But in spite of the fact that he takes over the Lockean way of ideas so wholeheartedly, in spite of the fact that some of the later utilitarian writers professed to be inspired by him,[38] he doesn't take up a thorough stance of disengagement. In a curious way, he remains close to Hutcheson, from whom he borrows the language of moral sentiments, but also more.

We can see Hume as exploring one possible response to the loss of the providentialist world-view. If we can no longer think of our ordinary fulfilments as made significant by being part of a divine design, we can suppress altogether the issue of significance (although we continue to live by an answer to it), and objectify the natural domain with a view to maximum efficacy. This is the utilitarian response. But we can also explore a way of seeing our normal fulfilments as significant even in a non-providential world. The significance would lie simply in the fact that they are ours; that human beings cannot help, by their very make-up, according significance to them; and that the path of wisdom involves coming to terms with, and accepting, our normal make-up.

Of course, this is an interpretation of Hume which by its very nature can't find direct warrant in the text. Hume was like the radical Aufklärer in that the issues that I am describing as those of significance were not acknowledged. The available languages to do so were precisely those of providence or the traditional ethic, and Hume wanted to take his distance from both of them. We are left trying to puzzle out the spirit with which he undertook his inquiries into human nature. It certainly seems to me to be different from the disengaged search for efficacy of the radical Aufklärer.

But it is easier to say what it isn't than what it is. As with the Aufklärer, we can perhaps gauge it best by the pattern of what Hume opposes. Like them, he opposes religion and much of traditional metaphysics. But the ground of this opposition seems to be that these views lead us to depreciate and hence tyrannize our own nature. This is close to the radical Aufklärer, and there is a similar acknowledgement of our sensual nature. But where their avowed goal was to achieve a disengaged grasp of our nature as a neutral domain, permitting control, Hume seems to have had in mind from the start that his inquiries would serve the end of self-acceptance.

This is what aligns him with Hutcheson, and against Locke. The end of self-exploration is not disengaged control but engagement, coming to terms with what we really are. It is thus in a very Hutchesonian spirit that he uses the language of moral sentiments. True, the whole providential framework has been dropped; and this is not a small difference. But the anatomization of moral sentiments is not undertaken in order to free outselves of them, to stand outside them, noting their ultimately arbitrary nature in order to be able to suspend them or change them. We are so accustomed to the disengaged stance of the Enlightenment that we can hardly fail to read Hume's anatomy of the passions and moral sentiments in this spirit. But this seems not to have been his. The aim was to show the house that as humans we had to live in. We anatomize the moral sentiments, in all their ultimate metaphysical arbitrariness, could-have-been-otherwiseness, in order to accept them, endorse them, know what address we are living at. Even the disengagement serves the end of an ultimate engagement.

Hume's sources were classical, and mainly Epicurus and Lucretius. For all the invocation of these two by Enlightenment utilitarians,[39] they were in some ways far from their spirit. It is possible to interpret the Enlightenment mainly as "the rise of modern paganism",[40] accentuating its ancient and particularly its Epicurean sources. And there is a lot of truth in this. Some of the French *'libertins'*, like Saint-Evremond, were almost exclusively inspired by pre-Christian thought. Shaftesbury, as we have seen, was largely an ancient Stoic; this appears more clearly in his *Philosophical Regimen*[41] than in his published works. But there was also much which came specifically from Christian sources, or was specifically modern—as are the three major goods I cited above. In utilitarianism above all the emphasis on active benevolence, on making the world into a happy place, had no ancient parallels, and certainly wasn't Epicurean.

But what *was* profoundly Epicurean-Lucretian was the notion that the metaphysical views which tie us to a larger moral order destroy our peace of mind, our psychic equilibrium, in the name of an illusion—that they impose extraneous demands which can only distract us from the true road to happiness and tranquillity. The belief that the gods concern themselves with us can only inspire fear. We have to turn away from this preoccupation with the moral order and take ourselves as we are, find our pleasures as we can, in the right order which fits with our nature.

In other words, we reject the "gods" not in order to be disengaged self-remoulders but to be able to take our lives as they are, without fear. Besides Epicurus and Lucretius among the ancients, this stance had a modern defender in Montaigne. It recognizes the crushing burdens laid on humans by their great spiritual aspirations, by what I called earlier 'hypergoods', and by the sacrifices which are demanded of ordinary human fulfilments in their name (section 4.2). "A quoy faire ces pointes eslevées de la philosophie sur lesquelles aucun estre humain ne se peut rassoir?" ("To what purpose are these heaven-looking and nice points of philosophy, on which no humane being can establish and grounde itselfe?")[42]

In refusing these demands, the neo-Lucretian stance resembles closely the radical Enlightenment in its rebuttal of the calumnies against nature of religion and traditional ethics. And indeed, the two are allied against these common enemies. But there is a subtle difference. Where a writer like Holbach or Condorcet wants to proclaim the innocence of nature and ultimately the benevolence of humans properly educated, thus opening for us the exciting prospect of a restored humanity, the neo-Lucretian spirit is content to remove the burden of impossible aspirations. The liberation is not to a marvellous remaking but more like a home-coming to a garden, a grateful acceptance of a limited space, with its own irregularities and imperfections, but within which something can flower. The moral inspiration comes not from the prospect of transformation but from the hard-won ability to cherish this circumscribed space.

> Fänden auch wir ein reines, verhaltenes, schmales
> Menschliches, einen unseren Streifen Fruchtlands
> zwischen Strom und Gestein.

> If only we too could discover a pure, contained,
> human place, our own strip of fruit-bearing soil
> between river and rock.[43]

This stance may also have Christian roots, as Montaigne shows. But those who adopt it have usually identified themselves as "pagans". What they see themselves as striving to undo is precisely the Judaeo-Christian call to "holiness", to a life on God's terms. What they want to restore is the pagan sense that man is and must remain below the gods. The lines I just quoted from Rilke are preceded by these, reflecting on the figures on Attic tombs:

> Gedenkt euch der Hände,
> wie sie drucklos beruhren, obwohl in den Torsen die Kraft steht.
> Diese Beherrschten wussten damit: so weit sind wirs,
> dieses ist unser, uns *so* zu beruhren; stärker
> stemmen die Götter uns an. Doch dies ist Sache der Götter.

> Remember the hands,
> how weightlessly they rest, though there is power in the torsos.
> These self-mastered figures know: "We can go this far,
> and this is ours, to touch one another this lightly; the gods
> can press down harder upon us. But that is the gods' affair.

I have obviously been constructing an 'ideal type' here, which fits no one exactly. But I think Hume was close to this spirit, closer at any rate than to the radical Enlightenment. Within the context of eighteenth-century culture, with its utterly different psychology, its commitment to politics, its morality of benevolence, he was striving to reformulate something analogous to this neo-Lucretian idea. We explore from within the human life form. We find that within this form, humans are irresistibly given to accord certain things significance. Certain matters are the invariable objects of moral sentiments, which are by their nature marked off from others by their unique significance.

It used to be thought that without some kind of ontological warrant in the very fabric of things, this significance would be illusory; and now it looks as though the universe cannot provide such a warrant (at least, it looked that way to Hume). But this doesn't matter. We don't need it. What is important is to recognize this form and accept it, cherish it, and learn to live within it.[44]

We have here in Hume, I think, the germ of an issue which comes more naturally to formulation in our century, although it is still difficult, masked as it is by the continuing influence of Enlightenment naturalism. But some have claimed to see in Wittgenstein's work the same combination of insights, that a way of life is both arbitrary and nevertheless something that we have to embrace. The question of the limits of our capacity to accept the basic lineaments of our form of life, the issue of what rides on this acceptance, are just now being formulated and explored.[45] But they have their roots as well in the Enlightenment, in its rejection of the notion of a providential order, and in its countervailing continuing affirmation, however implicit, however self-concealed, of the significance of ordinary life.

19.3

There is another facet of the spiritual significance of naturalism which it's worth mentioning here, because it's been a continuing force in modern culture. The belief that thinking beings are part of a vast physical order can awaken a kind of awe, wonder, even natural piety. The reflection which moves us is that thought, feeling, moral aspirations, all the intellectual and spiritual heights of human achievement, emerge out of the depths of a vast physical universe which is itself, over most of its measureless extent, lifeless, utterly insensitive to our purposes, pursuing its path by inexorable necessity. The awe is awakened partly by the tremendous power of this world which overshadows us—we sense our utter fragility as thinking reeds, in Pascal's phrase; but we also feel it before the extraordinary fact that out of this vast blind silence, thought, vision, speech can evolve.

We who think and see have a glimpse of how deep the roots are of our fragile consciousness, and how mysterious and strange its emergence is. This spiritual attitude is in flat contradiction to the Cartesian. There the dominant idea is of the purity of thinking being, of its utter heterogeneity from blind physical nature, and of its transcendently higher status. Cartesian dualism was very widely held in the seventeenth and eighteenth centuries. It seemed to many inseparable from a belief in immortality. And the proof that the soul was a separate kind of incorruptible stuff from matter seemed to establish beyond doubt that we were immortal. I spoke in the previous chapter about the intuitive certainty that many people had in this age about the existence of

God and a future life. To the extent that the latter was rationalized in terms of soul-body dualism, this philosophical doctrine too could seem secure.

What was almost an aside by Locke in the *Essay,* concerning the possibility that thought could after all be a property of matter,[46] set off a series of metaphysical battles. It started almost immediately, when his work was attacked by Edward Stillingfleet, Bishop of Worcester, as opening the door to unbelief. The attitude of Stillingfleet was shared by most other thinkers in the succeeding century. The very suggestion that there could be a materialist account of thought seemed to them both bizarre—wasn't it just evident that thinking was utterly different from extended matter?—and also quite gratuitously subversive of religion and morality.

Those who were drawn to materialism often strengthened the latter impression. They were indeed concerned to subvert traditional religion and morality. What could easily fail to be noticed was that this new/old philosophy was not just the negation of all spiritual stances to human life, but involved its own characteristic one. It was easy to miss, because of the self-imposed inarticulacy of Enlightenment naturalism concerning its moral sources.

But this stance, and the conflict around it, is well captured by a writer of our day. Douglas Hofstadter recognizes that certain people

> have an instinctive horror of any "explaining away" of the soul. I don't know why certain people have this horror while others, like me, find in reductionism the ultimate religion. Perhaps my lifelong training in physics and science in general has given me a deep awe at seeing how the most substantial and familiar of objects or experiences fades away, as one approaches the infinitesimal scale, into an eerily insubstantial ether, a myriad of ephemeral swirling vortices of nearly incomprehensible mathematical activity. This in me evokes a cosmic awe. To me, reductionism doesn't "explain away"; rather, it adds mystery.[47]

We don't find such an openly articulate statement in an eighteenth-century author. But just as with the significance of human life, the spiritual inspiration can be sensed where it isn't stated.

Thus Holbach's materialism sees all beings alike as tending to a "gravitation sur soi",[48] as driving to maintain themselves in their being. This involved a break with the Cartesian conception of matter as fundamentally inert. This conception figured in a standard argument for the existence of God: he had to be invoked to explain how movement starts. Holbach replaces it with a picture of nature as the locus of force, a picture with depth, which awakens our awe and which can conceivably be the locus from which thought emerges, something unthinkable with the Cartesian variant.

But as usual it is Diderot in whose prose the spiritual impact registers most forcefully. In his *Rêve de d'Alembert,* he describes playfully the genesis of d'Alembert himself from a pre-embryonic condition, and then he finishes with this tableau of the rise and fall of genius, emerging from

> des agents matériels dont les effets successifs seraient un être inerte, un être sentant, un être pensant, un être résolvant le problème de la précession des équinoxes, un être sublime, un être merveilleux, un être vieillissant, dépérissant, mourant, dissous et rendu à la terre végétale.

> material factors, the successive stages of which would be an inert body, a sentient being, a thinking being and then a being who can resolve the problem of the precession of the equinoxes, a sublime being, a miraculous being, one who ages, grows infirm, dies, decomposes and returns to humus.[49]

This spiritual attitude isn't new. It has Epicurean roots. Lucretius also offers a picture of our emerging from the larger universe, which he represents as nourishing us, as unconsciously beneficent, so that we can look at heaven as our father and at earth as our mother.[50] And he too expresses his awe before this vast whole: seeing it laid out before him fills him with a kind of divine delight and shuddering.[51]

But in a context where dualism was deeply intricated with the most important religious and metaphysical beliefs, materialism seemed shocking and novel. One of the important changes of the eighteenth century and since is that this perspective generally ceases to be an outlandish, outside view, even becoming in our century the orthodox outlook in certain circles. So that even the struggle of which Hofstadter speaks between reductionists and their opponents rarely opposes Cartesian dualists to materialist views;[52] rather, reductionism is opposed by a picture of nature as consisting of different levels of being, very often accompanied by some notion of "emergence".[53]

These theories have some of their roots in Romantic thought, and this gives us some clue as to why this emergentist spiritual stance makes such headway against the Cartesian in the late eighteenth century. It was the stance not only of materialists but also of the different varieties of anti-dualist thought, moved by a sense of nature as the locus of a great current of life, which went to make up Romanticism, as well as the "Weimar classicism" of Goethe and Schiller. The sense that our thought and feeling emerge from nature gives them depth and potential force, indeed, introduces a new notion of 'depth', as we shall see in the next chapter. Although Romantic expressivism can be opposed to materialism, the two can also be very fruitfully interwoven.

The advance of this new stance to nature, whether inspired by materialism or proto-Romanticism, helped to foster a new sense of cosmic time. The classical cosmos of meaningful order had been eternal but basically unchanging. The biblical universe was historical but of a relatively short duration, a few thousand years, something that felt immense at the time but that the imagination could easily encompass. In either case, to be in the universe was to be in an ordered whole whose extent and limits could be grasped.

The eighteenth century sees the dawning of a real sense of geological time: that is, not only of the immense time scale in which the universe has evolved, but also of the cataclysmic changes which have filled these aeons. This change was partly a matter of scientific discovery, leading up to the eventual formulation and general acceptance of Darwin's theory. Buffon and others made some steps in this direction from the mid-eighteenth century. But it also reflected a change in the imagination and in the sense of our place in nature. Diderot leapt well beyond the available evidence when he wrote:

> Qu'est-ce que notre durée en comparaison de l'éternité des temps? . . . Suite indéfinie d'animalcules dans l'atome qui fermente, même suite indéfinie dans l'autre atome qu'on appelle la Terre. Qui sait les races d'animaux qui nous ont précédés? qui sait les races d'animaux qui succéderont aux nôtres?

> What is the duration of our time compared with eternity? . . . Just as there is an infinite succession of animalculae in one fermenting speck of matter, so there is the same infinite succession of animalculae in the speck called earth. Who knows what animal species preceded us? Who knows what will follow our present ones?[54]

The new feeling for nature, which I described in Chapter 17, moved beyond the English garden, beyond the valleys of Switzerland where the wilderness touches human habitation and which Rousseau made famous, and comes finally to the inhospitable heights, where it meets in awe an immensity which seems utterly indifferent to human life. Ramond journeyed into these regions, and his books gave expression to this exaltation before the vastness of the untamed heights. They place us before the unchartable immensity of time.

> Tout concourt à rendre les méditations plus profondes, à leur donner cette teinte sombre, ce caractère sublime qu'elles acquièrent, quand l'âme, prenant cet essor qui la rend contemporaine de tous les siècles, et coexistante avec tous les êtres, plane sur l'abîme du temps.

> Everything works together to make our meditations deeper, and to give them this sombre hue, this sublime character which they acquire, when the soul, taking the leap which makes it contemporary with all centuries, and coexistent with all beings, soars over the abyss of time.[55]

Charles Rosen quotes Ramond's descriptions of the Alps and Pyrenees, which bring to immediate visibility, as it were, in the accounts of different layers of rock and ice, the widely separated ages of their genesis.[56] Some startling findings of learned men combine here with the Romantic temper to produce a new sensibility, which has come to dominate our world.

19.4

We stumble here across one of the many ways in which our conceptions of moral sources are bound up with the kind of narrative structures in which we make sense of our lives. The close interconnection between these, as well as with our notions of self and society, was mentioned in Part I. But more needs to be said on this score. Enlightenment naturalism didn't only have an effect on our conceptions of cosmic time; it also generated its own forms of personal and historical narration.

To understand these, we have to take account of the full extent of its moral sources, avowed and unarticulated. I have tried to organize these around the three main poles mentioned above: the dignity of self-responsible reason, the significance of the ordinary impulses of nature, and the imperative of benevolence.

These notions of reason and nature define a certain perfection for human beings, where the full exercise of self-responsible reason yields the fullest clarity about their own nature and its significance. This in turn defines the contrasting predicament, the one in which humans, alas, find themselves, where reason is hobbled or blinded, and nature as a consequence inadequately or distortively recognized.

The actual experience of Enlightenment is that of a struggle through this condition of blindness towards perfection. A crucial feature of the narrative, both of individual lives and of history, within which this struggle makes sense is that it must somehow account for the fall into blindness and error as well as trace the path of our gradual rise out of them. With a certain parallel to the Christian story, we have a human prehistory which sees us fall victim to error, as imposture and superstition take hold of our minds, and then a long struggle of liberation.

The nodal point of this narrative of struggle is the exercise of unchained reason leading to the unmasking of error, which in turn acknowledges and hence releases the dignity of nature. Biographically, this is how the Aufklärer understands his or her own growth, the break with an earlier religious, Deistic, or metaphysical background, the release of his or her own natural powers. And historically, this is how we are to understand the human story in which we fit. Insofar as we can look optimistically on the human story, it must be one of progress, of the successive unchainings of reason, leading to successive discoveries of truth, and hence overcomings of error.

This is how the Aufklärer's own life gets its significance, by his or her taking a place, playing a role in this chain of progress. And this is how he or she can become part of the community of a restored and perfected humanity which will one day be: by having contributed somewhere along the line to bringing it about. This membership is acknowleged in the recognition, the gratitude of future generations towards the lonely fighters of today. And so correlative to the sense of obligation to work for this fulfilled humanity (so hard to understand purely on grounds of the harmony of interests) is an expectation of fame and gratitude from our posterity. The community of interest which is not there on the level of concrete human fulfilments, between me and the happy future community for which I sacrifice my present well-being, is restored on the level of the meaning of our lives, by their recognition of my signal contribution to what they have all come to define as what makes human life significant.

And so it is not surprising that posterity is repeatedly evoked by the Aufklärer. Its recognition is their great consolation. Their posthumous fame was their immortality.[57] Diderot invoked it constantly. In his later years, he wrote his most penetrating works entirely for readers of the future, and didn't even try to publish them in his lifetime. In his *Refutation* of Helvétius' *de l'Homme,* just after the passage I quoted above, in which he shows how absurd it is to explain the heroism of contemporary philosophes in terms of physical pleasure, Diderot formulates what he thinks their real motivation is:

> Ils se flattent qu'un jour on les nommera, et que leur mémoire sera éternellement honorée parmi les hommes ... Ils jouissent d'avance de la douce mélodie de ce concert lointain de voix à venir et occupées à les célébrer, et leur coeur en trésaille de joie.

> They flatter themselves that one day we will acclaim them, and that their memory will be forever honoured among men ... They rejoice in advance in the sweet melody of the distant concert of voices, which will come to celebrate them, and their heart quivers with joy.[58]

Holbach, in his *Essai sur les préjugés,* makes a great declaration of faith in the future of Enlightenment:

> Malgré tous les efforts de la tyrannie, malgré les violences et les ruses du sacerdoce, malgré les soins vigilants de tous les ennemis du genre humain, la race humaine s'éclairera; les nations connaîtront leurs véritables intérêts; une multitude de rayons assemblés formera quelque jour une masse immense de lumière qui échauffera tous les coeurs, qui éclairera tous les esprits.

Despite all the efforts of tyranny, despite the violence and trickery of the priesthood, despite the vigilant efforts of all the enemies of mankind, the human race will attain enlightenment; nations will know their true interests; a multitude of rays, assembled, will form one day a boundless mass of light that will warm all hearts, that will illuminate all minds.

And from this he concludes:

Ainsi, sages, . . . vous n'êtes point les hommes de votre temps; vous êtes les hommes de l'avenir, les précurseurs de la raison future. Ce ne sont ni les richesses, ni les honneurs, ni les applaudissements du vulgaire que vous devez ambitionner: c'est l'immortalité.

And so, wise men . . . you are not men of your times; you are men of the future, the precursors of future reason. It is not wealth, nor honour, nor vulgar applause that you should aim for: it is immortality.[59]

Certainly the greatest and fullest statement of the philosophy of history of the unbelieving Enlightenment is Condorcet's *Esquisse,* taking us through ten ages of human existence, the tenth being the anticipated radiant future of mankind. The whole picture is there: the decline into servitude and superstition under the imposture of the educated classes, the alliance between despotism and superstition, the countervailing struggle of reason, aided by science, the progressive strengthening of reason in the modern age aided by technology, particularly the art of printing. The result is a progress in knowledge and mores which gathers speed over the immediately past centuries, and becomes irreversible with the firm establishment of the principles of modern epistemology;[60] gentler ways replace the hardness and barbarism of earlier laws and practices.[61]

The closing passage of the book, coming after a description of the future which awaits the human race, reads:

Combien ce tableau de l'espèce humaine, affranchie de toutes ces chaînes, soustraite à l'empire du hasard, comme à celui des ennemis des ses progrès, et marchant d'un pas ferme et sûr dans la route de la vérité, de la vertu et du bonheur, présente au philosophe un spectacle qui le console des erreurs, des crimes, des injustices dont la terre est encore souillée, et dont il est souvent la victime! C'est dans la contemplation de ce tableau qu'il reçoit le prix de ses efforts pour le progrès de la raison, pour la défense de la liberté. Il ose alors les lier à la chaîne des destinées humaines: c'est là qu'il trouve la vraie récompense de la vertu, le plaisir d'avoir fait un bien durable, que la fatalité ne détruira plus par une compensation funeste, en ramenant les préjugés et l'esclavage. Cette contemplation est pour lui un asile, où le souvenir de ses persécutions ne peut le poursuivre;

où, vivant par la pensée avec l'homme rétabli dans les droits comme dans la dignité de sa nature, il oublie celui que l'avidité, la crainte ou l'envie tourmentent et corrompent; c'est là qu'il existe véritablement avec ses semblables, dans un élysée que sa raison a su se créer, et que son amour pour l'humanité embellit des plus pures jouissances.

How this portrait of mankind, free of all these chains, no longer under the rule of chance, or the enemies of progress, and walking with a sure and certain step on the path of truth, of virtue and happiness, presents to the philosopher a sight which consoles him for the errors, the crimes, the injustices which still sully the earth, and of which he is often the victim! In the contemplation of this portrait he receives the reward for his efforts towards the progress of reason and the defence of liberty. He then dares to bind these efforts to the chain of human destiny: there he finds virtue's true reward, the pleasure of having created an enduring good, which fate will no longer destroy with a deadly compensation, by bringing back prejudice and slavery. This contemplation is a refuge for him, where the memory of his persecutions cannot follow; where, living in thought with a humanity re-established in the rights and dignity of its nature, he forgets the one which is corrupted and tormented by greed, fear, or envy; it is there that he exists in reality with those like him, in an Elysium which his reason knows how to create, and which his love for humanity has embellished with the purest enjoyments.[62]

This passage takes on additional poignancy when one reflects that it was written in 1793, when its author was in hiding in Paris, with a warrant for his arrest by the Jacobin-controlled Committee of Public Safety as a suspected Girondin, and that he in fact had only a few months more to live. There were, indeed, "errors, crimes, injustices" for which he needed consolation. And it adds to our awe before his unshaken revolutionary faith when we reflect that these crimes were no longer those of an ancien régime, but of the forces who themselves claimed to be building the radiant future.

20

NATURE AS SOURCE

20.1

Enlightenment naturalism has obviously been tremendously important in forming our contemporary society and culture. But just as obviously, it has been contested and criticized. The counter-Enlightenment, the ecological movement, and the radical anti-utilitarian-technologist left are living forces today as well. The late eighteenth century saw a number of reactions to rationalist Deism and naturalism which opened the way for these counter-movements, and which also helped to transform modern culture very profoundly.

I want to talk about some of these in this chapter. They are rather diverse: I will be discussing both Kant and Romanticism, for instance. But there is a point in common, a guiding thread. I mentioned at the beginning of the last chapter that there were two widely held objections to the standard Deism of the eighteenth century. The first was an anti-Panglossian one, against its rather rosy, optimistic view of the world; the second was an anti-levelling one, against a too simple view of the human will, intent simply on happiness. Good and evil became a matter of training, knowledge, enlightenment; they were no longer the fruit of radically different qualities of the human will. "Pleasure, or wrong or rightly understood / Our greatest evil, or our greatest good".[1]

Enlightenment naturalism took up the anti-Panglossian objection. It broke the dependence on a doctrine of providence—even though one could still complain that it retained a pretty optimistic view of the human prospect. But it made, if anything, the anti-levelling objection even more relevant. It pushed further the denial of any qualitative distinction in the will; all was desire; in the more radical variants, even physical desire.

The common thread between the currents of thought and feeling that I want to talk about here is their espousal of this anti-levelling objection—their resistance to a one-dimensional picture of the will and their recovery of the sense that good and evil are in conflict in the human breast. There is one thinker who is famous for articulating this objection in the eighteenth century, and that is Rousseau. He is a crucial influence for virtually all the writers and currents I want to mention.

Rousseau started off as a friend of the Encyclopaedists—especially of Diderot—and ended up their enemy. This was partly a matter of personalities—to say that Rousseau was hard to get on with would be to make the understatement of the eighteenth century. But there was also a solid core of real philosophical disagreement. We can formulate this by saying that Rousseau was drawn to a moral view in which there was place for a real notion of depravity. Human evil was not the kind of thing which could be offset by any increase of knowledge or enlightenment. Indeed, the belief that it could be was itself part of the moral distortion, and reliance on it could only aggravate things. What was needed was a transformation of the will.

Rousseau brought back into the world of eighteenth-century Deism the fundamentally Augustinian notion that humans are capable of two loves, of two basic orientations of the will. This Deism was in a sense an offshoot of Erasmian Christianity, as I argued above; while the doctrine of the two loves, although common to all strands of Christian thought, was a major theme of what I have called hyper-Augustinianism. Rousseau was disconcerting to the philosophes, because he seemed so much of the time to be going over to the enemy.

Rousseau on the philosophes sometimes awakens echoes of Pascal on Descartes, and of the Jansenist reaction to Cartesianism in general. There is a similar mixture of closeness and distance. Pascal was one of the leading thinkers of the new mathematics and a proponent of the new science. Cartesian dualism was taken up by many of the Jansenists, for instance by Antoine Arnauld and Pierre Nicole, as a framework for their moral and theological views. But what couldn't be assimilated was the Cartesian confidence in man's own powers to achieve the good, the sense that the muddle and confusion of embodied thinking, which Arnauld and Nicole see as a consequence of the Fall,[2] could be overcome just by our own intellectual efforts.

With this goes a shift in self-interpretation. The muddle and confusion are no longer seen as simply the result of negligence and bad habits, something which a little resolution and proper understanding can clear up. Indeed, the Cartesian idea that we are in principle transparent to ourselves, and only fail to know ourselves through confusion, is abandoned. The Jansenist writers, in fully Augustinian fashion, insist that we don't know the depths of our own hearts. We are constantly giving ourselves spiritual marks which we may not deserve. No one knows if his inclination to pray really comes from grace, or perhaps from some self-serving end. We have "une inclination naturelle de l'amour propre . . . ", says Nicole, "à croire que nous avons dans le coeur tout ce qui nage sur la surface de nostre esprit." But "il y a toujours en nous un certain fond, et une certain racine qui nous demeure inconnu et impénétrable toute nostre vie" ("a natural inclination of pride . . . to believe that we have in our hearts all that is floating on the surface of our minds . . . but . . . there are always certain depths within, certain roots that remain unknown and impenetrable to us all of our lives").[3]

For Pascal, I am a "monstre incompréhensible". We are full of contradictions. Far from being self-transparent, our self is a mystery to us. "Où est donc ce moi?" he asks.[4] What alone can bring some order in this, can give some (relative) self-understanding, is grace, which transforms the terms of our inner conflicts.

This denial of self-transparency will be taken up again and will be crucial to the expressivist followers of Rousseau. But what is more relevant to my immediate purpose is the way that Rousseau transposes this way of thinking to integrate it into Deism.

In the orthodox theory, the source of the higher love is grace; it is the God of Abraham, Isaac, and Jacob. For Rousseau (without entirely ceasing to be God, at least of the philosophers), it has become the voice of nature. The doctrine of original sin, in its orthodox understanding, has been abandoned.[5] Nature is fundamentally good, and the estrangement which depraves us is one which separates us from it. An Augustinian picture of the will has been transposed into a doctrine which denies one of the central tenets of Augustine's theology.

"Posons pour maxime incontestable que les premiers mouvements de la nature sont toujours droits; il n'y a point de perversité originelle dans le coeur humain" ("Let us lay it down as an incontrovertible rule that the first impulses of nature are always right; there is no original sin in the human heart").[6] But there has been a Fall; perversity has come upon us. Humans have done this to themselves. "Tout est bien sortant des mains de l'Auteur des choses", is Rousseau's opening line of Book I of *Emile;* "tout dégénère entre les mains de l'homme" ("God makes all things good; man meddles with them and they become evil").[7] The original impulse of nature is right, but the effect of a depraved culture is that we lose contact with it. We suffer this loss because we no longer depend on ourselves and this inner impulse, but rather on others and on what they think of us, expect from us, admire or despise in us, reward or punish in us. We are separated from nature by the dense web of opinion which is woven between us in society and can no longer recover contact with it.

Rousseau sometimes has recourse to an aural image (these images were important for him, no doubt in part because he was a musician): nature is likened to a voice within. Conscience, our inner guide, "speaks to us in the language of nature". It speaks to everyone, but very few hear it. The prejudices which usurp its place are its worst enemies. "Leur voix bruyante étouffe la sienne et l'empêche de se faire entendre; le fanatisme ose la contrefaire, et dicter le crime en son nom. Elle se rebute enfin à force d'être éconduite; elle ne nous parle plus" ("Their noisy voices drown her words, so that she cannot get a hearing; fanaticism dares to counterfeit her voice and to inspire crimes in her name. She is discouraged by ill-treatment; she no longer speaks to us").[8]

To regain contact with this voice would be to transform our motivation, to have a wholly different quality of will. Rousseau cannot accept the Enlightenment naturalist notion that what we need to become better is more reason, more learning, more "lumières". His First Discourse, on the arts and sciences, rebuts the suggestion that this kind of progress makes us better. On the contrary, it is all too often accompanied by moral decline. Our interest, well understood, is not the source of benevolence in us. This "abominable philosophy" has no place for virtuous actions, but must find a base motivation for them. It debases Socrates and calumnies Regulus. It is hard even to concede that its partisans can be in good faith.[9]

On the contrary, the progress of this calculating reason is one of the signs of corruption. It flourishes only where conscience is stifled, as the Savoyard curate makes clear in his impassioned invocation:

> Conscience! Conscience! instinct divin, immortelle et céleste voix; guide assuré d'un être ignorant et borné, mais intelligent et libre; juge infaillible du bien et du mal, qui rends l'homme semblable à Dieu, c'est toi qui fais l'excellence de sa nature et la moralité de ses actions; sans toi je ne sens rien en moi qui m'élève au-dessus des bêtes, que le triste privilège de m'égarer d'erreurs en erreurs à l'aide d'un entendement sans règle et d'une raison sans principe.

> Conscience! Conscience! Divine instinct, immortal voice from heaven; sure guide for a creature ignorant and finite indeed, yet intelligent and free; infallible judge of good and evil, making man like to God! In thee consists the excellence of man's nature and the morality of his actions; apart from thee, I find nothing in myself to raise me above the beasts— nothing but the sad privilege of wandering from one error to another, by the help of an unbridled understanding and a reason which knows no principle).[10]

This opposition of morality and "progress" was easy to interpret in a primitivist sense. And so Rousseau has been interpreted, in his time and ours. But Rousseau's actual idea, which is not primitivist, is much more challenging and has actually been more influential. Though his popular image has often been of the admirer of the "noble savage", where his influence really counted—on other thinkers who themselves had a tremendous impact—he was not misunderstood. We have only to think of Kant, of the writers of the Sturm und Drang, and the Romantic period.

The view Rousseau himself propounded—or the views, because it may be hard to make *Emile* consistent in the end with the *Social Contract*—did not involve going back to the precultural or presocietal stage. Rather the idea of a recovery of contact with nature was seen more as an escape from calculating other-dependence, from the force of opinion and the ambitions it engendered, through a kind of alignment or fusion of reason and nature, or in other terms, of culture/society on one hand, and the true élan of nature on the other. Conscience is the voice of nature as it emerges in a being who has entered society and is endowed with language and hence reason.[11] The general will represents the demands of nature, free from all distortion due to other-dependence or opinion, in the medium of publicly recognized law.

What is often mistaken for primitivism in Rousseau is his undoubted espousal of austerity against a civilization of increasing needs and consumption. Rousseau often speaks in the language and evokes the principles of the ancient Stoics. True strength involves having few needs, being content with the essential. "L'homme est très fort quand il se contente d'être ce qu'il est; il est très faible quand il veut s'élever au-dessus de l'humanité" ("When man is content to be himself he is strong indeed; when he strives to be more than man he is weak indeed"). It is our dependence on others, on appearances, on opinion which multiplies our wants, and thus in turn makes us even more dependent. "Otez la force, la santé, le bon témoignage de soi, tous les biens de cette vie sont dans l'opinion; ôtez les douleurs du corps et les remords de la conscience, tous nos maux sont imaginaires" ("Health, strength, and a good conscience excepted, all the good things of life are a matter of opinion; except bodily suffering and remorse, all our woes are imaginary"). True freedom is found only in austerity:

> O homme! resserre ton existence au dedans de toi, et tu ne seras pas misérable. Reste á la place que la nature t'assigne dans la chaîne des êtres, rien ne t'en pourra faire sortir . . . Ta liberté, ton pouvoir, ne s'étendent qu'aussi loin que tes forces naturelles, et pas au delà; tout le reste n'est qu'esclavage, illusion, prestige.

> Oh man! live your own life and you will no longer be wretched. Keep to your appointed place in the order of nature and nothing can tear you from it . . . Your freedom and your power extend as far and no further than your natural strength; anything more is but slavery, deceit, and trickery.[12]

This austere freedom from excess wants is common to both the models that Rousseau seems to be offering of the return to nature. It is essential to being an integral and free human being on one's own, the road that *Emile* mainly explores. It is here that Rousseau sounds closest to the ancient Stoics. But it is also crucial to the political formula of self-obedience through a commonly established law, which he lays out in the *Social Contract*. Here Rousseau takes up one of the common themes of the civic humanist tradition, which warns of the corrupting effects of wealth and ease on civic virtue.

These very familiar ancient themes of austerity as a condition of true virtue become woven by Rousseau into a modern one, the affirmation of ordinary life. In educating Emile so he will eventually be able to make his way in the world, Rousseau wants first to make him identify himself with Robinson Crusoe. He must be taught an honest, useful trade. A central fulfilment of his life will be his relation to Sophie, who will become his wife.

Of course, this fits more easily with Rousseau's portrait of the restored individual than it does with his vision of mankind restored to nature through the polity. Civic humanism is not easy to combine with the ethic of ordinary life. But Rousseau does his best to separate the goods of honour and glory from their traditional association with a higher realm of activity, distinct from the nurture and continuation of life. The good political community is bound together by a sentiment which is an extension of the joy that humans feel in each others' company even in the most ordinary and intimate contexts.[13] There is for Rousseau no Aristotelian or Arendtian hiatus between the life of the citizen and the pursuit of the means of life. That is why for him, unlike for Aristotle or Arendt, the actual activity of deliberation is not very important; what matters is the unity. In the best kind of simple condition, "le bien commun se montre partout avec évidence" ("the common good will then be everywhere evident") and doesn't need elaborate debate and deliberation. Laws are few, and when new ones are needed,

> cette nécessité se voit universellement. Le premier qui les propose ne fait que dire ce que tous ont déjà senti, et il n'est question ni de brigues ni d'éloquence pour faire passer en loi ce que chacun a déjà résolu de faire, sitôt qu'il sera sûr que les autres le feront comme lui.

> the necessity is perceived universally. He who proposes them only says what all have already felt, and neither faction nor eloquence is required to obtain the passage of a measure which each person has already resolved to adopt, as soon as he is sure that others will act with him.

The happiest people are groups of peasants who settle their affairs under an oak.

Quand on voit chez le peuple le plus heureux du monde des troupes de paysans régler les affaires de l'Etat sous un chêne et se conduire toujours sagement, peut-on s'empêcher de mépriser les raffinements des autres nations, qui se rendent illustres et misérables avec tant d'art et de mystère?

When we see, among the happiest people in the world, groups of peasants directing affairs of state under an oak, and always acting wisely, can we help but despise the refinements of those nations which render themselves illustrious and miserable by so much art and mystery?[14]

Rousseau's borrowings from the standard Deism of the eighteenth century, in particular from the moral sense school, are evident enough. The Savoyard curate articulates a position whose main lines had become commonplace: we infer from the order of things to the existence of a good God. There must be a will to move matter,[15] and an intelligence to coordinate it. Our freedom implies the spirituality of the soul; and the injustice of rewards and punishments in this world argues that there is a future one where this will be redressed. As with other Deist thinkers, the goodness of God is identified with that of his order,[16] and it is unreasonable to demand or expect that this will be interrupted by miracles or any special help to humans in their striving to be good.[17] We even find some of the arguments familiar from Hutcheson against the extrinsic theory, that people love virtue ultimately out of enlightened self-interest. Why then do we admire the great ancients like Cato, who can't conceivably do us any good?[18]

But for all this continuity, a major tranposition has taken place. The bland assurance that all interests harmonize, that we above all need to understand that beneficence is the best road to happiness, that self-love and social are the same, has been replaced by a keen sense of the polarity of good and evil, of the depravity and necessary transformation of the human will.

On the face of it this might seem like a return to an earlier position, nourished by Stoic and Christian sources. But these too have been transposed into a thoroughly modern position. For the distinction of vice and virtue, of good and depraved will, has been aligned with the distinction between dependence on self and dependence on others. Goodness is identified with freedom, with finding the motives for one's actions within oneself. Although drawing on ancient sources, Rousseau is actually pushing the subjectivism of modern moral understanding a stage further. This is what has made him so tremendously influential.

I described in Part III how the eighteenth-century ethic of following nature represented an internalization relative to the ancient one. The providential design of nature takes the place of the hierarchical order of reason as the constitutive good.[19] This design becomes evident to us partly through our own motivations and feelings. The good is discovered partly through a turning within, consulting our own sentiments and inclinations, and this helped bring about a philosophical revolution in the place of sentiment in moral psychology.

Rousseau carries this revolution farther. In a sense, he is the crucial figure in its being carried to its modern term, whether for good or ill. For a moral sense theorist like Hutcheson, our own moral feelings are an important source of understanding of the good, but they only serve in combination with our grasping our setting within a providential order. This allows us to see how our instinctive approval of benevolence serves to bring about our own and the universal good. Rousseau's notion of the voice of nature within seems to be saying something much stronger. True, the Savoyard curate relies on the vision of providential order too. But the definition of conscience as an inner sentiment could be taken in a much stronger sense. Not just that I have, thanks be to God, sentiments which accord with what I see through other means to be the universal good, but that the inner voice of my true sentiments *define* what is the good: since the élan of nature in me *is* the good, it is this which has to be consulted to discover it.

Rousseau never took the radical step to this much more subjectivist position. He ran his inner voice in tandem with the traditional way of understanding and recognizing universal good. But he was the crucial hinge figure, because he provided the language, with an eloquence beyond compare, which could articulate this radical view. All that was needed was for the inner voice to cut loose from its yoke fellow and declare its full moral competence. A new ethic of nature arises with Romantic expressivism, which takes this step.

Rousseau immensely enlarged the scope of the inner voice. We now can know from within us, from the impulses of our own being, what nature marks as significant. And our ultimate happiness is to live in conformity with this voice, that is, to be entirely ourselves. "J'aspire au moment", says the Savoyard curate, "où, délivré des entraves du corps, je serai *moi* sans contradiction, sans partage, et n'aurait besoin que de moi pour être heureux" ("I long for the time when, freed from the fetters of the body, I shall be myself, at one with myself, no longer torn in two, when I myself shall suffice for my own happiness").[20] This is a rather startling statement in a declaration of religious faith; and highly significant in a writer who stands in other respects in an Augustinian tradition, and whose autobiography contains so many echoes of that of the Bishop of Hippo, beginning with the title.[21] The source of unity and wholeness which Augustine found only in God is now to be discovered within the self.

Rousseau is at the origin point of a great deal of contemporary culture, of the philosophies of self-exploration, as well as of the creeds which make self-determining freedom the key to virtue. He is the starting point of a transformation in modern culture towards a deeper inwardness and a radical autonomy. The strands all lead from him, and I want now to explore some of these. Inwardness I want to take up later. But first, I will look at the new notion of autonomy, and for this will turn to Kant.

20.2

Kant too rebels against standard Deism along the lines of the anti-levelling objection. Enlightenment naturalism and utilitarianism make things worse, in his view. They leave no place for a moral dimension at all. For Kant, this means leaving no place for freedom, for freedom has to have a moral dimension. This not in virtue of a less radical, more restrictive notion of freedom. Rather Kant follows Rousseau in defining freedom and morality essentially in terms of each other.

Morality is not to be defined in terms of any specific outcomes. The moral action is not marked as such by its outcome, but rather by the motive for which it was undertaken. Because it is not defined in terms of outcomes, this motive is spoken of by Kant as 'formal'. What the moral person wants above all is to conform his action to the moral law. That is his ultimate purpose. He will take whatever outcome that dictates, and bring it about. But this won't be done for the sake of the outcome itself, but because that's what conforming to the law amounts to here.[22]

This amounts to freedom, because acting morally is acting according to what we truly are, moral/rational agents. The law of morality, in other words, is not imposed from outside. It is dictated by the very nature of reason itself. To be a rational agent is to act for reasons. By their very nature, reasons are of general application. Something can't be a reason for me now, without being a reason for all agents in a relevantly similar predicament. So the truly rational agent acts on principles, reasons which are understood to be general in their application. But this is what Kant means by acting according to the law. The moral law, as I said above, isn't defined in terms of specific outcomes. It is defined merely formally, by the principle of law-following itself. When I decide to act according to law, when I determine for instance that I will not act unless I can will that the maxim of my action be universally followed, I am simply living up to my true nature as a rational agent.

So if the decision to act morally is the decision to act with the ultimate purpose of conforming my action to universal law, then this amounts to the determination to act according to my true nature as a rational being. And acting according to the demands of what I truly am, of my reason, is freedom. This is why merely following the dictates of de facto desire is a kind of heteronomy for Kant. He transforms the Enlightenment humanist notion of what truly emanates from us. Just being a de facto desire, even a physiological need, of mine doesn't make a purpose count as emanating from me. What is truly so is what reason produces, and what reason demands is that one live by principles.

This is a more radical definition of freedom, which rebels against nature as what is merely given, and demands that we find freedom in a life whose normative shape is somehow generated by rational activity. This idea has been a powerful, it is not overstated to say revolutionary, force in modern civilization. It seems to offer a prospect of pure self-activity, where my action is determined not by the merely given, the facts of nature (including inner nature), but ultimately by my own agency as a formulator of rational law. This is the point of origin of the stream of modern thought, developing through Fichte, Hegel, and Marx, which refuses to accept the merely "positive", what history, or tradition, or nature offers as a guide to value or action, and insists on an autonomous generation of the forms we live by. The aspiration is ultimately to a total liberation.

Kant thus follows Rousseau in his condemnation of utilitarianism. Instrumental-rational control of the world in the service of our desires and needs can just degenerate into organized egoism, a capitulation before the demands of our lower nature, "le triste privilège de m'égarer d'erreurs en erreurs à l'aide d'un entendement sans règle et d'une raison sans principe", of which the Savoyard curate spoke.

And just as with Rousseau, however much this may sound like a return to an earlier ethical outlook, it is in fact radically new. Kant gives a firm but quite new base to the subjectivization or internalization of moral sources which Rousseau inaugurates. The moral law is what comes from within; it can no longer be defined by any external order. But it is not defined by the impulse of nature in me either, but only by the nature of reasoning, by, one might say, the procedures of practical reasoning, which demand that one act by general principles.

Kant explicitly insists that morality can't be founded in nature or in anything outside the human rational will. This is a root and branch rejection of all ancient moralities. We cannot accept that the cosmic order, or even the order of ends in human "nature", should determine our normative purposes. All such views are heteronomous; they involve abdicating our responsibility to generate the law out of ourselves. In spite of some resemblances to ancient Stoicism, Kant's theory is really one of the most direct and uncompromising formulations of a modern stance.

And, like Descartes, at the centre of his moral view is a conception of human dignity. Rational beings have a unique dignity. They stand out against the background of nature, just in that they are free and self-determining. "Everything in nature works according to laws. Only a rational being has the capacity of acting according to the conception of laws, i.e., according to principles".[23] Everything else in nature, in other words, conforms to laws blindly. Only rational creatures conform to laws that they themselves formulate. This is something incomparably higher.

That is why rationality imposes obligations on us. Because we have this status which is incomparably higher than anything else in nature, we have the obligation to live up to it. In a way, we could formulate the fundamental principle underlying Kant's whole ethical theory somewhat like this: live up to what you really are, viz., rational agents. Because it is something higher, rationality commands our respect. And so we experience moral commands as higher than the demands of nature. The moral law commands our respect *(Achtung)*.

"Rational nature", says Kant, "exists as an end in itself".[24] It is the only thing which does so. Everything else in the universe can be treated as a mere means to our goals, whatever they are. For these other things have no unconditional worth. Their value is only instrumental, but "man and, in general, every rational being exists as an end in himself and not merely as a means to be arbitrarily used by this or that will. In all his actions, whether they are directed to himself or to other rational beings, he must always be regarded at the same time as an end".[25] Or as he puts it later: other things have a price, only rational agents have dignity *(Würde)*.[26] In a sense, our obedience to the moral law is simply the respect that this dignity commands from us. The sources of the good are within.[27]

Kant's debt to Augustine is as obvious as Rousseau's. Everything depends on a transformation of the will. Indeed, the moral man may be engaged in exactly the same external activity as the non-moral one. Kant underlines the fact that each may seek exactly the same outcomes. Two shopkeepers may avoid shortchanging their customers, but for one this will be a prudential measure to keep his trade, while to the other it is what the moral law requires.[28] The moral person may lead the same external life as the non-moral one, but it is inwardly transformed by a different spirit. It is animated by a different end.

There is thus nothing wrong with the life of instrumental reason, dedicated to rational control. Indeed, Kant clearly thinks that this is also a facet of rationality, and he argues in his historical works that the development of instrumental reason, which is imposed on humans by nature if they are to survive, serves to bring them to rationality in a broader sense.[29] The error of Enlightenment naturalism is to have misunderstood the spirit in which life is to be lived, the basic end which should preside over it all. This is not happiness, but rationality, morality, and freedom. Man may in fact attain a high level of civilization, without becoming truly moral. Here Kant agrees with Rousseau. "Alles Gute aber, das nicht auf moralisch-gute Gesinnung gepropft ist, ist nichts als lauter Schein und Schimmerndes Elend" ("But all good enterprises which are not grafted onto a morally good attitude of mind are nothing but illusion and outwardly glittering misery").[30]

Kant thus draws heavily on Augustine's model of the two loves, the two directions of human motivation. Indeed, the influence of Augustinian thinking on Kant is at times overpowering, via its Protestant and Pietist formulations. Kant had a lively sense of human evil, of the distorted and crooked state of human nature.[31] He speaks of the 'radical evil' in human nature,[32] which surprised and shocked some of his contemporaries in such a prominent defender of the Enlightenment.[33]

The theory has deep roots in Christian theology, and Kant remained a believing Christian. But his conception is radically anthropocentric. The proximate source of this transformation of the will is not God, but the demands of rational agency itself which lie within me. The fact that ultimately, in Kant's view, it is God who designed things this way doesn't mitigate the central status given to human dignity.

Kant remained a man of the Enlightenment. But he gave it a new definition. In the Anglo-French-Scottish conception, progress in enlightenment meant both the advance of self-responsible reason and of the arrangements which ensure human happiness. Kant's definition of enlightenment focusses on the first line of march exclusively. His well-known essay on the subject opens: "Aufklärung ist der Ausgang des Menschen aus seiner selbst verschuldeten Unmündigkeit" ("Enlightenment is man's emergence from his self-incurred immaturity"). And he continues a few lines on: "Sapere aude. Habe Muth dich deines eigenen Verstandes zu bedienen! ist also der Wahlspruch der Aufklärung!" ("The motto of enlightenment is therefore: Sapere aude! Have courage to use your *own* understanding!")[34] The crucial issue is the growth in moral freedom and responsibility.

But this new definition enables Kant to give a clear and explicit basis to one of the central assumptions of Enlightenment thinking, the belief that the growth in rationality brought along with it an increase in benevolence, that it somehow releases a fund of benevolence in us. We saw that this assumption seems already present with Locke, and is strongly if confusedly and half-implicitly operative in the writings of the naturalists. For these latter, it was hard to give it a clear and justified place.

In Kant, what takes the place of universal benevolence is something closer to a principle of universal justice, the determination to act only by universal maxims and to treat all rational beings as ends. But now it is quite clear why *this* flows inseparably from the growth of reason. It is the central demand of reason in its practical use. Becoming more rational means coming to this determination. What could only be implicitly and half-consciously invoked by the naturalist Enlightenment can now be made central: human beings are capable of a universal will to beneficence or justice, which is part of their make-up as rational beings, and which comes to be released in its full power by their acceding to self-responsible reason. There is a kind of secularized variant of *agapē* implicit in reason itself, which cannot but grow stronger with the development of enlightenment.

Some belief of this kind, sometimes in a Christianized variant, sometimes in radically secular form, has bulked large in the self-consciousness of moderns over the last two centuries, and has fed our faith in ourselves as a reforming civilization, capable of reaching higher moral goals than any previous age has. The stupendous humanitarian efforts of the nineteenth and twentieth centuries, the great efforts at political reconstruction after wars, especially Woodrow Wilson's dream of a new world order, were fed and sustained by it. Our growing inability to hold on to it creates something like a spiritual crisis in our civilization.

This faith is part of the legacy of the Enlightenment, even where it lacked the terms to make sense of it. Kant did at least manage to give it a clear, if fragile, basis in the conception of a noumenal rational agent.

21

THE EXPRESSIVIST TURN

21.1

Kant offers one form of modern internalization, that is, a way of finding the good in our inner motivation. Another comes with that family of views in the late eighteenth century that represents nature as an inner source. I am speaking about views which arise with the German Sturm und Drang and continue developing thereafter through the Romantic period, both English and German. Rousseau is naturally its point of departure, and its first important articulation comes perhaps in the work of Herder; thereafter it is taken up not only by Romantic writers but by Goethe and, in another way, by Hegel and becomes one of the constituent streams of modern culture.

The philosophy of nature as source was central to the great upheaval in thought and sensibility that we refer to as 'Romanticism', so much so that it is tempting to identify them. But as the mention of Goethe and Hegel shows, this would be too simple. My claim is rather that the picture of nature as a source was a crucial part of the conceptual armoury in which Romanticism arose and conquered European culture and sensibility. The word has a bewildering number of definitions; and some have even doubted that there is such a unified phenomenon, as against simply a conceptual muddle hidden in a single term.[1]

There is, indeed, one popular picture of what Romanticism is, which seems rather disconnected from any doctrine about nature. This sees the movement as a rebellion against the construction of neo-Classical norms in art and especially literature. Against the classical stress on rationalism, tradition, and formal harmony, the Romantics affirmed the rights of the individual, of the imagination, and of feeling. There is a lot of truth in this description, particularly applied to the wave of French Romanticism in the early nineteenth century. In France the hold of neo-Classicism was always strong, and it took a revolutionary movement to displace it.

If we define Romanticism in this way, then its relation to the philosophies of nature as source can be clearly stated. This notion of an inner voice or impulse, the idea that we find the truth within us, and in particular in our feelings—these were the crucial justifying concepts of the Romantic rebellion in its various forms. They were indispensable to it. That is why Rousseau is so often their starting point. Sometimes the voice or impulse is seen as particular to the person himself; it is the voice of one's self; this was perhaps more common among the French writers like Lamartine or Musset, who sought in their poetry to give authentic expression to their feelings. Sometimes it is also seen as the impulse in us of nature, as the larger order in which we are set. This was the case with some English writers, like Blake and in a different way also Wordsworth.[2] But this idea was much further elaborated in Germany. Herder offered a picture of nature as a great current of sympathy, running through all things. "Siehe die ganze Natur, betrachte die grosse Analogie der Schöpfung. Alles fühlt sich und seines Gleichen, Leben wallet ze Leben" ("See the whole of nature, behold the great analogy of creation. Everything feels itself and its like, life reverberates to life"). Man is the creature who can become aware of this and bring it to expression. His calling as "an epitome and steward of creation" is "dass er Sensorium seines Gottes in allem Lebenden der Schöpfung, nach dem Masse es ihm verwandt ist, werde" ("That he become the organ of sense of his God in all the living things of creation, according to the measure of their relation to him").[3] This is the picture which was taken up by the German writers of the 1790's, e.g., Hölderlin, Schelling, and Novalis.[4]

This philosophy of nature as source seems essential to Romanticism, but the converse is not the case. It can continue to inform the vision of writers, even when they have put Romanticism—defined as the rejection of classic order—behind them. This was the case with Goethe,[5] for instance, and with Hegel.[6]

All these writers see human beings as set in a larger natural order, often conceived as a providential order, with which they should be in harmony. In this respect, they are at one with earlier Deism. And indeed, for German writers, Shaftesbury was often an important source, as well as Rousseau. What I want to get at in speaking of nature as an inner source is the subtle but important difference with the earlier views which resides in the Rousseauian notion that our access to this order is primarily inward.

The Deist providential order showed human life and its ordinary fulfilments to be marked as significant, so that both attaining these fulfilments for oneself and securing them for others took on a higher importance and were strongly valued as endorsed by the Divine plan. We come to appreciate this by seeing the order of things and inferring its divine origin. This in turn makes sense of and justifies our moral sentiments, if these figure in our theory (as they do not, let us remember, on the Lockean variant).

On the views I now want to consider the sense of this significance comes from within. It is an inner impulse or conviction which tells us of the importance of our own natural fulfilment and of solidarity with our fellow creatures in theirs. This is the voice of nature within us.

In their external tenets the doctrines may seem to be the same. Herder, for instance, held views about the natural order as harmonious and providentially created which were not greatly at odds with those of, say, Hutcheson. It may appear that only the mode of access to the truth has changed; that the shift is towards a less intellectual view, which no longer places such reliance on proofs of divine creation from design but which can ground all this instead in inner conviction.[7]

But of course this change in the mode of access already implies some change in the idea of what it is to acknowledge the providential significance of things. To have a proper moral stance towards the natural order is to have access to one's inner voice. We can't think of it as an identical message, available either by external argument from design or by inner intuition. The medium is here integral to the message: those who haven't grasped the significance of things inwardly, those who have only a cold, external understanding of the world as providential, haven't really got the point at all. We can think of the change in these terms: any theology includes some notion of how we can come in contact with God or his purposes; a radical change in this latter doctrine means an alteration in our understanding of God and creation as well.

This is the more evident, in that the opposition between the cold, external understanding and the inner grasp of things was a polemical one for these theories. They follow Rousseau in propounding a two-loves view: the inner voice is our mode of access, but we can lose contact with it; it can be stifled in us. And what can stifle it is precisely the disengaged stance of calculating reason, the view of nature from the outside, as a merely observed order. The filiation with earlier theories of grace is evident. Nature stands as a reservoir of good, of innocent desire or benevolence and love of the good. In the stance of disengagement, we are out of phase with it, cut off from it; we cannot recover contact with it.

In this stance we may believe, with Enlightenment naturalism, that all people are similarly motivated, that all desire alike is for happiness, and that what matters is how enlightened or misguided our search for it is. But in fact, our will needs to be transformed; and the only thing that can do it is the recovery of contact with the impulse of nature within us. We must open ourselves up to the élan of nature within, as we had to open ourselves to God's grace on the orthodox theory. There is more than an analogy here; there is also a filiation. And indeed, a theory of nature as a source can be combined with some form of Christian faith, following the lead of Deism in which God's relation to us passes mainly through his order, as we can see in Rousseau, and later in the German Romantics. Thus in Schiller's "Ode to

Joy", the great current of life which flows through nature, revivifying us and restoring us to fraternity, is first addressed in a rather "pagan" image: "Freude, schöner Götterfunken, Tochter aus Elysium". But later the whole order is seen to presuppose the loving father: "Uber fernem Sternenzelt / Muss ein lieber Vater wohnen"; quite in line with standard Deism, or even theism. The slide from an orthodox view to a secularized variant of this religion of nature could be made through a series of intermediate stages almost without noticing the break.

But plainly a slide was now possible, even easy. Some theorists subscribed to the basic orthodox, or at least Deistic, doctrines about the world as a providential creation. I have already tried to show how even in these cases, a subtle but important change was already introduced. But once one admits that access to the significance of things is inward, that it is only properly understood inwardly, one can quietly slip one's moorings in orthodox formulations. What is primary is the voice within or, according to other variants, the élan running through nature which emerges inter alia in the voice within. Orthodoxy is believable, for those who believe it, ultimately as the best interpretation of this voice or élan. This is in any case the ultimate logic of a theory of nature as inner source, even if this was not entirely appreciated at its inception.

God, then, is to be interpreted in terms of what we see striving in nature and finding voice within ourselves. A slide to a kind of pantheism is all too easy, and this we see in the Romantic generation with the early Schelling, for instance, and later in another form with Hegel. This slide can go further and take us outside of properly Christian forms, until we get a view like Goethe's, for instance, or the views which were reflected in the widespread invocations of Spinoza in the Romantic period.

We can go further again, and ultimately come close to joining with the explorations of naturalism that I adumbrated in the previous chapter: the significance of things is one that emerges out of physical nature and our own material being. But at the time which I'm now discussing, any convergence of materialism and the view of nature as a source is still well in the future, and will require, as we saw, some loosening of the close connection between materialism and the disengaged stance.

The philosophy of nature as a source, while it goes beyond the Deism of Shaftesbury and Hutcheson, obviously stands with them in their critique of Locke and the extrinsic theory. It stands with them in giving a central and positive place to sentiment in the moral life. It is through our feelings that we get to the deepest moral and, indeed, cosmic truths. "Das Herz ist der Schlüssel der Welt und des Lebens", says Novalis ("The heart is the key to the world and life"). For Herder, all passions and sensations "can and must be operative, precisely in the highest knowledge, for this grew out of them all and can only live in them". Wordsworth concurs with Aristotle that: "Poetry is the most philosophic of all writing: . . . its object is truth, not individual and local, but general and operative; not standing upon external testimony, but carried alive into the heart by passion; truth which is its own testimony".[8] Indeed, this philosophy takes the centrality of sentiment to unheard-of lengths. From this perspective, a central part of the good life must consist in being open to the impulse of nature, being attuned to it and not cut off from it. But this is inseparable from how I feel, from my having sentiments of a certain sort. By itself, this is not new. We might even argue that it is the Enlightenment theories which are exceptional in making moral obligation reside so exclusively in actions and cutting out motivation altogether, as I discussed in Part I. For Aristotle, virtue consisted in having dispositions to do the good willingly. For Plato, for Christian theology, the love of the Good or of God is at the very centre of the good life. The requirement in this new philosophy that I be in tune with the impulse of nature could be seen just as another demand of love: now the nature which speaks through me is the good which must be cherished.

But there is something disanalogous to all these precedents in the philosophy of nature as source. This places a value on our sentiments for themselves, as it were. Unlike the Aristotelian ethic it doesn't define certain motivations as virtuous in terms of the actions they move us to. It is more directly concerned with how we feel about the world and our lives in general. This makes the analogy with Plato's love of the Good. But unlike this, what is required is not the love of some transcendent object but rather a certain way of experiencing our lives, our ordinary desires and fulfilments, and the larger natural order in which we are set. To be in tune with nature is to experience these desires as rich, as full, as significant—to respond to the current of life in nature. It really is a matter of having certain *sentiments* as well as of aiming at or doing certain things.

The difference with Aristotle is this: the "sentiments" valued on the Aristotelian perspective are defined in terms of the mode of life or actions they move us to, while for nature as source we might just as well say that the way of life or action is defined by the sentiments. Certain feelings, such as our sense of oneness with humanity or a response of joy and reverence to the spectacle of untamed nature, are just as, if not more, fundamental in defining the good life as any actions. The good life is originally defined partly in terms of certain sentiments. This is why late-eighteenth-century sentimentalism, when it moved beyond the early influential formulations of Rousseau, found its natural home in the philosophies of nature as a source.

The difference in relation to the Platonic model is that here the "sentiments" are defined by the transcendent object of love, the Good. We can believe that we can attain a description of this object independent of our feelings, although the object properly understood must command our love and awe. But we come to define what nature is as a source in the course of articulating what it inclines us to. If we think of nature as a force, an élan running through the world, which emerges in our own inner impulses, if these impulses are an indispensable part of our access to this force, then we can only know what it is by articulating what these impulses impel us to. And this articulation must be partly in terms of sentiment, as we have seen. So once again, our sentiments are integral to our most original, underived definition of the good.

The first difference above, that in relation to the Aristotelian model, gives rise to another slide, analogous to the one away from orthodox theology. If the good life is defined partly in terms of certain sentiments, then it can also slip its moorings and depart from the traditional ethical codes. At first, the appropriate sentiments are defined very much in congruence with the ethic of ordinary life and benevolence, following moral sense theory. Benevolence and sympathy are seen as natural, as were the traditional limits on sensual fulfilment by, say, Rousseau or Herder. But the way is open for a redefinition. Renewed contact with the deep sources in nature can be seen as conferring a heightened, more vibrant quality to life. This can be interpreted in a way which abandons the usual restraints on sensual fulfilment. In partial attunement to the outlook of Enlightenment materialism, sensuality can itself be made significant. The good life comes to consist in a perfect fusion of the sensual and the spiritual, where our sensual fulfilments are experienced as having higher significance.[9] The journey along this path takes us beyond the period now being discussed. We have perhaps come to the end of this road only in our own time, with the "flower generation" of the 1960's.

Similarly, the source which gives heightened vibrancy to our lives can be detached from benevolence and solidarity. But this, too, happens later. It is eventually articulated most memorably by that great anti-Romantic, Nietzsche.

This slide, along either of these paths, tends to dissolve the distinction between the ethical and the aesthetic. The category of the aesthetic itself develops in the eighteenth century, along with a new understanding of natural and artistic beauty, which focussed less on the nature of the object, and more on the quality of the experience evoked. The very term 'aesthetic' points us to a mode of experience. And this tended to be the focus of various theories of the century, developed by, inter alia, the Abbé du Bos, Baumgarten, and Kant.[10] Now that ethics came to be defined partly in terms of sentiments, the lines become easier to fudge. We usually think it is easy to distinguish ethical and aesthetic objects or issues. But when it is a matter of sentiments; and when, moreover, the 'ethical' ones are redefined in a way which abandons the traditional virtues of temperance, justice, and beneficence, then the lines seem difficult to draw. Is there any more point in drawing them? If we disregard Nietzsche's polemic against the 'moral' and just try to classify his superman ideal for ourselves, would we call it ethical or aesthetic? Doesn't this opposition turn out to be false here?

21.2

If our access to nature is through an inner voice or impulse, then we can only fully know this nature through articulating what we find within us. This connects to another crucial feature of this new philosophy of nature, the idea that its realization in each of us is also a form of expression. This is the view that I have called elsewhere 'expressivism'.[11] I am focussing on particular features of expression in using this term. To express something is to make it manifest in a given medium. I express my feelings in my face; I express my thoughts in the words I speak or write. I express my vision of things in some work of art, perhaps a novel or a play. In all these cases, we have the notion of making something manifest, and in each case in a medium with certain specific properties.

But to talk of 'making manifest' doesn't imply that what is so revealed was already fully formulated beforehand. Sometimes that can be the case, as when I finally reveal my feelings that I had already put in words for myself long ago. But in the case of the novel or play, the expression will also involve a formulation of what I have to say. I am taking something, a vision, a sense of things, which was inchoate and only partly formed, and giving it a specific shape. In this kind of case, we have difficulty in distinguishing sharply between medium and 'message'. For works of art, we readily sense that being in the medium they are is integral to them. Even when it is clear that they are saying something, we sense that we cannot fully render this in another form. Richard Strauss may write a tone poem *Also Sprach Zarathustra*. But even had he intended it to, this couldn't be an adequate rendition of Nietzsche's work into another medium, not in the way that 'ne pas fumer' adequately renders the instruction 'no smoking' into French.

And so for this kind of expressive object, we think of its "creation" as not only a making manifest but also a making, a bringing of something to be. This notion of expression is itself modern. It grows at the same time as the understanding of human life that I am trying to formulate. Indeed, it is one facet of it. I use it only because it is more generally recognizable to us in this field of artistic works.

My claim is that the idea of nature as an intrinsic source goes along with an expressive view of human life. Fulfilling my nature means espousing the inner élan, the voice or impulse. And this makes what was hidden manifest for both myself and others. But this manifestation also helps to define what is to be realized. The direction of this élan wasn't and couldn't be clear prior to this manifestation. In realizing my nature, I have to define it in the sense of giving it some formulation; but this is also a definition in a stronger sense: I am realizing this formulation and thus giving my life a definitive shape. A human life is seen as manifesting a potential which is also being shaped by this manifestation; it is not just a matter of copying an external model or carrying out an already determinate formulation.

This conception reflects the return in force of biological models of growth, as against the mechanistic ones of association, in the account of human mental development, models which Herder articulated so well and so effectively in this period. This obviously owes a great deal to Aristotle's idea of nature which actualizes its potential. But there is an importantly different twist. Where Aristotle speaks of the nature of a thing tending towards its complete form, Herder sees growth as the manifestation of an inner power (he speaks of '*Kräfte*'), striving to realize itself externally. Nature is now within. In fact, the Aristotelian concepts have been interwoven with the modern notion of expression as an articulation which both manifests and defines. This is closely tied to the idea of a self, a subject. It is no longer some impersonal 'Form' or 'nature' which comes to actuality, but a being capable of self-articulation. Leibniz was an important source for expressivism. His notion of a monad already effected the connection between the Aristotelian idea of nature and a subject-like particular. The monad was a proto-self.

Expressivism was the basis for a new and fuller individuation. This is the idea which grows in the late eighteenth century that each individual is different and original, and that this originality determines how he or she ought to live. Just the notion of individual difference is, of course, not new. Nothing is more evident, or more banal. What is new is the idea that this really makes a difference to how we're called on to live. The differences are not just umimportant variations within the same basic human nature; or else moral differences between good and bad individuals. Rather they entail that each one of us has an original path which we ought to tread; they lay the obligation on each of us to live up to our originality.

Herder formulated this idea in a telling image: "Jeder Mensch hat ein eignes Mass, gleichsam eine eigne Stimmung aller seiner sinnlichen Gefühle zu einander" ("Each human being has his own measure, as it were an accord peculiar to him of all his feelings to each other").[12] Each person is to be measured by a different yardstick, one which is properly his or her own.

We can see ideas in the tradition which prepared the way for this—for instance, the Christian notion of a variety of gifts which is correlative to the variety of vocations, which we see expressed in St. Paul, and then taken up again by the Puritans. Here we have the notion that the good life for you is not the same as the good life for me; each of us has our own calling, and we shouldn't exchange them. Following you may be betraying my own calling, even though you are being faithful to yours. What the late eighteenth century adds is the notion of originality. It goes beyond a fixed set of callings to the notion that each human being has some original and unrepeatable "measure". We are all called to live up to our originality.

This radical individuation was obviously facilitated by expressivism and the notion of nature as a source. What the voice of nature calls us to cannot be fully known outside of and prior to our articulation/definition of it. We can only know what realizing our deep nature is when we have done it. But if this is true for human beings in general, why should it not also be true for each human being in particular? Just as the manifestations of the great current of life in the rest of nature can't be the same as its realization in human life, so its realization in you may be different from its realization in me. If nature is an intrinsic source, then each of us has to follow what is within; and this may be without precedent. We should not hope to find our models without.

This has been a tremendously influential idea. Expressive individuation has become one of the cornerstones of modern culture. So much so that we barely notice it, and we find it hard to accept that it is such a recent idea in human history and would have been incomprehensible in earlier times. In addition, this notion of originality as a vocation holds not only between individuals. Herder also used it to formulate a notion of national culture. Different *Völker* have their own way of being human, and shouldn't betray it by aping others. (In particular, Germans shouldn't ape Frenchmen. But Herder was also a passionate, and early, anti-colonialist.) This is one of the originating ideas of modern nationalism.

The expressive view of human life went along naturally with a new understanding of art. If expression defines in a double sense, i.e., both formulates and shapes, then the most important human activity will partake of this nature. The activity by which human beings realize their nature will also define in this double sense.

It is art which comes to fill this niche. In our civilization, moulded by expressivist conceptions, it has come to take a central place in our spiritual life, in some respects replacing religion. The awe we feel before artistic originality and creativity places art on the border of the numinous, and reflects the crucial place that creation/expression has in our understanding of human life.

But in thus being made central, art was also reinterpreted. If to define myself is to bring what is as yet imperfectly determined to full definition, if the paradigm vehicle for doing this is artistic creation, then art can no longer be defined in traditional terms. The traditional understanding of art was as mimesis. Art imitates reality. This of course left a number of crucial questions open: in particular, the question of what kind and level of reality was to be imitated. Was it the empirical reality surrounding us? Or the higher reality of the Forms? And what was the relation between them? But on the new understanding, art is not imitation, but expression in the sense discussed here. It makes something manifest while at the same time realizing it, completing it.

This is the shift which M. H. Abrams described so well in *The Mirror and the Lamp*.[13] The move from mimesis to expression was under way well before the Romantic period, throughout the eighteenth century in fact. It fed on a host of things: in part, the new valuation of sentiment gave a higher significance to its expression; in part also, the new conceptions of the origins of language and culture in the expressive cry lent colour to the view that the earliest speech was poetical, that early people spoke in tropes because they spoke from the heart and the natural expression of feeling is poetry. This could easily combine with the primitivist sentiment that the earliest, most primitive poetry was also the purest. Admiration for early, rugged, unspoilt, strongly expressive poetry grew in the second half of the eighteenth century, and turned people towards folk poetry (Herder played a particularly important role here) as well as towards Homer, the Hebrew Bible, and even the entirely invented writer 'Ossian'. In the 1770's, influential writers on aesthetics, like Sir William Jones and J. G. Sulzer, could declare Aristotle's mimesis theory erroneous as far as poetry was concerned.[14] But something further was needed to produce the conception of art of the Romantic age and that was what I have been calling the idea of nature as a source. This goes beyond the doctrine that poetry is primarily an expression of feeling. It takes this up in a revolution of moral ideas which confers tremendous significance on this expression. It is now what realizes and completes us as human beings, what rescues us from the deadening grip of disengaged reason. This revolution not only extends the expressive interpretation beyond poetry (and of course also music, where it had always had a footing) to art in general but also gives art its new and exalted status in human life. The expressive theory of art is given a crucially human and even cosmic significance, in being taken up into the expressivist conception of mankind and nature.

A cosmic dimension intrudes to the extent that we see the source not just as nature in us but as linked with the larger current of life or being, as most of the great writers did in the Romantic epoch. The theme which had been developing since the Renaissance of the artist as creator is taken up with a new intensity. The artist doesn't imitate nature so much as he imitates the author of nature. The artist creates not in imitation of anything phenomenally pre-existing. By analogy, the work of art now doesn't so much manifest something visible beyond itself as constitute itself as the locus of manifestation. Shelley draws on the language of Renaissance neo-Platonists in saying that poetry is "the creation of actions according to the unchangeable forms of human nature . . . It makes us inhabitants of a world to which the familiar world is a chaos . . . It creates anew the universe after it has been annihilated in our minds by the recurrence of impressions blunted by reiteration".[15] The creation here is also a manifestation, or a transfiguration. And something similar is indicated by Wordsworth when he speaks of

> How exquisitely the individual Mind
> . . . to the external World
> is fitted:—and how exquisitely too
> . . . . .
> The external World is fitted to the Mind;
>
> And the creation (by no lower name
> Can it be called) which they with blended might
> Accomplish[16]

Herder puts it too bluntly: "The artist is become a creator God".[17] Perhaps an image for the Romantic artist which captures better the blend of making and revealing was that of the soothsayer or seer. Through art, what is hidden and unrevealed in nature becomes manifest. "Jeder Künstler ist Mittler für alle übrigen" ("Every artist is a mediator for all others").[18] For Shelley, the poet "strips the veil of familiarity from the world, and lays bare the naked and sleeping beauty which is the spirit of its forms".[19] As a mediator of spiritual reality to humans, the artist can be likened to a priest, as Schleiermacher sees it,

> ein wahrer Priester des Höchsten, indem er ihn [Gott] denjenigen näher bringt, die nur das Endliche und Geringe zu fassen gewohnt sind, er stellet ihnen das Himmlische und Ewige dar als ein Gegenstand des Genusses und der Vereinigung.
>
> a true priest of the Highest in that he brings Him [God] closer to those who are used to grasping only the finite and the trifling; he presents them with the heavenly and eternal as an object of pleasure and unity.[20]

But as I argued above, this revelation involved not just a copying of what was already formulated; manifestation required articulation. That is why the writers of this period give such a central role to the creative imagination. It is in the eighteenth century that the distinction arises between the merely reproductive imagination, which simply brings back to mind what we have already experienced, perhaps combined in novel ways, on one hand, and the creative imagination which can produce something new and unprecedented, on the other. This distinction becomes of vital importance in the Romantic period. Coleridge formulated it in his celebrated opposition between 'fancy' (which merely reproduces) and the imagination proper.

> The primary IMAGINATION I hold to be the living Power and prime Agent of all human Perception, and as a repetition in the finite mind of the eternal act of creation in the infinite I AM.[21]

This creative imagination is the power which we have to attribute to ourselves, once we see art as expression and no longer simply as mimesis. Manifesting reality involves the creation of new forms which give articulation to an inchoate vision, not simply the reproduction of forms already there. This is why the Romantic period developed its particular concept of the symbol. The symbol, unlike allegory, provides the form of language in which something, otherwise beyond our reach, can become visible. Where the allegorical term points to a reality which we can also refer to directly, the symbol allows what is expressed in it to enter our world. It is the locus of a manifestation of what otherwise would remain invisible. As A. W. Schlegel put it: "Wie kann nun das Unendliche auf die Oberfläche zur Erscheinung gebracht werden? Nur symbolisch, in Bildern und Zeichen" ("How then can the infinite be brought to manifestation on the surface? Only symbolically, in pictures and signs").[22] And Coleridge takes up the same idea. He defines the symbol as "characterized by a translucence of the special in the individual, ... above all by the translucence of the eternal through and in the temporal".[23] It can't be separated from what it reveals, as an external sign can be separated from its referent. It "always partakes of the Reality which it renders intelligible; and while it enunciates the whole, abides itself as a living part of that Unity, of which it is the representative".[24] Or again, the perfect symbol "lives within that which it symbolizes and resembles, as the crystal lives within the light it transmits, and is transparent like the light itself".[25]

This concept of the symbol is what underlies the ideal of a complete interpenetration of matter and form in the work of art. Coleridge's image of translucence makes this connection understandable. In a perfect work of art, the "matter"—the language of a poem or the material of a sculpture—should be entirely taken up in the manifestation; and reciprocally, what is manifested ought to be available only in the symbol, and not merely pointed to as an independent object whose nature could be defined in some other medium. One of the sources for this conception of the perfect symbol was Kant's third critique and his notion of the aesthetic object as manifesting an order for which no adequate concept could be found. This was an idea which deeply influenced Schiller, and through him the aesthetics of an entire generation.[26]

It is tempting to see the new understanding of art as arising in order to fill its niche in the new expressivist conception of human life. But other changes concurred. In particular, there is the gradual fading of a believable notion of cosmic order, whose nature could be specified and understood independently of the realization/manifestation of the current of nature in our lives. The old order based on the ontic logos was no longer acceptable. Even the more recent, eighteenth-century order of interlocking purposes became harder to credit. This was partly due to factors mentioned in the previous chapter: the force of the anti-Panglossian objection; the rise of materialist views; the new scientific discoveries that placed the universe in a time scale of cataclysmic changes which dwarfed the earlier, cosier pictures of harmony.

But there were also reasons particular to the Romantic and expressivist outlooks. The interlocking universe was bound up with the notion of a harmony of premoral purposes which was part of an Enlightenment humanist picture of things; and this was less and less acceptable to those who felt the inadequacy of this kind of humanism. What replaced the interlocking order was the Romantic notion of a purpose or life coursing through nature.

In a way, the Romantic idea developed out of the Deist order of harmonized natures. We saw in Chapter 16 how with Pope this concordance and harmony of ends could be poetically expressed as love.[27] And in this Pope shows the roots of this outlook, through Shaftesbury back to Ficino and Florentine Platonism, the roots also of the Romantic vision of nature. But for Pope, love ties together an order whose principle of coherence is already evident enough to dispassionate reason. It is the circle of nature where each thing serves as grist to the mill of some other ("see dying vegetables life sustain").[28] The Romantic order, in contrast, was not organized on principles which could be grasped by disengaged reason. Its principle of order was not exoterically available. Rather it was itself an enigma, and one could only understand it fully by participating in it. The love is such that one has to be initiated into it to see it. The old idea of a rationally evident harmony of natures gives way to a new one of a current of love or life, which is both close to us and baffles understanding. "Nah ist / Und schwer zu fassen der Gott" ("Near is / And difficult to grasp, the God").[29]

But if the order of things is not exoterically there to be imitated by art, then it must be explored and made manifest through the development of a new language, which can bring something at first esoteric and not fully seen to manifestation.

Earl Wasserman has shown how the decline of the old order with its established background of meanings made necessary the development of new poetic language by the Romantics. Pope, for instance, in his *Windsor Forest,* could draw on the age-old views of the order of nature as a commonly available source of poetic images. For Shelley, this resource is no longer available; the poet must articulate his own world of references, and make them believable.

> Until the end of the eighteenth century there was sufficient intellectual homogeneity for men to share certain assumptions . . . In varying degrees, . . . man accepted . . . the Christian interpretation of history, the sacramentalism of nature, the Great Chain of Being, the analogy of the various planes of creation, the conception of man as microcosm . . . These were cosmic syntaxes in the public domain; and the poet could afford to think of his art as imitative of "nature" since these patterns were what he meant by "nature".
>
> By the nineteenth century these world-pictures had passed from consciousness . . . The change from a mimetic to a creative conception of poetry is not merely a critical or philosophic phenomenon; . . . Now, . . . an additional formulative act was required of the poet . . . Within itself the modern poem must both formulate its own cosmic syntax and shape the autonomous poetic reality that the cosmic syntax permits: "nature", which was once prior to the poem and available for imitation, now shares with the poem a common origin in the poet's creativity.[30]

The Romantic poet has to articulate an original vision of the cosmos. When Wordsworth and Hölderlin describe the natural world around us, in *The Prelude, The Rhine,* or *Homecoming,* they no longer play on an established gamut of references, as Pope still could in *Windsor Forest.* They make us aware of something through nature for which there are as yet no adequate words.[31] The poems themselves are finding the words for us. In this "subtler language"—the term is borrowed from Shelley—something is defined and created as well as manifested. A watershed has been passed in the history of literature.

Something similar happens in painting in the early nineteenth century. Caspar David Friedrich, for instance, distances himself from the traditional iconography. He is searching for a symbolism in nature which is not based on the accepted conventions. The ambition is to let "the forms of nature speak directly, their power released by their ordering within the work of art".[32] Friedrich too is seeking a subtler language; he is trying to say something for which no adequate terms exist and whose meaning has to be sought in his works rather than in a pre-existing lexicon of references.[33] He builds on the late-eighteenth-century sense of the affinity between our feelings and natural scenes, but in an attempt to articulate more than a subjective reaction. "Feeling can never be contrary to nature, is always consistent with nature".[34]

21.3

I have been looking at two responses to the felt inadequacies of Enlightenment naturalism: the autonomy theory of Kant, and the diffuse movement of thought which comes to see nature as a source. Both react to what seems like the lack of a proper moral dimension in standard Deism and naturalism. But they react in different, incompatible ways.

Kant wants to recover the integrity of the moral, which he sees in an entirely different quality of motivation. To be moved by this is freedom, but it also entails a radical break with nature, a disengagement in a sense more radical than the naturalistic Enlightenment had envisaged. The understanding of nature as source takes a different path. It is also meant to rescue the moral dimension, but this is now to be discovered in the élan of nature itself, from which we have cut ourselves off. The two are on incompatible courses: Kant's division of nature from reason seems as much a denial of nature as source as the standard Enlightenment view; and the exaltation of nature as a source must seem as heteronomous as utilitarianism, in the eyes of a Kantian. And yet, there is also a profound affinity between the two, and a need was felt to combine them. One can see signs of this in Kant himself. His third critique was both a response to the growing aesthetic of expression and an important seminal work in its development. And the ambition becomes general in the 1790's: autonomy must be reconciled with unity with nature, Kant and Spinoza must be united; these were the watchwords. The young Schelling, for instance, saw his task in these terms. I want to look briefly at both the opposition and the aspiration to unity.

Both views are reactions to the felt inadequacies of standard Enlightenment Deism and naturalism. What seemed common to them was that they lacked a proper moral dimension, as I said above. This could be described in a way which has become popular today, by saying that they were 'one-dimensional'.[35] But this doesn't necessarily mean that there were differences on substantive moral questions or political options. Kantians as well as utilitarians tend to liberal views and believe in humanitarian and liberal policies, and so did a great many of those who espoused the view of nature as a source. There was a reactionary wing among the Romantics; and major questions about the nature of freedom—whether it should be seen as 'positive' or 'negative'—divide the followers of Rousseau from those of Hobbes and Locke and Bentham. These political differences build on metaphysical ones, but they aren't entailed in them. We see in Humboldt a spirited defence of individual freedom from an expressivist viewpoint.[36] And Comtean positivism was a great source of reactionary thought in the nineteenth century.

To see the standard Enlightenment view as one-dimensional is to see no place in it for what makes life significant. Human life seems a matter merely of desire-fulfilment, but the very basis for strong evaluation, for there being desires or goals which are intrinsically *worth* fulfilling, seems missing. Naturalism is especially vulnerable, because it explicitly attempts to subvert the traditional distinctions which have grounded earlier forms of strong evaluation. As I argued in the previous chapter, it relies strongly on its own implicit recognition of the significance of human life, but there are great resistances to the open articulation of this significance.

In the wake of this modern naturalism, and its supposed debunking of the traditional bases of strong evaluation, it has become common to wonder whether there is any such basis at all. It seems a propos to ask if the very notion that certain human fulfilments have a special significance is not a comfortable fiction, a projection of our feelings onto reality, whether this arises as a detached philosophical conjecture or as an anguished existential issue. And yet the whole Enlightenment ethic demands some such notion of significance.

The Kantian view finds its second dimension in the notion of a radical autonomy of rational agents. The life of mere desire-fulfilment is not only flat but also heteronomous. This critique has been the point of origin of a family of theories which have defined human dignity in terms of freedom. The fully significant life is the one which is self-chosen.

Expressivist views find their second dimension in nature as a source. The life of instrumental reason lacks the force, the depth, the vibrancy, the joy which comes from being connected to the élan of nature. But there is worse. It doesn't just lack this. The instrumental stance towards nature constitutes a bar to our ever attaining it.

The instrumental stance involves our objectifying nature, which means, as I described earlier, that we see it as a neutral order of things. That is, no facts about how things stand in this order amount to a consideration by itself in favour of one or other definition of the good life, but only, if at all, in combination with some value premiss drawn from elsewhere. In objectifying or neutralizing something, we declare our separation from it, our moral independence. Naturalism neutralizes nature, both without us, and in ourselves.

This stance of separation is what blocks us. It prevents us from opening ourselves to the élan of nature, both within and without. One of the great objections against Enlightenment disengagement was that it created barriers and divisions: between humans and nature;[37] and perhaps even more grievously, within humans themselves; and then also, as a further consequence, between human and human. This last seems to follow both because of the atomist affinities of naturalism and because the purely instrumental stance to things allows for no deeper unity in society than that of sharing certain common instruments.

And so among the great aspirations which come down to us from the Romantic era are those towards reunification: bringing us back in contact with nature, healing the divisions within between reason and sensibility, overcoming the divisions between people, and creating community. These aspirations are still alive: although the Romantic religions of nature have died away, the idea of our being open to nature within us and without is still a very powerful one. The battle between instrumental reason and this understanding of nature still rages today in the controversies over ecological politics. Behind the particular issues about the dangers of pollution or resource depletion, these two spiritual outlooks are in confrontation. One sees the dignity of man in his assuming control of an objectified universe through instrumental reason. If there are problems with pollution or ecological limits, they will themselves be solved by technical means, by better and more far-reaching uses of instrumental reason.

The other sees in this very stance to nature a purblind denial of our place in things. We ought to recognize that we are part of a larger order of living beings, in the sense that our life springs from there and is sustained from there. Recognizing this involves acknowledging a certain allegiance to this larger order. The notion is that sharing a mutually sustaining life system with other creatures creates bonds: a kind of solidarity which is there in the process of life. To be in tune with life is to acknowledge this solidarity. But this is incompatible with taking a purely instrumental stance towards this ecological context.

Or to take the argument in the reverse direction, taking up an instrumental stance is a denial of the need for this attunement. It is a kind of separation, a statement a priori of our moral independence, of our self-sufficiency.

The battle between these spiritual outlooks, which starts in the eighteenth century, is still going on today. This in spite of the fact that the Romantic doctrines about the current of life, or the All of nature, have just about totally disappeared. Just as Enlightenment humanism is no longer extant in its Deist form, but survives in naturalism, so the idea of nature as a source no longer refers to a God or cosmic spirit in the world, but the demand remains very much alive that we be open to or in tune with nature in ourselves and outside. The loss of belief in a spirit in nature has itself, of course, been the occasion of crisis and doubt, but the understanding of nature as a source still survives, although what underlies it is very uncertain and problematic.

This dispute between spiritual outlooks is deeply embedded in the inner conflicts of advanced industrial, capitalist societies. Instrumental reason plays such a large role in their institutions and practices that whatever shakes our confidence in it as a spiritual stance also causes deep malaise in contemporary advanced societies. There is a circular causal relation between the other crises and difficulties of capitalism and this spiritual malaise, which I have tried to trace elsewhere.[38]

I've been developing at some length the expressivist criticism of Enlightenment naturalism. But we can see from this account that expressivism will also be in conflict with the Kantian critique. This too could be accused of dividing us from nature without, and from our own nature within. Indeed, these two charges seem to apply with even greater force to the Kantian view, which marks such a sharp separation and opposition between freedom and nature. And in fact, Kant is severely taken to task for this in the Romantic period.

But what is just as noticeable is the attempt somehow to combine the two critiques. And there are good reasons for this which go just as deep into the roots of both. It is not only that they both start off from the same point, the shallowness of the standard Enlightenment. They also have important affinities. Both are internalizations. Both try to place the sources within. Both therefore show their Rousseauian heritage and make freedom a central good. And because they do, both render themselves vulnerable to the critique of the other.

Just because it is a theory of freedom, the Kantian moral philosophy finds it hard to ignore the criticism that the rational agent is not the whole person. This didn't lead Kant to want to alter his definition of autonomy, but he did see that the condition of polar opposition between reason and nature was somehow non-optimal; that the demands of morality and freedom point towards a fulfilment in which nature and reason would once more be in alignment. Such a condition is defined, for instance, by the summum bonum of the second critique, where virtue and happiness come to be coordinated.[39] And a reunion of another kind is pointed to in these lines from the "Conjectural Beginning of the Human Race" where, after speaking of the strife we now see between culture and nature, Kant speaks of a future in which "vollkommene Kunst wieder Natur wird: als welches das letzte Ziel der sittlichen Bestimmung der Menschengattung ist" ("Perfected art becomes nature again; which is the final goal of the moral destiny of the human race").[40]

And yet, also because it is a theory of freedom, the view of nature as a source can't ignore the point that mere sinking into unity with nature would be a negation of human autonomy. That is why the great thinkers who emerged out of the expressivist stream in this period all strove to unite radical autonomy and expressive unity, as we see with Schiller, Hölderlin, and Hegel, for instance.

The notion developed that the breach of reason with nature was a necessary one; that man had to make it in order to develop his powers of reason and abstraction. Schiller makes this point in his *Letters on the Aesthetic Education of Man*,[41] as does Hölderlin in his *Hyperion Fragment*.[42] The belief was that the human destiny was to return to nature at a higher level, having made a synthesis of reason and desire. The original single unity makes its way through divided paths, in reason and in nature, and then comes to fruition in a reconciliation. Hölderlin evokes this return of unity in this passage from *Hyperion*:

> Wie der Zwist der Liebenden, sind die Dissonanzen der Welt. Versöhnung ist mitten im Streit und alles Getrennte findet sich wieder. Es scheiden und kehren im Herzen die Adern und einiges, ewiges, glühendes Leben ist Alles.

> Like lovers' quarrels are the dissonances of the world. Reconciliation is in the midst of strife and all things separated come together again. The veins separate and return in the heart and everything is one unified, eternal glowing Life.[43]

The expressivist philosophies of nature as a source tended to develop a theory of history which saw it as resembling a spiral, from a primitive undifferentiated unity, to a conflictual division between reason and sensibility, human and human, to a third and higher reconciliation, in which the gains of the second period, reason and freedom, were fully retained. This structure has its roots very obviously in the Christian picture of salvation history, from original Paradise, through a Fall, to ultimate Redemption. But it is connected more immediately to millenarist developments out of Judaeo-Christian thought, which were just then acquiring new political relevance.

For in the late eighteenth century there is a third development which also owed something to Rousseau and which introduced a polarization between good and evil into Enlightenment thinking. That is what has been called modern political messianism.[44] I'm thinking of the spirit which was in evidence, for instance, at the height of the fervour of the French Revolution— the sense that a new epoch was dawning, reflected in the adoption of a new calendar.

Millenarism, as it is better called, has a long history in Western civilization. Its beginnings go back to the Middle Ages and the writings of Joachim of Fiore, who foretold that a third age would dawn, the age of the Holy Ghost, succeeding the first two: that of the Father (the time of the Old Testament) and that of the son. It would be an age of spirituality, of a higher form of human life, in preparation for the consummation of all things. A certain body of millenarist expectations, that is, a certain set of notions of what the last things would look like, built up in the Middle Ages, and from time to time these were activated by sects. The scenario usually included a battle between the forces of light and the forces of darkness, between Christ and anti-Christ; after which there would be a reign of the just for a thousand years, before the final consummation.[45]

The millenarist scenario describes a moment of crisis, one in which acute conflict is about to break out, one in which the world is polarized as never before between good and evil. It is a moment in which the suffering and tribulation of the good dramatically increases. But at the same time, it promises an unprecedented victory over evil, and hence a new age of sanctity and happiness unparalleled in history.

The sources of this scenario, of course, lie deep in the religious tradition of Judaism and Christianity, and in the messianic expectations which have always been harboured there. They take shape in mediaeval Europe from time to time and define a consciousness of crisis and revolt, and an expectation of radical new beginnings. Nor does this end with the Middle Ages. Millenarist expectations also played a role in the Reformation—in the revolt at Münster in the 1530's, for instance. They came again to the fore among some of the participants in the English Civil War. The Fifth Monarchy men were defining themselves according to another biblical prophecy, from the Book of Daniel: the reign of God succeeds that of the world empires.

What we see in the French Revolution is something like the same framework of expectations, but for the first time secularized. Once again, the picture is of a crisis, brought about by an unprecedented polarization between the forces of good and evil, building up to a decisive conflict, which will usher in an era of unprecedented good. In the short term, however, our tribulations sharply increase as an inescapable result of the crisis and conflict.

Some of the secular content for these expectations was provided by Enlightenment humanism. The new age would be one of reason and benevolence, of freedom and humanitarianism, of equality and justice and self-rule. But they required something richer than Enlightenment naturalism as a basis. The picture of polarization required a strong notion of good and evil, not one that turned only on the difference between enlightened and unenlightened self-interest. And so we find Rousseauian language coming to the fore at the height of the Revolution. The battle is between virtue, patriotism, and freedom, on one side, and vice, treason, and tyranny, on the other. The Revolution offers the hope of a new epoch, not because it proposes to engineer society at last in a rational form; rather the hope is that it can at last call forth the great benevolence latent in virtuous men, once the corrupt servants of tyranny have been swept aside. There is a Rousseauian trust in the goodness of uncorrupted nature in the revolutionary time, without Rousseau's acute, even despairing, sense of how impossible it was to recover contact with this nature in large modern states:

These millenarist expectations, which are more a mood than a doctrine, arise in the heat of the revolutionary struggle. And not only in France: they were, indeed, more articulately voiced in England and Germany, which had stronger, more recent millenarist traditions. Southey, in his more conservative later years, described how he had felt at the moment of the Revolution: "Old things seemed passing away, and nothing was dreamt of but the regeneration of the human race". Priestley, the radical and Unitarian, saw in it the fulfilment of biblical prophecies, and foresaw the advent of "the millennium, or the future peaceable and happy state of the world".[46]

And it is in Germany, where actual revolution takes place simply as an import, along with the invading French armies, that the millenarist expectations are philosophically elaborated. In the process they are transposed, reflecting not so much the hopes of the radical Enlightenment as those of the expressivist theory of nature as source. What emerges is the spiral view of history I described above, in which we break out of our original integration into the great current of life, to enter a phase of division and opposition, followed by a return to unity at a higher level.

We find this view elaborated in Schiller and then taken up by a number of others, including Schelling, Hölderlin, and Hegel. At first this led to very immediate expectations of dramatic change. This philosophy combined with a sense of crisis and new possibility engendered by the French Revolution, which indeed had partly inspired it. It defined the perspective of a new politics and a new culture, of which Germany would be the initiator. We can see some expectation of this kind glowing through the lines of Hegel's *Phänomenologie des Geistes* of 1807, though the transformation is seen in quite apolitical terms. In later Hegel, the sense of imminent radical transformation is gone. But what remains is the notion of a new and higher age, which has already dawned, and which is now seeing the unfolding of a new and higher political form, and the religious and philosophical culture which goes with it.

Hegel incorporates the whole traditional scenario of Western millenarism, but in á transposed, philosophical form. There are the three ages of world history, the crisis of heightened conflict at the entry of the new age (fortunately now behind us, in the form of the Revolution and its resulting wars), and the new higher resolution. Lost in the philosophical transposition, of course, is the final battle between good and evil, resulting in the total victory of the former. The Hegelian battle is never between good and bad, but between two requirements of the good; and it issues in synthesis, not total victory.

But Marx reinstates this element of polarization and total victory in his version of the spiral; and this is the form in which political millenarism has become a major force in modern civilization and history. I have tried to show elsewhere[47] how Marx's theory of alienation and his perspective on liberation are based not only on Enlightenment humanism but also on Romantic expressivism, and hence ultimately on the idea of nature as a source.

21.4

The expressivist theories of nature as source thus develop their own conceptions of history and of the narrative forms of human life, both in how an individual life unfolds towards self-discovery and in how this life fits into the whole human story. One such form is the spiral I've just been describing. But the critique of modern Enlightenment civilization as fragmented and dessicated could also generate a pessimistic sense that the world had declined, perhaps irreversibly, from an earlier, richer time. It could inspire a nostalgia for a past age of integrity—often identified with the Middle Ages.

Both forms broke with Enlightenment narrations. Even the 'optimistic' spiral view, in some ways similar to the belief in progress, was in other ways diametrically opposed. It is similar to the extent that it points towards a higher, better future; but very different in its polarization, in the drama of separation and reunion. The linear picture of progress that Condorcet offers is utterly denied. Those things that can progress in a linear fashion—scientific knowledge, technological know-how, riches—are far from being accepted as unadulterated goods.

And the picture of the growth of a life is utterly different in the central place it gives to self-discovery. The expressivist revolution constituted a prodigious development of modern post-Augustinian inwardness, in its self-exploratory branch. Insofar as one of the main themes of Part IV has been the attempt to explain our modern sense of inner depths, it is only now that we can fully see what underlies it. We certainly saw the bases for a strong orientation to inwardness in the transpositions wrought on Augustine by Descartes and Montaigne, and in the practices of disengaged self-remaking, and religious and moral self-exploration, which arise in the early modern period. But only with the expressivist idea of articulating our inner nature do we see the grounds for construing this inner domain as having *depth*, that is, a domain which reaches farther than we can ever articulate, which still stretches beyond our furthest point of clear expression.

That examining the soul should involve the exploration of a vast domain is not, of course, a new idea. The Platonic tradition would concur. But this domain is not an 'inner' one. To understand the soul, we are led to contemplate the order in which it is set, the public order of things. What is new in the post-expressivist era is that the domain is within, that is, it is only open to a mode of exploration which involves the first-person stance. That is what it means to define the voice or impulse as 'inner'.

Of course, Augustine had a notion of something 'inner' which similarly stretched beyond our powers of vision: our 'memory'. But at the base of this is God; to penetrate to the depths of our memory would be to be taken outside ourselves. And this is where we achieve our ultimate integrity as persons, in the eye of God, from the outside. Augustine's inwardness leads to the higher, as we said. In the philosophy of nature as source, the inexhaustible domain is properly within. To the extent that digging to the roots of our being takes us beyond ourselves, it is to the larger nature from which we emerge. But this we only gain access to through its voice in us. This nature, unlike Augustine's God, cannot offer us a higher view on ourselves from beyond our own self-exploration. The modern, post-expressivist subject really has, unlike the denizens of any earlier culture, "inner depths".

This concept of an inexhaustible inner domain is the correlative of the power of expressive self-articulation. The sense of depth in inner space is bound up with the sense that we can move into it and bring things to the fore. This we do when we articulate. The inescapable feeling of depth comes from the realization that whatever we bring up, there is always more down there. Depth lies in there being always, inescapably, something beyond our articulative power. This notion of inner depths is therefore intrinsically linked to our understanding of ourselves as expressive, as articulating an inner source.

The subject with depth is therefore a subject with this expressive power. Something fundamental changes in the late eighteenth century. The modern subject is no longer defined just by the power of disengaged rational control but by this new power of expressive self-articulation as well—the power which has been ascribed since the Romantic period to the creative imagination. This works in some ways in the same direction as the earlier power: it intensifies the sense of inwardness and leads to an even more radical subjectivism and an internalization of moral sources. But in other respects these powers are in tension. To follow the first all the way is to adopt a stance of disengagement from one's own nature and feelings, which renders impossible the exercise of the second. A modern who recognizes both these powers is constitutionally in tension.

I said in Chapter 19 that modern culture has diversified our moral sources and added two frontiers of exploration to the original theistic one: nature and our own powers. Plainly both of these have been transformed by the entry of expressivist theories into our culture. Nature is now conceived also as a source, and our powers have been added to. Moreover, expressivism relates these two frontiers differently than does Enlightenment humanism, in that the exploration of self and nature can be run together. This both greatly complicates and enriches the modern moral predicament.

PART V

Subtler Languages

22

OUR VICTORIAN
CONTEMPORARIES

22.1

These two big and many-sided cultural transformations, the Enlightenment and Romanticism with its accompanying expressive conception of man, have made us what we are. I don't mean this as a causal hypothesis, of course. As I have often said, the order of causation is difficult to trace in this domain. If we were looking for causes, we would have to mention a great many other things like the industrial revolution and the rise of modern nationalism. What I mean is rather that our cultural life, our self-conceptions, our moral outlooks still operate in the wake of these great events. We are still visibly working out their implications or exploring possibilities which they opened up for us. We still await another such large-scale cultural upheaval which might carry us out of their orbit, as we sense ourselves to have already departed from the orbit of Deism, Lockean or Hutchesonian, let alone such seventeenth-century notions as the divine right of kings. It is not just that we no longer believe these doctrines: we are not all unanimous about the defining doctrines of the Enlightenment or about expressivism. Rather it is that these earlier views have become strange to us; it is hard to recapture in imagination what they could ever have had going for them. Some watershed has been passed.

Perhaps we are now going over another such watershed, though I have my doubts. But even if this is what is occurring, we are still too much involved in it to see it clearly. We still instinctively reach for the old vocabularies, the ones we owe to Enlightenment and Romanticism.

That is why the Victorians are so close to us. In some ways we naturally think ourselves to have evolved away from them, beyond them. This is particularly true when we consider whatever we believe to be the most characteristic beliefs or practices of modernity, and then note with satisfaction that we have taken these further than our forebears of the last century. Universal equality is more radically understood, as twentieth-century social reforms, anti-colonialism, and feminism all attest; democracy is more integrally applied. All this is true. But what is remarkable is that the basic moral

393

and political standards by which we congratulate ourselves were themselves powerful in the last century. Even more strikingly, the very picture of history as moral progress, as a 'going beyond' our forebears, which underlies our own sense of superiority, is very much a Victorian idea.

Of course, there were resistances. And what I have been saying is tendentious, because it involves reading these as holdovers from an earlier time. From within nineteenth-century societies, one might argue, it wasn't always evident that, say, the remaining expressions of hierarchy were doomed relics of the past and that the concessions to equality were the wave of the future. What is more, those who were affected by the Enlightenment and by Romanticism were at the outset a minority, drawn from the educated classes of Europe and America, and were an even smaller proportion of these classes as one proceeded eastward, where these in turn were less significant in their societies. Our history since 1800 has been the slow spreading outward and downward of the new modes of thought and sensibility to new nations and classes, with the transfer in each case involving some kind of adapting transformation of the ideas themselves.

It would be a mistake, a typical example of retrospective illusion, to regard this march as inevitable. But whatever the causes, through whatever battles that might have turned out differently, there is a remarkable continuity between ourselves and those nations and classes affected by the new ways from the end of the eighteenth century on. This, of course, especially applies to the Anglo-Saxon countries.[1]

I want to look first at some of these continuities, before turning to see the ways in which the ideas of the Enlightenment and the Romantic era have been modified and developed, built on and fought against, in the last two centuries.

Certain moral ideas emerge from this crucial period which still form the horizon of our moral outlook. One thing the Enlightenment has bequeathed to us is a moral imperative to reduce suffering. This is not just a sensitivity to suffering, a greater squeamishness about inflicting it or witnessing it. It is true that this undoubtedly has occurred, as we can see it a host of ways, especially in the softening of penal codes which the Enlightenment helped bring about, partly under the influence of Beccaria and Bentham. But beyond this, we feel called on to relieve suffering, to put an end to it. Hence the tremendous impact of campaigns for famine relief, for instance, in our time. We routinely grumble about our lack of concern and note disapprovingly that it requires often spectacular television coverage of some disaster to awaken the world's conscience. But this very critique supposes certain standards of universal concern. It is these which are deeply anchored in our moral culture.[2]

We see here the joint force of two moral ideas whose development we have been tracing through the modern period: the significance of ordinary life and the ideal of universal benevolence. The first has made the issues of life itself and the avoidance of suffering of supreme importance; the second imposes the obligation to secure them universally.

Another major idea we have seen developing is that of the free, self-determining subject. This is a freedom defined negatively by the decline or erosion of all those pictures of cosmic order which could claim to define substantively our paradigm purposes as rational beings. But it is also defined positively by the reflexive powers which are central to the modern subject, those which confer the different kinds of inwardness on him or her, the powers of disengaged reason, and the creative imagination. The various conceptions of freedom, "negative" and "positive", are grounded on different stances towards, and definitions of, these powers, "positive" theories being generally based on some notion of an inner source, and "negative" theories being generally highly critical of all such notions.[3] But beyond these disagreements, what is universal in the modern world is the centrality of freedom as a good.

This, together with the ideal of universal benevolence, has generated another deeply entrenched moral imperative, to universal justice, which has found expression in our century in the various universal declarations of rights. The language of subjective rights offers a way of formulating certain important immunities and benefits which also builds in some idea of the dignity of a free subject, for it expresses these immunities and benefits as a kind of property of the subject, which can be invoked by the subject in his or her own cause.

And of course these ideas of freedom and dignity, in association with the promotion of ordinary life, have steadily eroded hierarchy and promoted equality—and that in all sorts of dimensions, between social classes, races, ethnic and cultural groups, and the sexes. Most notably, it has helped to bring about the steady rise in democracy as a legitimate form of political rule, to the point where it has become in the late twentieth century the inescapable source of legitimacy: everyone, even its most flagrant enemies, from Enver Hoxha to Agusto Pinochet, has been forced to claim some kind of democratic endorsement in "elections" or "plebiscites". Everyone would now agree, whatever their real feelings, with Jefferson's final judgement on his Declaration of Independence, delivered near the end of his life, that it "will be (to some parts sooner, to others later, but finally to all) the signal of arousing men to burst the chains under which monkish ignorance and superstition had persuaded them to bind themselves, and to assume the blessings and security of self-government". It is based on "the palpable truth, that the mass of mankind has not been born with saddles on their backs, nor a favoured few booted and spurred, ready to ride them legitimately, by the grace of God".[4]

However unsuccessful mankind has been in attaining "the blessings and security of self-government", no other aspiration ultimately incompatible with this is now avowable.

All these ideas seem to have come into their full force in the twentieth century. They were clearly at work in the Anglo-Saxon societies, however, from the beginning of the last century. Consider the great crusade in England for the suppression of the slave trade, and later for the abolition of slavery itself. The first objective was achieved in 1807, and the second in 1833. One has to recognize that the timing of these measures also depended on economic developments, that Britain benefited from its self-appointed position as guardian of international morality in giving a free hand to its navy to intervene in Africa and Latin America. But taking all this into account, we still should remark the arrival of a quiet new phenomenon which has become almost banal in our contemporary world: the mobilizing of a large-scale citizens' movement around a moral issue, with the intent of effecting political change. People were well aware at the time that something new was happening. In a statement of 1823, the recently founded Liverpool Society for the Abolition of Slavery attributed its unprecedented success in achieving moral "improvement" to "the practice of combining society itself in intellectual masses, for the purpose of attaining some certain, defined, and acknowledged good, which is generally allowed to be essential to the well-being of the whole".[5]

This is a formula which has been repeated continually, through the U.S. abolitionist crusade, countless temperance movements, to the great American civil rights movement of the 1960's and beyond. These movements reflect, and have helped to propagate and intensify, the imperatives of universal benevolence and justice and the sense that a recognition of these is integral to our civilization.

This recognition is of great importance, because it appears that the new moral consciousness has been inseparable from a certain sense of our place in history. Once again notions of the good are interwoven with modes of narrative. The imperative of benevolence carries with it the sense that this age has brought about something unprecedented in history, precisely in its recognition of this imperative. We feel that our civilization has made a qualitative leap, and all previous ages seem to us somewhat shocking, even barbarous, in their apparently unruffled acceptance of inflicted or easily avoidable suffering and death, even of cruelty, torture, to the point of revelling in their display. This sense of historical innovation was also there at the beginning of the last century. The statement of the Liverpool Society I quoted from above considered "the present age . . . remarkable beyond any that has preceded it, for the rapid and surprising improvement which has taken place in the moral character and disposition of mankind".[6]

We still share today that sense of moral exceptionalism relative to the long human past and over the whole range of moral ideas I sketched above. We are perhaps shier and more hesitant about stating it than the Liverpudlians of 1823, in part because we have been shaken by our own savagery in this century. But this hasn't shattered the idea that higher standards in the relevant regards are built into the moral culture of our civilization;[7] rather it has impressed us with the ease with which this civilization can be shaken off. The publics of North Atlantic societies still apply an implicit double standard to the atrocity stories that their media bombarded them with: the even minor lapses of some societies provoke shock and outrage, while much greater crimes elsewhere are almost shrugged off as all that one can expect. Syria's president, Assad, massacres several thousand people in Hama while suppressing a revolt of the Muslim Brotherhood, and the Western world barely turns a hair. Israel's indirect involvement in the massacres at Sabra and Chatila refugee camps during the war in Lebanon arouses moral condemnation, which significantly enough almost omits from its scope the Lebanese Forces which actually did the killing. Israelis often complain about this double standard, without appreciating that they are the object of an ethnocentric compliment or, more deeply, the beneficiaries of the historically exceptionalist view we hold about our civilization.

And of course we also differ from our Liverpudlian predecessors in having steadily raised the demands that flow from these moral imperatives. For most educated people today, capital punishment is a practice which ought to be relegated to the unenlightened past. The requirements of modernity have escalated, while the sense of being a qualitative exception remains constant.

It is too easy just to make the intellectual gesture of wiping this aside as a bit of prideful illusion. There is no doubt lots of pride and illusion in our self-image. But it is still true that the civilization which grew out of western Europe in modern times (certain aspects of which now extend well beyond Europe) has given an exceptional value to equality, rights, freedom, and the relief of suffering. We have somehow saddled ourselves with very high demands of universal justice and benevolence. Public opinion, concentrating on some popular or fashionable "causes" and neglecting other equally crying needs and injustices, may apply these standards very selectively. Those defending the unconscionable always try to point this out, as though the existence of other blackguards somehow excuses them. South African apologists sound the alarm over communism, and defenders of Communist regimes ask their critics why they don't attack military dictatorships. The premiss of all this special pleading is that our commitment really is to *universal* justice and well-being. Hence the unsettling ploy of accusing us of unjust selection, even when we attack what is obviously a flagrant injustice.

Nor does the recognition of this commitment have to involve the chauvinism that we frequently see in doctrines of historical exceptionalism. These have generally been insufferably ethnocentric in two respects: first, because they attributed to us a very high score on the standards which our civilization has made central; they breathed a serene self-satisfaction about how democratic or free or equal or universally benevolent we are. And second, because they couldn't recognize that there could be other goods which other civilizations had more fully recognized and more intensely sought than we have. One can correct for both these errors, however, and still recognize that the civilization that grew out of western Europe has defined goods which others have not, and recognize as well that these if taken seriously make rather extreme demands.

We can take a jaundiced or cynical view of these demands, look on them as a bit of hypocrisy which is built into our way of life, a posture of self-congratulation about which we're not really serious. Or we can look on them in a Nietzschean way, as seriously enough meant, but in fact motivated by envy and self-hatred. Or we can while approving them neutralize them as a distant ideal, an idea of reason never to be integrally realized in this world. Some degree of this latter is probably necessary to keep our balance. And taking the demand in this more modest form, we may feel some security in the fact that the practices of beneficence are built into the modern bureaucratic administration of society: in the form of universal provision of various benefits, for example, as well as mechanisms for appeal, recovery of rights, and the like. Indeed, much of the effort of what we often loosely call social democracy has gone into building universal concern, as it were, into the very fabric and procedures of our societies.

But this sense of security is unlikely to have survived the recognition, more and more borne in on us in recent years, that bureaucracy creates its own injustices and exclusions and that a great deal of suffering is not so much relieved as rendered invisible by it. There is no established procedure which can meet the demand for universal concern. If we are to take it seriously, that is, as a call to keep ever on the move towards meeting it, there is a question which can't be avoided: What can sustain this continuing drive? What can enable us to transcend in this way the limits we normally observe to human moral action? These limits are obvious enough. They include our restricted sympathies, our understandable self-preoccupation, and the common human tendency to define one's identity in opposition to some adversary or out group.

I think this is one of the important questions we have to ask ourselves today, and I want to return to it in the conclusion. But what is important for my purpose here is the recognition that any doctrine of historical exceptionalism, any belief that we can and ought to lay stronger demands on ourselves than prevailed in the past, must contain at least implicitly some answer to this question. In some cases, the answer will be quite unarticulated, because of the reluctance of the unbelieving Enlightenment to face the issue of moral sources. But we must at least assume that there is some answer if we are to take the demands seriously.

There are in fact several answers, and they reflect the different views about moral sources which have partly shaped each other and partly been opposed to each other over the last two centuries. In order to get a clearer view on them and their relationship, we have to return to the nineteenth century. This development assumed different forms; and most notably there was a radical divergence between the Anglo-Saxon and French societies. In the latter the sense of progress was militantly 'lay', and was largely opposed by those who sided with the church. But in England and America, exceptionalism was a blend of Christian and Enlightenment ideas. The notion of progress and the emphasis on rationally planned improvement came from the Enlightenment. But the inspiration and driving force still came largely from Christian faith, and the sense of exceptionalism attached to Christian (or often to Protestant) civilization.[8]

Indeed, the anti-slavery crusade originated in part in a revival movement, initiated by William Wilberforce and the Clapham Sect, that was an attempt to revivify evangelical Christianity in face of the growing infidelity of the educated classes. Wilberforce thought he discerned in contemporary France where this kind of degeneration could lead: "manners corrupted, morals depraved, dissipation predominant, above all, religion discredited". But Christianity could only be revived from its heart, "practical benevolence".[9] In fact, this revival succeeded. The Victorian era was in general more pious and more concerned about the state of religion than was the eighteenth century. But the faith which emerged from this renewal was significantly different— among other ways, in its intense practical concern—from what had existed before the Enlightenment.

These moral crusades, starting with the anti-slavery movement, cast some light on the complex relation between theistic and secular moral sources, at least in Anglo-Saxon cultures. We have already seen how the demands of Christian faith were redefined to incorporate a heavy dose of social reform, often conceived in terms of utilitarian calculation. This change built on an already existing tradition in English Protestantism which went back to the strong Calvinist link between godliness, regeneration, and an ordered social life. This had always incorporated a strong element of practical charity, which needed only to be extended in keeping with the allegedly new findings and capacities of the Enlightened age. The roots in Puritanism account for that peculiar amalgam of radicalism, social reform, and moral rigourism which was typical of English-speaking movements. The success of abolition in the United States found a lot of the same people later working in temperance movements. The sense of exceptionalism of the new Christian age linked together such things as cruelty, torture, coarseness, drunkenness, and general physical disorder as features that the new times must transcend.[10]

But beyond this the movements show us something of the complex and bi-directional relationship between Christian and secularized moral sources. On one hand, the driving force of both the British anti-slavery movement and American abolitionism was religious. It is difficult indeed to imagine these movements attaining the same intensity of commitment, the same indomitable purpose, or the same willingness to sacrifice in the English-speaking societies of that time outside of this religious mode. Although the philosophes were generally against slavery, many of them toyed with racist theories. Hume, for instance, was of the opinion that blacks were inferior. Allowing for such racial differences seemed just another way of dethroning the Bible to make room for empirical science. It had for the moment no important practical consequences, and seemed only motivated as an anti-Christian demonstration. It was later in the nineteenth and early twentieth centuries that this scientism would produce some real monsters, which have been since invoked with horrifying effect.[11]

But back in the eighteenth century it was believers who felt called upon to defend passionately the unity of the human race. And it was Christians who were the driving force in the abolitionist cause on both sides of the Atlantic.

The movements themselves, however, could be the occasions of heterodoxy, if not secularization. This was partly because those who engaged in them frequently became embroiled with their own more cautious and conservative co-religionaries, themselves often in positions of power. For those deeply involved in the crusade, anti-slavery was essential to Christianity, and any compromise was betrayal. The reticence or condemnation of the establishment would thus often drive the committed abolitionist to rebellion.

In fact, something of the same dialectic was at work within the churches as had originally helped to generate the unbelieving Enlightenment. From one Calvinist perspective, too great an identification with the cause could lead to the Papist error of seeking salvation in works. From the perspective of a committed abolitionist, anything less than full commitment was backsliding. The two views could barely coexist. But to the extent that the hyper-Augustinian view comes to be accepted as the definition of Christian faith, that it comes to be generally accepted that wholesale dedication to secular reform sits uneasily with this faith, to that degree those committed to the cause may feel forced outside orthodox Christianity by the very force of that commitment. The paradox is that a religious impulse and vision may sometimes drive people out of religious belief.

Something of these pressures can be seen in the career of the American abolitionist minister Henry Clarke Wright. "Christ is the Prince of moral reformers . . . as well as the Prince of Peace", he affirmed. But he was outraged by the establishment's complicity in slavery and its persecution of William Lloyd Garrison, and he began to evolve towards more heterodox views. He wrote a tract entitled: "The Bible, if Opposed to Self-Evident Truth, is Self-Evident Falsehood". And he declared, "In spirit and in practice, Voltaire was nearer the kingdom of heaven than the slaveholding clergy of America".[12]

We can see here a slide towards a mutually supportive opposition, in which hyper-Augustinian Christianity strengthens the moral credentials of unbelief; and this in turn deepens the suspicions of hyper-Augustinian believers about secular reform. Something like this polarization is evident in the French Enlightenment. And the slide towards it has been visible among socially committed Christians since—witness, for example, the China missionaries in our own day who ended up Communists.

Something very important happened in the nineteenth century when these reformers and others stepped outside the boundaries of belief. But it would be a mistake to think of this as part of a smooth, continuing, unidirectional move towards 'secularization'.[13] The initial impulse underlying reform was a deeply religious one, and something of this remains. It is not just that this can in a sense sacralize the secular cause. It is also that the religious impetus may be very much in evidence again in later waves of reform which are in some sense the inheritors of the early anti-slavery crusades; as we see with a leader like William Jennings Bryan late in the century and even more strikingly in the civil rights movement of the 1960's, in which ministers took such a leadership role, and whose major figure was Martin Luther King. Even in a much more secularized Britian, the leader of the Campaign for Nuclear Disarmament was until recently a monsignor. Of course the same secularizing slide occurred among some of the originally believing young people in the civil rights movement. But what should also be remarked is the recurrence of religious leadership in these causes that call for deep moral commitment.

22.2

Still, something important and irreversible did happen in the latter part of the nineteenth century with the rise of unbelief in the Anglo-Saxon countries. It was then that they moved from a horizon in which belief in God in some form was virtually unchallengeable to our present predicament in which theism is one option among others, in which moral sources are ontologically diverse. Latin societies had perhaps already made the break; in France, the Enlightenment and Revolution saw the crucial change. But in England and the United States, this came in the second half of the nineteenth century. In the earlier part of the century, the tide there moved back strongly towards orthodoxy—the evangelicals of the Clapham Sect were indeed part of that move—and Deism became less fashionable for a while. When the tide of orthodoxy ebbs again in the latter part of the century, it goes further than Deism. Atheism, or 'agnosticism', is now an option.

Examining this change as it occurs in England and America will help to clarify our present predicament. We can see here re-enacted something of the same reactions that underlay the unbelieving Enlightenment, as I described in Chapter 19. And as I said then, our understanding of the moral nature of these reactions is clouded by the widespread notion that the loss of religious belief flowed somehow as an inevitable consequence from the rise of 'science' or the development of the modern economy. Something like this story is what many unbelievers think, and this certainly reflects their outlook, as we shall see, but it doesn't really illuminate it.

Explanations of these two kinds are often given today. Belief either gave way before scientific rationality, or else it fell victim to industrialization and the development of our mobile, technological society. Or the two explanations may be combined. Leslie Stephen, one of the great pioneers of Victorian unbelief, held something like this view. He thought that a kind of scientific rationality must eventually win out. "If the race gradually accommodates itself to its environment, it should follow that the beliefs of the race gravitate towards that form in which the mind becomes an accurate reflection of the external universe". Religion must ultimately wither. Yet he also recognized that other factors were at play: "But great forces may work slowly; and it is only after many disturbances and long continued oscillations that the world is moved from one position of equilibrium to the other".[14]

In fact these two accounts, let us call them the scientistic and the institutional, are easy to combine, because they share certain premises. This comes clear when one probes them further.

It should be obvious that the institutional account is inadequate. This is not to say that the big changes in society haven't had important consequences for what we believe. How could they not? Industrialization, urbanization, concentration, the rise of technological society, what one could call 'secularization' in a narrow sense—i.e., not the whole change of outlook which we're trying to explain, but the shift which has taken so many facets of social life out of the purview of church institutions over the last centuries: all these have transformed our lives. They could not but change the way we see things. But what is questionable is the thesis that they are sufficient conditions of the loss of religious belief. Whether they have this result has to depend on what else is happening in the culture: the meaning of religious belief, the nature of the possible alternatives to it, the strains to which it is subject. The simple correlation behind the institutional account is perhaps already being refuted as these societal changes are spreading beyond the West and producing different consequences elsewhere.

What would make the simple correlation true? If religious faith were like some particulate illusory belief, whose erroneous nature was only masked by a certain set of practices, then it would collapse with the passing of these and their supersession by others; as perhaps certain particular beliefs about magical connections have. This then is the assumption which often underpins the institutional account. But this is just about exactly what is assumed in the scientistic account; and that is why they go well together. We might put it this way. Any institutional explanation of a change in outlook needs to be supplemented by some account of the cultural background. The simple scientistic premiss that religion withers in face of scientific rationality is what does duty for background to the institutional account. If this is incredible, we need something to put in its place.

But crude as it is, the scientistic thesis gets some colour of credibility from the actual drama which unfolded in the Victorian era. There was, indeed, a battle between Theology and Science, which the former lost. And many Victorians felt themselves forced, against their deepest longings, to abandon the faith. Our outlook on the relation between belief and unbelief in English-speaking countries is still marked by this founding battle and is in many ways obscured by our misunderstanding of it.

The battle over science was real enough. Tremendous strides were made in the last century in our understanding of geology, particularly of the immense age of the earth, and even more significantly, in our understanding of biology. In the latter case, the possibility of an explanation in depth, even a mechanistic one, opens up for the phenomena of life. A new sense grows of the nature we inhabit as immense in several dimensions: not only in space but also in time, and then further in the dimension of its micro-constitution. The new time perspective as well as the new direction in biology were combined in the explosive impact of the publication of Darwin's theory in 1859. This continues into our century with the somewhat similar impact of Freud's theories a half century later.

Darwin had devastating consequences for belief because of the intellectual structures in which faith had come to be cast, mainly but not only in Protestant countries. In the previous two centuries there had been an immense investment in the argument from design as a certain proof of the existence of the Deity. We saw how central this was for Deism, but it came to affect virtually all tendencies in the church. Even a hyper-orthodox figure like Cotton Mather could say early in the eighteenth century that "a BEING that must be *superior* to *Matter*, even the *Creator* and *Governor* of all *Matter*, is every where so conspicuous" that "*Atheism* is now for ever chased and hissed out of the World".[15] Darwin, by showing how there could be design without a Designer, blew a gaping hole in this whole way of reasoning.

Adding to the vulnerability had been the drift towards biblical literalism in Protestant churches and the crucial apologetic significance given to Christ's miracles as the proof of his credentials, which Locke and others had stressed. These and other factors too made certain findings of nineteenth-century science seem utterly contrary to Christian faith in a manner that hardly seems so evident today.

These were aggravating circumstances, but they don't provide the whole explanation for that certainty of collision between science and religion that was after all even stronger among the unbelievers. What made them so sure? Intellectually, it was some thesis of the kind I indicated with the word 'scientism', which one could formulate perhaps as the belief that the methods and procedures of natural science, as they were then being codified, suffice to establish all the truths we need to believe. And what made them believe this? Not conclusive reasons, because there aren't such. Nothing assures us that all the issues on which we have to formulate some creed are arbitrable in this fashion. Scientism itself requires a leap of faith.

What powers this faith is its own moral vision. Here we come closer to an undistorted picture of the great Victorian drama of unbelief. Not the simple replacement of non-science by science, but a new militant moral outlook growing out of the old and taking its place beside it as a fighting alternative.

This outlook is one of the major constituents of contemporary culture. Central to it is an "ethics of belief" (the title of an influential book of the late Victorian period).[16] One *ought* not to believe what one has insufficient evidence for. Two ideals flow together to give force to this principle. The first is that of self-responsible rational freedom, which I have frequently discussed in these pages. We have an obligation to make up our own minds on the evidence without bowing to any authority. The second is a kind of heroism of unbelief, the deep spiritual satisfaction of knowing that one has confronted the truth of things, however bleak and unconsoling.

This theme recurs constantly in the writings of the period. Samuel Putnam, a former minister, was ready to look at "the infinite abyss" in which humanity will ultimately vanish without a single "gleam of hope". Religion revolted him: "O the weakness, the falsehood of religion in view of this terrific destiny!" He would have no truck with this "cry of the child against the night", this "coward's sentimentality".[17] "The very moment man recognizes the evil of his lot, that very moment the grandeur of his being arises. For he can love; he can endure; he can perish without terror". And Victorians frequently spoke of the "manliness" required to face the bare truth.[18]

If one couldn't believe, then honesty required that one speak out. Here the agnostics showed their filiation to evangelical Christianity, from which many of them descended.[19] Charles Eliot Norton accused believers of committing "the great sin" of "insincere profession". And Thomas Huxley based his confidence for the future on this thought: "However bad our posterity may become, so long as they hold by the plain rule of not pretending to believe what they have no reason to believe because it may be to their advantage so to pretend, they will not have reached the lowest depths of immorality".[20]

An ethic of this kind calls for something like scientism, a sharp boundary between what one has good reason to give credence to and what goes beyond this limit. A universe in which the most important questions were truly surrounded with mystery would undercut this clear moral call. Ideally, one needs clear principles, like those of scientific method, which can divide the sheep from the goats among the beliefs which try to nestle in our minds. This utterly clear sense of the boundary between permissible and impermissible is another powerful mark of their evangelical legacy. Epistemology and moral fervour are mutually supporting.

The ethics of belief is linked through science to a third major force, the demand of benevolence. Just as in the case of the unbelieving Enlightenment, science was linked for the Victorians with progress in technology and hence in human betterment, a tradition which goes back to Bacon. Thus the turn from religion to science not only betokened a greater purity of spirit and greater manliness but also aligned them with the demands of human progress and welfare. Indeed, the courage to face the unhallowed universe could be thought of as a sacrifice which agnostics were willing to make for human betterment. In the words of an American unbeliever, their "grand philosophy" taught them "to lose sight of ourselves and our burdens in the onward march of the human race". And indeed, as we saw with Bentham and the unbelieving Enlightenment, many cherished the notion that facing the Godless universe liberated reserves of benevolence in us. In the words of another American, "the moment that one loses confidence in God, or immortality in the universe", one becomes "more self-reliant, more courageous, and the more solicitous to aid where only human aid is possible".[21]

Some of these themes come together in a moving statement in a letter by Thomas Huxley. He speaks about his immoral youth and later reform, and asks what brought this about: "The hope of immortality or of future reward?" This played no role:

No, I can tell you exactly what has been at work. Carlyle's *Sartor Resartus* led me to know that a deep sense of religion was compatible with the entire absence of theology. Secondly, science and her methods gave me a resting place independent of authority and tradition. Thirdly, love opened me up to a view of the sanctity of human nature and impressed me with a deep sense of responsibility.[22]

This is the powerful alternative morality that knocked such a breach in Victorian religion. It was not some supposedly logical incompatibility between science and faith but this imperious moral demand not to believe which led many Victorians to feel that they had to abandon, however sorrowfully, the faith of their fathers.

The illusion of scientism was strong not just because of the particular field on which this drama of unbelief was played out in the last century. It is also generated by the ethics of belief itself, as I have tried to show. This pushes us towards some or other variant of scientism and hence tends to obscure its own deeper motivations. These are still more or less on the surface in the works of the founders, and that is why it repays us to return to them. But for many of their twentieth-century followers, any recognition of the moral dimension has been utterly suppressed.

A striking example is the sociobiologist Edward O. Wilson. In his *On Human Nature*, the scientism has quite swallowed up the morality; indeed, we are offered a crassly reductive account of this latter. Natural selection wires in certain propensities to react, certain "gut feelings", which are "largely unconscious and irrational".

> Like everyone else, philosophers measure their personal emotional responses to various alternatives as though consulting a hidden oracle.
> That oracle resides in the deep emotional centers of the brain, most probably within the limbic system . . . Human emotional responses and the more general ethical practices based on them have been programmed to a substantial degree by nature selection over thousands of generations.[23]

Or again,

> Human behavior—like the deepest capacities for emotional response which drive and guide it—is the circuitous technique by which human genetic material has been and will be kept intact. Morality has no other demonstrable ultimate function.[24]

A reductive position of this sort is, of course, in a very deep sense untenable; that is, no one could actually live by it, and hence the best available account of what we actually live by cannot but be different. This surfaces towards the end of the book, where Wilson, with sublime indifference to inconsistency, gives us his moral vision. He confesses himself deeply moved by the "evolutionary epic", and particularly by the extraordinary story of man's rise through ingenuity and clear-sighted instrumental reason. What inspires respect for man is not just his success, but his having risen to this success by extending his knowledge and broadening his vision. "The true Promethean spirit of science means to liberate man by giving him knowledge and some measure of dominion over the physical environment".

This greater knowledge and vision in turn can transform his aspirations. He constructs an overall view linking his past trajectory to the future he aspires to. The scientific age, having cast off mankind's traditional myths,

> constructs the mythology of scientific materialism, guided by the corrective devices of the scientific method, addressed with precise and deliberately affective appeal to the deepest needs of human nature, and kept strong by the blind hopes that the journey on which we are now embarked will be farther and better than the one just completed.

To do this successfully, we have to break free from our particular, parochial allegiances and attachments; we have to be able to see ourselves as part of the big picture.

> Human nature bends us to the imperatives of selfishness and tribalism. But a more detached view of the long-range course of evolution should allow us to see beyond the blind decision-making process of natural selection and to envision the history and future of our genes against the background of the entire human species. A word already in use intuitively defines this view: nobility. Had the dinosaurs grasped the concept they might have survived. They might have been us.[25]

Wilson's 'nobility' incorporates some of the ideals I was describing above. It involves our having the courage to detach ourselves from the limited perspective, the flattering or consoling myth, to see the age-long struggle for survival as a whole, and then to be moved to go beyond narrow egoism to carry it on to greater heights. It is a kind of self-responsible freedom, a transcendence of particularity, which underlies our efficacy and which we should cultivate. The moral vision burns at the heart of the epistemology.

Wilson's 'nobility' also brings to the fore something else. What the Victorians called the 'manliness' which enables us to face the truth also has another side. We not only transcend our craven desire for comfort and assurance; we also rise beyond our narrow perspective and can take in the whole. We become so filled with awe of it that we can step outside our own limited concerns. There is something in the modern ethic of scientific reason which is continuous with earlier Stoicism and which resonates with themes already evoked by Descartes.[26] Bertrand Russell articulated this in our century. In "The Essence of Religion", he distinguishes two natures in human beings, one "particular, finite, self-centred; the other universal, infinite and impartial". The infinite part "shines impartially":

Distant ages and remote regions of space are as real to it as what is present and near. In thought, it rises above the life of the senses, seeking always what is general and open to all men. In desire and will, it aims simply at the good, without regarding the good as mine or yours. In feeling, it gives love to all, not only to those who further the purposes of the self. Unlike the finite self, it is impartial; its impartiality leads to truth in thought, justice in action, and universal love in feeling.[27]

On a more personal level, he says in a letter:

The endless battle within me makes me like what acts without inward battling: that is why I like necessity & the laws of motion & the doings of dead matter generally. I can't imagine God not full of conflict . . . So I prefer no God. Life seems to me essentially passion, conflict, rage; moments of peace are brief and destroy themselves. A God must be calm like Spinoza's, merely the course of nature. All this is autobiography, not philosophy.[28]

What came about for the Anglo-Saxon cultures in the Victorian crisis of faith was that for the first time an alternative moral horizon was available to belief in God. Henceforth, belief and unbelief exist in contrast and tension with each other, and both are made problematic by the fact that they exist in this field of alternatives, as I said earlier (Chapter 18). Neither can benefit from the unchallenged security which religious faith enjoyed in the earlier epoch. Moral sources can be sought not only in God but in the two new "frontiers": the dignity which attaches to our own powers (at first those of disengaged reason only, but now also including the creative imagination); and the depths of nature within and without.

But the scientific ethic of (un)belief is only one way in which these alternative sources can be drawn on. There was also the gamut of positions which descended from Romanticism. This could offer its own roads to unbelief, but those who travelled them were very critical of scientism. The movement out of theism was more gradual here, passing through a number of intermediate positions, and in some cases not quite consummated. Ralph Waldo Emerson hovered on the borders where theism, pantheism, and non-theism all meet.

But when people did move out along these paths, what actuated them was not so much the difficulties with science, though that also played a role in this period, but more something inherent to the notion of nature as a source which Romanticism had bequeathed to them (often, as in the cases of Emerson and Arnold, through the influence of Coleridge). Goethe gave the most influential articulation to this. It was the sense that the ideal of expressive integrity fitted better with the 'pagan' outlook of the ancients than with the transcendent aspirations of Christianity. The identification of the Greeks with harmonious unity was a major theme of the German Romantics. And Arnold took up something of the same idea in opposing 'Hebraism' and 'Hellenism'. The former impels us to moral perfection; but the latter has given us the idea of perfection as the "harmonious expansion of *all* the powers which make the beauty and worth of human nature".[29] We need both to be full beings.

Leslie Stephen was a paradigm case of one who took the scientistic road to unbelief. Matthew Arnold, however, travelled at least part of the way along a Goethean path. He went not without regret. As "the Sea of Faith" ebbs, it leaves only

> Its melancholy, long, withdrawing roar,
> Retreating, to the breath
> Of the night wind, down the vast edges drear
> And naked shingles of the world.[30]

And there is some question whether he went all the way. He still speaks of God as "the power not ourselves that makes for righteousness", and prayer as an "energy of aspiration".[31] But he went as far as he did, impelled not by the "ethics of belief" so much as by the felt necessity to find a better, more serviceable religion for a democratic age. In other words, he too was looking for moral sources for the demands, both narrowly moral and for a wider perfection, that modernity makes on us. And he found these sources, notoriously, in culture.

Culture, for Arnold, unites reason with the "moral and social passion for doing good". It is "reason involving the whole personality", as Lionel Trilling formulates his doctrines.[32] Culture is what can replace religion, and must do so if the decline of belief is not to have impoverishing consequences.

Arnold is exploring here a third path, neither faith in God of a normally recognized kind nor scientistic agnosticism. It is an aspiration towards wholeness, towards a fulness of joy where desire is fused with our sense of the deepest significance. Its source is the Romantic ideal of self-completion through art. One way of drawing the map of possible moral sources in our day is to see it as divided between these three domains. These are the alternatives which are usually in tension, influencing each other and making each other problematic. But great power accrues to a philosophy which can claim plausibly to unite two of the three; this has been one reason for the immense drawing power of Marxism over the last century. In one interpretation at least, it seems to combine scientistic materialism with the aspiration to expressive wholeness.[33] This mixture exercises a tremendous attraction.

22.3

I want to return now to the question which sent me off into the long excursus on the nineteenth century and the crisis of faith: What underlies our sense of historical exceptionalism, that we recognize and can meet very stringent demands of universal justice and benevolence? Not surprisingly, the possible answers to this question can be at least loosely fitted onto the tripartite "map" of moral sources which we have inherited from the nineteenth century.

The original root of the demand that we seek universal justice and well-being is of course our Judaeo-Christian religious tradition. In broad terms, this is obvious, and I have been tracing some of the more detailed connections in the preceding pages. The orthodox Christian understanding of this universal concern is *agapē*, or 'charity'; and the answer to the question of what makes it possible is grace. This may not be linked to any exceptionalist view of a society, since nothing guarantees that whole societies will be transformed by grace. Christianity has always had a very ambivalent relationship to the societies in which it has existed, and the very concept of Christendom is fraught with theological tension.[34]

But when the commitment to universal concern takes on non-theistic definition, something else has to play the role of grace. This question is frequently occluded, because of the general reluctance of the unbelieving Enlightenment to raise the entire issue about moral sources. But it is often implicitly addressed. Exceptionalist self-portraits all have to contain an implicit answer to this question, indicating what they think in fact is making it possible for us to be more 'civilized' (equal, democratic, concerned, etc.) than others have been. What have these answers been?

I have already discussed one in connection with the Enlightenment, the belief that as we achieve the fulness of disengaged reason and detach ourselves from superstitions and parochial attachments, we should as a matter of course be moved to benefit mankind. This seems to be taken for granted by Bentham in his own case in the cri de coeur I quoted earlier.[35] And we see a pervasive belief in our scientific culture that scientific honesty and detachment itself inclines one to fairness and beneficence in dealing with people. Freud in his own way seems to have been quite confident too of his own good intentions.[36] Something stronger seemed to come to the surface among the pioneer agnostics of the nineteenth century: the idea that the step beyond the comfortable world of illusion, the manly confronting of the universe in its vast indifference, itself frees us from our petty egoism to devote ourselves to the universal welfare. Perhaps one can come closest to a sense of what is involved here by looking at a twentieth-century work of literature like Albert Camus's *La Peste*, where the hero, Dr. Rieux, embodies the link between the utter dissolution of all the illusions of religious belief and a dogged unshakeable commitment to relieve human suffering.

Dostoyevsky, in a remarkable passage in *A Raw Youth*, also gives us a sense of some such connection. Versilov presents the vision of a day when humans will awake and find that they are utterly alone in the universe, that there is no God or immortality, that they have only themselves. And the result will be such a degree of mutual tenderness and care that the world will be transformed into a paradise.[37]

But here we are already entering the terrain of another family of answers, those which descend from Rousseau. Rousseau built on another great theme of eighteenth-century thought, that of sympathy. The 'natural' human being has sympathy of an animal kind; is troubled at the sight of suffering and moved to help. In society, this can all too easily be stifled.[38] But to the extent that human beings become social and rational in an undistorted way, both pity and self-love are transmuted into conscience, and this, far from being a harsh voice of duty opposed to feeling, ideally speaks to their hearts and moves them to benevolence.[39]

Rousseau suggested a picture of human nature characterized by a great fund of benevolence, whose sources were as natural and spontaneous in us as any of our normal desires. It is nothing but the normal, undistorted transmutation by reason of something which is instinctive in our animal nature. This can be stifled by the depraved kind of reason, but it is there like a deep source waiting to be tapped. The substitute for grace is the inner impulse of nature.

This idea was taken up in a host of different forms. It is continued in one way by Romantic theories of nature as a source, in the picture of a restored being whose spontaneous feelings, even sensual desires have become infused with benevolence, like those "drunk with fire" who enter the sanctuary of Joy in Schiller's early poem or the Empedocles figure of Hölderlin's early drafts.[40] And the idea continues right up to the present time, its latest, most spectacular manifestation being in the student revolts of 1968 and in a more diffuse way, in the 1960's "flower generation" as a whole.

But Kant also found a basis for the idea of a good will within us, one that turned altogether away from natural desires to our status as rational agents and the awe we cannot but experience before the demands that this lays on us. Here we return to the Enlightenment view that it is the development of reason which makes this will effective; it is now no longer instrumental rationality which transforms us, however, but rather the demands of universality.

And thus as an alternative to the naturalist faith in scientific reason, we have a family of views in the late eighteenth century which see a great source of benevolence within us, either in our natural desires or in our noumenal being—or perhaps also in a fashion which cannot be distributed between these alternatives. We have only to think of the Temple of Sarastro in Mozart's *Magic Flute*. Here is a source of goodness, of benevolent will, radiating out from undistorted human nature. "In diesen heiligen Hallen", discord and hatred give way to forgiveness and love. The music convinces us where the words never could.

All of these possible substitutes for grace—the clear vision of scientific reason, the Rousseauian or Romantic inner impulse of nature, the Kantian good will, Sarastrian goodness—have helped to ground a confidence that we can meet the demands of universal benevolence. In the actual life of modern culture, they have not been treated as alternatives to or seen as incompatible with religious faith. Nineteenth-century exceptionalist views in the English-speaking world sometimes combined virtually all of them: there was less perhaps of the Rousseauian-Romantic, but there was frequently a combination of Christian faith with a sense of the progress of modern society in enlightened and rational control. This in turn could consist with a Kantian or Sarastrian sense that inner sources of benevolence have been released by enlightened education. The resulting amalgam, occurring in different proportions at different times, gives one something of the mood which has surrounded the great endeavours of human improvement in English-speaking societies in the last two centuries: from temperance campaigns through educational reforms, to the great efforts at world reconstruction which followed the two world wars. Rather different, 'lay' mixtures were in evidence in France, with a heavier reliance on the Kantian and Sarastrian, and even in some cases, a peculiarly French scientistic transposition of Romantic holism, which descends in the tradition from Saint-Simon through Comte to Durkheim and beyond.

Just as in the case of our conceptions of the good, our ideas about our moral motivation show a confusing mixture of fusion, mutual influence, and rivalry among the different sources. Belief and unbelief have been complexly related to each other. It is not just that the secular replacements issue historically from the Christian notion of grace; they in turn have influenced it. Modern notions of *agapē* have been affected by the ideal of austere and impartial beneficence which emerges from disengaged reason. This was already evident in Hutcheson and becomes salient in Christian utilitariansim. But they have also been transformed by Romantic conceptions of spontaneous feeling, of a goodness which flows from inner nature. At the same time, this influence has not been uncontested. Proponents of different streams in Christian spirituality have bitterly combated what they see as foreign intrusions. The hyper-Augustinian cast of thought retains its suspicion of unredeemed nature and of unreserved commitment to activist reform. And then the different influences, Romantic and Enlightenment, clash within Christian churches as well as everywhere else in the culture.

On top of that, these different pictures of grace and its substitutes are rivals. We can take our stand in one in order to reject the others. Because each of them is vulnerable, as we shall see later, because each can be brought to crisis, a complex interplay arises in which each can be at some moment strengthened by the weakness exposed in the others. The belief in a unilinear process called 'secularization' is the belief that the crisis only affects religious beliefs, and that the invariable beneficiaries are the secular ones. But this is not an adequate view of our situation.

22.4

I have been mapping our moral landscape as it emerges from the nineteenth century and have been taking as my thread the typically modern moral demands and the moral sources which feed them. But there is another major issue, which intruded towards the end, and that is the battle between the Enlightenment and Romanticism as it continues to develop. This battle is still going on throughout our culture, as the struggle between the technologically and the ecologically oriented today attests. The two strands have been at odds from the beginning; expressive theories emerge partly in criticism of the one-dimensionality of instrumental reason. But they have also come in curious ways to coexist within our culture. In order to understand this better, we should look closer at the impact and then at the successive transformations of Romantic expressivism.

Romantic expressivism arises in protest against the Enlightenment ideal of disengaged, instrumental reason and the forms of moral and social life that flow from this: a one-dimensional hedonism and atomism. The protest continues throughout the nineteenth century in different forms, and it becomes ever more relevant as society is transformed by capitalist industrialism in a more and more atomist and instrumental direction. The charge against this way of being is that it fragments human life: dividing it into disconnected departments, like reason and feeling; dividing us from nature; dividing us from each other. Schiller made the charge in the sixth of his *Aesthetic Letters;* we find it taken up again by Arnold.[41] It is also accused of reducing or occluding meaning: life is seen one-dimensionally as the pursuit of homogeneous pleasure; no goal stands out as being of higher significance.

But there was a third line of criticism, more explicitly political, that atomism—that is, a condition in which everyone defines his or her purposes in individual terms and only cleaves to society on instrumental grounds—

undermines the very basis of cohesion which a free, participatory society needs to maintain itself. Again, this point was given influential formulation in Schiller's sixth *Letter*. But it was taken up on a more sophisticated level by Tocqueville, who connected it to the whole tradition of thought on republican regimes. Tocqueville pursues the old notion that a too great interest in self-enrichment is a danger for public liberty, which demands that we orient ourselves to public life instead of being absorbed by a preoccupation with individual welfare, which we pursue by merely instrumental reason.

A love of liberty is essential to citizens, he writes:

> Seule elle est capable de les arracher au culte de l'argent et aux petits tracas journaliers de leurs affaires particulières pour leur faire apercevoir et sentir à tout moment la patrie au-dessus et à côté d'eux; seule elle substitue de temps à autre à l'amour du bien-être des passions plus énergiques et plus hautes, fournit à l'ambition des objets plus grands que l'acquisition des richesses.

> Freedom alone is capable of lifting men's minds above mere mammon worship and the petty personal worries which crop up in the course of everyday life, and of making them aware at every moment that they belong each and all to a vaster entity, above and around them—their native land. It alone replaces at certain critical moments their natural love of material welfare by a loftier, more virile ideal; offers other objectives than that of getting rich.[42]

From Schiller, from Tocqueville, from Humboldt also, and from Marx in his own way, Romanticism was part source of an important range of alternative political visions, critical of the instrumentalist, bureaucratic, and industrial society which was growing in the West. One line of these, through Tocqueville, was grafted onto the civic humanist tradition and has helped keep it in contention right into the twentieth century.

But another fruit of Romanticism in modern politics is nationalism. Perhaps it is necessary to reiterate here that to say this is not to offer a causal explanation. If we sought to explain nationalism, we would have to take account of the functional requirements of new societies which had cut loose from the old notions of hierarchical order, had seen the traditional local communities eroded, and needed to find a new basis of cohesion among supposedly free and equal individuals. Or we would have to look at the same factors from another angle, that of the aspirations of bourgeois elites or intellectuals to build a new anti-hierarchial political entity. Factors of this kind can help explain why nationalism spread and became a powerful force in European civilization in the nineteenth century. But they don't explain the peculiar features of nationalism as a moral and political outlook. These have their roots first in Rousseau's notion that the locus of sovereignty must be a people, that is, an entity constituted by a common purpose or identity, something more than a mere "aggregation".[43] This root idea is developed further in Herder's conception of a *Volk*, the notion that each people has its own way of being, thinking, and feeling, to which it ought to be true; that each has a right and a duty to realize its own way and not to have an alien one imposed on it.[44]

In the first wave of modern nations like the United States, France, and in its own peculiar way Britain, all built prior to Herderian nationalism, the basis of cohesion was the political nation and a certain ideal of citizenship. But in the next wave of catch-up, reactive nation-building, the dominant principle became language, in European societies at any rate. Language is the obvious basis for a theory of nationalism founded on the expressivist notion of the special character of each people, language conceived in Herderian fashion, that is, in terms of an 'expressive' theory.[45] It is a concept which roots the plurality of states in the nature of things, but not in a natural order conceived in the old hierarchical mode. It claims to find the principle of a people's identity—what makes it more than an aggregation—as something already given, not arbitrarily determined, but rooted in its being and past; while at the same time this principle is no external allegiance but something constitutive of the people's autonomous humanity, something essential to being human. Language is obviously a prime candidate for this constitutive, essence-defining role, especially in a Herderian perspective. That is why it can serve to bring cohesion to modern societies. But to understand just how it is meant to bring this cohesion, we have to see it in expressivist terms.

This brings us to one of the ways in which the Enlightenment and expressivist strands in modern culture can be brought to co-exist. The uglier side of modern nationalism frequently combines a chauvinistic appeal to the national personality or will with a drive to power which justifies recourse to the most effective industrial and military means. The extreme case of this repulsive phenomenon was Nazi Germany. Here was a regime brought to power partly by appeals to expressive integrity against instrumental reason. It to some degree emerged out of *Wandervögel* youth groups, and it glorified sturdy peasants. Its practice was a ruthless application of instrumental reason, which broke even the bounds of the thinkable as hitherto defined. This combination unfortunately works. Nationalism in its chauvinist mode can destroy its original justification in Herderian expressivism.

Like other offshoots of Romantic expressivism, nationalism also inseparably involves certain narrations, often wildly fictitious and anachronistic, sometimes approaching mystification when rather arbitrary acts of political construction are shrouded in a bogus antiquity. But in one way or another, a nation in order to have an identity requires and develops a certain picture of its history, genesis, development—its sufferings and its achievements. These stories envelop us and form our pictures of ourselves and our past, more than we are usually aware. This is one extremely important way in which expressivism has shaped our world.[46]

But the Romantic-expressive cast of thought and sensibility, whether in politics, art, or theories of culture, or just as raw protest against instrumental society, undergoes an important transformation in the nineteenth century. We can best trace this by following two related changes.

1. The first was in the picture of nature. The Romantics developed an expressive view of nature, sometimes seen as a great current of life running through everything, and emerging also in the impulses we feel within. As we see it apostrophized by Schiller as Joy or theorized by Schelling as Spirit, this picture owed a great deal to the traditional notion of a providential order. Indeed, it managed to reintegrate something of the older notion of a meaningful order. Schelling and his contemporaries drew on neo-Platonic sources, on Ficino, on Renaissance theories of correspondence. Schelling acknowledges his affinity with Giordano Bruno. But this picture was transposed by expressivism and the new idea of the creative imagination.

Thus in Schelling's *Naturphilosophie,* different natural phenomena correspond to different levels of realization of spirit in nature. Nature is "visible Spirit".[47] This certainly resembles the old neo-Platonic theories of the Renaissance, where the physical reality around us is also the embodiment of the Ideas. What has changed is the very notion of embodiment. It is no longer the manifestation in the flux of an impersonal Form; it is rather understood on the model of the self-realization of a subject, completing and defining itself in the process of self-manifestation. The order of nature has gone through a subjectivist twist. It follows that our access to it essentially turns on our own powers of expressive self-definition, the artistic imagination as the early Schelling conceives it; or 'reason' in the peculiar sense Hegel gives this term.

But in the nineteenth century, this vision of cosmic order began to erode just as its predecessors had. Partly this was due, no doubt, to the development of natural science, which presented a universe much vaster and more bewildering in space, time, and evolution than the earlier orders had envisaged and rationalized. And to this we must add the developments in biology in the latter half of the century, which introduced natural science into the very depths of inner nature that the Romantics had originally made part of the European self-consciousness. The result for us has been a split-screen vision of nature. On one side is the vast universe which scientific discovery continually reveals, huge and in some ways baffling, stretching far beyond our imaginative powers in both the gigantic and the minuscule; indifferent to us and strangely other, though full of unexpected beauty and inspiring awe. On the other side is the nature whose impulse we feel within, with which we can feel ourselves out of alignment and with which we can aspire to be in attunement. How these two are to be related is deeply problematical. This is one respect in which our cultural predicament is utterly different from what existed before the eighteenth century, where the scientific explanation of the natural order was closely aligned with its moral meaning, as we see both with Plato and with the Deist conceptions of order. For us, the two have drifted apart, and it is not clear how we can hope to relate them.

One way to deal with the problem is simply to suppress one of these terms as irrelevant or illusory. This is the response of disengaged naturalism, which recognizes only the order of scientific explanation. But if we don't take this quick way with it, we can recognize an area of puzzlement and uncertainty in modern culture. The different ways of meeting this puzzlement have had a lot to do with our changing understanding of the creative imagination and its role in our moral life.

But for those who retained a sense of the inner impulse of nature, its meaning began to change. This came partly from the scientific developments. And partly too, it was the continuing force of what I called above the anti-Panglossian objection to all notions of providential order, that they made the structure of all things a bit too tidy and harmonious for our experience. There were other factors as well, which I will discuss in the next chapter.

The shift finds one of its expressions in the philosophy of Schopenhauer. For those who went through this change, the great current of nature to which we belong is no longer seen as something comprehensible, familiar, closely related to the self, and benign and comes more and more to be seen as vast, unfathomable, alien, and amoral, until we get reflections like those of Conrad's narrator Marlowe in *Heart of Darkness,* as he sees the natives dancing on the shores of the river:

> The earth seemed unearthly . . . and the men were—No, they were not inhuman. Well, you know, that was the worst of it,—this suspicion of their not being inhuman. It would come slowly on one. They howled and leaped, and spun, and made horrid faces; but what thrilled you was just the thought of their humanity—like yours—the thought of your remote kinship with this wild and passionate uproar. Ugly. Yes, it was ugly enough; but if you were man enough you would admit to yourself that there was in you just the faintest trace of a response to the terrible frankness of that noise, a dim suspicion of there being a meaning in it which you—you so remote from the night of first ages—could comprehend. And why not? . . . What was there after all? Joy, fear, sorrow, devotion, valour, rage—who can tell?—but truth—truth stripped of its cloak of time.[48]

2. The second change is obviously related. In its reflections in civic humanist thought and nationalism, in Arnold's theory of culture, Romantic expressivism was seen as closely interwoven with the moral aspirations I discussed above: as their major source of support or as their normal complement. But the very notion of fulfilment through art contained, as we have seen, the seeds of a possible breach. This breach came about for influential strands of our culture in the nineteenth century, and we are still living with the consquences. In order to see this, we have to trace the epiphanies of the creative imagination over this period.

23

VISIONS OF THE
POST-ROMANTIC AGE

23.1

The idea of the creative imagination, as it sprang up in the Romantic era, is still central to modern culture. The conception is still alive among us of art—of literature, in the first place, and especially of poetry—as a creation which reveals, or as a revelation which at the same time defines and completes what it makes manifest.

There are strong continuities from the Romantic period, through the Symbolists and many strands of what was loosely called 'modernism', right up to the present day. What remains central is the notion of the work of art as issuing from or realizing an 'epiphany', to use one of Joyce's words in a somewhat wider sense than his. What I want to capture with this term is just this notion of a work of art as the locus of a manifestation which brings us into the presence of something which is otherwise inaccessible, and which is of the highest moral or spiritual significance; a manifestation, moreover, which also defines or completes something, even as it reveals.

A work of this kind is not to be understood simply as mimesis, even though it may involve a descriptive component. In fact there are two different ways in which a work can bring about what I'm calling an epiphany, and the balance over the last century has shifted from one to the other. In the first, which dominated with the Romantics, the work does portray something—unspoilt nature, human emotion—but in such a way as to show some greater spiritual reality or significance shining through it. The poetry of Wordsworth or the paintings of Constable and Friedrich exemplify this pattern. In the second, which is dominant in the twentieth century, it may no longer be clear what the work portrays or whether it portrays anything at all; the locus of epiphany has shifted to within the work itself. Much modernist poetry and non-representational visual art is of this kind.

But even with the first pattern, which I will call epiphanies of being, a purely mimetic understanding of the work is no longer enough. Because the aim is not just to portray but to transfigure through the representation, to render the object "translucent". And so here too, the epiphany can only be brought about through the work, which remains a 'symbol' in the Romantic sense of that term. That is, we can't understand what it is qua epiphany by pointing to some independently available object described or referent. What the work reveals has to be read in it. Nor can it be adequately explained in terms of the author's intentions, because even if we think of these as definitive of a work's meaning, they themselves are properly revealed only in the work. And that being so, the work *must* be understood independently of whatever intentions the author has formulated in relation to it. As Oscar Wilde put it, "When the work is finished it has, as it were, an independent life of its own, and may deliver a message far other than that which was put into its lips to say".[1] No explication or paraphrase can do it justice. Its meaning must be found in itself. We might say that it exists in and for itself, "self-begotten", to use an expression from Yeats.[2]

Another expression which is often used here is 'auto-telic'. But this term is properly applied only to the second pattern I described above, and perhaps only to an extreme variant at that. An influential strand of thought from the Symbolists on has conceived of the work not as an epiphany of being, either of nature or of a spiritual reality beyond nature. They have tried to detach it from all relation to what is beyond it and yet, paradoxically, to retain the epiphanic quality. The work remains the locus of revelation, and of something of ultimate significance, but it is also utterly self-contained and self-sufficient. Mallarmé, who is one of the paradigm figures of this line of thought, liked to speak (following, he thought, Hegel) of 'nothingness': "After I found nothingness I found beauty".[3]

This is certainly one of the possibilities, extreme and in some ways baffling as it is, which has been opened up by modern epiphanic art. It has remained an important part of modern culture, and it reflects a rejection of the world and of being which I will discuss below. But it would be a mistake to confound the genus with the species. There are a host of other writers, from Wordsworth to Yeats and beyond, who have produced works which are not 'auto-telic' in this stringent Mallarméan sense, but which strive towards an epiphany.[4]

The terms which were coined in the Romantic era still apply to the epiphanic art of the twentieth century. That time developed a rich organic language to talk about the organic unity of the work of art, about the process of artistic creation—Coleridge likened it, indeed saw it as related to the process of growth in nature—and, by extension, to talk about undistorted, fulfilled human life, as against the cramping and fragmenting categories of mechanism. The biological images of early expressivism, as we see very clearly with Herder, for instance, were directed against the dualism of mind and body, of reason and sensibility. For Schiller, beauty brings form and matter into a perfect unity. 'Play', through which we aim at beauty, unites form and life within us; and the object of true beauty exhibits a perfect fusion of its content and its form. There is nothing in its content which is irrelevant to its form; and the form reciprocally is not separable from this embodiment, is not something which could be expressed integrally elsewhere.

There is something paradoxical here. 'Form' for Schiller is linked to the universal. The term is partly used to designate the moral drive in us, which tries to give universally valid form to our lives; and partly it derives from the notion of a concept, which is a universal term in contrast to its particular instantiations. Morality and general concepts are closely linked in Schiller, because he is very much influenced by Kant. And yet in the work of art, the universal term is inseparable from, is identified with, its instantiation. A beautiful object is a particular which carries universal import.[5]

Categories of this kind continue to be used for epiphanic art. A work manifests something, has significance, and yet this is somehow inseparable from its embodiment—or at least inseparability is the condition that art aspires to. It was said of Pater, "His ideal is the kind of art where thought and its sensible embodiment are completely fused". As Wilde put it, "Like Aristotle, like Goethe after he had read Kant, we desire the concrete, and nothing but the concrete can satisfy us". In Art, "the body is the soul".[6] This inseparability, this particularity with universal significance, is also conveyed in Yeats's images of the tree and the dancer. Something like Schiller's aspiration to a condition beyond the forceful imposition of form on matter, and a fusion of the two in beauty, is still alive in these lines:

> Labour is blossoming or dancing where
> The body is not bruised to pleasure soul,
> Nor beauty born out of its own despair,
> Nor blear-eyed wisdom out of midnight oil.
> O chestnut tree, great-rooted blossomer,
> Are you the leaf, the blossom, or the bole?
> O body swayed to music, O brightening glance,
> How can we know the dancer from the dance?[7]

This ideal of fusion is what underlies the Romantic idea of the symbol as the translucence of the eternal in the temporal, in Coleridge's terms. The symbol remains central to epiphanic art, and not only in the school which was called 'Symbolist'. Carlyle spoke of the symbol as "an embodiment and revelation of the infinite". Yeats took up the Romantic contrast of symbol with allegory: "A symbol is indeed the only possible expression of some invisible essence, a transparent lamp about a spiritual flame; while allegory is one of many possible representations of an embodied thing or a familiar principle . . . : the one is a revelation, the other an amusement".[8] The "image" that Pound and his generation sought partakes of the same nature. The image is a concrete manifestation; it is not meant to be understood as discourse about something. Music, the clearly non-discursive, non-representative art, is the model. Symbolists and Imagists, like Pater, think that all art should aspire to the condition of music.[9]

Quite understandably, the Romantic image of the poet as a seer continues, explicitly in Baudelaire, but implicitly in the quality of admiration and awe which surround the makers of epiphanies up to our day. There is a kind of piety which still surrounds art and artists in our time, which comes from the sense that what they reveal has great moral and spiritual significance; that in it lies the key to a certain depth, or fulness, or seriousness, or intensity of life, or to a certain wholeness. I have to use a string of alternatives here, because this significance is very differently conceived, and often—for reasons which have to do with the very nature of epiphanic art and which I will discuss below—is not clearly conceived at all. But for many of our contemporaries art has taken something like the place of religion.

In contrast to the fulness of epiphany is the sense of the world around us, as we ordinarily experience it, as out of joint, dead, or forsaken. The world "in disconnection dead and spiritless",[10] or the world as seen through Blake's vegetative eye, has some affinity with the Waste Land of Eliot. There is a continuing thread here, a critique of the mechanistic and instrumental, as a way of seeing, and as a way of living, and then as the very principle of our social existence, which runs through an immense variety of different articulations, interpretations, and suggested remedies. An allegiance to epiphanic art has almost invariably been accompanied by a strong hostility to the developing commercial-industrial-capitalist society, from Schiller to Marx to Marcuse and Adorno; from Blake to Baudelaire to Pound and Eliot.

But just speaking of the moral significance of epiphanic art leaves an important ambiguity unexamined. The relation to morality of the wholeness or intensity it promises is very problematic. Already Schiller, in his famous *Letters on the Aesthetic Education of Man,* seems to offer two incompatible views of the relation of beauty to morality. On one view, play and the beauty it creates is an aid to the moral will. This will defines the content of human perfection, and beauty is an auxiliary, even though an indispensable one, in attaining this.[11] But another view is constantly suggested through the work, and occasionally formulated: play and the aesthetic offer a higher fulfilment than the merely moral, because the moral only realizes one side of us, form and not matter, while beauty can make us whole, give us harmony and freedom.[12]

Morality here is understood in the terms of the eighteenth century, where justice and benevolence, and the control of the desires by reason, constitute its essence. The new thought emerging in Schiller's text is that beauty might offer us a higher goal. At least on Schiller's version this would incorporate morality and be fully compatible with it. The harmonized, free being who plays would spontaneously want to be good in the accepted senses; he would just have something more than the stern follower of duty. But the worrisome possibility is now open that this higher fulfilment might take us outside the received morality; it might lead us to turn aside from it, as Pater feared;[13] or it might even demand that we repudiate it, as Nietzsche affirms of the ethic of benevolence.

The germ was there in the new aesthetic which developed in the eighteenth century. It defined the beautiful in terms of a certain kind of feeling or subjective reaction. Kant gave a new and powerful articulation to this in his third critique. The beautiful was defined in terms of a certain kind of pleasure. It is of the essence of this, following Shaftesbury, that it be 'disinterested'. What the object of beauty gives us is something quite distinct either from utilitarian satisfactions or from the fulfilment of moral demands.[14] The basis is there for a declaration of independence of the beautiful relative to the good.

But Kant doesn't take this step. The beautiful turns out to be another way that we are in touch with the supersensible in us. It is a "symbol of the morally good".[15] It is thus related and firmly subordinated to our moral destiny. He originates the first of the two theories I discerned above in Schiller's work. It took the expressivism of the Romantic period to give a higher normative significance to the aesthetic and open the way for a full-scale challenge to the primacy of morality. A line from Wilde shows how the Kantian doctrine has been transmuted into modern counter-morality: "All the arts are immoral except those baser forms of sensual or didactic art that seek to excite to action of evil or good".[16]

Thus a view has come down to us from the Romantics which portrays the artist as one who offers epiphanies where something of great moral or spiritual significance becomes manifest—and what is conveyed by this last disjunction is just the possibility that what is revealed lies beyond and against what we normally understand as morality. The artist is an exceptional being, open to a rare vision; the poet is a person of exceptional sensibility. This was a commonplace among the Romantics.

But this also opens the artist to exceptional suffering. In part this was thought to lie in the very fact of a rare sensibility, which must open one to great suffering as well as great joy. But in part it comes from the idea that the artist's vocation forces him or her to forgo the ordinary satisfactions of life in the world, to forgo successful action and fulfilled relationships. This is the predicament which D. H. Lawrence in a comment on Beethoven's letters called "the crucifixion into isolate individuality".[17]

Being cut off from ordinary fulfilments can also mean being cut off from other people, on the margins of society, misunderstood, despised. This has been a recurring picture of the fate of the artist in the last two centuries, whether presented in forms of maudlin self-pity, as a successor to Wertherian Weltschmerz, or seen steadily and without self-dramatization as an inescapable predicament.

The opposition of the visionary artist and the blind, or "philistine", "bourgeois" society brings together this vision of an exceptional fate and the hostility to commercial capitalist civilization. United to a historical narrative of advancing discovery, it can yield the idea or myth of the avant-garde. Some are destined to move ahead of the huge advancing column, to strike out on their own. Their work is not, cannot be understood in their time. But much later, the rest will catch up, and the original few will be recognized and celebrated after death.

This image expresses the opposition between artist and society—his exclusion. But it also allows for the connection, one might also say the collusion between them. For it contains the idea that the others catch up—to where the earlier trail-blazers were, that is; a new wave will have since gone beyond the general comprehension and been misunderstood in its turn. Moreover, once this image becomes generally accepted; once it becomes not just the self-image of the misunderstood artist, but the socially accredited stereotype, the collusion between bourgeois and artist finds a language.

Students of nineteenth-century "Bohemia" in Paris have remarked how ambivalent the relations were between the bourgeois world and the demi-monde of the artist.[18] It was not just that some later well-established bourgeois passed a period of their youth in "Bohemia". It was also that it fed the bourgeois imagination, as the success of a host of works, including Murger's novel and Puccini's opera, attests.[19] Even those who operate fully within commercial civilization, who run their lives by disengaged, instrumental reason, want to have some part in the epiphanies of the creative imagination. These must be confined; they cannot be allowed to break out and realize their full, often anti-moral and usually anti-instrumental, intent. But they must be there.

Nor should this be surprising. Only rather exceptional and austere souls can live entirely by the moral sources of disengaged reason. The conforming mass of nineteenth-century middle-class society certainly didn't try. They lived mostly by their religion. And when this failed, or began itself to be transformed by Romanticism or the cult of sentiment, they also turned to the new sources of spiritual nourishment. Hence this ambivalence towards a world and works which were a negation of and sometimes a threat to their values, but that many of them also saw as a preserve, which protected and intensified many of the things which gave life meaning.

The opposition was necessary, because the life forms of expressive fulfilment and instrumental-rational discipline were partly *defined* in contrast to each other. Many people couldn't confine themselves to one side. As Jerrold Seigel[20] shows, the ambivalence was also to be found in Bohemia, where many writers and artists dreamed of eventual recognition by the bourgeois world, and others (or some of the same) submitted to the most demanding discipline in the name of their art.

The paradox and irony is that the popular image of "La Bohème" plays down this serious side. Not the dedicated creators of works, but "those for whom art meant living the life"[21] entered the stereotype popular in "straight" society: amateurs like Rodolphe, destined to return to the bourgeois world after his youthful wanderings end with the death of Mimi. The identification of art with feeling and sentiment becomes the popular bourgeois view,[22] in contrast to the major creative figures of the Romantic period and after. Not surprisingly, the fashionable image screened out that current in Bohemia which was sympathetic to the political challenge to the established order, and which contributed its part to the revolutionary floods of 1848 and 1871.

The ambivalent relationship continues up to our day, and has become in the context of the contemporary mass media and art market an almost open collusion between supposedly revolutionary artists or performers and the mass public. The decent distance in the nineteenth-century relation between bourgeois and Bohemia depended on each side preserving its integrity; it required that the bourgeois world stand by its values and that the genuine avant-garde stay clear of the Murger-Puccini game of playing up to the bourgeois world. But now that free self-expression and polymorphous perversity offer ideas for advertising slogans and thus help to turn the wheels of commerce, and the media, as the late Andy Warhol put it, can make anyone a celebrity for a quarter of an hour, the distance is hard to maintain. When the collusion becomes so close, a certain corruption has set in.

23.2

I have been arguing that a certain understanding of art has run continuously through the modern world since the Romantic era. It is the conception I've been calling epiphanic, and it encompasses not only an aesthetic of the work of art but also a view about its spiritual significance and about the nature and situation of the artist. It is a view not only about art but about the place of art in life, and its relation to morality. It is in fact an exaltation of art; for this becomes the crucial locus of what I have been calling moral sources. Realizing an epiphany is a paradigm case of what I called recovering contact with a moral source. The epiphany is our achieving contact with something, where this contact either fosters and/or itself constitutes a spiritually significant fulfilment or wholeness.

Nor is this view of art the property of a minority or a coterie only. The individual instantiations of this view are indeed held by a minority in each case, sometimes a little-known one. But the general understanding of the place of art is very widespread and deep in our culture, and this corresponds to a widely shared sense that the creative imagination is an indispensable locus of moral sources, as the paradoxical and ambivalent relation between minority art and mass public I have just described attests.

This general conception has been through a number of transformations and taken a great many forms. It has brought about successive revolutions in poetics and engendered styles of poetry very different from those of the Romantics. But what often inspired these changes was this very notion of the epiphanic. Wordsworth shows us what is spiritually significant in the ordinary, both people and things. At the same time, his poetry contains a realistic description of these people and things, and straightforward expressions of feeling. But the lines of modern poetry which flow from Baudelaire have detached themselves from the straightforwardly mimetic and expressive. What underlay this separation was the sense that the revelatory power of the symbol depends on a break with ordinary discourse. Mallarmé speaks of the poet as "ceding the initiative to words" and allowing the poem to be structured by their inherent, interacting forces, "mobilized by the shock of their inequality".[23] For the Imagists, "the proper and perfect symbol is the natural object".[24] The poetic image is opaque, non-referential. Here the Romantic contrast between the symbolic and the referential has intensified into the attempt to achieve epiphany by deranging reference—to give power to symbols by taking language beyond discourse. What was united in the Romantics is here rigorously opposed. So the principle of unity of Pound's *Cantos* is utterly different from that of Wordsworth's *Prelude*. It is no longer narrative, but the interlocking images, which unify.

I will be looking at some of the developing understandings of the creative imagination in the last two centuries, not in respect of poetical styles but in an aspect complexly related to these. I want to examine the notions of moral (including im-, a-, and non-moral) sources that have emerged in these transformations. Within the continuities of epiphanic art, this is a history of ruptures and oppositions. In fact, some of the important disputes, fought out in earlier epochs between strands of traditional ethics or interpretations of Christian theology, recur in this new medium.

But before I launch into this story, there is an objection which has to be faced. It goes against the whole cadre of continuity that I have set up to tell it, the view of modern epiphanic art as in continuity with the Romantic era, as indeed, striving in some ways to intensify some defining features of Romantic art. What about all those whose work is undoubtedly epiphanic in my sense, but who have declared themselves as anti-Romantics? T. E. Hulme, for instance, in some sense the founder of Imagism, thought of himself as a 'classicist' rather than a Romantic, precisely because he wanted to repudiate the centring on the subject, the striving after self-expression which he identifies with the Romantics. For Hulme, the highest art is an epiphany of something which is impersonal, 'life-alien'.[25] Eliot seems to have been influenced by Hulme in his own self-declaration as a 'classicist'. And then we think of the more austere Symbolists, of Mallarmé and Rimbaud, for instance, whose epiphanies were most decidedly 'life-alien', and who tried to move beyond self-expression utterly. Can we look at these as in continuity with the Romantics?

In important respects, no. These important respects concern precisely what is being revealed in the epiphany, and this has important relevance to the moral sources in question. This is the story I want to tell. But it is a muddle to think that the decisive break occurs over the issue of self-expression versus impersonality. Most of the great Romantic poets saw themselves as articulating something greater than themselves: the world, nature, being, the word of God. They were not concerned primarily with an expression of their own feelings; as indeed, I showed in Chapter 21.[26]

Where subjectivism enters in is in the view of nature as a source, as I called it. For this involves the idea that an indispensable route of access to the world or nature or being we want to articulate is the impulse of nature or the intimations of the spirit within. "Nach innen geht der geheimnisvolle Weg", says Novalis ("Inward goes the way full of mystery").[27] This is what makes a clear distinction between writers like Schelling, Novalis, Baudelaire, on one hand, and the great thinkers of Renaissance neo-Platonism and magical thought, like Bruno, on the other, despite all the debt which the first owed to the second. This debt was in fact considerable, and acknowledged, as in Schelling's invocation of Bruno and in Baudelaire's use of the language of the 'correspondences' and images of alchemy.

Bruno and Paracelsus, for instance, though they may have thought of their knowledge as esoteric, saw themselves as grasping the unmediated spiritual order of things. It may take secret and not widely available lore to uncover it, but it doesn't have to be revealed through an articulation of what is in us. It is in this sense a public order that it is available unmediated by our powers of creative articulation.

It is this kind of public order, a tableau of the spiritual significance of things, which is no longer possible for us. It is not only the rise of science and of disengaged reason which has taken it beyond reach. It is also our understanding of the role of the creative imagination. Moderns certainly can conceive of a spiritual order of correspondences: Baudelaire did, and Yeats did, and millions have read them and been moved by their poetry. But what we cannot conceive is such an order which we wouldn't have to accede to through an epiphany wrought by the creative imagination; which would be somehow available unrefracted through the medium of someone's artistic creation.

But an order which can only be attained thus refracted is a fundamentally different thing. The unmediated order existed, as it were, *an sich,* to use anachronistic post-Kantian language. It made sense to raise issues about what plants or animals really bore the signature of the planet Saturn. If Bruno and Paracelsus disagreed, at least one of them had to be wrong. But with the orders refracted in the imagination, these questions have no place. Does Byzantium "really" have the significance it takes on the Yeats's poems? Must a quite different invocation of it in the quite independent language of another poet be wrong? This sounds absurd.

Whatever is true of our scientific theories, the visions of our poets have to be understood in a post-Kantian fashion. They give us reality in a medium which can't be separated from them. That is the nature of epiphany. This is not to say that we can't discriminate. Plainly we think some deeper, more revealing, truer than others. Just what these judgements are based on is very hard to say. But it plainly isn't correspondence to a reality unmediated by exactly the forms which are at issue.

The moral or spiritual order of things must come to us indexed to a personal vision. The two important factors I mentioned above dovetail to lock us into this predicament, to render any unmediated order beyond our reach: the detachment of the spiritual order from the order of nature we explore in natural science, which had to render the former problematic, is compensated for and complemented by our post-Romantic notion of the creative imagination. Both together spell the end of unmediated orders.

But this means that a certain subjectivism is inseparable from modern epiphanies. We can try to take our distance from the Romantic notion, encapsulated in the quote from Novalis, that we should seek the key to the order of things within. And this is not an unimportant change. It may be vital to alter the focus of attention; something like what Rilke did in his "Neue Gedichte", when he tried to articulate things from within themselves, as it were. But what we can't escape is the mediation through the imagination; we are always articulating a personal vision. And the connection of articulation with inwardness remains for this reason unsevered and unbreakable. Just because we have to conceive of our task as the articulation of a personal refraction, we cannot abandon radical reflexivity and turn our back on our own experience or on the resonance of things in us.

Thus in one of the most successful of his New Poems, "The Panther", Rilke beautifully evokes the animal pacing in his cage through its own inwardness: "Ihm ist, als ob es tausend Stäbe gäbe/und hinter tausend Stäbe keine Welt" ("It seems to him there are a thousand bars; and behind the bars, no world"). The images which can enter him from this alien surrounding run through the "tensed stillness of his limbs", but "cease to be" when they reach his heart. Rilke has indeed taken us into the panther, but this turns out to be inseparable from making the panther an emblem of our own alienated inwardness.[28]

The "anti-Romantic" move into "classicism" of someone like Hulme or Eliot thus cannot be a move back to the invocation of unmediated orders. It remains epiphanic and in that way in profound continuity with the whole movement from the Romantics. It is a caricature to present the Romantics as concerned only with self-expression; and it is an illusion to think one can bypass the imagination and hence the inwardness of personal vision. But just because of this, there is a point in striving to avoid the merely subjective. Indeed, this is in some ways the central issue of epiphanic art.

The very fact that there can only be refracted visions means that we cannot separate what is manifested from the medium which we have created to reveal it. But this means that there are forms of subject-centredness which don't consist in talking directly about the self. There is the venerable and familiar one that weaves a language of self-absorption in which the vision of reality is constantly clouded by our own reactions. And there is the specifically modern temptation that the epiphany will become primarily a celebration of our own powers of creative articulation. This self-affirmatory thrust can be more or less avowed, as with futurism, or it can hover ambiguously, as with surrealism, or be altogether self-concealed. The very nature of epiphanic art can make it difficult to say just what is being celebrated: the deep recesses beyond or below the subject, or the subject's uncanny powers. It has been remarked[29] that some of the same artists were excited by both primitivism and Futurism in the period before the First World War.

Subject-centredness is a much more insidious thing than the thematic penchant for self-expression. And because, for a host of reasons which I will discuss below, a lot in our modern culture pushes us towards it, overcoming it is a major task, both moral and aesthetic, of our time. But we make the task speciously easy for ourselves if we fail to see how in both the aspirations and the dangers there is a deep continuity between us and the Romantic era.

23.3

The starting point from which I want to discern the derivations and departures is the moral vision which was widespread among Romantic writers. These celebrated the goodness of nature. They were at one in this respect with the Deists and the naturalistic Enlightenment, in that they saw the created order as a great source of goodness. They broke from the one-dimensionality of the earlier thinkers, and saw human motivation not as uniform but as capable of qualitative transformation. They followed Rousseau in his opposition between the corrupt and undistorted will, which in turn goes back as we saw to Augustine's doctrines of the two loves. But they identified the source of "grace" as nature within. We have to return to full contact with the great current which runs through all and which also resonates within us.

Of course, in one influential variant, they recognized that a rupture with nature was necessary for us to attain reason and freedom. But the goal was to recover a higher unity in which these would be reconciled with nature, what Schiller saw for instance in our play with beauty, which became a paradigm idea for the whole Romantic generation of the 1790's. In this spiral vision, the Fall, however necessary, is the break with nature. Coleridge, deeply influenced by this strand of German thought, defined "Redemption" as a "Reconciliation from this Enmity with Nature".[30] 'Reconciliation' (Versöhnung) was a key term for Hegel.

Meanwhile the great world of nature around us was a source of solace and strength. One form of epiphany lay in showing the spiritual goodness, the source of healing in the natural world, which has been rendered banal or dead by our estrangement from it. Novalis aimed at a transmutation of this kind, and this is what poetry does for Shelley, when "it creates anew the universe, after it has been annihilated in our minds by the recurrence of impressions blunted by reiteration".[31] This is also what Wordsworth was about, in showing the spiritual significance of ordinary things and people, in his elevation of the ordinary, and his recovery of "a sense sublime/Of something far more deeply interfused".[32] Constable followed him, in choosing the unexceptional, and in trying "to make something out of nothing". He could declare "I never saw an ugly thing in my life",[33] something, that is, which his art could not transfigure.

The transfiguration of the ordinary was indeed, one important theme of Romantic art, and the image of alchemy frequently returns.[34] All this was grounded in a profound sense of the goodness of nature.

There were three important transformations of this Romantic vision in the nineteenth century, which involved negating crucial features of it, but in other ways carried it forward.

(a) The first was called 'realism', sometimes 'naturalism', a subset of the many strands called by these names. I am thinking first of all of the variants which turn up in France from about mid-century: e.g., the writings of Zola, and in a different way of Flaubert; the paintings of Courbet and Manet. These writers and painters seemed to accept the outlook of Enlightenment naturalism, to deny altogether the notion of a spiritual reality beyond or behind things, and in particular to deny all notions of a great current of nature, the crux of so much Romantic writing and painting (with, for instance, Constable or Friedrich). This would seem to be a counter-epiphanic art par excellence, one which was determined to show things in their crude, lowly reality and to dispel any illusion of a deeper meaning inhabiting them—the very reverse of a transfiguration.

But the continuity with Romanticism is not that abruptly broken. The premiss of realism then and now is that we somehow in the normal course of things fail to see things aright, that we grasp them only through a veil of illusion which lends them a false enhancement or significance, woven by our fears and self-indulgence. It takes courage and vision to see them as they are; but more than this, it takes the resources of art. We live surrounded by this reality but don't really see it, because our vision is shaped—and clouded—by our falsely consoling modes of representation. It takes a new, fiercely veridical portrayal to break through the veil.

This kind of art may involve no epiphany of translucence, as we might call it, where something deeper shines through the real, but it does involve an unveiling, a revelation of the real face of things, and this requires a transfiguration of a kind. We might take Flaubert's *Madame Bovary* as an example. In this work, there is no desire to bestow dignity of any sort on the characters or to show a deeper significance to their action. Indeed, the deflationary effect comes from the pitiless portrayal of the illusion of deeper meaning in Emma's romantic longings. It all ends up as something unspeakably banal and ordinary, however lofty the dream. The goal seems to be to depict quite unremittingly the tawdriness of the mediocre. The power of the work as art lies in its extraordinary ability to capture this banality, where the almost irresistible drift of the inherited modes of representation had been to enhance or idealize. But why does this move either the writer or the reader? Not just as a tour de force, but in the sense of power and freedom from this banality which is inseparable from the capturing of it as an object of contemplation.

There is a kind of transfiguration here; not the kind which reveals meaning, but rather that which gives the meaningless and banal unhappiness the closure and shape of fate. Charles Rosen and Henri Zerner, in their interesting book on realism and Romanticism, speak of the "determinism" of Baudelaire, which "allows the facts to speak for themselves without comment: the inevitablity is an aesthetic quality. It is not merely a substitute for beauty, but is to be considered absolutely beautiful in itself".[35]

So the unveiling of things in their meaninglessness involves its own kind of transfiguration. The joy we take in this has something to do with our own power to confront the truth and acknowledge it; and this power crucially depends on the closure which makes the entrapment in banality and emptiness a kind of fate which we can contemplate. It is being able to contemplate it which frees us from the entrapment, and this freedom is the condition of the sense of power and joy. Realist art relies on its own form of transfiguration in stripping things of meaning.

It is a kind of transfiguration which tends to exalt more the creative power of the artist. But realism contains more than this. Not all of it was so resolutely counter-epiphanic. There was another strand in which something does after all shine through the subject. Courbet provides an example.

Naturalism expressed itself in the context of French painting in a rejection of the traditional distinctions of genres and definition of subjects, which depended heavily on a hierarchy of the proper objects of painting, which itself was justified by notions of order and spiritual significance: traditional views gave sacred subjects a high place, ranked history over landscape, and put "genre" painting on subjects of daily life below these. Courbet turned to painting ordinary people, workers, peasants, rural bourgeois. But these were sometimes given the monumental scope that ought to have been reserved for history painting. Realism meant the "disappearance of the subject", in the sense of a scene or event already made canonical by history or religion or classical culture which the painting is intended to represent. But ordinary events without this established meaning are given the dignity of treatment previously confined to those endowed with it. This was self-consciously a rejection of hierarchy and in a certain sense of displacement. These new 'subjects' were taking the place of the old; an affirmation was being made about their dignity.

But Courbet didn't try to dress these up like the classical themes. That is one possible strategy for a reversal of hierarchy: to take a scene from ordinary life and idealize it by using the whole rhetoric of gesture, pose, and composition which had been evolved in neo-Classical art. Rosen and Zerner[36] show an example of this by one of Courbet's contemporaries. But Courbet and the more austere realists turned their back on this rhetoric, and on any attempt to idealize what they depicted.

In its tough-minded materialism, realism seems to be the negation of Romanticism. But the continuity is there in the transfiguratory intent which is undeniable in some of these pictures. The transfiguration is partly effected by the very levelling move which puts ordinary people in the place of the historical or sacred personages. As Courbet himself said, "Le fond du réalisme c'est la négation de l'idéal" ("The basis of realism is the negation of the ideal"). Through this negation, he claimed, "J'arrive en plein à l'émancipation de l'individu, et finalement, à la démocratie" ("I come right to the emancipation of the individual, and finally to democracy").[37] As Rosen and Zerner put it, in their discussion of the *Burial at Ornans,* "A genre scene is raised, by this aggression and by the life size of the figures, to the dignity of an historical painting. The infinitely repeatable scene of a village funeral is given the singularity of an important historical event".[38] A statement is being made about ordinary people; about the dignity of all humans.

But there was something deeper. If one views these paintings without a sense of their immediate historical context, as we do now, something of the transfiguration still comes through. That is because they carry something of the power and titanic force of raw nature, a force which declares irrelevant all judgements made on this nature as crude or imperfect from more refined and spiritual points of view. Rosen and Zerner in their discussion of the *Burial* point to "the aggressive presence of the personages".[39] A force resides in these people, even for those unfamiliar with the earlier hierarchy of genres. And similarly Courbet's *Stonebreakers* portrays not only deprivation; it also captures the strain, the concentrated exertion to the very limit, of hard physical labour. There is force and not only misfortune here.

The affirmation of raw nature, which is in effect a declaration of its independence from the depreciatory judgements of "higher" standpoints, takes up one of the basic themes of the naturalist Enlightenment. There it was a matter of affirming the innocence of nature. Here it has become something more ambiguous, already affected by the nineteenth-century transposition in the sense of nature which I discuss below, but basically similar in its moral purport. In these and other paintings of Courbet, as also in some of Manet's outstanding works—*Le Déjeuner sur l'Herbe*, *Olympia*—the sense comes through that unrefined nature, basic desire, doesn't have to be seen as a dead weight holding us back from spiritual ascent, but is to be wholeheartedly embraced, perhaps even rejoiced in. What was once a basic thesis of the materialist philosophers now inhabits the canvas. This is a naturalist transfiguration.

We could even speak here of a naturalist epiphany. There seem to be two strands of realism, one of which focusses on the power of the artist, the other on the dignity and force of the subject. But in fact they appear to be closely connected; it seems to have been possible to run them together; and even the epiphanic kind in its own way testifies to the power of the artist. The thoroughgoing naturalist disenchantment of the world throws into relief the creative work of the imagination in transfiguring it. All this emerges in a short passage of Emile Zola's appreciation of the painting *Jallais Hill, Pointoise* by Camille Pissaro:

This is the modern countryside. One feels the passage of man, who digs up the earth, cuts it up, saddens the horizon. This valley, this hillside manifest a simplicity and an heroic frankness. Nothing could be more banal, were nothing greater. The painter's temperament has drawn a rare poem of life and force from ordinary reality.[40]

Here the arch-priest of deflating naturalism speaks of a transmutation of the banal in poetry.

The paradox of the interpenetration of these two strands of naturalism is matched by the close relations between realism and Impressionism, which I will return to in the next chapter. Rosen and Zerner point out the multiple connections which hold—paradoxical as this seems—between realism and the later explorations of the artist's own transforming of the real, or of the way things appear: the connections with Impressionism, for instance.[41] It can seem, after all, part of a more radical and thoroughgoing realism to make the painting manifest itself as a representation, instead of trying to make it recede unobtrusively before a subject supposedly effortlessly there in its objective being.

23.4

(b) We find a negation of a quite different kind, though with some strange points of contact, in Baudelaire. Here there is no rejection of the spiritual. On the contrary, Baudelaire constantly affirms it. What is denied is rather nature, that is, the Romantic belief that the highest spiritual reality courses through nature. Baudelaire utterly rejects the Rousseauian belief that man is by nature good. In spite of his strange and rather ambiguous relation to Catholic orthodoxy, Baudelaire enthusiastically affirms the doctrine of original sin; he strongly endorses de Maistre. He admires Poe for declaring "the natural wickedness of man".[42]

> La plupart des erreurs relatives au beau naissent de la fausse conception du dix-huitième siècle relative à la morale. La nature fut prise dans ce temps-là comme base, source et type de tout bien et de tout beau possibles. La négation du péché originel ne fut pas pour peu de chose dans l'aveuglement général de cette époque . . . La nature ne peut conseiller que le crime . . . [Dans] toutes les actions et les désirs du pur homme naturel, vous ne trouverez rien que d'affreux.

> Most errors relating to beauty are born of eighteenth-century misconceptions concerning morality. Nature was taken in that time as base, source, and model of all possible beauty and good. The denial of original sin was not without significance in the general blindness of this period . . . Nature cannot but counsel that which is criminal . . . [In] all the actions and desires of the purely natural man, you will find nothing that is not ghastly.[43]

If Romanticism, like Deism, grew out of an Erasmian Christianity, here is an authentic statement of the most extreme Augustinian pessimism, no longer even Christian in its one-sidedness: closer in fact to Manichaeism. Thus Baudelaire was fascinated by sexual desire, but at the same time experienced it as something base, dragging us downward, a source of melancholy and regret:

> Il y a dans toute homme, à toute heure, deux postulations simultanées, l'une vers Dieu, l'autre vers Satan. L'invocation à Dieu, ou spiritualité, est un désir de monter en grade; celle de Satan, ou animalité, est une joie de descendre. C'est à cette dernière que doivent être rapportées les amours pour les femmes et les conversations intimes avec les animaux, chiens, chats, etc.

> There are in all men, at all times, two simultaneous postulations, one towards God, the other towards Satan. The invocation to God, or spirituality, is a desire to raise oneself higher; that towards Satan, or animality, is the joy of descent. To the latter belong the love of women, and intimate conversations with animals, dogs, cats, etc.[44]

Baudelaire had no time for the Romantic reverence for extra-human nature, either:

> Je suis incapable de m'attendrir sur les végétaux . . . mon âme est rebelle à cette singulière religion nouvelle, qui aura toujours, ce me semble, pour tout être *spirituel* je ne sais quoi de *shocking*. Je ne croirai jamais que *l'âme des Dieux habite dans les plantes,* et quand même qu'elle y habiterait, je m'en soucierais médiocrement, et considérerais la mienne comme d'un bien plus haut prix que celle des légumes sanctifiés. J'ai même toujours pensé qu'il y avait dans *La Nature,* florissante et rajeunie, quelque chose d'impudent et d'affligeant.

> I am incapable of sympathizing with vegetation . . . my soul rebels against this singular new religion, that will always have, it seems to me, for any *spiritual* being, something *shocking*. I will never believe that *the soul of the Gods inhabits plants,* and even if it did, it would concern me but little, and I would consider my own soul as of much higher value than that of such sanctified vegetables. And moreover I have always found in *Nature,* flourishing and renewed, something shameful and distressing.[45]

Just as the Rousseauian outlook was associated with liberalism and democracy, so Baudelaire, though basically apolitical, had reactionary sympathies, in spite of some temporary wobbles which saw him for instance involved in the first phases of 1848. But this didn't mean that he had any sympathy for bourgeois commercial civilization. On the contrary, he considered the age one of decadence. The reason for the wobbles to the left lay precisely in this hostility to the status quo.

What Baudelaire held up in opposition to his world was an ideal of aristocracy, one of the spirit and sensibility. Dandyism was one of the forms it took. The dandy is continuous with the aristocrat; something of the style has often sprung up in aristocratic castes. What defines the aristocrat is what moves him and what fails to move him. The warrior is concerned not at all for life, but very much for his honour; so the warrior-aristocrat will espouse and play out this pattern of concern by rituals of punctiliousness, even carrying to absurd length the sacrifice of safety or wealth, as when one hazards one's life in a duel for a triviality. Indeed, it is just the absurdity which makes the point.

Something of this heroism is reflected in the dandy. It is the very absurdity of giving such a priority to one's appearance and dress which distinguishes him. The unshakeable attachment through all obstacles to what seems trivial is the mark of his exceptional nature. He may be deathly ill, but he will still maintain his style. In this case, "il souffrira comme le Lacédémonien sous la morsure du renard". Keeping to this inflexible demand will "fortify the will and discipline the soul". Baudelaire likens him to a stoic.[46]

In his rejection of nature, Baudelaire is anti-Romantic, and in his aristocratism, he stands against the most famous poets of the Romantic era. But he is one with them in his hatred of commercial/instrumental civilization, and certainly follows them in seeking the antidote in art.

It is an art closely linked to religion; or perhaps which itself takes the place of religion. Certain of the things Baudelaire says make it sound familiar enough. Behind the fallen natural world stands a spiritual world, and art can bring this to epiphany. Nature is ugly, but the imagination of the artist allows him "de saisir les parcelles du beau égarées sur la terre, de suivre le beau à la piste partout où il a pu glisser à travers les trivialités de la nature déchue" ("to seize upon the bits of beauty scattered about the earth, to follow beauty's trail wherever it has managed to slip in admist the trivialities of fallen nature").[47] Baudelaire often refers to this spiritual world whose fragments the artist thus gathers in the traditional terms of Renaissance neo-Platonism, in terms of 'correspondences', as though things had a spiritual significance which linked them in chains of equivalence:

> La Nature est un temple où de vivants piliers
> Laissent parfois sortir de confuses paroles;
> L'homme y passe à travers des forêts de symboles
> Qui l'observent avec des regards familiers.

> Nature is a temple whose living colonnades
> Breathe forth a mystic speech in fitful sighs;
> Man wanders among symbols in those glades
> Where all things watch him with familiar eyes.[48]

But other things that Baudelaire says, and much of his poetry, don't fit very well with this picture of the poet gathering shards and hints of supernatural beauty. There are quite other kinds of epiphany, in which we are thrown headlong into evil and ugliness and decay. In part this reflects Baudelaire's ambivalent stance towards the Manichaean universe he sees: Satanism, to plunge into evil to the point of intoxication, of releasing a "frisson galvanique", seems as valid a response as askesis—perhaps even an alternative route to the same goal. What must be avoided at all costs is banality and the dead, inert time of ordinary ugliness.

> Il faut toujours être ivre. Tout est là: c'est l'unique question. Pour ne pas sentir l'horrible fardeau du Temps qui brise vos épaules et vous penche vers la terre, il faut vous enivrer sans trêve. Mais de quoi? De vin, de poésie ou de vertu, à votre guise. Mais enivrez-vous.

> One should alway be drunk. That's the great thing; the only question. Not to feel the horrible burden of Time weighing on your shoulders and bowing you to the earth, you should be drunk without respite. Drunk with what? With wine, with poetry, or with virtue, as you please. But get drunk.[49]

And Baudelaire can conclude "que le plus parfait type de Beauté virile est *Satan*—à la manière de Milton" ("that the most perfect model of virile Beauty is Satan—in the manner of Milton").[50]

But what emerges in the plunge into evil and ugliness is very often neither the frisson nor the fragments of spiritual beauty, but a kind of fierce undefinable joy. It has something to do with the very power of the human spirit to stand in these abandoned regions, in full possession of itself and of its capacity to transmute even this into a symbol of its plight.[51] Baudelaire's most terrible poems often end with a surge of power, an affirmation of the poet's full possession of the meaning unshaken by the horror. "Une Charogne" ends:

> Alors, ô ma beauté! dites à la vermine
>   Qui vous mangera de baisers,
> Que j'ai gardé la forme et l'essence divine
>   De mes amours décomposés!

> Speak, then, my Beauty, to this dire putrescene,
>   To the worm that shall kiss your proud estate,
> That I have kept the divine form and the essence
>   Of my festered loves inviolate!

And the last stanza of "Un Voyage à Cithère" reads:

Dans ton île, ô Vénus! je n'ai trouvé debout
Qu'un gibet symbolique où pendait mon image ...
—Ah! Seigneur! donnez-moi la force et le courage
De contempler mon coeur et mon corps sans dégout!

On your isle, Venus, I saw but one thing standing,
gallows-emblem from which my shape was hanging ...
God! give me strength and will to contemplate
heart, body—without loathing, without hate.[52]

Similarly, Baudelaire's descriptions of Paris, as a kind of infernal city of mists and suffering, sometimes attain a terrible beauty, but which is closer to what Kant understood as the sublime, because the beauty is inseparable from this sense of our own power to stand and contemplate the full meaning of this forsaken world.

This is one with our power to disengage from the organic, the merely natural, which for Baudelaire is the realm of evil, ugliness, chaos. We surmount it by artifice. The task of art is to correct nature. Imagination breaks up the creation; it "decomposes" it, "separates" it, and puts it together by its own laws, so that nature emerges "corrigée, embellie, refondue" ("corrected, embellished, reformed").[53] His dream is not the old Edenic one of a garden, but on the contrary of a city which is totally man made, which has banished the organic altogether, as in the poem "Rêve parisien", where

J'avais banni de ces spectacles
Le végétal irrégulier,

Et, peintre fier de mon génie
Je savourais dans mon tableau
L'enivrante monotonie
Du métal, du marbre et de l'eau.

To banish, as irregular,
All vegetation from that land;

And, proud of what my art had done,
I viewed my painting, knew the great
Intoxicating monotone
Of marble, water, steel and slate.[54]

The dream which remakes things can be "perfect as a chrystal"; for Baudelaire the inorganic is higher than the organic, which is a realm of chaos.[55]

Thus this poet, who is in some ways utterly opposed to naturalism, who rejects its materialism and demands that art remake reality, nevertheless wreaks his own transfigurations, not even of the ordinary, but of the hideous and terrible. He is also an alchemist, and saw himself in this light, as these lines attest:

> Car j'ai de chaque chose extrait la quintessence,
> Tu m'as donné ta boue et j'en ai fait de l'or.

> For I have from each thing extracted its quintessence,
> You have given me mud and I have made of it gold.[56]

And for all Baudelaire's spiritualist protestations, these transfigurations often yield a God-forsaken world. The difference with the realists I mentioned above is that there is no affirmation of the goodness of being. The light comes from the poet's own imaginative powers. All else is darkness. But this too could become the basis for a humanist self-affirmation, and despite the differences, Baudelaire's influence couldn't remain confined to the misanthropic right.

But for my purposes here, what is important is Baudelaire as the originator of an epiphanic art which is against nature. Baudelaire brings into the Romantic-expressive stream the opposite spirtuality from its point of origin, not that with its roots in Erasmian Christianity, but the one rooted in Jansenism and the acute sense of human fallenness. It is hard to understand this just as a theological option. Baudelaire was too far out of the orbit of Christian faith, too much actuated by quite non-Christian ideas, for this to be a satisfying explanation. Rather he gave expression to an option within the religion of art itself.

If we think of art as something higher, as the way in which humans recover wholeness, or at least escape degradation and fragmentation, then we can imagine a sensibility for which anything belonging to nature seems too inert, disordered, opaque, banal, to be the source of art. The Romantic exaltation of nature seems a profanation, a surrender to the merely given, the ordinary, the mediocre mass. Art can only fulfil its mission if it breaks with this and builds a realm entirely apart.

The roots of this spiritual attitude go far back, into an issue about moral sources distinct from that which divided the different strands of Christian faith. It is an issue that seems to divide Aristotle from Plato. It concerns the place of the ensemble of "physical" desires and needs, for food, for drink, for sex—the desires we share with the animals—in the moral life. From one standpoint, the morally good life contains a comfortable niche for these, although they must remain subordinate to other goods like contemplation and the citizen life, and mustn't overflow their appointed limits. The other view is more extreme. It concedes the need to grant some place to the "necessary" desires,[57] but sees them as potential sources of impurity. The most perfect life leans to asceticism; it would concede these desires only the smallest possible space.

The attractions of the first, Aristotelian view are that it overcomes inner division, and gives a place in the moral life to all facets of our being. But the force of 'Platonism' comes from the transcendent aspiration to purity, which is won through a denial of mere desire. Its power lies in the sense that the good is something far beyond the mere needs of life, and something to which one can soar only by escaping from the toils of the bodily.

This issue is in logic quite distinct from that between Erasmian and hyper-Augustinian Christianity. Erasmus himself was a Platonist. And the Calvinist divines I quoted earlier who saw the ordinary fulfilments of life as potentially spiritual followed the Aristotelian road. But both the naturalist Enlightenment and Romanticism grew out of the extreme Erasmian wing of Christianity, while at the same time they went further than ever before in integrating physical fulfilment into the moral life.

This constellation creates in a sense a fusion between the two issues. Henceforth those of a 'Platonist' bent tend also to adopt a dark vision of mankind's fallen nature.

Transposed into the religion of art, this gives us Baudelaire's notion of art as an anti-nature, coupled with a lively sense of human evil. This obviously fits well with his aristocratic, anti-levelling stance. This is a position which recurs in the following century. We will see it for instance in T. E. Hulme, one of the influential thinkers of early Modernism. Hulme in rejecting Romanticism precisely defined it as the view that man was by nature good, the view introduced by Rousseau.[58] Hulme's Augustinianism by contrast dictates an art in which "there is nothing vital", which arises from "disgust with the trivial and accidental characteristics of living shapes", and seeks "a perfection and rigidity which vital things can never have". It seeks it in life-alien, "geometric" forms.[59]

M. H. Abrams has noted the widespread existence in modern literature of a constellation which combines dogmatic theological orthodoxy (or what is meant to be such), political and social conservatism, and an anti-Romantic poet; it may be called 'classical' but in fact justifies avant-garde art.[60] This is the legacy of Baudelaire.

The rejection of nature gives a certain sense to the slogan 'l'art pour l'art', which was not Baudelaire's invention and which he didn't really espouse, but one sense of which does capture his outlook. In a way, whoever follows a religion of art takes the second of the two views which Schiller offered and sees art as offering a higher human realization than morality, that is, makes art an end in itself. But in Schiller's formulation, beauty in completing human life helps realize all the other recognizably moral goals. It brings not only wholeness to each person but unity to society.[61] It is equally true to say that art is for humans, or for life.

But when Baudelaire says "la poésie . . . n'a pas d'autre but qu'Elle même" ("poetry . . . has no other end but itself"),[62] something important has changed. He hastens to add that he doesn't want to say that poetry doesn't improve us; it does. But it must be pursued utterly for its own sake. Even this, of course, could be agreed to by all Romantic poets, indeed, by all artists of our time, if it means just the exclusion of works designed with didactic purpose. But when one sees the gulf which has opened in Baudelaire's view between art and the search for human natural fulfilment, it is clear that the self-sufficiency of art has now become an exclusive rather than an inclusive doctrine.

Baudelaire inspired the heroic, almost self-destructive attempt to create an art of total self-suffiency, the "pure" art of Mallarmé and the Symbolists. Mallarmé, far from trying to imitate nature in his poetry, strives rather to free himself from it. Ordinary things are volatilized and rendered absent or unreal ('abolition' is a word which frequently recurs in Mallarmé). Moreover, poetry ought to be purified of any personal thoughts and feelings of its creator. This is the ideal of the 'auto-telic' work, the prosecution of which Mallarmé carried to (literally) unthinkable lengths, to truly glacial heights, in search of a purity he had to identify with Nothing:

> Je te dirai que depuis un mois dans les plus purs glaciers de l'Esthétique— qu'après avoir trouvé le Néant, j'ai trouvé le Beau,—et que tu ne peux t'imaginer dans quelles altitudes lucides je m'aventure.

> I tell you after a month in the pure glaciers of the Aesthetic—that after having found Nothingness, I found Beauty,—and you cannot imagine the lucid heights I explore.[63]

This nothing is the place of the logos, and Mallarmé's straining after it is also an attempt to bend poetry back onto itself, to bring to light and celebrate the power of the word. This has made him one of the great trail-blazers of twentieth-century poetry and philosophy.

23.5

(c) But along with an art of despiritualized nature in Realism and an art of the epiphanies of anti-nature, there is a third important form that the negation of Romanticism takes in the nineteenth century, and that is an art which relates to the wild energy of an amoral nature.

This turn arises from the philosophy of Schopenhauer, not entirely in ways that he intended. Baudelaire here found his match in misanthropy. The greatest, the most influential misanthrope of the nineteenth century—the great "pessimist"—was Schopenhauer. In a sense what Schopenhauer offered was an expressivism with the value signs reversed. For he took the idea of nature as a source, a power which comes to expression in things. This power 'objectified' itself in the different realities we see around us, and these 'objectifications' constituted a hierarchy, all the way from the lowest, most inanimate level to conscious beings at the summit.

This all-pervading power is the Schopenhauerian will. But it is not a spiritual source of good. On the contrary, it is nothing but wild, blind, uncontrolled striving, never satisfied, incapable of satisfaction, driving us on, against all principles, law, morality, all standards of dignity, to an insatiable search for the unattainable. The will strives only to perpetuate itself and its objectifications; and what we think are our desires are in a sense only its unconscious strategies to achieve this end. We love and we try to attain happiness, but sexual desire is by its very nature incapable of bringing happiness. It is only another device of the will to perpetuate itself through us.

Schopenhauer's reversal of sign relative to Romantic expressivism is strangely reminiscent of the hyper-Augustinian reactions to Christian humanism. Indeed, the notion of a spiritual force uniting nature plainly descends from Renaissance neo-Platonism and its doctrine of love. Ficino is one of the ancestors of expressivism, as we have seen. Continuing this parallel, we can say that what the Jansenists were to St. François de Sales or Camus, Schopenhauer was to Schelling and Hegel. Within their expressivist metaphysic, he introduces radical vitiation. The source from which all reality flows as expression is poisoned. It is not the source of good, but of insatiable desire, of an imprisonment in evil, which makes us miserable, exhausts us, and degrades us.

The parallel with Baudelaire is evident. Within the categories of Romantic expressivism, the spiritual and moral outlook recurs that these categories were originally meant to exclude. It testifies in a way to the force of the expressivist understanding of self and world, that it could slide from being the reflection of only one of the spiritual strands of our civilization to become the common background in which both confront one another. Now the moral sensibility which holds the good to be utterly other than a natural existence, which it quite transcends, finds a post-Romantic formulation.

What are the attractions of this outlook? Partly, as I said in connection with Baudelaire, that the degrading of empirical reality is a way of underlining the transcendent purity of the good. One senses in the passages in which Plato most strongly condemns and degrades the life of the desires that this is intrinsically linked with a sense of the exalted purity of a life focussed on the good, that what moves him to debase the first is in part the sharp contrast thus marked with the second, by which alone it can shine forth in resplendent clarity. And behind the acute sense of our sinfulness and impotence is Calvinism or Jansenism in the corresponding exaltation of the transcendent sovereignty of God, and his gratuitous mercy.

Another motive may also be at work in Schopenhauerian pessimism. The notion of a harmony between freedom and nature, of a spontaneous alignment of desire and reason, the kind of thing which Schiller describes with his notion of beauty, is very heady and inspiring. It is easy to imagine our finding this union unrealizable, even incredible, in our own experience of life. And then one has the choice either to see oneself as in some way especially depraved or out of tune, or to cast doubt on the whole theory and attribute the lack of attunement to the very nature of things. It is not only easier on oneself, but can appear more plausible, to take the latter course.

And this can be liberating. Just as for the hyper-Augustinian sensibility of Luther, the sense of sin as our general plight and of redemption as outside our power liberated him from a crushing sense of personal depravity; so the Schopenhauerian view can allow us to cast off the impossible burdens of Schillerian optimism, which crush us under a sense of our own inadequacy.

This is, of course, another side to the Lutheran liberation. I not only unload the burden from myself, not only recognize the general plight of depravity; I also rejoice in the confidence that liberation comes from elsewhere. These two steps, the recognition of my helplessness and lowliness, and the sense of my salvation, are closely bound together. Is there something analogous to this in Schopenhauer?

Yes, there is, but it takes us very far away from Luther. Schopenhauer is definitely breaking with any form of Christian or post-Christian thought. He explicitly espouses a Buddhist outlook, and sees our liberation not in a transfiguration of ordinary life, far from it, but in an escape from the self and the will altogether.

And yet—Schopenhauer also offered something else, and this was what turned out to be widely influential. He had a notion of transfiguration, through art. Although we do not achieve the total liberation of nirvana, we can manage to quiet the will in us when we grasp the Ideas, the eternal forms which underlie the particular examples we meet in the world of objectifications of the will on their various levels. We encounter these principally in art. And we attain this stilling and contemplation most directly in music, because this is not merely a picture of the will's objectifications but in some way a direct picture of the will itself.[64]

Schopenhauer takes from Kant the key doctrine that aesthetic contemplation is disinterested, and translates that as a disengagement from the pressure of the will. It

> suddenly raises us out of the endless stream of willing, and snatches knowledge from the thraldom of the will . . . Then all at once the peace, always sought but always escaping us . . . comes to us of its own accord, and all is well with us. It is the painless state, prized by Epicurus as the highest good and as the state of the Gods; for that moment we are delivered from the miserable pressure of the will. We celebrate the Sabbath of the penal servitude of willing; the wheel of Ixion stands still.[65]

So Schopenhauer too offers a notion of the transfiguration of the real through art, a reality which itself is worthless and degraded. Schopenhauer's philosophy—not as he intended it, but as it took effect on the culture of late-nineteenth-century Europe—was the basis of a family of theories of transfiguration through creative expression. Schopenhauer's philosophy itself was a revolt against the whole Christian-inspired requirement that we affirm the goodness of what is. He wanted to throw off once and for all this terrible burden that Christian civilization has laid on us; to declare reality evil once and for all, and have done with it. But he opened the path by which the great majority of those who were inspired by him returned to the original framework. This is a testimony to its strength in our civilization.

Schopenhauer had an immense influence on the thought and art of late-nineteenth-century Europe: in Germany, Austria, also France, even Russia. Most of the great writers, composers, and thinkers were deeply affected by his thought, imprinted with it: Wagner, Nietzsche, Mahler, Thomas Mann—one could greatly extend this list. But what was common to these figures was not Schopenhauer's notion of release from the ego but his idea of transfiguration through art.

Thus Nietzsche, who starts off as a Schopenhauerian, and whose *Birth of Tragedy* was influential in creating the Schopenhauerian mould of thought, speaks of art as "justifying" reality: "Only as an aesthetic product can the world be justified to all eternity".[66] The transfiguration through art is no longer a mere repose for the tortured being on its way to full release; it is somehow the end and purpose of things. In *Schopenhauer as Educator*, Nietzsche talks of nature coming to self-knowledge through man, of its reaching its consummation in the day when a man will finally come to be "who feels himself infinite in knowing and living, in seeing and ability, and who with all his being is part of nature".[67]

A lot has survived of the original expressivist constellation after the Schopenhauerian transmutation—much more than Schopenhauer had wanted. True, the sense of nature as a source of goodness, of the spirit, is definitively rejected. The driving force of the will can only mean suffering. But what is great, what makes it all worthwhile, what can therefore almost be seen as its justification, as the end for which it exists, is the transfiguration. Of course, Nietzsche rejected all this later on, but what he then espoused represented even less a return to the original philosophy of Schopenhauer.

The young Nietzsche enthusiastically followed Wagner in the latter's hope to create a new and more vibrant German culture. The Wagnerian *Gesamt-kunstwerk* was to be a major instrument of this. Wagner drew heavily on Schopenhauer's theories of art, particularly music—there are passages of Wagner where one really feels the force of the idea that music is a direct picture of the will. But all this was in aid not of an escape from willing, but of a new reformation of German culture and politics. The world is to be remade; life is to be made once more significant. It will be transfigured through tragedy.

In Mahler's Third Symphony we have one of the great expressions in music of Schopenhauer's theory of the will. In the first movement, in particular, we sense the force of the will emanating in nature. But as we reach the higher levels and our redemption from the will, this comes to be portrayed in Christian terms. The consciousness of the insatiable and unstoppable will is the consciousness of sin; and the miracle which takes us beyond is a redemption of love. Once more, as with Wagner and the young Nietzsche but even more markedly, Mahler seems to be saying that the development of the will through its fragmented phase was for the sake of this crowning achievement, in which we accede to the vision of oneness with the All.

Once again, in spite of the negation, we find that a lot has remained of the original Romantic-expressive constellation. One thing is a sense of nature as a great reservoir of force, one that we need to regain contact with. It is no longer seen as a domain of spirit, of goodness; quite the contrary. But to be cut off from it is to fall into desiccation, emptiness, dullness, a narrow and shrivelled life, egoism, and cowardice. This is Nietzsche's claim in *Schopen-hauer as Educator,* and we find it often repeated among Schopenhauerians.[68] We cannot cut ourselves off from this fermenting source of power, from the "Dionysian", as we all too easily do in our civilization based on 'reason'; for we find that our lives shrivel and dry up to insignificance. But at the same time, we dare not plunge too deeply, too precipitately, too unguardedly into it, because it is wild, formless, unreason itself.

This idea of nature as a great reservoir of amoral force, with which we must not lose contact, is one of the important bequests of the post-Schopenhauerian period to twentieth-century art and sensibility. We find echoes of it in a host of places, in Fauvism, Surrealism, D. H. Lawrence.[69] But it is also a moral vision; and this too has had its effects, some of them catastrophic on a world scale.

Another important legacy, and here there is a convergence with the other negations/continuations of Romanticism, is the enhanced sense of our own expressive powers. It is through the articulations of the creative imagination that the will is tapped and transmuted into beauty. The power of the human imagination to refract and transfigure reality emerges magnified out of the Schopenhauerian turn. And in this it pushes in the same direction as the art of anti-nature and even ultimately as the transfigurations of realism. In different but parallel ways, they emphasize that the epiphanies of art involve a *transmutation* of what is there: despiritualized reality, or fallen nature, or the amoral will; rather than the revelation of a good which is ontically independent of us—even if it needs us to come to epiphany. This is not true of the Baudelaire who speaks of the 'correspondences'; nor is it true of Schopenhauer himself, who sees the artist as contemplating the Ideas. But it is true of those who followed in their wake, as these vestiges of (neo)Platonism disappeared, encouraged in part by some of Baudelaire's own poetic practice.

The temptation thus grows to an epiphanic art which will primarily celebrate our own powers, the self-centred and subjectivist art I spoke about above. I want to return to this issue below.

A third legacy of Schopenhauer is a further enrichment of our sense of the inner depths of a human being, a renewed sense of our link with the whole of nature, but as a great reservoir of unbridled power, which underlies our mental life. This has been elaborated by a great number of writers and artists—and not least in the passage from Conrad's *Heart of Darkness* that I quoted at the end of the last chapter—who have added to the force and imaginative reach of this picture of ourselves.

And not just writers of literature; also men of science: one of the important authors deeply influenced by the Schopenhauerian climate of thought was Freud. It is a commonplace how Schopenhauer anticipated the Freudian doctrines of the unconscious determination of our thought and feeling. Even more important, the Schopenhauerian will was the ancestor to the Freudian id. But rather than taking the engaged stance in an attempt to renew contact, Freud takes a Cartesian stance to this inner world. The aim is by objectifying it to gain a disengaged understanding of it and, as a consequence, to liberate us from its obsessions, terrors, compulsions.

Freud's is a magnificent attempt to regain our freedom and self-possession, the dignity of the disengaged subject, in face of the inner depths. This is not to say that Freud's project didn't overlap at all with that of the post-Schopenhauerian artists. The very terms of Freudian science and the language of his analyses require an articulation of the depths. And Freud certainly had a sense of the great power of the human symbolic capacity, even imprisoned as it most often is in the gigantic conflict of instincts, and distorted as it is by condensations and displacements. It may turn out that Freud's project, a kind of natural science of the mind, is impossible in the stringent terms in which he conceived it. The exploration may be nearer to art and literature than he would have been willing to concede.

But there is no doubt that as self-interpretation the Freudian theory has its power, along with others which are offered without benefit of science; and if no more for all its scientific trappings, then no less either. And for those who have been able to assume it, shape has sometimes been given to their lives which has allowed them in effect to gain some distance, some self-possession, in face of the inner obsessions, fears, and strivings of the Schopenhauerian world.

23.6

I have been looking at three ways in which the Romantic understanding of epiphanic art was transformed, continued yet negated, in the nineteenth century. What I have been looking for is the changes in underlying moral vision. These were related to changes in the theory and practice of the arts, and above all to an enhanced sense of the powers of the creative imagination.

But they also had other effects: in particular, on our understanding of our moral predicament; and as these moral visions have gained a deeper and wider hold in our civilization, largely through the art they inform, these effects have become more palpable.

I want to speak of one very important effect here. We face an issue today which doesn't have an exact precedent in earlier times. It is the issue of what I want to call self-affirmation.

We can see it arising in the wake of the developments described above. I described the outlooks of Baudelaire and Schopenhauer as a recovery of an older spiritual tradition within a new context of thought and sensibility. They found a way to give voice to the sense of fallen nature within a context shaped by Romantic expressivism and also to some degree by the fading of Christian theism as the unchallengeable framework of moral thinking, even though expressivism and disbelief originally emerged out of a quite opposite spiritual orientation. But their views had their own impact and contributed to creating a new climate of thought, one in which the original Romantic vision of spiritualized nature was not as easily believable. The continuing development of a natural scientific view of nature and the 'disenchantment' brought about by industrial civilization undoubtedly also contributed to this change.

In a sense, the shoe now began to be on the other foot. For those who stood in the tradition affirming the goodness of nature, it became necessary to find new languages to say what they wanted to say. This was the more necessary in that the new articulations of fallen nature, being partly or wholly outside the Christian theological framework, were much more stark and total. Within Christian theology, it is never possible to escape altogether the notion that the creation is ultimately good. The semi-Manichaean outlook of Baudelaire was less restrained in this respect, and the theory of Schopenhauer not at all.

But the position which affirms the goodness of nature isn't a marginal one. It has all the depth in our civilization of the combined weight of Christianity and Platonism. It is the basis of the most widespread secular ethics and political views, those which descend from the Enlightenment as well as those in full continuity with the original Romantics. And it is the necessary basis for a family of life goods which is widely recognized in our civilization, those related to benevolence. The pessimists seemed to be undermining the grounds on which universal benevolence was seen as a good, the value of human life and happiness.

In different ways, all three of the developments away from Romanticism, while exalting art and our transfigurative powers, can raise questions about the goodness of being. This is obvious for Baudelaire and Schopenhauer; but it can also arise with naturalistic realism, not because of any intention to paint nature and mankind as bad, but just because the stark rejection of any spiritual dimension may easily engender a sense that the affirmation is insufficiently based, that there isn't that much to affirm after all. For those committed to the goodness of being and benevolence—and plainly that still means the vast majority of us in this civilization—this can open a crisis, a crisis of affirmation.

One can try to meet this crisis by returning to the older creeds: either a Christian faith, or some Enlightenment doctrine of reason and freedom, or a Romantic-inspired view of nature as a source. But another dimension has now entered as well. Romanticism, followed by the three developments I've just described, has made us aware of the power of the creative imagination in transfiguring ordinary reality, even base and repulsive reality, in the case of Baudelaire. This cannot but suggest an analogous role in the recovery of the capacity to affirm goodness.

In other words, it becomes possible for us to see a crisis of affirmation as something which we may have to meet through a transfiguration of our own vision, rather than simply through a recognition of some objective order of goodness. The recovery may have to take the form of a transformation of our stance towards the world and self, rather than simply the registering of external reality. Put in yet other terms, the world's being good may now be seen as not entirely independent of our seeing it and showing it as good, at least as far as the world of humans is concerned. The key to a recovery from the crisis may thus consist in our being able to "see that it is good".

The Judaeo-Christian origins of this whole notion ring in the phrase I've just used. In effect, there are two different bases to the deep commitment of

Jewish, Christian, and Muslim civilizations to goodness of being. One lies in the Greek philosophy they have all taken in, principally in Plato, where the goodness of reality is a feature of its own ordering, something we grasp by contemplation. But the other basis comes from the doctrine of creation, and is there in the first chapter of Genesis. The goodness of the world is not something quite independent from God's seeing it as good. His seeing it as good, loving it, can be conceived not simply as a *response* to what it is, but as what *makes* it such. There is, of course, an age-old debate in all three traditions about the relations between what God sees and what he makes, his intellect and his will. For the vast majority of theologians it has been basic that these two can't be separated and related in God the way they are in us.

What we have in this new issue of affirming the goodness of things is the development of a human analogue to God's seeing things as good: a seeing which also helps effect what it sees. This can mean, of course, that the self-attribution of this power is a resolutely atheist doctrine, the arrogation to man of powers formerly confined to God. This will be so with Nietzsche, whom we'll look at in a minute. But this doesn't have to be so. One of the most insightful thinkers to explore this power is Dostoyevsky, who sees it in a Christian perspective.

In fact the notion of a transformation of our stance towards the world whereby our vision of it is changed has been traditionally connected with the notion of grace. Augustine holds that in relation to God, love has to precede knowledge. With the right direction of love, things become evident which are hidden otherwise. What is new is the modern sense of the place and power of the creative imagination. This is now an integral part of the goodness of things, and hence the transformation of our stance and thus our outlook helps to bring about the truth it reveals.

Now this idea may but doesn't have to be given an atheist formulation. Whether it does or not depends on whether we go on seeing ourselves as dependent on God for this transformation. But those who affirm this dependence, like Dostoyevsky, just as those who do not, like Nietzsche, have a thoroughly modern conception of what the transformation involves. This conception has its roots in the post-Romantic notion of the creative imagination, which helps complete what it reveals. Let us turn briefly to three influential nineteenth-century writers who illustrate this issue of self-affirmation: Kierkegaard, Dostoyevsky, and Nietzsche.

In *Either/Or*, Kierkegaard lays out the idea of an aesthetic transfiguration of life, only to trump it with a higher form, the ethical. The ethical we attain by choosing ourselves in the light of infinity. As against the aesthetic man, who is carried on from one finite thing to another and is fully occupied with these, who in a sense makes no choices, or only chooses among finite things in finite contexts, the ethical man truly chooses himself. He chooses himself infinitely; that is, the choice is not for the sake of any finite thing but, on the contrary, all finite things get their value and significance from this choice.

This change of stance which Kierkegaard calls choosing ourselves brings about a reversal which can be called a transfiguration. All the elements in my life may be the same, but they are now transfigured because chosen in the light of the infinite. In a sense, we renounce all the finite things when we renounce the aesthetic stance and go to the ethical. But we receive them all back, now no longer as absolutes, as the determinants of our final ends, but as relative to our life project. None of the detail of one's life changes. We now live for the infinite. But this change is in a sense purely inward. Indeed, in a sense it transforms a merely outward life and gives it inwardness.[70] But the extraordinary person who has gone through this is outwardly perfectly ordinary.

This choosing of ourselves, this placing ourselves in the infinite, lifts us out of despair and allows us to affirm ourselves. The aesthetic man lives in dread, because he is at the mercy of external finite things and their vicissitudes. But he also lives in despair, despair of himself, because he cannot but sense that he is meant for something higher; he is not meant to be the plaything of the finite. In choosing myself, I become what I really am, a self with an infinite dimension. We choose our real selves; we become for the first time true selves. And this lifts us out of despair. Or rather, what we now despair of is the merely finite. And with this infinite choice and despairing of the finite we overcome dread. And through this, we sense ourselves for the first time as worthy to be loved and chosen. Through choice we attain self-love, self-affirmation.

There are clear echoes here of Kant. The self-choosing infinite self is what we truly are, a dignity which we should live up to, and our failing to do so induces in us a sense of our degradation. But this higher being which we really are has quite a different shape from Kant's. It is not the rational agent, who generates a law out of himself which he must obey. He doesn't realize his dignity by submitting nature to law. Rather he transforms his life by seeing/living it in a new dimension, that of infinite choice. There is a parallel, because the shift to the moral law, just as that to infinite choice, relativizes all the particular goals in my life; they are now valid only subject to, conditional on, a higher end. But for Kierkegaard this higher end is not obeying a rational law but living in the dimension of infinite choice. I accede to it not by submitting my nature to reason but by a radical shift in stance towards life.

Kierkegaard in his later writings evolved beyond this definition of the ethical, which came to be seen as a stage which was in turn trumped by the religious. But this retains some of the features of B's position in *Either/Or*. In particular, the idea remains of a transformation which depends on a new stance towards oneself, overcoming despair and dread. Only now it is made clearer how this depends on our relation to God.[71]

Dostoyevsky in his early life was deeply influenced by the German Romantics, in particular by Schiller. Visions of this kind are still articulated by characters in later novels. I am thinking, for instance, of the picture of a restored humanity in *Raw Youth*, matched by Stavrogin's dream in the appendix to *The Devils*. It also comes out in his sympathy for the elder Verkhovensky in that novel. Moreover, in the great statement of Zossima in *The Brothers Karamazov*, we have a picture of grace as a current flowing through nature, which marries certain traditional themes of Christian thought and the Romantic vision.

But one of Dostoyevsky's central insights turns on the way in which we close or open ourselves to grace. The ultimate sin is to close oneself, but one's reasons for doing so can be of the highest. In a sense, the person who is closed is in a vicious circle from which it is hard to escape.

We are closed to grace, because we close ourselves to the world in which it circulates; and we do that out of loathing for ourselves and for this world. But paradoxically, the more noble and sensitive and morally insightful one is, the more one is liable to feel this loathing. It is one of Dostoyevsky's noble and deeply moral characters, Ivan Karamazov, who most strongly expresses this rejection. He wants to give God back "his ticket" to this world of unacceptable suffering; and he wants this so firmly because he has the moral sensitivity to feel that the ultimate happiness of the whole of mankind isn't worth the tears of an innocent child.

But this is to close oneself in a vicious circle. Rejecting the world seals one's sense of its loathsomeness and of one's own, insofar as one is part of it. And from this can only come acts of hate and destruction. Moreover, these radiate out from one in a chain, a kind of negative apostolic succession, as one inspires others through this loathing to loathe in their turn. Ivan's noble attitude ultimately issues in the crime of his half-brother Smerdyakov. And in *The Devils*, Dostoyevsky explores how this reverse apostolic succession brings about violence and terror. Radiating out from Stavrogin are various lines of rejection of the world. Dostoyevsky, even in spite of the elements of caricature in this novel, gives an acute understanding of how loathing and self-loathing, inspired by the very real evils of the world, fuel a projection of evil outward, a polarization between self and world, where all the evil is now seen to reside. This justifies terror, violence, and destruction against the world; indeed, this seems to call for it. No one, I believe, has given us deeper insight into the *spiritual* sources of modern terrorism or has shown more clearly how terrorism can be a response to the threat of self-hatred.

Dostoyevsky's rejectors are "schismatics" *(raskolniki)*, cut off from the world and hence grace. They cannot but wreak destruction. The noblest wreak it only on themselves. The most base destroy others. Although powered by the noblest sense of the injustice of things, this schism is ultimately also the fruit of pride, Dostoyevsky holds. We separate because we don't want to see ourselves as part of the evil; we want to raise ourselves above it, away from the blame for it. The outward projection of the terrorist is the most violent manifestation of this common motive.

What will transform us is an ability to love the world and ourselves, to see it as good in spite of the wrong. But this will only come to us if we can accept being part of it, and that means accepting responsibility. Just as 'no one is to blame' is the slogan of the materialist revolutionaries, so 'we are all to blame' is of Dostoyevsky's healing figures.[72] Loving the world and ourselves is in a sense a miracle, in face of all the evil and degradation that it and we contain.[73] But the miracle comes on us if we accept being part of it. Involved in this is our acceptance of love from others. We become capable of love through being loved; and over against the perverse apostolic succession is a grace-dispensing one: from Markel to Zossima to Alyosha to Grushenka; matching that from Ivan to Smerdyakov, or that from Stavrogin to Pyotr Verkhovensky and through him to his terrorist followers.

Dostoyevsky brings together here a central idea of the Christian tradition, especially evident in the Gospel of John, that people are transformed through being loved by God, a love that they mediate to each other, on one hand, with the modern notion of a subject who can help to bring on transfiguration through the stance he takes to himself and the world, on the other. From this point of view, it doesn't matter that Dostoyevsky saw himself as opposing much of the modern tradition—he once identified Descartes's cogito as the root of the modern evil. What he was opposing was the belief that humans affirm their dignity in separation from the world. In this Dostoyevsky was being faithful to his Romantic roots. What is significant here is the way in which the modern identity, with its transforming powers, has become incorporated in Dostoyevsky's vision, even while he opposes it. It is not an accident that Dostoyevsky's positive figures have to go through the experience of modernity. "The absolute atheist stands on the last rung but one before most absolute faith".[74] Dostoyevsky's healing grace lies beyond the modern identity, not anterior to it.

With Nietzsche, we have a totally different vision, and yet with some strange points of contact—the character Kirillov in *The Devils* sounds in some respects like a fictional anticipation of Nietzsche. The profoundly Christian resonance which remains paradoxically in Nietzsche in spite of his virulent opposition to Christianity lies in his aspiration to affirm the whole of reality, to see it as good, to say 'yes' to it all. This is an aspiration which wouldn't have been comprehensible outside of Judaeo-Christian culture.

But this is meant to be achieved *against* Christianity, and against the moralities which spring from it. Nietzsche's break with Schopenhauer's pessimism didn't turn on his having a higher vision of the cosmos and the forces at work in it. On the contrary, everything is will to power, and humans only a more intense objectification of this will. The aspiration is realized by a victory over oneself, a kind of 'self-overcoming', in which one is able to affirm the world, even though it remains the domain of blind, unspiritual, chaotic forces. This is impossible for the moral consciousness, which issues from Christianity. It can only bear the universe if it sees it as the seat of rationality, or as undergoing some progress in ethics and civilization, or as destined for the ultimate salvation. Against all this, Nietzsche opposes his myth of the eternal return: there will be no resolution, no rising higher, no compensation for suffering, no ultimate reconciliation, no way out. This is the vision which separates all-too-humans from supermen. Only the latter can bear it, can look it in the eye and still say 'yes' to everything.

Nietzsche is talking about a kind of transformation, a transfiguration of the world: a vision which doesn't alter any of its contents but the meaning of the whole. But in contrast to Kierkegaard and Dostoyevsky, the strength to make this transformation comes entirely from within us, from a self-overcoming.

Morality demanded a kind of self-overcoming in its way. And perhaps one can say (or is this introducing a kind of Hegelian vision of stages into Nietzsche?) that it was a necessary step.[75] Morality brought us to the notion of something pure and great and infinitely worth affirmation and love—only it wasn't us as we are, but the negation of our essential being, the denial of the will to power. What we have to do, while hanging onto that sense of the magnificent, of the categorically affirmable, of the infinitely worthy of love,[76] is overcome the force of morality and find the strength to rise above its demands, which sap our strength and fill us with the poison of self-hatred. What emerges from this struggle with ourselves is not a loss of but a reversal in this categorical affirmation. This power to affirm does indeed repose in us. And in the struggle we discover that it makes no sense to turn it against us. Rather what really commands affirmation is this very power itself and the whole matrix within which it is set, and which is essential to it. What commands affirmation is the universe of the will to power which engenders and contains such affirmation. We can say 'yes' to all that is.

But this is immensely hard, because the sense that there is something higher goes so easily with, and tends to engender again, the sense of our unworthiness and the condemnation of ourselves and others, not to speak of the false ideals of mildness and benevolence and the unmanning emotion of pity. These are the forces which make the all-too-human; and these are the forces which have to be overcome on the hard path to the superman.

Nietzsche wanted to put behind him the doctrine of aesthetic transfiguration which he drew from Schopenhauer, and which marks his early work. He wanted to go beyond "justifying" the world through its manifestation in art and really affirm it. But some aspect of aesthetic transfiguration remains. What in the universe commands our affirmation, when we have overcome the all-too-human, is not properly called its goodness but comes close to being its beauty. It is perhaps not reducible to, but cannot be quite separated from, aesthetic categories. Part of what makes Nietzsche's vision compelling is the beauty of his language, especially in *Zarathustra*. But the beauty is not just ancillary, not just part of the presentation or simply an aesthetic response to a good which could be specified in other terms. Part of the heroism of the Nietzschean superman is that he can rise beyond the moral, beyond the concern with good, and manage in spite of suffering and disorder and the absence of all justice to respond to something like the beauty of it all. Hence the affirmation cannot be fully separated from an aesthetic transfiguration. Zarathustra is inseparably visionary and poet.

As with Baudelaire's poems on the horrible and ugly, the beauty is inwardly connected to the stance of unflinching acceptance. The beautiful light which bathes certain passages of *Zarathustra* is not separable from the soaring spirit of Zarathustra himself, which through its overcoming reaches deeply into the far landscape of human moral striving, like the slanting rays of the late afternoon sun. But the connection goes both ways: the overcoming is only possible in the vision of beauty.

I have tried to draw out of these three authors something which I think they have in common, viz., the idea of changed stance towards self and world, which doesn't simply recognize a hitherto occluded good, but rather helps to bring this about. The new stance enables me to overcome dread and despair; or to stand in the stream of love; or to accede to the full unity of total self-affirmation of the superman. In the case of Dostoyevsky and Nietzsche, the change involves something like the recognition of reality as good, but this at the same time helps to bring about this goodness. Accepting to be part of the world contributes to healing it for Dostoyevsky; affirming the will to power carries the will to a higher potency for Nietzsche. As in Genesis, seeing good makes good.

One could say that seeing good empowers, and that it thus functions as what I have been calling a moral source. We have here a further step in the process I have called the internalization of moral sources. Alongside the sense of our dignity as disengaged, free, reasoning subjects, alongside our sense of the creative imagination as a power of epiphany and transfiguration, we have also this idea of an affirming power, which can help realize the good by recognizing it.

Of course, none of these powers need to be seen as exclusively within. In particular, the second and third are frequently understood as related to nature as a source or to God. But unlike previous conceptions of moral sources in nature and God, these modern views give a crucial place to our own inner powers of constructing or transfiguring or interpreting the world, as essential to the efficacy of the external sources. Our powers must be deployed if these are to empower us. And in this sense the moral sources have been at least partly internalized.

The internalization is in a sense more complete in the atheist or naturalist theories, more complete for Nietzsche than for Dostoyevsky. But Nietzsche's theory presents a paradox (perhaps more than one!). One of the things that makes a doctrine of our affirming power so necessary is just our commitment to an ethic of benevolence, which is why an inability to affirm the goodness of human beings can be threatening. But Nietzsche wins through to his total yea-saying precisely by jettisoning the ethic of benevolence, which is inextricably linked in his view with self-negating morality. He presents us a cruel dilemma. Is it one we have to face?

24

EPIPHANIES OF MODERNISM

24.1

All these developments have helped to create an epiphanic art in the twentieth century which is in some respects very different from the Romantic prototype. The forms which dominate our century are often loosely collected under the title 'modernist'. Two differences are striking in relation to the great Romantics, features which paradoxically go together although they seem to be opposed. Twentieth-century art has gone more inward, has tended to explore, even to celebrate subjectivity; it has explored new recesses of feeling, entered the stream of consciousness, spawned schools of art rightly called 'expressionist.' But at the same time, at its greatest it has often involved a decentring of the subject: an art emphatically not conceived as self-expression, an art displacing the centre of interest onto language, or onto poetic transmutation itself, or even dissolving the self as usually conceived in favour of some new constellation.

There seems to be a slide to subjectivism and an anti-subjectivist thrust at the same time. These should be opposed, and they are certainly in tension. But in their genesis they belong together, and this may not be too difficult to explain.

The modernists found themselves in opposition to their world for reasons which were continuous with those of the Romantics. The world seen just as mechanism, as a field for instrumental reason, seemed to the latter shallow and debased. By the twentieth century the encroachments of instrumental reason were incomparably greater, and we find the modernist writers and artists in protest against a world dominated by technology, standardization, the decay of community, mass society, and vulgarization. There was, indeed, a minority, like the Futurists, which took a positive stance towards technology and wanted to celebrate its creative potentialities; but they too were appalled at the passivity and ugliness which they saw as the actual consequences of mass industrial society.

For the Romantics, the counterweight to the world deformed by mechanism and the utilitarian stance was the real world of nature and undistorted human feeling. Wordsworth looked to find this in the country and among simple folk. To the German Romantics, followed by Coleridge, the world was an emanation of spirit. Poetry can restore us to this world by showing what is really there behind it, making it shine through nature. In Blake's vision, we liberate ourselves from the "vegetative eye" and see the true spiritual reality. And Shelley says of poetry that "it creates anew the universe, after it has been annihilated in our minds by the recurrence of impressions blunted by reiteration".[1]

The epiphany which will free us from the debased, mechanistic world brings to light the spiritual reality behind nature and uncorrupted human feeling. Epiphanic art can take the form of descriptions of these which make this reality shine through, as Wordsworth and Hölderlin, Constable and Friedrich do, each in his own way. But this recourse is no longer available in the early twentieth century, at least not in this direct way—for a host of overlapping reasons.

The change was partly due to the prodigious development of industrial society. In an urbanized, technological society, nature is marginalized. There are no more peasants living in symbiosis with it. The landscapes painted by Constable are being obliterated. Machines and a human environment designed to cope with anonymous masses dominate our world. What remains outside all this is wilderness; but this we have come to understand in terms rather different from the Romantics. Our understanding of it is shaped by another change, which was especially important in the second half of the nineteenth century. This was the progress of a scientific, mechanistic worldview, no longer based simply in mechanics but claiming to englobe the life sciences as well.

These two changes furthered and were facilitated by a shift in the sense of nature as a force, which came to be less and less captured by Romantic notions of spiritual reality, and more and more matched a vision like Schopenhauer's: nature as a great reservoir of amoral power. Changes in society, scientific theory, and the images articulating sensibility came together to make the old Romantic outlook virtually untenable.

It was untenable on two levels: first, it was no longer fully believable; but second, it was also repudiated. Many modernists defined themselves as anti-Romantic. The Romantic outlook seemed compromised by its co-option into the 'bourgeois' world—just as 'modernism' appears in our day to some 'post-modernists'. We can easily see why this was so. I described in the last chapter the collusive relation that develops between bourgeois and avant-garde. The creative imagination and the horizons of emotional fulfilment that it opens become an indispensable part of spiritual nourishment—even for those who staff the world of power and commerce. We see this not only in the popularity in the 'straight' world of works about 'la vie de Bohéme' but also on a more serious, philosophical level in a synthesis such as that wrought by J. S. Mill. Mill suffered deeply in his own life from the conflict between the demands of the most austere disengaged reason and the need for a richer sense of meaning, which he ultimately found through the Romantic poets. He had somehow to integrate Bentham and Coleridge, and he put together a synthesis, which one sees in such works as *Utilitarianism* and the *Essay on Liberty*, which combines a disengaged, scientistic utilitarianism with an expressivist conception of human growth and fulfilment, and which owes a lot to German Romanticism, through Coleridge and Humboldt. Whether this synthesis is consistent or not is another issue; what is important here is that it represents one form of a widespread attempt to integrate Romantic notions of personal fulfilment into the private lives of the denizens of a civilization run more and more by the canons of instrumental reason.

To the extent that this synthesis becomes believable, Romantic models of fulfilment can contribute to the self-justification of this civilization. We can see this in a widespread justificatory notion of late capitalism today: the wheels of industry turn in order to give individuals the means for a rich and satisfying private life. Late Victorian self-congratulation turned more on a sense of the fulfilments of family life. Here Romantic notions had helped to give further body to the ideal of the family as the haven of warm sentiment in an otherwise cooling world. The Wordsworthian picture of the child, for instance, as a being of unspoilt innocence, could be taken up by Dickens in a critical spirit against the society that left them prey to exploitation and degradation; but it also could serve as a ground for self-esteem as higher living standards allowed more and more families to provide safe, respectable homes.

Victorian piety and sentimentality seemed to have captured the Romantic spirit. For those who saw this whole world as spiritually hollow and flat, Romanticism could appear as integral to what they rejected as instrumentalism was. It merely offered trivialized, ersatz, or inauthentic meanings to compensate for a meaningless world. For those who hungered after some purer, deeper, or stronger moral source that the world of disengaged reason couldn't provide, the expression of simply personal emotion or the celebration of routinized fulfilments was a travesty. And so the modernists as heirs to the Romantics turned against what they saw as Romanticism. The breach with their world had to be more thoroughgoing. They couldn't turn for solace to merely subjective feeling or to the confidence that the world emanates from the spirit.[2]

That is why many of the path-breaking modernist writers had less in common with the stance of the great Romantics than with that of a Baudelaire, whose stance seeks the epiphany no longer in a fallen nature but somehow beyond or outside it. And that is why they frequently found themselves in sympathy with the Nietzschean appeal to the heroic virtues, against what they saw as the comfortable, flabby humanitarianism of their time.[3] Hulme, who drew from both these sources, attacked Romanticism for its denial of original sin; he correctly saw the origins of this denial in Rousseau and in the doctrines of nature as source, and wanted to repudiate the one with the other. Romanticism was just "spilt religion";[4] its error was to have elided religion and nature, where they should have been kept strictly apart, It failed "to realize that there is an absolute, and not a relative, difference between humanism (which we can take to be the highest expression of the vital) and the religious spirit. The *divine* is not *life* at its intensest. It contains in a way an almost *anti-vital* element".[5] To take this stance was to reject what I called earlier the epiphanies of being. This can produce a poetics which strips the aura from things. Early Eliot is a striking example, precisely under the influence of Baudelaire and T. E. Hulme.

But we see a parallel development in rather different terms with Thomas Mann, this time under a Schopenhauerian influence. Hans Castorp's epiphany in the "Snow" passage of *The Magic Mountain* shows how the harmonious beauties of the sunlit classical world are built on the horrors of old age, decay, and human sacrifice. And in *Death in Venice* what irresistibly attracts Gustav von Aschenbach, that highly controlled and disciplined craftsman, admirer of Frederick the Great, to the effortlessly incarnate beauty of Tadzio is also drawing him ineluctably towards disease and death. The epiphanies of being for Mann have this profoundly ambiguous character. As for Proust, the revelation of time restored is bought at the cost of a pitiless destruction of the illusions of love.[6]

All this can help explain the particular form of the modernist turn to interiority. Thinkers in the early twentieth century were exercised by a problem which is still posed today: What is the place of the Good, or the True, or the Beautiful, in a world entirely determined mechanistically? Hulme, for instance, took materialism as a serious challenge, identifying it through this statement by Munsterberg:

> Science is to me not a mass of disconnected information, but the certainty that there is no change in the universe, no motion of an atom, and no sensation of a consciousness which does not come and go absolutely in accordance with natural laws; the certainty that nothing can exist outside the gigantic mechanism of causes and effects; necessity moves the emotions in my mind.[7]

To counter the imperial claims of an all-embracing mechanism, strengthened by the march of an advancing technology, the recourse couldn't simply be an epiphanic *description* of nature. For not only had this very mechanism made this response problematic, and Schopenhauer's vision undermined it; but the recoil from the epiphanies of being branded it as wrong. It did not provide a genuine alternative to the instrumental world which generated the mechanist outlook, which offered to reduce even our sensations and feelings to its exceptionless laws. The obvious recourse against this all-pervasive levelling was interiority: that the lived world, the world as experienced, known and transmuted in sensibility and consciousness, couldn't be assimilated to the supposedly all-encompassing machine. Bergson, with his doctrine of the irreducibility of experience to external explanation, of durée to the spatialized time of physical explanation, was the great source of liberation for Hulme.

This kind of move, which brings philosophers together with artists and critics in an attempt to recover what has been suppressed and forgotten in the conditions of experience, has been repeated many times in the twentieth century. Hulme later took up Husserl as he had Bergson. And the banner under which Husserl sailed, 'phenomenology', has been appropriated for the distinct but parallel enterprises of Heidegger and Merleau-Ponty, while in quite different terms, similar revolutions in thought and sensiblility have been inspired by the late writings of Wittgenstein, or have been attempted by Michael Polanyi.

Each one of these moves has been accompanied, for those who took part in them, by the same sense of exhilaration that Hulme felt.[8] This comes from the retrieval of the lived experience or creative activity underlying our awareness of the world, which had been occluded or denatured by the regnant mechanistic construal. The retrieval is felt as a liberation, because the experience can become more vivid and the activity unhampered through being recognized, and alternatives open up in our stance towards the world which were quite hidden before.

In Hulme's early theory poetry restores a living contact with reality. In a mechanistic, utilitarian world we come to deal with things in a mechanical, conventionalized way. Our attention is turned away from things to what we are getting done through them. Ordinary prose reflects this. It deals in dead counters, which allow us to refer to things without really seeing them. In prose "we get words divorced from any real vision".[9] Poetry is meant to break through this abstraction. "It always endeavours to arrest you, and to make you continuously see a physical thing, to prevent you gliding through an abstract process".[10] The poetic image breaks away from a language of counters and gives us a fresh intuitive language which restores our vision of things.

One can see immediately the close parallel with Heidegger. Our ordinary interests focus us on objects as "present-at-hand" (vorhanden); we forget altogether the way in which objects are primarily there for us as "ready-to-hand" *(zuhanden)*. There is a steady tendency towards the "forgetfulness of Being," which has to be reversed by an existential analytic, a study which brings to light the forgotten being of things and opens us to the meaning of Being, which has been obscured and covered over in our modern world-view.[11]

Through whatever important differences, a line of affiliation links all these philosophical overturnings to the basic concerns of the Romantics. They all aim to combat the hold of mechanistic-utilitarian categories on our lives; they all have some debt to philosophies of vitalism and expressivism: Wittgenstein to Schopenhauer, Heidegger to Dilthey.[12] And they all stand close to facets of modernist consciousness in their rejection of the hegemony of disengaged reason and mechanism.

So where the original Romantics turned to nature and unadorned feeling, we find many moderns turning to a retrieval of experience or interiority. This is the inward turn I have described. But what about the anti-subjectivism we find so frequently in Pound and Eliot, in Rilke, and in Heidegger as well? This is the feature which is so often articulated as an opposition to Romanticism (as with Hulme), or as 'classicism' (Eliot), or even as an anti-humanism (Wyndham Lewis, and again later Heidegger).

This paradoxically has some of the same roots. The original Romantic belief in nature held for nature within us as well. The spiritual reality which emanated in the world which surrounds us was also within. The Spirit in nature comes to consciousness in man, for Schelling and Hegel. Coleridge sees nature in terms of life; everything grows, and shapes itself from within. The artist's imagination works by the same principle. The artist doesn't imitate mere nature as *natura naturata,* but is rather forming nature as *natura naturans.* But that is because of the bond between the spirit of nature and the human soul. The spirit is also at work in us.

Early Romanticism developed out of the notion that I have called nature as a source, whose paradigmatic early statement was in Rousseau. We can discover how to be at one with nature, how to unlock its secrets, by turning within. "Inward goes the way full of mystery", as Novalis puts it.[13] Goethe affirmed that "human nature knows itself one with the world. Mankind can be sure that the outer world is an answering counterpoint to the sensations of the inner world". And Wordsworth in the Preface to the *Lyrical Ballads* states as the poet's essential faith that "he considers man and nature as essentially adapted to each other, and the mind of man as naturally the mirror of the fairest and most interesting qualities of nature".[14] Self-articulation can thus be in harmony with, can further the revelation of, the spirit in things.

That is, of course, what gives rise to the denigrating picture of Romanticism as concerned simply with self-expression, which emerges too easily in its condemnations in the mouth of a Hulme or an Eliot. This is a calumny, as

I pointed out above; though the charge is properly levelled at some of the sub-Paterian post-Symbolism of the turn of the century, it is not true of the great Romantics.[15] But in the very pre-established harmony between self- and world-articulation lies the pretext for the false accusations.

This harmony is no longer compatible, however, with a picture of inner and outer nature which has absorbed the impact of scientific biology and Schopenhauer. And it must be even less acceptable to those in the Baudelairean stream who, like Hulme, have set their faces against the 'Romantic' belief in the inherent goodness of man and nature. That harmony was the foundation of the Romantic epiphanies of being, which for the modernists became just as unacceptable when they reposed on the supposed goodness of inner impulse as when they were based on the alleged expression of spirit in nature.

What remained was the post-Nietzschean notion of nature as an immense amoral force, with which we ought to recover contact, which was evident in different forms in Fauvism, for instance, or in early Stravinsky, or in D. H. Lawrence. But this, except perhaps in the extreme case of Surrealism, couldn't be identified with the whole self, instinct and creative imagination together. Indeed, what was gone was the alignment between these two, between inner nature and reason, that the Romantics had seen as proper to a restored humanity.

And so a turn inward, to experience or subjectivity, didn't mean a turn to a *self* to be articulated, where this is understood as an alignment of nature and reason, or instinct and creative power. On the contrary, the turn inward may take us beyond the self as usually understood, to a fragmentation of experience which calls our ordinary notions of identity into question, as with Musil, for example; or beyond that to a new kind of unity, a new way of inhabiting time, as we see, for instance, with Proust.

Indeed, we can see how the notion could arise that an escape from the traditional idea of the unitary self was a condition of a true retrieval of lived experience. The ideals of disengaged reason and of Romantic fulfilment both rely in different ways on a notion of the unitary self. The first requires a tight centre of control which dominates experience and is capable of constructing the orders of reason by which we can direct thought and life. The second sees the originally divided self come to unity in the alignment of sensibility and reason. Now to the extent that both of these come to be seen as facets of a world and an outlook whose claims to embrace everything we want to escape, to the degree that we adopt a post-Schopenhauerian vision of inner nature, the liberation of experience can seem to require that we step outside the circle of the single, unitary identity, and that we open ourselves to the flux which moves beyond the scope of control or integration.

Nietzsche had already explored this dizzying thought, that the self might not enjoy a guaranteed, a priori unity.[16] That is one of the things which makes him one of the main forerunners and inspirers of twentieth-century modernism. D. H. Lawrence was giving voice to a "Dionysiac" conception of life when he said: "Our ready-made individuality, our identity, is no more than an accidental cohesion in the flux of time".[17] But there is an echo from what we think of as the diametrically opposed, "classical", and hierarchical pole of modernism in Hulme's rejection of a belief in "the substantial unity of the soul", as another part of our erroneous humanist heritage.[18] And similar ideas echo through other modernist writers: Musil, as just mentioned; Proust also says that we are "plusieurs personnes superposées".[19] And Joyce in *Finnegan's Wake* explores a level of experience in which the boundaries of personality become fluid.

The need for an escape from the restrictions of the unitary self has indeed become an important recurring theme in this century, and all the more so in what is sometimes referred to as 'post-modernism', as we see in one way in Foucault's attack on the disciplinary or the confessing self, and in another way in the work of Lyotard.[20]

There is a parallel modernist attack on the time-consciousness and modes of narrativity associated with disengaged instrumental reason and Romanticism. The critique of the first is more in evidence. The objectified view of the world that disengaged reason produces involves a spatialization of time. Time is seen as a series of discrete moments, states of the universe at an instant, between which certain causal chains can be traced—the "homogeneous, empty time" of Benjamin. The ideal understanding of this world of time-space, as conceived by late-nineteenth-century scientism,[21] is unhooked from any time-perspective. It could be, for instance, the perfect understanding of a Laplacean omniscient predictor before the whole thing started just as well as it could be the retrospective comprehension of a scientific mind surveying the completed record after it ends. In such a comprehensive, ordered view, the moments are grasped together; they coexist; hence the image that often recurs in reproach: that time is 'spatialized'.

This is the point of attack for many of the most influential reactions to mechanism. They protest in the name of lived time. Bergson is the earliest. But Heidegger makes time the crucial issue of his early work. He rebels against a view of time in which the present is the dominant dimension, in other words, the spatialized view, in favour of one which is founded on the "three ek-stases", and which gives primacy, if it gives any at all, to the future. Heidegger's time is lived time, organized by a sense of the past as the source of a given situation, and the future as what my action must co-determine. This organization is inseparable from the agent's inhabiting his moment, his epoch; it disappears as soon as one takes the Laplacean perspective from outside. Heidegger recurs in different ways throughout his work to the central thesis that it is a fundamental error to consider Laplacean time alone real, and the time of 'events' *(Er-eignis)* as merely epiphenomenal. To construct an ordered world-view on this premiss is always to court incoherence and to deny part of reality.[22]

We also find this critique of modern mechanism and instrumentalism taken up on behalf of Marxism by Lukács. In the general 'reification' wrought by capitalism, time also becomes a homogeneous item of calculation. It "sheds its qualitative, variable, flowing nature; it freezes into an exactly delimited, quantifiable continuum filled with quantifiable 'things' . . . : in short, time becomes space".[23]

Modernist writers took up this critique of the spatialization of time. But their challenge went deeper: it touched the basic modes of narrativity of disengaged reason, *and* of Romanticism. The first spawned a view of history as progress, in which the development of reason and science leads to ever-greater instrumental control and hence well-being. The second often presents history as decline, but it also has an optimistic variant: of history as growth through a spiral, moving in the end towards a reconciliation of reason and feeling. The modernist consciousness tended to be estranged from both the "optimistic" construals. Some of the major writers we think of as modernist carry us quite outside the modes of narration which endorse a life of continuity or growth with one biography or across generations.[24]

Hans Castorp, in *The Magic Mountain*, finds the time of ordered management, of cumulative control, even the time of organic growth, slipping away from him. In the sanatorium one drifts into a kind of timelessness, where all measures are lost and time loses it shape. Just as it was with the unitary self, this kind of slippage from our normal sense of measured time is the essential condition for a deeper experience which opens another dimension of life.

Proust's epiphany in the last volume of *A la recherche du temps perdu* also involves a short-circuiting of our usual mode of narrativity. Outside of this epiphany, and prior to it, his life can't be brought together into the usual story of achievement, where one creates a succession of works and thus becomes a "writer". It is so much 'temps perdu' in the double sense of wasted time on its way to joining the unrecoverable past. Only by cohering in a way which cuts across time, which joins widely separated epiphanic moments through memory, can it be given a sense, which can then be the basis for an oeuvre of the recognized kind. The recovery of the past stops the wasting of time.

Or consider the uses of history in the poetry of Eliot and Pound. Theirs could sometimes be mistaken for the familiar Romantic stance, yearning after a richer past, one fuller of meaning, from the standpoint of an empty or shallow present. The implicit narration here is of history as decline, and the longing to recapture the earlier reality is doomed from the start, what is gone can only be invoked in nostalgia.

But on examination, this doesn't seem at all to be what is afoot in Pound's 'poems including history' or in Eliot's comparable work. The present age is indeed spiritually indigent. We in our time need to recover the past in order to attain fulness. But this is not so much because history has meant decline, as because the fulness of meaning isn't available with the resources of a single age. And what is more, Pound and Eliot seem to hold that we *can* recapture the past or, rather, make the great moments and achievements of other times come alive again in ours, to bring the long-dead back to speech. Again the goal here seems to be a kind of unity across persons, or across time, such as is realized in the Tiresias figure of *The Waste Land* or in the juxtapostions in Pound's *Cantos*, which runs athwart our usual time of narrated successions.[25]

The modernist retrieval of experience thus involves a profound breach in the received sense of identity and time, and a series of reorderings of a strange and unfamiliar kind. These images of life have reshaped our ideas in this century of what it is to be a human being.

As a result of this, the epiphanic centre of gravity begins to be displaced from the self to the flow of experience, to new forms of unity, to language conceived in a variety of ways—eventually even as a "structure". An age starts of 'decentring' subjectivity, which reaches its culmination, or perhaps its parody, in certain recently fashionable doctrines from Paris. For all the genuine discoveries which we have made in this mode, the impetus to enter it is in large part the same as that which turned us inward. Decentring is not the alternative to inwardness; it is its complement.

As a result of these two changes, the language of poetry, as also that of visual art, has undergone a further change, has become 'subtler' in a stronger sense than that of the Romantics. Earlier (section 21.2) in commenting on Wasserman's invocation of the term 'subtler language' from Shelley, I pointed to the gap that separates Pope from Wordsworth, for instance, in their descriptions of nature. Where Pope could call on the established gamut of references which the great chain of being afforded, Wordsworth or Hölderlin are finding new words by which something can become manifest to us through nature. And something similar could be said about Friedrich relative to traditional iconography in painting. But it is still through a description, or a representation of a landscape, that the epiphany occurs.

Much modern poetry is no longer descriptive in this sense. There is no unambiguously defined matter referred to or portrayed. Images are not simply introduced as simile or metaphor to characterize a central referent, story, or object. From the Symbolists on, there has been a poetry which makes something appear by juxtaposing images or, even harder to explain, by juxtaposing words. The epiphany comes from between the words or images, as it were, from the force field they set up between them, and not through a central referent which they describe while transmuting.

We can sometimes still work out a central reality a poem is "about". "The Love Song of J. Alfred Prufrock" is presumably "about" the etiolated, pusillanimous life of contemporary man, or one such. But much of the poem neither describes nor clearly expresses such a man. Who speaks and who is addressed in the opening lines?

> Let us go then, you and I,
> When the evening is spread out against the sky
> Like a patient etherized upon a table.

We triangulate to the meaning through the images.

It is obvious that an analogous, even stronger point could be made about twentieth-century non-representational visual art. Roger Shattuck has spoken of the way that criticism in all the arts has settled on the term 'juxtaposition' "to convey the idea of how the parts of a modern work of art are put together ... The twentieth century has addressed itself to arts of juxtaposition as opposed to earlier arts of transition".[26]

24.2

What does this mean for the epiphanic art of the modernists? In some cases, with their rejection of the epiphanies of being, they seem to be lining up with the counter-epiphanic strand of naturalism. Consider the lines of Eliot just quoted, where the sudden shift to the simile evoking illness and the sterilized artifice of medicine brutally disappoints the expectation of an epiphany in nature which the image about the evening seemed to promise. D. H. Lawrence turned against 'depth', the freighting of things with meanings, and in a passage from *Aaron's Rod* likens the liberation from the weight of this experience of obligatory significance to the escape from "a horrible enchanted castle, with wet walls of emotions and ponderous chains, of feelings and ghastly atmosphere".[27] Another moment of liberation is evoked in *Kangaroo*:

> No home, no tea. Insouciant carelessness. Eternal indifference. Perhaps it is only the great pause between carings. But it is only in this pause that one finds the meaninglessness of meanings—like old husks which speak dust. Only in this pause that one finds the meaninglessness of meanings, and the other dimension. The reality of timelessness and nowhere ... nothing is so meaningless as meanings.[28]

Something like the same refusal of depth seems to underly Pound's understanding of Imagism. The aim was to make the particular thing come alive before us. Two of Pound's three "rules" prescribed: "direct treatment of the 'thing' " and "to use absolutely no word that did not contribute to the presentation".[29] The *Imagist Manifesto* states as its goal: "To present an image. We are not a school of painters, but we believe that poets should render particulars exactly and not deal with vague generalities. To produce poetry that is hard and clear, never blurred and indefinite".[30]

The emphasis was on the hard-edged presentation of the thing, its clear delineation. Instead of being allowed to interpenetrate as they partake of the same meaning, the things portrayed are to be sharply circumscribed. They stand out as distinct. "The proper and perfect symbol is the natural object".[31] Above all, we have to avoid the sloppy modes of thought and perception that make boundaries fluid and allow things to flow into each other. For Pound, if literature had any function for society, it was to contribute this clarity. "When this work goes rotten ... when the very medium, the very essence of their work, the application of word to thing goes rotten, i.e., becomes slushy and inexact, or excessive and bloated, the whole machinery of social and individual thought and order goes to pot".[32]

The emphasis on clarity and distinctness was in a sense counter-epiphanic in intent. It was part of the refusal of the overlay of inauthentic meaning, of the accretions of the instrumental society and the inauthentic and etiolated feelings it generated. To cleanse these and allow reality its full force, to retrieve genuine experience, it was necessary to return to the surface of things. As so often with a theme in modernism, this one was already anticipated by Nietzsche, in his famous remark about the Greeks who were deep enough to stay at the surface of things.[33]

This counter-epiphanic side of some modernist authors seems to link them with naturalism. And in fact, the relations are complex. For naturalism itself tended to slide towards a retrieval of experience, as one can perhaps see best of all in the development of painting through Impressionism. The slide comes quite normally from the paradoxical fact, discussed above (section 23.3), that in order to reveal things in their meaninglessness, they have to undergo a certain transfiguration in art. An uncompromising realism can then seem to demand that this process of transmutation be itself brought to light. This would mean to lay bare the way that reality can be captured in a representation which itself then allows us to see this reality in its truth. And this involves us in a reflexive turn, exploring the way that things come to be for us in appearance.

Realist painting can do what it does because of the crucial fact that painting can make us see things differently. Painting can bring to the fore patterns, lines of force, whole aspects of things, which are certainly there in our visual field but overshadowed, made recessive, by our normal way of attending to and apprehending things. There is a vast latent content to our awareness of things, and indefinite multiplicity of patterns only tacitly there, unthematized relations in our 'pre-objective world', as Merleau-Ponty says; or connections which we attend from in order to attend to what is focal for us, as Polanyi describes it.[34]

To explore the way in which painting can shape our perception is inseparable from an exploration of the pre-objective world. It means bringing to light the merely tacit patterns and connections on which we usually lean unnoticing as we construe our normal world. It opens us up to the way things 'look', which means seeing some facet on which we normally rely, but which we would never really see until we stop rushing past it to fix things in their normal everyday presence for us. Impressionist painting made some of this suppressed tacit 'look' of things visible, and began an exploration of the power of painting which was itself a signal exercise of this power.

But what takes place in this exploration is precisely a retrieval of experience, which opens us up to the usually hidden appearances of things, facets that we too quickly move by in our ordinary workaday dealings with them. It does what Hulme says poetry is supposed to do, makes us see things with a freshness and immediacy which our ordinary routine way of coping with the world occludes.

Thus Cézanne, arguably the greatest of the early post-Impressionists, brought to expression the meaningful forms and relationships which undergird our ordinary perception, as they emerge and take shape from the materiality of things. To do this he had to forge a new language, abandoning linear and aerial perspective and making the spatial dispositions arise from the modulations of colour. He "recaptures and converts into visible objects what would, without him, remain walled up in the separate life of each consciousness: the vibration of appearances which is the cradle of things".[35]

The realist impulse thus leads by an understandable route to a recovery of lived experience, one of the recurring goals of modernist art and twentieth-century philosophy. And through this, this originally counter-epiphanic thrust opens up new fields for epiphanic art. And how could it be otherwise? What Impressionism made thematic was the power of art to transfigure ordinary reality. It involved an unprecedented exploration of this power. But the naturalist portrayal of the profane and banal is only one of the uses of transfiguration. This can also serve to manifest the emotion that invests things or the deeper meaning behind them, or to explore the mysterious nature of experience itself.

And so it is not surprising that the Impressionists prepare the ground for 'post-Impressionists' like Cézanne, Gauguin, Van Gogh, and the expressionist painters, who give us again epiphanies of translucence. But something important has changed. We are not back with the Romantics, with the familiar epiphanies of being. There is a gap in the works of some of these painters between the object portrayed and what is showing through it which is qualitatively new. With the expressionists, for instance, there is no pretence that the figures in the painting could ever look like that in life, however much perception has been shaped by art. There is a self-conscious awareness that what is appearing here isn't to be found reflected through the surface of ordinary things. The epiphany is of something only indirectly available, something the visible object can't say itself but only nudges us towards. With the move to non-representational art, this feature of twentieth-century painting becomes central and obtrusive.

The epiphany is indirect. This phrase might capture in a nutshell a great deal of modernist art. Returning to literature, we can see that the counter-epiphanic thrust of the writers I cited wasn't meant to put an end to epiphany. On the contrary, it founds a possibility of a quite new kind. This comes about through the projection of a frame onto reality. But to see this better, we have to bring in another facet of the intellectual background of the age.

I have mentioned the widespread aspiration to retrieve experience from the deadening, routinized, conventional forms of instrumental civilization. But what exactly was involved in gaining access to a richer experience? Did it mean simply throwing off the old forms and achieving a kind of unmediated contact with the fulness of life?

For some, it did. The aspiration took two seemingly opposed but related forms. One consisted in embracing the new industrial civilization, by making it an instrument of untrammelled transforming will. This was the road taken by Marinetti and the Italian Futurists. We regain unity by submitting the world entirely to our creative power. Technology is what makes this possible. Futurism offers hymns to technology:

> We will sing of great crowds excited by work, by pleasure, and by riot; . . .
> we will sing of the vibrant nightly fervour of arsenals and shipyards
> blazing with violent electric moons; greedy railway stations that devour
> smoke-plumed serpents; factories hung on clouds by crooked lines of their
> smoke; bridges that stride the rivers like giant gymnasts . . . adventurous
> steamers that sniff the horizon.[36]

Marinetti and his followers threw themselves into a fervent celebration of man's creative power. They glorified speed, audacity, violence. They enjoyed, even cultivated the intoxication of power. The term recurs: "I now declare that lyricism is the exquisite faculty of intoxicating oneself with life, of filling life with the inebriation of oneself".[37] Or again: "Our art will probably be accused of tormented and decadent cerebralism. But we shall merely answer that we are, on the contrary, the primitives of a new sensitiveness, multiplied hundredfold, and that our art is intoxicated with spontaneity and power".[38]

The other form, seemingly opposed, called for an abandonment of control. It aspired to open us fully to the deep unconscious forces within. This was the road of Surrealism, which developed out of Dada after the First World War. André Breton stated its goals while he still identified with the earlier movement: "DADA, recognizing only instinct, condemns a priori all meaning. According to DADA, we must give up all control over ourselves. There can no longer be any question of the dogmas of morality and taste".[39]

The old Romantic aspiration to overcome fragmentation, to break down the repressive barriers between unconscious and conscious, irrational and rational, imagination and reason, recurs. But unlike with the great Romantics, the goal was not so much a synthesis in difference as a merging of the separated rational ego into the deeper flux. They called for "la descente, vertigineuse en nous" ("a dizzying descent into ourselves"),[40] a liberation of the power of dreaming within, a negation of all rational control. Breton's aim was to get from himself "un monologue de débit aussi rapide que possible, sur lequel l'esprit critique du sujet ne fasse porter aucun jugement, qui ne s'embarasse, par conséquent, d'aucune réticence, et qui soit aussi exactement que possible la *pensée parlée*" ("a monologue to be spoken as rapidly as possible without any intervention on the part of the critical faculties, a monologue consequently unencumbered by the slightest inhibition").[41]

Other writers had come close to this, without going all the way:

Mais nous, qui ne nous sommes livrés à aucun travail de filtration, qui nous sommes faits dans nos oeuvres les sourds réceptacles de tant d'échos, les modestes *appareils enregistreurs* qui ne s'hypnotisent pas sur le dessein qu'ils tracent, nous servons peut-être encore une plus noble cause.

We, who have made no effort whatsoever to filter, who in our works have made ourselves into simple receptacles of so many echoes, modest *recording instruments* who are not mesmerized by the drawings we are making, perhaps we serve an even nobler cause.[42]

The total abandonment to instinctual depths may seem strange in writers of the post-Schopenhauerian era, who claimed to be influenced by Freud and for whom in consequence the original Romantic notion of nature as an emanation of spirit was no longer available. But their trust in these depths was as total as that of the most naive Romantic. They strove to "éclairer la partie non révélée et pourtant révélable de notre être où toute beauté, tout amour, toute vertu que nous ne connaissons à peine luit d'une manière intense" ("cast light upon the unrevealed and yet revealable portion of our being wherein all beauty, all love, all virtue that we can scarcely recognize in ourselves shine with great intensity").[43]

We can understand this stance of trust if we see it in the tradition of the radical Enlightenment, which I described in an earlier chapter. It is a declaration of the innocence of nature against the false calumnies heaped on it by religion and morality with their supposedly "higher" spiritual demands. In throwing over "the dogmas of morality and taste," we embrace raw, unspiritual nature and thereby affirm its goodness. This, of course, can itself lead to something like a religious attitude and experience. The extremes tend to touch.

In taking this stance, Surrealists naturally saw themselves as on the extreme left. They thought of themselves as allies of the Communist party, in spite of the half-comic, half-brutal incomprehension they experienced from this body, rigidly controlled by hard-bitten philistines. Overcoming the barrier between reason and the instinctual depths was also breaking down the division between art and life. It promised a new restored existence, and not just new modes of artistic expression. Art redeems life. The Schillerian hope is recovered in a much more radical form, which has its roots perhaps in Rimbaud, and its further fruits in our day in May 1968.

This is a tradition of art which is avant-garde in a more than aesthetic sense. The Surrealists saw themselves in this light. The term here is fully appropriate: they were supposedly the advanced detachment of a new form of life, helping to lead people in a struggle to attain it. Hence the affinity they felt with Bolshevism. They saw themselves and their world in terms of a similar narrative of historical struggle and revolution, where small detachments of brave fighters throw themselves ahead of the main body, and take heavy losses while turning the tide to victory.

Politically, they seem antipodal to the Futurists, who ended up joining Mussolini's Fascists after the First World War.[44] But there are affinities. Both go after an unmediated unity: in one case, the world is subsumed under the will; in the other, the ego merges with nature in the form of inner depths. Each of these formulae stands close to merging with the other. The titanic exaltation of the will, negating all tradition, religion, and morality, can come to affirm itself as an upsurge of instinct. The religion of the will then fuses paradoxically with a celebration of the animal, of race, as we see with Nazism. The unmediated merging with nature, on the other hand, makes its impulses into my will, which must be given untrammelled expression. The opposites meet.[45]

The common features of the two movements reflect this. Both take up the poetics of juxtaposition in a polemical spirit. They see it as a way of cracking the forms and hence of breaking the hold of repressive traditions. The destructive intent is as usual stated in more violent language by Marinetti, who in order to free words will "begin by brutally destroying the syntax";[46] but the idea of a liberating break is common to the two, as also the sense that this break suffices to allow the unity sought to come about through its own inherent power. For the Surrealists, juxtaposition is meant to bring us closer to the deep subconscious processes, the dream work, which leap between seemingly unconnected elements without the transitions of logic.[47] But the Futurists, with their emphasis on unreflecting immediacy, on the surge of unconsidered power, were not far away from them: "Up to now literature has exalted a pensive immobility, ecstasy, and sleep. We intend to exalt aggressive action, a feverish insomnia, the racer's stride, the mortal leap, the punch and the slap".[48] For both, the unity itself is understood as something momentary, experienced in a high state of excitement. Paralleling Marinetti's talk of 'intoxication' and 'insonnia febbrile' is Breton's slogan: "La beauté sera CONVULSIVE ou ne sera pas!"[49]

24.3

This kind of search for immediate unity, whether through a celebration of our own power or through a merging in the depths, can be called subjectivist. Against this, the main figures of high modernism remained aware of inescapable duality, and uncollapsible distance between agent and world, between thinker and instinctual depths. Indeed, although Bergson might have been interpreted as calling for an unmediated unity, the artists who made modernism were aware that there was something contradictory in a goal so described. Implicit in what Impressionism was exploring was the insight that we only see the world through the forms we construct to grasp it. That is why it takes a painting to transform our way of seeing. Unmediated experience was an impossibility.

This in fact connected to an understanding which was once more gaining ground in the philosophy of this period. An age of empiricism was giving away again to a revival of the thought of Kant, in Germany and in France. But this neo-Kantianism was aware, as the master had not been, of the historical and cultural variation in the forms whereby we structure experience. And this sense was made all the more acute by the climate of post-Schopenhauerian thought, as crystallized in particular by Nietzsche. Nietzsche stressed the utter lack of order in original, raw experience, "the formless unformulable world of the chaos of sensations".[50] In order to live at all in this world, we have to impose some order on it.

This general understanding of the indispensable mediating role of form underlay the most influential philosophies of science of the period. But it posed a special problem for those who sought the retrieval of experience, for this was generally conceived as a return to the concrete, to the immediate, to the fulness of lived reality, as against the abstract, the mediated, the merely conceptualized. If there was no unmediated experience, then wasn't this ambition quite illusory?

What was needed was a distinction between forms which gave us experience deadened and etiolated, and those which brought it back vivid and full. Hulme provided one such in his contrast between prose and poetry, as we saw above. All language starts in images, but with use these become routinized and end up as mere counters, which allow us to deal with things without really noticing them. Poetry, by using fresh visual images, attempts to arrest us and make us actually see the physical things, as against sliding past "through an abstract process":

> A poet says a ship 'coursed the seas' to get a physical image, instead of the counter word 'sailed'. Visual meanings can only be transferred by the new bowl of metaphor; prose is an old pot which lets them leak out. Prose is in fact the museum where the dead images of verse are preserved.[51]

Pound developed a deeper view of the relation of form to experience, one which took explicit account of the tension between the concrete particulars we encounter and the abstract general terms we use. A good place to see this is in Pound's theory of the ideogram, which he took over from Fenellosa. The Chinese ideogram is superior to Western script, because it embeds within it the step from particular to universal. To make the character for red, the Chinese have put together abbreviated pictures of rose, iron rust, cherry, and flamingo. Built into the sign for the general term is therefore a continuing mention of the particulars from which it was abstracted.[52] The process of forgetting the original images, which deadens and flattens our language into counters, is arrested. Pound thought that the ideogram, by making the etymology visible, could restore immediacy to language. Moreover, it could preserve the past in the present, something which had a crucial importance for him.[53]

Of course, as a view about the quality of consciousness in Chinese readers, this is nonsense. But a crucial feature of Pound's poetics crystallizes around this wrong idea. Just as the rose, iron rust, cherry, and flamingo point past themselves to redness, so the diverse cultural fragments and "luminous details" of history assembled in the *Cantos* can in their juxtaposition frame an insight. But this time what the fragments make present is something for which we have no words, something we couldn't simply grab onto while letting the fragments drop.

Here is a way of giving form to experience that doesn't involve general terms, whose continued use relegates to oblivion the particular experiences from which they derive. As a theory of how language in general might work, it is obviously flawed, as I have just indicated. But as a view of how poetry can say the otherwise unsayable, it has been immensely fertile and influential. In juxtaposing thoughts, fragments, images, we reach somehow between them and thus beyond them.

Juxtaposition also governs Pound's use of the image, and metaphor. Pound himself described the struggle to write his poem:

IN A STATION OF THE METRO

The apparition of these faces in the crowd;
Petals on a wet, black bough.

The original experience came as he was getting out of the Metro at La Concorde, and "saw suddenly a beautiful face, and then another and another, and then a beautiful child's face, and then another beautiful woman, and I tried all that day to find words for what they had meant to me, and I could not find any words that seemed to me worthy, or as lovely as that sudden emotion". After more than a year and a number of false starts, Pound wrote the poem. As Kenner says, every word, even those of the title, is essential. The title and first line describe the occasion of that remarkable experience. But only the juxtaposition with the last line can recover "that sudden emotion".[54]

Pound's notion of metaphor partakes of the same idea. The true metaphor is 'interpretive', not just 'ornamental'. It has the "precision" that comes from the attempt "to reproduce exactly the thing which has been clearly seen". But this itself is a visionary pattern which transfigures the world as it usually appears. The metaphor recaptures it by superimposing an image or pattern on the scene. The same is true of the Japanese haiku, which places one object against another; and a similar point can be made of the geometric forms of Vorticism, which structure our experience. In all these cases, as in the Metro poem, the vision emerges from the contact of scene and image, from the way one reaches out to shape the other. The vision is their joint products.[55]

But should we speak of epiphany here? Pound sometimes speaks as though the point of these juxtapositions was just to see reality undistorted. "[Art] means constatation of fact. It presents. It does not comment". Or "the arts, literature, poesy, are a science, just as chemistry is a science . . . Bad art is inaccurate art. It is art that makes false reports". At other times he speaks as though it were a matter of capturing an emotion as in the Metro poem, or where he describes art as above all the "expression of emotional values".[56] Apart from the fact that these two accounts seem incompatible, neither seems to take epiphany—that is, the revelation of something higher, not reducible simply to a subjective response through the work or what it portrays—as the central point. Some of the New Critics, whose theories were heavily influenced by the poetic practice of Pound and Eliot, e.g., I. A. Richards, sometimes talk as though the point of the poetry were the emotion it captures. But such a reductive view isn't right for Pound, and of course, not for Eliot either.

In Pound's case, this becomes clear once we resolve the apparent contradiction in his explanations above. The reality we are meant to report accurately on is not the bare scene, but the scene transfigured by emotion. And the emotion, in turn, is not simply personal or subjective; it is a response to a pattern in things which rightly commands this feeling. It is this pattern which is the "thing which has been clearly seen", and which the "precise interpretive metaphor" captures. The poetry which strives to be "accurate" is thus not simply mimetic. It liberates us from the constricting conventional ways of seeing, so we can grasp the patterns by which the world is transfigured.[57] Pound's image, the 'vortex' that he later took up along with Wyndham Lewis, his "ideogrammatic method" in the *Cantos,* all exhibit a poetry that makes something appear, brings it into our presence. But it doesn't work like the old epiphanies of being, where the object portrayed expresses a deeper reality. It doesn't come to us *in* the object or image or words presented; it would be better to say that it happens *between* them. It's as though the words or images set up between them a force field which can capture a more intense energy.

This is the image used by Hugh Kenner to describe Pound's poetics.[58] He finds images of this range in Pound himself, as in this quote from 1913:

> We might come to believe that the thing that matters in art is a sort of energy, something more or less like electricity or radio-activity, a force transfusing, welding, and unifying. A force rather like water when it spurts up through very bright sand and sets it in swift motion.[59]

What art captures can be likened to energy. But what is this energy, and how is it captured? Pound in 1912 offered the image of words like great hollow cones "charged with a force like electricity":

> Thus three or four words in exact juxtaposition are capable of radiating this energy at a very high potentiality; ... This particular energy which fills the cones is the power of tradition, of centuries of race consciousness, of association; and the control of it is the 'Technique of Content' which nothing short of genius understands.[60]

The cone image was later replaced by that of the vortex: "The image ... is a radiant node or cluster; it is what I can, and must perforce call a VORTEX, from which, and through which, and into which, ideas are constantly rushing".[61]

The work of art as vortex is a cluster; it is a constellation of words or images which sets up a space which draws ideas and energy into it. Or we could say that it concentrates energies that are otherwise diffuse, and makes them available at one spot/moment: "An 'Image' is that which presents an intellectual and emotional complex in an instant of time".[62] This is the nature of the Poundian epiphany; it happens not so much in the work as in a space that the work sets up; not in the words or images or objects evoked, but between them. Instead of an epiphany of being, we have something like an epiphany of interspaces. Hence the recourse Pound has in these years to metaphors from electricity and radioactivity. And much later on, in 1934, he will still speak of artists as "the antennae of the race".[63] But whatever the metaphor, something like this understanding of the epiphanic is at work in Pound's mature work, in the *Cantos*. The concatenation of images draws towards itself, and makes present for us, an "energy" which can be more closely identified as something of "the power of tradition, of centuries of race consciousness". The highest moments of artistic intensity and understanding are re-created and made contemporary by a poetry which can recapture the energy held in the great creations of the past, whether from ancient China or Homeric Greece, and transpose them into our language. So the first two lines of Canto I connect us again with the eleventh book of the *Odyssey*, as Odysseus and his companions sail away from Circe towards the land of the dead:

> And then went down to the ship,
> Set keel to breakers, forth on the godly sea

where Odysseus, like Pound, will make the great shades of the past speak.

This 'interspatial' mode of epiphany replaces the Romantic epiphany of being. It can no longer be understood in expressivist terms. 'Expressivism', as I first introduced it a few chapters ago, denotes a certain view of human nature. It is one which draws on Aristotle, but with the new twist that the move from potentiality to actuality must be understood also as a kind of self-expression and therefore involves some element of self-definition. This view tended to give art a newly central place in human life. Art becomes one of the, if not the, paradigm medium in which we express, hence define, hence realize ourselves.

This helps to set a paradigm of epiphanic art, based on this model of expression. We complete ourselves through expressions which reveal and define us. If we then think of nature as the emanation of some spiritual reality, the same model applies. Nature as "visible Spirit", in Schelling's phrase, must also be understood in expressive terms. We come to read nature as the embodiment of ideas or divine purposes; but no longer after the model of Deism, where the purposes, purely instrumental, can be identified independently of what fulfils them. Rather the purpose or idea only comes to full definition in its embodiment. We read the former in the latter in the manner of an expression. Bringing about the epiphany consists in showing what is expressed or embodied in reality. We have an epiphany of being.

Obviously the interspatial mode I am trying to discern in Pound is very different. The image may bring some object before us, as the opening lines of

Canto I bring us sailors launching their ship, and indeed the point of Imagist poetry was to make the object stand vividly before us. The epiphany comes through the presentation. But this is not to say that the object expresses anything. Pound's metaphors point to a quite different relation: e.g., that of a receiving set to radio signals (artists are "the antennae of the race"), or of an electro-magnetic field to electrical energy. The epiphanic object brings these forces into our presence and makes them operative among us, but this is not an expressive relation; indeed, energies (unlike purposes or ideas) are not the kind of thing which can be expressed. It is this non-expressive relation that I am trying to grope for when I say that the object sets up a kind of frame or space or field within which there can be epiphany.

From within this model of epiphany, we can see the point of insisting on a hard-edged, clear, highly particularizing portrayal of the object. When we're dealing with an expressive object, we strive to see through it, for it is infused with the deeper meaning. But when the object serves to frame an epiphanic space, it must stand out distinctly, in its full opacity: the more defined the frame, the more distinct the message. And we can understand the modernist refusal of depth: what is rejected is the depth of expressed meanings. There is of course another kind of depth which remains, as I will indicate.

And of course with this kind of epiphany, there doesn't need to be a determinate object at all. Words can do the framing or the concatenation of half-coherent images they deploy for us. Much of modern poetry works in this way. There may not be a succession of clearly defined images, but the very disruption and tension in what is evoked sets up an epiphanic field. This poetry has strong analogies to contemporary non-representative visual art.[64]

24.4

I have been looking at the particular case of Pound's poetics; and obviously something analogous could be said about Eliot.[65] But the general idea of an interspatial or framing epiphany has wide resonances throughout twentieth-century culture. The connections are not only with the scientific developments which Pound picked up on for his metaphors. There is also a parallel in the Saussurian theory of meaning, which is said to inhere not so much in the words but in the oppositions between them.[66]

But there are closer parallels in the aesthetics and artistic practice of other twentieth-century writers. Theodor Adorno is an interesting case in point. Adorno, through his background in Marx, Hegel, and Schiller, still held in some way to the original Romantic ideal of a full reconciliation of reason and sensibility, a pleroma of happiness in which sensual desire and the search for meaning would be fulfilled in perfect alignment. But he also belonged to the post-Schopenhauerian age, and he shared the modernist sensibility, which saw in the breaking of old aesthetic forms a liberation of concrete experience. He sees a link between the process of reification of human activity in capitalist society, denounced by Lukács, the domination and forced unification of the self under the instrumental ego, and the canonical "meanings" which late Romantic art attributes to things. Modernist art has an emancipatory potential because it involves a "negation of objectively obligating meaning". The rebellion against the canonical notions of the unity of a work of art is linked to the rebellion against the dominant idea of the unity of the ego. It opens a place for everything in the individual's experience which these repressive totalities of meaning can't allow. Modern art is a "Prozess gegen das Kunstwerk als Sinnzusammenhang" ("indictment of the work of art as a totality of meaning"), and hence operates as a powerful principle of individuation and promotes the development of particularity.[67]

Adorno's model of total fulfilment comes from the old expressivist source, via Marx and Lukács. But he was enough of a post-Schopenhauerian, and lived through such a traumatic period of disappointment of the Marxist hope, that he ceased to conceive full reconciliation as a live possibility. What we can look for, and what the best art can give us, are hints and intimations of full "redemption", in addition to a keenly critical eye for the shortcomings of the present reality.

Thus fulfilment or reconciliation is understood in expressivist terms: it would mean the full flowering of particularity, its integral recognition. This is something which can only take place through articulation in concepts, in universals. The reconciliation eludes us, because universal concepts always suppress from sight something of the reality of the particular. The perfect, non-distorting, non-reductive appellation would be the 'name', a term drawn by Adorno from the Cabbalist tradition. We have lost the power truly to name things.

But we can approximate to it, we can strive after this kind of grasp of things; and here Adorno borrows a key idea from Walter Benjamin. Unable to "name' things, we can nevertheless frame them in 'constellations', clusters of terms and images whose mutual affinity creates a space within which the particular can emerge. This doesn't realize the full reconciliation, but points towards it, gives it a kind of presence in our lives, and constitutes a sort of messianic premonition, in Benjamin's religious language.

The Benjamin-Adorno constellation is another form of interspatial or framing epiphany. Its elements don't express what they indicate; they frame a space, and bring something close which would otherwise be infinitely remote.

This casts light on Benjamin's preference for allegory over symbol and his affinity with baroque tragedy. This was a reversal of the central ordering of the Romantic age. The symbol was the vehicle of a higher art than allegory, because it presented something which was not accessible in any other way; and it was thus otherwise inaccessible, because the symbol was inseparable from what it revealed. Coleridge expressed this second point by saying that the symbol "always partakes of the Reality which it renders intelligible; and while it enunciates the whole, abides itself as a living part of that Unity, of which it is the representative".[68] It was this doctrine of the consubstantiality of symbol and meaning that made Benjamin turn to the allegory as a model. For like many modernist writers, he was conscious of the gap between language and what it invoked. Allegory preserves the character of language as a sign; it recognizes the distance, the alterity, between sign and signified. He takes in his own way the counter-expressive stance of modernism.

But this example also brings to the fore the continuities with Romanticism. The symbol as consubstantial is rejected. But the other basic idea, that it reveals something otherwise inaccessible, stands. This is just as true of Benjamin's constellation, and of framing epiphanies in general, as of the earlier expressivist ones. In this fundamental sense, modernism is still on the side of symbol against allegory. There is no simple reversal of Romanticism; there is a dissociation of what it had linked together. Art still remains the unsubstitutable locus of epiphany, even though this is no longer conceived as expressive.

There is something analogous to this framing in Proust as well, although here one might better speak of an 'intertemporal' epiphany. The Proustian epiphany is connected to an experience like the madeleine or the uneven pavement, but it doesn't arise simply on the occasion of this experience. It comes when a recurrence, or something sufficiently close, triggers off the memory. Proust himself says that when the original experience occurs, it hinders the epiphany; it dominates our attention and obstructs the vision behind it, as it were. Only when we recall it in memory can we see behind it to what was revealed through it. Here again, the epiphany can't be seen *in* an object but has to be framed *between* an event and its recurrence, through memory.

One could go on.[69] But I don't want to claim that all the writers that we think of as modernist have striven for framing epiphanies. The ways of modernism are many. What does seem to be more widespread is the turn away from epiphanies of being, which I can now characterize more clearly by three features: they (1) show some reality to be (2) an expression of something which is (3) an unambiguously good moral source. Framing epiphanies negate (2); they are not expressions of anything. But there are other ways of turning from epiphanies of being; for instance, the post-Schopenhauerian path explored by Thomas Mann, in which the feature negated is (3). The disease which is epidemic in Venice and eventually overcomes Gustav von Aschenbach is indeed expressive of something deeper. As with all true symbols it defies characterization; but it has to do with sensual fascination of effortless incarnate beauty which saps the will to impose form. This, however, is far from unambiguously good; indeed, there is nothing in Mann's universe which bears that description.

Again, in the case of the expressionist painters I mentioned, above, not only (3) but also (1) seem negated; the claim to accurate representation is also being dropped.

In whatever form, this common negative trait of modernists issues in another, which has both a negative and a positive side. This is an awareness of living on a duality or plurality of levels, not totally compatible, but which can't be reduced to unity. We recur here to the earlier discussion of different models of the self. The self of disengaged reason is and ought to be a single centre of strategic calculation. The Romantic expressive outlook points to an ideal of perfect integration, in which both reason and sensuality, the impulse within and nature without, are harmonized. But in the post-Schopenhauerian world of Thomas Mann there is no single construal of experience which one can cleave to exclusively without disaster or impoverishment. *The Magic Mountain* presents two radically incombinable modes of time-consciousness, one which approaches timelessness and another which is constituted by the calendar of real events, of achievements and failures in the world. Hans Castorp is drawn irresistibly into the first on the mountain, but he is also inevitably called back to the second by the imperious demands of world history, as war breaks out in 1914. One can't live by either one alone, but neither can they be combined or synthesized. Human life is irreducibly multilevelled. The epiphanic and the ordinary but indispensable real can never be fully aligned, and we are condemned to live on more than one level —or else suffer the impoverishment of repression.

This brings us back to the inward turn which I mentioned at the outset. The recognition that we live on many levels has to be won against the presumptions of the unified self, controlling or expressive. And this means a reflexive turn, something which intensifies our sense of inwardness and depth, which we have seen building up through the whole modern period. This can be misunderstood, because a frequently evoked theme among modernists is just the rejection of subjectivism, of a subjective expressivism, and the turning to structures outside the self: either the various transforms of the timeless and unindividuated Schopenhauerian will, or a deeper, impersonal mythic consciousness, or else the constellations of words or objects themselves which frame an epiphany.

In particular those who focus on these constellations have seen themselves as getting outside the subject again, to something "out there", public and impersonal, the power of language. But this in no way cancels the radically reflexive nature of the modernist enterprise. The reflexive move comes first in the fact that we unveil the power of language by turning back onto it from our ordinary unthinking focus on things. We have to stop seeing language as simply an inert instrument whereby we can deal more effectively with things. It involves becoming aware of what we do with words.

But beyond this, we run into the structural fact that I have already invoked here a number of times: in the post-Enlightenment world, the epiphanic power of words cannot be treated as a fact about the order of things which holds unmediated by the works of the creative imagination. That Canto I captures the energy that runs through Homer isn't a truth like that (as we used to believe) Saturn is linked to melancholy or that (as we believe now) DNA controls heredity. Discoveries like Pound's come to us indexed to a personal vision. Indeed, many of the references in the images of Pound, Eliot, and other poets come from their own personal experience. The fragments that Eliot "shores against his ruin" in *The Waste Land* are an idiosyncratic collection. To be moved by the poem is also to be drawn into the personal sensibility which holds all these together. The deeper, more general truth emerges only through this.[70]

For this reason, inwardness is as much a part of the modernist sensibility as of the Romantic. And what is within is deep: the timeless, the mythic, and the archetypical that are brought forth by Mann or Joyce—or Jung, whose work is fully a product of the modernist sensibility—may be transpersonal. But our access to it can only be within the personal. In this sense, the depths remain inner for us as much as for our Romantic forebears. They may take us beyond the subjective, but the road to them passes inescapably through a heightened awareness of personal experience.[71]

The modernist multilevelled consciousness is thus frequently 'decentred': aware of living on a transpersonal rhythm which is mutually irreducible in relation to the personal. But for all that it remains inward; and is the first only through being the second. The two features are inseparable.

This connects to a third feature. The Romantics made the poet or artist into the paradigm human being. Modernists have only accentuated this. The bringer of epiphanies cannot be denied a central place in human life. But the denial of the epiphanies of being has made the very process of bringing them problematic and mysterious. There is a new reflexive turn, and poetry or literature tends to focus on the poet, the writer, or on what it is to transfigure through writing. It is amazing how much art in the twentieth century has itself for its subject, or is on one level at least thinly disguised allegory about the artist and his work.

This doesn't have to be rampant subjectivism. The epiphanic is genuinely mysterious, and it possibly contains the key—or a key—to what it is to be human. We can even argue, as Heidegger does, that the way to overcome subjectivism is precisely to understand its true nature, which he approaches through his notion of the 'clearing'. One of the poets Heidegger draws on, Rilke, exhibits this third feature at its best and least self-indulgent. Both decentring and inwardness are fully recognized in the images of the ninth *Duino Elegy*. Transfiguration is a task laid on us by the world.

> Und diese, von Hingang
> lebenden Dinge verstehn, dass du sie rümst; vergänglich,
> traun sie ein Rettendes uns, den Vergänglichsten, zu.
> Wollen, wir sollen sie ganz im unsichtbarn Herzen verwandeln
> in—o unendlich in uns! Wer wir am Ende auch seien.
>
> Erde, ist es nicht dies, was du willst: unsichtbar
> in uns erstehn?—Ist es dein Traum nicht,
> einmal unsichtbar zu sein?

> And these Things,
> which live by perishing, know you are praising them; transient,
> they look to us for deliverance: us, the most transient of all.
> They want us to change them, utterly, in our invisible heart,
> within—oh endlessly—within us! Whoever we may be at last.
>
> Earth, isn't this what you want: to arise within us,
> *invisible*? Isn't it your dream
> to be wholly invisible someday?[72]

Rilke has taken us beyond expressivism, beyond the post-Schopenhauerian myths, and beyond any temptation to a mere celebration of our epiphanic power, to the central issue of the nature of epiphany, not just as our action, but as a transaction between ourselves and the world.

24.5

We live still in the aftermath of modernism; indeed, we are still in the aftermath of almost everything I have been talking about in these pages, of the Enlightenment, of Romanticism, of the affirmation of ordinary life. But in particular, modernism shapes our cultural world. Much of what we live today consists of reactions to it and, more, of the dissociation and prolongation of the strands it united.

Let us look at some of these. In Hulme, for instance, who himself went through a number of phases as Levenson shows,[73] several things come together: a reaction against subjectivism, a poetry of mere self-expression; a reaction against Rousseauian humanism, the denial of original sin; a rejection of organic forms in favour of the geometric; a recoil from epiphanies of being. All this combined with his own view of the epiphanic as the recovery of experience, which beyond this had some religious source. For Hulme, many of these stands were indissociable: the repudiation of subjectivism *was* the repudiation of humanism, and this was indissolubly linked with the turn away from the organic.

But it is possible to see how a different sensibility could dissociate these, and unite them with quite different ones. There is a well-known and much discussed link between modernism, understood as the reaction against instrumental civilization and co-opted Romanticism, multilevelled consciousness, and framing epiphanies, on one hand; and political reaction, on the other. The ascendancy of Pound and Eliot, with a partial assist from Yeats and Stevens, have made this very obtrusive. It is the amalgam we find in Hulme. Some of the reactions to modernism are coloured by it. But this synthesis is not written in the very logic of things. The strands have also been dissociated. One might argue that almost everybody writing poetry in English, and perhaps in most other European languages as well, has been influenced by the poetics of this great pair. Many share the opposition to industrial civilization; but not all by any means concur in the politics. Adorno and Horkheimer show early on how some of the key features of this modernism can be integrated into a stance on the left.

The reactions and prolongations differ greatly depending on what they associate and dissociate. There is a kind of response which associated the epiphanies of 'pure' auto-telic poetry with reaction and anti-humanism, and which tries to recover a public poetry, one which could be part of a conversation between poet and the broader public of a nation or class. This poetry turns away from epiphany; it aims to reveal, or celebrate, or make more intense and vivid some dimension of public experience. Something of this impetus made Auden write:

> All I have is a voice
> To undo the folded lie,
> The Romantic lie in the brain
> Of the sensual man-in-the-street
> And the lie of Authority
> Whose buildings grope the sky;
> There is no such thing as the State
> And no one exists alone;
> Hunger allows no choice
> To the citizen or the police;
> We must love one another or die.[74]

Brecht in another way was moved by this to a more aggressive rejection of 'pure poetry'. What these writers have taken from modernism is a facet of its negative movement, the pitiless stripping of Romantic illusion and confronting us with a hard-edged reality. Like the modernists they retrieve and release a certain experience; but it is not so much the inner dimension of meaning which is restored to vividness as common realities and hopes, pains and fulfilments.

In the same vein in 1935 Pablo Neruda called for an "impure poetry", one which was to be "ravaged by the labour of our hands as by an acid, saturated with sweat and smoke, a poetry that smells of urine and white lilies, a poetry on which every human activity, permitted or forbidden, has imprinted its mark". Later, when he joined the Communist party, he supplemented this with a ringing attack on "Gidean intellectualists, Rilkean obfuscators of life, specious existentialist jugglers, surrealist poppy flowers, bright only in your graves, europeanizing modish carcasses, pale maggots in the cheese of capitalism".[75]

But the anti-Romantic, anti-aesthetic thrust of modernism can also be taken up for quite different reasons which have nothing to do with the Marxist Left or the proletariat. The search for a stark and austere poetry of reality deserted by the spirit can come from the need to find words for a devastated world, as one sees with certain German and Polish poets in the wake of the war and under the press of Stalinism. Tadeusz Różewicz rejects the myths and archetypes which were so central to the language of modernist epiphany in Joyce, Pound, Eliot, and Mann. Of his own poems, he says: "I have fashioned them out of a remnant of words, salvaged words, out of uninteresting words, words from a great rubbish dump, the great cemetery". Różewicz seemed to be trying to free himself, after the war, from the forms and turns of the cultural tradition, to achieve a kind of nakedness, in which the meanings of simple words could be recovered:

> After the end of the world
> after my death
> I found myself in the middle of life
> I created myself
> constructed life
> people animals landscapes
>
> this is the table I was saying
> this is the table
> on the table are lying the bread the knife
> the knife serves to cut the bread
> people nourish themselves with bread[76]

From a somewhat different standpoint, Zbigniew Herbert also repudiated the dominant aesthetic:

The romantic conception of the poet who lays bare his wounds, who intones his own unhappiness, still has many adherents today, despite the changes in style and literary taste. They believe that it is the artist's sacred right to be self-centred and to exhibit his sore ego ... Beyond the poet's ego there extends a different, obscure real world. One should not cease to believe that we can grasp this world in language and do justice to it.[77]

One of the things that came to the fore in this austere postwar poetry was a striving which had been partly latent in the earlier naturalism. It grows from the insight that to capture the most degraded or devastated reality in poetry involves a transfiguration whereby it can be confronted, and borne without flinching, by the human spirit. I argued this in Chapter 23 in connection with nineteenth-century realism, but it becomes more palpable with some of the stripped-down anti-poetry of recent decades. Finding a language for horror and destruction can be part of a fight for spiritual survival.

But the devastation can also be faced quite differently, by a return to classical sources or, as with Herbert, by an appeal beyond the present disordered age, even beyond the conflicted and twisted human to the perfection of the inanimate.

> The stone
> is a perfect creature
>
> equal to itself
> obedient to its limits
>
> filled exactly
> with a stony meaning[78]

This negation borders on something else again, a purpose beyond stoic lucidity of vision. As with the *via negativa* in theology, the counter-epiphanic can be embraced not in order to deny epiphany altogether, not just in order to find a place for the human spirit to stand before the most complete emptiness, but rather to force us to the verge of epiphany. This is one way of reading the work of Samuel Beckett, perhaps also a way of understanding some of the work of Paul Celan.

> Weggebeizt vom
> Strahlenwind deiner Sprache
> das bunte Gerede des An-
> erlebten—das hundert-
> züngige Mein-
> gedicht, das Genicht.
>
> Etched away from
> the ray-shot wind of your language
> the garish talk of rubbed-

off experience—the hundred-
tongued pseudo-
poem, the noem.[79]

The resolute turning away from the lived, from a poetry of the self, bespeaks
an extreme denuding, a stripping down of language, which goes with the
image of the glacier in the stanza following the one just quoted. These winter
images, which seem parallel to Herbert's 'stone', recur in Celan's work:

Kein Halbholz mehr, hier,
in den Gipfelhängen,
kein mit-
sprechender
Thymian.

Grenzschnee und sein
die Pfähle und deren
Wegweiser-Schatten
aushorchender, tot-
sagender
Duft.

No more half-wood, here,
on the summit slopes,
no col-
loquial
Thyme

Border snow and
its odour that
auscultates the posts and
their road-sign shadows,
declaring them
dead.[80]

But this uncompromising austerity seems to be aimed at reaching the edge of
a farther epiphany, beyond all the negations, hinted at in certain poems, like
"Hütenfenster" ("Tabernacle Window"), or this one from *Atemwende:*

Fadensonnen
über der grauschwarzen Ödnis.
Ein baum-
hoher Gedanke
greift sich den Lichtton: es sind
noch Lieder zu singen jenseits
der Menschen.

Thread suns
above the grey-black wilderness.
A tree-
high thought
tunes in to light's pitch: there are
still songs to be sung on the other side
of mankind.[81]

Another path leads in a diametrically opposite direction to the austere
relevance of impure poetry. The framing epiphany focusses attention on the
work. Unlike with the expressive, the work which points beyond itself
maintains its distinct existence and is expressly not consubstantial with what
it reveals, in the manner of the Coleridgean symbol. It can induce us to take
it on its own, as an 'auto-telic' work, as though it could yield up its secrets if
we examined it in isolation, without relating it to the world or human life
from which it emerges. We can concentrate on the rich internal relations that
the elements of the frame bear to each other, and extract certain formal
properties. The Russian Formalists opened an influential line of study of this
kind. Roman Jakobson even developed a thesis about the distinction between
prose and poetry: prose is transparent, and carries us through to the domain
described; poetry focusses our attention on the medium. In poetry, the words
themselves become obtrusive.[82]

These studies have revealed something interesting, but as a global
understanding of the great modernist works, any formalist approach is
gravely defective. It leaves out entirely the epiphanic dimension. It seems most
plausible with non-expressive, non-mimetic art, such as non-representational
painting. But even here, this approach fails to appreciate the way in which
non-mimetic art has aimed to transform our vision of things; and how the
negation of epiphanies of being has often been just a step towards the new
kind of epiphany.

The focus on the isolated text has latterly been strengthened from another
quarter. The counter-epiphanic and decentring strands of modernism have
recently combined in a climate of thought which has had some vogue in
philosophy and criticism, even if it has been relatively sterile in literature
itself.[83] The vogue emanates from Paris, and is associated in criticism with
'deconstruction', while in philosophy the authors concerned have been
influenced by a certain reading of Nietzsche as well as by the decentring
strand of modernism. The authors are also rather different from each other.
To take the best-known two: Derrida has been influenced by Heidegger,
various forms of structuralist thought, and Lévinas, and presents a picture of
a subject who is enfolded in language which he can neither oversee nor

escape; while the later Foucault draws more directly on Nietzsche for a picture of the self as constructed through relations of power and modes of discipline. Foucault's filiation to the anti-Romantic strand of modernism comes out in his critique of the notion that the self has "depth". This he considers just another factitious notion, belonging to one of the possible constructions of the self and connected with the modern forms of control through the helping professions, paradigmatically the therapy of psychoanalysis. Building on a long tradition of control through the confessional, this form of power depends on inculcating in us the understanding that we have depths in ourselves to be revealed, which we imperfectly understand and need help to decipher and do justice to.[84]

Both these philosophies, different as they are, draw on a certain reading of Nietzsche which has been popular in France in recent decades. It is a reading which focusses on Nietzsche's sense of the arbitrariness of interpretation, on interpretation as an imposition of power, but completely neglects the other facet of this baffling thinker, the Dionysian vision of the "eternal return" which makes possible the all-englobing affirmation of "yea-saying". As a result, both philosophies have taken up the negative thrust of modernism—its anti-Romanticism, its suspicion of the supposed unity and transparency of the disengaged self, of the alleged inner sources of the expressive self—while neglecting its opening to epiphany.

Both want to disclaim any notion of the good. What they end up celebrating instead, not entirely by design, is the potential freedom and power of the self. The Derridian insight into the illusions of the philosophies of "presence" opens the way to an endless free play, unconstrained by a sense of allegiance to anything beyond this freedom. Derridian deconstruction claims to undo certain hierarchical distinctions, such as that between abstraction and concrete experience, misreadings as against true readings, confusion versus clarity, and the like. The general method is to show that the traditionally privileged term depends on, or is a special case of, the 'lower' one, e.g., that all readings are misreadings.[85]

There is a Nietzschean background to this, but there is also a contemporary liberationist attempt involved in it. The undermining of hierarchies seems a step towards a world of equals in mutual recognition. Derrida himself places his work in relation to women's liberation by speaking of "phallogocentrism", an entrenched position in which two forms of specious hierarchy maintain a mutually supportive complicity.[86] And Richard Bernstein has warmly appreciated the liberating intent he reads in Derrida.[87]

But this intent seems undercut by Derrida's supposed stance outside of any affirmation of good. It is not just that his egalitarianism sits ill with his Nietzschean heritage; perhaps Nietzsche's own affirmation, his *amor fati,* wasn't all that consistent with his original 'deconstruction' of morality, in at least some of its formulations. It is rather that Derrida doesn't have the saving inconsistency of Nietzsche, for whom there emerged, out of the uncompromising recognition of the flux, something which deserved unconditional affirmation, yea-saying. For Derrida there is nothing but deconstruction, which swallows up the old hierarchical distinctions between philosophy and literature, and between men and women, but just as readily could swallow up equal/unequal, community/discord, uncoerced/constrained dialogue, and the like. Nothing emerges from his flux worth affirming, and so what in fact comes to be celebrated is the deconstructing power itself, the prodigious power of subjectivity to undo all the potential allegiances which might bind it; pure untrammelled freedom. The poverty of this position comes out perhaps most starkly when it is compared with the religious philosophy of Lévinas, from whom Derrida derived some of his key terms.

Foucault for his part seems to have dropped the stance of neutrality at the end of his life. In his very last interviews, he espoused the ideal of the aesthetic construction of the self as a work of art.[88] There is a deep problem here because of the difficulty of detaching a notion of the aesthetic from the other strands in modern thought that Foucault still wanted to repudiate. But what is striking again is the kind of unrestrained, utterly self-related freedom that this ideal entails.

The very claim not to be oriented by a notion of the good is one which seems to me to be incredible, for reasons outlined in the first part of this book. But it also reflects that the underlying ideal is some variant of that most invisible, because it is the most pervasive, of all modern goods, unconstrained freedom.

To the extent that this kind of freedom is held up as the essence of 'post-modernity', as it is by Jean-François Lyotard,[89] it shows this to be a prolongation of the least impressive side of modernism. There seem to be three kinds of spiritual profile which emerge from this whole movement. (1) One result can be that modernism leads to an even higher estimate of the unrestricted powers of the imagination than the Romantics had, and thence to a celebration of these powers. The Futurists clearly trod this path, and as we saw, this was closely related to the attempt to merge the ego into the stream of life, as we find with the Surrealists. (2) A second outcome can be that one move through the critique to a new form of epiphany, as the greats of early Modernism—Proust, Pound, Joyce, Eliot, Mann—all did. (3) A third way is towards an austere discipline of the imagination, which renounces the comforting and beautifying images in the attempt to find a language for what is horrible, degraded, or devastated in our time, to "grasp this world in language and do justice to it", as Herbert puts it.

The second and third paths can command respect and hold our allegiance over time. We still read and admire the great early moderns. But the subjectivist self-celebration of the first is shallow, and this profile invariably plays itself out. Wave after wave passes, without holding more than historical interest. More, we can say that the subjectivism of self-celebration is a standing temptation in a culture which exalts freedom and puts such a value on the creative imagination. Even profiles 2 and 3 are thus in danger of sliding into this, and sometimes do in their degenerate forms. We can have supposedly epiphanic art which is merely portentous or bombastic, boosting the writer. And we have trivialized variants of the third profile—in pop art, for instance, which justified itself as a serious attempt to extend the language of art, but was often just an attention-grabbing gimmick.

The 'post-modernism' of Lyotard turns out to be an overelaborated boost for the first spiritual profile of modernism, in the name of unrestricted freedom. The work of Derrida and Foucault, albeit weightier—in Foucault's case, incomparably so—also fits within this first profile. They offer charters for subjectivism and the celebration of our own creative power at the cost of occluding what is spiritually arresting in this whole movement of contemporary culture.[90]

But we're entering here into a discussion of the spiritual possibilities in today's culture, and this is what I would like to take up, all too briefly, in the Conclusion. But before I embark on this, I want to say another word about the role modernist art has played in defining these possibilities.

24.6

I have been looking at modernism, its epiphanies and its counter-epiphanic thrusts, from a certain angle. I have seen them as changes wrought on the aspiration, which originates in the Romantic era, to recover contact with moral and spiritual sources through the exercise of the creative imagination. These sources may be divine, or in the world, or in the powers of the self. They may be seen as new, hitherto untouched, or as in the case of Pound and Eliot, the aim may be to restore the power of old ones which have been lost. The aspiration, however conceived, is usually made more urgent by the sense that our modern fragmented, instrumentalist society has narrowed and impoverished our lives.[91] This also is in striking continuity with the Romantics, for all the reversals modernism brought.

That is why the great works of modernism resist our understanding them in subjectivist fashion, as mere expressions of feeling or as ways of ordering the emotions. Recovering moral sources opens us to something which empowers. It does more than rearrange the furniture of the psyche. I. A. Richards, one of the founders of the New Criticism, put forward a basically psychologistic view of modern poetry. As Stephen Spender sums it up, poetry for Richards "is a means of arranging the order of our internal lives by making a harmonious pattern of extremely complex attitudes, once thought to refer to an external order of metaphysics but now seen to be a symbolic ordering of our inner selves".[92] But such a self-enclosed reading manifestly will not do: not for Eliot or Pound, but not either for Thomas Mann, or D. H. Lawrence, or Joyce, or Proust, or Rilke—if I can be allowed a rather wide reading of 'poetry'.

Richards was on to something, however, when he pointed out that beliefs or dogmas play a very different role among moderns. This is the point I have been trying to make in speaking of the 'subtler language'. It is not that one can simply factor out the mythology or metaphysics or theology of Yeats, Mann, Lawrence, or Eliot and consider them just as an elaborate set of instruments to reorder their psyches. But something has undoubtedly changed since the era of the great chain of being and the publicly established order of references. I have tried to express this by saying that the metaphysics or theology comes indexed to a personal vision, or refracted through a particular sensibility.

What is it to have a publicly established order of references? It is not just to share *beliefs* with everybody else, but something rather more fundamental. This is what Wittgenstein explores in *On Certainty,*[93] where he speaks of the error of speaking of a 'belief' or 'assumption' that the world started more than five minutes ago, or that the ground will stay solid under our feet. These are matters on which we will not normally have formulated a belief; not because we doubt them, but because we're too busy relying on them, leaning on them as it were, as we go about believing and doubting other things. They are part of the tacit background of objects of reliance, of things that are 'ready-to-hand', in Heidegger's language.[94]

The analogy is not complete, of course. The belief in God in an "age of faith", or the belief in the hierarchy of beings in the great chain, could never remain at the level of total inarticulacy of our reliance on the solidity of the earth. These beliefs are formulated, and belief may even be demanded of us as a duty. But in earlier ages they also sank into the background. In our public and private life of prayer, penance, devotion, religious discipline, we lean on God's existence, use it as the pivot of our action, even when we aren't formulating our belief, as I use the stairs or the bannister in the course of my focal action of getting down to the kitchen to cook a meal. Or again, in writing and painting, the references of the chain of being, the great events of sacred and profane history, are there for me also as something I have to count with, realities I have to accommodate, as I concentrate perhaps on my rhyme scheme or on the contrast of my colours.

Virtually nothing in the domain of mythology, metaphysics, or theology stands in this fashion as publicly available background today. But that doesn't mean that there is nothing in any of those domains that poets may not want to reach out to in order to say what they want to say, no moral sources they descry there that they want to open for us. What it does mean is that their opening these domains, in default of being a move against a firm background, is an articulation of personal vision. It is one that we might come to partake in as well, as a personal vision; but it can never become again an invoking of public references, short of an almost unimaginable return—some might say 'regression'—to a new age of faith.

The hunger for a 'public poetry' has certainly been felt in the twentieth century, and very much in reaction to the great modernists.[95] But this has required precisely a turning away from the metaphysical to everyday things and the common experiences of life, politics, and war, as in early Auden or in writers of the Left like Brecht.

Perhaps the contrast can be seen most starkly if we think of how we can also call on individual intuitions in order to map a public domain of references. Linguistics may make use of our linguistic intuitions of grammaticality. To make these available usually requires a reflexive turn. I ask myself: Can you say 'she don't got a cent'? and I answer negatively. But there is no call to talk here of a 'personal vision'. What I am mapping is precisely a bit of the publicly available background, what we all lean on and count with while we communicate. By contrast, what Eliot or Pound or Proust invites me to has an ineradicably personal dimension.

Richards is wrong to talk about the beliefs being irrelevant. But there is a difference from the old days. It is not just that they are more tentative than the old public creeds. It is also that what I call their personal index makes them a different kind of thing. We know that the poet, if he is serious, is pointing to something—God, the tradition—which he believes to be there for all of us. But we also know that he can only give it to us refracted through his own sensibility. We cannot just detach the nugget of transcendent truth; it is inseparably imbedded in the work—this is the continuing relevance of the Romantic doctrine of the symbol.

How can I formulate the epiphany which opens through *The Waste Land*? Going through the critical apparatus may facilitate the epiphany, but doesn't yield a formulation of it. Well, I can write another poem myself, index it to *my* personal vision. Otherwise, I can only indicate what it is by directing you to the poem itself. The beliefs remain embedded and interwoven in one person's vision and sensibility and even in his memory and biography, if we reflect how Pound and Eliot's works often gain clarity and force when we understand some of the personal allusions in the fragments that make them up.

That is why the centre of gravity is displaced onto the words in so much modern poetry. The roots of poetry go deep into the invocative uses of language; those whereby we bring something about or make something present by what we say. These have played a big part in religious life from the earliest days up to the reciting of the Quran or the saying of Mass. But they also exist in secular life, in performatives or in the most banal forms, such as when we open a conversation.

In the normal invocative uses, we lean on the words, we attend from them to what is being invoked. But with the poetry of, say, Pound, a strange shift takes place. Some 'energy' is being captured in these words, but the only way to define it is precisely to attend to the words. It is analogous to a religion in which the crucial definitions attach to the ritual rather than to the theology. Some writers argue that this is the case for many 'primitive' religions, which opens a line of comparison to which many modernists have been sympathetic.

All this gives some colour to Richards's sidelining of belief or Roman Jakobson's theory of poetry as arising where the words become salient; but neither of these does justice to the epiphanic nature of much modern art. The interweaving of the subjective and the transcendent is perhaps best expressed in these lines of Wallace Stevens:

The world about us would be desolate except for the world within us.

The major poetic idea in the world is and always has been the idea of God.

After one has abandoned a belief in God, poetry is the essence which takes its place as life's redemption.[96]

25

CONCLUSION: THE CONFLICTS OF MODERNITY

25.1

It is time to tie the preceding discussion of modernism into the portrait of the modern identity that I have been assembling. I have examined modernism in the context of the conflict in our culture over the disengaged and instrumental modes of thought and action which have steadily increased their hold on modern life. Modernism succeeds Romantic expressivism both in protest against these and in the search for sources which can restore depth, richness, and meaning to life. But in the process, the place of this conflict relative to the other tensions in contemporary culture has been altered. In order to explain this, I want to return to the picture I was beginning to draw in Chapter 22, in describing how our present moral outlook develops from the Victorian age.

There I started with an attempt to encapsulate the moral imperatives which are felt with particular force in modern culture. These emerge out of the long-standing moral notions of freedom, benevolence, and the affirmation of ordinary life, whose development I traced at some length from the early modern period through their Deist and Enlightenment forms. We as inheritors of this development feel particularly strongly the demand for universal justice and beneficence, are peculiarly sensitive to the claims of equality, feel the demands to freedom and self-rule as axiomatically justified, and put a very high priority on the avoidance of death and suffering.

But under this general agreement, there are profound rifts when it comes to the constitutive goods, and hence moral sources, which underpin these standards. The lines of battle are multiple and bewildering, but in these pages I have been sketching a schematic map which may reduce some of the confusion. The map distributes the moral sources into three large domains: the original theistic grounding for these standards; a second one that centres on a naturalism of disengaged reason, which in our day takes scientistic forms; and a third family of views which finds its sources in Romantic expressivism or in one of the modernist successor visions. The original unity of the theistic horizon has been shattered, and the sources can now be found on diverse frontiers, including our own powers and nature.

The different families of modern views draw on these frontiers in different ways, and they combine what they take from our powers and from nature in characteristic fashion. The disengaged view obviously leans heavily on our powers of disengaged reason. This is the source which powers the austere ethic of self-responsible freedom, the courageous ethics of belief. But a conception of nature also enters into its ethic of benevolence—albeit this is hard to avow openly—if only in the rather minimal way, as we saw with E. O. Wilson, of enthusiasm at man's "evolutionary epic". Romantic or modernist views make more of our powers of creative imagination and generally draw on a much richer conception of nature, which has an inner dimension.

The fact that there is so much agreement about the standards, over deep divisions about the sources, is one of the motivations for the kind of moral theory, widespread today, which tries to reconstruct ethics without any reference to the good, as I discussed in section 3.3. It is in fact often possible to start from agreed intuitions about what is right, even across the gaps that separate the three families. But modern proceduralist ethics are also motivated by quite other considerations. In some cases, they spring from the disengaged family, and they share its reluctance or metaphysical embarrassment at open avowal of moral sources, or they may even believe that freedom requires their denial. Proceduralism can put a good face on this. And then again, as I tried to show in section 3.3, proceduralist ethics are sometimes motivated by a strong commitment to the central modern life goods, universal benevolence and justice, which they wrongly believe can be given a special status by segregating them from any considerations about the good. In this they fit foursquare within the tradition of Enlightenment naturalism: the very austerity about the goods of the spirit enables us to dedicate ourselves so much more single-mindedly to universal beneficence. They continue in the line of Bentham's cri de coeur about the love of humankind, of the agnostic's austere commitment to progress, of the struggle of Camus's Dr. Rieux to relieve suffering in a disenchanted world.

Of course, my map is overschematic. For one thing, the three domains don't stay the same; they are continually borrowing from and influenced by each other. For another, there have been attempts to straddle the boundaries and combine more than one. I mentioned Marxism as a marriage of Enlightenment naturalism and expressivism. But third, we need to see the map in a temporal dimension. Not everyone is living by views which have evolved recently. Many people live by pre-modernist forms of Romantic expressivism. In some respects, the actual goals which inspired the students' revolt of May 1968 in Paris, for all the borrowing of modernist forms from Situationism, Dada, Surrealism, avant-garde cinema, and the like,[1] were closer to Schiller than to any twentieth-century writer. The picture of a restored harmony within the person and between people, as a result of 'décloisonnement', the breaking down of barriers between art and life, work and love, class and class, and the image of this harmony as a fuller freedom: all this fits well within the original Romantic aspirations. The basic notions could have been drawn from the sixth of Schiller's *Aesthetic Letters*. This picture comes close at times to a pre-Schopenhauerian perspective.

Then again, many of the ideas of "human potential" movements in the United States also go back to the original expressivism, partly through the indigenous American line of descent, including Emerson and Whitman. These movements often incorporate post-Freudian psychology, but frequently (as Europeans often remark) without the tragic sense of conflict which was central to Freud. Their notion of expressive fulfilment is very much "pre-Schopenhauerian". Consider this personal credo:

> BE GENTLE WITH YOURSELF. You are a child of the Universe no less than the trees and the stars. You have a right to be here. And whether or not it is clear to you, no doubt the universe is unfolding as it should. Therefore be at peace with God, whatever you conceive Him to be. And whatever your labors and aspirations, in the noisy confusion of life, keep peace in your soul. With all its sham, drudgery and broken dreams, it is still a beautiful world.[2]

Or again, there are strands of American evangelical Protestantism which in some respects are continuous with the spirituality of the Great Awakening. This is not to say that there have not been important changes: predestination has been forgotten, modern technology has been fully mobilized for revival—in all sorts of ways this religion has been contaminated by the modern world. But there has been no willing and express acceptance of Romantic expressivism or modernism. The emphasis is still on the saving power of grace and on the order which this alone can put in one's life.

My point here is not at all to depreciate these views, as though the later ones were bound to be better; only to show how understanding our society requires that we take a cut through time—as one takes a cut through rock to find that some strata are older than others. Views coexist with those which have arisen later in reaction to them. This is to oversimplify, of course, because these rival outlooks go on influencing and shaping each other. Born-again Christians in the United States cannot help being somewhat influenced by expressive individualism. Indeed, some of them went through the latter, during the 1960's, for instance, and ended up joining a strict evangelical church. Something had to rub off.[3] But the outlooks are *defined* in polar opposition.

This is one reason why I have had to assemble the portrait of the modern identity through its history. An instantaneous snapshot would miss a great deal. Another reason is that only through adding a depth perspective of history can one bring out what is implicit but still at work in contemporary life: the Romantic themes still alive in modernism, masked sometimes by the anti-Romantic stance of modernists; or the crucial importance of the affirmation of ordinary life, which is in some ways too pervasive to be noticed; or the spiritual roots of naturalism, which modernism usually feels forced to suppress.

And only in this way was it possible to show the connections between the modern moral outlook and its multiple sources, on one hand, and the different evolving conceptions of the self and its characteristic powers, on the other; and to show also how these concepts of the self are connected with certain notions of inwardness, which are thus peculiarly modern and are themselves interwoven with the moral outlook. And I hope some light has been cast as well on the relation between these concepts and certain modes of narration of biography and history, as well as certain conceptions of how we hang together in society. It is this whole complex that I want to call the modern identity.

What can one hope to get out of drawing this portrait, beyond the satisfactions of greater self-understanding if one draws it right? Well, certainly this self-understanding has been one of my motives. But I also think that getting this straight can give one insight into issues that are hotly debated in our time. In particular, one can understand better the standing areas of tension or threatened breakdown in modern moral culture.

I believe there are three such. The first is the one I mentioned at the beginning of this chapter: underneath the agreement on moral standards lies uncertainty and division concerning constitutive goods. The second great zone of tension contains the conflict between disengaged instrumentalism and the Romantic or modernist protest against it. The rise of modernism has made a difference in this conflict. The short way of explaining this is to say that it has transformed one of the forces in contest. Our conception of the creative imagination, of epiphany, and of the realities they give us access to has been transformed in the last century, and this has altered our view of the alternatives to disengaged reason. But in addition to the changes they have wrought in this second zone of tension, the developments over the last century which issued in modernism have also opened a breach between the first zone and the second.

The original Romantic expressivism, for all its tendency to exalt art, saw expressive fulfilment as compatible with morality, defined in terms of the modern standards. For Schiller, the full development of the play drive would make it possible to be spontaneously moral; we would no longer have to impose rules on our unwilling desires. But subsequent developments, through Schopenhauer, through the Baudelairean repudiation of nature, call this pre-established harmony into question and, through this, raise the issue whether an aesthetically realized life would also, could also, be moral. Nietzsche offers the most direct challenge: the way to the harmony of yea-saying passes through the repudiation of the ethic of benevolence. But in less dire ways, anyone in the post-Schopenhauerian stream has at least to raise the question whether artistic epiphany draws us to the same things that morality demands. Writers like Pound and Lawrence answer this question positively, but it obviously now remains a question; and when we consider some of the things they say, and Pound's politics in particular, one can wonder whether they themselves didn't fail to see the conflict implicit in their own views.

And so a third zone of potential conflict opens up: beyond the question about the sources of our moral standards, and the one which opposes disengaged instrumentalism to a richer fulfilment, there is the question whether these moral standards are not incompatible with that fulfilment; whether morality doesn't exact a high price from us in terms of wholeness. This is a question which has come to the fore with certain contemporary 'post-modern' writers, influenced by Nietzsche, like Jacques Derrida and Michel Foucault. We can call these conflicts, respectively, (1) the issue about sources, (2) the issue about instrumentalism, and (3) the issue about morality.

25.2

I want to look briefly at these from the standpoint of the picture of the modern identity I have drawn. Of course, this discussion really demands another book (at least) to do justice to it. But my goal here is less to contribute to the debate than it is to clarify further my portrait of the modern identity by indicating what this view inclines one to say, and I will take the licence of a prospectus to be terse and dogmatic, to offer a number of beliefs without fully adequate proof. I hope to trace a path through the controversies about modernity which is distinct from some of the most travelled ones of our time. Perhaps one day I'll be able to return to this question to show why one *has* to tread this path.

Let us begin with the second issue, the controversy about the disengaged instrumental mode of life, because that has been the centre of the most influential theories of modernity over the last two centuries.

From the Romantic period, the drift towards this mode of life in modern society has been attacked. The attack has been on two levels, as I mentioned in Chapter 21: that the disengaged, instrumental mode empties life of meaning, and that it threatens public freedom, that is, the institutions and practices of self-government. In other words, the negative consequences of instrumentalism are allegedly twofold, experiential and public.

Again and again, in a host of different ways, the claim has been made that an instrumental society, one in which, say, a utilitarian value outlook is entrenched in the institutions of a commercial, capitalist, and finally a bureaucratic mode of existence, tends to empty life of its richness, depth, or meaning. The experiential charge takes various forms: that there is no more room for heroism, or aristocratic virtues, or high purposes in life, or things worth dying for—Tocqueville sometimes talked like this, and he somewhat influenced Mill to have the same fears. Another claim is that nothing is left which can give life a deep and powerful sense of purpose; there is a loss of passion. Kierkegaard saw "the present age" in these terms;[4] and Nietzsche's "last men" are an extreme case of this decline, having no aspiration left in life but to a "pitiable comfort".[5]

The instrumental society may bring this about through the images of life it offers and celebrates, just by occluding deeper meanings and making them hard to discern. This is a criticism frequently made today of the mass media. Or it may do so by inducing and facilitating a merely instrumental stance, or even an overriding concern with a "pitiable comfort". This is a criticism frequently levelled at consumer society.

But the society's action can also be seen as more direct and forceful. The charge may be that the instrumental mode of life, by dissolving traditional communities or driving out earlier, less instrumental ways of living with nature, has destroyed the matrices in which meaning could formerly flourish. Or the action may be quasi-coercive, as we see, for instance, in Max Weber's notion of modern society as an "iron cage"[6] or Marx's theory of capitalism (from which Weber borrowed). Here the exigencies of survival in capitalist (or technological) society are thought to dictate a purely instrumental pattern of action, which has the inevitable effect of destroying or marginalizing purposes of intrinsic value.

The loss of meaning can be formulated in other ways. Weber, picking up a theme from Schiller, talks of the 'disenchantment' (Entzauberung) of the world. The world, from being a locus of 'magic', or the sacred, or the Ideas, comes simply to be seen as a neutral domain of potential means to our purposes.

Or else it can be formulated in terms of division or fragmentation. To take an instrumental stance to nature is to cut us off from the sources of meaning in it. An instrumental stance to our own feelings divides us within, splits reason from sense. And the atomistic focus on our individual goals dissolves community and divides us from each other. This is a theme we've seen before, articulated by Schiller. But it was also taken up by Marx (at least in his early work), and later by Lukács, Adorno, and Horkheimer, and Marcuse, as well as in the student movement of May 1968.

Or people speak of a loss of resonance, depth, or richness in our human surroundings; both in the things we use and in the ties which bind us to others. "All that is solid melts in air", Marx said; Marshall Berman has echoed this line from the *Communist Manifesto* in the title of his influential book.[7]

On the one hand, the solid, lasting, often expressive objects which served us in the past are being set aside for the quick, shoddy, replaceable commodities with which we now surround ourselves. Albert Borgman speaks of the 'device paradigm', whereby we withdraw more and more from "manifold engagement" with the things surrounding us, and instead request and get products designed simply to deliver some circumscribed benefit. He contrasts what is involved in heating our houses with the contemporary central heating furnace, and what this same function entailed in pioneer times, when the whole family had to be involved in cutting and stacking the wood, feeding the stoves or fireplace, and the like.[8] Hannah Arendt focussed on the more and more ephemeral quality of modern objects of use. She argued that "the reality and reliability of the human world rest primarily on the fact that we are surrounded by things more permanent than the activity by which they are produced." This comes under threat in a world of modern commodities.[9]

And Rilke in the seventh of the *Duino Elegies* links the need to transmute the world into interiority to the loss of substance of our contemporary man-made world.

> Nirgends, Geliebte, wird Welt sein, als innen. Unser
> Leben geht hin mit Verwandlung. Und immer geringer
> schwindet das Aussen. Wo einmal ein dauerndes Haus war,
> schlägt sich erdachtes Gebild vor, quer, zu Erdenklichem
> völlig gehörig, als ständ es noch ganz im Gehirne.
> . . . . .
> ... Ja, wo noch eins übersteht,
> ein einst gebetetes Ding, ein gedientes, geknietes—,
> hält es sich, so wei es ist, schon ins Unsichtbare hin.

> Nowhere, beloved will world be but within us. Our life
> passes in transformation. And the external
> shrinks into less and less. Where once an enduring house was,
> now a cerebral structure crosses our path, completely
> belonging to the realm of concepts, as though it still stood in the
>   brain

. . . . .
... Where one of them still survives,
a Thing that was formerly prayed to, worshipped, knelt before—
just as it is, it passes into the invisible world.[10]

On the other hand, the individual has been taken out of a rich community life and now enters instead into a series of mobile, changing, revocable associations, often designed merely for highly specific ends. We end up relating to each other through a series of partial roles.

So much for the experiential consequences. But public consequences are also frequently charged against instrumentalist society. One long-standing one, which I have already discussed, is that it tends to destroy public freedom. Tocqueville has offered one variant of this, in his notion that atomic, instrumental society both saps the will to maintain this freedom and at the same time undermines the local foci of self-rule on which freedom crucially depends. There is another variant which Marx puts forward, this time directed specifically at capitalist society, in his charge that it generates unequal relations of power which make a mockery of the political equality which genuine self-rule presupposes. More recently another realm of public consequences has entered the debate. Instrumental society is accused of ecological irresponsibility, which places the long-term existence and well-being of the human race in jeopardy. This is the range of political issues on which the moral and spiritual struggle around instrumentalism now primarily focusses.

25.3

My aim in setting out this sketch of the charges is to help illustrate my conception of the modern identity by describing the perspective it offers on them. There is a temptation, to which I will yield, to do this polemically, by showing what I think is wrong with the familiar and widely held perspectives. But one general point can be made at the outset. What emerges from the picture of the modern identity as it develops over time is not only the central place of constitutive goods in moral life, hence illustrating my argument in Part I, but also the diversity of goods for which a valid claim can be made. The goods may be in conflict, but for all that they don't refute each other. The dignity which attaches to disengaged reason is not invalidated when we see how expressive fulfilment or ecological responsibility has been savaged in its name. Close and patient articulation of the goods which underpin different spiritual families in our time tends, I believe, to make their claims more palpable. The trouble with most of the views that I consider inadequate, and that I want to define mine in contrast to here, is that their sympathies are too narrow. They find their way through the dilemmas of modernity by invalidating some of the crucial goods in contest.

This is aggravated by the bad meta-ethic I discussed in Part I, which wants to do without the good altogether and hence makes this kind of selective denial easier. Worse, by putting forward a procedural conception of the right, whereby what we ought to do can be generated by some canonical procedure, it accredits the idea that what leads to a wrong answer must be a false principle. It is quick to jump to the conclusion that whatever has generated bad action must be vicious (hence nationalism must be bad because of Hitler, communitarian ethics because of Pol Pot, a rejection of instrumental society because of the politics of Pound and Eliot, and so on). What it loses from sight is that there may be genuine dilemmas here, that following one good to the end may be catastrophic, not because it isn't a good, but because there are others which can't be sacrificed without evil.

Moreover, now that I'm allowing myself the licence of bald statement, I want to make an even stronger claim. Not only are these one-sided views invalid, but many of them are not and cannot be fully, seriously, and unambivalently held by those who propound them. I cannot claim to have proved this, but what I hope emerges from this lengthy account of the growth of the modern identity is how all-pervasive it is, how much it envelops us, and how deeply we are implicated in it: in a sense of self defined by the powers of disengaged reason as well as of the creative imagination, in the characteristically modern understandings of freedom and dignity and rights, in the ideals of self-fulfilment and expression, and in the demands of universal benevolence and justice.

This should perhaps be a banal truism, but it isn't. And it isn't because there are strong and varied inducements to repudiate one or another aspect of the "package" I have just outlined. These include the tensions within the modern identity itself, like that between its 'disengaged' and 'expressive' aspects which I'll be discussing in a minute; or the rebellion against the stringent demands of benevolence which Nietzsche denounced so effectively, and which I will also look at later. Another important source of obscurity is the uneasiness of Enlightenment naturalism with any notion of the good, including its own. This has greatly contributed to the credence given to the proceduralist ethics I just mentioned.

All this, in a context of historical ignorance, helps to accredit the oversimple and almost caricatural readings of one or another strand of modernity. Such readings make various facets of modernity seem easy to repudiate. Narrow proponents of disengaged reason point to the irrational and anti-scientific facets of Romanticism and dismiss it out of hand, blithely unaware of how much they draw on a post-Romantic interpretation of life as they seek 'fulfilment' and 'expression' in their emotional and cultural lives. On the other hand, those who condemn the fruits of disengaged reason in technological society or political atomism make the world simpler than it is when they see their opponents as motivated by a drive to "dominate nature" or to deny all dependence on others, and in fact conveniently occlude the complex connections in the modern understanding of the self between disengagement and self-responsible freedom and individual rights, or those between instrumental reason and the affirmation of ordinary life. Those who flaunt the most radical denials and repudiations of selective facets of the modern identity generally go on living by variants of what they deny. There is a large component of delusion in their outlook. Thus, to take other examples, defenders of the most antiseptic procedural ethic are unavowedly inspired by visions of the good, and neo-Nietzscheans make semi-surreptitious appeal to a universal freedom from domination.

A proof of these charges would have to consider them case by case.[11] But an exploration of the modern identity like that I have attempted here should prepare us to see their validity by taking us beyond caricatural, one-sided readings and giving us a sense of how pervasive this identity is, and how implicated we are in all its facets.

I think it is important to make this point, because these various repudiations and denials are not just intellectual errors. They are also modes of self-stultification, if an acknowledgement of the good can empower. The retrieval of suppressed goods is not only valuable on the Socratic grounds that if we are going to live by the modern identity, it better be by an examined version of it. It is also a way in which we can live this identity more fully. Of course, whether this is an unmixed good depends on whether the identity is a self-destructive one, which is itself one of the major points at issue in the debate about modernity. I will return to this in the final sections. But right now, after these preliminary remarks, I propose to examine different readings of the dispute over instrumentalism, whose terms I laid out in the previous section.

The protagonists of disengaged reason are often totally dismissive of these complaints. The alleged experiential consequences are illusory. Those who complain lack the courage to face the world as it is, and hanker after the comforting illusions of yesteryear. The supposed loss of meaning reflects merely the projection of some confused emotions onto reality. As for the public consequences, these may be real enough, but they can only be faced by tackling the problems of democracy and ecology as technical questions and searching for the best solutions through the application of the relevant sciences, social and natural.

From my standpoint, this position involves a massive blindness to the goods which underlie the negative charges I just outlined, e.g., the recognition of some intrinsically valuable purpose in life beyond the utilitarian; expressive unity; the fulfilment of one's expressive potential; the acknowledgement of something more than instrumental meaning to the natural environment; a certain depth of meaning in the man-made environment. It is not part of my brief to argue this here, because my purpose is to illustrate my position rather than establish it. But the lines of argument are obvious enough.

Goods, as I said in Part I, can't be demonstrated to someone who really is impervious to them. One can only argue convincingly about goods which already in some way impinge on people, which they already at some level respond to but may be refusing to acknowledge. The order of argument is in a sense ad hominem, and involves showing that there is what Ernst Tugendhat calls a "way of experience"[12] which leads from one's interlocutor's position to one's own via some error-reducing moves, such as the clearing up of a confusion, the resolving of a contradiction, or the frank acknowledgement of what really does impinge.[13]

I don't think it would be hard to find such in the case of the extreme proponents of disengaged reason. If they are orthodox utilitarians, and if my arguments in Part I are valid, they will have an untenable meta-ethic to start with. In addition, as I have just indicated, there is plenty of evidence that in their lives they are not impervious to such goods as expressive unity and integrity. Romanticism has shaped just about everyone's views about personal fulfilment in our civilization. The apologists of instrumentalism suppress their awareness of this when it comes to espousing their explicit ideology. They simplify their moral world by deliberately narrowing their sympathy. Or so I would wish to argue.

Moreover, the instrumentalist reading of the public consequences is badly off target. There is an important set of conditions of the continuing health of self-governing societies, well explored by Tocqueville. These include a strong sense of identification of the citizens with their public institutions and political way of life, and may also involve some decentralization of power when the central institutions are too distant and bureaucratized to sustain a continuing sense of participation by themselves. These conditions are under threat in our highly concentrated and mobile societies, which are so dominated by instrumentalist considerations in both economic and defence policies. What is worse, the atomist outlook which instrumentalism fosters makes people unaware of these conditions, so that they happily support policies which undermine them—as in the recent rash of neo-conservative measures in Britain and the United States, which cut welfare programmes and regressively redistribute income, thus eroding the bases of community identification. Atomism has so befogged our awareness of the connection between the act and consequence in society that the same people who by their mobile and growth-oriented way of life have greatly increased the tasks of the public sector are the loudest to protest paying their share of the costs of fulfilling them. The hegemony of this outlook in our politics, further entrenched by irresponsible bureaucracy, also represents a standing threat to our ecological well-being. Such would be my claim.[14]

There is another family of views which comes to the fore when one has rejected the instrumentalist reading. These are views which share with instrumentalism common roots in Enlightenment naturalism. They are as thoroughly human-centred, but they espouse some notion of expressive fulfilment. On one reading, Marxism is such a view; and certainly the various theories of the earlier Frankfurt school, of Adorno and Horkheimer in one way, and of Marcuse in another, fit this description. They may be optimistic about the human prospect, as Marxism is, or rather pessimistic, as the thinkers of the Frankfurt school tended to be. Indeed, it appears almost as if Adorno saw the human problem as insoluble in history. But what he nevertheless hung onto was a notion of integral expressive fulfilment, in which the demands of sensual particularity would be fully harmonized with those of conceptual reason, and in which the domination and suppression of the former by the latter would be overcome. This remains a critical standard, even where it cannot be integrally realized.

Obviously, I have much greater sympathy for this position, particularly in its "pessimistic" variants, where it comes close to an undistorted recognition of conflict between goods. But from the standpoint of the modern identity as I understand it, this view still remains too narrow. It is still entirely anthropocentric, and treats all goods which are not anchored in human powers or fulfilments as illusions from a bygone age. In this it shows its filiation to the radical Enlightenment. This means not only that it is closed to any theistic perspective, but that it can't even have a place for the kind of non-anthropocentric exploration of sources which has been an important part of modernist art, be it in Rilke, Proust, Mann, Eliot, or Kafka. It is forced in the end to offer a rather reductive account of these explorations, and to relate them to the search for an expressive fulfilment of the subject. It is tied in this sense to subjectivism.

Even leaving the issue of theism aside, what is striking is the fact that the modernist works and experiments which are most deeply convincing and moving, those which have lasted, have been precisely those which went beyond subjectivism—e.g., among others, the works of the five I just mentioned. And many of these writers set their face against a subjectivist art—this was very often part of what was involved in their anti-Romanticism. It seems an arbitrary act, an excessive reliance on an ideological allegiance to the naturalist Enlightenment, to negate all this a priori.

Too, a certain subjectivist expressivism has won its way into contemporary culture, and its limitations seem obvious. In the human potential movement in the contemporary United States, and in other writings of similar tenor, there is a set of ideals which come from Romantic expressivism, in large part through indigenous American roots: Emerson and Transcendentalism, and Walt Whitman. The goals are self-expression, self-realization, self-fulfilment, discovering authenticity. But the present climate is much more impregnated with naturalism than were its nineteenth-century sources.

One thing this climate derives from Enlightenment naturalism is the stance of defending nature and ordinary desire from what are seen as specious spiritual demands, which lay the external standards of tradition on the self and threaten to stifle its authentic growth and fulfilment. Another thing it inherits is the belief in science and technique, which naturally has particularly strong roots in the United States. This emerges in the great importance given to methods of therapy and the sciences which supposedly underpin them: psychoanalysis, psychology, sociology. These two together, the subordination of some of the traditional demands of morality to the requirements of personal fulfilment, and the hope that this can be promoted by therapy, make up together the cultural turn which has been named "the triumph of the therapeutic".[15]

As critics have pointed out, the modes of life which this outlook encourages tend to a kind of shallowness. Because no non-anthropocentric good, indeed nothing outside subjective goods, can be allowed to trump self-realization, the very language of morals and politics tends to sink to the relatively colourless subjectivist talk of 'values'.[16] To find the meaning to us of "our job, social class, family and social roles", we are invited to ask questions like this: "In what ways are our values, goals, and aspirations being invigorated or violated by our present life system? How many parts of our personality can we live out, and what parts are we suppressing? How do we *feel* about our way of living in the world at any given time?"[17]

But our normal understanding of self-realization presupposes that some things are important beyond the self, that there are some goods or purposes the furthering of which has significance for us and which hence can provide the significance a fulfilling life needs. A total and fully consistent subjectivism would tend towards emptiness: nothing would count as a fulfilment in a world in which literally nothing was important but self-fulfilment.

What is more, the primacy of self-fulfilment reproduces and reinforces some of the same negative consequences as instrumentalism. Community affiliations, the solidarities of birth, of marriage, of the family, of the polis, all take second place. Here is advice on how to deal with the midlife crisis from the same influential book of the mid-1970's I just quoted.

You can't take everything with you when you leave on the midlife journey. You are moving away. Away from institutional claims and other people's agenda. Away from external valuations and accreditations, in search of an inner validation. You are moving out of roles and into the self. If I could give everyone a gift for the send-off on this journey, it would be a tent. A tent for tentativeness. The gift of portable roots . . .

    . . . the delights of self-discovery are always available. Though loved ones moved in and out of our lives, the capacity to love remains.[18]

We may attain expressive fulfilment by this route (subject to the caveat about subjectivism in the previous paragraph), but in a world of changing affiliations and relationships, the loss of substance, the increasing thinness of ties and shallowness of the things we use, increases apace. And the public consequences are even more direct. A society of self-fulfillers, whose affiliations are more and more seen as revocable, cannot sustain the strong identification with the political community which public freedom needs.

    Robert Bellah and his co-authors probe this erosion of the political in their *Habits of the Heart*. The primacy of self-fulfilment, particularly in its therapeutic variants, generates the notion that the only associations one can identify with are those formed voluntarily and which foster self-fulfilment, such as the 'life-style enclaves' in which people of similar interests or situation cluster—e.g., the retirement suburbs in the South, or revocable romantic relationships.[19] Beyond these associations lies the domain of strategic relations, where instrumental considerations are paramount. The therapeutic outlook seems to conceive community on the model of associations like Parents without Partners, a body which is highly useful for its members while they are in a given predicament, but to which there is no call to feel any allegiance once one is no longer in need.[20] The ethic generated beyond self-fulfilment is precisely that of procedural fairness, which plays a big role in the instrumentalist outlook. Politically, this bit of the 'counter-culture' fits perfectly into the instrumental, bureaucratic world it was thought to challenge. It strengthens it.

    There can also be more sinister or threatening offshoots of this culture. The "triumph of the therapeutic" can also mean an abdication of autonomy, where the lapse of traditional standards, coupled with the belief in technique, makes people cease to trust their own instincts about happiness, fulfilment, and how to bring up their children. Then the "helping professions" take over their lives,[21] a process described by Foucault but perhaps not adequately explained by him. And the extreme mobility and provisional nature of relationships can lead to a shrinking of the time sense, a feeling of inhabiting a narrow band of time, with an unknown past and a foreshortened future.[22] But enough has been said on this score to sketch the case against this subjectivist expressivism.

    The logical place to turn would be to an anti-subjectivist reading of this conflict, one that had a place for goods which are not simply centred on the individual or on human fulfilment, a view equally critical of instrumentalism and of subjective expressivism. But the difficulty is that views of this kind are frequently themselves one-sided; they have their own form of narrowness, their own blind spots. Thus the book *Habits of the Heart,* on which I have drawn a great deal, seems itself to offer a too simple view of our predicament. Bellah and his collaborators often write as though the principal issue were what I have called the public consequences. They see the threat that first utilitarian, and now also expressive individualism pose for our public life. They search for ways to recover a language of commitment to a greater whole. But without ever saying so, they write as though there were not really an independent problem of the loss of meaning in our culture, as though the recovery of a Tocquevillian commitment would somehow also fully resolve our problems of meaning, of expressive unity, of the loss of substance and resonance in our man-made environment, of a disenchanted universe. A crucial area of modern search and concern has been elided.

In a rather different way, there is a parallel elision in the work of Jürgen Habermas. In his *Theorie des kommunikativen Handelns,*[23] he takes Adorno to task for his pessimistic judgement on modernity. The sense of an impossible conflict between instrumental reason and expressive fulfilment comes, Habermas thinks, from the faulty conception of the agent. Adorno is still operating with the old 'consciousness theory' model of traditional philosophy, which construes our predicament in terms of a relation of subject to object; whereas in fact, the agent is constituted by language, hence by exchange between agents, whose relationship thus escapes the subject/object model. The significant others (Habermas has borrowed a great deal from George Herbert Mead) are not simply external to me; they help constitute my own selfhood.

Habermas reasons that Adorno, thinking as he does in terms of the subject/object relation, can only construe the advance of Enlightenment reason as involving an increasing instrumental domination of object by subject. But once we see that agents are constituted by exchange, we understand that reason also advances in another dimension, that of the rational search for consensus through argument.

Habermas's speech model certainly gives us reason to be less pessimistic about democracy and self-management than Adorno was, because we can see how the advance of instrumental control over nature doesn't *have* to mean a parallel growth of instrumental control over people. Habermas thus corrects Adorno's estimate of the public consequences of instrumentalism. But why should this alter our view of the experiential consequences? The fact that the self is constituted through exchange in language (and, as I indicated in Part I, I strongly agree with Habermas on this) doesn't in any way guarantee us against loss of meaning, fragmentation, the loss of substance in our human environment and our affiliations. Habermas, rather like Bellah and his associates, elides the experiential problem under the public, as though the two could be solved for the price of one.

What gets lost from view here is not the demands of expressive fulfilment, because Habermas does take account of these—they have their own differentiated sphere of modern rationality, alongside the moral-practical and the cognitive-instrumental. Rather, what cannot be fitted into his grid is what the last two chapters have been mainly occupied with, the search for moral sources *outside* the subject through languages which resonate *within* him or her, the grasping of an order which is inseparably indexed to a personal vision.

Habermas's conception of modernity, which is partly inspired by Weber, is in this respect in line with a widespread view. It allows that there was a premodern sense that humans were part of a larger order, but it sees the development of modern rationality precisely as showing the incoherence of this view. It has differentiated the varied strands of reason, and the old sense of order falls between the strands. Now there can be (1) a scientific attempt to know the world as objectified, i.e., as no longer seen in terms of its meanings for us; (2) the attempt of practical reason to determine the right; and (3) explorations of subjective expressive integrity and authenticity.[24] But there is no coherent place left for an exploration of the order in which we are set as a locus of moral sources, what Rilke, Pound, Lawrence, and Mann were doing in their radically different ways. This is not (1) because they are not trying to objectify this order; on the contrary. It is not (2) because Habermas has a procedural conception of practical reason. It is not (3) because that is concerned purely with subjective expression. It falls between the holes in the grid.

We can easily see why. It is not the exploration of an 'objective' order in the classical sense of a publicly accessible reality. The order is only accessible through personal, hence 'subjective', resonance. This is why, as I argued earlier, the danger of a regression to subjectivism always exists in this enterprise. It can easily slide into a celebration of our creative powers, or the sources can be appropriated, interpreted as within us, and represented as the basis for 'liberation'. But at its best, in full integrity, the enterprise is an attempt to surmount subjectivism. It is just that this remains a continuing task, which cannot be put behind us once and for all, as with the public order of former times.

This exploration of order through personal resonance fares no better at the hands of another class of views, even more strongly anti-subjectivist than the ones just examined. These are views, like those of the followers of Leo Strauss, which are critical of the whole modern turn, both in its disengaged-instrumental and in its Romantic-expressive forms. The sympathies of this type of outlook tend to be rather narrow, and their reading of the varied facets of the modern identity unsympathetic. The deeper moral vision, the genuine moral sources invoked in the aspiration to disengaged reason or expressive fulfilment tend to be overlooked, and the less impressive motives—pride, self-satisfaction, liberation from demanding standards—brought to the fore. Modernity is often read through its least impressive, most trivializing offshoots.[25]

But this distorts. The most frivolous and self-indulgent forms of the human potential movement in the United States today can't give us the measure of the aspiration to expressive fulfilment as we find it, for instance, in Goethe or Arnold. And even the most frivolous manifestation may reflect more than we can see at a glance. Above all, we have to avoid the error of declaring those goods invalid whose exclusive pursuit leads to contemptible or disastrous consequences. The search for pure subjective expressive fulfilment may make life thin and insubstantial, may ultimately undercut itself, as I argued above. But that by itself does nothing to show that subjective fulfilment is not a good. It shows only that it needs to be part of a 'package', to be sought within a life which is also aimed at other goods. This can be the basis, of course, for a cruel dilemma, in which the demands of fulfilment run against these other goods—one which thousands of divorcing or near-divorcing couples are living through in our time, for instance. But a dilemma doesn't invalidate the rival goods. On the contrary, it presupposes them.

I have been looking at different readings of the dispute over instrumentalism: from the standpoints of disengaged reason and subjective expressivism; then through the eyes of certain writers who contain subjectivism by assuming the experiential problem under the moral and political; finally through eyes critical of the whole modern turn, with its rejection of the public cosmic order of meanings. My claim is that they are all too narrow. They are all too quick and dismissive in denying certain goods whose validity emerges, I want to argue, if one does a close study of the modern identity as it has developed. These are goods, moreover, by which we moderns live, even those who believe they deny them: as disengaged rationalists still puzzle through their personal dilemmas with the aid of notions like fulfilment; and anti-moderns will themselves invoke rights, equality, and self-responsible freedom as well as fulfilment in their political and moral life.

But what has emerged from this quick survey is that, although they are narrow in different ways and they dismiss different goods, one class seems to be the especially unlucky target of all of them, and that is what I called the exploration of order through personal resonance. It falls through all the grids. The exclusion goes even wider than I have indicated. I haven't mentioned Weber, principally because I have many fewer criticisms to make of his theory. His is one of the most profound and insightful, in my view, not less because it has a lively sense of the conflict among goods. But even Weber, under the influence of a subjectivist interpretation of Nietzsche, has no place for this exploration.

This is a major gap. It is not just the epiphanic art of the last two centuries which fails to get its due by this dismissal. We are now in an age in which a publicly accessible cosmic order of meanings is an impossibility. The only way we can explore the order in which we are set with an aim to defining moral sources is through this part of personal resonance. This is true not only of epiphanic art but of other efforts, in philosophy, in criticism, which attempt the same search. This work, though it obviously fails of any epiphanic quality, falls into the same category. I have throughout sought language to clarify the issues, and I have found this in images of profound personal resonance like 'epiphany', 'moral sources', 'disengagement', 'empowering', and others. These are the images which enable me to see more clearly than I did before. They could, I believe, be the animating ideas of an epiphanic work, but that would require another kind of capacity. The great epiphanic work actually can put us in contact with the sources it taps. It can *realize* the contact. The philosopher or critic tinkers around and shapes images through which he or another *might* one day do so. The artist is like the race-car driver, and we are the mechanics in the pit; except that in this case, the mechanics usually have four thumbs, and they have only a hazy grasp of the wiring, much less than the drivers have. The point of this analogy is that we delude ourselves if we think that philosophical or critical language for these matters is somehow more hard-edged and more free from personal index than that of poets or novelists. The subject doesn't permit language which escapes personal resonance.

We either explore this area with such language or not at all. That is why the dismissal of this kind of exploration has important moral consequences. Proponents of disengaged reason or of subjective fulfilment embrace these consequences gladly. There are no moral sources there to explore. Root-and-branch critics of modernity hanker after the older public orders, and they assimilate personally indexed visions to mere subjectivism. Stern moralists, too, want to contain this murky area of the personal, and tend as well to block together all its manifestations, whether subjectivist or exploratory. Morality is held to be distinct from all this, independent of it, and imperiously binding. One way of making this kind of claim (seem to) stick is by adopting a proceduralist conception of morality. Habermas and Hare, for instance, have theories of this kind. A similar containment can be brought about by a certain theological outlook. Our commands come from God, and we can bypass and subordinate the area of personal sensibility.

But a study of the modern identity ought to make one dissatisfied with all these positions. It is not that the basic moral standards of modernity, concerning rights, justice, benevolence, depend on this exploration; they depend rather on goods to which we don't have access through personal sensibility. But there are other important issues of life which we can only resolve through this kind of insight; for instance, why it matters and what it means to have a more deeply resonant human environment and, even more, to have affiliations with some depth in time and commitment. These are questions which we can only clarify by exploring the human predicament, the way we are set in nature and among others, as a locus of moral sources. As our public traditions of family, ecology, even polis are undermined or swept away, we need new languages of personal resonance to make crucial human goods alive for us again.

And this exploration is not only important for its experiential relevance. It would greatly help in staving off ecological disaster if we could recover a sense of the demand that our natural surrounding and wilderness make on us. The subjectivist bias that both instrumentalism and the ideologies of personal fulfilment make almost inescapable makes it almost impossible to state the case here. Albert Borgman points out[26] how much of the argument for ecological restraint and responsibility is couched in anthropocentric language. Restraint is shown as necessary for human welfare. This is true and important enough, but it is not the whole story. It doesn't capture the full extent of our intuitions here. Our ideological milieu constitutes a force field in which even doctrines of a quite different intent are bent to conformity.

To read, for instance, Rilke is to get an articulation of our farther, stronger intuitions, of the way the world is not simply an ensemble of objects for our use, but makes a further claim on us. Rilke expresses this claim in images of 'praising' and 'making inward', which seem to lay a demand of attention, of careful scrutiny, of respect for what is there. And this demand, though connected with what we are as language beings, is not simply one of self-fulfilment. It emanates from the world. It is hard to be clear in this domain, just because we are deep into a language of personal resonance. But something extremely important to us is being articulated here through whatever groping and fragmentary one-sidedness. To declare this whole kind of thinking without object is to incur a huge self-inflicted wound.

25.4

I have discussed the conflict over instrumentalism at some length because it has been in the forefront of the discussion of modernity for a couple of centuries. My intent was to clarify the modern identity by providing a reading of the conflict in which it provides the context, and I hope that something has been gained by this. What emerges is a perspective critical of most of the dominant interpretations for being too narrow, for failing to give full recognition to the multiplicity of goods and hence to the conflicts and dilemmas they give rise to.

What also emerges from this discussion and that of earlier chapters is the way in which various sorts of selective blindness are entrenched and aggravated by philosophical considerations. As we saw with Descartes and Locke, the developing power of disengaged, self-responsible reason has tended to accredit a view of the subject as an unsituated, even punctual self. This is from one perspective quite understandable: it involves reading the stance of disengagement, whereby we objectify facets of our own being, into the ontology of the subject, as though we were by nature an agency separable from everything merely given in us—a disembodied soul (Descartes), or a punctual power of self-remaking (Locke), or a pure rational being (Kant). The stance is thereby given the strongest ontological warrant, as it were.

But however understandable, the move is erroneous. I haven't had space to pursue this here, but much of the most insightful philosophy of the twentieth century has gone to refute this picture of the disengaged subject.[27] What is important to note here is that this is not just a wrong view of agency; it is not at all necessary as a support to self-responsible reason and freedom. These ideals can and do have their validity (however limited by others); we can still recognize the development of this power (within proper bounds) as an important achievement of modernity, even when we cast off this invalid anthropology.

However, it is one of those facts about the current distribution of the onus of argument, about which I spoke in Chapter 9, that the case against disengaged subjectivity always has to be made anew; and similarly for the understanding that this case doesn't invalidate (though it may limit the scope of) self-responsible reason and freedom. The way the debate normally goes, it is all too easy for it to polarize into two camps. On one side are the holders of the ideals of self-responsible reason and freedom, who feel they therefore must take on the disengaged anthropology. Very often, this comes about through their attachment to an empiricist epistemology, whose omni-competence does presuppose something like the Lockean view of the subject.[28] On the other side are protesters against this somewhat desiccated outlook, who therefore feel that they have to reject altogether these ideals of reason and freedom.

In a similar—understandable but invalid—way, the radical Enlightenment accredited a philosophy which denied strong evaluation; and in its own fashion, the developing power of creative imagination has tended to lend colour to philosophies of subjective self-expression. These have also given rise to polarized debates in which the important insights get lost.

All of this points to the crucial importance of the strands of philosophy I mentioned above, which have been trying to lift us out of the preconceptions we easily slide into and to develop anthropologies of situated freedom.

The other two zones of tension I mentioned at the outset are not as widely recognized as the one I have been discussing. Rather their contours become evident only through the picture of the modern identity that I have been drawing.

The one I listed first contained the issue about sources. There doesn't seem to be an important conflict here. We agree surprisingly well, across great differences of theological and metaphysical belief, about the demands of justice and benevolence, and their importance. There are differences, including the stridently debated one about abortion. But the very rarity of these cases, which contributes to their saliency, is eloquent testimony to the general agreement. To see how much our consensus embraces, we need only compare any strand in our culture with basic beliefs held earlier and outside it: we may think, for instance, of judicial torture, or mutilation for crimes of theft, or even of an openly declared (as against hidden and unavowed) racism.

So why worry that we disagree on the reasons, as long as we're united around the norms? It's not the disagreement which is the problem. Rather the issue is what sources can support our far-reaching moral commitments to benevolence and justice.

In our public debates standards which are unprecedentedly stringent are put forward in respect of these norms and are not openly challenged. We are meant to be concerned for the life and well-being of all humans on the face of the earth; we are called on to further global justice between peoples; we subscribe to universal declarations of rights. Of course, these standards are regularly evaded. Of course, we subscribe to them with a great deal of hypocrisy and mental reservation. It remains that they are the publicly accepted standards. And they do from time to time galvanize people into action—as in the great television-inspired campaigns for famine relief or in movements like Band-Aid.

To the extent that we take these standards seriously (and that varies from person to person), how are they experienced? They can just be felt as peremptory demands, standards that we feel inadequate, bad, or guilty for failing to meet. No doubt many people, probably almost all of us some of the time, experience them this way. Or perhaps we can get a 'high' when we do sometimes meet them, from a sense of our own worth or, more likely, from the momentary relief from the marginal but oppressive sense we usually have of failing to meet them. But it is quite a different thing to be moved by a strong sense that human beings are eminently *worth* helping or treating with justice, a sense of their dignity or value. Here we have come into contact with the moral sources which originally underpin these standards.

These sources are plural, as we saw. But they have in common that they all offer positive underpinning of this kind. The original Christian notion of *agapē* is of a love that God has for humans which is connected with their goodness as creatures (though we don't have to decide whether they are loved because good or good because loved). Human beings participate through grace in this love. There is a divine affirmation of the creature, which is captured in the repeated phrase in Genesis 1 about each stage of the creation, "and God saw that it was good". *Agapē* is inseparable from such a "seeing-good".

The different, more or less secularized successor notions all incorporate something similar. Thus Enlightenment naturalism, as I argued above, is in part motivated by the sense that in rejecting religion it is for the first time doing justice to the innocence of natural desire, that it is countering the calumny implicit in ascetic codes.

High standards need strong sources. This is because there is something morally corrupting, even dangerous, in sustaining the demand simply on the feeling of undischarged obligation, on guilt, or its obverse, self-satisfaction. Hypocrisy is not the only negative consequence. Morality as benevolence on demand breeds self-condemnation for those who fall short and a depreciation of the impulses to self-fulfilment, seen as so many obstacles raised by egoism to our meeting the standard. Nietzsche has explored this with sufficient force to make embroidery otiose. And indeed, Nietzsche's challenge is based on a deep insight. If morality can only be powered negatively, where there can be no such thing as beneficence powered by an affirmation of the recipient as a being of value, then pity is destructive to the giver and degrading to the receiver, and the ethic of benevolence may indeed be indefensible. Nietzsche's challenge is on the deepest level, because he is looking precisely for what can release such an affirmation of being. His unsettling conclusion is that it is the ethic of benevolence which stands in the way of it. Only if there is such a thing as *agapē*, or one of the secular claimants to its succession, is Nietzsche wrong.

There are other consequences of benevolence on demand which Nietzsche didn't explore. The threatened sense of unworthiness can also lead to the projection of evil outward; the bad, the failure is now identified with some other people or group. My conscience is clear because I oppose them, but what can I do? They stand in the way of universal beneficence; they must be liquidated. This becomes particularly virulent on the extremes of the political spectrum, in a way which Dostoyevsky has explored to unparalleled depths.

In our day as in his, many young people are driven to political extremism, sometimes by truly terrible conditions, but also by a need to give meaning to their lives. And since meaninglessness is frequently accompanied by a sense of guilt, they sometimes respond to a strong ideology of polarization, in which one recovers a sense of direction as well as a sense of purity by lining up in implacable opposition to the forces of darkness. The more implacable, even violent the opposition, the more the polarity is represented as absolute, and the greater the sense of separation from evil and hence purity. Dostoyevsky's *Devils* is one of the great documents of modern times, because it lays bare the way in which an ideology of universal love and freedom can mask a burning hatred, directed outward onto an unregenerate world and generating destruction and despotism.

The question which arises from all this is whether we are not living beyond our moral means in continuing allegiance to our standards of justice and benevolence. Do we have ways of seeing-good which are still credible to us, which are powerful enough to sustain these standards? If not, it would be both more honest and more prudent to moderate them. And in this connection, the issue I raised briefly in Chapter 19 recurs. Is the naturalist seeing-good, which turns on the rejection of the calumny of religion against nature, fundamentally parasitic? This it might be in two senses: not only that it derives its affirmation through rejecting an alleged negation, but also that the original model for its universal benevolence is *agapē*. How well could it survive the demise of the religion it strives to abolish? With the 'calumny' gone, could the affirmation continue?

The question might arise in another form, following the discussion in section 23.6: perhaps the original Enlightenment affirmation was indeed confident, based on a highly idealized, immediately post-providential vision of nature. But can this affirmation be sustained in face of our contemporary post-Schopenhauerian understanding of the murkier depths of human motivation? Is there somewhere a transfigurative power to see these as good, without paying Nietzsche's price?

Or must benevolence ultimately come to be conceived as a duty we owe ourselves, somehow required by our dignity as rational, emancipated moderns, regardless of the (un)worth of the recipients? And to the extent that this is so, how close will we have come to the world Dostoyevsky portrays, in which acts of seeming beneficence are in fact expressions of contempt, even hatred?

Perhaps another question might be put here as well. Is the naturalist affirmation conditional on a vision of human nature in the fullness of its health and strength? Does it move us to extend help to the irremediably broken, such as the mentally handicapped, those dying without dignity, fetuses with genetic defects? Perhaps one might judge that it doesn't and that this is a point in favour of naturalism; perhaps effort shouldn't be wasted on these unpromising cases. But the careers of Mother Teresa or Jean Vanier seem to point to a different pattern, emerging from a Christian spirituality.

I am obviously not neutral in posing these questions. Even though I have refrained (partly out of delicacy, but largely out of lack of arguments) from answering them, the reader suspects that my hunch lies towards the affirmative, that I do think naturalist humanism defective in these respects—or, perhaps better put, that great as the power of naturalist sources might be, the potential of a certain theistic perspective is incomparably greater. Dostoyevsky has framed this perspective better than I ever could here.

But I recognize that pointed questions could be put in the other direction as well, directed at theistic views. My aim has been not to score points but to identify this range of questions around the moral sources which might sustain our rather massive professed commitments in benevolence and justice. This entire range is occluded by the dominance of proceduralist meta-ethics, which makes us see these commitments through the prism of moral obligation, thereby making their negative face all the more dominant and obtrusive[29] and pushing the moral sources further out of sight. But the picture I have been drawing of the modern identity brings this range back into the foreground.

25.5

I want now to look very briefly at the third zone. What emerged from the discussion of the critique of instrumentalism was the need to recognize a plurality of goods, and hence often of conflicts, which other views tend to mask by delegitimizing one of the goods in contest. Instrumentralists can ignore the cost in expressive fulfilment or in the severing of ties with nature, because they don't recognize these. Critics of modernity are frequently just as dismissive about these goods, which for their part they dismiss as subjectivist illusion. Proponents of subjective fulfilment allow nothing to stand against 'liberation'.

And the discussion we have just finished about the sources of benevolence brought us also to a crucial conflict, which has been illuminatingly explored in rather different ways by Nietzsche and Dostoyevsky: the demands of benevolence can exact a high cost in self-love and self-fulfilment, which may in the end require payment in self-destruction or even in violence.

And indeed, there has been some awareness of this for some centuries now in our culture. The naturalist rebellion against the ascetic demands of religion and the earlier quiet rejection of Christianity by discreet individuals in the name of paganism reflect at least in part the recognition that a terribly high cost was being demanded.

In our day, the conflict has been further articulated by writers who have drawn on Nietzsche. One of the important themes one can find in the work of the late Michel Foucault is the understanding of the way in which high ethical and spiritual ideals are often interwoven with exclusions and relations of domination. William Connolly has formulated this aspect of Foucault's thought very aptly.[30] And contemporary feminist critique has also contributed greatly to this understanding, in showing how certain conceptions of the life of the spirit exclude women, accord them a lesser place, or assume their subordination.[31] The sense that in this and other ways hypergoods can stifle or oppress us has been one of the motives for the naturalist revolt against traditional religion and morality, as I argued in Part I (sections 3.2–3).

From all these examples, in my view, a general truth emerges, which is that the highest spiritual ideals and aspirations also threaten to lay the most crushing burdens on humankind. The great spiritual visions of human history have also been poisoned chalices, the causes of untold misery and even savagery. From the very beginning of the human story religion, our link with the highest, has been recurrently associated with sacrifice, even mutilation, as though something of us has to be torn away or immolated if we are to please the gods.

This is an old theme, well explored by Enlightenment thinkers, and particularly by those with what I called the 'neo-Lucretian' outlook (section 19.3). But the sad story doesn't end with religion. The Kharkov famine and the Killing Fields were perpetrated by atheists in an attempt to realize the most lofty ideals of human perfection.

Well, then, one might say, the danger attends religion, or else millenarist ideologies which are somewhat similar to religion in putting moral passion before hard evidence. What we need is a sober, scientific-minded, secular humanism.

But in spite of the richness, as yet not fully explored, of the neo-Lucretian stance, this still seems to me too simple. And the reason lies in the crucial difference between the perspective I have been exploring here and the various naturalist and Nietzschean critiques of self-immolation. Characteristically, these take the self-destructive consequences of a spiritual aspiration as a refutation of this aspiration. They make once again what I believe is the cardinal mistake of believing that a good must be *invalid* if it leads to suffering or destruction.

Thus Enlightenment naturalism thought it was refuting Christianity in showing the cost of asceticism; Nietzsche often gives a picture of 'morality' which shows it to be merely envy, or a device of the weak, or ressentiment, and which thus deprives it of all claim on our allegiance.[32] Foucault in his writings seemed to be claiming (I believe) impossible neutrality, which recognized no claims as binding.

But I have argued that this way of reasoning is deeply mistaken. Not only can some potentially destructive ideals be directed to genuine goods; some of them undoubtedly are. The ethic of Plato and the Stoics can't be written off as mere illusion. And even non-believers, if they don't block it off, will feel a powerful appeal in the gospel, which they will interpret in a secular fashion; just as Christians, unless immured in blinkered self-sufficiency, will recognize the appalling destruction wrought in history in the name of the faith.

That is why adopting a stripped-down secular outlook, without any religious dimension or radical hope in history, is not a way of *avoiding* the dilemma, although it may be a good way to live with it. It doesn't avoid it, because this too involves its 'mutilation'. It involves stifling the response in us to some of the deepest and most powerful spiritual aspirations that humans have conceived. This, too, is a heavy price to pay.

This is not to say, though, that if we have to pay some price, this may not be the safest. Prudence constantly advises us to scale down our hopes and circumscribe our vision. But we deceive ourselves if we pretend that nothing is denied thereby of our humanity.

Is this the last word? Does something have to be denied? Do we have to choose between various kinds of spiritual lobotomy and self-inflicted wounds? Perhaps. Certainly most of the outlooks which promise us that we will be spared these choices are based on selective blindness. This is perhaps the major point elaborated in this book.

But I didn't undertake it in this downbeat a spirit. The kind of study I have embarked on here can be a work, we might say, of liberation. The intuition which inspired it, which I have recurred to, is simply that we tend in our culture to stifle the spirit. We do this partly out of the prudence I have just invoked, particularly after the terrible experiences of millenarist destruction of our century; partly because of the bent of modern naturalism, one of our dominant creeds; partly because of partisan narrowness all around. We have read so many goods out of our official story, we have buried their power so deep beneath layers of philosophical rationale, that they are in danger of stifling. Or rather, since they are our goods, human goods, *we* are stifling.

The intention of this work was one of retrieval, an attempt to uncover buried goods through rearticulation—and thereby to make these sources again empower, to bring the air back again into the half-collapsed lungs of the spirit.

Some readers may find this overblown (though these will probably have stopped reading long ago). And perhaps I am merely overreacting to a narrowness of the academy which has little effect on the world outside—although I don't think this is so. Others may accuse me with greater apparent justice of inconsistency—or even irresponsibility. If the highest ideals are the most potentially destructive, then maybe the prudent path is the safest, and we shouldn't unconditionally rejoice at the indiscriminate retrieval of empowering goods. A little judicious stifling may be the part of wisdom.

The prudent strategy makes sense on the assumption that the dilemma is inescapable, that the highest spiritual aspirations must lead to mutilation or destruction. But if I may make one last unsupported assertion, I want to say that I don't accept this as our inevitable lot. The dilemma of mutilation is in a sense our greatest spiritual challenge, not an iron fate.

How can one demonstrate this? I can't do it here (or, to be honest, anywhere at this point). There is a large element of hope. It is a hope that I see implicit in Judaeo-Christian theism (however terrible the record of its adherents in history), and in its central promise of a divine affirmation of the human, more total than humans can ever attain unaided.

But to explain this properly would take another book. My aim in this Conclusion has only been to show how my picture of the modern identity can shape our view of the moral predicament of our time.

NOTES

INDEX

NOTES

1. INESCAPABLE FRAMEWORKS

1. Iris Murdoch, *The Sovereignty of Good* (London: Routledge, 1970).
2. See my "What Is Human Agency?" in Charles Taylor, *Human Agency and Language* (Cambridge: Cambridge University Press, 1985). A good test for whether an evaluation is 'strong' in my sense is whether it can be the basis for attitudes of admiration and contempt.
3. J. L. Mackie, *Ethics: Inventing Right and Wrong* (Harmondsworth: Penguin Books, 1977).
4. See the discussion below in section 3.2 and also my "Explanation and Practical Reason" (forthcoming).
5. For a good example of this, see E. O. Wilson, *On Human Nature* (Cambridge, Mass.: Harvard University Press, 1978).
6. See Leszek Kołakowski, *Religion* (London: Fontana, 1982).
7. Michel Foucault, *Surveiller et punir* (Paris: Gallimard, 1975).
8. See Marcel Proust, *A l'ombre des jeunes filles en fleur* (Paris: Gallimard, 1954), p. 438, on this inescapable sense of and concern for our appearance in public space.
9. See A. W. H. Adkins, *From the Many to the One* (Ithaca: Cornell University Press, 1970), pp. 9–10.
10. See *The Gay Science*, para. 125. All translations are by Gretta Taylor or by myself, unless otherwise specified.
11. See Alasdair MacIntyre, *After Virtue* (Notre Dame: University of Notre Dame Press, 1984), pp. 203–204.
12. See the perceptive discussion of this crisis of Luther as what we moderns would call a crisis of "identity" in Erik Erikson, *Young Man Luther* (New York: Norton, 1958).
13. Paul Tillich, in *The Courage to Be* (New Haven: Yale University Press, 1952), has described the difference between the age of the Reformation and our own in something like these terms.
14. See Christopher Lasch, *The Culture of Narcissism* (New York: Norton, 1979), pp. 80–81; and also Janet Malcolm, *Psycho-analysis: The Impossible Profession* (New York: Knopf, 1981).

2. THE SELF IN MORAL SPACE

1. See Heinz Kohut, *The Restoration of the Self* (New York: International University Press, 1977), pp. 153–154.
2. Erik Erikson, *Young Man Luther* (New York: Norton, 1958).
3. C. G. Gallup, Jr., "Chimpanzees: Self-Recognition", *Science,* 6 June 1983, pp. 86–87.
4. See the articles by Susan Hales and by A. Pratkanis and A. Greenwald in the special issue on the "rediscovery of the self" of the *Journal for the Theory of Social Behaviour* 15 (1985).
5. See my "Understanding and Human Science", *Review of Metaphysics* 34 (1980), 25–38. Bernard Williams also offers an account of this requirement, inter alia, in his *Descartes* (Harmondsworth: Penguin Books, 1978). The term 'absolute' here is borrowed from his discussion. Another description of the requirement, as one for 'objectivity', figures in Thomas Nagel's *The View from Nowhere* (New York: Oxford University Press, 1986).
6. I have discussed this in *Human Agency and Language* (Cambridge: Cambridge University Press, 1985), chaps. 1, 2, 4; and in *Philosophy and the Human Sciences* (Cambridge: Cambridge University Press, 1985), chap. 1. The point in the contemporary discussion generally owes a great deal to Heidegger and his thesis that understanding is the mode of being; see *Sein und Zeit* (Tübingen: Niemeyer, 1927), div. I, chap. 5, sect. A. Cf. Bert Dreyfus's commentary in *Being in the World* (Cambridge, Mass.: MIT Press, 1988), and the point that *Dasein* is "interpretation all the way down". Cf. also the work of H. G. Gadamer, especially *Wahrheit und Methode* (Tübingen: Mohr, 1975).
7. Ernst Tugendhat, in his *Selbstbewusstsein und Selbstbestimmung* (Frankfurt: Suhrkamp, 1979), makes a point parallel to this, but in his case the foil is the Fichte-derived philosophy of Dieter Henrich, with its discussion of our relation to ourselves as the limiting case of a subject-object relation where the two are identical. Tugendhat's point is that the self we know in self-knowledge can't be construed as an object. Being a self is a matter of how things matter to us. Tugendhat has also drawn on Heidegger in his very interesting and penetrating discussion.
8. This is, of course, the taking-off point for "post-structuralist" discussions of the end of subjectivity and the impossibility of lucid self-consciousness. But these arguments fundamentally misunderstand the nature of language. Cf. note 12 below on Humboldt.
9. See my "Theories of Meaning" in Taylor, *Human Agency and Language.*
10. See Jerome Bruner, *Child's Talk* (New York: Norton, 1983). Brunner shows the tremendous importance of game-like "formats", modes of communicative interaction between parent and child, in providing the context and support system in which children learn to speak. And these in turn are preceded by and build on the establishing and enjoyment and celebration of sustained eye-to-eye contact. This original, prelinguistic communion provides

the indispensable context for the development of common spaces around objects of references, often through the use of standardized gestures and intonations: e.g., 'see the pretty dolly'; ibid., pp. 70–71.

11. *Philosophical Investigation*, I, para. 242.

12. George Herbert Mead is usually credited with making a point of this kind, about the social genesis of the self. See his *Mind, Self, and Society* (Chicago: University of Chicago Press, 1962). But Mead is still too close to a behaviourist view, and doesn't seem to take account of the constitutive role of language in the definition of self and relations. Wilhelm von Humboldt is the most perspicuous theorist in the tradition. He understood the way in which language is made and remade in conversation, but he also saw how the very nature of a conversation requires a recognition of individual speakers and their different perspectives. The speech situation cannot be thought of as built out of causally related monologues; but neither can it be thought of as the deployment of a supersubject or the unfolding of a structure. Common space is constituted by speakers who join their perspectives, and to this end speakers must remain ever at least tacitly aware of them. 'Shifter' words like 'I', 'you', 'here', 'there' play a crucial role in inaugurating and maintaining common space. It is interesting that children learn these very easily and early (see Jerome Bruner, "The Transactional Self", in his *Actual Minds, Possible Worlds*, Cambridge, Mass.: Harvard University Press, 1986, p. 60). An interesting discussion of these expressions occurs in Gareth Evans, *The Varieties of Reference* (Oxford: Oxford University Press, 1982). The Humboldtian understanding of language and the speech situation shows what is confused in the dramatic utterances of "post-structuralists" about the loss or unreality of subjectivity.

13. The close connection between identity and interlocution also emerges in the place of *names* in human life. My name is what I am "called". A human being *has* to have a name, because he or she has to be *called*, i.e., addressed. Being called into conversation is a precondition of developing a human identity, and so my name is (usually) given me by my earliest interlocutors. Nightmare scenarios in science fiction where, e.g., the inmates of camps no longer have names but just numbers, draw their forces from this fact. Numbers tag people for easy reference, but what you use to address a person is his name. Beings who are just referents and not also addressees are ipso facto classed as non-human, without identity. It is not surprising that in many cultures the name is thought in some way to capture, even to constitute, the essence or power of the person. Thus in some societies one's real name is kept secret from outsiders. And in certain religious traditions—our own being a striking example—the name of God takes on a central importance. God's revelation of his name to Moses was both a crucial and enigmatic event; and this name subsequently couldn't be used directly to refer to God, but was spelled by the Tetragrammaton and spoken as 'Adonai', or 'Lord'. To praise God was also to praise his Name.

14. One can perhaps understand the importance of friendship for Epicureanism

partly in relation to the essential importance of this close circle for those who strove to liberate themselves from what they thought to be the errors of the many.

15. Our "conversation" with the absent and dead is, of course, mediated by the works of oral and written culture, by sayings, sacred writings, works of thought, poetry, and works of art in general. These are originally conceived as figuring in a conversation. They are destined to be taken up and heard again or read repeatedly. The hermeticism of much modern art may make us think the contrary. But a reflection on artistic form might overcome this impression. All of our central art forms emerge out of earlier modes of social celebration or rite, be they tribal dance, liturgies, original Greek theatre, or sacred painting. I believe that further reflection and study would show that what we class as artistic form even today—that is, what allows us to recognize some collection of words as a poem or some pattern of colours as a painting, and the like—is closely connected with the property of encapsulating or revealing something (in principle) for anyone. In this way, they retain their connection with the original context of the most "primitive" art, a context of social enactment. One thing a work of art is in its essence, I would say, is a bit of "frozen" potential communication. I wish I could say more at present to make this view convincing.

16. See my "Language and Human Nature" in Taylor, *Human Agency and Language*.

17. Robert Bellah, et al., *Habits of the Heart* (Berkeley: University of California Press, 1985), pp. 56–62.

18. Sudhir Kakar, *The Inner World* (Delhi: Oxford University Press, 1978), p. 86.

19. Ibid., pp. 86–87.

20. We are also ethnocentric, or at least too narrow in our understanding and sympathy, if we take it as axiomatic that a self is what we ought to want to have or be. There are influential spiritual outlooks which want to have us escape or transcend the self. Buddhism is the best known. But there are also certain strands of modern Western culture, for whom the demands in any case of the Western identity of the disengaged and independent agent have seemed unreal, or intolerably restricting, or oppressive. There is a literature of escape from the self, to which Nietzsche has contributed, and also, in another way, Musil, Bataille, and also Foucault, and in another way again figures like Derrida. These may be temporarily allied to, but must be distinguished from, attempts to reconnect the self with some larger reality, to overcome the slide towards subjectivism in modern culture, as we see with Heidegger, and in a quite different way with, say, Alasdair MacIntyre, or Robert Bellah. Transcending the self in terms of the model I'm working with here is to escape identification with a particular voice in the conversation, no longer to be the one who stands in a certain perspective in moral space. There is no doubt that we have the imaginative power to step beyond our own place and to understand ourselves as playing a part in the whole. If we didn't, we

wouldn't be able to set up with other human beings what I have been calling 'common space', because that requires that we see ourselves as one perspective among others. So we can also see ourselves "from the perspective of the whole"; we can see the self in imagination as simply an aspect of a larger system, activated by it. What is not clear is to what degree one can actually *assume* that standpoint and live it. To weigh this we need a finer discussion of our moral possibilities. Half-baked reflections on language and the impossibility of full presence don't suffice.

I am very sceptical whether contemporary neo-Nietzschean doctrines of overcoming the self or the "subject" can meet this test. Quite different are attempts to overcome modern subjectivism which purport to reconnect us with some larger reality, social or natural. Those based, for instance, on the recognition that some of the most crucial human fulfilments are not possible even in principle for a sole human being, that they involve a good in which more than one participate in complementary fashion, whose emblem would be less the lonely affirmation of freedom and more, e.g., the dance; these are less adequately described as negations of the self than they are as ways of understanding its embedding in interlocution. Unlike the neo-Nietzschean positions, views of this kind don't attempt to do altogether without a notion of the good. Indeed, they require some conception of the human good as something realized *between* people rather than simply within them. In this category belong various socialist theories, civic humanist conceptions of politics, and theories of sex complementarity. For the last, see Prudence Allen, *The Concept of Woman* (Montreal: Eden Press, 1985).

21. Marcel Proust, *A la recherche du temps perdu* (Paris: Gallimard, 1919).
22. John Dunne, *The City of the Gods* (New York: Macmillan, 1965).
23. Thucydides, *The Peloponnesian War*, II.43.
24. See Heidegger, *Sein und Zeit*; P. Ricoeur, *Temps et récit*, 3 vols. (Paris: Seuil, 1983–1985); A. MacIntyre, *After Virtue* (Notre Dame: University of Notre Dame Press, 1984); Bruner, *Actual Minds, Possible Worlds*.
25. For instance, in the works mentioned in note 24 by MacIntyre, Ricoeur, and Bruner.
26. *Sein und Zeit*, Div. II, chaps. 3, 4.
27. MacIntyre, *After Virtue*, pp. 203–204.
28. Derek Parfit, *Reasons and Persons* (Oxford: Oxford University Press, 1984), chaps. 14, 15.
29. Parfit, *Reasons and Persons*, chaps. 10–13. Locke relies on the case of minds "switching bodies"; Parfit puts particular weight on division of a person into two.
30. See John Locke, *An Essay concerning Human Understanding*, ed. P. H. Nidditch (Oxford: Oxford University Press, 1975), 2.27.9.
31. "For it being the same consciousness that makes a Man be himself to himself, personal Identity depends on that only, whether it be annexed only to one individual Substance, or can be continued in a succession of several Substances"; ibid. Parfit wants to sidetrack the old issue of personal identity,

but what takes its place is a kind of psychological connectedness or continuity, which is a descendant of Locke's criterion; see Parfit, *Reasons and Persons,* pp. 204–209.

32. "We must consider what Person stands for; which, I think, is a thinking intelligent Being, that has reason and reflection, and can consider it self as it self, the same thinking thing in different times and places"; Locke, *Essay,* II.27.9.

33. Parfit, *Reasons and Persons,* p. 216.

34. Heidegger, *Sein und Zeit,* div. II, chaps. 3, 4.

35. Of course there is one major modern philosopher, Nietzsche, who seemed to protest against any retrospective conferring of meaning on the past by the future. This is one of the meanings of his otherwise obscure doctrine of the eternal recurrence. See Alexander Nehamas, *Nietzsche: Life as Literature* (Cambridge, Mass.: Harvard University Press, 1985), chap. 5. But it is Nietzsche himself who speaks of 'redemption' in these terms: "To redeem the past and to transform every 'It was' into an 'I wanted it thus'—that alone do I call redemption", *Thus Spake Zarathustra* (Harmondsworth: Penguin Books, 1961), p. 161.

36. Marcel Proust, *Le Temps retrouvé* (Paris: Gallimard, 1954), p. 237.

37. If we took Parfit seriously, so that deeming "my" childhood to be that of a separate person meant that the rules of interpersonal morality now operate, then we could say that by this repudiation I forever condemn *his* chances for a meaningful life, which would indeed be a heinous offence.

38. This is not to say that the horrendous scenarios imagined by Locke and Parfit would not destroy or put in question the unity of a life. They certainly alert us to necessary conditions of this unity. But they fail altogether to engage with the narrative unity I have been talking about here. Suppose you criticized a movement of someone's symphony as lacking thematic unity, and a philosophical discussion then ensued as to just what the unity of a movement consists in. Someone points out that you can't have a unified piece if half the orchestra plays in Montreal and the other half in Toronto. True enough, we were taking performance in a single hall for granted; but if somebody thought that the unity we were talking about turned simply on such questions of spatial contiguity, he or she would have grievously missed the point.

3. ETHICS OF INARTICULACY

1. See Bernard Williams, *Ethics and the Limits of Philosophy* (London: Fontana, 1985).

2. 'Projection' is a term used by John Mackie; see his *Ethics* (Harmondsworth: Penguin Books, 1977), p. 42. Simon Blackburn speaks of 'projectivism'; see his "Errors and the Phenomenology of Value", in *Morality and Objectivity,* ed. Ted Honderich (London: Routledge, 1985).

3. See R. M. Hare, *Freedom and Reason* (Oxford: Oxford University Press, 1963).

4. See E. O. Wilson, *On Human Nature* (Cambridge, Mass.: Harvard University Press, 1978).
5. Mackie uses this analogy in his claim that values "are not part of the fabric of the world" in *Ethics*, p. 15; see also his discussion, pp. 19–20. Others have pointed out the disanalogies; e.g., see Blackburn, "Errors and the Phenomenology of Value"; John McDowell, "Values and Secondary Qualities", in *Morality and Objectivity*, ed. Honderich; and Williams, *Ethics and the Limits of Philosophy*, chap. 8. Not all the disanalogies are necessarily fatal to the projective view. Indeed, there is at times some uncertainty in the debate as to which "side" ought to be drawing the analogy.
6. Williams, *Ethics and the Limits of Philosophy*, chap. 8. The point has also been effectively argued by John McDowell. See his "Are Moral Requirements Hypothetical Imperatives?" *Proceedings of the Aristotelian Society*, supp. vol. (1978), and idem, "Virtue and Reason", *Monist* 62 (1979), 331–350.
7. Williams, *Ethics and the Limits of Philosophy*, pp. 141–142.
8. See Williams's discussion in ibid., pp. 149–150.
9. See Williams's *Descartes* (Harmondsworth: Penguin Books, 1978), and also his *Ethics and the Limits of Philosophy*.
10. See, inter alia, my *Philosophy and the Human Sciences* (Cambridge: Cambridge University Press, 1985), chaps. 1–3.
11. I have tried to show the essential continuity of these languages in "Neutrality in Political Science", in Taylor, *Philosophy and the Human Sciences*.
12. See B. F. Skinner, *Beyond Freedom and Dignity* (New York: Knopf, 1971).
13. See the dismissal of certain considerations as "mere phenomenology" by proponents of a computer model of the mind, for instance. See Ned Block's discussion of appeals to 'intuition' in "What Intuitions and Homunculi Don't Show", a reply to John Searle's "Minds, Brains and Programs", in *Behavioral and Brain Sciences* 3 (1980), 425–426.
14. See "Mental Events" in Donald Davidson, *Essays on Action and Events* (Oxford: Oxford University Press, 1980), p. 216.
15. See Richard Wollheim, *The Thread of Life* (Cambridge, Mass.: Harvard University Press, 1984), chap. 1, for a discussion of what is involved in 'living' or 'leading' one's life.
16. Mackie, *Ethics*, p. 38.
17. See Simon Blackburn, "Rule Following and Moral Realism", in *Wittgenstein: To Follow a Rule*, ed. S. Holtzman and C. Leich (London: Routledge 1981), and Blackburn, "Errors and the Phenomenology of Value".
18. Blackburn, "Errors and the Phenomenology of Value", p. 4.
19. Because of this, there has been a tendency for non-realists to stay away from the terms of thick moral decription designating particular goods and to found their theories on an analysis of highly general terms, like 'good' and 'right'. Elizabeth Anscombe noted this a number of decades ago (see her "Modern Moral Philosophy", *Philosophy* 33, 1958). Recently the point has been taken up in an illuminating way by Susan Hurley, who names this focus on the general 'centralism', the view that "the general concepts, *right* and *ought*, are . . . logically prior to and independent of the specific concepts,

such as *just* and *unkind"* ("Objectivity and Disagreement", in *Morality and Objectivity*, ed. Honderich, p. 56). She has developed convincing arguments against centralism in her writings; see idem, *Natural Reasons* (forthcoming), chaps. 2, 3.

20. Blackburn, "Errors and the Phenomenology of Value", pp. 19–20.
21. I. Kant, *The Critique of Practical Reason*, book I, part I, sect. 7; *Foundations of the Metaphysics of Morals*, p. 433 (page numbering of the Berlin Academy edition).
22. J. Habermas, *Theorie des kommunikativen Handelns*, 2 vols. (Frankfurt: Suhrkamp, 1981), I, chap. 3; and idem, *Moralbewusstsein und kommunikatives Handeln* (Frankfurt: Suhrkamp, 1983), chaps. 3, 4.
23. See Williams, *Ethics and the Limits of Philosophy*, chap. 10.
24. G. W. F. Hegel, *The Philosophy of Right*, para. 141.
25. See R. M. Hare's definition of the moral partly in terms of its 'overriding" other considerations; *Freedom and Reason*, 9.3; and *Moral Thinking* (Oxford: Oxford University Press, 1981), pp. 24, 55.
26. F. Nietzsche, *Ecce Homo*, "Morgenröte", sect. 1.
27. This notion of 'internal' good is close to Alasdair MacIntyre's concept of goods 'internal' to practices, as he expounds this in *After Virtue* (Notre Dame: University of Notre Dame Press, 1984), chap. 14. I expounded another version of the idea in "Justice after Virtue" (forthcoming).
28. See Williams, *Ethics and the Limits of Philosophy*, chap. 8. I think that Williams adopts a version of what I am calling "sophisticated naturalism" in this section; if so, his is certainly a highly sophisticated variant.
29. See e.g., McDowell, "Are Moral Requirements Hypothetical Imperatives?" and idem, "Virtue and Reason".
30. I have tried to make this case in a number of places. See particularly *Human Agency and Language* (Cambridge: Cambridge University Press, 1985), chaps. 2, 5, 7.
31. See Prudence Allen, *The Concept of Woman* (Montreal: Eden Press, 1985), chap. 5.
32. See Michel Foucault, *Surveiller et punir* (Paris: Gallimard, 1975), and idem, *Histoire de la sexualité*, vol. 1 (Paris: Gallimard, 1976).
33. See Foucault, *Surveiller et punir*.
34. See Frantz Fanon, *Les Damnés de la terre* (Paris: Maspéro, 1968).
35. See, for instance, Hare, *Freedom and Reason;* and idem, *Moral Thinking*.
36. See my "Explanation and Practical Reason" (forthcoming).
37. Ernst Tugendhat, in *Selbstbewusstsein und Selbstbestimmung* (Frankfurt: Suhrkamp, 1979), p. 275, presents a view of this kind. He speaks of a "way of experience" (*Erfahrungsweg*) which may be available from A to B, but not vice versa. I have borrowed from his interesting analysis.
38. See Hare, *Freedom and Reason*.
39. John Rawls, *A Theory of Justice* (Oxford: Oxford University Press, 1972), chap. 1, sect. 7; Mill uses the same expression for something similar in *Utilitarianism*, chap. 1. Of course, Rawls is here talking not of the whole of morality, but only of justice.

40. I have argued against this tendency in "The Diversity of Goods" in Taylor, *Philosophy and the Human Sciences*.

41. See Wilson, *On Human Nature*, pp. 6, 38.

42. See Mackie, *Ethics*.

43. Williams, *Ethics and the Limits of Philosophy*, chap. 10.

44. Hare, *Moral Thinking*, I.9, pp. 16–17.

45. Habermas, *Moralbewusstsein*, pp. 76, 103.

46. Clifford Geertz, *The Interpretation of Cultures* (New York: Basic Books, 1973), chap. 1. Geertz acknowledges the earlier coining of the term by Gilbert Ryle in his *Concept of Mind* (London: Hutchinson, 1949), but it is Geertz whose illuminating use of it has given the term its resonance.

47. The term, of course, could have a number of other equally justified uses, some of them designating doctrines that I heartily concur in; just as there are anti-naturalist views which deserve to be rejected. But I need some short handy term for this particular view about science and human nature.

48. See Gail Sheehy, *Passages: Predictable Crises of Adult Life* (New York: Bantam Books, 1976).

49. See Francis Oakley, "Christian Theology and the Newtonian Science", *Church History* 30 (1961), 433–457.

50. See Robert Lenoble, *Mersenne et la naissance du mécanisme* (Paris: J. Vrin, 1943).

51. "Whatsoever is the object of a man's appetite or desire, that is it which he for his part calleth good"; *Leviathan*, ed. M. Oakeshott (Oxford: Blackwell, n.d.), chap. 6, p. 32.

52. "The pacts and covenants, by which the parts of the body politic were at first made, set together, and united, resemble that *fiat*, or the *let us make man*, pronounced by God in the creation"; ibid., introduction, p. 5.

53. "Nothing in the world—indeed nothing even beyond the world—can possibly be conceived which could be called good without qualification except a *good will*". This is the opening sentence of Kant's *Foundations of the Metaphysics of Morals*.

54. Ibid., p. 435.

55. Iris Murdoch, *The Sovereignty of Good* (London: Routledge, 1970), p. 80.

56. F. Bacon, *Novum Organum*, I. 73; trans. from *Francis Bacon: A Selection of His Works*, ed. Sidney Warhaft (Toronto: Macmillan, 1965).

57. Thus Bentham in *On the Principles of Morals and Legislation*, chap. II, paras. 5–6, takes the moral high ground with his opponents and explains the adoption of the 'principle of asceticism' from the motives of pride and "fear, the offspring of superstitious fancy."

58. Habermas, *Moralbewusstsein*, pp. 113–114, 117–119.

59. Williams, *Ethics and the Limits of Philosophy*, chap. 10. The chapter is entitled "Morality, the Peculiar Institution", which sufficiently indicates Williams's attitude to this aspiration to purity.

60. See Habermas, *Moralbewusstsein*, chap. 3, and idem, *Theorie des kommunikativen Handelns*, vol. I, chap. 3. An influential trend in contemporary thought has been to apply this proceduralist move to political theory, as

distinct from ethics, to try to develop norms of social justice or fairness, norms governing the coercive actions of political authorities. Thus Ronald Dworkin, who explicitly recognizes some notion of the good life (or at least of a life worth living) as crucial to moral choice, wants to exclude any considerations about the good life from political deliberations in order to be true to what he understands as the (defining liberal) principle of treating citizens as equals ("Liberalism", in *Public and Private Morality,* ed. Stuart Hampshire, Cambridge: Cambridge University Press, 1978; and also Dworkin, "What Liberalism Isn't", in *New York Review of Books,* 20 January 1983, pp. 47–50). Rawls's celebrated theory again concerned social justice. And views in this domain about the neutralizing of some of our ends for the purposes of political deliberation have been put forward by T. M. Scanlon ("Contractualism and Utilitarianism" in *Utilitarianism and Beyond,* ed. A. Sen and B. Williams, Cambridge: Cambridge University Press, 1982) and Thomas Nagel ("Moral Conflict and Political Legitimacy", *Philosophy and Public Affairs* 16, 1987).

This is obviously a distinct issue from the one I am discussing in this section, although obviously these political doctrines are influenced by procedural views in morals; and the two have developed together since Hobbes and Grotius. But it is quite possible to be strongly in favour of a morality based on a notion of the good but lean to some procedural formula when it comes to the principles of politics. There is a lot to be said for this, precisely for the sake of certain substantive goods, e.g., liberty and respect for the dignity of all participants. Procedural norms have certainly been one of the crucial arms of liberal democracy. In the work of Rousseau himself, often thought the progenitor of "totalitarian democracy" (J. L. Talmon, *The Origins of Totalitarian Democracy,* London: Gollancz, 1952), the procedural requirements—common deliberation, the participation of all—have offered the strongest bulwark against the dangerous unanimist or "Jacobin" thrust of his thought. If in the end I cannot quite agree with some such procedural view as the sufficient definition of the principals of liberal democracy, this is not because I don't see its force. The political issue is, indeed, quite distinct from that of the nature of moral theory.

61. See Hare, *Freedom and Reason,* 9.3; and idem, *Moral Thinking,* pp. 24, 55.
62. See Habermas, *Moralbewusstsein,* chap. 4; also his *Theorie des kommunikativen Handelns.*
63. Hare, *Moral Thinking,* chap. 11.
64. See Rawls, *A Theory of Justice,* chap. 7, sect. 60.
65. See Michael Sandel, *Liberalism and the Limits of Justice* (Cambridge: Cambridge University Press, 1982).
66. In fact there are three separate theses which are advanced at different times under the slogan of the priority of the right over the good. The first two are the ones I have been discussing in the text: (a) the Kantian thesis that moral obligation can't be made derivative from the 'good' as utilitarians conceive it, i.e., all and any objects of people's desires; and (b) the thesis that morality is concerned only with what actions are obligatory and not with qualitative

distinctions. I have argued that this second thesis is based on a deep misapprehension about the nature of morality. But there is a third possible meaning: (c) the thesis that what is important in ethical life is the obligation we have to others, e.g., to fair dealing and benevolence, and that these are incomparably more weighty than the requirements of a good, or fulfilled, or valuable, or worthwhile life. This third thesis is certainly not based on a fundamental mistake about the nature of morality. It turns on a real distinction, in that we can discern these different kinds of demands in our ethical life. It corresponds roughly to that between the first two axes of my discussion in section 1.4. We might say that what distinguishes the two demands is that the relation between virtue and obligation is reversed.

In one case, I acknowledge a demand laid on me, say, by other human beings (to respect their rights), or perhaps by God (to observe the Torah). From this I derive a qualitative distinction between different modes of life, in which the virtue terms are respectively, here, justice and piety. But what these amount to is defined by the nature of the demand. They consist in devotion to the performance of what the demand enjoins: just dealing or the Law. In the other case, the primitive concept is that of a good or fulfilled life. Here the qualitative distinction is primary. The demands on my action or, if you like, my "obligations", flow from this; they are defined in terms of the excellence which this life-form exhibits, say, integrity or expressive fulfilment.

The distinction here is real, and so it is a conceivable ideal to cleave to the first rather than the second, to obligations as against fulfilments. In this, form (c) of the right over the good differs from form (b), which is based on a confusion. But nevertheless I think there would be something hubristic and self-destructive in the attempt to carry this exclusive choice consistently through, a forgetfulness of self which aspires beyond human powers. Williams offers strong arguments against this kind of aspiration in his *Ethics and the Limits of Philosophy*.

67. I have discussed this in "The Diversity of Goods" in Taylor, *Human Agency and Language*.
68. Williams, *Ethics and the Limits of Philosophy*, chap. 10.

4. MORAL SOURCES

1. Nor does it mean that these articulations are final. Our moral traditions are always being transformed by new articulations. But these find their basis in, would be impossible without, those already made.
2. Loving the good can't be considered merely a contingent aid to doing good, hence only conditionally enjoined—as one might argue, for instance, that a lifeguard ought to remain in good physical condition, in case he needed to exert himself to save someone. Loving the good can't be considered merely *instrumental* to doing good. This is because doing the morally good always has *some* restriction as to motive. It can't *just* consist in a pattern of behaviour, regardless of why it is exhibited. Even highly consequentialist "ethics of responsibility", in Weber's phrase, have to lay down something

534 · Notes to Pages 93–102

about the agent's motives: e.g., he should be *concerned* for the consequences, and not just for the "purity" of his means. To love the constitutive good (however conceived) is to be strongly motivated in just that way which is defined as part of doing the good (on that conception). That is why being good involves *loving* something and not just *doing* something.

3. Nietzsche claimed that Kant was still too much of a Christian and Platonist. See *The Gay Science*, para. 355.

4. Iris Murdoch, *The Sovereignty of Good* (London: Routledge, 1970), p. 74. Or as she writes later, "If there were angels they might be able to define good but we would not understand the definition," p. 99. Anyone who has read Murdoch's book will see the extent of my debt to her in what I have written here.

5. Murdoch, *Sovereignty of Good*, pp. 91–92.

6. See Michael Walzer, *Exodus and Revolution* (New York: Basic Books, 1985).

7. Northrop Frye, *The Great Code* (Toronto: Academic Press, 1982).

8. Walzer, *Exodus*, p. 3.

9. See the discussion of Kraus in S. Toulmin and A. Janik, *Wittgenstein's Vienna* (London: Weidenfeld, 1973).

10. See Michel Foucault, "What is Enlightenment?", in *The Foucault Reader*, ed. Paul Rabinow (New York: Pantheon Books, 1984); and Hubert Dreyfus and Paul Rabinow, "What is Maturity? Habermas and Foucault on 'What is Enlightenment?' ", in *Foucault: A Critical Reader*, ed.; David Hoy (Oxford: Blackwell, 1986).

11. See F. Nietzsche, *Die fröhliche Wissenschaft*, sects. 110, 179, 246, 265, 301, 307, 333, 344, 354, 355, 373, 374.

12. See my "Foucault on Freedom and Truth", in *Philosophy and the Human Sciences* (Cambridge: Cambridge University Press, 1985).

13. "A Master Within", in F. Schiller, *Letters on the Aesthetic Education of Man*, letter VI.

14. See Carole Gilligan, *In a Different Voice* (Cambridge, Mass.: Harvard University Press, 1982), who argues that the conception of ethical development through stages inspired by Piaget and developed by Lawrence Kohlberg in fact depreciates certain modes of ethical thinking which women find more congenial.

15. Murdoch, *Sovereignty of Good*, p. 85.

16. See Albert Borgman, *Technology and the Character of Contemporary Life* (Chicago: University of Chicago Press, 1984), chap. 22.

17. Mandelstam's poem, which he composed without writing it down, and read in a few small gatherings in Moscow in 1933 among friends, one of whom betrayed him, goes in part like this:

> We live, deaf to the land beneath us,
> Ten steps away no one hears our speeches,
> All we hear is the Kremlin mountaineer,
> The murderer and peasant-slayer.

(This is the first version, the one which got into the hands of the secret police.) Nadezhda Mandelstam, *Hope against Hope* (London: Collins, 1971), p. 13.

18. I add this concession because of the strand of utilitarian theory which (with good warrant in Bentham) includes animals in the calculation when it comes to fulfilling the injunction to maximize happiness and minimize suffering. See, e.g., Peter Singer, *Animal Liberation* (New York: Random House, 1975).

19. I have discussed this in "Philosophy and Its History", in *Philosophy in History,* ed. Richard Rorty, J. B. Schneewind, and Quentin Skinner (Cambridge: Cambridge University Press, 1984).

20. Benedict Anderson, *Imagined Communities* (London: Verso, 1983).

21. I have discussed this in "The Moral Topography of the Self", in *Hermeneutics and Psychological Theory,* ed. Stanley Messer, Louis Sass, and Robert Woolfolk (New Brunswick: Rutgers University Press, 1988).

22. I have made this argument at great length, in connection with a certain range of examples in "Humanismus und moderne Identität", in *Der Mensch in den modernen Wissenschaften,* ed. Krzysztof Michalski (Stuttgart: Klett-Cotta, 1985).

5. MORAL TOPOGRAPHY

1. I have discussed the relationship between these localizations and the sense of moral sources at greater length in "The Moral Topography of the Self", in *Hermeneutics and Psychological Theory,* ed. Stanley Messer, Louis Sass, and Robert Woolfolk (New Brunswick: Rutgers University Press, 1988).

2. This is what Heidegger was getting at in his famous formulation about *Dasein,* that its being is "in question". *Dasein* is an entity (*ein Seiendes*) which is "dadurch ontisch ausgezeichnet, dass es diesem Seienden in seinem Sein *um* dieses Sein selbst geht"; *Sein und Zeit* (Tübingen: Niemeyer, 1927), p. 12.

3. See Mircea Eliade, *Le Chamanisme* (Paris: Gallimard, 1968), p. 179.

4. Aristotle speaks of a friend as "another self" in a famous passage of the *Ethics,* 1169b7, but this doesn't have the same force as our present description of human agents as 'selves', as will be evident below.

We sometimes translate texts from a quite different culture with expressions like 'the self'. This is the case, for instance, with Upanishadic literature, where one might find English translations with phrases like 'the Self and Brahman are one'. To what extent this involves an ethnocentric assimilation, or to what extent it captures a real feature of this religious outlook, cannot be decided a priori. But we should notice that the word translated '*atman*', like our 'soul', 'spirit', 'psyche', is a term for what is essential to the agent etymologically linked to an expression for breathing.

The relation of our modern Western notion of the self to a radically different doctrine and cultural outlook, like the 'no-self' ('*anatta*') view of Theravada Buddhism, is still a baffling and difficult subject, at least for me.

But perhaps a study of this kind, of the genesis of the modern Western notion, might help prepare the ground for an illuminating comparison, along with interpretations of the Theravadan view, such as Steven Collins, *Selfless Persons* (Cambridge: Cambridge University Press, 1982).

5. "From the Native Point of View", in *Interpretive Social Science,* ed. P. Rabinow and W. M. Sullivan (Berkeley: University of California Press, 1979), p. 230.
6. Ibid.
7. Thus Geertz says that the *batin* or "inside" domain is "considered to be, at its roots at least, identical across all individuals, whose individuality it thus effaces"; ibid.

6. PLATO'S SELF-MASTERY

1. At 444B in the *Republic,* injustice is described as a kind of civil war, or a revolt of one part of the soul against the whole.
2. I use this periphrasis here because there is some evidence that the historical Plato was not unambivalent about manic inspiration. There is not only the reference I quoted in the *Apology,* but also a seemingly favourable treatment in the *Phaedrus.* For my purposes, I don't need to resolve these ambiguities. I am tracing here a very influential moral view, one of whose prime sources was the *Republic,* which does take a rather hard line both with the warrior ethic and with inspiration (see for instance 403A, where *mania* is associated with uncontrolled sexual passion). It doesn't matter to my enterprise whether this reflects the 'real' Plato. My aim is to capture the tradition-setting doctrine laid down in the *Republic,* however great the ironic distance might be its author took to it. The name 'Plato' in my text is shorthand for the propounder of this doctrine. Those who don't see it as Plato's should endow the name with invisible inverted commas each time it appears.
3. Bruno Snell, *The Discovery of the Mind* (Cambridge, Mass.: Harvard University Press, 1953), chap. 1.
4. Richard Onians, *The Origins of European Thought* (Cambridge: Cambridge University Press, 1951).
5. A. W. H. Adkins, *From the Many to the One* (Ithaca: Cornell University Press, 1970), p. 27.
6. See, for instance, Hugh Lloyd-Jones, *The Justice of Zeus* (Berkeley: University of California Press, 1971), p. 9.
7. Plato in fact rarely uses the language of 'inside' or the 'inward' to make a moral point—surprisingly rarely in view of the way that we moderns in expounding Plato are naturally inclined to reach for these terms. There are a couple of places in the *Republic* where they do occur: (1) at 401D, Socrates says that "education in music is the most sovereign, because more than anything else rhythm and harmony find their way to the inmost soul [eis to entos tēs psychēs] and take the strongest hold of it"; (2) at 443D, Socrates says that true justice is not just "in regard to the doing of one's own business externally [peri tēn exō], but with regard to that which is within [peri tēn

entos] and in the true sense concerns oneself". The second use foreshadows Augustine and comes close to a usage familiar today. The first seems to be using the term to say something a little different: that rhythm and harmony penetrate the soul through and through, as against touching it superficially. And (3), at 589A–B he speaks of "ho entos anthrōpos", but this is in connection with his rather weird image of a composite being, resembling a man but containing a lion and a many-headed beast as well as a little man within.

7. "IN INTERIORE HOMINE"

1. See *On Free Will*, II.viii.24 and II.xi.30ff.
2. The demand is "ut omnia sint ordinatissima" *On Free Will*, I.vi.15, quoted in E. Gilson, *The Christian Philosophy of Saint Augustine* (London: Gollancz, 1961), p. 130. "Lex vero aeterna est ratio divina vel voluntas Dei, ordinem naturalem conservari jubens, perturbari vetans"; quoted in ibid., p. 307, n. 7.
3. "Talis est quisque, qualis ejus dilectio est. Terram diligis? Terram eris. Deum diligis? quid dicam, Deus eris"; quoted by Gilson, *Saint Augustine*, p. 250, n. 24.
4. There were, of course, transition thinkers. To dramatize the contrast, I have leapt from Plato to Augustine. But one already sees the language of inwardness in Plotinus, for instance. Augustine, however, gave it a more central place; he was concerned not just with a turn away from what is outside, but with a search within. Augustine's was the influential formulation for the Christian thought which succeeded him in the West. There are analogies with Gregory of Nyssa's doctrines, particularly the in-dwelling of the Word, which helped shape the spirituality of the Eastern Church, as well as all subsequent forms of Christian mysticism. See Jean Daniélou, *Platonisme et théologie mystique: Doctrine spirituelle de Saint Grégoire de Nysse* (Paris: Aubier, 1953), part III, chap. 2
5. *De vera Religione*, XXXIX.72.
6. Quoted in Gilson, *Augustine*, p. 65.
7. "*Epimeleia heautou*"; see Foucault's *Histoire de la sexualité*, vol. 3, *Le Souci de soi* (Paris: Gallimard, 1984).
8. See Thomas Nagel, *The View from Nowhere* (New York: Oxford University Press, 1986); and idem, "What Is It Like to Be a Bat?" in *Mortal Questions* (Cambridge: Cambridge University Press, 1979).
9. *On Free Will*, II.iii.7.
10. Gilson, *Saint Augustine*, pp. 41–42, points to six places in Augustine's works where he invokes the cogito argument.
11. Although we see another proto-Cartesian argument in *de Trinitate*, X.x.13ff.
12. *On Free Will*, II.vi.13.
13. Ibid., II.x.28.
14. Ibid., II.xii.34.
15. Ibid., II.xiv.37.

16. "Lucem illam incorpoream . . . , qua mens nostra quodammodo irradiatur, ut de his omnibus recte judicare possumus"; *de Civitate Dei*, XI.xxvii.2.

17. "Commemoratur, ut convertatur ad Dominum tamquam ad eam lucem qua etiam cum ab illo averteretur quodam modo tangebatur"; *de Trinitate*, XIV.xv.21, quoted in Gilson, *Saint Augustine*, p. 104.

18. Man does not see the eternal rules "in sua natura"; Gilson, *Saint Augustine*, p. 94.

19. Gilson, *Saint Augustine*, p. 20.

20. *Confessions*, III.vi.11.

21. "Ut vita carnis anima est, its beata vita hominis Deus est"; *de Civitate Dei*, XIX.26. Cf. also the *Confessions*, VII.i.2, where God is described as "vita vitae mei". See also Gilson, *Saint Augustine*, pp. 132, and 308–309, n. 16: "Quia vero vita ejus est Deus, quo modo cum ipsa est in corpore, praestat illi vigorem, decorem, mobilitatem, officia membrorum, sic cum vita ejus Deus in ipsa est, praestat illi sapientiam, pietatem, justitiam, caritatem".

22. *De Trinitate*, IXf.

23. See Charles Kahn: "Discovery of the Will: From Aristotle to Augustine", in *The Question of Eclecticism*, ed. J. M. Dillon and A. A. Long (Berkeley: University of California Press, 1988). I have drawn a great deal from this interesting discussion.

24. *Confessions*, VII.xxi.27.

25. Ipse ibi modus est sine modo amare"; quoted in Gilson, *Saint Augustine*, p. 139. This formula is actually from a friend and disciple of Augustine, but it sums up his view. Augustine himself says that when God is the object, "modus diligendi est sine modo diligere"; see Gilson, *Saint Augustine*, p. 311, n. 9.

26. "Deus lumen cordis mei, et panis oris intus animae meae, et virtus maritans mentem meam et sinum cogitationis meae"; *Confessions*, I.xiii.21.

27. "Car comment serait-il possible que je pusse connaître que je doute et que je désire, c'est-à-dire qu'il me manque quelque chose et que je ne suis pas tout parfait, si je n'avais en moi aucune idée d'un être plus parfait que le mien, par la comparaison duquel je connaîtrais les défauts de ma nature"; *Méditations*, in *Descartes: Oeuvres et lettres*, ed. André Bridoux (Paris: Gallimard, Bibliothèque de la Pléiade, 1953), p. 294.

28. "Et cogenda rursus, ut sciri possint, id est velut ex quadam dispersione colligenda, unde dictum est cogitare"; *Confessions*, X.xi.18.

29. "Sicut imago ex anulo et in ceram transit, et anulum non relinquit"; *de Trinitate*, XIV.xv.21.

8. DESCARTES'S DISENGAGED REASON

1. Letter to Gibieuf, 19 January 1642; *Descartes: Philosophical Letters*, trans. Anthony Kenny (Oxford: Oxford University Press, 1970), p. 123 [hereafter *Letters*].

2. Second rule, *Discours de la méthode,* IIe Partie, in *Oeuvres de Descartes,* ed. Charles Adam and Paul Tannery (Paris: Vrin, 1973), VI 18 [hereafter A&T]; and *The Philosophical Works of Descartes,* trans. E. S. Haldane and G. R. T. Ross (Cambridge: Dover, 1955), I 92 [hereafter H&R]. Cf. also the *Regulae,* XII: "Ne traitant ici des choses qu'autant qu'elles sont perçues par l'entendement, nous n'appelons simples que celles dont la connaissance est si claire et si distincte que l'esprit ne les puisse diviser en un plus grand nombre dont la connaissance soit plus distincte"; *Descartes: Oeuvres et lettres,* ed. André Bridoux (Paris: Gallimard, Bibliothèque de la Pléiade, 1953), p. 81 [hereafter Pléiade].

3. *Discours de la méthode,* A&T, VI 18–19; H&R, I 92. Cf. the *Regulae,* X, which enjoins us to "l'observation constante de l'ordre qui existe dans la chose elle-même, ou de celui qu'on a ingénieusement imaginé"; Pléiade, p. 70.

4. Augustine himself made this point, stressing the etymological link between *'cogitare'* and *'cogere', Confessions,* X.xi.18.

5. *Méditations,* A&T, IX-1 26; H&R, I 157.

6. That the step from the ordinary embodied to the disengaged perspective is what generates clarity and distinctness in this domain of sensations and secondary properties is made evident by Descartes on a number of occasions. Consider the following: from *Méditations* III, A&T, IX-1 34: "les idées que i'ay du froid & de la chaleur sont si peu claires & si peu distinctes"; from *Principles,* I.68, A&T, IX-2 56: "nous connoissons clairement et distinctement la douleur, la couleur & les autres sentimens, lors que nous les considerons simplement comme ... des pensées"; from *Méditations* VI, A&T, IX-1 66, where he talks of "ces sentiments ou perceptions des sens n'ayant esté mises en moy que pour signifier à mon esprit quelles choses sont convenables ou nuisibles au composé dont il est partie, & iusques là estant assez claires & assez distinctes". See Alan Gewirth's discussion in his "Clearness and Distinctness in Descartes", in *Descartes: A Collection of Critical Essays,* ed. William Doney (Garden City, N.Y.: Doubleday, 1967), p. 260, n. 33. In other words, grasped from the outside, as body-to-mind causal connections with a survival function, these obscure experiences become clear.

7. Cf., for example, the letters to Elisabeth of 5 May and 4 August 1645. In the latter, Descartes makes the Epictetan distinction between the things that depend on us and those which don't. Among things which can make us happy there are "celles qui dependent de nous, comme la vertu & la sagesse, & ... celles qui n'en dependent point, comme les honneurs, les richesses & la santé"; A&T, IV 264. One can be entirely happy with the first kind of good: "comme un petit vaisseau peut estre aussy plein qu'un plus grand, encore qu'il contiene moins de liqueur, ainsy, prenant le contentement d'un chascun pour la plenitude & l'accomplissement de ses desirs reglez selon la raison, ie ne doute point que les plus pauvres et les plus disgraciez de la fortune ou de la nature ne puissent estre entierement contens et satisfaits,

aussy bien que les autres, encore qu'ils ne iouissent pas de tant de biens"; A&T, IV 264.

8. 20 November 1647; A&T, V 85; *Letters,* p. 228. See also *Traité des passions de l'âme* [hereafter *TPA*], art. 152.

9. See his letter to Elisabeth of the 15 September 1645, where he says that we should "recevoir en bonne part toutes les choses qui nous arrivent, comme nous estant expressement envoyées de Dieu; & pour ce que le vray obiet de l'amour est la perfection, lorsque nous élevons nostre esprit a le considerer tel qu'il est, nous nous trouvons naturellement si enclins a l'aymer, que nous tirons mesme de la ioie de nos afflictions, en pensant que sa volonté s'execute en ce que nous les recevons"; A&T, IV 291–292. Cf. the letter to Chanut of 1 February 1647.

10. Epictetus, *Discourses,* I.11, LV.11.

11. Letter to Chanut of 15 June 1646; A&T, IV 441; *Letters,* p. 196.

12. *Discours de la méthode,* VI, A&T, VI 61–62; H&R, I 119.

13. *TPA,* art. 36–40.

14. Ibid., art. 52, A&T, XI 372; H&R, I 358.

15. Letter to Elisabeth of 18 May 1645, A&T, IV 202 (trans. here, and elsewhere unless otherwise attributed, by G. Taylor).

16. Letter to Elisabeth of 1st September 1645, A&T, IV 286–287; *Letters,* p. 170. This endorsement even of "excess" is perhaps a rhetorical flourish to allow him to finish his letter with a nice compliment: "Ie n'en auray iamais de plus excessive, que celle qui me porte au respect & a la veneration que je vous doy". But the underlying thesis, that passion can and should be strong provided its direction is controlled, is seriously meant.

17. Letter to Elisabeth of 18 May 1645, A&T, IV 202.

18. See, for instance, the quotations in note 9 above.

19. Peter Berger in his "On the Obsolescence of the Concept of Honor", in *Revisions,* ed. Stanley Hauerwas and Alasdair MacIntyre (Notre Dame: University of Notre Dame Press, 1983), makes what I take to be a converging point about the modern concept of dignity, in contrast to honour, that it "always relates to the intrinsic humanity divested of all socially imposed rules or norms" (p. 176); it is a property, in other words, of a disengaged humanity.

20. Cf. the letter to Elisabeth of 1 September 1645, A&T, IV 283–284: "Tout nostre contentement ne consiste qu'au tesmoignage interieur que nous avons d'avoir quelque perfection". Cf. also the reference to "les grandes âmes" in the letter of 18 May 1645, ibid., p. 203. They are ready to risk their lives to help their friends, because "le témoignage que leur donne leur conscience, de ce qu'elles s'acquittent en cela de leur devoir, & font une action löuable & vertueuse, les rend plus heureuses, que toute la tristesse, que leur donne la compassion, ne leur afflige".

21. Letter to Elizabeth of 4 August 1645, A&T, IV 264.

22. Epictetus, *Discourses,* I.4.

23. Seneca, *de Ira,* III.vi; *de beata Vita,* IX.4.

24. Letter to Christina of 20 November 1647, A&T, V 85; *Letters,* p. 228.

25. Letter to Elisabeth of 18 May 1645, A&T, IV 202.
26. Cicero, in Book II of the *Tusculan Disputations*, calls for self-control in face of pain. Everyone has some weakness. We have to rule it, as a master does a slave, or a commander a soldier, or a parent a child ("vel ut dominus servo vel ut imperator militi vel ut parens fillio", II.47–48). He repeatedly calls on our sense of manly dignity to steel us to bear pain with equanimity: "Virorum esse fortium et magnanimorum et patientium et humana vincentium, toleranter dolorem pati" (II.43). 'Virtue', he reminds us, comes from *'vir'* = man (as against woman), and the peculiar excellence of men is fortitude, scorning pain and death. So men should face pain with courage and do nothing in a despondent, cowardly, slothful, servile, or womanish spirit ("ne quid abjecte, ne quid timide, ne quid ignave, ne quid serviliter mulieriterque faciamus", II.55). The centrality of the command relation, and the exalting of men over women are redolent of the warrior/honour ethic.
27. Letter to Elisabeth of 18 August 1645; the statement to Christina is in the letter to her of 20 November 1647: it is the best disposition of the will, "si l'on a tousiours une ferme & constante resolution de faire exactement toutes les choses que l'on iugera estre les meilleures, & d'employer toutes les forces de son esprit à les bien connoistre"; Pléiade.
28. *TPA*, art. 48, A&T, XI 367; H&R I 354.
29. Guillaume du Vair, who in a number of ways is almost a transitional figure, foreshadowing some Cartesian formulations while in the Stoic tradition (indeed, identified as one of the main authors of the 'neo-Stoic' revival), also speaks of the good of man as "l'usage de la droite raison, qui est à dire . . . la vertu, laquelle n'est autre chose que la ferme disposition de nostre volonté, à suivre ce qui est honneste et convenable"; *La Philosophie morale des Stoiques,* in *Oeuvres,* reproduction of the 1641 edition (Geneva: Slatkine, 1970), p. 256. It is significant that du Vair was an active political figure, one of the architects of the compromise which ended the wars of religion with the accession of Henri IV.
30. The evolution of both terms is a symptom of the general cloud under which the honour ethic begins to fall in European culture shortly after this time, and is one of the most important developments of modernity. Cf. Albert Hirschman, *The Passions and the Interests* (Princeton: Princeton University Press, 1977). In the seventeenth century, the terms were near synonyms. Cf. e.g., Corneille's *Polyeucte,* III.v.1034: "quoiqu'il soit généreux, quoiqu'il soit magnanime". Descartes explains (*TPA*, art. 161) why he uses 'generosity' and not 'magnanimity'. See note 32.
31. See Gustave Lanson, "Le Héros cornélien et le 'généreux' selon Descartes", in *RHLF* (1895), and also Ernst Cassirer, *Descartes, Corneille et Christine de Suède* (Paris, 1942).
32. I say 'virtually', because the sense retains for Descartes some link with good birth. Hence his use of 'generosity' and not 'magnanimity'. In *TPA*, art. 161, he says that there is no virtue to which "la bonne naissance contribuë tant, qu'á celle qui fait qu'on ne s'estime que selon sa juste valeur", A&T, XI 453. But nevertheless, good education can work wonders. The well-born have a

head start, not a monopoly. Cf. also his letter to Elisabeth of 18 May 1645, where he distinguishes "les grandes ames" from "les ames basses et vulgaires".

33. *TPA,* art. 153, A&T, XI 445–446; H&R, I 401–402.
34. *TPA,* art. 161, A&T, XI 454; H&R, I 406. See also arts. 156 and 203.
35. *Méditations* III, A&T, IX-1 38; H&R, I 167.
36. Antoine Arnauld and Pierre Nicole's *La Logique ou l'art de penser,* recent edition (Paris: Flammarion, 1970), is a profoundly Cartesian work, written by two of the major figures of Port Royal. The force of original sin is visible, inter alia, in the all-too-human penchant for obscure and confused ideas and for vanity, and in other sources of illusion and error. See, e.g., part I, chaps. 9–11.
37. One can see Pascal's reaction to the whole project of Descartes in the *Entretien avec M. de Sacy,* in *Oeuvres de Blaise Pascal,* ed. L. Brunschvicg, P. Boutroux, and F. Gazier (Paris: Hachette, 1904–1925), IV, 43.

9. LOCKE'S PUNCTUAL SELF

1. This whole development is very well described in Gerhard Oestreich, *Neo-Stoicism and the Early Modern State* (Cambridge: Cambridge University Press, 1983); and Marc Raeff, *The Well-Ordered Police State* (New Haven: Yale University Press, 1983).
2. Michel Foucault, *Surveiller et punir* (Paris: Gallimard, 1975).
3. See Francis Oakley, "Christian Theology and the Newtonian Science", *Church History* 30 (1961), 433–457.
4. See his letter to Mersennes of 15 April 1630, A&T, I 145.
5. *Discours de la méthode,* VI, A&T VI 62.
6. See Chapter 8, note 6.
7. Maurice Merleau-Ponty, *La Phénoménologie de la perception* (Paris: Gallimard, 1945), introduction; Michael Polanyi, *The Tacit Dimension* (New York: Doubleday, 1966), chap. 1.
8. *Discours de la méthode,* II, A&T, VI 13.
9. Aristotle, *Posterior Analytics,* II 19, 101a 10–14.
10. Ralph Cudworth, *Concerning Eternal and Immutable Morality* (London, 1731), book IV, chap. 1, p. 126.
11. Ibid., p. 287. Cudworth's book, although it was only published in 1731, well after his death in 1688, was actually written before Locke's *Essay* appeared, with its famous description of the Mind as originally "white Paper, void of all Characters" (2.1.2). He is not responding directly to Locke here, nor did Locke to him. But the opposition could not have been clearer if they had been in direct polemic with each other.
12. Ibid., p. 242.
13. References in parentheses are to Locke's *An Essay concerning Human Understanding,* ed. P. H. Nidditch (Oxford: Clarendon Press, 1975). Numbers refer to the book, chapter, and section respectively, except in the case of the introductory Epistle, where the reference is to page number.

14. Edmund Husserl, *Cartesianische Meditationen* (The Hague: Mouton, 1950), p. 47.
15. *"Logon didonai", Republic,* 534B.
16. See James Tully, "Governing Conduct", in *Conscience and Casuistry in Early Modern Europe,* ed. E. Leites (Cambridge: Cambridge University Press, 1986). I am indebted to James Tully's work for much of my understanding not only of Locke but of the whole movement of modern politics and thought which starts with the neo-Stoics and lays the groundwork for Locke.
17. There seems even to be something incoherent in Locke's notion of the self whose identity depends on the consciousness it has of this identity. For any issue, whether p holds or not, to be a real issue, which turns on some fact of the matter, there has to be a distinction between p's being true and its appearing to me that p is true. But Locke's consciousness criterion just seems to make the fact that my identity incorporates experiences E *consist in* my consciousness that these experiences belong together as mine. Butler was one of the first to put forward this objection; see the discussion by John Mackie, *Problems from Locke* (Oxford: Oxford University Press, 1976), pp. 186–187. Even if Locke can be cleared of this charge, it seems plain that our pretheoretical sense of the fact of the matter can't be captured by his criterion. Among other things, it would make the relation 'same person as' intransitive. I would be the same person as the teenager who graduated from high school, because I still remember my graduation; and he would be the same as the five-year-old who had a birthday party, because he remembered the birthday party; but I would not be the same as the five-year-old, because over the years I've forgotten the party.
18. *Essay,* 2.27.12ff; Derek Parfit, *Reasons and Persons* (Oxford: Oxford University Press, 1984), chap. 10–13.
19. Locke describes this particular case (2.27.15) in the traditional fairytale language of "the soul" of the prince entering and informing the body of the cobbler. Using substance language here gives the supposition its seeming clarity and definiteness. The issue, of course, is whether that whole conception of the soul is defensible, given the embodied nature of human agency. Merleau-Ponty and others in our time have made a convincing case for the negative.

   The whole phenomenon of paramnesia, where a person remembers, or seems to remember, someone else's experience, poses an insurmountable problem for Locke. Does this sense of remembering as my own experience Napoleon's thoughts at the battle of Jena make me the same person as he? Locke does at one point (2.27.13) face this possibility: "Why one intellectual substance may not have represented to it, as done by itself, what *it* never did, and was perhaps done by some other agent . . . will be difficult to conclude from the nature of things". But having looked into the abyss, he immediately turns away: the difficulty can "best be resolved into the goodness of God; who as far as the happiness or misery of any of his sensible creatures is concerned in it, will not, by a fatal error of theirs, transfer from one to another that consciousness which draws reward or punishment with it". As Mackie very acutely points out (*Problems,* pp. 184–185), even this evasion begs the crucial question. If my identity with X just *consisted* in my consciousness of this identity, then I *would* be Napoleon, and God would be doing no injustice in punishing me for his sins. As Mackie says, "There would be no error . . . that the goodness of God can be invoked to prevent". Once again, Locke stumbles on our prereflective sense of identity, which his consciousness criterion crucially fails to capture.

20. See Parfit, *Reasons and Persons.*

21. I am thinking mainly of the behaviouralist school from Watson to Hull and Skinner, who interpret learning as the acquisition of associated connections between 'stimulus' and 'response'.

22. See, e.g., D. Dennett and D. Hofstadter, *The Mind's "I"* (New York: Basic Books, 1981).

23. '*Epimeleia heautou*', Foucault's *Histoire de la sexualité,* vol. 3, *Le Souci de soi* (Paris: Gallimard, 1984).

10. EXPLORING "L'HUMAINE CONDITION"

1. *Essais,* I.viii, in *Les Essais de Michel de Montaigne,* ed. Pierre Villey, re-ed. V. L. Saulnier, 2 vols. (Paris: PUF, 1978), I 33 [hereafter V/S]; *The Essayes of Montaigne,* Florio translation (New York: Modern Library, 1933), 24 [hereafter F]. I have drawn on the interesting discussion in M. Screech, *Montaigne and Melancholy* (London: Duckworth, 1984).

2. *Essais,* I.viii, V/S I 33; F 24.

3. *Essais,* II.xii, V/S I 601; F 545.

4. *Essais,* III.ii, V/S II 804; F 725.

5. *Essais,* III.ii, V/S II 805; F 726.

6. *Essais,* I.i, V/S I 302; F 261.

7. *Essais,* III.xii, V/S II 1059; F 958.

8. *Essais,* III.ii., V/S II 809; F 730.

9. *Essais,* III.v, V/S II 841; F 756.

10. *Essais,* III.ix, V/S II 989; F 896.

11. *Essais,* III.xii, V/S II 1039; F 939.

12. *Essais,* III.xiii, V/S II 1106; F 1003.

13. *Essais,* III.xiii, V/S II 1115; F 1012.

14. *Essais,* III.viii, V/S II 930; F 840.

15. *Essais,* III.xiii, V/S II 1114; F 1011. See also II.xvii V/S I 639: "Ceux qui veulent desprendre nos deux pieces principales et les sequestrer l'une de l'autre, ils ont tort. Au rebours, il les faut r'accoupler et rejoindre. Il faut ordonner à l'ame non de se tirer à quartier, de s'entretenir à part, de mespriser et abandonner le corps (aussi ne le sçauroit elle faire que par quelque singerie contrefaicte), mais de se r'allier à luy, de l'embrasser, le cherir, luy assister, le contreroller, le conseiller, le redresser et ramener quand il fourvoye, l'espouser en somme et luy servir de mary . . . Les Chrestiens ont

une particuliere instruction de cette liaison: car ils sçavent que la justice divine embrasse cette société et jointure du corps et de l'ame".

16. *Essais*, III.ii, V/S II 811; F 731.
17. "Descartes legt ein sauberes Netz der Klassifizierung ... über die Seele"; Hugo Friedrich, *Montaigne* (Frankfurt: Francke, 1967), p. 166.
18. *Essais*, II.17, V/S I 657; F 596.
19. *Essais*, II.xviii, V/S I 665; F 602. See also III.ix, V/S II 980: "Je sens ce proffit inesperé de la publication de mes meurs qu'elle me sert aucunement de regle. Il me vient par fois quelque consideration de ne trahir l'histoire de ma vie. Cette publique declaration m'oblige de me tenir en ma route, et à ne desmentir l'image de mes conditions".
20. *Essais*, III.ix, V/S II 983, n. 4.
21. *Essais*, III.xiii, V/S II 1115; F 1013.
22. P. Miller and T. H. Johnson, *The Puritans* (Cambridge, Mass.: Harvard University Press, 1924), p. 461.
23. Lawrence Stone, *The Family, Sex and Marriage in England, 1500–1800* (London: Weidenfeld, 1977), p. 228.
24. Ian Watt, *The Rise of the Novel* (London: Chatto & Windus, 1957), chap. 3.

11. INNER NATURE

1. 'Ex toto velle', *Confessions*, VIII.9.
2. Luther will not hear of the idea that the especially demanding norms of the Sermon on the Mount are "counsels of perfection" addressed to the few, while the Decalogue applies to all. "Darum müssen wir anders dazu reden, dass Christi Worte jedermann gemein bleiben, er sei 'vollkomen' oder 'unvollkommen'. Denn Vollkommenheit und Unvollkommenheit steht nicht in Werken, macht auch keinen besondern äusserlichen Stand unter den Christen, sondern steht im Herzen, im Glauben und Liebe, dass, wer mehr glaubt und liebt, der ist vollkommen, er sei äusserlich Mann oder Weib, Fürst oder Bauer, Mönch oder Laie. Denn Liebe und Glaube machen keine Sekten noch Unterschiede äusserlich"; *Von weltlicher Obrigkeit,* in *Luther,* ed. K. G. Steck and H. Gollwitzer (Frankfurt: Fischer, 1955), pp. 145–146.
3. *De Anima*, 430a20, 431a1.
4. Ibid., 425b26-27.
5. I have discussed this transition in epistemological theory in "Overcoming Epistemology", in *After Philosophy: End or Transformation?* ed. Kenneth Baynes, James Bohman, Thomas McCarthy (Cambridge, Mass.: MIT Press, 1987).
6. Walter Ong, *Ramus, Method and the Decay of Dialogue* (Cambridge, Mass.: Harvard University Press, 1958), p. 278.
7. Ibid., p. 279.
8. Hence the *Gloria* of the Latin Mass contains the line "glorificamus te", and then, shortly after, "gratias agimus tibi propter magnam gloriam tuam".

9. Raymond Klibansky, Erwin Panofsky, and Fritz Saxl, *Saturn and Melancholy* (London: Nelson, 1964).

10. See, for instance, Herbert Feigl, "The 'Mental' and the 'Physical' " in *Minnesota Studies in the Philosophy of Science* (Minneapolis: University of Minnesota Press, 1956), vol. II.

11. Keith Thomas, *Religion and the Decline of Magic* (London: Weidenfeld, 1971), p. 51.

12. See Quentin Skinner, *The Foundations of Modern Political Thought,* 2 vols. (Cambridge: Cambridge University Press, 1978), II, part II, chap. 4.

13. Quoted from the Puritan preachers John Dod and Robert Cleaver by Michael Walzer, *The Revolution of the Saints* (Cambridge, Mass.: Harvard University Press, 1965), p. 187.

14. See Walzer, *Revolution,* pp. 183–198.

15. See the discussion in John Plamenatz, *Man and Society,* 2 vols. (New York: McGraw-Hill, 1963), I, chap. 5.

16. For instance, John Rawls, *A Theory of Justice* (Cambridge, Mass.: Harvard University Press, 1971); Robert Nozick, *Anarchy, State and Utopia* (Oxford: Blackwell, 1974); Bruce Ackerman, *Social Justice in the Liberal State* (New Haven: Yale University Press, 1980).

17. C. B. Macpherson, *The Political Theory of Possessive Individualism* (Toronto: University of Toronto Press, 1962).

18. Skinner, *Foundations,* I, part II.

19. I have discussed this in "Social Theory as Practice", in my *Philosophy and the Human Sciences* (Cambridge: Cambridge University Press, 1985). The modern identity is also linked in a complex way to citizen consciousness. I have tried to describe the way this identity underpins our contemporary political understanding of ourselves as equal bearers of rights, who are also citizens and producers, in "Legitimation Crisis", in ibid. The recessiveness of citizen consciousness is just one, but very crucial, case in which a widespread background understanding makes it hard for us to grasp crucial dimensions of our practice, and hence cramps and distorts this practice itself. These issues have been further explored in Mimi Bick, "The Liberal-Communitarian Debate: A Defence of Holistic Individualism", D. Phil. thesis, Oxford University, 1987.

20. See Hobbes, *Leviathan,* chap. 4; and Locke, *Essay,* III.3.1–4.

21. *Essai sur l'origine des connoissances humaines* (Paris: A. Colin, 1924), part I, sect. ii, chap. 4. I have dealt with this issue at greater length in "Language and Human Nature", in my *Human Agency and Language* (Cambridge: Cambridge University Press, 1985).

12. A DIGRESSION ON HISTORICAL EXPLANATION

1. Quoted from "On the Dignity of Man" in E. Cassirer, P. O. Kristeller, and J. H. Randall, Jr., *The Renaissance Philosophy of Man* (Chicago: University of Chicago Press, 1948), pp. 224–225.

2. Ibid.

3. E. Cassirer, *Individuum und Kosmos in der Philosophie der Renaissance* (Leipzig and Berlin: Bibliothek Warburg, 1927), chap. 1; Eugene F. Rice, *The Renaissance Idea of Wisdom* (Cambridge: Cambridge University Press, 1958), chap. 5. The sources of this new understanding of the human role in the cosmos were Christian. They lay in the traditional theological idea that humans were called to be God's helper in finishing the creation, a notion which one finds in some of the Fathers, e.g., Origen, Basil, Gregory of Nyssa. St. Ambrose presents man under the image of a farmer, improving the earth in partnership with God. Man is the being who brings nature back to God. In the Renaissance, this notion was given additional force by the revived emphasis on man as a microcosm, which we see in Nicholas of Cusa, in Ficino, in Bovillus. This is what lies behind the Paracelsan theory that nature as it exists before us is not something already finished, but meant to be completed by humans. All things have been given by God to man "in order that he may bring them to the highest development, just as the earth does with all that it brings forth . . . It is not God's will that His secrets should be visible: it is His will that they should become manifest and knowable through the works of man who has been created in order to make them visible" (quoted in Clarence S. Glacken, *Traces from the Rhodian Shore,* Berkeley: University of California Press, 1976, pp. 466–467). Vulcan, god of fire and forge, the archetypal artisan, is called on to complete creation.
4. "La natura é piena d'infinite vagioni que non furono mai in isperienza"; quoted in Cassirer, *Individuum,* p. 62.
5. "Perfetta cognizione dell'obiette intelligibile"; quoted in E. Panofsky, *Idea* (Berlin: Hessling, 1960), p. 38.
6. Ibid., pp. 62–63.
7. Panofsky sees the development of free-standing sculpture coming already with late Gothic; see his *Renaissance and Renascences in Western Art* (Stockholm: Almquist & Wiksells, 1965), pp. 60ff.
8. E. Gombrich, *Art and Illusion* (London: Phaidon, 1959).
9. Panofsky, *Renaissance and Renascences,* p. 120: "Quando empiono de colori e luoghi descritti niun altra cosa cercarsi se non che in questa superficie se presentono le forme delle cose vedute, non altrimenti, que se essa fusse de vetro tralucente"; "scrivo uno quadrangolo di retti angoli quanto grando io voglio, el quale reputo essere una finestra aperta per donde io miri quello que quivi sará dipinto".
10. "Zugleich das Objekt veregegenständlicht und das Subjekt verpersönlicht"; Panofsky, *Idea,* p. 26.
11. This Albertian perspective dominates European painting up to the end of the last century, up to, say, Cézanne. And the move outside it can be seen as an attempt to undo the distance between the painter and his subject, to explore and articulate the experience of vision, rather than the distal object. I shall return to this below in Chapter 24.
12. This is reflected in the use of the term 'creation' for artistic making. This begins in the Renaissance and then takes on new importance and centrality in the last two centuries, with the new, enhanced status of art in the

post-Romantic period. Leonardo sees both science and art as "creations": "La scienza è una seconda creazione fatta col discorso, la pittura è una seconda creazione fatta colla fantasia"; quoted in Cassirer, *Individuum,* p. 170.

13. Max Weber, *Economy and Society* (Berkeley: University of California Press, 1978), I, 11.

14. See Louis Althusser and Etienne Balibar, *Lire le Capital* (Paris: Maspéro, 1968).

15. See E. P. Thompson, *The Making of the English Working Classes* (London: Gollancz, 1964).

13. "GOD LOVETH ADVERBS"

1. I want to argue later (Chapter 21) that the image of inner depths is connected with a notion of self-exploration as the articulation of a domain which we can never fully exhaust. The term rarely appears before the Romantic period. But not surprisingly, the image does occur in Montaigne, who with his acute sense of particularity almost at times seems a contemporary of Herder and Humboldt. In *Essais* 11.6, p. 48, he says: "C'est une espineuse entreprinse, et plus qu'il ne semble, de suyvre une alleure si vagabonde que celle de nostre esprit; de penetrer les profondeurs opaques des replis internes."

2. See above, section 1.3.

3. *Politics,* III, 1280b; "a state is a partnership of families and clans in living well [eu zēn], and its object is a full and independent life [zōēs teleias kai autarkous]", 1280b35.

4. See Ian Hacking, *The Emergence of Probability* (Cambridge: Cambridge University Press, 1975), p. 39.

5. Quentin Skinner, *The Foundations of Modern Political Thought,* 2 vols. (Cambridge: Cambridge University Press, 1978), I. See also John Pocock, *The Machiavellian Moment* (Princeton: Princeton University Press, 1975).

6. See Erich Auerbach, *Mimesis* (Princeton: Princeton University Press, 1953), p. 134.

7. We can find a twentieth-century reformulation of this idea of the superiority of the life of honour/glory over that of mere production in Hannah Arendt's portrayal of the ancient polis in *The Human Condition* (Chicago: University of Chicago Press, 1958). The life of action, which is concerned with how agents appear in public space, is contrasted to lives of mere work, and even lower, of labour. There was a hierarchy here, and I want very much to follow Arendt in her claim that modern culture is based on its overthrow, although my formulation of this will be somewhat different.

8. From *Valerius Terminus,* quoted in B. Farrington, *Francis Bacon* (New York: Lawrence and Wishart, 1962), p. 142.

9. F. Bacon, *Novum Organum,* I.73; trans. from *Francis Bacon: A Selection of His Works,* ed. Sidney Warhaft (Toronto: Macmillan, 1965), pp. 350–351.

10. Quoted in Farrington, *Francis Bacon,* pp. 148–149.

11. Thus Boyle held that "artificers" had given the world many more useful inventions, like the compass, than the "speculative Devisers of new Hypotheses, whose Contemplations aiming but for the most part at the solving, not the encreasing or applying, of the Phaenomena of Nature, it is no wonder they have been more ingenious than fruitful, and have hitherto more delighted than otherwise benefitted Mankind"; *Certain Philosophical Essays* (London, 1661), p. 18. In a rush towards humility, Boyle wanted to describe himself as an "Underbuilder" (p. 17), inaugurating a new fashion: Locke speaks of himself as an "under-labourer" (Epistle to the *Essay*, p. 14).

12. Albert Hirschman, *The Passions and the Interests* (Princeton: Princeton University Press, 1976), pp. 9–12.

13. Ibid., pp. 56–63.

14. This was not, of course, the end of the matter. The ethic of honour gains ground again in a different form in connection with the rising ideal of citizenship, which makes its way first in the Anglo-Saxon countries and then elsewhere. And in a sense, the task of doing justice to both of these notions of the good becomes a major problem for those reflecting on politics and the development of society, as one sees in different ways with Ferguson, Adam Smith, and the framers of the American Constitution.

15. *Phaedo*, 118A.

16. See Rabbi Joseph B. Soloveitchik, *Halakhic Man,* trans. Lawrence Kaplan (Philadelphia: Jewish Publication Society of America, 1983), part I, sect. viii, where Soloveitchik contrasts 'Halakhic Man' with 'homo religiosus', stressing that the former is focussed on making holy the world men live in.

17. Quoted from Urian Oakes, *A Seasonable Discourse,* in E. S. Morgan, *The Puritan Family* (New York: Norton, 1966), p. 14.

18. Quoted from Thomas Hooker, *The Application of Redemption,* in Morgan, *The Puritan Family,* p. 14.

19. Quoted from a sermon by Thomas Leadbeater in Morgan, *The Puritan Family,* p. 16.

20. Quoted in Perry Miller, *The New England Mind: The Seventeenth Century* (Cambridge, Mass.: Harvard University Press, 1967), p. 41.

21. Thus William Perkins attacks "Popish vows" as "a meere will-worship"; quoted in John Dunn, *The Political Thought of John Locke* (Cambridge: Cambridge University Press, 1969), p. 224, n. 2.

22. Robinson, quoted in Charles H. George and Katherine George, *The Protestant Mind of the English Reformation* (Princeton: Princeton University Press, 1961), p. 124.

23. Quoted from Richard Sibbes, *The Saints Cordials* (1637), in ibid., pp. 124–125.

24. Increase Mather, quoted in Miller, *New England Mind,* p. 42.

25. Richard Sibbes, quoted in George and George, *Protestant Mind,* p. 125.

26. Max Weber, *The Protestant Ethic and the Spirit of Capitalism,* trans. Talcott Parsons (New York: Scribner, 1958), pp. 170–171.

27. Increase Mather, quoted in Miller, *New England Mind,* p. 42.

28. John Cotton, quoted in ibid., pp. 42–43.
29. John Dod, quoted in George and George, *Protestant Mind*, p. 130.
30. Joseph Hall, quoted in ibid., p. 139n. William Perkins also makes the same point: "Now the works of every calling, when they are performed in an holy manner, are done in faith and obedience, and serve notably for God's glory, be the calling never so base . . . The meaneness of the calling, doth not abase the goodnesse of the worke: for God looketh not at the excellence of the worke, but at the heart of the worker. And the action of a sheepheard in keeping sheep, performed as I have said, in his kind, is as good a worke before God, as in the action of a Judge, in giving sentence or a Magistrate in ruling, or a Minister in preaching"; George and George, *Protestant Mind*, p. 138.
31. Quoted from William Perkins, *Works*, in George and George, *Protestant Mind*, p. 139.
32. Richard Sibbes, quoted in William Haller, *The Rise of Puritanism* (New York: Harper, 1939), p. 161.
33. Quoted from John Dod and Robert Cleaver, *Household Government*, in Michael Walzer, *The Revolution of the Saints* (Cambridge, Mass.: Harvard University Press, 1965), p. 216.
34. Quoted from Robert Sanderson, *Sermons*, in George and George, *Protestant Mind*, pp. 130–131.
35. William Perkins, quoted in George and George, *Protestant Mind*, p. 136.
36. Joseph Hall, quoted in ibid.
37. Ibid.
38. William Perkins, quoted in ibid., p. 128; emphasis added.
39. Perkins quoted in ibid., p. 136.
40. Robert Bolton, quoted in ibid., p. 136.
41. Lawrence Stone, *The Family, Sex and Marriage in England 1500–1800* (London: Weidenfeld, 1977), p. 136.
42. Ibid., pp. 136–137; Morgan, *The Puritan Family*, p. 48.
43. Stone, *The Family*, p. 137.
44. John Cotton, quoted in Morgan, *The Puritan Family*, p. 48.
45. *Paradise Lost*, VIII, ll. 192–194.
46. Quoted in Walzer, *Revolution*, pp. 24–25.
47. See ibid., p. 213. We can see here how well Calvinism could fuse with the neo-Stoic spirit, where rigorous personal discipline was linked to purposeful and constructive social reorganization. It was not an accident that the first fruits of this spirit in the new military methods and discipline came about under William of Orange in the Netherlands' revolt against Spain. See above, Chapter 9.
48. Quoted from John Field and Thomas Wilcox, *An Admonition to Parliament*, in Walzer, *Revolution*, p. 220.
49. See Christopher Hill, *Intellectual Origins of the English Revolution* (Oxford: Clarendon Press, 1965), and R. F. Jones, *Ancients and Moderns* (New York: Dover, 1982).

50. Quoted in Foster R. Jones, *Ancients and Moderns* (Berkeley: University of California Press, 1965), p. 102.
51. Hill, *Intellectual Origins*.
52. Quoted in Jones, *Ancients and Moderns*, p. 94.
53. George and George, *Protestant Mind*, p. 125.
54. Samuel Mather, quoted in Miller, *New England Mind*, p. 180.
55. See ibid., pp. 162–180.

14. RATIONALIZED CHRISTIANITY

1. For instance, Edward Stillingfleet, Bishop of Worcester, took exception to the *Essay*, as undermining the principles of Christianity. Locke also had to defend his *Reasonableness of Christianity* against attack as highly unorthodox.
2. See *Two Treatises of Government*, ed. Peter Laslett (Cambridge: Cambridge University Press, 1967), II.5.
3. *Of the Law of Nature and Nations*, orig. Latin ed. (Lund, 1672), Eng. trans (London, 1710), II.iii.20
4. References in parentheses in this chapter, unless otherwise indicated, are to Locke's *An Essay concerning Human Understanding*, ed. P. H. Nidditch (Oxford: Oxford University Press, 1975); numbers refer respectively to book, chapter, and section. 'Epistle' stands for the introductory 'Epistle to the Reader', followed by the page number in this edition.
5. Pufendorf has a similar conception. See *Law of Nature*, I.vi.5
6. *The Reasonableness of Christianity* (London, 1695), p. 215.
7. The whole debate about the relation between God's commands and reason is transformed once we see reason not as vision of a substantive order but as instrumental. In the first case, something can only be an injunction of unaided reason if it is good in virtue of the inherent bent of nature. But then God is no longer able to alter the good at will. But if God's command makes it right by making it the instrumentally rational thing to do, then the conflict disappears.
8. See *Two Treatises*, I.86.
9. This case is made in some detail in *Reasonableness*, pp. 256–282.
10. *Reasonableness*, pp. 287–289. To be fair, we should take into account that Locke was not alone in embracing this repugnant view in his time. Bossuet justified his vigorous persecution of Fenelon's doctrine of *'amour pur'* by arguing that God's law has to hold us at least partly by our own self-interest.
11. See Shaftesbury's letter to Ainsworth of 3 June 1709 in *Life, Unpublished Letters, and Philosophical Regimen of Anthony, Earl of Shaftsbury*, ed. Benjamin Rand (London: S. Sonnenschein & Co., 1900), pp. 403–404: "It was Mr. Locke that struck the home blow: for Mr. Hobbes's character and base slavish principles in government took off the poison of his philosophy. 'Twas Mr. Locke that struck at all fundamentals, threw all order and virtue out of the world, and made the very ideas of these ... *unnatural* ... Thus virtue,

according to Mr. Locke, has no other measure, law, or rule, than fashion and custom". A very uncharitable interpretation coming from an ex-pupil! John Yolton has described how common this reaction was; see *John Locke and the Way of Ideas* (Oxford: Oxford University Press, 1956), chap. 2.2.

12. See Shaftesbury, *Life*; and the discussion in Yolton, *John Locke*, chap. 2.

13. *Two Treatises*, II.6; see also II.135; and *Some Thoughts concerning Education*, para. 116.

14. *Two Treatises*, I.86.

15. I have drawn a lot on the discussion of this point by John Dunn in his *The Political Thought of John Locke* (Cambridge: Cambridge University Press, 1969), chaps. 16–18.

16. *Two Treatises*, II.26.

17. Ibid., II.34.

18. Ibid., II.37.

19. "I think every one, according to what way Providence has placed him in, is bound to labour for the public good, as far as he is able, or else he has no right to eat"; Locke's letter to William Molyneux of 19 January 1694, quoted in Dunn, *John Locke*, p. 251.

20. Dunn, *John Locke*, p. 254.

21. Neal Wood, *The Politics of Locke's Philosophy* (Berkeley: University of California Press, 1983), p. 115.

22. In *The Reasonableness of Christianity*, pp. 1–2, Locke distances himself from two extreme views. The first is that of those who "would have all Adam's posterity doomed to eternal infinite punishment, for the transgression of Adam, whom millions had never heard of, and no one had authorized to transact for him, or be his representative; this seemed to others so little consistent with the justice or goodness of the great and infinite God, that they thought there was no redemption necessary . . . ; and so made Jesus Christ nothing but the restorer and preacher of pure natural religion; thereby doing violence to the whole tenour of the New Testament". Locke neatly keeps his distance from Deism, but by making it the inevitable reaction to orthodox Calvinism, he separates himself from this as well.

23. *Some Thoughts concerning Education*, paras. 104, 105.

24. *Reasonableness*, p. 216.

25. Dunn, *John Locke*, pp. 193ff.

26. Perkins attacked the "Popish vows" of monasticism as a "meere Will-worship"; quoted in Dunn, *John Locke*, p. 224, n. 2.

27. Locke, following Bacon, frequently sees the issue between himself and his opponents in terms of pride versus a realistic sense of human possibility. This is true in particular of proponents of the metaphysics he attacks. One of the goals of the *Essay* is described as "to break in upon the Sanctuary of Vanity and Ignorance" (Epistle, p. 10). By contrast, he described his own work with seeming humility as that of an "under-labourer" (ibid., p. 14).

28. Richard Cumberland, *de Legibus Naturae* (London, 1672).

29. John Yolton, *John Locke*, p. 64, sees Locke as articulating the position that is embraced by "the new forms of natural religion which were growing in

popularity towards the end of the century. In the minds of these sympathizers with Deism and Unitarianism, rationality was substituted for innateness as a basis for morality and religion."

30. I have been trying to give an account of the moral sources of Locke's position and rescue them from the misrepresentation of his contemporary adversaries and today's naturalist climate of thought. But can we say that Locke already embarks on a covering over of his moral sources? And that this partly explains the misperception? Disengagement brings about an objectification of self and world, which presents them as neutral domains open to control. But the more they appear in this light, the more we occlude the constitutive goods that provide our moral sources. This process of occlusion will be taken much further by the thinkers of the naturalist Enlightenment in the next century. The moral vision powering the movement ends up being virtually unexpressed in the body of the doctrine. It is embedded implicitly in the rhetorical appeal and in the polemics.

31. Mathew Tindal, *Christianity as Old as the Creation* (London, 1730), p. 14.

32. John Toland, *Christianity Not Mysterious* (London, 1696), p. 15.

33. Ibid., pp. 28–29.

34. "Non tollit gratia naturam sed perficit naturam"; *Summa Theologica*, Ia Pars, quest. 1, art. 8, ad secund.

35. *Reasonableness*, p. 289.

36. Ibid., p. 193.

37. Locke is rightly not classed as a full Deist, because the ultimate position which usually goes by this name, as we see it in Lessing and others, went a step further. Not only grace but even historical revelation was sidelined. We see this full-blooded position with, e.g., Tindal and Shaftesbury. Christ becomes just a particularly persuasive teacher of natural religion. Locke expressly repudiates this position in *Reasonableness*, p. 2.

15. MORAL SENTIMENTS

1. See above, Chapter 9.

2. Hobbes, *Leviathan*, ed. M. Oakeshott (Oxford, Blackwell, n.d.), chap. 6, p. 32.

3. Ibid., part II, chap. 17, p. 112. This connection has been commented on by Ernst Cassirer, *The Platonic Renaissance in England* (Edinburgh: Nelson, 1953), chap. 3.

4. See discussion in Cassirer, *Platonic Renaissance*.

5. John Smith, quoted in Cassirer, *Platonic Renaissance*, p. 164.

6. Ibid., p. 163.

7. Ibid., p. 164.

8. Ibid., p. 165.

9. Ibid.

10. Benjamin Whichcote, *Sermons*, quoted in ibid., p. 82.

11. Cudworth, for instance, shows the influence of Plotinus' emanation theory, as mediated through Ficino, in his *True Intellectual System*, where he affirms

that things in the Universe "Descend and Slide down from Higher to Lower, so that the first Original of all things, was not the most Imperfect, but the most Perfect Being", quoted in Cassirer, *Platonic Renaissance,* pp. 137–138.

12. Though Cudworth did come to accept Cartesian mechanism as far as the world of matter was concerned. See his *Eternal and Immutable Morality* (London, 1731). But the attempt to graft this onto a Platonic-Plotinan theory of forms makes for a very odd physics.

13. *Philosophical Regimen,* in *Life, Unpublished Letters, and Philosophical Regimen of Anthony, Earl of Shaftesbury,* ed. Benjamin Rand (London: S. Sonnenschein & Co., 1900), p. 54.

14. *An Inquiry concerning Virtue or Merit,* in Shaftesbury, *Characteristics of Men, Manners, Opinions, and Times* (London, 1711; New York: Bobbs-Merrill, 1964), I.279.

15. *The Moralists,* in Shaftesbury, *Characteristics,* II.20–22.

16. Shaftesbury, *Philosophical Regimen,* in *Life and Letters,* ed. Rand, pp. 23–24. See also the statement further on in this work that what makes pain unbearable is wrong dogmata; p. 158.

17. Ibid., p. 30.

18. Ibid., p. 232; emphasis in original.

19. See ibid., pp. 7–8; also *Miscellaneous Reflections,* in Shaftesbury, *Characteristics,* II.280.

20. Shaftesbury, *Philosophical Regimen,* in *Life and Letters,* ed. Rand, p. 262; see also *The Moralists,* in Shaftesbury, *Characteristics,* p. 43. The original image is in Epictetus' *Discourses,* II.i.39.

21. Shaftesbury, *Philosophical Regimen,* in *Life and Letters,* ed. Rand, pp. 256–257.

22. Shaftesbury, *Characteristics,* pp. 110, 112.

23. *The Moralists,* in Shaftesbury, *Characteristics,* II.106.

24. Shaftesbury, *Characteristics,* I.240.

25. *The Moralists,* in Shaftesbury, *Characteristics,* II.99–100.

26. *A Letter concerning Enthusiasm,* in Shaftesbury, *Characteristics,* I.28.

27. *Inquiry,* in Shaftesbury, *Characteristics,* I.269.

28. *The Moralists,* in Shaftesbury, *Characteristics,* II.55; see also *Sensus Communis,* II.iii, III.iii, in *Characteristics,* I.65–69, 77–81.

29. *Advice to an Author,* in Shaftesbury, *Characteristics,* I.227; see also II.139–140, II.293–294. In II.78–84, Shaftesbury has the old man in the dialogue, a rather unpleasant, hostile creature, briefly defend the view that men were not naturally in society, but had to contract out of a state of nature. He is roundly squelched. The alignment of Locke with Hobbes comes in Shaftesbury's letter to Michael Ainsworth, June 3, 1709 (*Life and Letters,* ed. Rand, p. 403): "It was Mr. Locke that struck the home blow: for Mr. Hobbes's character and base slavish principles in government took off the poison of his philosophy. 'Twas Mr. Locke that struck at all fundamentals, threw all order and virtue out of the world, and made the very ideas of these . . . unnatural, and without foundation in our minds".

30. *Advice,* in Shaftesbury, *Characteristics,* II.227.

31. Some other places in Shaftesbury's work where this analogy appears are: *Characteristics*, I.214, 251–252, 314, II.129, 177; *Philosophical Regimen*, in *Life and Letters*, ed. Rand, p. 54.
32. Shaftesbury, *Characteristics*, I.136.
33. Ibid., I.216.
34. *Miscellaneous Reflections*, in Shaftesbury, *Characteristics*, II.177.
35. Samuel Clarke, *Discourse of Natural Religion*, in *British Moralists, 1650–1800*, ed. D. D. Raphael (Oxford: Oxford University Press, 1969), sects. 225–226, 230–232; William Woolaston, *Religion of Nature Delineated*, in *British Moralists*, ed. Raphael, sects. 274–290.
36. "Natural Law [*jus naturale*] is the dictate of right reason, showing the moral turpitude, or moral necessity, of any act from its agreement or disagreement with a rational nature, and consequently that such an act is either forbidden or commanded by God", Grotius, *de Jure Belli ac Pacis*, I.i.10; "anything is unjust which is repugnant to the nature of society established among rational creatures", ibid., I.i.3.
37. In the *Letter concerning Enthusiasm*, in *Characteristics*, I.39, Shaftesbury proposes that, in assessing the claims of enthusiasts, "to judge of the spirits whether they are of God, we must antecedently judge our own spirit, whether it be of reason and sound sense; whether it be fit to judge at all, by being sedate, cool, and impartial, free of every biassing passion, every giddy vapour, or melancholy fume".
38. See Peter Gay, *The Enlightenment: An Interpretation*, vol. 1, *The Rise of Modern Paganism* (New York: Knopf, 1966).
39. See, e.g., Shaftesbury, *Philosophical Regimen*, in *Life and Letters*, ed. Rand, pp. 1–10.
40. See, e.g., *Inquiry*, in Shaftesbury, *Characteristics*, I.255, 259–260.
41. See Chapter 5.
42. For instance: "My own concern is for truth, reason, and right *within myself*"; Shaftesbury, *Philosophical Regimen*, in *Life and Letters*, ed. Rand, p. 232, emphasis in original. A bit later he warns us not to be concerned only to create beautiful surroundings for ourselves, but to "remember ever the garden and groves within", where all is often "Gothic and grotesque", p. 247. In *Advice*, he speaks of "interior numbers", *Characteristics*, I.214; see also II.143, 177. The calls to turn inward are frequent: see, e.g., *Characteristics*, I.29, 31, II.274–275.
43. For uses of 'self', see, e.g., *The Moralists*, in Shaftesbury, *Characteristics*, II.105, and idem, *Philosophical Regimen*, in *Life and Letters*, ed. Rand, pp. 129, 136, 150, 255.
44. '*Lichtung*'; the word appears in *Sein und Zeit*, but it is used more frequently by Heidegger in later works to speak of the background to all phenomena, what makes it possible that things appear. See the discussion in Charles Guignon, *Heidegger and the Problem of Knowledge* (Indianapolis: Hackett, 1983), p. 70.
45. Thus in Plato's *Phaedo*, Socrates gives an exposition of the theory of ideas as representing the correct reading of Anaxagoras' famous dictum that *nous* is

at the basis of all things. For Aristotle, in knowledge the *eidos* of the object is the same as that in the *nous* of the knower.

46. See *Inquiry*, in Shaftesbury, *Characteristics*, I.262.
47. Epictetus, *Encheiridion*, XVI, recommends that we show sympathy with a friend who has suffered some loss, but that we not lament internally.
48. Shaftesbury, *Philosophical Regimen*, in *Life and Letters*, ed. Rand, p. 54.
49. *The Moralists*, in Shaftesbury, *Characteristics*, II.144.
50. Francis Hutcheson, *An Essay on the Nature and Conduct of the Passions and Affections, with Illustrations upon the Moral Sense*, facsimile reproduction of the third edition, 1742 (Gainesville: Scholars Facsimile Reprints, 1969), intro., pp. 210–211. Hereafter *Illustrations*.
51. Francis Hutcheson, *An Essay on the Nature and Conduct of the Passions and Affections*, facsimile reproduction of the 1742 edition (Gainesville: Scholars Facsimile Reprints, 1969), preface, p. vi [hereafter *Essay*]. See also *Illustrations*, p. 211: "Ingenious speculative Men, in their straining to support an Hypothesis, may contrive a thousand subtle selfish Motives, which a kind generous Heart never dreamed of".
52. Hutcheson, *Essay*, pp. 200–201.
53. John Locke, *An Essay concerning Human Understanding*, ed. P. H. Nidditch (Oxford: Oxford University Press, 1975), 2.2.2.
54. A sense is "every determination of our Minds to receive Ideas independently on our Will, and to have Perceptions of Pleasure and Pain"; Hutcheson, *Essay*, p. 4.
55. Francis Hutcheson, *An Inquiry into the Original of Our Ideas of Beauty and Virtue*, facsimile reproduction of the edition of 1725 (Hildesheim: Georg Olms, 1971), p. 106.
56. See John Mackie, *Ethics* (Harmondsworth: Penguin Books, 1977), chap. 1.
57. E.g., in Hutcheson, *Illustrations*, p. 289, where he makes the analogy to colour.
58. Hutcheson, *Inquiry*, p. 274.
59. Hutcheson, *Essay*, p. 182. An analogous point is made about the ultimately arbitrary basis of the sense of beauty in idem, *Inquiry*, p. 42: "There is an infinity of Tastes or Relishes of Beauty possible."
60. Hutcheson comes face to face with this issue in *Illustrations*, p. 237. But he then proceeds to duck it. In fact, it seems insoluble on his terms. If we answer that we judge God good because he is benevolent, and we are programmed to approve benevolence, it could be replied that if he had made us approve cruelty, and as a result we were (as Hutcheson believes we would be) all miserable, we would judge him cruel and hence still find him good. Hutcheson plainly thinks he is making some kind of judgement *between* these two scenarios; but this requires a sense of 'good' independent of the brute deliverances of our moral sense as it happens to be constituted. In the language I used above in section 1.1, Hutcheson describes our moral judgements in a psychology of brute reactions, but he wants to go on treating them as responses to proper objects. He doesn't feel the discomfort that we might think he ought, because his basic convictions—about the goodness of

benevolence and the bountiful providence of God—in fact have an absolute status for him, not contingent on his psychology (however hard this might be to square with that psychology). From this absolute standpoint, the two scenarios are easily distinguished, and the existing dispensation triumphantly endorsed.

61. "Happiness denotes pleasant Sensation of any kind, or a continued State of such sensations", Hutcheson, *Illustrations*, p. 207; "Happiness consists in the highest and most durable Gratifications of, either all our Desires, or, if all cannot be gratified at once, of those which tend to the greatest and most durable Pleasures, with exemption either from all Pains and Objects of Aversion, or at least from those which are most grievous", idem, *Essay*, p. 114.

62. Hutcheson, *Inquiry*, pp. 150, 165. In *Essay*, pp. 118–120, Hutcheson launches a direct attack on the ideal of *apatheia* of the Stoics.

63. Francis Hutcheson, *A System of Moral Philosophy*, facsimile reproduction of the posthumous 1755 edition (Hildesheim: Georg Olms, 1969), p. 222. Hutcheson tries a similar reduction of the cardinal four virtues in *Inquiry*, pp. 126–127: "So that these four Qualities, commonly call'd Cardinal Virtues, obtain that Name, because they are Dispositions universally necessary to promote publick Good, and denote Affections towards rational Agents"; cf. also ibid., p. 272.

64. Hutcheson, *Essay*, pp. 204–205. Some of Hutcheson's arguments that the world is for the best might seem a trifle overdrawn even to Dr. Pangloss. He consoles his (middle- and upper-class) readers, for the impression they might have that the lot of the labouring classes is one of "miserable slavery", with the consideration that the lower orders are tougher and don't mind it all that much (*System*, pp. 196–197). Other arguments, showing the universality of benevolent sentiments, are almost moving in the naive good nature they reveal in their author. "Human Nature seems scarce capable of malicious disinterested Hatred, or a sedate Delight in the Misery of others", *Inquiry*, p. 132: this sentence could not even be framed in our century. Similar points are made in *System*, pp. 156–157; and *Essay*, p. 141. Hutcheson even invokes "a natural, kind Instinct, to see Objects of Compassion", to explain why people flock to public executions and to see gladiators; *Inquiry*, pp. 217–218. Even if the Marquis de Sade did live at the other end of the eighteenth century, Hutcheson appears sometimes like the holy fool of moral philosophy, too good for this terrible world.

65. Hutcheson, *Illustrations*, pp. 227–228.

66. Hutcheson, *Inquiry*, p. 274.

67. "To represent these motives of Self-Interest, to engage men in publickly useful Actions, is certainly the most necessary Point in Morals"; Hutcheson, *Illustrations*, p. 283. See also idem, *Inquiry*, pp. 227–228.

68. David Fate Norton, *David Hume* (Princeton: Princeton University Press, 1982), chaps. 1, 2.

69. Hutcheson, *Inquiry*, pp. 252–253. See also idem, *Essay*, pp. viii–ix.

70. Hutcheson, *Essay*, pp. iv–v.

71. Hutcheson, *Inquiry*, p. 161. See also idem, *Illustrations*, p. 327: "Opinion of Goodness in the Deity and our Fellows, increases good Affection, and improves the Temper: Contrary Opinion of either, by raising frequent Aversions, weakens good Affections, and impairs the Temper".
72. Hutcheson, *Essay*, p. 88.
73. Ibid., p. 205.
74. Hutcheson, *System*, p. 216.
75. Hutcheson, *Inquiry*, p. 164. See also idem, *Essay*, p. 202: The "perfection of our Kind" consists, inter alia, in this: "to form the most extensive Ideas of our own true Interests, and those of all other Natures, rational and sensitive; to abstain from all Injury; to pursue regularly and impartially the most universal absolute Good, as far as we can".
76. Hutcheson, *System*, pp. 206–208. See also idem, *Inquiry*, pp. 272, 276.
77. Hutcheson, *Inquiry*, pp. 168ff.
78. Hutcheson, *Illustrations*, p. 226. In this argument Hutcheson makes the point for which Hume later became famous with his unforgettable statement: "Reason is and ought to be the slave of the passions".
79. Hutcheson, *Essay*, pp. 179–180.

16. THE PROVIDENTIAL ORDER

1. Francis Hutcheson, *A System of Moral Philosophy*, fascimile reproduction of the posthumous 1755 edition (Hildesheim: Georg Olms, 1969), p. 217.
2. See Chapter 15.
3. According to the traditional Catholic catechism of a few decades ago, man was created "to serve and love God".
4. Robin Lane Fox, *Pagans and Christians* (New York: Knopf, 1986), pp. 109–117, 259.
5. Ibid., p. 129.
6. David Hartman, *A Living Covenant* (New York: Macmillan, 1985), p. 46.
7. The link of the holy with what is set apart seems very widespread. Separateness seems to be part of the root meaning of *'kadosh'*, as also of the sense of *'hagios'*; see A. J. Festugière, *La Sainteté* (Paris: PUF, 1949), chap. 1. And what was made *'sanctus'* by the Roman was thereby set apart.
8. Thus Philo in his *On Abraham* also presents the story of the patriarch in an allegorical dimension, where for example his departures into the wilderness symbolize the different stages of knowledge, from materialistic pantheism to self-knowledge, and then from this in turn to the apprehension of God. I owe this point to Gretta Taylor.
9. See Philippians 2:7, where Paul speaks of Christ "emptying himself" to take the form of a slave.
10. See Benjamin Whichcote in *The Cambridge Platonists*, ed. C. A. Patrides (Cambridge: Cambridge University Press, 1980), p. 131; also John Smith talks of "those Servile spirits which are not acquainted with God and his Goodness, may be so haunted by the frightfull thoughts of a Deity, as to scare and terrifie them into some worship and observance of him. They are apt to

look upon him as an hard master . . . they cannot truly love him." See also Ernst Cassirer, *The Platonic Renaissance in England* (Edinburgh: Nelson 1953), p. 163.

11. Matthew Tindal, *Christianity as Old as the Creation* (London, 1730), chap. 4.

12. Whichcote in *Cambridge Platonists*, ed. Patrides, pp. 70–71, 167. The Cambridge Platonists drew heavily on the Greek fathers, and in particular espoused their concept of *"theiōsis"*, that humans are destined to be drawn through the incarnation to participate in the divine nature.

13. Tindal, *Christianity as Old as the Creation*, p. 14.

14. Ibid., p. 16.

15. See, e.g., Matthew 9:2, Mark 2:5, Luke 5:20.

16. Hutcheson, *System*, p. 184.

17. Ibid., p. 186. Naturally, this conception of providential order made Deism even more directly vulnerable to some of the traditional difficulties of theodicy. The Lisbon earthquake had an unpredecentedly large intellectual impact in the eighteenth century precisely because it conflicted so grievously with the upbeat picture of benevolent order.

18. *Lessings Werke*, ed. J. Pedersen and W. von Olshausen (Berlin-Leipzig, 1924), XXIII, 47.

19. G. E. Lessing, *Die Erziehung des Menschengeschlechts* (Bern: Lang, 1980).

20. Moses Mendelssohn, *Jerusalem*, trans. A. Jospe (New York: Schocken, 1969), p. 65.

21. Alexander Pope, *An Essay on Man*, I.237–241, 267–268.

22. A. O. Lovejoy, *The Great Chain of Being* (Cambridge, Mass.: Harvard University Press, 1936).

23. Pope, *Essay on Man*, I.244–246.

24. See John Locke, *An Essay concerning Human Understanding*, ed. P. H. Nidditch (Oxford: Oxford University Press, 1975), 3.6.12; and Hutcheson, *System*, p. 183.

25. G. W. Leibniz, *Essais de Théodicée* (Paris: Garnier-Flammarion, 1969), part I, paras. 8ff., pp. 108ff.

26. Pope, *Essay on Man*, I.289.

27. Pope also used other parts of the traditional repertoire of notions about cosmic order in his *Windsor Forest*, e.g., the *coincidentia oppositorum*. Earl R. Wasserman discusses this in *The Subtler Language* (Baltimore: Johns Hopkins University Press, 1968).

28. Pope, *Essay on Man*, III.7–8.

29. Ibid., III.9–26, 109–14.

30. G. W. Leibniz, in *Philosophische Schriften*, ed. C. I. Gerhardt, 7 vols. (Berlin: Weidmann, 1875–1890), IV, 499.

31. Pope, *Essay on Man*, III.295–302.

32. Ibid., I.289–294. The concluding slogan is repeated at IV.145.

33. Ibid., II.53, 82–92, 101–110.

34. Ibid., IV.396.

35. Ibid., IV.353–360.

36. See discussions in Francis Hutcheson, *An Essay on the Nature and Conduct of the Passions and Affections, with Illustrations upon the Moral Sense,* facsimile reproduction of the third edition, 1742 (Gainesville: Scholars Facsimile Reprints, 1969), pp. 237–239; and idem, *An Inquiry into the Original of Our Ideas of Beauty and Virtue,* facsimile reproduction of the edition of 1725 (Hildesheim: Georg Olms, 1971), p. 94, II.i.8.

37. The distinction I've been drawing between Deism of extrinsic law and calculation, on the one hand, and one of sentiment, on the other, is obviously one of ideal types. Each had its perfect instantiation (Locke and Hutcheson, respectively), but it was not impossible to mix elements of both. They shared the central idea of a providential interlocking universe which harmonized interests. So the importance of moral sentiment could be recognized, while the ultimacy in the order of explanation which Hutcheson gave it could be dropped: moral sentiments were explained by the more fundamental notion of sympathy by Adam Smith in *The Theory of Moral Sentiments* (London, 1759), ed. D. D. Raphael and A. L. Macfie (Oxford: Oxford University Press, 1976), part VII, sect. III, chap. 3; or explained partly by sympathy and partly by utility, as in Hume's account of justice in *A Treatise of Human Nature* (London, 1739), book III, part II, chaps. 1, 2; and *An Enquiry concerning the Principles of Morals* (London, 1777), chap. 3.

   Smith as a matter of fact makes a conscious effort to synthesize what he thinks are the one-sided theories of his predecessors. Alongside the "gentle" and "amiable" virtues of benevolence, he allows for the "awful and respectable" ones of self-command (*Theory,* part I, sect. I, chap. 5, p. 23), which were central for the ancients and were given renewed saliency in the neo-Stoic climate, which was reflected as we saw in the theories of Descartes and Locke. In addition to stressing the importance of calculation, Smith sees an important place for that identification with the whole which was crucial to ancient Stoicism and which Shaftesbury and Hutcheson had given new life to, each in his own way. Smith writes: "The idea of that divine Being, whose benevolence and wisdom have, from all eternity, contrived and conducted the immense machine of the universe, so as at all times to produce the greatest possible quantity of happiness, is certainly of all the objects of human contemplation by far the most sublime"; *Theory,* part VI, sect. II, chap. 3, p. 236. Smith, like Shaftesbury, was obviously inspired by Stoicism. But he transposed this inspiration much more thoroughly into the forms of modern Deism. Not only is the universe a "machine" and contrived "to produce the greatest possible quantity of happiness", but our identification with it takes the form of the internalized "impartial spectator", which figures in a very modern (and reductive) theory of conscience.

38. Hutcheson, *Illustrations,* pp. 239–240, 286ff.

17. THE CULTURE OF MODERNITY

1. Albert Hirschman, *The Passions and the Interests* (Princeton: Princeton University Press, 1977), pp. 56–63.

2. John Pocock, *The Machiavellian Moment* (Princeton: Princeton University Press, 1975).
3. See Louis Dumont, *Homo Aequalis* (Paris: Gallimard, 1977).
4. Erich Auerbach, *Mimesis* (Princeton: Princeton University Press, 1953), chaps. 7, 8, 11, 12.
5. Ian Watt, *The Rise of the Novel* (London: Chatto & Windus, 1957), pp. 87–88.
6. Ibid., chap. 1.
7. For instance, Erwin Panofsky, *Renaissance and Renascences in Western Art* (Stockholm: Almquist & Wiksells, 1965); Benedict Anderson, *Imagined Communities* (London: Verso, 1983), pp. 28–29.
8. A. C. Charity, *Events and Their Afterlife* (Cambridge: Cambridge University Press, 1966).
9. Auerbach, *Mimesis*, p. 73–74.
10. Walter Benjamin, *Illuminations* (New York: Schocken, 1969), p. 261.
11. Anderson, *Imagined Communities*, pp. 30–31.
12. Watt, *Rise of the Novel*, pp. 34–35.
13. Historians of the family, like Philippe Ariès in his *L'Enfant et la vie familiale sous l'ancien régime* (Paris: Seuil, 1973), p. 460, have brought home to us how the earlier hierarchical, organic society has been undermined and disaggregated as much by the aspiration to family intimacy as by 'individualism', in the usual sense of a centring on the rights or purposes of individuals. In fact, these two forces have worked in close tandem. It is only in the late twentieth century that they begin to threaten each other, that an ideology of 'self-fulfilment' militates against family life. Tocqueville was well aware of this. He spoke of an individualism "which disposes each member of the community to sever himself from the mass of his fellows and to draw apart with his family and his friends, so that after he has thus formed a little circle of his own, he willingly leaves society at large to itself"; *Democracy in America*, 2 vols. (New York: Knopf, 1983), II, 98.
14. *Julie; ou La Nouvelle Héloïse*, 3e partie, Lettre XI; *New Eloise* (University Park: Pennsylvania State University Press, 1962), II, 171–172.
15. Ariès, *L'Enfant*, p. 450; *Centuries of Childhood*, trans. R. Baldick (New York: Knopf, 1962), p. 398. Ariès (*L'Enfant*, p. xvi) also mentions an earlier development in fifteenth-century Florence, where the palazzi of prominent citizens were built on a new design, permitting greater privacy of the family. But the segregation of intimate space wasn't carried as far as in the northern countries in the eighteenth century.
16. As Ariès puts it: "Cette conscience de l'enfance et de la famille . . . postulait des zones d'intimité physique et morale qui n'existaient pas auparavant"; *L'Enfant*, p. 450.
17. Ariès makes the point well in speaking of the earlier emergence of the family as a locus of spiritual life in the fifteenth and sixteenth centuries. Speaking of the "floraison iconographique" of family themes in these centuries, he says: "Désormais la famille est non seulement discrètement vécue, mais reconnue comme une valeur et exaltée par toutes les puissances de l'émotion"

(*L'Enfant*, p. 406). Of course, the family had always existed as "réalité vécue . . . Mais elle n'existait pas comme sentiment ou comme valeur" (p. 460).

18. The title of a book by Christopher Lasch (New York: Basic Books, 1977).

19. J. Fliegelman, *Prodigals and Pilgrims* (Cambridge: Cambridge University Press, 1982), pp. 260ff.

20. Ariès, *Centuries of Childhood*, p. 413.

21. Jan Lewis, *The Pursuit of Happiness* (Cambridge: Cambridge University Press, 1983), chaps. 5 and 6; quotes from pp. 171, 212.

22. Ibid., p. 81. Ariès has also commented on the nineteenth-century conceptualization of heaven as an eternal family reunion; see *The Hour of Our Death*, trans. H. Weaver (New York: Knopf, 1981), p. 611.

23. Rousseau can include among the benefits of the higher life that man gains in society, where he becomes a moral being, that as a result, "ses sentiments s'ennoblissent"; *Du Contrat social*, I.8. In the *Essai sur l'origine des langues* (Paris: Bibliothèque du Graphe, 1976), we have another picture of men becoming human through society, again in terms of an alteration in feeling: "On se rassemble autour d'un foyer commun, on y fait des festins, on y danse . . . et sur ce foyer rustique brûle le feu sacré qui porte au fond des coeurs le premier sentiment de l'humanité" (p. 132).

24. Daniel Mornet, *Le Sentiment de la nature en France de J.-J. Rousseau à Bernardin de Saint-Pierre* (Paris: Hachette, 1907; reprinted New York: B. Franklin, 1971), p. 202.

25. Daniel Mornet, *Le Romantisme en France au XVIIIe siècle* (Paris: Hachette, 1912), p. 128.

26. Ibid., p. 34.

27. Ibid., 145–146.

28. Mornet, *Sentiment*, part II, book I, chap. 1. For a general account of these developments, see also ibid., part I, and John McManners, *Death and the Enlightenment* (Oxford: Oxford University Press, 1981), chap. 10.

29. Mornet, *Sentiment*, part II, book II, chap. 2.

30. Ibid., p. 248.

31. Ibid., p. 210.

32. Ibid., p. 269.

33. Ibid., pp. 238, 240.

34. *Macbeth*, 2.3.56, 2.4.17–18.

35. M. H. Abrams, "Structure and Style in the Greater Romantic Lyric", in *From Sensibility to Romanticism: Essays Presented to F. A. Pottle*, ed. F. W. Hilles and H. Bloom (New York: Oxford University Press, 1965), p. 537.

36. T. S. Eliot, *The Sacred Wood* (London: Methuen, 1950), p. 100.

37. Boileau, cited in L. Furst, *Romanticism in Perspective* (New York: Macmillan, 1969), p. 252.

38. The eighteenth-century account of the sublime as developed by Burke and later by Kant is linked with this new aesthetic of subjective response. Burke sees the source of the sublime in our reactions to pain and danger. Kant's notion of the sublime presents it very much as an 'objective correlative' of our own being as agents of practical reason. The sublime is so, because it

awakens a sense of our own unbounded moral power. But here, of course, the response is no longer defined as sentiment. See E. Burke, *A Philosophical Enquiry into the Origin of Our Ideas of the Sublime and the Beautiful* (London, 1757; 2nd edition, 1759), reprint edited by J. T. Boulton (London: Routledge, 1958), part I, sect. vii; and I. Kant, *Critique of Judgement*, first part, first division, second book.

39. Mornet, *Romantisme*, p. 47. It is an irony of history that Mme. Necker's daughter, Mme. de Staël, was one of the decisive figures in the later introduction of German Romanticism into France.

40. Mornet, *Sentiment*, p. 255.

41. Quoted in Abrams, "Structure and Style", pp. 551–552.

42. See Earl Wasserman, *The Subtler Language* (Baltimore: Johns Hopkins University Press, 1968).

43. Laurence Sterne, *Sentimental Journey*, ed. Herbert Read (London: Scholastic Press, 1929), p. 125.

44. See Philip Greven, *The Protestant Temperament* (New York: Knopf, 1977), chap. 2.

45. As Jan Lewis argues for the case of Virginia; *The Pursuit of Happiness*, pp. 222–223.

18. FRACTURED HORIZONS

1. Louis Dumont, in *Essais sur l'individualisme* (Paris: Gallimard, 1983), has perceptively discussed the particular case of Germany, taking in and transforming the British-French Enlightenment. I have also talked about this in my *Hegel* (Cambridge: Cambridge University Press, 1975), chap. 1.

2. We shall see in the concluding chapter how crippling it can be to lose sight of this distinction and simply *identify* a given cultural development with a particular philosophy. Rational insightful discussion about, e.g., the ideals of self-responsible reason and freedom, becomes almost impossible when they are seen as indissolubly linked to, e.g., a Lockean theory of the punctual self. This means either that those who espouse these ideals feel bound to embrace the theory; or that those who cannot abide the theory feel bound to reject the ideals. Since the ideals have some validity and the theory is (I believe) terribly wrong, this identification is bound to lead us astray, whichever way it works.

3. See H. G. Gadamer, *Wahrheit und Methode* (Tübingen: Mohr, 1975).

4. I have been discussing the relation betwen philosophical formulations and broad movements of culture, which are reflected among other places in literature. But something of the same circular relation holds between these currents and the important formulations in literature themselves. Daniel Mornet in his *Le Sentiment de la nature en France de J.-J. Rousseau à Bernardin de Saint-Pierre* (Paris: Hachette, 1907; reprinted New York: B. Franklin, 1971), discusses this relation very insightfully (see the Conclusion). On the one hand, Rousseau's *La Nouvelle Héloïse* made the new philosophy of sentiment, and the related feeling for nature, into a powerful force on the French cultural scene. But this is not to say that a climate of

feeling had not been developing in this direction before. On the other hand, the pre-existence of this climate shouldn't make us lose from view the way in which Rousseau shaped the new outlook—e.g., the peculiarly Rousseauian sense of the nobility of feeling, its relation to natural goodness, and a doctrine of freedom, as well as the particular natural settings which Rousseau made paradigmatic. *La Nouvelle Héloïse* prompted people to travel in droves to the Swiss mountains and valleys.

5. Robert Lenoble, *Mersenne et la naissance du mécanisme* (Paris: J. Vrin, 1943), p. 171.
6. Benjamin Whichcote, quoted in *The Cambridge Platonists*, ed. C. A. Patrides (Cambridge: Cambridge University Press, 1980), pp. 46–47.
7. Peter Gay, *The Enlightenment: An Interpretation*, vol. 1, *The Rise of Modern Paganism* (New York: Knopf, 1966), pp. 400–401.
8. And, of course, something similar went for immortality, which also seemed obvious and unquestionable to our ancestors. It was interwoven with belief in God, and it too was supported by an inward and outward "route". The fact that we had a soul which was higher than and would survive the body seemed inseparable from our having a higher nature, being capable of reason, reflection, moral purpose. The various post-Cartesian "proofs" of immortality through the immateriality and indivisibility of the soul represent one line of rational articulation of this deep-lying belief. And at the same time, immortality seems so obviously a part of any providential scheme, since it alone would allow for ultimate justice in rewards and punishments as well as the completion of our spiritual growth. Bishop Butler and Kant offer arguments which articulate this route—albeit late in the day, when the edifice of rooted belief has begun to crumble.
9. Philip Greven, *The Protestant Temperament* (New York: Knopf, 1977).
10. Ibid., pp. 328, 324.
11. See D. P. Walker, *The Decline of Hell* (London: Routledge, 1964); John McManners, *Death and the Enlightenment* (Oxford: Oxford University Press, 1981), pp. 176–190; Bernard Semmel, *The Methodist Revolution* (New York: Basic Books, 1973), chap. 2.

19. RADICAL ENLIGHTENMENT

1. 'Aufklärer', meaning 'thinker (or proponent) of the Enlightenment'. Unfortunately, there seems to be no single noun carrying this sense in English. So, with some apologies, I have used the German word. I am relieved to say that there is precedent for this. Peter Gay, in his justly celebrated study *The Enlightenment: An Interpretation*, 2 vols. (New York: Knopf 1966, 1969), met the same problem by using the French word 'philosophe'. I could have followed him, but I feared that the ordinary sense of this word, which is both wider and narrower than the special use, might confuse things. Hence my recourse to this Germanism.
2. J. Bentham, *On the Principles of Morals and Legislation*, chap. 1, para. 2.
3. The list is from Bentham's *Principles*, chap 2, para. 14, note d.

4. Helvétius, *de l'Homme,* V.iii.12.

5. Bentham, *Principles,* chap. 1, para. 1.

6. Quoted in Arthur M. Wilson, *Diderot* (Oxford: Oxford University Press, 1972), pp. 210, 237. See also Condorcet, *Esquisse d'un tableau historique des progrès de l'esprit humain* (Paris: Editions Souales, 1970), p. 159: "Il fut enfin permis de proclamer hautement ce droit si longtemps méconnu, de soumettre toutes les opinions à notre propre raison, c'est-à-dire, d'employer, pour saisir la vérité, le seul instrument qui nous ait été donné pour la reconnaître. Chaque homme apprit, avec une sorte d'orgueil, que la nature ne l'avait pas absolument destiné à croire sur la parole d'autrui".

7. *Discours de la méthode,* IIIe partie, in *Oeuvres de Descartes,* ed., Charles Adam and Paul Tannery (Paris, Vrin, 1973), VI 22.

8. Cf. Paul Hazard, *La Crise de la conscience européenne* (Paris: Fayard, 1961), and P. Chaunu, *La Civilisation de l'Europe des lumières* (Paris: Flammarion, 1971). Even more anachronistic is the view that Descartes was already a secret unbeliever, and just declared his belief for reasons of prudence. Straussians tend to hold this view.

9. See Descartes's proof of God in the third Meditation.

10. Holbach, *Le Systéme de la nature,* facsimile reproduction, 2 vols. (Hildesheim: Georg Olms, 1966), I, 3.

11. Ibid., I, 58–59.

12. Ibid., I, 2.

13. Ibid., II, 408–409.

14. Helvétius, *de l'Homme,* II.vi, pp. 146–147.

15. Bentham, *Principles,* chap. 2, paras. 5–6.

16. Whichcote and Smith both denounce those who project their own faults onto God, and portray him as "some Peevish and Self-will'd thing, because themselves are such"; Ernst Cassirer, *The Platonic Renaissance in England* (Edinburgh: Nelson, 1953), p. 165. "Those, who are Revengeful, think; the Goodness of God permits Him to be Cruel", as Whichcote puts it in *Aphorisms,* no. 388.

17. John Smith, quoted in *The Cambridge Platonists,* ed. C. A. Patrides (Cambridge: Cambridge University Press, 1980), p. 140.

18. Diderot, *Supplément au voyage de Bougainville,* in *Oeuvres philosophiques* (Paris: Garnier, 1964), p. 476.

19. See also Condorcet, *Esquisse,* p. 97.

20. Diderot, *Oeuvres,* p. 510. Diderot seems to throw himself into a full-scale primitivism in this work, opposing 'natural' man to 'artificial' man (p. 511). But this was far from being his unequivocal position. Later in the same dialogue (p. 513), he abruptly points out that civilized people live longer than savages. This evokes his lapidary argument against Rousseau in his refutation of Helvétius' *de l'Homme:* "La durée moyenne de la vie de l'homme policé excède la durée moyenne de la vie de l'homme sauvage. Tout est dit" (Diderot, quoted p. 513, n. 2). Diderot was aware of the tension in his position, but he still preferred it to Rousseau's, which he repudiates in the following lines with almost insulting force: "J'aime mieux la vice raffiné sous

un habit de soie que la stupidité féroce sous une peau de bête. J'aime mieux la volupté entre les lambris dorés et sur la mollesse des coussins d'un palais, que la misère, pâle, sale et hideuse, étendue sur la terre, humide et malsaine" (quoted in Ira Wade, *The Structure and Form of the French Enlightenment*, 2 vols., Princeton: Princeton University Press, 1977, I, 276).

21. Holbach, *Politique naturelle* (Tours, 1796), p. 118.

22. Condorcet, *Esquisse*, p. 226.

23. Ibid., pp. 226–227.

24. Quoted in Ross Harrison, *Bentham* (London: Routledge, 1983), p. 276.

25. The way in which the earlier conceptions of order could justify the terrible punishments of earlier times is well illustrated in the opening passages of Foucault's *Surveiller et punir* (Paris: Gallimard, 1975), where, as noted earlier, he relates the execution of Damiens, guilty of attempted regicide, in the middle of the eighteenth century, the time of Enlightenment itself. I have discussed this in my "Foucault on Freedom and Truth", in *Philosophy and the Human Sciences* (Cambridge: Cambridge University Press, 1985).

26. The expression 'impartial spectator' is Adam Smith's (*The Theory of Moral Sentiments*, London, 1759), but the ideal of impartial benevolence is general throughout the Deist and naturalist Enlightenment. We saw above (Chapter 14) that Locke had some similar notion that rising from passion to reason frees us from egoism and destructiveness. And in our day too, we see examples of the same kind of moral reflection. Thus Derek Parfit, after establishing (to his satisfaction) his reductive theory of personal identity, which relativizes the issue of our continued existence as the same person, says: "Is the truth depressing? Some may find it so. But I find it liberating, and consoling. When I believed *the non-reductive view* I seemed imprisoned in myself. My life seemed like a glass tunnel, through which I was moving faster every year, and at the end of which there was darkness. When I changed my view, the walls of the glass tunnel disappeared. I now live in the open air . . . Other people are closer. I am less concerned about the rest of my own life, and more concerned about the lives of others"; *Reasons and Persons* (Oxford: Oxford University Press, 1984), p. 281.

27. Bentham, *Principles*, chap. 2, para. 4.

28. Holbach, *Système*, II, chap. 12.

29. Diderot, *Réfutation suivie de l'ouvrage d'Helvétius intitulé l'Homme*, in *Oeuvres philosophiques*, p. 573.

30. Holbach, *Système*, II, chap. 10, quoted in Pierre Naville, *D'Holbach et la philosophie scientifique au XVIIIe siècle* (Paris: Gallimard, 1967), p. 362. Diderot makes a similar charge in his *Essai sur les règnes de Claude et Néron*, Assézat edition, III, p. 217; quoted in Naville, *D'Holbach*.

31. Paul Bénichou, *Morales du grand siècle* (Paris: Gallimard, 1948).

32. See Daniel Mornet, *La Pensée française au XVIIIe siècle* (Paris: Hachette, 1912), p. 152.

33. As Holbach does in his *Système*, II, chap. 10.

34. Marquis de Sade, *Juliette*, I.89, quoted in Naville, *D'Holbach*, pp. 367–368.

35. Bentham, *Principles*, chap. 1, para. 1.

36. Harrison, *Bentham,* chap. 10.
37. See, for instance, Diderot's refutation of Helvétius' *De l'homme,* cited in note 29.
38. Bentham speaks of him as one of his sources.
39. Bentham, *Principles,* chap. 2, para. 7.
40. See Peter Gay, *The Enlightenment: An Interpretation,* vol. 1, *The Rise of Modern Paganism* (New York: Knopf, 1966).
41. *Philosophical Regimen,* in *Life, Unpublished Letters, and Philosophical Regimen of Anthony, Earl of Shaftesbury,* ed. Benjamin Rand (London: S. Sonnenschein & Co., 1900).
42. *Essais,* III.ix, in *Les Essais de Michel de Montaigne,* ed. Pierre Villey, re-ed. V. L. Saulnier, 2 vols. (Paris: PUF, 1978), II 989; *The Essayes of Montaigne,* Florio translation (New York: Modern Library, 1933), 896.
43. Rilke, *Duino Elegies,* II; *The Selected Poetry of Rainer Maria Rilke,* trans. Stephen Mitchell (New York: Vintage, 1984), p. 161.
44. Thus I would argue that Hume's humbling of the claims of reason through his sceptical arguments is meant not to induce a kind of epistemic despair but to lead us to discover and accept our limits. He freely admits that no one can really *be* a sceptic and suspend belief: "Nature, by an absolute and uncontroulable necessity has determined us to judge as well as to breathe and feel"; *A Treatise of Human Nature,* Selby-Bigge edition (Oxford: Oxford University Press, 1888), p. 183. The point of the argument is to show us "that belief is more properly an act of the sensitive, than of the cogitative part of our nature" (ibid.). This insight should liberate us from the vain strivings to an impossible self-grounded certainty. I have been helped a great deal in my discussion by Barry Stroud's *Hume* (London: Routledge, 1977), although he might easily find my view here unacceptable.
45. See, for instance, Sabina Lovibond, *Realism and Imagination in Ethics* (Oxford: Blackwell, 1983), for an interesting development of Wittgenstein's ideas in this connection. Heidegger also opened up lines of exploration of an issue which can also be seen as one of accepting what we are, i.e., the place of *Lichtung.*
46. Locke, *An Essay concerning Human Understanding,* ed. P. H. Nidditch (Oxford: Oxford University Press, 1975), 4.3.6.
47. Douglas Hofstadter, "Reductionism and Religion" (reply to John Searle), *Behavioural and Brain Sciences* 3 (1980), 434.
48. Holbach, *Système,* I, 59.
49. Diderot, *Le Rêve de d'Alembert, in Ouevres philosophiques,* p. 266; and in *Rameau's Nephew and D'Alembert's Dream,* trans. L. W. Tancock (Harmondsworth: Penguin Books, 1966)..
50. Lucretius, *de Rerum Natura,* II.991ff.
51. *"Divina voluptas"* and *"horror",* de Rerum Natura, III.28–29.
52. Although this is sometimes the case: see K. Popper and J. Eccles, *The Self and Its Brain* (New York: Springer, 1977).
53. See Marjorie Grene, *The Knower and the Known* (Washington, D.C.: University Press of America, 1984), for a statement of an anti-reductivist

theory of levels of being which is also quite anti-dualist. Merleau-Ponty is also famous for having developed a theory of this kind. See *La Structure du comportement* (Paris: PUF, 1953), and *La Phénoménologie de la perception* (Paris: Gallimard, 1945).

54. Diderot, *Rêve*, in *Oeuvres*, p. 299; and *D'Alembert's Dream*, p. 174.
55. Quoted in Daniel Mornet, *Le Sentiment de la nature en France de J.-J. Rousseau et Bernardin à Saint-Pierre* (Paris: Hachette, 1907; reprinted New York: B. Franklin, 1971), p. 283. Mercier was moved to similar feelings up in the Jura: "Ainsi quand l'imagination s'enfonce dans la succession rapide des années et des siècles, . . . lorsqu'elle considère ces milliers d'hommes qui sont tombés et qui tombent, cette multitude de faits écoulés, ces troncs ensevelis, dont il reste à peine la mémoire, l'âme éprouve un certain frémissement; . . . et la réflexion court se perdre avec les heures dans l'abîme des choses éternelles"; quoted in Daniel Mornet, *Le Romantisme en France au XVIIIe siècle* (Paris: Hachette, 1912), pp. 175–176.
56. Charles Rosen, "Now, Voyager", in *The New York Review of Books*, 6 November 1986, p. 58.
57. This turn towards an immortality of fame was one of the points of affinity between the French Enlightenment and the political culture of the ancients. The Encyclopaedists played their part in the return in force of classical models in French culture of the latter half of the eighteenth century, after the rococo interlude of the Regency. The background is being laid down against which the thought and rhetoric of the Revolutionary period will arise. The link between ancient Roman leader and modern philosophe-revolutionary is forged iconographically in the great tableaux of David. It is not an accident that the great shrine of the Revolution, which still retains symbolic force in the Republican tradition, is the Panthéon.
58. Diderot, *Réfutation*, in *Oeuvres philosophiques*, p. 574.
59. Holbach, *Essai sur les préjugés*, from chap. 14, quoted in Naville, *D'Holbach*, pp. 359–360.
60. Condorcet, *Equisse*, p. 157.
61. Ibid., pp. 161, 164.
62. Ibid., pp. 238–239.

20. NATURE AS SOURCE

1. Alexander Pope, *An Essay on Man*, II.91–92.
2. Antoine Arnauld and Pierre Nicole, *La Logique ou l'Art de penser*, Flammarion "Science de l'homme" (Paris: Flammarion, 1970), part I, chaps. 9, 10.
3. Pierre Nicole, quoted in Paul Bénichou, *Morales du grand siècle* (Paris: Gallimard, 1948), pp. 140–142.
4. Pascal, quoted in ibid., p. 420, 323.
5. See J.-J. Rousseau, *Lettre à Mgr. de Beaumont* (Paris: Editions Garnier, 1962) pp. 445–448.

6. J.-J. Rousseau, *Emile* (Paris: Editions Garnier, 1964), book II, p. 81; *Emile*, trans. Barbara Foxley (London: Dent, 1911), p. 56. Almost the same words appear in the *Lettre à Mgr. de Beaumont*, p. 444, and in the beginning of *Rousseau, Juge de Jean-Jacques*, in *Oeuvres Complètes*, Pléiade edition, 2 vols. (Paris: Gallimard, 1959), I, 668.

7. *Emile*, p. 5; Foxley trans., p. 5.

8. *Emile*, p. 355; Foxley trans., p. 254. See also the First Discourse (Paris: Edition Garnier-Flammarion, 1971), p. 59: "O vertu! . . . ne suffit-il pas pour apprendre tes lois de rentrer en soi-même et d'écouter la voix de sa conscience dans le silence des passions?"

9. *Emile*, p. 353; Foxley trans., p. 253.

10. *Emile*, pp. 354–355; Foxley trans., p. 254.

11. "Or c'est du système moral formé par ce double rapport à soi-même et à ses semblables que naît l'impulsion de la conscience. Connaître le bien, ce n'est pas l'aimer: l'homme n'en a pas la connaissance innée, mais sitôt que sa raison le lui fait connaître, sa conscience le porte à l'aimer: c'est ce sentiment qui est inné"; *Emile*, p. 354.

12. *Emile*, pp. 65, 64, 68; Foxley trans., pp. 45, 47.

13. See his description of the scene he witnessed as a boy, where the soldiers and officers of the Saint-Gervais regiment dance together after their military exercise and are joined by their wives and families. Public and domestic celebration flow into each other, with no hiatus. "Il résulta de tout cela un attendrissement général que je ne saurois peindre". Rousseau is profoundly moved. As is his father. "Mon pére . . . fut saisi d'un trésaillement que je crois sentir et partager encore. 'Jean-Jacques, . . . aime ton pays' "; in J.-J. Rousseau, *Lettre à M. d'Alembert sur les spectacles* (Paris: Editions Garnier, 1962), p. 232n.

14. J.-J. Rousseau, *Du Contrat social*, book IV, chap. 1; *The Social Contract*, trans. Charles Frankel (New York: Hafner, 1947), p. 92.

15. *Emile*, pp. 329–330. This was, of course, exactly the point where Holbach and Diderot hotly contested the Deist argument. Rousseau declares their theory incomprehensible. "J'ai fait tous mes efforts pour concevoir une molécule vivante, sans pouvoir en venir à bout. L'idée de la matière sentant sans avoir de sens me paraît inintelligible et contradictoire"; p. 329n.

16. "La bonté de l'homme est l'amour de ses semblables, et la bonté de Dieu est l'amour de l'ordre"; *Emile*, p. 347.

17. "Que lui demanderais-je? qu'il changeât pour moi le cours des choses, qu'il fît des miracles en ma faveur? Moi qui dois aimer par-dessus tout l'ordre établi par sa sagesse et maintenu par sa providence, voudrais-je que cet ordre fût troublé pour moi? Non, ce voeu téméraire mériterait d'être plutôt puni q'exaucé"; *Emile*, p. 359.

18. *Emile*, p. 350.

19. Chapter 16.

20. *Emile*, p. 358, emphasis in original; Foxley trans., p. 257.

21. Ann Hartle, *The Modern Self in Rousseau's Confessions* (Notre Dame, Ind.:

University of Notre Dame Press, 1983), has explored the parallelisms between Augustine's and Rousseau's books. It enables her to bring out the contrast between the two, and the crucial role played in Rousseau's autobiographical exploration by the self.

22. Of course, it is crucial to Kant's position that the formal criterion *does* dictate particular outcomes in given circumstances; otherwise his morality would be without content. The various formulations of the categorical imperative, particularly the one in terms of universalizability, are supposed to generate this content. One can be sceptical whether they really do, but for the sake of my discussion here, I want to overlook these objections.

23. I. Kant, *Foundations of the Metaphysics of Morals* (Indianapolis: Bobbs-Merrill, 1969), p. 412 (I have quoted from the Lewis White Beck translation, but for ease of reference across editions, page references are to the Berlin Academy edition, usually given in the margin or in square brackets in translations of this work).

24. Ibid., p. 429.

25. Ibid., p. 428.

26. Ibid., p. 434.

27. See my discussion in "Kant's Theory of Freedom", in *Philosophy and the Human Sciences* (Cambridge: Cambridge University Press, 1985), pp. 318–337.

28. Kant, *Foundations*, p. 397.

29. I. Kant, *Idee zu einer allgemeinen Geschichte in weltbürgerlicher Absicht*, in *Kants Werke*, Berlin Academy edition (Berlin: Walter de Gruyter, 1968), VIII, 19–22.

30. Ibid., p. 26g; *Kant's Political Writings*, trans. Hans Reiss (Cambridge: Cambridge University Press, 1970), p. 49.

31. "Aus so krummen Holze, als woraus der Mensch gemacht ist, kann nichts ganz Gerades gezimmert werden"; Kant, *Idee*, p. 23.

32. *Die Religion innerhalb der Grenzen der blossen Vernunft*, First Part, in *Kants Werke*, Berlin Academy edition, VI, 17–44.

33. Goethe on reading this passage spoke of how Kant had "spoilt his philosophical bib".

34. "Was ist Aufklärung?", *Kants Werke*, Berlin Academy edition, VIII, 35; *Kant's Politcal Writings*, p. 54.

21. THE EXPRESSIVIST TURN

1. See A. O. Lovejoy, "On the Discrimination of Romanticisms", in his *Essays in the History of Ideas* (Baltimore: Johns Hopkins University Press, 1948). The literature which attempts to define Romanticism is very vast. I have found very useful Lilian Furst's *Romanticism in Perspective* (New York: Macmillan, 1969). See also her "The Contours of European Romanticism" in her collection of the same title (London: Macmillan, 1979); and also René Wellek, "The Concept of Romanticism in Literary History", in *Concepts of*

Criticism, ed. Stephen G. Nichols, Jr. (New Haven: Yale University Press, 1963).

2. See Wordsworth, "Tintern Abbey":

> For I have learned
> To look on nature, not as in the hour
> Of thoughtless youth; but hearing oftentimes
> The still, sad music of humanity,
> Nor harsh nor grating, though of ample power
> To chasten and subdue. And I have felt
> A presence that disturbs me with the joy
> Of elevated thoughts; a sense sublime
> Of something deeply interfused,
> Whose dwelling is the light of setting suns,
> And the round ocean and the living air,
> And the blue sky, and in the mind of man;
> A motion and a spirit, that impels
> All thinking things, all objects of all thought,
> And rolls through all things.

3. Johann Gottlob Herder, *Vom Erkennen und Empfinden der menschlichen Seele,* in *Herders Sämtliche Werke,* ed. Bernard Suphan, 15 vols. (Berlin: Weidmann, 1877–1913), VIII, 200. Coleridge, who was very influenced by German thought, expresses a similar idea: "Everything has a life of its own . . . and we are all *One Life*"; quoted in M. H. Abrams, *The Mirror and the Lamp* (Oxford: Oxford University Press, 1953), p. 65. Shelley also invokes an image similar to that of the great current in things, through the metaphor of the Aeolian lyre which is made to sound by the wind. This becomes the image for poets who, if they have "been harmonized by their own will . . . give forth divinest melody, when the universal breath of being sweeps over their frame"; quoted in Abrams, *Mirror,* p. 61.

4. F. Hölderlin, in *Hyperion,* book I, second letter, speaks of a longing "Eines zu sein mit Allem, was lebt, in seliger Selbstvergessenheit wiederzukehren ins All der Natur". Of course, this is not our ultimate destiny; we have to return to a higher unity which incorporates thought and freedom. But this 'All' is the reality in which we are set. Novalis for his part asks: "Gehören Tiere, Pflanzen und Steine, Gestirne und Lüfte nicht auch zur Menschheit und ist sie nicht ein blosser Nervenknoten in dem unendlich verschieden laufende Fäden sich kreuzen?" Quoted in Furst, *Romanticism in Perspective,* p. 84.

5. Michael Beddow, *The Fiction of Humanity* (Cambridge: Cambridge University Press, 1982), chap. 2, has shown how Goethe in his classical period drew on the same expressivist conception he had drawn from Herder earlier. He shared the view that the poet articulates not just his own self, but a larger reality. "Just so with the poet. So long as he only speaks out his few subjective feelings, he deserves not the name; but as soon as he knows how

to appropriate to himself and express the world, he is a poet"; quoted in Abrams, *Mirror*, p. 344, n. 29.

6. See my *Hegel* (Cambridge: Cambridge University Press, 1975), chaps. 1 and 2, for Hegel's relation to the Romantic generation.

7. This is the move the Savoyard curate makes when he argues that, though he can't prove his theory of the primacy of conscience, his opponents cannot prove the opposite; and so "quand nous affirmons qu'il existe, nous sommes tout aussi bien fondés qu'eux, et nous avons de plus le témoignage intérieur, et la voix de la conscience qui dépose pour elle-même"; *Emile* (Paris: Editions Garnier, 1964), p. 354.

8. Novalis, *Sämtliche Werke* (Heidelberg: Verlag Lambert Schneider, 1953), VI, 379; Herder, *Vom Erkennen*, in *Sämtliche Werke*, VIII, 199; Wordsworth, *Preface to the 'Lyrical Ballads'*, in *Poetical Works*, II, 394–395.

9. This kind of immediate unity between the sensual and the spiritual, for which the Romantic generation found inspiration in Rousseau, is celebrated in some of Hölderlin's very early poems, like the "Hymne an die Göttin der Harmonie". Later the unity was reinterpreted as a higher synthesis, incorporating reason, and the immediate unity is seen as inspiring and yet suicidal, a combination captured in the figure of Empedocles:

> Das Leben suchst du, suchst, und es quillt und glänzt
> Ein göttlich Feuer tief aus der Erde dir,
> Und du in schauderndem Verlangen
> Wirfst dich hinab, in des Ätna Flammen

Friedrich Hölderlin: Poems and Fragments, ed. Michael Hamburger (London: Routledge, 1960), p. 30.

10. The Abbé du Bos, in *Réflexions critiques sur la poësie et sur la peinture* (Paris, 1719), refers the judgement of beauty to the senses, rather than reason. In this his work came together with Hutcheson's *Inquiry* of 1725 to create a new climate of thought, which defined beauty in terms of our responses. Our propensity to react with a particular form of pleasure became a primitive in the explanation of beauty. This is the form which later came to be called 'aesthetic', in part under the influence of Baumgarten (*Aesthetica*, 2 vols., Frankfurt an der Oder, 1750–1758). Burke, in his *A Philosophical Enquiry into the Origin of Our Ideas of the Sublime and the Beautiful* (London, 1757; 2nd edition, 1759), reprint edited by J. T. Boulton (London: Routledge, 1958), builds on this in his celebrated and influential definition of the sublime, in terms of our responses to pain, danger, and the terrible. Kant (*Kritik der Urteilskraft*, 1790) drew on this, but of course he distanced himself from the aesthetic sense theory just as he had from the moral sense theory. Nevertheless, both beautiful and sublime are defined in terms of the response of the subject, and their relation to his faculties.

11. See Taylor, *Hegel*, chap. 1.

12. Herder, *Ideen*, vii.1, in *Sämtliche Werke*, XIII, 291.

13. (New York: Oxford University Press, 1953).
14. See Abrams, *Mirror,* chap. 4, for a discussion of these developments.
15. Quoted in Abrams, *Mirror,* p. 282.
16. Preface to "The Excursion", ll. 63–71.
17. Quoted in T. Todorov, *Théories du symbole* (Paris: Seuil, 1977), p. 185.
18. F. Schlegel, *Ideen* 44, in *Kritische Schriften,* p. 91; trans. Lilian R. Furst, quoted in Furst, *Romanticism in Perspective,* p. 321, n. 18.
19. Shelley, *Defense of Poetry,* in *Complete Works* (New York: Gordian Press, 1965), VII, 137. Novalis also sees himself as lifting the veil on the world of the spirit, but he also stresses that the poet remakes, transforms, transfigures this world through the imagination. "Ich bin der Mittelpunkt, der heilige Quell"; *Heinrich von Ofterdingen,* in *Sämtliche Werke,* I, 321–322.
20. F. Schleiermacher, *Über die Religion* (Berlin: Realschulbuchhandlung, 1806), p. 9; Furst, *Romanticism in Perspective,* p. 335, n. 83.
21. Coleridge, *Biographia Literaria* (London: Oxford University Press, 1954), I 202.
22. A. W. Schlegel, *Vorlesungen über dramatische Kunst und Literatur* (Heidelberg: Mohr & Winter, 1817), p. 91.
23. *Statesman's Manual: Political Tracts of Wordsworth, Coleridge and Shelley* (Cambridge: Cambridge University Press, 1953), p. 25.
24. From *The Statesman's Manual,* quoted in M. H. Abrams, *The Correspondent Breeze* (New York: Norton, 1984), p. 221.
25. Quoted in Charles Rosen and Henri Zerner, *Romanticism and Realism* (New York: Norton, 1984), p. 26.
26. See Schiller's *Letters on the Aesthetic Education of Man,* bilingual ed., ed. and trans. E. M. Wilkinson and C. A. Willoughby (Oxford: Oxford University Press, 1967). Furst, in her *Romanticism in Perspective,* makes the interesting observation that the same emphasis on the imagination was not in evidence among French Romantic writers as it was among their German and English counterparts. This undoubtedly had to do with their focus on the unforced depiction of nature and the expression of authentic feeling, as against the articulation of a larger reality in nature. The symbol didn't play a key role for them. But Furst points out that in some regards the Symbolist writers of the latter part of the century—Nerval, Baudelaire, Mallarmé, Rimbaud—were the first to have fully transposed English and German Romanticism into French culture, while making it the basis for a new departure of their own. Baudelaire, unlike his earlier Romantic compatriots, gave the imagination a central place, like Novalis; see ibid., pp. 287–288. See also H. G. Gadamer's discussion on the development of this notion of symbol is his *Wahrheit und Methode* (Tübingen: Mohr, 1975), pp. 66–77. For a critique of the view that the symbol is central to post-Romantic literature, see Paul de Man, "The Rhetoric of Temporality", in his *Blindness and Insight* (Minneapolis: University of Minnesota Press, 1983).
27. Alexander Pope, *An Essay on Man,* III.7–26.
28. Ibid., III.15.

29. The opening lines of Hölderlin's "Patmos"; English from *Friedrich Hölder-erlin: Poems and Fragments,* trans. Michael Hamburger (London: Routledge, 1966), p. 463.
30. Earl Wasserman, *The Subtler Language* (Baltimore: Johns Hopkins University Press, 1968), pp. 10–11.
31. Thus Wordsworth tells of how he

> would stand,
> If the night blackened with a coming storm,
> Beneath some rock, listening to notes that are
> The ghostly language of the ancient earth,
> Or make their dim abode in distant winds.
> ("The Prelude", II.307–311)

The poet himself has to forge the images through which we come to hear this "ghostly language".
32. Rosen and Zerner, *Romanticism,* p. 58. This chapter (2) contains an excellent discussion of the Romantic aspiration to a natural symbolism.
33. Ibid., pp. 68ff.
34. Quoted in ibid., p. 67. Rosen and Zerner relate this to a statement by Constable: "For me, painting is only another word for feeling".
35. Herbert Marcuse, *One-Dimensional Man* (Boston: Beacon Press, 1964).
36. Wilhelm von Humboldt, *On the Limits of State Action* (London: Cambridge University Press, 1969).
37. "The groundwork, therefore, of all true philosophy is the full apprehension of the difference between . . . that intuition of things which arises when we possess ourselves, as one with the whole . . . and that which presents itself when . . . we think of ourselves as separated beings, and place nature in antithesis to the mind, as object to subject, thing to thought, death to life"; Wordsworth, *The Friend,* 3 vols. (London, 1818), III, 261–262.
38. See my "Legitimation Crisis?", in *Philosophy and the Human Sciences* (Cambridge: Cambridge University Press, 1985).
39. Kant, *Kritik der praktischen Vernunft,* second book, first section, in *Kants Werke,* Berlin Academy edition, V, 107–110.
40. Kant, "Muthmasslicher Anfang der Menschengeschichte", *Kants Werke,* Berlin Academy edition, VIII, 116n.
41. Schiller, *Letters,* VI, para. 6.
42. I have discussed this at greater length in *Hegel,* chap. 1.
43. Quoted in Richard Unger, *Hölderlin's Major Poetry* (Bloomington: Indiana University Press, 1975), p. 21; trans. Unger.
44. See J. L. Talmon, *The Origins of Totalitarian Democracy* (London: Secker & Warburg, 1952), and idem, *Political Messianism* (London: Secker & Warburg, 1960); although Talmon casts his net somewhat wider than I do.
45. See Norman Cohn, *The Pursuit of the Millennium* (London: Secker & Warburg, 1957).
46. Quotations from Abrams, *Mirror,* pp. 47, 51.
47. See my *Hegel,* chap. 20.

22. OUR VICTORIAN CONTEMPORARIES

1. All this doesn't mean that the tendentious reading is entirely false. What is remarkable is that hierarchy did erode; and that moreover, the societies in which equality was more advanced came to be more and more recognized as pace-setters culturally, although this had also something to do with their being generally the most advanced economically. So liberalism began to erode resistance even in Tsarist Russia. Wilhelmine Germany looked for justification in thoroughly 'modern' ideologies, like nationalism, and a vulgar-Hegelian view of the state, for its own special preliberal institutions. The Austrian state progresssively lost confidence in itself.

   What we see everywhere is the demise of an earlier political structure of modernization, which started with the wave of absolutist regimes in the seventeenth century and was inspired in part by the neo-Stoic philosophy. See Gerhard Oestreich, *Neostoicism and the Early Modern State* (Cambridge: Cambridge University Press, 1982); Marc Raeff, *The Well-Ordered Police State* (New Haven: Yale University Press, 1983); Perry Anderson, *Lineages of the Absolutist State* (London: NLB, 1974). This model was particularly effective in Germany and Russia, and lasted longest there. It called for control and reorganization from the top/centre with a view to increasing efficiency and productivity, but all this was predicated on a society of orders and hierarchy. This only appears inconsistent in hindsight (though it may ultimately have been self-defeating). At the time, this hierarchy seemed indissolubly linked with the very principle of sovereignty that unified these societies and justified the activist policy, both in that a society of orders supposedly required some supreme authority to harmonize and coordinate them, and in that royal power was seen as the apex of the hierarchy. Baroque display of monarchical power was an essential part of the political formula of these societies. See Raeff, *Police State*, pp. 147–149.
2. Nietzsche, of course, reads this as a hyper-sensitivity to suffering, a weakness. The modern age is "eins allesamt im Schrei und der Ungeduld des Mitleidens, im Todhass gegen das Leiden überhaupt, in der fast weiblichen Unfähigkeit, Zuschauer dabei bleiben zu können, leiden *lassen* zu können" (*Jenseits von Gut und Böse*, 202). This is a weakness from which the superman must free himself. But for all the appeal of Nietzsche's philosophy, we somehow find it as a culture impossible to free ourselves from this concern. Even after the gruesome attempt of Nazism to negate this ethic, Europe has returned to it.
3. For the origins of the contemporary debate about theories of freedom, see Isaiah Berlin, "Two Concepts of Liberty", in *Four Essays on Liberty* (Oxford: Oxford University Press, 1969). For the relation to different views of the subject, see my "What's Wrong with Negative Liberty", in *Philosophy and the Human Sciences* (Cambridge: Cambridge University Press, 1985).
4. Quoted in Fawn Brodie, *Thomas Jefferson: An Intimate History* (New York: Norton, 1974), p. 468.
5. Quoted in David Bryon Davis, *Slavery and Human Progress* (Oxford: Oxford University Press, 1984), p. 115.

6. Ibid. James Turner, in *Without God, Without Creed* (Baltimore: Johns Hopkins University Press, 1985), pp. 204, 206, quotes two nineteenth-century figures who also saw their age as setting a new standard in its sensitivity to suffering. W. E. B. DuBois, somewhat hyperbolically, declared the nineteenth century "the first century of human sympathy". And Oliver Wendell Holmes, Jr., said in 1895: "We have learned the doctrine that evil means pain, and the revolt against pain in all its forms has grown more and more marked. From societies for the prevention of cruelty to animals up to socialism, we express in numberless ways the notion that suffering is a wrong which can be and ought to be prevented, and a whole literature of sympathy has sprung into being".

It can be argued that the heightened historical consciousness and concern that the Victorians showed, in comparison with their predecessors, and that we share with them, is connected to this issue of moral exceptionalism. The question of their (and our) place in history is very important to them (us). And not only because they/we may sense some higher moral standards in ours, but also because of the uneasy sense that something very valuable has been sacrificed in the process. Looking back may chart progress or articulate irretrievable loss; and often it does both. For either reason, history becomes an abiding obsession.

7. Moral exceptionalism is just one facet in the complex idea of civilization, which has been an essential notion in the collective self-narration of our culture over the last two centuries. As it develops in the Enlightenment, 'civilization' designates the condition we have evolved to, mainly through the development of the arts and sciences. It is part of the newly developed story of the genesis of our culture against the background of the homogeneous time of nature, which relates this culture to institutional and social change over centuries. Ferguson is one of the important authors in this regard. The link between 'civilization' and highly developed technical prowess is still one we make today, although this has also been challenged since the Romantic period—or the two have been bundled together in a common negation, as in the distinction popular in Germany early in the century between '*Zivilisation*' and '*Kultur*'. See Norbert Elias, *The Civilizing Process*, trans. E. Jephcott (New York: Urizen Books, 1978), chap. 1, part 1.

But from the very beginning, the concept was not confined to the scientific-technological-economic domain. The notion was current that progress in the arts, sciences, and commerce brought with it a softening of mores. '*Le doux commerce*' "civilizes" us. '*Douceur des moeurs*' and '*politesse*' originally centre around a refinement of manners and sensibility, captured by the term '*civilité*'. But in the eighteenth century 'civilization' comes to englobe the new moral sensitivity to suffering and concern for general well-being. This is the moral dimension I have been dealing with in this chapter. See ibid.

In addition, there is a third facet: 'civilization' is thought to involve a sense of ourselves as individuals in the triple sense I described earlier. "Civilized" people are capable of taking an objectifying distance from their society, culture, and history, precisely the distance that these modern development stories presuppose and require. And indeed, there is a sense in which we find the writers of the last two centuries familiar and understandable just because we share this stance with them, in a way we cannot extend to people of other times and cultures.

8. Turner, *Without God,* pp. 86–88, points out how far some American evangelicals went in accepting the idea of progress and the exceptionalist vocation of the United States. The "post-millennial" belief in a golden age before the Second Coming became very widespread in the early part of the nineteenth century.

9. Ibid., p. 140.

10. See ibid., p. 212.

11. See Stephen Jay Gould, *The Mismeasure of Man* (New York: Norton, 1981).

12. Quoted in Davis, *Slavery,* p. 142.

13. See the discussion in ibid., pp. 142ff.

14. Leslie Stephen, *English Thought in the Eighteenth Century,* 2 vols. (London: J. Murray, 1902), I, 17.

15. Quoted in Turner, *Without God,* p. 57.

16. W. K. Clifford, *The Ethics of Belief and Other Essays,* ed. Leslie Stephen and Frederick Pollock (London: Watts, 1947).

17. Quoted in Turner, *Without God,* p. 216.

18. Quoted in ibid., p. 235.

19. See Noel Annan's *Leslie Stephen* (London: Weidenfeld, 1984), chap. 5, for the influence of evangelicalism. Annan points out that a great many of the early agnostics in England came from evangelical backgrounds, as Stephen himself did. Turner, *Without God,* points out something analogous for the United States. A great many of the early pioneers of unbelief had themselves been clergy or came from clerical backgrounds.

20. Quoted in Turner, *Without God,* pp. 216, 217.

21. Quoted in ibid., p. 238. In this chapter, I have been focussing on developments in the Anglo-Saxon world, but this connection between atheism and humanist benevolence was even more explicitly made by certain Continental thinkers. Indeed, it was trumpeted by Feuerbach. Man has squandered all his treasures on God; by becoming atheist he takes them back. Unbelief releases these treasures (I would say 'moral sources') for human self-affirmation. The practical intent of Feuerbach's work comes out clearly in this statement, made in 1848: "The purpose of my writings, as also of my lectures, is to turn men from theologians into anthropologists, from theophilists into philanthropists, from candidates for the hereafter into students of the here and now, from religious and political lackeys of the heavenly and earthly monarchy into free, self-confident citizens of the world"; L. Feuerbach, "Vorlesung über das Wesen der Religion", in *Gesammelte Werke,* vol. 6 (Berlin: Dietz, 1967), pp. 30–31. The impact of this position on Marx is well known. See F. Engels, "Ludwig Feuerbach und der Ausgang der klassischen deutschen Philosophie", in *Marx-Engels-Werke,* vol. 21 (Berlin: Dietz, 1962), p. 272.

22. Quoted in Stephen, *English Thought,* p. 240.
23. *On Human Nature* (Cambridge, Mass.: Harvard University Press, 1978), pp. 38, 6.
24. Ibid., p. 167.
25. Ibid., pp. 201, 209, 197.
26. See Descartes's letter to Elisabeth of 15 September 1645, in *Descartes: Oeuvres et lettres,* ed. André Bridoux (Paris: Gallimard, Bibliothèque de la Pléiade, 1953).
27. Quoted in Ronald Clark, *Bertrand Russell* (London: Cape, 1975), p. 190.
28. Quoted in ibid., p. 174.
29. Matthew Arnold, *Culture and Anarchy,* ed. Dover Wilson (Cambridge: Cambridge University Press, 1932), p. 48; quoted in Lionel Trilling, *Matthew Arnold* (New York: Norton, 1939), p. 268.
30. From Matthew Arnold, "Dover Beach", ll. 25–28.
31. Quoted in Trilling, *Matthew Arnold,* p. 321.
32. Arnold, *Culture and Anarchy,* p. 45, quoted in Trilling, *Matthew Arnold,* p. 266; Trilling, *Matthew Arnold,* p. 265.
33. I have discussed this interpretation of Marx in *Hegel* (Cambridge: Cambridge University Press, 1975), chap. 20.
34. See Emmanuel Mounier, *Feu la Chrétienneté* (Paris: Seuil, 1950).
35. See section 19.1 above. I quoted from Ross Harrison's *Bentham* (London: Routledge, 1983), p. 276.
36. "Das Moralische ist selbstverständlich". Freud endorses this statement in a letter to James Putnam; see Ernest Jones, *The Life and Work of Sigmund Freud,* vol. 2, *Years of Maturity* (New York: Basic Books, 1955), p. 417.
37. F. Dostoyevsky, *A Raw Youth,* trans. Constance Garnett (London: Heinemann, 1916), part III, chap. 7, sects. 2, 3, pp. 462, 466–467; There is a somewhat similar passage in the addendum to *The Possessed,* where Stavrogin recounts his dream of a world in which the final recognition of uncompromising naturalism leads to a paradisiac condition. Stavrogin, like Versilov, was inspired to his vision of the Golden Age by the painting of Claude Lorraine, "Acis and Galatea". See *The Devils,* trans. David Magarshack (Harmondsworth: Penguin, 1971), pp. 695–696.
38. "C'est la raison qui engendre l'amour-propre, et c'est la réflexion qui le fortifie; c'est elle qui replie l'homme sur lui-même; . . . c'est la philosophie qui l'isole; c'est par elle qu'il dit en secret à l'aspect de l'homme souffrant: péris si tu veux, je suis en sûreté. Il n'y a plus que les dangers de la société entière qui troublent le sommeil du philosophe, et qui l'arrachent de son lit. On peut impunément égorger son semblable sous sa fenêtre; il n'a qu'à mettre ses mains sur ses oreilles et s'argumenter un peu pour empêcher la nature qui se révolte en lui de l'identifier avec celui qu'on assassine. L'homme sauvage n'a point cet admirable talent; et faute de sagesse et de raison, on le voit toujours se livrer étourdiment au premier sentiment de l'humanité"; *Discours sur l'origine de l'inégalité parmi les hommes* (Paris: Garnier-Flammarion, 1971), p. 198.
39. J.-J. Rousseau, *Emile* (Paris: Classiques Garnier, 1964), pp. 354–355.

40. Schiller, "Ode to Joy"; where the wings of joy tarry, "alle Menschen werden Brüder"; Hölderlin's "Empedocles" ode and the early drafts of "Der Tod des Empedokles" reflect the same spirit. See Richard Unger, *Hölderlin's Major Poetry* (Bloomington: Indiana University Press, 1975), chap. 4.

41. See Trilling, *Matthew Arnold*, p. 32.

42. Alexis de Tocqueville, *L'ancien régime et la Révolution* (Paris: Editions Gallimard, 1967), p. 52; *The Old Regime and the Revolution* (Garden City: Doubleday, 1955), p. xiv. Later in the same work Tocqueville speaks of "cette espèce de passion du bien-être qui est comme la mère de la servitude", p. 203.

43. See J.-J. Rousseau, *Du Contrat social*, book I, chap. 5.

44. "Denn jedes Volk ist Volk; es hat seine Nationale Bildung wie seine Sprache"; Herder quoted in Benedict Anderson, *Imagined Communities* (London: Verso, 1983), p. 66.

45. For a discusssion of 'expressive' theories of language, see my "Language and Human Nature", in *Human Agency and Language* (Cambridge: Cambridge University Press, 1985). I have discussed some of the bases of modern linguistic nationalism in "Why Do Nations Have to Become States?" in *Confederation,* ed. Stanley French (Montreal: Canadian Philosophical Association, 1980).

46. I have learnt a great deal from Benedict Anderson's penetrating work *Imagined Communities,* and also his "Narrating the Nation", *Times Literary Supplement,* 13 June 1986, p. 659.

47. "Die Natur soll der sichtbare Geist, der Geist die unsichtbare Natur sein", Schelling, in *Ideen zu einer Philosophie der Natur,* in *Werke* (Leipzig: F. Eckhart, 1907), II, 55.

48. Joseph Conrad, *Heart of Darkness* (New York: Dell, 1960), p. 70.

23. VISIONS OF THE POST-ROMANTIC AGE

1. Quoted in Frank Kermode, *The Romantic Image* (London: Routledge, 1961), p. 46. I have found this study very helpful in formulating the continuities from the Romantic period through to today.

2. Ibid., p. 56.

3. Quoted in Michael Hamburger, *The Truth of Poetry* (London: Weidenfeld, 1969), p. 29, from a letter to Henri Cazalis of July 1866; see S. Mallarmé, *Propos sur la poésie,* ed. Henri Mondor (Monaco, 1953), p. 77.

4. The auto-telic work is also connected in a complex way with the whole tendency of 'l'art pour l'art'. This too is obviously a possible development of the whole post-Romantic conception of art as the locus of the highest human fulfilment. But here too, we mustn't confuse species with genus. I will discuss this below.

The contemporary trend in criticism to treat texts as self-sufficient or as only related to other texts is a strange endeavour to treat all works as though they were auto-telic, in total disregard of two distinctions, that between the epiphanic and the non-epiphanic, and that between epiphanic works which were and those which were not intended as auto-telic. As always, treating a work by alien canons turns up interesting insights, but the wild claims to omnicompetence of this approach only darken the scene.

5. See J. C. F. Schiller, *Letters on the Aesthetic Education of Man,* bilingual edition, ed. and trans. E. M. Wilkinson and C. A. Willoughby (Oxford: Oxford University Press, 1967). Schiller is also drawing on Kant here. See the *Critique of Judgement,* part I, sect. I, book I, para. 9, where Kant says that a judgement of taste is always particular, because the beautiful object cannot be related to a general concept. It is significant that in this work Kant treats both aesthetic objects and organic beings, thereby reflecting in his own way the affinity which the age saw between them.

6. Quoted in Kermode, *Romantic Image,* pp. 21, 46.

7. W. B. Yeats, "Among Schoolchildren", ll. 57–64.

8. Quoted in Kermode, *Romantic Image,* pp. 109, 113.

9. Ibid., pp. 65, 134. The return to allegory as a source of models by some twentieth-century writers and critics—Walter Benjamin, for example—is only an apparent exception to this continued force of the Romantic symbol. As we shall see below, a crucial continuity holds. But the change has a lot to do with the shift away from the epiphanies of being in the twentieth century, which was anticipated by Mallarmé.

10. Ibid., p. 45.

11. Schiller, *Letters,* XXIII, XXIV.

12. Ibid., XXVII; see also letters XIV and XV, which contains the memorable line: "der Mensch spielt nur, wo er in voller Bedeutung des Worts Mensch ist, und er ist nur da ganz Mensch, wo er spielt".

13. Kermode, *Romantic Image,* pp. 20–21.

14. Kant, *Critique of Judgement,* part I, sect. I, book I, paras. 2–5.

15. Ibid., part I, sect. I, para. 59.

16. Quoted in Kermode, *Romantic Image,* p. 44.

17. Quoted in ibid., p. 6.

18. See Jerrold Seigel, *Bohemian Paris* (New York: Penguin Books, 1986).

19. Murger, *Scènes de la vie de Bohème;* Puccini, *La Bohème.*

20. Seigel, *Bohemian Paris,* part I.

21. Ibid., p. 58.

22. Ibid., p. 120.

23. Quoted in M. H. Abrams, *The Correspondent Breeze* (New York: Norton, 1984), p. 119.

24. Pound, quoted in ibid., p. 118.

25. See Kermode, *Romantic Image,* chap. 7.

26. This is one of the drawbacks to my term 'expressivism', that it is often taken for a view which privileges *self*-expression. Needless to say, this is not the sense in which I intend it. But I recognize that this misunderstanding will probably keep arising until I can think of a better term.

27. Novalis, *Schriften,* ed. P. Kluckhohn and R. Samuel (Stuttgart: Klett-Cotta, 1960–1975), II, 419.

28. This point is made in Michael Hamburger's *The Truth of Poetry* (London:

Weidenfeld, 1969), p. 30. Translation of "The Panther" by Stephen Mitchell, in *The Selected Poetry of Rainer Maria Rilke* (New York: Vintage, 1984), p. 25.

29. See Roger Shattuck, "Catching Up with the Avant-Garde", *New York Review of Books*, 18 December 1986, p.72.

30. Quoted in Abrams, *Correspondent Breeze*, p. 125.

31. Quoted in M. H. Abrams, *The Mirror and the Lamp* (Oxford: Oxford University Press, 1953), p. 282.

32. "Tintern Abby", ll. 95–96. Similarly, Wordsworth writes in *The Prelude*, XIII, ll. 367–372:

> and I remember well
> That in life's every-day appearances
> I seemed about this time to gain clear sight
> Of a new world—a world, too, that was fit
> To be transmitted, and to other eyes
> Made visible . . .

And in the Preface to *Lyrical Ballads,* he says: "Humble and rustic life was generally chosen, because, in that condition, the essential passions of the heart find a better soil in which they can attain their maturity, . . . and speak a plainer and more emphatic language; . . . and . . . because in that condition the passions of men are incorporated with the beautiful and permanent forms of nature"; *Poetical Works,* II, 386–387. Coleridge described his purpose thus: "Mr Wordsworth . . . was to propose to himself as his object to give the charm of novelty to things of everyday, and to excite a feeling analogous to the supernatural, by awakening the mind's attention from the lethargy of custom, and by directing it to the loveliness and the wonders of the world before us"; in *Biographia Literaria*, chap. 14, quoted in Lilian Furst, *Romanticism in Perspective* (London: Macmillan, 1969), pp. 245–246.

33. Quoted in Hugh Honour, *Romanticism* (London: Allen Lane, 1979), pp. 68, 92.

34. Shelley, in his *Defense of Poetry,* says of it that "it transmutes all it touches, and every form moving within the radiance of its presence is changed by wondrous sympathy to an incarnation of the spirit which it breathes; its secret alchemy turns to potable gold the poisonous waters which flow from death through life"; in *Complete Works*, VII, 137, quoted in Furst, *Romanticism and Perspective,* pp. 160–161. See the same place for an analogous quote from Tieck. Palmer speaks of his paintings as visions of nature "passed thro' the intense purifying separating transmuting heat of the soul's infabulous alchymy"; quoted in Honour, *Romanticism,* p. 86.

35. Charles Rosen and Henri Zerner, *Romanticism and Realism* (New York: Norton, 1984), p. 157. I have drawn a great deal from the penetrating discussion in this book. From this point of view, Charles Bovary's last words in the novel, "C'est la faute de la fatalité!", on one level give one more crowning expression to the inarticulate, uncomprehending banality of his life

and earn the contempt of his interlocutor, Rodolphe, but nevertheless on another level, by an ironic turn, capture a profound truth about Emma's life and death.

36. See the discussion of Jean-Pierre Alexandre Antigna's *The Fire* in Rosen and Zerner, *Romanticism and Realism*, p. 166.

37. *Gustave Courbet*, catalogue of the exposition held at the Grand Palais, Paris, 30 September 1977 to 2 January 1978 (Paris, 1977), p. 36.

38. Rosen and Zerner, *Romanticism and Realism*, p. 165.

39. Ibid.

40. Quoted from the explanation under the painting, which hangs in the New York Metropolitan Museum of Art.

41. Rosen and Zerner, *Romanticism and Realism*, chap. 6; the authors point out that in the mature work of Courbet, the painted surface becomes obtrusive. He rejected the standard of the academic 'fini', and made the painting stand out as a representation; pp. 151–152, 223.

42. Quoted in Abrams, *Correspondent Breeze*, p. 121.

43. Charles Baudelaire, quoted in Abrams, *Correspondent Breeze*, p. 127.

44. From *Mon coeur mis à nu*, quoted in Pascal Pia, *Baudelaire* (Paris: Seuil, 1952), p. 61.

45. Quoted in Pia, *Baudelaire*, p. 98.

46. From *Peintre de la vie moderne*, quoted in Pia, *Baudelaire*, p. 68–69.

47. Quoted in Abrams, *Correspondent Breeze*, p. 122.

48. Trans. Richard Wilbur, in Charles Baudelaire, *The Flowers of Evil*, ed. Marthiel Matthews and Jackson Matthews (Norfolk, Conn.: New Directions, 1962), p. 12.

49. Quoted in Pia, *Baudelaire*, p. 77; trans. Louise Varèse, in Charles Baudelaire, *Paris Spleen* (New York: New Directions, 1970), p. 74.

50. Quoted in Pia, *Baudelaire*, p. 88.

51. In this respect there seems to be an affinity between Baudelaire and the kind of realism exemplified by Flaubert in the discussion above.

52. Trans. Allen Tate and Frederick Morgan, respectively, in Baudelaire, *Flowers of Evil*, pp. 38, 161.

53. Hugo Friedrich, *Die Struktur der modernen Lyrik* (Hamburg: Rowohlt, 1967), pp. 55–56; Abrams, *Correspondent Breeze*, p. 128.

54. Trans. Edna St. Vincent Millay, in Baudelaire, *Flowers of Evil*, p. 129.

55. Friedrich, *Struktur*, p. 54.

56. Quoted in Hamburger, *Truth of Poetry*, p. 267.

57. See *Republic*, 558–559.

58. T. E. Hulme, *Speculations*, ed. Herbert Read (London: K. Paul, 1924), pp. 116–118; see also pp. 255–256.

59. Ibid., pp. 9, 53. See Abrams, *Correspondent Breeze*, pp. 129–130.

60. See Abrams, *Correspondent Breeze*, pp. 123–124. And of course the theological element can drop out. The sources for this stance include a passionately anti-Christian thinker, Nietzsche. Hulme was influenced by him as well—e.g., in his espousal of the 'heroic' values. See Hulme, *Further Speculations*, ed. Sam Hynes (Minneapolis: University of Minnesota Press,

1955), pp. 199–200. (But see also his critique of Nietzsche for not going far enough in his anti-Romanticism; *Speculations,* p. 62.) Hulme also admired Sorel's *Réflexions sur la violence* and translated it into English. The rest of the aggressively right-wing constellation that Abrams outlines survives the excision of Christianity in, e.g., Pound and Wyndham Lewis.

61. Schiller, *Letters,* XXVII.
62. Quoted in Pia, *Baudelaire,* p. 118.
63. Quoted in Abrams, *Correspondent Breeze,* p. 139, from letter to Henri Cazalis of July 1866; see Mallarmé, *Propos sur la poésie,* ed. Mondor, p. 27.
64. "Ein Abbild des Willens selbst"; A. Schopenhauer, *The World as Will and Representation,* third book, sect. 52. Trans E. F. J. Payne, 2 vols. (New York: Dover, 1969).
65. Ibid., third book, sect. 38; Payne trans., I, 196.
66. F. Nietzsche, *Die Geburt der Tragödie,* sect. 5; *The Birth of Tragedy,* trans. Francis Golffing (New York: Doubleday, 1956), p. 42.
67. Quoted in William J. McGrath, *Dionysian Art and Populist Politics in Austria* (New Haven: Yale University Press, 1974), p. 66.
68. See McGrath, *Dionysian Art,* especially chapter 4, where he describes a number of minor plays of the period in Vienna.
69. It also echoes in the preoccupation with evil, decadence, and untamed instinctual energy, which was one strand of the fin-de-siècle fascination for Bohemia. See Seigel, *Bohemian Paris,* chap. 10.
70. S. Kierkegaard, *Either/Or,* trans. W. Lowrie and D. Johnson, 2 vols. (Garden City: Doubleday, 1959), II, 255. See also *The Sickness unto Death,* trans. W. Lowrie (Garden City: Doubleday, 1954).
71. I owe a great deal in my discussion of Kierkegaard to Jane Rubin, whose book, *Too Much of Nothing: Modern Culture and the Self in Kierkegaard's Thought* (forthcoming), has not been adequately reflected in these pages. Although it was left behind in his later work, the position that Kierkegaard develops in *Either/Or* provided the kernel idea which Heidegger made into his notion of resoluteness, of the choice of life in face of death, which defines his notion of 'authenticity'. See *Sein und Zeit,* div. II, chaps. 1–2.
72. See F. Dostoyevsky, *The Devils,* trans. David Magarshack (Harmondsworth: Penguin Books, 1971), part III, chap. 5, sect. 3, p. 580, and chap. 7, sect. 2, p. 638.
73. See the remark by Ivan in *The Brothers Karamazov,* trans. David Magarshack (Harmondsworth: Penguin Books, 1958), p. 277.
74. Said by Father Tikhonov in "Stavrogin's Confession", appendix to *The Devils,* p. 679.
75. See F. Nietzsche, *Jenseits von Gut und Böse,* para. 188.
76. It is a mistake to think that Nietzsche wanted to set this sense aside. Losing it is precisely what he calls 'nihilism'. See *Die fröhliche Wissenschaft,* para. 346; and *Zur Genealogie der Moral,* I, sect. 12: "Hier eben liegt das Verhängnis Europas—mit der Furcht vor dem Menschen haben wir auch die Liebe zu ihm, die Ehrfurcht vor ihm, die Hofnung auf ihn, ja den Willen zu ihm eingebüsst. Der Anblick des Menschen macht müde—was ist heute

Nihilismus, wenn er nicht *das* ist . . . ?" The great danger of modern morality is precisely that its steady self-undermining of its own credibility may end us up in nihilism.

24. EPIPHANIES OF MODERNISM

1. Quoted in M. H. Abrams, *The Mirror and the Lamp* (Oxford: Oxford University Press, 1953), p. 282.
2. Ricardo Quiñones in his *Mapping Literary Modernism* (Princeton: Princeton University Press, 1985), chap. 4, speaks of the "counter-Romanticism" of Modernism.
3. "Before Copernicus, man was not the centre of the world; after Copernicus he was. You get a change from a certain profundity and intensity to that flat and insipid optimism which, passing through its first stage of decay in Rousseau, has finally culminated in the state of slush in which we have the misfortune to live"; T. E. Hulme in *Speculations,* ed. Herbert Read (London: K. Paul, 1924), p. 80. Ford Madox Ford expressed something of the same sentiments less prudently in January 1914: "What we want most of all in the literature of today is religion, is intolerance, is persecution, and not the mawkish flap-doodle of culture, Fabianism, peace and good will. Real good religion, a violent thing full of hatreds and exclusions"; quoted in Michael Levenson, *A Genealogy of Modernism* (Cambridge: Cambridge University Press, 1984), p. 59. The twentieth century has lavishly indulged this request, only forgetting to confine the consequences to literature.
4. Hulme, *Speculations,* p. 118.
5. Ibid., p. 8; emphasis in original.
6. Yeats of course doesn't fully fit this pattern. But in a sense Yeats, who was older than the great modernist generation which comes into creativity in the first two decades of this century, could be considered a transition figure.
7. Quoted in Hulme's "Notes on Bergson", in *Further Speculations,* ed. Sam Hynes (Minneapolis: University of Minnesota Press, 1955), p. 47.
8. For Hulme, reading Bergson "put an end to an intolerable state"; "I had been released from a nightmare which had long troubled my mind"; it was "an almost physical sense of exhilaration, a sudden expansion, a kind of mental explosion"; ibid., pp. 29–30. See also Levenson, *Genealogy of Modernism,* p. 40.
9. Hulme, *Further Speculations,* p. 78.
10. Ibid., p. 10.
11. See M. Heidegger, *Sein und Zeit* (Tübingen: Niemeyer, 1927), introduction, chap. 2, sects. 5, 6.
12. This latter link has been well argued by Charles Guignon in his *Heidegger and the Problem of Knowledge* (Indianapolis: Hackett, 1983), chap. 2.
13. Novalis, *Schriften,* ed. P. Kluckhorn and R. Samuel (Stuttgart: Klett-Cotta, 1960–1975), II, 419.
14. Quoted in Quiñones, *Mapping Literary Modernism,* p. 129.
15. See H. Kenner, *The Pound Era* (London: Faber, 1972), pp. 173–191.

16. See the interesting discussion on this question in Alexander Nehamas, *Nietzsche: Life as Literature* (Cambridge, Mass.: Harvard University Press, 1985), esp. chaps. 5 and 6.
17. Quoted in Quiñones, *Mapping Literary Modernism*, p. 93.
18. Quoted in ibid., p. 146.
19. From *Contre Sainte-Beuve*, quoted in Quiñones, *Mapping Literary Modernism*, p. 146.
20. See Michel Foucault, *Surveiller et punir* (Paris: Gallimard, 1975); idem, *La Volonté de savoir* (Paris: Gallimard, 1976); Jean-François Lyotard, *La Condition post-moderne* (Paris: Seuil, 1979).
21. The situation changes, of course, with relativity and quantum mechanics. Some modernist writers thought they found support in the new concepts of twentieth-century physics for their critique of the dominant late-Victorian time-consciousness.
22. See Heidegger, *Sein und Zeit*, div. II, chaps. 3–4. But the same basic idea is also argued in other ways through a great many other works by Heidegger.
23. György Lukács, *History and Class Consciousness*, trans. R. Livingstone (Cambridge, Mass.: MIT Press, 1971), p. 90.
24. Quiñones, in *Mapping Literary Modernism*, offers a "map" of literary modernism largely based on the shifts in its conceptions of time. I have learned a great deal from his discussion.
25. See Eliot's note to *The Waste Land:* "Tiresias, although a mere spectator and not indeed a 'character', is yet the most important personage in the poem, uniting all the rest. Just as the one-eyed merchant, seller of currants, melts into the Phoenician Sailor, and the latter is not wholly distinct from Ferdinand Prince of Naples, so all the women are one woman, and the two sexes meet in Tiresias"; *The Complete Poems and Plays of T. S. Eliot 1909–1950* (New York: Harcourt Brace, 1962), p. 52. See also the discussion in James Longenbach, *Modernist Poetics of History: Pound, Eliot, and the Sense of the Past* (Princeton: Princeton University Press, 1987), chap. 10 and passim.
26. See Roger Shattuck, *The Banquet Years* (New York: Vintage, 1968), p. 332. Hulme, in *Further Speculations*, p. 73, speaks of the "piling up and juxtaposition of distinct images in different lines".
27. Quoted in Quiñones, *Mapping Literary Modernism*, p. 141.
28. Quoted in ibid., pp. 143–144.
29. Quoted in Kenner, *The Pound Era*, p. 178.
30. Quoted in Michael Hamburger, *The Truth of Poetry* (London: Weidenfeld, 1969), p. 189.
31. Quoted in M. H. Abrams, *The Correspondent Breeze* (New York: Norton, 1984), p. 118.
32. Quoted in Hamburger, *The Truth of Poetry*, p. 39.
33. *The Gay Science*, preface, sect. 4. Hamburger, *The Truth of Poetry*, p. 39, also points to a parallel with Karl Kraus, who also wanted to purge language of self-delusion and false sentiment, by clearly separating what was too easily confused.
34. See Maurice Merleau-Ponty, *La Phénoménologie de la perception* (Paris:

Gallimard, 1945); and Michael Polanyi, *The Tacit Dimension* (Garden City: Doubleday, 1966).

35. Maurice Merleau-Ponty, "Cézanne's Doubt", in *Sense and Nonsense,* trans. Hubert and Patricia Dreyfus (Chicago: Northwestern University Press, 1964), pp. 17–18.

36. "Noi cantaremo le grandi folle agitate dal lavoro, del piacere o dalla sommosa: cantremo le maree multicolori e polifoniche delle rivoluzioni nelli capitali moderne; cantaremo il vibrante fervore notturno degli arsenali e dei cantieri incendiati da violente lune elettriche; le stazioni ingorde, divoratrici de serpi che fumano; le officine appese all nuvole pei conorti fili dei loro fumi; i ponti simili a ginnasti giganti que scalvano i fiumi . . ."; from the "Manifesto del Futurismo", of which a French version appeared in *Le Figaro* on 20 February 1909, para. 11; reprinted in *Il Futurismo italiano,* ed. Isabella Gherarducci (Rome: Riuniti, 1976), p. 28. The English version is quoted in Charles Russell, *Poets, Prophets and Revolutionaries* (Oxford: Oxford University Press, 1985), p. 91.

37. Marinetti, as quoted in Russell, *Poets,* pp. 91–92. Point 4 of the "Manifesto del Futurismo" reads in part: "Noi affermiamo che la magnificenza del mondosi è arrichita di una belleza nuova: la belleza della velocità . . . un automobile ruggente, . . . è piú bello della *Vittoria di Samotracia*"; in *Il Futurismo italiano,* ed. Gherarducci, p. 27.

38. From a Futurist manifesto of 1910, quoted in *Il Futurismo italiano,* ed. Gherarducci, p. 93.

39. From Breton's "Deux manifestes Dada", quoted in ibid., p. 126.

40. André Breton, "Second Manifeste du Surréalisme" (1930), in *Manifestes du Surréalisme* (Paris: Gallimard, 1973), p. 92; translation quoted in Russell, *Poets,* p. 133.

41. From the "Manifeste du Surréalisme" (1924), in *Manifestes,* p. 34; translation quoted in Russell, *Poets,* p. 142. In the "Second Manifeste", Breton talks about "ces produits de l'activité psychique, aussi distraits que possible de la volonté de signifier, aussi allégés que possibles des idées de responsabilité toujours prêtes à agir comme freins, aussi indépendants que possible de tout ce qui n'est pas *la vie passive de l'intelligence*"; *Manifestes,* p. 121.

42. From Breton's "Manifeste du Surréalisme", *Manifestes,* p. 40; translation quoted in Russell, *Poets,* pp. 142–143.

43. André Breton, from the "Second Manifeste", *Manifestes,* p. 121n; translation quoted in Russell, *Poets,* p. 133.

44. In fact, the Futurists' political views were rather repellent from the beginning. Here are some quotes from the founding Manifesto:

> 9. Noi vogliamo glorificare la guerra—sola igiene del mondo—il militarismo, il patriotismo, il gesto distruttore dei libertari, le belle idee per cui si muore e il disprezzo della donna.

> 10. Noi vogliamo distruggere i musei, le bibilotecche, le accademie d'ogni specie, e combattere contro il moralismo, il femminismo e contro ogni viltà opportunistica o utilitaria.

    9. We will glorify war—the world's only hygiene—militarism, patriotism, the destructive gesture of freedom-bringers, beautiful ideas worth dying for, and scorn for women.

   10. We will destroy the museums, libraries, academies of every kind, will fight moralism, feminism, every opportunistic or utilitarian cowardice.

Il Futurismo italiano, ed. Gherarducci, p. 28; translation quoted in Russell, *Poets,* p. 89. The mitigating circumstances to be cited are that all this happened in the age of innocence before the First World War, when it might still be half taken as a joke.

45. Violence was not far from the surface in Surrealism, either. As Breton said in his "Second Manifeste" of 1930; "L'acte surréaliste le plus simple consiste, revolver aux poings, à descendre dans la rue et à tirer au hasard, tant qu'on peut, dans la foule. Qui n'a pas eu, au moins une fois, envie d'en finir de la sorte avec le petit système d'avilissement et de crétinisation en vigueur a sa place toute marquée dans cette foule, ventre à hauteur de canon"; *Manifestes,* p. 78.

    To speak of another affinity, Roger Shattuck notes the close relation between the reception of primitive art in the prewar period and the seemingly anithetical fascination with technology. "The embracing of primitive art by Picasso, Matisse, Derain, Apollinaire, Stravinsky, and many others coincided with a widespread affirmative response by artists and writers to science and technology. Futurism in Italy and Russia gave that response a name and a doctrine. The same artists and writers who welcomed the unfamiliar forms and magical content of African Sculpture also reveled in powerful automobiles; they went to movies, speculated about airplane flight and the fourth dimension ... Yet primitivism and futurism are usually treated separately". From "Catching Up with the Avant-Garde", *New York Review of Books,* 18 December 1986, p. 72.

46. Marinetti, "Destruction of Syntax—Imagination without Strings—Words-in-Freedom", quoted in Russell, *Poets,* p. 92.

47. See Shattuck, *The Banquet Years,* p. 341.

48. "La letteratura esaltò fino ad oggi l'immobilità pensosa, l'estasi e il sonno. Noi vogliamo esaltare il movimento aggressivo, l'insonnia febrile, il passo di corsa, il salto mortale, lo schiaffo ed il pugno". Point 3 of the "Manifesto del Futurismo", *Il Futurismo italiano,* ed. Gherarducci, p. 27; translation quoted in Russell, *Poets,* p. 88.

49. André Breton, *Nadja,* p. 215; quoted in Russell, *Poets,* p. 147.

50. F. Nietzsche, *The Will to Power,* trans. Walter Kaufmann and R. J. Hollingdale (New York: Random House, 1968), p. 307.

51. Hulme, *Further Speculations,* p. 10. See also *Speculations,* pp. 134–135. Sanford Schwartz, *The Matrix of Modernism* (Princeton: Princeton University Press, 1985), whose discussion of the philosophical background in modernism I have found extremely helpful, points to analogous theories about the flux of experience in Bergson, William James, and F. H. Bradley, which were also very influential around this time.

52. See the discussion in Schwartz, *Matrix*, pp. 87–88.
53. See ibid., p. 91.
54. I have drawn on the discussion in Kenner, *The Pound Era*, pp. 184–185.
55. Quotations drawn from the discussion in Schwartz, *Matrix*, pp. 92–93.
56. Quoted in ibid., p. 66.
57. See the discussion in ibid., pp. 105–108. Eliot propounds a parallel position later in his critical works. He castigates realism which "ends its course in the desert of exact likeness to the reality which is perceived by the most commonplace mind". The artist must rather "intensify the world to his emotions". But this emotion is not personal. Rather by his "continual extinction of personality", the artist produces a work that expresses a "new art emotion" (quotations from Schwartz, *Matrix*, pp. 174, 171).
58. Kenner, *The Pound Era*.
59. Ibid., pp. 154–155.
60. Ibid., p. 160.
61. Ibid., p. 185.
62. Ibid.
63. Ibid., p. 156.
64. Joseph Frank, in his "Spatial Form in Modern Literature" (in *The Widening Gyre,* New Brunswick, N.J.: Rutgers University Press, 1963), has shown the link between what I have been calling a framing epiphany, with its revelation by juxtaposition, often of elements widely separated in time, and the rise of the time-consciousness I discussed earlier, which denies linearity, and unites widely separated moments either in a timeless present or through the archetypes of myth. Both reflect a move away from ordinary narration to a "spatialization" of time, which Frank relates in an interesting way to the spiritual condition of contemporary culture. Needless to say, this is very different from the 'spatialization' I spoke of above in connection with a Laplacean world-view. Unlike this, the spatializing of time in modernist literature is very much situated. It grows out of and does not cancel our situation in time.
65. Eliot speaks of the poet's mind as "constantly amalgamating disparate experience; . . . in the mind of the poet these experiences are always forming new wholes" (quoted in Schwartz, *Matrix*, p. 96). There are, of course, great differences between Eliot and Pound, not least in their substantive religious and metaphysical beliefs. But I think they were similar not only in their recourse to what I have been calling 'framing epiphanies' but also in their uses of history. These are also characteristically modernist, both building on and departing from the romantics. Like these latter, Eliot and Pound are both critical of the modern age for what it has lost: Eliot speaks of the "dissociation of sensibility" it has undergone. But at the same time, they break quite decisively with the Romantic modes of narrative, which place us somewhere between a lost golden age and a possible harmonious future synthesis. The aim of epiphany is not so much to bring us close to an unrecoverable past or to hasten a more integrated future, but rather to realize a transhistorical unity, connecting us to the highest spiritual articulations of

different ages (which were, of course, not the same for Eliot as for Pound, though there is a lot of overlap). The epiphany opens us to something perennial, and allows it to radiate again in our time. For Eliot, the perennial came to be identified with the timeless, in the religious vision that informs the *Four Quartets:* "In my beginning is my end". From this point of view, Donald Davie's attempt to distinguish Pound from Eliot (*Ezra Pound: Poet as Sculptor,* New York: Oxford University Press, 1964, pp. 173–177), on the grounds that Pound is attentive to the particularity of things existing in their own right, but Eliot (like Yeats) is ever ready to appropriate them as symbols and emblems, seems to me overdrawn. It makes Eliot sound subjectivist in a way that he is not, and seems to downplay the epiphanic in Pound.

66. Ferdinand de Saussure, *Cours de linguistique générale* (Paris: Payot, 1978), pp. 155–156.

67. See the discussion in Albrecht Wellmer's "Wahrheit, Schein, Versöhnung", in his *Zur Dialektik von Moderne und Postmoderne* (Frankfurt: Suhrkamp, 1985), p. 27.

68. From *The Statesman's Manual,* quoted in Abrams, *Correspondent Breeze,* p. 221.

69. The poetics of juxtaposition can also serve to establish a new stance in time. Against a sense of time as a disconnected succession of instants, where our previous experiences and even identity are carried away without remainder, the juxtaposing of images holds together past and future in a single instant. The dimensions of the present are extended. The moment is intensified into a kind of continuous present, an ephemeral eternity. This seems to have been in part what Apollinaire's "simultanism" was aimed at. See Shattuck, *The Banquet Years,* pp. 345–350; and Russell, *Poets,* pp. 65–86. The breakdown of a meaningful narrative of life, which normally guards against this kind of disconnection, makes this new stance all the more urgent. This is an example of the kind of spatialization of time of which Frank speaks (see note 64).

70. Kenner, in *The Pound Era,* pp. 171–172, relates the particular story which gave rise to one of Pound's lines: "eucalyptus that is for memory".

71. Thus Eliot says that poetry "may make us from time to time a little more aware of the deeper, unnamed feelings which form the substratum of our being, to which we rarely penetrate"; quoted in Schwartz, *Matrix,* p. 155.

72. Translation by Stephen Mitchell in *The Selected Poetry of Rainer Maria Rilke* (New York: Vintage, 1984), pp. 201–202.

73. Levenson, *Genealogy of Modernism,* chaps 3, 6.

74. From the earliest version of "September 1, 1939", reproduced in *Poetry of the Thirties,* ed. Robin Skelton (London: Penguin, 1964), p. 283.

75. Quoted in Hamburger, *Truth of Poetry,* pp. 221, 223.

76. Quoted in Czesław Miłosz, *The History of Polish Literature* (New York: Macmillan, 1969), pp. 462–463. This poem, as well as the one cited below by Herbert, was drawn to my attention by Alba Taylor.

77. Quoted in Hamburger, *Truth of Poetry,* pp. 247, 251–252.

78. Quoted in Miłosz, *History,* pp. 471–472.

79. Paul Celan, "Weggebeizt", from the collection *Atemwende,* in *Gesammelte*

Werke (Frankfurt: Suhrkamp, 1983), II, 31; trans. Michael Hamburger in *Poems of Paul Celan* (New York: Persea Books, 1988), p. 230.

80. Paul Celan, "Kein Halbholz", from the collection *Lichtzwang*, in *Gesammelte Werke*, II, 296; trans. M. Hamburger in *Poems of Paul Celan*, p. 300.

81. Paul Celan, "Fadensonnen", from *Atemwende*, in *Gesammelte Werke*, II, 26; trans. M. Hamburger in *Poems of Paul Celan*, p. 226.

82. Roman Jakobson, *Questions de poétique* (Paris: Seuil, 1973).

83. Unless one wants to consider as belonging to the same movement certain powerful contemporary novelists of disintegration and imprisonment like William Burroughs and Thomas Pynchon.

84. See Michel Foucault, *La Volonté de savoir* (Paris: Gallimard, 1976), passim; also Hubert L. Dreyfus and Paul Rabinow, *Michel Foucault: Beyond Structuralism and Hermeneutics* (Chicago: University of Chicago Press, 1983), chap. 8.

85. See Jonathan Culler, *On Deconstruction* (Ithaca: Cornell University Press, 1982), pp. 175–179.

86. See ibid., p. 172.

87. See Richard Bernstein, "Serious Play: The Ethical-Political Horizon of Jacques Derrida", *Journal of Speculative Philosophy* (forthcoming).

88. See Dreyfus and Rabinow, *Michel Foucault*, afterword.

89. Jean-François Lyotard, *La Condition post-moderne* (Paris: Minuit, 1979).

90. In its own very different way, Derrida's philosophy illustrates the link I was trying to make in relating Futurism and Surrealism. A philosophy which supposedly negates subjectivity, self-possession, and full presence and which sees thought as perpetually dispersed and "deferred" in a field of infinite substitutions also exalts the indefinite freedom of play, and presents itself as a liberating doctrine. Engulfment and extreme subjectivism come together here in a notion of free play, which in its anti-humanism is antipodal to Schiller's. It offers a mode of thinking which "affirms free play and tries to pass beyond man and humanism, the name man being the name of that being, who throughout the history of metaphysics or of ontotheology—in other words, through the history of all of his history—has dreamed of full presence, the reassuring foundation, the origin and end of the game"; "Structure, Sign, and Play in the Discourse of the Human Sciences", in *The Structuralist Controversy*, ed. Richard Macksey and Eugenio Donato (Baltimore: Johns Hopkins University Press, 1972), pp. 264–265.

91. As Stephen Spender puts it, "There runs through modern criticism the fantasy of a Second Fall of Man ... The Second Fall seems to result from the introduction of scientific utilitarian values and modes of thinking into the world of personal choice between good and evil, with the result that values cease to be personal and become identified with the usefulness or destructiveness of social systems and material things"; in his *The Struggle of the Modern* (London: Hamish Hamilton, 1963), p. 26. Spender speaks here of an outlook which stretches "from Carlyle, Ruskin, Morris and Arnold, to T. E. Hulme, Ezra Pound, Yeats, Eliot, Lawrence and Leavis". But he could also have gone back to the original Romantics.

92. Spender, *Struggle*, p. 17.
93. Ludwig Wittgenstein, *On Certainty*, G. E. M. Anscombe and G. H. von Wright (Oxford: Blackwell, 1977), paras. 84ff.
94. For a discussion of this notion of the 'background', see Hubert Dreyfus, *What Computers Can't Do* (New York: Harper, 1979), part III; John Searle, *Intentionality* (Cambridge: Cambridge University Press, 1983), chap. 5; Michael Polanyi, *The Tacit Dimension* (Garden City: Doubleday, 1966).
95. See the discussion in Hamburger, *Truth of Poetry*, chap. 8.
96. From his *Opus Posthumus*, quoted by Spender in *Struggle*, p. 39.

25. CONCLUSION: THE CONFLICTS OF MODERNITY

1. See A. Willener, *L'Image-Action de la société* (Paris: Seuil, 1970), part IV.
2. Quoted in Robert Bellah et al., *Habits of the Heart* (Berkeley: University of California Press, 1985), p. 63.
3. See Steven M. Tipton, *Getting Saved from the Sixties* (Berkeley: University of California Press, 1982).
4. S. Kierkegaard, *Two Ages: The Age of Revolution and the Present Age, A Literary Review*, trans. H. V. and E. H. Hong (Princeton: Princeton University Press, 1978).
5. "Erbärmliches Behagen"; *Also Sprach Zarathustra*, Zarathustra's Preface, sect. 3. Albert Borgman, *Technology and the Character of Contemporary Life* (Chicago: University of Chicago Press, 1984), seems to echo this in showing how the original liberating promise of technology can degenerate into "the procurement of frivolous comfort" (p. 39).
6. Max Weber, *The Protestant Ethic and the Spirit of Capitalism*, trans. Talcott Parsons (New York: Scribner, 1958), p. 181.
7. Marshall Berman, *All That Is Solid Melts into Air* (New York: Verso, 1982).
8. Borgman, *Technology*, pp. 41–42.
9. Hannah Arendt, *The Human Condition* (Garden City: Doubleday, Anchor Edition, 1959), p. 83.
10. The Seventh Elegy, trans. Stephen Mitchell, in *The Selected Poetry of Rainer Maria Rilke* (New York: Vintage, 1984), p. 189.
11. I have tried to show the impossibility of some of the repudiations made by Michel Foucault in my "Foucault on Freedom and Truth", in *Philosophy and the Human Sciences* (Cambridge: Cambridge University Press, 1985); and I have tried to make the more general point in "Humanismus und moderne Identität" in *Der Mensch in den modernen Wissenschaften*, ed. Krzysztof Michalski (Stuttgart: Klett-Cotta, 1985). Richard Bernstein in "Serious Play: The Ethical-Political Horizon of Jacques Derrida", *Journal of Speculative Philosophy* (forthcoming), shows how much the appeal of Derrida's work turns on its apparent commitment to an ethic of non-domination.
12. See Ernst Tugendhat, *Selbstbewusstsein und Selbstbestimmung* (Frankfurt: Suhrkamp, 1979), p. 275.
13. I have discussed this at greater length in "Explanation and Practical Reason" (forthcoming).

14. I have argued these Tocquevillian theses at some length in various places, e.g., "Social Theory as Practice", and "Legitimation Crisis?", in *Philosophy and the Human Sciences* (Cambridge: Cambridge University Press, 1985); also "Alternative Futures", in *Constitutionalism, Citizenship and Society in Canada,* ed. Alan Cairns and Cynthia Williams (Toronto: University of Toronto Press, 1985); "The Politics of the Steady State", in *Beyond Industrial Growth,* ed. Abraham Rotstein (Toronto: University of Toronto Press, 1976), and "Algunas condiciones para una democracia viable", *Democracia y Participación,* eds. R. Alveyey and C. Ruiz (Santiago: CERC, 1988). Bellah et al., *Habits,* gives a Tocquevillean reading of the moral languages of contemporary America. See also Michael Sandel, "The Procedural Republic and the Unencumbered Self", *Political Theory* 12 (February 1984), 81–96.

15. See the original work by Philip Rieff, *The Triumph of the Therapeutic* (New York: Norton, 1966). The concept is now widely invoked. Christopher Lasch makes use of it in his *Culture of Narcissism* (New York: Norton, 1979), and *The Minimal Self* (New York: Norton, 1984). Alasdair MacIntyre has drawn on it in sketching his 'characters' of the emotivist era, *After Virtue* (Notre Dame: University of Notre Dame Press, 1984), chap. 3; and Bellah et al. also invoke it in *Habits,* chap. 5.

16. See, e.g., Bellah et al., *Habits,* pp. 80, 131–133.

17. Gail Sheehy, *Passages: Predictable Crises of Adult Life* (New York: Bantam Books, 1976), p. 30.

18. Ibid., pp. 364, 513.

19. Ibid., chap. 3.

20. Ibid., chap. 5. Steven Tipton, one of the co-authors of *Habits,* in his *Getting Saved from the Sixties,* chap. 5, shows how some of the milieus in the human potential movement, as well as certain sects, make it possible for people to integrate an expressive private life with an instrumental work and public life, although in their original 1960's posture the first was undermining the second.

21. Christopher Lasch, chap. 7 passim, p. 387; idem, chap. 1.

22. Lasch, *Narcissism,* chap. 1; idem, *Self,* chap. 2.

23. Jürgen Habermas, *Theorie des kommunikativen Handelns,* 2 vols. (Frankfurt: Suhrkamp, 1981), I, chap. 4.

24. Ibid., chap. 1.

25. This is a pattern it is easy to fall into. Even Bellah et al. sometimes present their subjectivist respondents in a largely negative light. Or perhaps the pattern is there in the mind of the reader. In any case, a penetrating book like Alasdair MacIntyre's *After Virtue* can create the impression in some readers of dismissing the 'Enlightenment project' as simply a mistake.

26. Borgman, *Technology,* chap. 11.

27. See, for instance, Maurice Merleau-Ponty, *La Phénoménologie de la perception* (Paris: Gallimard, 1945); Martin Heidegger, *Sein und Zeit* (Tübingen: Niemayer, 1927); the works of the later Wittgenstein can also, I think, be seen in this light; as also Michael Polanyi's *Personal Knowledge* (New

York: Harper, 1964); and *The Tacit Dimension* (Garden City: Doubleday, 1966).

28. I have discussed this at greater length in "Overcoming Epistemology", in *After Philosophy: End or Transformation?* ed. Kenneth Baynes, James Bohman, and Thomas Macarthy (Cambridge, Mass.: MIT Press, 1987).

29. Bernard Williams, in his *Ethics and the Limits of Philosophy* (London: Fontana, 1985), chap. 10, shows the centrality of the notion of obligation to the dominant meta-ethic. Williams's chapter is entitled "Morality, the Peculiar Institution", and this gives some indication of its bent.

30. See, e.g., William Connolly, "Taylor, Foucault and Otherness," *Political Theory* 13, no. 3 (August 1985), 365–376.

31. See, e.g., the discussion of the tradition of political theory in Jean Bethke Elshtain, *Public Man, Private Woman* (Princeton: Princeton University Press, 1981).

32. But Nietzsche's thought is, as always, more many-sided and complex than this. See the section "Was bedeuten asketische Ideale?" in *Jenseits von Gut und Böse*.

INDEX

Abrams, M. H., 377, 440
Adams, Henry, 233
Adkins, A. W. H., 118
Adorno, Theodor, 422, 477, 478, 483, 501, 506, 509–510
Akiva, Rabbi, 268
Alberti, Leon Battista, 200, 201
D'Alembert, Jean le Rond, 349
Anderson, Benedict, 106, 288
Aquinas, Thomas, 141, 143, 192, 220, 235, 258
Arendt, Hannah, 360, 501
Ariès, Philippe, 291, 293
Aristotelianism, 13, 148, 190, 277, 372, 373, 440
Aristotle, 125, 164, 186, 188, 230; ethics and the good, 66, 76, 86, 137, 138, 148, 278, 283; the good life, 82, 125, 211, 212, 372, 439; practical wisdom, 125, 126; modern notions of nature, 189, 372, 375
Arnauld, Antoine, 157, 356
Arnold, Matthew, 408, 409, 413, 418, 511
Atomism, 82, 161, 193, 195–197, 207, 383, 413, 500, 504–506
Auden, W. H., 483, 492
Auerbach, Erich, 286, 287
Aufklärer, 321, 322, 329–331, 344, 351, 352, 564n1
Augustine, 93, 121, 127–143, 148, 152, 156, 177, 185, 214, 220, 256, 390, 449
Augustinianism, 140, 141, 185, 324; in modern theology, 18, 128, 214, 220, 221, 356; in modern moral outlooks, 83, 356, 357, 362, 366, 434, 440; inwardness, 137, 163, 184, 251, 315; Descartes, 140, 141, 143, 156, 157, 311; Montaigne, 163

Autonomy, 14, 55, 245, 285, 290, 305, 306, 308, 363, 382, 383, 385, 508

Bacon, Francis, 85, 161, 212, 213, 230–232, 234, 240, 242, 258, 264, 405
Baconian model, 164, 192, 200, 213, 230–232
Basic reason, 76, 77, 89
Baudelaire, Charles, 422, 426, 427, 431, 434–442, 446–448, 454, 458, 459
Baumgarten, Alexander, 373
Beccaria, Cesare, 318, 394
Behaviourism, 58, 113, 525n12
Bellah, Robert, 39, 508–510
Benevolence, 31, 64, 78, 84, 85, 258, 448, 458; ethic of, 255, 334, 405, 496, 516; Hutcheson, 259–268, 556n60; Deism, 265, 267, 281, 282, 566n26; universal benevolence, 305, 322, 335, 395, 412, 422; and the Enlightenment, 329–333, 336, 337, 366, 370, 387, 560n37; and Nietzsche, 343, 423, 455, 518–519; and Rousseau, 358, 362, 373, 411; and justice, 395–397, 410, 517, 518; and nature as source, 411, 412
Benjamin, Walter, 463, 478, 479
Bentham, Jeremy, 87, 308, 318, 319, 323, 328, 331, 332, 337, 338, 394, 410
Berman, Marshall, 501
Bernstein, Richard, 488
Best account principle (BA principle), 58, 59, 68, 69, 71–74, 76, 99, 106, 257
Blackburn, Simon, 59, 60
Blake, William, 369, 422, 457
Block, Ned, 513, 520
Boileau, Nicolas, 299
Bolton, Robert, 225